THE HOLT HANDBOOK

fifth edition

THE HOLT HANDBOOK

fifth edition

LAURIE G. KIRSZNER
PHILADELPHIA COLLEGE OF PHARMACY AND SCIENCE

STEPHEN R. MANDELL
DREXEL UNIVERSITY

HARCOURT BRACE COLLEGE PUBLISHERS

FORT WORTH PHILADELPHIA SAN DIEGO NEW YORK
ORLANDO AUSTIN SAN ANTONIO
TORONTO MONTREAL LONDON SYDNEY TOKYO

Publisher	Earl McPeek
Acquisitions Editor	Julie McBurney
Product Manager	Charlie Watson
Developmental Editor	Camille Adkins
Project Editor	Denise Netardus
Art Director	Vicki Whistler
Production Manager	Linda McMillan

ISBN: 0-15-507904-2
Library of Congress Catalog Card Number: 97-80825

Address for Orders: Harcourt Brace College Publishers, 6277 Sea Harbor Drive, Orlando, FL 32887-6777
1-800-782-4479

Address for Editorial Correspondence: Harcourt Brace College Publishers, 301 Commerce Street, Suite 3700, Fort Worth, TX 76102

Web Site Address
http://www.hbcollege.com

Harcourt Brace College Publishers will provide complimentary supplements or supplement packages to those adopters qualified under our adoption policy. Please contact your sales representative to learn how you qualify. If as an adopter or potential user you receive supplements you do not need, please return them to your sales representative or send them to: Attn: Returns Department, Troy Warehouse, 465 South Lincoln Drive, Troy, MO 63379.

Printed in the United States of America

8 9 0 1 2 3 4 5 6 7   039   9 8 7 6 5 4 3 2 1

Harcourt Brace College Publishers

Our goal for the fifth edition of *The Holt Handbook* is the same as it was for the first: to create a writer's handbook that serves as a classroom text, as a comprehensive reference, and as a writer's companion. In preparing the first edition, we concentrated on making the book inviting, accessible, useful, and clear for both teachers and students. In the fifth edition, we have kept these goals in mind, adding distinctive new design features and fine-tuning established ones in order to make information even easier to locate than before.

A **guide to the plan of the book** now appears on the inside front cover to facilitate reference. Yellow **close-up boxes,** which appear throughout the text, focus on special problems and are identified by a magnifying glass icon. **Checklists,** designed to provide concise guidance and review for writers, are also yellow; these are further distinguished by a check mark icon. Light blue **computer boxes,** new to this edition, highlight information students will use as they compose and revise papers on their computers, and blue lines enclose **boxed lists and charts** and other information students are likely to refer to on a regular basis. **Cross-references,** which direct users to related discussions in other parts of the book, are indicated by small blue "buttons" in the margin keyed to "hypertext" links (blue, underlined in blue) in the text. Throughout the text, we have taken special care to make headings clear and descriptive and to position them logically on the page. We believe the result is a highly accessible reference work that enables writers to find and use information quickly and easily.

Although *The Holt Handbook*, Fifth Edition, is grounded in the most up-to-date research in composition, it is also informed by our many years of classroom experience. As teachers, we continue to search for what works for our students, giving them what they need to succeed in college and beyond. Our hope is that this book continues to reflect our commitment to our teaching and to our students—some of whose writing appears on its pages. With its logical organization, its process approach, its emphasis on revision, its encouraging tone, and its focus on student writing, we believe that *The Holt Handbook* remains both a writing-centered text and a student-centered text.

As we began this revision of *The Holt Handbook,* our goal was to retain the features that have made the book so satisfying to users, while adding new material and new features to make it a more valuable reference text and writing guide. Thoughtful and incisive comments from users of the first four editions and our own classroom experience with the book led us to make a number of significant changes in the fifth edition.

THE FIFTH EDITION AT A GLANCE

- **New exercise sets**   The handbook includes forty new sets and another forty new to the Annotated Instructor's Edition. As in earlier editions, **Student Writer at Work** exercises reinforce the connection between the material discussed in the chapters and student writing.

- **Extensive revision of Part 1, "Composing an Essay"**   In the fifth edition, all prewriting activities and written drafts related to the student essay, "My Problem: Escaping the Stereotype of the 'Model Minority,'" appear together in a **new Chapter 4, "Writer's Notebook: Composing an Essay."**

- **New Chapter 5, "Essay Patterns and Purposes"**   This chapter, unique in college-level writing handbooks, includes eight short student essays. It briefly explains and illustrates how to develop narrative, descriptive, exemplification, process, cause and effect, comparison and contrast, division and classification, and definition essays.

- **Special focus on grammar "hot spots"**   In Part 4, where our focus is on sentence-level problems, we provide especially full treatment of the problems teachers and students struggle with most: sentence fragments; comma splices and fused sentences; faulty modification; faulty parallelism; and awkwardly worded sentences.

- **New Chapter 40, "Using the Internet for Research"**   A new chapter introduces students to the Internet and the World Wide Web as research tools.

- **New Chapter 42, "Avoiding Plagiarism"**   A full chapter on the issue of plagiarism underscores its importance for students and helps them understand the ethics as well as the mechanics of using sources.

- **Extensive revision of Chapter 43, "Documentation"**   Expanded discussions of the most current MLA, Chicago, APA, and CBE documentation styles, including the newest formats for electronic sources, make this chapter more comprehensive as well as completely up to date.

- **New Chapter 45, "Research Notebook: A Student's Process"**   A separate chapter is now devoted to one student's prewriting and research activities, as well as her commentary on her progress, concluding with a model student paper, "Athletic Scholarships: Who Wins?"

- **New drama paper in Chapter 51, "Writing about Literature"** A student paper on the one-act play *Trifles* has been added to Chapter 51, which already includes student papers on a short story and a poem.

- **Expanded material on using computer technology integrated throughout the text** In addition to the new computer boxes, many other discussions reflect the importance of electronic resources in the research and writing processes, considering the role of this new technology in everything from doing computer-based research, to using correct formats for documenting electronic sources, to creating attractive documents, to using a spell checker.

- **Extensively revised Appendix A, "Document Design and Manuscript Guidelines"** Formerly titled "Preparing Your Papers," this appendix now discusses document design—the use of headings, lists, and visuals (tables, graphs, diagrams, and photographs)—as well as MLA and APA guidelines for manuscript preparation.

- **Newly revised Appendix B, "English for Speakers of Other Languages (ESOL)"** This appendix (formerly Chapter 26) offers students a context for understanding English grammar rules by contrasting them to those of their own language. This unique approach gives the section appeal for native as well as nonnative English speakers.

THE FIFTH EDITION IN DETAIL

Part 1 of *The Holt Handbook*, Fifth Edition, now includes two new chapters. The treatment of the writing process in Chapters 1 through 3 is more lucid and easier to follow now that all the student's prewriting activities and drafts, as well as his commentary on his progress, appear in a new Chapter 4, "Writer's Notebook: Composing an Essay." This revision eliminates breaks in the discussion of the writing process in Chapters 1 through 3 and creates in Chapter 4 a freestanding narrative that students can follow as they write their own papers. We have also expanded and clarified the discussion of thesis and support, and this relationship is further developed in the new Chapter 5, "The Essay: Patterns and Purposes." Here we explain the uses of each of eight patterns of development and illustrate each with an annotated student essay.

Because critical thinking is such an important part of the writing process, we devote all of Part 2 to this subject. Chapter 7, "Reading Critically and Writing Critical Responses," includes a discussion of active reading strategies as well as a discussion of critical reading. Chapter 8, "Thinking Logically," which explains the principles of inductive and deductive reasoning, also includes discussions of the Toulmin model and Rogerian argument, thus enabling instructors to supplement their discussions of traditional logic with these approaches. In addition, this chapter includes a helpful summary box that compares inductive and deductive reasoning. Chapter 9, "Writing an Argumentative Essay," spotlights a student paper, "The Returning Student: Older Is Definitely Better," that uses sources (including electronic sources) to support an argumentative thesis.

Throughout Parts 3 through 7 we have edited and redesigned our presentations of style, grammar, punctuation, and mechanics so that definitions, guidelines, and key concepts are emphasized visually as well as stylistically. We have carefully scrutinized every example and exercise in these sections and have edited, revised, eliminated, or replaced material when necessary. In addition, headings have been reworded, redesigned, or relocated to make information more accessible. Particularly detailed coverage has been given to those areas students and teachers have identified as most important to them: sentence fragments; comma splices and fused sentences; faulty modification; faulty parallelism; awkwardly worded sentences; and comma use. Although we have streamlined material in other sections of the text, here we have been careful to retain the detailed coverage and numerous examples and exercises that students and teachers want.

Part 8, "Writing with Sources," has received especially close attention in past editions, and we have continued to fine-tune the seven chapters in this section to make it even more useful. Chapter 39, "Research for Writing," opens with a helpful chart that presents a clear overview of the research process, and material reflecting recent developments in computer-based research has been highlighted throughout. A new chapter, "Using the Internet for Research" (Chapter 40), supplements the research section with vital, up-to-date information on how to use the Internet and the World Wide Web as research tools. A newly configured Chapter 41, "Summarizing, Paraphrasing, Quoting, and Synthesizing," now includes a section on synthesizing ideas, and we have expanded our discussion of plagiarism (formerly part of this chapter) and highlighted it in a new chapter, "Avoiding Plagiarism" (Chapter 42). Chapter 43, "Documentation," which has been significantly updated and expanded, now includes the formats presented in the fourth edition of the *MLA Handbook for Writers of Research Papers* (including the 1998 guidelines for documenting electronic sources), the fourteenth edition of the *Chicago Manual of Style,* and the fourth edition of the *Publication Manual of the American Psychological Association.* Chapter 43 also devotes careful attention to how to cite a variety of different kinds of electronic sources, following the most current MLA, APA, Chicago, and CBE guidelines.

In Part 9, "Writing in the Disciplines," we have updated the discussions of each of the disciplines to include the most current print and electronic resources. Sample research papers in each discipline have been edited to conform to the latest conventions of style, format, and documentation. In addition, a new student literature paper, "Breaking through the Boundaries: Acts of Defiance in *Trifles*," has been added to Chapter 51, "Writing about Literature," which now includes three model student papers—one on a short story, one on a poem, and one on a play. Chapter 52, "Writing for the Workplace," now includes information on communicating by E-mail and fax.

The text concludes with two appendices, "Document Design and Manuscript Guidelines" and "English for Speakers of Other Languages (ESOL)," both significantly expanded and updated from the previous edition.

In its fifth edition, *The Holt Handbook* continues to approach writing as a recursive process, giving students the opportunity to practice planning, shaping, writing, and revising. This approach encourages students to become involved with every stage of the process and to view revision as a natural and ongoing part of writing. The style, grammar, and mechanics and punctuation chapters present clear, concise definitions of key concepts followed by examples and exercises that gradually increase in difficulty and sophistication. (Whenever possible, sentence-level skills are reinforced in groups of related sentences that focus on a single topic instead of in isolated sentences.) Thus, students learn incrementally, practicing each skill as it is introduced. In this way they begin to recognize and solve sentence-level problems within longer units of discourse, replicating the way they must actually interact with their own writing. This approach has been useful to hundreds of thousands of students who have used the first four editions, and we continue to believe strongly in its effectiveness.

The Holt Handbook, Fifth Edition, is writing centered, and it puts writing first. It is a classroom text, a reference book, and—above all—a writing companion that students can turn to again and again for advice and guidance as they write in college and beyond. Our goal for each edition has remained the same: to combine the best of current composition research with our instincts as experienced teachers. We continue to believe that we have the obligation to give not just the rule but the rationale behind it. Accordingly, we are careful to explain the principles that writers must understand if they are to make informed choices about grammar, usage, rhetoric, and style. The result is a book that students and instructors can continue to use with ease, confidence, and (we hope) pleasure.

ANCILLARY PACKAGE

With this edition, an even more comprehensive ancillary package is available for students and instructors.

The following support materials for instructors and students are available to adopters of *The Holt Handbook*, Fifth Edition. Instructors should contact their Harcourt Brace representatives for more information.

For Instructors

Annotated Instructor's Edition—The full text of the student edition, plus answers to exercises in the handbook, additional exercises with answers, abstracts of articles, suggestions for relating theory and scholarship to classroom activities, computer and Internet tips, quotations, classroom activities, and teaching strategies

Diagnostic Test Package—A complete testing program, cross-referenced to *The Holt Handbook*, Fifth Edition, including general grammar proficiency tests and diagnostic tests, as well as practice tests for CLAST, TASP, and the Tennessee Proficiency Examination

The Harcourt Brace Guide to Teaching First-Year Composition—An introduction to the basics of teaching writing, with essay examples from students, and a comprehensive bibliography for further study

The Harcourt Brace Guide to Teaching Writing with Computers—Techniques for teaching writing in networked and non-networked computer environments, including tips for teaching Internet research

The Harcourt Brace Guide to Writing across the Curriculum—A brief history of Writing across the Curriculum, plus strategies for launching a WAC program, including tips for designing writing assignments

The Harcourt Brace Sourcebook for Teachers of Writing—A collection of articles by composition scholars, considering such rhetoric and composition issues and trends as analyzing audience, teaching community-based writing, and assigning expressive essays

Transparencies—A collection of eighty images from *The Holt Handbook*, Fifth Edition

For Students

The Harcourt Brace Guide to Documentation and Writing in the Disciplines—Full introductions to writing in the humanities, the social sciences, and the natural sciences, with model papers typical of the work students will be expected to submit in each discipline

Supplementary Exercises—A collection of grammar and composition exercises for students who need reinforcement of basic skills; designed for use with *The Holt Handbook*, Fifth Edition

The Holt Composition Workbook, Form A—A full-length workbook intended for first-year students; designed for use with *The Holt Handbook*, Fifth Edition, or on its own

The Holt Composition Workbook, Form B—A full-length workbook intended for developmental as well as first-year students; designed for use with *The Holt Handbook*, Fifth Edition, or on its own

The Holt Guide to the Internet—An overview of the Internet, its components, and its purposes, including but not limited to research

The Writing Circle—A guide for student writers working constructively in small groups, intended to make each group session productive and satisfying for all participants

The Harcourt Brace Guide to Peer Tutoring—A Guide for Writers and Peer Editors—An introduction to peer consulting pedagogy and practice, with readings from such rhetoricians and composition theorists as Kenneth Bruffee, Peter Elbow, and Mina Shaughnessey

Preparing for the TASP—A guide that enables students to connect sample test material to explanations and exercises available in the handbook

Preparing for the CLAST—A guide that enables students to connect sample test material to explanations and exercises available in the handbook

Electronic Supplements

The Holt Handbook, Fifth Edition, CD-ROM—The full text of *The Holt Handbook*, Fifth Edition, plus NoteTaker and Biblogen

ExaMaster+ Test Bank—Four exams of two hundred questions each for skills development, diagnostic evaluation, and state exam preparation

Writing Tutor V—A self-paced tutorial program of forty modules offering practice in grammar, punctuation, mechanics, parts of speech, correction of sentence errors, editing, and revision

ACKNOWLEDGMENTS

We thank the following colleagues for their help in the development of the fifth edition:

Reviewers

Michel de Benedictis, Miami-Dade Community College

Kay Bosgraaf, Montgomery College

Beth Brunk, University of Texas at Arlington

Daniel Butcher, Southeastern Louisiana University

Linda Daigle, Houston Community College Central

Dani Day, University of Texas at Arlington

Eleanor Gaunder, University of North Alabama

Jacqueline Goffe-McNish, Dutchess Community College

Stephen Harding, University of Texas at Arlington

Sydney Harrison, Manatee Community College

Peggy Jolly, University of Alabama at Birmingham

Quentin Martin, Loyola University of Chicago

Nellie McCrory, Gaston College

Nancy McGee, Detroit College of Business

Audrey Wick, University of Texas at Arlington

Consultants

Patricia Arnott, University of Delaware (Library issues)

Clyde Moneyhun, Youngstown State University (ESOL issues)

Carol Clark Powell, University of Texas at El Paso (Web issues)

Contributors to the Annotated Instructor's Edition

Larry Bromley, University of Texas at Arlington

Scott Douglass, Chattanooga State Technical Community College

Lori Gravley, Western New England College

Michael Lèger, University of Texas at Arlington

Richard Louth, Southeastern Louisiana University

Judy Pearce, Montgomery College

Russ Pottle, Southeastern Louisiana University

Jeff Wiemelt, Southeastern Louisiana University

We also thank the following reviewers for their sound advice on the development of the fourth edition: Henry Castillo, Temple Junior College; Laurie Chesley, Grand Valley State University; Scott Douglass, Chattanooga State Technical Community College; Maurice R. Duperre, Midlands Technical College; Nancy Ellis, Mississippi State University; Jane Frick, Missouri Western State University; G. Dale Gleason, Hutchinson Community College; Maureen Hoag, Wichita State University; Susan B. Jackson, Spartanburg Technical College; Anne Maxham-Kastrinos, Washington State University; J. L. McClure, Kirkwood Community College; John Pennington, St. Norbert College; Robert Perry, Lock Haven University of Pennsylvania; Robbie C. Pinter, Belmont University; Mary Sue Ply, Southeastern Louisiana University; Linda Rollins, Motlow State Community College; Laura Ross, Seminole Community College; Anne B. Slater, Frederick Community College; Connie White, Salisbury State University; Karen W. Willingham, Pensacola Junior College.

We express our appreciation to the following reviewers of the third edition: Lynne Diane Beene, University of New Mexico, Albuquerque; Elizabeth Bell, University of South Carolina; Jon Bentley, Albuquerque Technical-Vocational Institute; Debra Boyd, Winthrop College; Judith Burdan, University of North Carolina/Chapel Hill; Phyllis Burke, Hartnell College; Sandra Frisch, Mira Costa College; Gerald Gordon, Black Hills State University; Mamie Hixson, University of West Florida; Sue Ellen Holbrook, Southern Connecticut State University; Linda Hunt, Whitworth College; Rebecca Innocent, Southern Methodist University; Gloria John, Catonsville Community College; Gloria Johnson, Tennessee State University; Suzanne Liggett, Montgomery College; Richard Pepp, Massasoit Community College; Nancy Posselt, Midlands Technical College; Robert Peterson, Middle Tennessee State University; Randy Popkin, Tarleton State University; George Redmond, Benedict College; Terry Roberts, University of North Carolina/Chapel Hill; Linda Rollins, Motlow State Community College; Gary Sattelmeyer, Trident Technical College; Father Joseph Scallon, Creighton University; Emily Seelbinder, Queens College; Cynthia Smith, University of West Florida; Bill Stiffler, Harford Community College; Nancy Thompson, University of South Carolina/Columbia; Kathleen Tickner, Brevard Community College; Warren Westcott, Frances Marion College; Connie White, Salisbury State University; and Helen Yanko, California State University/Fullerton.

We also thank the following colleagues for their valuable comments on the development of the first and second editions: Chris Abbott, University of Pittsburgh; Virginia Allen, Iowa State University; Stanley Archer, Texas A & M University; Lois Avery, Houston Community College; Rance G. Baker, Alamo Community College; Julia Bates, St. Mary's College of Maryland; John G. Bayer, St. Louis Community College/Meramec; Larry Beason, Texas A & M University; Al Bell, St. Louis Community College at Florissant Valley; Debra Boyd, Winthrop College; Margaret A. Bretschneider, Lakeland Community College; Pat Bridges, Grand Valley State College; Alma Bryant, University of South Florida; Wayne Buchman, Rose State College; David Carlson, Springfield College; Patricia Carter, George Washington University; Faye Chandler, Pasadena City College; Peggy Cole, Arapahoe Community College; Sarah H. Collins, Rochester Institute of Technology; Charles Dodson, University of North Carolina/Wilmington; Margaret Gage, Northern Illinois University; Sharon Gibson, University of Louisville; Owen Gilman, St. Joseph's University; Margaret Goddin, Davis and Elkins College; Ruth Greenberg,

University of Louisville; George Haich, Georgia State University; Robert E. Haines, Hillsborough Community College; Ruth Hamilton, Northern Illinois University; Iris Hart, Santa Fe Community College; John Harwood, Penn State University; Michael Herzog, Gonzaga University; Clela Hoggatt, Los Angeles Mission College; Keith N. Hull, University of Wyoming/Laramie; Anne Jackets, Everett Community College; Zena Jacobs, Polytechnic Institute of New York; LaVinia Jennings, University of North Carolina/Chapel Hill; D. G. Kehl, Arizona State University; Philip Keith, St. Cloud State University; George Kennedy, Washington State University; William King, Bethel College; Edward Kline, University of Notre Dame; Susan Landstrom, University of North Carolina/Chapel Hill; Marie Logye, Rutgers University; Helen Marlborough, DePaul University; Nancy Martinez, University of New Mexico/Valencia; Marsha McDonald, Belmont College; Vivien Minshull-Ford, Wichita State University; Robert Moore, SUNY/Oswego; George Murphy, Villanova University; Robert Noreen, Califomia State University/Northridge; L. Sam Phillips, Gaston College; William Pierce, Prince George's Community College; Robbie Pinter, Belmont College; Nancy Posselt, Midlands Technical College; Robert Post, Kalamazoo Valley Community College; Richard N. Ramsey, Indiana University/Purdue University; Mike Riherd, Pasadena City College; Emily Seelbinder, Wake Forest University; Charles Staats, Broward Community College/North; Frank Steele, Westem Kentucky University; Barbara Stevenson, Kennesaw College; Jim Stick, Des Moines Area Community College; James Sodon, St. Louis Community College at Florissant Valley; Josephine K. Tarvers, Rutgers University; Kathleen Tickner, Brevard Community College/Melbourne; George Trail, University of Houston; Daryl Troyer, El Paso Community College; Ben Vasta, Camden County Community College; Connie White, Salisbury State College; Joyce Williams, Jefferson State Junior College; Branson Woodard, Liberty University; and Peter Zoller, Wichita State University.

Among the many people at Harcourt who contributed to this project, we would like to single out Michael Rosenberg for his energy and vision as well as Julie McBurney for carrying forward Harcourt's extraordinary commitment to the book.

In addition, we want to acknowledge the very vital day-to-day (sometimes minute-to-minute) contributions of two amazing people: Camille Adkins and Denise Netardus. Camille, our friend as well as our developmental editor, brought to the project a winning combination: a delightfully droll sense of humor and a pragmatic yet creative editorial approach. Denise, our project editor, somehow managed to maintain both high standards and incredible patience. We couldn't have done it without them, and we hope we never have to.

Once again, we would like to thank our families—Mark, Adam, and Rebecca Kirszner and Demi, David, and Sarah Mandell—who gave us no editorial assistance, did not type the manuscript, and offered no helpful suggestions, but who managed to put up with the general chaos for the duration of another edition.

Finally, we would like to thank each other for making this book a collaboration in the truest sense.

CONTENTS

Contents

Contents

Contents

Contents

Contents

Contents

Contents

Contents

Contents

Contents

Contents

Contents

Contents

Contents

Contents

Contents

Contents

Contents

Contents

Contents

PART 1

COMPOSING AN ESSAY

CHAPTER 1

PLANNING AN ESSAY

1a Understanding the Writing Process

Writing is a process that enables writers to discover ideas, make connections, and see from new perspectives. In this sense, writing is a demanding, creative process of thinking and learning—about yourself, about others, and about your world. In another sense, writing is a tool that empowers you: it enables you to participate in the ongoing dialogue among people who "talk" to each other in letters, newsgroups, memos, petitions, reports, articles, editorials, and books. In short, writing is important because if you can write, you can communicate.

Writing is a constant process of decision making, of selecting, deleting, and rearranging material.

THE WRITING PROCESS

Planning: Consider your purpose, audience, and tone; choose your topic; discover ideas to write about.
Shaping: Decide how to organize your material.
Writing: Draft your essay.
Revising: "Re-see" what you have written; write additional drafts.
Editing: Check grammar, spelling, punctuation, and mechanics.
Proofreading: Check for typographical errors.

The neatly defined stages listed above communicate neither the complexity nor the flexibility of the writing process. Although we will examine these stages separately, they actually overlap: as you look for ideas, you may begin to shape your material; as you shape your material, you may begin to write; as you write a draft, you may reorganize your ideas;

as you revise, you continue to discover new material. Moreover, these stages are repeated over and over again throughout the writing process.

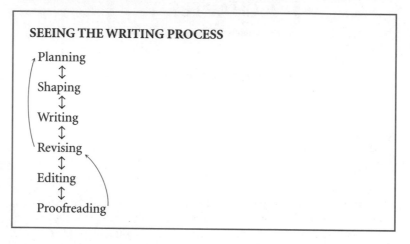

SEEING THE WRITING PROCESS

Planning
⇕
Shaping
⇕
Writing
⇕
Revising
⇕
Editing
⇕
Proofreading

During your college years and in the years that follow, you will develop your own version of the writing process and use it whenever you write, adapting it to the audience, purpose, and writing situation at hand.

EXERCISE 1

Write a paragraph in which you describe your own writing process. What do you do first? What steps do you return to again and again? Which stages do you find most enjoyable? Which do you find most frustrating?

1b Thinking about Writing

See
Pt. 2

Writing presents many situations in which you must **think critically**: make judgments, weigh alternatives, analyze, compare, question, evaluate, and engage in other decision-making activities. Virtually all writing demands that you make informed choices about your subject matter and about the way you present your ideas.

Planning your essay—thinking about what you want to say and how you want to say it—begins well before you actually put your thoughts on paper in any organized way. This planning is as important a part of the writing process as the writing itself.

(1) Determining Your Purpose

When we sit down to write, we often have a **purpose** in mind. For example, we may write *to express emotions,* exploring ideas and feelings in a diary or journal, an autobiographical memoir, or a personal letter; *to inform,* perhaps in a newspaper or magazine article, an encyclopedia entry, a reference text, or an instruction manual; or *to persuade,* trying to convince an audience to agree with a position on an issue in a proposal, an editorial, or an essay that takes a stand on a moral, ethical, political, or social issue.

Writing to Express Emotions

At the age of five, six, well past the time when most other children no longer easily notice the difference between sounds uttered at home and words spoken in public, I had a different experience. I lived in a world magically compounded of sounds. I remained a child longer than most; I lingered too long, poised at the edge of language—often frightened by the sounds of *los gringos,* delighted by the sounds of Spanish at home. I shared with my family a language that was startlingly different from that used in the great city around us.

(Richard Rodriguez, *Aria: A Memoir of a Bilingual Childhood*)

Writing to Inform

Most tarantulas live in the tropics, but several species occur in the temperate zone and a few are common in the southern U.S. Some varieties are large and have powerful fangs with which they can inflict a deep wound. These formidable-looking spiders do not, however, attack man; you can hold one in your hand, if you are gentle, without being bitten. Their bite is dangerous only to insects and small mammals such as mice; for man it is no worse than a hornet's sting.

(Alexander Petrunkevitch, "The Spider and the Wasp")

Writing to Persuade

Testing and contact tracing may lead to a person's being deprived of a job, health insurance, housing and privacy, many civil libertarians fear. These are valid and grave concerns. But we can find ways to protect civil rights without sacrificing public health. A major AIDS-prevention campaign ought to be accompanied by intensive public education about the ways the illness is *not* transmitted, by additional safeguards on data banks and by greater penalties for those who abuse HIV victims. It may be harsh to say,

5

but the fact that an individual may suffer as a result of doing what is right does not make doing so less of an imperative.

(Amitai Etzioni, "HIV Sufferers Have a Responsibility")

Your purpose determines the material you choose and the way you arrange and express it. For instance, a memoir written by an adult re-membering summer camp might *express emotions* about the difficulties experienced during a month away from home, exploring memories of mosquitoes, poison ivy, institutional food, shaving cream fights, and so on. A magazine article about summer camps could *inform*, explaining how camping has changed in the past twenty years, for example. Such an article would present facts and statistics straightforwardly, objectively describing such features as recreational programs and sports facilities. An advertising brochure designed to recruit potential campers could *persuade* by enumerating the benefits of the camping experience. Such a brochure would stress positive details—the opportunity to meet new friends, for example—and deemphasize the possibilities of homesick-ness and rainy weather. In each case, purpose determines what material is selected and how it is presented.

Whenever you write, you may be guided by one of these three general purposes—in college writing, for example, your purpose is most often to inform or to persuade—or you may have other, more specific aims or a combination of purposes.

✔ CHECKLIST: DETERMINING YOUR PURPOSE

Is your purpose

✔ to express emotions?	✔ to speculate?
✔ to inform?	✔ to warn?
✔ to persuade?	✔ to reassure?
✔ to explain?	✔ to take a stand?
✔ to amuse or entertain?	✔ to identify problems?
✔ to evaluate?	✔ to suggest solutions?
✔ to discover?	✔ to define causes?
✔ to analyze?	✔ to predict effects?
✔ to debunk?	✔ to reflect?
✔ to draw comparisons?	✔ to create?
✔ to make an analogy?	✔ to communicate?
✔ to define?	✔ to observe
✔ to criticize?	✔ to interpret?
✔ to satirize?	✔ to instruct?

(2) Identifying Your Audience

Writing is often such a solitary activity that it is easy to forget about your audience. But except for diaries and journals, everything you write addresses an **audience**—a particular set of readers.

At different times, in different roles, you address a variety of audiences. As a citizen, consumer, or member of a community, civic, political, or religious group, you may respond to pressing social, economic, or political issues by writing letters to a newspaper editor; to a public official; to a representative of a special interest group, business, or corporation; or to another recipient you do not know well or at all. In your personal life, you may write notes and letters to friends and family. As an employee, you may write letters, memos, and reports to your superiors, to staff members you supervise, or to workers on your level; you may also be called on to address customers or critics, board members or stockholders, funding agencies or the general public. As a student, you write essays, reports, and other papers addressed to one or more instructors and sometimes to other students or to outside evaluators.

As you move through the stages of the writing process, you shape your paper increasingly in terms of what you believe your audience needs and expects. Your assessment of your readers' interests, educational level, **biases**, and expectations determines not only the information you include but also your emphasis, the arrangement of your material, and the style or tone you choose.

See
7b3

The Academic Audience   As a student, you most often write for an audience of one: the instructor who assigns the paper. Instructors want to know what you know and whether you can express what you know clearly and accurately. They assign written work to encourage you to use **critical thinking** skills, so the way you organize and express your ideas can be as important as the ideas themselves.

See
Pt. 2

As a group, instructors have certain expectations. They expect correct information, standard grammar and correct spelling, a logical presentation of ideas, and some stylistic fluency. They also expect you to define your terms and to support your generalizations with specifics.

If you are writing in an instructor's academic field you can omit long overviews and basic definitions. Remember, however, that outside their areas of expertise, most instructors are simply general readers. If you think you may know more about a subject than your instructor does, be sure to provide background, supplying the definitions, examples, and analogies that will make your ideas clear.

The course for which you are writing should also influence your writing choices. If, for example, you decide to write about the underground mine fires that for years have been burning out of control near your hometown of Centralia, Pennsylvania, you would focus on different aspects of the topic for different courses.

Topic: Underground Fires

Course	Emphasis
Chemistry	Chemical analysis of fumes
Sociology	Relocation patterns of residents
Economics	Effects on local businesses and real estate market
Psychology	Emotional impact of fires on children
Political Science	Role of federal or state government

See
Pt. 9
Finally, keep in mind that different academic **disciplines** have their own formats, documentation styles, methods of collecting and reporting data, formulas and symbols, technical vocabularies, and stylistic conventions.

✔ CHECKLIST: IDENTIFYING YOUR AUDIENCE

Is your audience

- ✔ an individual?
- ✔ a member of a group?
- ✔ specialized?
- ✔ general?

Can you identify your audience's

- ✔ needs?
- ✔ expectations?
- ✔ educational level?
- ✔ biases?
- ✔ interests?

Do you need to supply your audience with

- ✔ definitions?
- ✔ overviews?
- ✔ examples?
- ✔ analogies?

What special conventions does your audience expect concerning

- ✔ format?
- ✔ documentation style?
- ✔ methods of collecting and reporting data?
- ✔ use of formulas and symbols?
- ✔ specialized vocabulary?
- ✔ writing style?

---

(3) Setting Your Tone

Tone conveys your attitude about your subject. The attitude, or mood, that you adopt as you write may be serious or frivolous, respectful or condescending, intimate or detached. Because tone tells your readers how you feel about your material, it must remain consistent with your purpose and your audience as you write and revise.

Your tone also reveals how you feel toward your readers—sympathetic or superior, concerned or indifferent, friendly or critical. For instance, if you identify with your readers or feel close to them, you use a personal and conversational tone. When you address a general reader indirectly or anonymously, you use a more distant, formal tone.

When your audience is an instructor and your purpose is to inform (as is often the case in college writing situations), you should use an objective tone, neither too personal and informal nor too detached and formal—unless you are told otherwise. The following paragraph from a student paper on the resistance to various drugs of a specific group of microorganisms achieves an appropriate tone for its audience (an instructor—and perhaps students—in a medical technology lab) and purpose (to report information).

> One of the major characteristics of streptococci is that they are gram-positive. This means that after a series of dyes and rinses they take on a violet color. (Gram-negative organisms take on a red color.) Streptococci are also nonspore forming and nonmotile. Most strains produce a protective shield called a capsule. They use organic substances instead of oxygen for their metabolism. This process is called fermentation.

An English composition assignment asking students to write a short, informal essay expressing their feelings about the worst job they ever had calls for an entirely different tone. In the next paragraph, the student's tone effectively conveys his attitude toward his job, and his use of the first person encourages audience identification. Sarcastic comments ("good little laborer," "Now here comes the excitement!") contribute to the informal effect.

> Every day I followed the same boring, monotonous routine. After clocking in like a good little laborer, I proceeded over to a gray file cabinet, forced open the half-caved-in doors, and removed a staple gun, various packs of size cards, and a blue ballpoint pen. Now here comes the excitement! Each farmer had a specific number assigned to his name. As his cucumbers were being sorted according to their particular size, they were loaded into two-hundred-pound bins, which I had to label with a stapled size card with the farmer's number on it. I had to complete a specific size card for every bin containing that size cucumber. Doesn't it sound wonderful? Any second grader could have handled it. And all the time I worked, the machinery moaned and rattled and the odor of cucumbers filled the air.

In a letter applying for a job, however, the same student would have different objectives. In this situation, his distance from his audience and his purpose (to impress readers with his qualifications and thereby persuade them to consider hiring him) would call for a much more objective and straightforward tone.

> My primary duty at Germaine Produce was to label cucumbers as they were sorted into bins. I was responsible for making sure each two-hundred-pound bin bore the name of the farmer who had grown those cucumbers and also for keeping track of the cucumbers' sizes. Accuracy was extremely important in this task.

EXERCISE 2

1. Focus on a book that you liked or disliked very much. How would you write about the book in each of the following writing situations? Consider how each writing situation would affect your content, style, organization, tone, and emphasis.

   - A journal entry recording your informal impressions of the book
   - An examination question that asks you to summarize the book's main idea
   - A book review for a composition class in which you evaluate the book's strengths and weaknesses
   - A letter in which you try to convince your local school board that the book should not be banned from the public high school's library
   - An editorial for your school newspaper in which you try to persuade other students that the book is worth reading

2. Choose one of the writing situations listed above, and write one paragraph in response to the specified assignment.

1c Getting Started

Before you begin writing, be sure you understand the exact requirements of your assignment. It is very important to keep these guidelines in mind as you write and revise. Don't make any guesses—and don't assume anything. Ask questions, and be sure you understand the answers.

✔ CHECKLIST: ANALYZING YOUR ASSIGNMENT

✔ Can you choose your own topic, or has your instructor assigned a topic?
✔ Are your choices limited in some way?
✔ What is the word, paragraph, or page limit?
✔ How much time do you have to complete your assignment?
✔ Must you do the assignment in class, or can you work on it at home?
✔ Can you do research?
✔ Will you be able to get feedback on your ideas for your paper in class discussion? In collaborative activities? In a conference with your instructor?
✔ If the assignment requires a specific format, do you know what its conventions are?

(1) Choosing a Topic

If your instructor permits you to choose your own topic, be sure to choose one you know something about—or, at least, one you want to learn about. Perhaps a class discussion or reading assignment will suggest a topic; maybe you have seen a movie or television special or had a conversation (or even an argument) about an interesting subject. If so, you are off to a good start. If not, your instructor may be able to help you choose a topic—or, you may be able to discover a promising topic during a collaborative brainstorming session.

Most of the time your instructor will give you an assignment that poses a question for you to answer or that gives a specific length, format, and subject or a list of subjects from which to choose.

How did the boundaries of Europe change after World War I? (Poses a question)

Write a two-page critical analysis of a film. (Specifies length, format, and subject area)

Write an essay explaining the significance of one of these court decisions: *Marbury* v. *Madison*, *Baker* v. *Carr*, *Brown* v. *Board of Education*, *Roe* v. *Wade*. (Gives list of specific subjects from which to choose)

Even if your instructor gives you a specific assignment, you cannot start to write immediately. First, you must narrow the assignment to suit your purpose, audience, and assignment.

NARROWING AN ASSIGNMENT

Course	Assignment	Topic
American History	Analyze the effects of a social program on one segment of American society.	How did the GI Bill of Rights affect American service-women?
Sociology	Identify and evaluate the success of one resource available to the homeless population of one major American city.	The role of the Salvation Army in meeting the needs of Chicago's homeless
Composition	Describe a place that is very important to you.	The Acoma Pueblo: my grandfather's home
Psychology	Write a three- to five-page paper assessing one method of treating depression.	Animal-assisted therapy for severely depressed patients

---

As you go through the process of deciding on a topic, keep your assignment, your audience, and your purpose in mind; also consider the things you know best and like best, those subjects that will give you a chance to convey a unique point of view. If your assignment is to write about a place that is important to you, don't write about your dorm room simply because it is the first thing you think of or about the Metropolitan Museum of Art just because you think the topic will impress your instructor. If, however, you see your dorm room as representing your independence from your family, and your essay is supposed to focus on the idea of making a fresh start, your room could be an ideal topic. Similarly, if you know the collections at the Metropolitan well and plan to study art, you may legitimately use your knowledge and interest in a paper about how your career goals developed.

EXERCISE 3

Read the following excerpt from Ron Kovic's autobiographical *Born on the Fourth of July.* Then list ten possible essay topics about your own childhood suggested by Kovic's memories of his. (Your purpose is to give your audience—your composition instructor—a vivid sense of what some aspect of your childhood was like.) Finally, choose the one topic that you feel best qualified to write about, and explain the reasons for your choice.

When we weren't down at the field or watching the Yankees on TV, we were playing whiffle ball and climbing trees checking out birds' nests, going down to Fly Beach in Mrs. Zimmer's old car that honked the horn every time it turned the corner, diving underwater with our masks, kicking with our rubber frog's feet, then running in and out of our sprinklers when we got home, waiting for our turn in the shower. And during the summer nights we were all over the neighborhood, from Bobby's house to Kenny's, throwing gliders, doing handstands and backflips off fences, riding to the woods at the end of the block on our bikes, making rafts, building tree forts, jumping across the streams with tree branches, walking and balancing along the back fence like Houdini, hopping along the slate path all around the back yard seeing how far we could go on one foot.

And I ran wherever I went. Down to school, the candy store, to the deli, buying baseball cards and Bazooka bubblegum that had the little fortunes at the bottom of the cartoons.

When the Fourth of July came, there were fireworks going off all over the neighborhood. It was the most exciting time of year for me next to Christmas. Being born on the exact same day as my country I thought was really great. I was so proud. And every Fourth of July, I had a birthday party and all my friends would come over with birthday presents and we'd put on silly hats and blow these horns my dad brought home from the A&P. We'd eat lots of ice cream and watermelon and I'd open up all the presents and blow out the candles on the big red, white, and blue birthday cake and then we'd all sing "Happy Birthday" and "I'm a Yankee Doodle Dandy." At night everyone would pile into Bobby's mother's old car and we'd go down to the drive-in, where we'd watch the fireworks display. Before the movie started, we'd all get out and sit up on the roof of the car with our blankets wrapped around us watching the rockets and Roman candles going up and exploding into fountains of rainbow colors, and later after Mrs. Zimmer dropped me off, I'd lie on my bed feeling a little sad that it all had to end so soon. As I closed my eyes I could still hear strings of firecrackers and cherry bombs going off all over the neighborhood. . . .

The whole block grew up watching television. There was Howdy Doody and Rootie Kazootie, Cisco Kid and Gabby Hayes, Roy Rogers and Dale Evans. The Lone Ranger was on Channel 7. We watched cartoons for hours on Saturdays—Beanie and Cecil, Crusader Rabbit, Woody Woodpecker—and a show with puppets called Kukla, Fran, and Ollie. I sat on the rug in the living room watching Captain Video take off in his spaceship and saw thousands of savages killed by Ramar of the Jungle.

I remember Elvis Presley on the Ed Sullivan Show and my sister Sue going crazy in the living room jumping up and down. He kept twanging this big guitar and wiggling his hips, but for some reason they were mostly showing just the top of him. My mother was sitting on the couch with her hands folded in her lap like she was praying, and my dad was in the other room talking about how the Church had advised us all that Sunday that watching Elvis Presley could lead to sin.

(2) Finding Something to Say

After you have a topic, you can begin to collect ideas for your paper, using one (or several) of the strategies discussed below. (Each of these strategies is illustrated in Chapter 4.)

USING COLLABORATIVE STRATEGIES

Many of the activities for finding something to say that are discussed in this section can be done collaboratively (with your instructor's permission). For example, you can **collaborate** (work in pairs or small groups) on brainstorming, clustering, and applying specific questions to a topic. Such group activity is often more enjoyable than solitary work, and it gives you the added benefit of doubling (or even tripling or quadrupling) the size of your pool of ideas.

See
3c1

Collaborative work can be useful at other stages of the writing process as well—for example, when you work on **revising** your essay.

See
Ch. 40

Reading and Observing   The best way to find material to write about is to open your mind to new ideas. As you read textbooks, magazines, and newspapers and as you browse the **Internet**, be on the lookout for ideas that pertain to your topic, and make a point of talking informally with friends or family about it.

You can also use material from books and articles as well as from nonprint sources such as films, television programs, interviews, telephone calls—and, of course, from the Internet. But be sure your instructor permits such research—and remember to document ideas that are not your own. If you do not, you will be committing **plagiarism**.

See
Ch. 42

Keeping a Journal Many professional writers keep **journals,** writing in them regularly whether or not they have a specific project in mind. Such a collection of thoughts and ideas can be a valuable resource when you run short of material. Journals, unlike diaries, do more than simply record personal experiences and reactions. In a journal you explore ideas; you think on paper, asking questions and drawing conclusions. You might, for example, analyze your position on a political issue, try to solve an ethical problem, or trace the evolution of your ideas about an academic assignment. You can also record quotations that have special meaning to you or make notes about your reactions to important news events, films, or conversations. A good journal is a scrapbook of ideas that you can leaf through in search of new material and new ways of looking at old material. The important thing is to *write regularly*—every day if possible—so that when a provocative idea comes along, you won't miss the opportunity to record it. (A sample journal entry appears on page 53.)

Freewriting Another strategy that can help you discover ideas is **freewriting.** Freewriting is comparable to the stretching exercises that athletes do to warm up. A relatively formless, low-key activity, it is also serious preparation for the highly focused, sometimes strenuous, work that lies ahead. When you freewrite, you let yourself go and write non-stop about anything that comes to mind, moving as quickly as you can. Give yourself a set period of time—say, five minutes—and don't stop to worry about punctuation, spelling, or grammar, or about where your mind is wandering. This strategy encourages your mind to make free associations; thus, it helps you to discover ideas you probably aren't even aware you have. When your time is up, look over what you have written and underline, bracket, or star the most promising ideas. You can then use each of these ideas as the centerpiece of a focused freewriting exercise.

When you do **focused freewriting,** you zero in on your topic. Here too you write without stopping to reconsider or reread, so you have no time for counterproductive reactions—no time to be self-conscious about style or form, to worry about the relevance of your ideas, or to count how many words you have and panic about how many more you think you need. At its best, focused freewriting can suggest new details, a new approach to your topic, or even a more interesting topic. (Sample freewriting exercises appear on page 54.)

Brainstorming One of the most useful ways to collect ideas is by brainstorming. This strategy enables you to recall pieces of information and to see connections among them.

When you **brainstorm,** you list all the points you can think of that seem pertinent to your topic, writing down ideas—comments, questions, single words, symbols, or diagrams—as quickly as you can, without pausing to consider their relevance or trying to understand their significance. (A sample brainstorming exercise appears on page 55.)

You can also do **collaborative brainstorming**—that is, you can brainstorm with your classmates in small groups that your instructor sets up or enlist a friend to help you explore ideas. Sometimes you can meet individually with your instructor to brainstorm about your paper. Collaborative brainstorming—invariably part discussion, part argument, and part dictation—can be very productive and enlightening. As ideas come up during the discussion, write them down quickly and uncritically, asking for clarification only if it is absolutely necessary. Don't stop to consider whether or not a particular idea will be useful or where in your paper you might use it. Even if an idea seems irrelevant, make a note of it. It may be just what you need later on.

Clustering **Clustering**—sometimes called *webbing* or *mapping*—is similar to brainstorming. As with brainstorming, you don't need to worry about writing complete sentences, and you jot down ideas quickly, without pausing to evaluate their usefulness or to analyze their logical relationships to other ideas. However, clustering encourages you to explore your topic in a somewhat more systematic (and more visual) manner.

You begin making a cluster diagram by writing your topic in the center of a sheet of paper. Then, you surround your topic with related ideas as they occur to you, moving outward from the general topic in the center and writing down increasingly specific ideas and details as you move toward the edges of the page. Eventually, following the path of one idea at a time, you create a diagram (often lopsided rather than symmetrical) that arranges ideas on spokes or branches radiating out from the center (your topic). If your clustering is a collaborative activity, you and one or more other students can even work on a single large sheet of paper, with each of you moving toward a different corner of the page. (A sample cluster diagram appears on page 56.)

USING YOUR COMPUTER TO GENERATE IDEAS

You can keep a computer journal, and you can also use your computer for freewriting and brainstorming.

continued on the following page

continued from the previous page
When you freewrite or write a journal entry, try turning down the brightness of the monitor, leaving the screen blank to eliminate distractions and to encourage spontaneity.

When you brainstorm, type your notes randomly. Later, after you print them out, you can add further notes and graphic elements (arrows, circles, and so on) to indicate parallels and connections.

Asking Journalistic Questions **Journalistic questions** offer a more structured way of finding something to say about your topic. (This process is illustrated on page 57.) The questions, along with your answers, will enable you to explore your topic in an orderly and systematic fashion.

This strategy involves asking six simple questions: *Who? What? Why? Where? When?* and *How?* Journalists often ask these questions to assure themselves that they have explored all angles of a story, and you can use them to see whether you have considered all aspects of your topic.

JOURNALISTIC QUESTIONS

Who?	Where?
What?	When?
Why?	How?

Asking In-Depth Questions If you have time, and if you want to generate ideas more systematically than you can with other strategies, you can ask a series of more focused questions about your topic. These in-depth questions not only can give you a great deal of information but also can suggest ways that you can eventually shape your ideas into paragraphs and <u>essays</u>.

See
Ch. 5

IN-DEPTH QUESTIONS

What happened? ⎫
When did it happen? ⎬ Suggest <u>narration</u> (an account
Where did it happen? ⎭ of your first day of school; a summary of Emily Dickinson's life)

continued on the following page

---

continued from the previous page

What does it look like? What does it sound like, smell like, taste like, or feel like?	Suggest <u>description</u> (of the Louvre; of the electron microscope)
What are some typical cases or examples of it?	Suggests <u>exemplification</u> (three infant day-care settings; four popular fad diets)
How did it happen? What makes it work? How is it made?	Suggest <u>process</u> (how to apply for financial aid; how a bill becomes a law)
Why did it happen? What caused it? What does it cause? What are its effects?	Suggest <u>cause and effect</u> (events leading to the Korean War; the results of Prohibition; the impact of a new math curriculum on slow learners)
How is it like other things? How is it different than other things?	Suggest <u>comparison and contrast</u> (of the popular music of the 1950s and the 1960s; of two paintings)
What are its parts or types? Can they be separated or grouped? Do they fall into a logical order? Can they be categorized?	Suggest <u>division and classification</u> (components of the catalytic converter; kinds of occupational therapy; kinds of dietary supplements)
What is it? How does it resemble other members of its class? How does it differ from other members of its class?	Suggest <u>definition</u> (What is Marxism? What is photosynthesis? What is schizophrenia?)

EXERCISE 4

List all the sources you encounter in one day (people, books, magazines, observations, and so on) that could provide you with useful information for the essay you are writing.

EXERCISE 5

Make a cluster diagram and brainstorming notes for the topic you selected in Exercise 3. If you have trouble thinking of material to write about, try freewriting. Then write a journal entry assessing your progress and evaluating the different strategies for finding something to say. Which strategy worked best for you? Why?

EXERCISE 6

Using the question strategies described on pages 17–18 to supplement the work you did in Exercises 4 and 5, continue generating material for a short essay on your topic from Exercise 3.

CHAPTER 2

SHAPING YOUR MATERIAL

2a | Grouping Ideas: Making a Topic Tree

After you have gathered material for your essay and begun to see the direction your ideas are taking, you start to sift through these ideas and choose those you can use in your essay. At this point you may find it useful to make a **topic tree,** a diagram that enables you to arrange material logically and to see relationships among ideas.

Begin by reviewing all your notes—from your freewriting, journal entries, brainstorming, and so on—and deciding on three or four basic headings under which to group your material. Write these headings across the top of a piece of paper. Then go through your notes again. This time select specific ideas or details and write each under the appropriate heading, drawing lines to connect each bit of specific information to the more general heading above. Continue going through your notes and adding related information, skipping details that do not fit into any of your categories. As you move down the page, move from general information to increasingly specific details.

When you complete your topic tree, you will see how your ideas are related. Understanding the nature of these relationships will help you **develop a tentative thesis** and organize supporting information in your essay. If you go on to prepare an **informal outline**, each branch of your topic tree will probably correspond to one of your outline's major divisions. (A sample topic tree appears on page 58.)

See
2b

See
2c

✔ CHECKLIST: MAKING A TOPIC TREE

✔ Review all your notes carefully.
✔ Decide on three or four general headings that best characterize your material.

continued on the following page

continued from the previous page
✔ Write or type these headings across the top of a piece of paper.
✔ Select ideas and details that fall within each category.
✔ List each idea under a relevant heading, moving from general information to increasingly specific details as you move down the page.
✔ Draw lines to connect specific information to general headings.

EXERCISE 1

Reread your notes from the work you did for Exercises 3, 5, and 6 in Chapter 1. Use this material to help you construct a topic tree.

2b   Developing a Thesis

Your **thesis** is the main idea of your essay, the central point that your essay supports.

(1)   Understanding Thesis and Support

The concept of **thesis and support**—stating the thesis, or main idea, and then supplying information that explains and develops it—is central to a good deal of the writing you will do in college.

As the following diagram illustrates, the essays you will write will consist of an **introductory paragraph**, which opens your essay and states

See 6f2

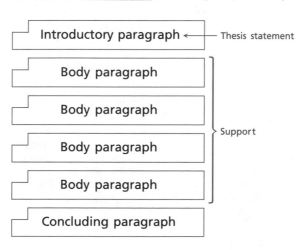

Introductory paragraph ← — Thesis statement

Body paragraph
Body paragraph
Body paragraph — Support
Body paragraph

Concluding paragraph

See
6f3
your thesis; a **concluding paragraph**, which closes your essay and gives it a sense of completion, perhaps restating your thesis; and a number of **body paragraphs,** which provide the support for your thesis statement.

(2) Defining an Effective Thesis Statement

An effective thesis statement has four characteristics.

An effective thesis statement clearly communicates your essay's main idea. It tells readers not only what your essay's topic is, but also how you will approach that topic and what you will say about it. Thus, your thesis statement reflects your essay's purpose. If your purpose is to persuade, your thesis will take a strong stand. If your purpose is to convey information, your thesis can present the specific points you will discuss or give an overview that suggests how the essay will be organized.

An effective thesis statement is more than a general subject, a statement of fact, or an announcement of your intent. Consider the differences among the following statements.

Subject	Statement of Fact	Announcement
The Draft	The United States currently has no peacetime draft.	In this essay I will reconsider our country's need for a draft.

Thesis statement   Once the military draft may have been necessary to keep the armed forces strong; however, today's all-volunteer force has eliminated the need for a draft.

Subject	Statement of Fact	Announcement
Intelligence Tests	Intelligence tests are used extensively in some elementary schools.	The paragraphs that follow will show that intelligence tests may be inaccurate.

Thesis statement   Although intelligence tests are widely used for placement in many elementary schools, they are not always the best measure of a student's academic performance.

continued on the following page

continued from the previous page

Subject	Statement of Fact	Announcement
Music Videos	Music videos can enhance record sales.	As I will argue in this paper, music videos are an important part of our culture.

Thesis statement   It may be true that music videos present stale images in place of listeners' original interpretations, but the shared images that these videos show us play an important role in establishing a common culture.

Subject	Statement of Fact	Announcement
Math Anxiety	Math anxiety is a problem for many young girls.	My paper will attempt to show why young girls have problems with mathematics.

Thesis statement   Young boys tend to outperform young girls in math classes not because of their superior ability but because girls may be afraid of being seen as unfeminine if they excel in math.

 DEFINING AN EFFECTIVE THESIS STATEMENT

Effective thesis statements should not include phrases such as "As I will show," "In my paper, I plan to demonstrate," and "It seems to me." These expressions tend to distract readers, calling attention to you rather than to your subject. Moreover, such meaningless phrases weaken your credibility by suggesting that your conclusions are based on opinion rather than on reading, observation, and experience.

An effective thesis statement is carefully worded. In order to communicate your main idea, an effective thesis statement should be clearly and accurately worded, with careful phrasing that makes your meaning apparent to your readers. Your thesis statement—usually expressed in a single, concise sentence—should be direct and straightforward and include no vague, abstract language, overly complex terminology, or unnecessary details that might confuse or mislead readers. Although your thesis statement cannot include every idea that your essay will develop, it may list your most important points; in any case, it should be specific enough to give readers a good idea of how you will develop your essay.

 CLOSE-UP **DEFINING AN EFFECTIVE THESIS STATEMENT**

Thesis statements are weakened by vague phrases such as *centers on, deals with, involves, revolves around, has to be, has a lot to do with,* and *is primarily concerned with.*

INEFFECTIVE THESIS STATEMENT: The real problem in our schools does not *revolve around* the absence of nationwide goals and standards; the problem *is primarily concerned with* the absence of resources with which to implement them.

EFFECTIVE THESIS STATEMENT: The real problem in our schools *is* not the absence of nationwide goals and standards; the problem *is* the absence of resources with which to implement them.

Finally, an effective thesis statement suggests your essay's direction, emphasis, and scope. Your thesis statement should not make promises that your essay will not fulfill. Ideally, it should help you visualize the most effective way to arrange your material and connect your thesis with your support, suggesting how your ideas are related, in what order your major points should be introduced, and where you should place your emphasis, as the following thesis statement does.

Widely ridiculed as escape reading, romance novels are becoming increasingly important as a proving ground for many never-before-published writers and, more significantly, as a showcase for strong heroines.

This thesis statement tells readers that the essay to follow will focus on two major new roles of the romance novel: providing markets for new writers and (more important) presenting strong female characters; it also suggests that the role of the romance novel as escapist fiction will be treated briefly. This effective thesis statement, as the diagram below shows, even suggests the order in which the various ideas will be discussed.

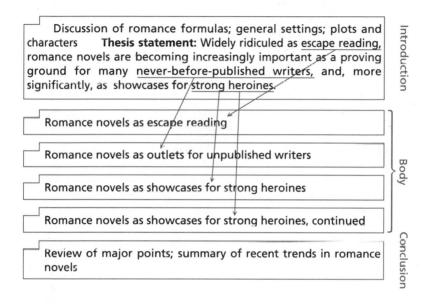

Discussion of romance formulas; general settings; plots and characters **Thesis statement:** Widely ridiculed as <u>escape reading</u>, romance novels are becoming increasingly important as a proving ground for many <u>never-before-published writers</u>, and, more significantly, as showcases for <u>strong heroines</u>.

Introduction

Romance novels as escape reading

Romance novels as outlets for unpublished writers

Romance novels as showcases for strong heroines

Romance novels as showcases for strong heroines, continued

Body

Review of major points; summary of recent trends in romance novels

Conclusion

CLOSE-UP DEFINING AN EFFECTIVE THESIS STATEMENT

One of the simplest kinds of thesis statements to write is also one of the dullest and most mechanical: the "three points" (or "four reasons" or "five examples") thesis. This thesis statement enumerates each of the specific points to be discussed ("Hot air ballooning is an exciting sport for three reasons: x, y, and z"), and the paper that follows goes on to cover each of these points, using the same tired language: "The first reason hot air ballooning is so exciting is x"; "Another reason is y"; "The most important reason is z." This kind of formulaic thesis statement can be a very useful strategy for a rough draft, but as you revise, you should try to substitute fresher, more interesting, and more original language.

✔ CHECKLIST: DEFINING AN EFFECTIVE THESIS STATEMENT

✔ Does your thesis statement clearly communicate your essay's main idea? Does it suggest the approach you will take toward your material? Does it reflect your essay's purpose?

✔ Is your thesis statement more than a subject, a statement of fact, or an announcement of your intent?

✔ Is your thesis statement carefully worded?

✔ Does your thesis statement suggest your essay's direction, emphasis, and scope?

---

(3) Stating Your Thesis

As a beginning writer, you should state your thesis early in your paper. This placement will immediately signal the focus of your discussion to your readers, and it will also serve as a reminder to you of your essay's direction, emphasis, and scope. Your thesis statement can appear anywhere in your essay, however, as long as it makes your essay's main idea clear to your readers. Where you state your thesis largely depends on the effect you wish your essay to have on a particular audience. In an **argumentative essay**, for example, you may have to lead your readers gradually to your controversial thesis instead of stating it at the outset. To do otherwise might alienate your audience. In **writing a research paper**, you may have to present several paragraphs of background material before your audience is able to understand your thesis.

See 9b

See Ch. 44

 STATING YOUR THESIS

Sometimes a thesis is not stated directly but rather is *implied* through the selection and arrangement of ideas. Like an explicit thesis, an implied thesis must convey the essay's main idea to readers. Professional writers often use this technique.

---

(4) Revising Your Thesis Statement

Occasionally—especially if you know a lot about your topic—you may begin writing with a thesis in mind. Most often, however, your thesis evolves out of the reading, questioning, and grouping of ideas that you do during the writing process.

The thesis statement that you develop as you plan your essay is only tentative. It gives you sufficient focus to guide you through your first draft, but you should expect to modify it in subsequent drafts. As you write and rewrite, you often think of new ideas and see new connections; as a result, you may change your essay's direction, emphasis, and scope several times, and if you do so, you must reword your thesis statement as well. Notice how the following thesis statements changed as the writers moved through successive drafts of their essays.

REVISING YOUR THESIS STATEMENT

Tentative Thesis Statement (rough draft)	Revised Thesis Statement (final draft)
Professional sports can easily be corrupted by organized crime.	Although proponents of legalized sports betting argue that organized crime cannot make inroads into professional sports, the way in which underworld figures compromised the 1919 World Series suggests the opposite.
Laboratory courses provide valuable educational experiences.	By providing students with the actual experience of doing scientific work, laboratory courses encourage precise thinking, careful observation, and creativity.
It is difficult to understand Henry James's short novel *The Turn of the Screw* without examining the personality of the governess.	A careful reading of Henry James's *The Turn of the Screw* suggests that the governess is an unreliable narrator, incapable of distinguishing appearance from reality.

---

(5) Using a Thesis Statement to Shape Your Essay

The wording of your thesis statement often suggests not only a possible order and emphasis for your essay's ideas, but also a specific

See
Ch. 5
pattern of development—narration, description, exemplification, process, cause and effect, comparison and contrast, division and classification, or definition. These familiar patterns may also shape individual paragraphs of your essay.

Thesis Statement	*Pattern of Development*
As the months went by and I grew more and more involved with the developmentally delayed children at the Learning Center, I came to see how important it is to treat every child as an individual.	Narration
Looking around the room where I had spent my childhood, I realized that every object I saw told me I was now an adult.	Description
The risk-taking behavior that characterizes the 1990s can be illustrated by the increasing interest and involvement in such high-risk sports as mountain biking, ice climbing, sky diving, and bungee jumping.	Exemplification
Armed forces basic training programs take recruits through a series of tasks designed to build camaraderie as well as skills and confidence.	Process
The exceptionally high birthrate of the post-World War II years had many significant social and economic consequences.	Cause and Effect
Although people who live in cities and people who live in small towns have some obvious basic similarities, their views	Comparison and Contrast

on issues like crime, waste disposal, farm subsidies, and educational vouchers tend to be
very different.

The section of the proposal   Division and Classification
that recommends establishing
satellite health centers is quite
promising; unfortunately, however, the sections that call for
the creation of alternative educational programs, job training, and low-income housing
are seriously flawed.

Until quite recently, most peo-   Definition
ple assumed that rape was an
act perpetrated by a stranger,
but today's wider definition encompasses acquaintance rape
as well.

EXERCISE 2

Analyze the following items and explain why none of them qualifies as
an effective thesis statement. How could each be improved?

1. In this essay, I will examine the environmental effects of residential and
   commercial development on the coastal regions of the United States.
2. Residential and commercial development in the coastal regions of
   the United States
3. How to avoid coastal overdevelopment
4. Coastal Development: Pro and Con
5. Residential and commercial development of America's coastal regions benefits some people, but it has some disadvantages.
6. The environmentalists' position on coastal development
7. More and more coastal regions in the United States are being
   overdeveloped.
8. Residential and commercial development guidelines need to be developed for coastal regions of the United States.
9. Coastal development is causing beach erosion.
10. At one time I enjoyed walking on the beach, but commercial and
    residential development has ruined the experience for me.

EXERCISE 3

For three of the following topics, formulate a clearly worded thesis statement.

1. A literary work that has influenced your thinking
2. Cheating in college
3. The validity of SAT scores as the basis for college admissions
4. Should women in the military serve in combat?
5. Private vs. public education
6. Should college health clinics provide birth control services?
7. Is governmental censorship of art ever justified?
8. The role of the individual in saving the earth
9. The portrayal of an ethnic group in film or television
10. Should smoking be banned from all public places?

EXERCISE 4

Read the following list of statements from "The Magnetic Tube" by John Leland. Then develop a thesis that will tie all the information together. Make sure your thesis statement is well constructed and conforms to the requirements outlined in **2b.**

1. "By the age of 2, American kids spend an average of 27 hours per week in front of the set."
2. "In nearly 40 years of study, researchers have found a correlation between children's TV habits and their levels of creativity, aggressiveness, and social skills."
3. "Because toddlers don't understand that a TV show is a production that happens elsewhere, they are often disoriented by its form: the changes of angle, cuts in time, the visual effects like zooming in and out."
4. "Even at age 2, says Joan Cantor, a professor of communication arts at the University of Wisconsin, children think things in the box could spill out. If there are monsters in the box, or scary animals, young children are not quite sure the monsters can't come out and get them."
5. "Jerome Singer, professor of psychology and child study at Yale, contends that TV preempts kids from doing what they ought to be doing—learning to create mini-worlds that they can control. Kids who can do this are more cooperative, more likely to become leaders, less likely to be overly aggressive."
6. "Toddlers who watch a lot of TV are also less likely to engage in fantasy play."
7. "The Academy of Pediatrics advises that parents should limit [children's] TV time to one to two hours a day."

EXERCISE 5

Review the topic tree you made in Exercise 1. Use it to help you to develop a thesis for an essay on the topic you chose in Exercise 3 in Chapter 1.

2c Preparing an Informal Outline

Once you have a thesis statement, you may want to prepare an informal outline. An **informal outline** is a blueprint for an essay, a plan that gives you more detailed, specific guidance than a thesis statement does. You need not always prepare such an outline; a short essay on a topic with which you are very familiar may require nothing beyond a thesis statement and a list of major divisions or main supporting points. More often, however, you will find that you need the additional help of an informal outline. With an informal outline, you can arrange your essay's main points and supporting ideas and details in an informal but orderly way to guide you as you write. (A sample informal outline appears on pages 59–60.)

✔ CHECKLIST: PREPARING AN INFORMAL OUTLINE

- ✔ Copy down the headings from your topic tree.
- ✔ Arrange the headings and the details in each category in the order in which you plan to discuss them.
- ✔ Expand the outline with additional material from your notes, adding any new points that come to mind.

For a short paper, an informal outline is usually sufficient. Sometimes, however—particularly when you are writing a long or complex essay—you will need to construct a **formal outline**.

See 3c3

EXERCISE 6

Read the following newspaper editorial. Then, prepare an informal outline that includes all the main ideas and supporting points.

The college football season is starting with a familiar flurry of resignations and probations.

At the University of Washington, Don James resigned as head coach after failing to notice that his quarterback owned three cars.

Of course, the athletic staff was not part of the money-lending scheme that ensnared the player and brought down the coach. It was one of those pesky "boosters" who always seem handy when blame is assigned.

So among big-time teams, Washington joined Auburn University on two-year probation. The NCAA is expected to add Texas A&M to the list as footballs are being teed up for the television cameras that provide the money that seduces universities into being willing co-conspirators in exploiting young athletes.

College football *is* a great show, and at its best, it still provides some of the emotion and spectacle missing in the cogwheel perfection of pro football. But big-time college football has a corruption at its center that can and must be cured. Why the nation's college presidents and boards of trustees, acting through the NCAA, have not taken the obvious steps is a mystery.

One such step is to limit participation rights from teams that fail to honor Principle VII of the Knight Foundation Commission on Intercollegiate Athletics. That principle says that athletes will graduate in the same proportion as nonathletes. The national graduation rate is around 50 percent. Five of the top twenty teams in *The Times* preseason poll—including reigning national champion Alabama—have graduation rates below 40 percent.

Starting immediately, the NCAA should set up standards so that private and public schools can be measured fairly against one another and then begin to punish schools that fail to graduate a proportionate number of athletes on time.

It should then do something about the money problem. Athletes make millions for their schools and receive piddling amounts for tuition and board. Their poverty in comparison to their market value as college players and potential earning power as pros make corruption inevitable.

A sensible first step is to lift student athletes out of poverty by giving them realistic scholarships based on the *entire* cost of keeping a student in school: tuition, housing, food, plus the allowances a parent would provide for clothes, transportation, social activities, and spending money.

With tuition alone at many NCAA schools running from $10,000 to $20,000, many middle-income families spend a total of $30,000 or more a year in after-tax dollars. And it is the total cost of keeping a student in comfortable style that an athletic scholarship should cover. Presently NCAA scholarships cover only tuition, room and board, books, and up to $2,400 in cash.

Nothing can bring back the era of pure amateurism in college football. But simple reforms could make it financially clean and academically respectable as well as entertaining.

EXERCISE 7

Prepare an informal outline for the paper you have been developing in Chapters 1 and 2.

CHAPTER 3

WRITING AND REVISING

3a Writing a Rough Draft

(1) Understanding Drafting

As its name implies, a rough draft is far from perfect; in fact, it usually includes false starts, irrelevant information, and seemingly unrelated details. At this stage, though, the absence of focus and order is not a problem. You write your rough draft simply to get your ideas down on paper so that you can react to them.

You will probably rewrite your essay several times, and you should expect to add or delete words, to reword sentences, to rethink ideas, and to reorder paragraphs. You should also expect to discover some new ideas—or even to take an unexpected detour. If this happens, don't panic. Your new direction may lead you to a more interesting essay than the one you have been planning.

When you write a rough draft, concentrate on the body of your essay, and don't waste time mapping out your introduction and conclusion. The effort to write appropriate and effective opening and closing paragraphs will slow you down; besides, these paragraphs are likely to change substantially in subsequent drafts. For now, focus on drafting the support paragraphs of your essay. (A sample rough draft appears on pages 60–62.)

(2) Developing Drafting Strategies

You will be revising much of what you write, and taking a practical and systematic approach to your first draft will greatly simplify the revision process.

STRATEGIES FOR WRITING A ROUGH DRAFT

- **Prepare your work area.** Once you begin to write, you should not have to stop because you need a sharp pencil, better lighting, important notes, or anything else.
- **Fight writer's block. Writer's block**—an inability to start (or continue) writing—is usually caused by fear that you will not write well or that you have nothing to say. If you really don't feel ready to write, take a short break. This may give your ideas time to incubate, which, in turn, may release new ideas. If you decide that you really don't have enough material to get you started, return to one of the strategies for **finding something to say**.
- **Get your ideas down on paper as quickly as you can.** Don't worry about sentence structure, about spelling and punctuation, or about finding exactly the right word—just write. Writing quickly helps you uncover new ideas and new connections between ideas. You may find that following an informal outline enables you to move smoothly from one point to the next, but if you find this structure too inhibiting or confining, go ahead and write without consulting your outline.
- **Take regular breaks as you write.** Try writing one section of your essay at a time. When you have completed a section—for example, one paragraph—take a break. Your mind may continue to focus on your assignment while you do other things. When you return to your essay, writing may be easier.
- **Leave yourself enough time to revise.** All writing benefits from revision, so be sure you have time to reconsider your work and to write as many drafts as you need.

See
1c2

You should always approach your rough draft (as well as all subsequent drafts before the one you hand in for a grade) as something you know you will revise. This means taking steps to make your draft physically receptive to revision.

- First, triple-space. (If you handwrite your draft, write on every other line.) This makes errors more obvious and also gives you plenty of room to add new material or to try out new versions of sentences.
- Second, if you do a handwritten draft, be sure you write on only one side of a sheet of paper so you can reread your pages side by side. Writing on only one side also permits you to cut and paste without destroying material on the other side of the page. This strategy gives

you the flexibility to keep reorganizing the sections or paragraphs of your paper until you find their most effective arrangement.

- Finally, develop a system of symbols, each designating a different type of revision. For instance, you can circle individual words or box longer groups of words (or even entire paragraphs) that you want to relocate. You can use an arrow to indicate the new location, or you can use asterisks or matching numbers or letters to indicate how you want to rearrange ideas. When you want to add words, use a caret like this.

 DRAFTING YOUR ESSAY

Because most people find it more difficult to see errors on the computer screen than on hard copy, it is a good idea to print out every draft so that you can revise on paper rather than on the screen, making revisions by hand on your printed draft and then returning to the computer to type in these revisions. If you prefer to revise directly on the computer screen, be careful not to delete any material that you may need later; instead, move this material to the end of your document so that you can assess its relevance later on. As you type your draft, get into the habit of including notes to yourself in parentheses or brackets, perhaps highlighting your comments and questions by using boldface or italic type.

 EXERCISE 1

Referring to the notes you generated during prewriting, write a rough draft of the essay you began planning in Chapter 1.

3b   Revising Your Drafts

(1)   Understanding Revision

Revision is a process you engage in from the moment you begin to discover ideas for your essay. As you work you are constantly rethinking your ideas and reconsidering their relevance, their relative importance, their logical and sequential relationships, and the patterns in which you arrange them. Revision is a creative part of the writing process, and everyone does it somewhat differently. You will have to experiment to find the techniques that work best for you.

Inexperienced writers sometimes believe that their first drafts should be perfect. Even when they do revise, they often do little more than refine word choices, correct grammatical or mechanical errors, or reprint their papers to make them neater. Experienced writers, however, expect to revise, and they expect revision to involve a major reworking of their papers, so they are willing to rethink a thesis statement or even to completely rewrite and rearrange an essay.

(2) Moving from Rough to Final Draft

Often, you write your rough draft without thinking much about your audience. When you revise, however, you should begin to make the kinds of changes that your readers need in order to understand and appreciate your ideas. Thus, revision should reflect not only your private criticism of your first draft but also your anticipation of your readers' needs and reactions.

✔ CHECKLIST: REVISING TO ACCOMMODATE YOUR READERS

✔ **Present one idea at a time and summarize when necessary.** When you overload your paper with more information than readers can take in, you lose their attention. Readers should not have to backtrack constantly to understand your message.

✔ **Organize your ideas clearly.** Readers expect your essay to do what your thesis statement says it will do, with major points introduced in a logical order and supported in your body paragraphs.

✔ **Provide clear signals to establish coherence.** Repeating key points, constructing clear topic sentences, using transitional words and phrases to link ideas logically, and providing verbal cues that indicate the precise relationships among ideas all help provide continuity and coherence.

As you revise successive drafts of your essay, you should shift your focus from larger elements, such as overall structure and content, to increasingly smaller elements. (You can see the progression of the revision process through several drafts in the work of the student writer in **4c**.)

Revising Your Rough Draft After you finish your rough draft, set it aside for a day if you can. When you return to it, you will probably notice problems that need attention, but keep in mind that you cannot solve every problem at once. It makes more sense to focus on only a few areas at a time, reworking your essay in several drafts. As you review this first draft, evaluate the thesis-and-support structure of your essay and your paper's general organization. Once you feel satisfied that your thesis statement says what you want it to say and that your essay's content supports this thesis and is logically arranged, you can turn your attention to other matters.

As you reread your draft, you may want to consult the questions on the "Revising the Whole Essay" checklist on page 48. If you have the benefit of a collaborative revision session or of a conference with your instructor, consider your readers' comments carefully, focusing for now on their suggestions about content, organization, and thesis and support.

Writing Additional Drafts   After you have read over your rough draft several times, marking it up with notes and outlining plans for revision, you are ready to write a second draft.

As you assess this draft, as well as any drafts that follow, you will narrow your focus to your essay's individual paragraphs, sentences, and words; if you like, you can use the "Revising Paragraphs," "Revising Sentence Style," and "Revising Word Choice" checklists on pages 48–50 to guide your revision.

 CLOSE-UP **FINDING A VOICE**

When we speak, each of us has a distinctive voice that others can recognize. As writers, we also try to achieve a unique voice, one that we can adjust depending on our audience and purpose and on our relationship to our subject.

As you move from rough to final draft, you should try to find a voice for your ideas. The first step toward finding your own voice is to state your own opinions and draw your own conclusions, not just echo ideas you have heard from friends or on talk radio. After all, you want your essay to sound as if it was written by you, not by some anonymous stranger. Moreover, stating your own ideas helps you to assume a voice of authority, and this sense of confidence and control goes a long way toward determining how readers respond to you.

Your voice emerges through your style (your choice of words and your way of constructing sentences) and through your tone, which reveals your attitude toward your subject. Using your own voice doesn't mean writing an essay full of colloquialisms and slang; what it does mean is using words you feel comfortable using, not those you think you should use. (This also means using a thesaurus only as a last resort.)

When you finish each draft of your essay, read it aloud. Does it sound natural? Does it sound like you? If not, keep revising.

Preparing a Final Draft   Once you have revised your drafts to your satisfaction, two final steps remain: editing and proofreading your paper.

Editing   When you **edit,** you concentrate on grammar and spelling, punctuation and mechanics. You will have done some of this work as you revised previous drafts of your paper, but now your *focus* is on editing. Approach your work critically, reading each sentence carefully. As you proceed, consult the items on the editing checklist on pages 50–51. Keep your preliminary notes and drafts and reference books (such as this handbook and a current dictionary) nearby as you edit.

 EDITING AND PROOFREADING

- As you edit and proofread, try looking at only a small portion of text at a time. If your software allows you to split the screen and create another window, create one so small that you can see only one or two lines of text. If you also use this technique, you can dramatically reduce the number of surface-level errors in your paper.

- Use the *search* or *find* command to look for words or phrases in usage errors to which your instructor has alerted you, or to look for errors you commonly make—for instance, confusing *it's* with *its*, *lay* with *lie*, *effect* with *affect*, *their* with *there*, or *too* with *to*. You can also locate inadvertent use of **sexist language** by searching for words like *he, his, him,* or *man.*

See 20f2

- Learn how to use the spell checker. Remember that it does not find "mistakes"; it simply identifies character strings it does not recognize. Thus, a spell checker will not recognize *there* in "They forgot there books on the table" as incorrect, nor will it spot the typographical error in "Whatever he wanted to do, he dad." You still must proofread your papers carefully.

- Keep in mind that neatness does not equal correctness. The computer's ability to produce neat-looking text can disguise flaws that might otherwise be readily apparent. Take special care to ensure that spelling and typographical errors do not slip by.

- Finally, remember that computer checks are only the beginning of the editing process. They can identify problem areas and offer suggestions, but the final editing decisions must be yours.

Proofreading After you have completed your editing, print a final draft. Now you must proofread, rereading every word carefully to make sure neither you nor your computer missed any errors. You must also make sure the final typed copy of your paper conforms to your instructor's format requirements.

 CHOOSING A TITLE

Most writers save choosing a title for last—until they see the final draft of their essay. As you try to decide on a title for your essay, keep the following guidelines in mind.

- A title should be descriptive, giving an accurate sense of your essay's focus. A key word or phrase central to your paper can make an especially effective title.

- A title's wording can echo the wording of your assignment, reminding you (and your instructor) that you have not lost sight of your focus.

- Ideally, a title should arouse interest, perhaps by using a provocative question or an apt quotation (or, if appropriate, by introducing a note of controversy).

Assignment: Write about a problem faced on college campuses today.

Topic: Free speech on campus

Possible titles:

- Free Speech: A Problem for Today's Colleges (descriptive; echoes wording of assignment and includes key words of essay)

- How Free Should Free Speech on Campus Be? (provocative question)

- The Right to "Shout 'Fire' in a Crowded Theater" (quotation)

- Hate Speech: A Dangerous Abuse of Free Speech on Campus (controversial position)

3c Using Revision Strategies

As you have seen, revising your drafts can be a complicated process. Learning how to use certain specific revision strategies, described on the pages that follow and illustrated in Chapter 4, can make revision a manageable, and even rewarding, process.

(1) Doing Collaborative Revision

Instead of trying to imagine an audience for your paper, you can engage in **collaborative revision** by addressing a real audience, asking friends, classmates, or family members to read your draft and comment on it (with your instructor's permission, of course). Their responses should tell you whether or not your essay has the effect you intended— and perhaps why it succeeds or fails. Collaborative revision can also be more formal. Your instructor may conduct the class as a workshop, assigning students to work in groups to critique other students' essays or asking students to exchange essays and write evaluations, perhaps answering questions such as the ones in the checklist below.

In any case, approach a fellow student's draft responsibly, and take the analysis of your own essay seriously. Collaborative revision, like all collaborative work, is a dialogue. You should always ask yourself what you can contribute—and what advice someone else can offer you.

✔ CHECKLIST: DOING COLLABORATIVE REVISION

✔ What is the essay about? Does the topic fulfill the requirements of the assignment?

✔ What is the main point of the essay? Is the thesis stated? If so, is it clearly worded? If not, how can the wording be improved?

✔ Is the essay arranged logically? Do the body paragraphs appear in an appropriate order?

✔ What ideas support the thesis? Does each body paragraph develop one of these ideas?

✔ Is any necessary information missing? Identify any areas that seem to need further development. Is any information irrelevant? If so, suggest possible deletions.

✔ Can you think of any ideas or examples from your own reading, experience, or observations that would strengthen the writer's essay?

continued on the following page

continued from the previous page

✔ Can you follow the writer's ideas? If not, would clearer connections between sentences or paragraphs be helpful? If so, where are such connections needed?

✔ Is the introductory paragraph interesting to you? Would another opening strategy be more effective?

✔ Does the conclusion leave you with a sense of completion? Would another concluding strategy be more effective?

✔ Is anything unclear or confusing?

✔ What is the essay's greatest strength?

✔ What is the essay's greatest weakness?

(2) Using Instructors' Comments

Instructors' comments—in correction symbols, in marginal comments, or in conferences—can also help you revise.

Correction Symbols Your instructor may indicate concerns about style, grammar, mechanics, or punctuation by using correction symbols listed on the inside back cover of this book. Instead of correcting a problem, the instructor will simply identify it and supply the number of the section in this handbook that deals with the error. After reading the appropriate section in the handbook, you should be able to make the necessary corrections on your own. For example, the symbol and number beside the following sentence referred a student to 20f2, the section in the handbook that discusses sexist usage.

Equal access to jobs is a desirable goal for all mankind. *Sexist Usage—see 20f2*

After reading section **20f2,** the student made the following change.

Equal access to jobs is a desirable goal for everyone.

(For examples of an instructor's use of correction symbols on a student paper, see **4c3.**)

Marginal Comments Instructors frequently make marginal comments on your essays to suggest changes in content or structure. Such comments may ask you to add supporting information or to arrange paragraphs differently within the essay, or they may recommend stylistic changes, such as more varied sentences. Marginal comments may also question your logic, suggest a more explicit thesis statement, ask for clearer transitions, or propose a new direction for a discussion. In some cases, you can consider these comments to be suggestions rather than corrections. You may decide to incorporate these ideas into a revised draft of your essay, and then again, you may not. In all instances, however, you should consider your instructor's comments seriously. After all, they are the product of years of teaching experience—and they represent a level of scrutiny that a beginning writer is seldom able to bring to his or her own draft. (A student draft with marginal comments appears in **4c3.**)

Conferences Many instructors require or encourage one-on-one conferences, and you should certainly take advantage of a conference if you can. (Some instructors also use **E-mail** to answer questions and offer feedback at various points in the writing process.) Your conference time should be tailored to your individual needs and to your paper's particular problems. During a conference, you can respond to your instructor's questions and ask for clarification of marginal comments. Sometimes your instructor will help you to revise a thesis statement so it says what you want it to say and help you decide how to support it effectively. If a certain section of your paper is a problem, use your conference time to focus on it, perhaps asking for help in sharpening an idea or choosing a more accurate word.

See
40b1

✔ CHECKLIST: PREPARING FOR A CONFERENCE

- ✔ **Make an appointment.** Make an appointment with your instructor before coming to his or her office, and arrive on time. Don't barge in and expect your instructor to drop everything to help you. (If you find you are unable to keep your appointment, call to reschedule.)
- ✔ **Read your paper carefully.** Before coming to the conference, review your notes and drafts, and go over all your instructor's comments and suggestions. Look up any correction symbols, and read the sections of the handbook to which each refers you. Then, make all the changes you can on your draft. (If you are coming to a conference to discuss ideas for a paper in progress, be sure your instructor is aware of this fact.)
- ✔ **Prepare a list of questions.** Don't expect your instructor to anticipate your questions; prepare a list in advance.
- ✔ **Bring your draft.** Come to the conference with a draft of your paper. Without it, both you and your instructor can talk only in generalities. If you have several drafts, you may want to bring them all, but be sure you bring the draft that has the instructor's comments on it.

continued on the following page

continued from the previous page

✔ **Take notes.** As you discuss your paper, write down any suggestions that you think will be helpful. Chances are that if you don't write down important suggestions at the time you hear them, you'll probably have forgotten them by the time you revise.

✔ **Participate actively.** A successful conference is an open exchange of ideas between you and your instructor. This means that you should be prepared to discuss your draft. Your instructor is there to help you clarify your thoughts and to answer your questions, but he or she doesn't expect to deliver a monologue.

(3) Making a Formal Outline

Making a formal outline can help you to plan and shape a draft before you write it, but an outline can also guide you as you check the structure of a draft that you have already completed. In fact, outlining is an extremely useful revision strategy.

Outlining can be helpful early in the revision process, when you are reworking the larger structural elements of your essay, or later on, when you are checking the logic of a completed draft. For example, a formal outline reveals at once whether points are irrelevant or poorly placed—or, worse, missing. It also reveals the hierarchy of your ideas—which points are dominant and which are subordinate.

A **formal outline** uses a system of letters and numbers to indicate the order of your ideas and the relationship of main ideas to supporting details. A formal outline is more polished and more detailed than an **informal outline.** It is more strictly parallel and more precise, pays more attention to form, and presents points in the exact order in which you plan to present them in your draft.

A formal outline may be a **topic outline,** in which each entry is a single word or a short phrase, or a **sentence outline,** in which each entry is a complete sentence. Each of these formats has advantages and disadvantages. A sentence outline is a more fully developed guide for your paper: you have a head start on your paper when you are able to use the sentences of your outline in your draft. Because it is so polished and complete, however, a sentence outline is more difficult and time consuming to construct, especially at an early stage of the writing process.

Formal outlines conform to specific conventions of structure, content, and style. If you follow the conventions of outlining carefully, your formal outline can help you to write a paper that covers all relevant ideas in an effective order, with appropriate emphasis, within a logical system of subordination.

See
2c

Write 3c

THE CONVENTIONS OF OUTLINING

Structure

- Outline format should be followed strictly.

    I. First major point of your paper
       A. First subpoint
       B. Next subpoint
          1. First supporting example
          2. Next supporting example
             a. First specific detail
             b. Next specific detail
    II. Second major point

- Headings should not overlap.
- No heading should have a single subheading. (A category cannot be subdivided into one part.)
- Each entry should be preceded by an appropriate letter or number, followed by a period.
- The first word of each entry should be capitalized.

Content

- Outline should include the paper's thesis statement.
- Outline should cover only the body of the essay, not the introductory or concluding paragraphs.
- Headings should be concise and specific.
- Headings should be descriptive, clearly related to the topic to which they refer.

Style

- Headings of the same rank should be grammatically parallel.
- Sentence outlines should use complete sentences, with all sentences in the same tense.
- In a sentence outline, each entry should end with a period.
- Topic outlines should use words or short phrases, with all headings of the same rank using the same parts of speech.
- In a topic outline, entries should not end with periods.

The pages that follow presents side-by-side topic and sentence outlines of this chapter. (An additional topic outline appears on pages 70–71; an additional sentence outline appears on pages 72–73.)

Topic Outline of Chapter 3—Writing and Revising

I.   Writing a rough draft
    A. Understanding drafting
    B. Developing drafting strategies
II. Revising your drafts
    A. Understanding revision
    B. Moving from first to final draft
        1. Revising your rough draft
        2. Revising additional drafts
        3. Preparing a final draft
            a. Editing
            b. Proofreading
III. Using revision strategies
    A. Doing collaborative revision
    B. Using instructor comments
        1. Using correction symbols
        2. Using marginal comments
        3. Using conferences
    C. Making a formal outline
    D. Using checklists

Sentence Outline of Chapter 3—Writing and Revising

I. Before you revise, you must write a rough draft.
    A. In a rough draft, your purpose is to get ideas down on paper.
    B. As you draft, take a practical and systematic approach to the process.
II. Once you have completed your first draft, you can begin to revise.
    A. Understand that revision is a natural part of the writing process.
    B. As you move from first to final draft, you narrow your focus.
        1. When you reread your rough draft, you focus on content and organization.
        2. When you revise additional drafts, you focus on paragraphs, sentences, and words.
        3. When you prepare your final draft, you focus on editing and proofreading.
            a. When you edit, you scrutinize grammar, punctuation, mechanics, and spelling.
            b. When you proofread, you check for typographical errors.
III. Certain specific strategies can aid the revision process.
    A. Collaborative revision is one useful revision strategy.
    B. Instructor comments can also guide your revision.
        1. Instructors often use correction symbols to refer you to specific sections of your handbook.
        2. Instructors also write marginal comments on your essays.
        3. Finally, instructors offer suggestions in conferences.
    C. A formal outline is another helpful revision strategy.
    D. Checklists can also help you to revise.

(4) Using Checklists

A **revision checklist**—one that your instructor prepares or one that you develop yourself—enables you to examine your writing systematically by helping you to focus on revising one element at a time. Depending on the problems you have and the time you have to deal with them, you can survey your paper using all the questions on a checklist or only some of them.

The four checklists that follow are keyed to sections of this text. They parallel the normal revision process, moving in stages from the most global to the most specific concerns. As your understanding of the writing process increases and you become better able to assess the strengths and weaknesses of your writing, you may want to add items to (or delete items from) one or more of the checklists. You can also use your instructors' comments to tailor these checklists to your own needs.

✔ CHECKLIST: REVISING THE WHOLE ESSAY

- ✔ Is your tone consistent with your purpose? **(See 1b3.)**
- ✔ Have you maintained an appropriate distance from your readers? **(See 1b3.)**
- ✔ Are thesis and support logically related, with each body paragraph supporting your thesis statement? **(See 2b1.)**
- ✔ Is your thesis statement clearly and specifically worded? **(See 2b2.)**
- ✔ Have you discussed everything promised in your thesis statement? **(See 2b2.)**
- ✔ Have you included any irrelevant points? **(See 2b2.)**
- ✔ Have you presented your ideas in a logical sequence? Can you think of a different arrangement that might be more appropriate for your purpose? **(See 2b5.)**
- ✔ Does your essay have a unique, genuine, and consistent voice? **(See 3b2.)**
- ✔ Do clear transitions between paragraphs allow your readers to follow your essay's structure? **(See 6c6.)**
- ✔ Does your essay follow a particular pattern of development? **(See Ch. 5.)**

✔ CHECKLIST: REVISING PARAGRAPHS

- ✔ Does each body paragraph have one main idea? **(See 6b.)**
- ✔ Are topic sentences clearly worded and logically related to your thesis? **(See 6c1.)**

continued on the following page

continued from the previous page

✔ Are your body paragraphs adequately developed? **(See 6e.)**
✔ Does your introductory paragraph arouse reader interest and prepare readers for what is to come? **(See 6f2.)**
✔ Does each body paragraph have a clear organizing principle? **(See 6c1.)**
✔ Are the relationships of sentences within paragraphs clear? **(See 6c2–5.)**
✔ Are your paragraphs arranged according to familiar patterns of development? **(See 6e.)**
✔ Does your concluding paragraph sum up your main points? **(See 6f3.)**
✔ Have you provided transitional paragraphs where necessary? **(See 6f1.)**

✔ CHECKLIST: REVISING SENTENCE STYLE

✔ Have you strengthened sentences with repetition, balance, and parallelism? **(See 12c–d, 18a.)**
✔ Have you avoided overloading sentences with too many clauses? **(See 13c.)**
✔ Have you used correct sentence structure? **(See Chs. 15 and 16.)**
✔ Have you placed modifiers clearly and logically? **(See Ch. 17.)**
✔ Have you avoided potentially confusing shifts in tense, voice, mood, person, or number? **(See 19a–d.)**
✔ Are your sentences constructed logically? **(See 19f–h.)**
✔ Have you used emphatic word order? **(See 12a.)**
✔ Have you used sentence structure to signal the relative importance of clauses in a sentence and their logical relationship to one another? **(See 12b.)**
✔ Have you eliminated nonessential words and needless repetition? **(See 13a–b.)**
✔ Have you varied your sentence structure? **(See Ch. 14.)**
✔ Have you combined sentences where ideas are closely related? **(See 14b.)**

✔ CHECKLIST: REVISING WORD CHOICE

✔ Is your level of diction appropriate for your audience and your purpose? **(See 20a–b.)**

continued on the following page

continued from the previous page

✔ Have you selected words that accurately reflect your intentions? **(See 20b1.)**

✔ Have you chosen words that are specific, concrete, and unambiguous? **(See 20b3–4.)**

✔ Have you enriched your writing with figurative language? **(See 20d.)**

✔ Have you eliminated jargon, neologisms, pretentious diction, clichés, ineffective figures of speech, and offensive language from your writing? **(See 20c, 20e–f.)**

✔ CHECKLIST: EDITING FOR GRAMMAR, PUNCTUATION, MECHANICS, AND SPELLING

GRAMMAR

✔ Have you used the appropriate case for each pronoun? **(See 24a–b.)**

✔ Are pronoun references clear and unambiguous? **(See 24c.)**

✔ Are verb forms correct? **(See 25a.)**

✔ Are tense, mood, and voice of verbs logical and appropriate? **(See 25b–k.)**

✔ Do subjects and verbs agree? **(See 26a.)**

✔ Do pronouns and antecedents agree? **(See 26b.)**

✔ Are adjectives and adverbs used correctly? **(See 27a–e.)**

PUNCTUATION

✔ Is end punctuation used correctly? **(See 28a–c.)**

✔ Are commas used correctly? **(See Ch. 29.)**

✔ Are semicolons used correctly? **(See Ch. 30.)**

✔ Are apostrophes used correctly? **(See Ch. 31.)**

✔ Are quotation marks used where they are required? **(See Ch. 32a–f.)**

✔ Are quotation marks used correctly with other punctuation marks? **(See 32e.)**

✔ Are other punctuation marks—colons, dashes, parentheses, brackets, slashes, and ellipses—used correctly? **(See Ch. 33.)**

MECHANICS

✔ Is capitalization consistent with standard English usage? **(See Ch. 34.)**

continued on the following page

continued from the previous page

✔ Are italics used correctly? **(See Ch. 35.)**

✔ Are hyphens used where required and placed correctly within and between words? **(See Ch. 36.)**

✔ Are abbreviations used where convention calls for their use? **(See Ch. 37.)**

✔ Are numerals and spelled-out numbers used appropriately? **(See Ch. 38.)**

SPELLING

✔ Are all words spelled correctly? (Run a spell check or check a dictionary if necessary.)

EXERCISE 2

Revise your rough draft, using one or more of the strategies for revision discussed in **3c**. At this point, it is probably most sensible to focus on the general concept of thesis and support and on content and arrangement of ideas. Try not to worry now about narrower stylistic issues, such as sentence variety and word choice.

EXERCISE 3

Review the second draft of your paper, this time paying attention not only to the way your thesis is worded and supported but also to paragraphing, topic sentences, and transitions, and to the way you structure your sentences and select your words. If possible, ask a friend to read your draft and to respond to the collaborative revision questions in **3c1**. Then revise your draft, incorporating any suggestions you find helpful.

EXERCISE 4

Using the revision checklists in **3c4** as a guide, create a customized checklist—one that reflects the specific concerns that you need to consider when you revise an essay. Then revise your essay according to this checklist.

EXERCISE 5

Edit your essay, and then prepare a final draft, being sure to proofread it carefully.

EXERCISE 6

Review your response to Exercise 1 in Chapter 1. How has your personal writing process changed since you wrote that response?

CHAPTER 4

WRITER'S NOTEBOOK: COMPOSING AN ESSAY

This chapter follows the writing process of Nguyen Dao, a first-year composition student. Nguyen's instructor gave the class the following assignment.

> Write a short essay about a problem you face that you believe is unique to you. Be sure your essay has a clearly stated thesis and helps readers to understand your problem and why it troubles you.

The instructor gave the class two weeks to complete the assignment and did not permit students to do research. She explained that she was going to require some collaborative work, so Nguyen knew that his classmates would read and react to his paper.

Because this paper was the class's first full-length assignment, the instructor asked students to take a systematic approach to the writing process, experimenting with many different kinds of activities designed to help them plan, shape, write, and revise their essays. Although not all of these strategies would work equally well for each student or each topic, she wanted students to discover which activities worked best for them. For this reason, she asked them to write a brief reaction to each activity after completing it. In addition to illustrating Nguyen Dao's writing process, the pages that follow include his comments (in italics) from his notebook.

4a Planning an Essay

(1) Choosing a Topic

Thinking up possible topics wasn't too hard. I've had plenty of problems lately. Some topics I thought about were specific things, like the trouble I had convincing my parents to let me live at school, and my decision to study political science and give up the idea of being a doctor. I also thought about more general, long-standing problems: dealing with my parents' strict rules and their limited English skills. I saw all these different problems as related to my being Asian-American. Then this made me think about the problem of how Asian-Americans are always stereotyped as family oriented, science oriented, or success oriented, which is not always true. Dealing with what people expect of me--because I'm supposed to be a "typical Asian" or "model minority"--is a problem I've always faced.

(2) Finding Something to Say

Reading and Observing

Writing about a problem I face that's unique to me isn't something I need to do any reading about. I know all about being stereotyped. I've had this problem for almost 19 years. I figured it would be a good idea to listen more closely to the kind of things people say about Asians all the time (the things I usually tune out) on TV or even right to my face. One thing I heard was the idea that Asians come to the US and take unskilled entry-level jobs away from American citizens. (Someone on talk radio was really steamed about this.) Maybe I can use this idea--maybe not.

Keeping a Journal

I really hated the idea of writing in a journal, but I guess it works. When I reread my first entry, it helped to remind me that my paper didn't have to be a confession or an argument about what's wrong with my life.

JOURNAL ENTRY

I'm not really comfortable writing about being Asian-American, but I have to admit it's a good topic for a paper about a problem I have. A lot of my problems seem to come from the ideas about what other people think Asians are supposed to do or be. But I don't want to get too personal because other people are going to read what I write, and it could get embarrassing. I don't want them to know about fights I have with my parents over what they think a good Asian son should be. It's like in that story where the Chinese mother tells her daughter there are two kinds of daughters--obedient ones and the other kind: "Americans." I don't feel like analyzing my whole family in public. What I want to do is write about just the pressures on Asians in general and mention a few things about my own life to support these general ideas.

Freewriting

I liked the idea about not having to worry about grammar, spelling, etc. Still, I felt pretty self-conscious doing freewriting, but I actually got one idea I might be able to use in my paper--the fact that Asians are expected to be certain things and not others.

FREEWRITING (EXCERPT)

I really don't want to do this freewriting, but I have to--I'm being forced--I have no choice, but it seems stupid. If I have ideas they'll come and if not they won't. I don't see why I need an idea anyway--I wish she'd just say write about your summer vacation like they did in high school, and I'd write about Colorado last summer and the mountains and that lake I can't remember the name but we had a boat and I could see--This is too hard. I need to write about Asians but there weren't any Asians in that town on that lake. People looked at me like someone from outer space half the time. I wonder what they thought, or who they thought I was.

FOCUSED FREEWRITING (EXCERPT)

Being Asian in the Colorado mountains--wondering whether people thought I was a Japanese tourist--Asian cowboy--Asian hiker/athlete/ mountain man. People never expect Asians to be athletes. Just engineers or violinists. Or maybe own fruit stands or be kung fu teachers. Being a teacher could be good for me--being a role model for kids, showing them other things to be.

Brainstorming

This is the way I like to think up ideas--moving around a page, starting and stopping when I feel like it instead of writing in sentences and paragraphs. It's good for me because I lose patience if I don't get ideas right away. I don't see anything I can use, though, except maybe the idea of the math/science stereotype.

BRAINSTORMING NOTES

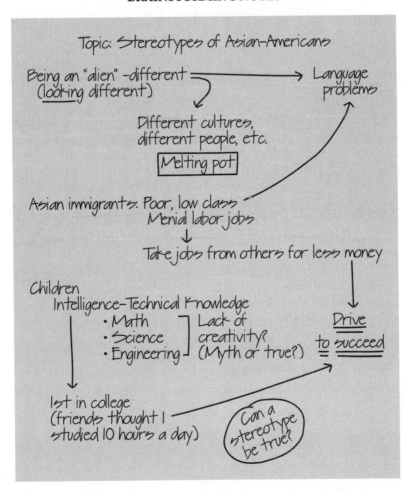

Clustering

This didn't take much time at all, and it showed me that I have basically three parts to my topic--stereotypes about Asian immigrants, stereotypes about their children, and ideas about myself. I'm not sure yet how this all fits together.

CLUSTER DIAGRAM

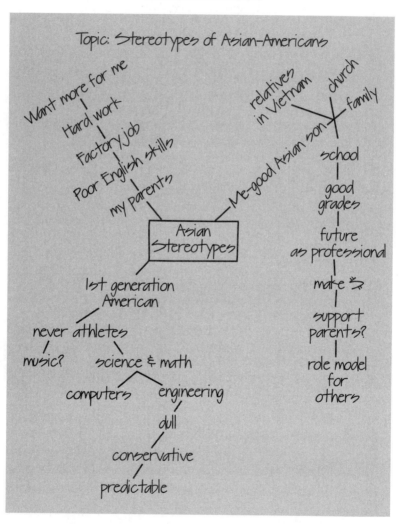

Asking Questions

These questions took a lot of time, but they did help me to see a possible shape for my essay. I thought the questions that explored the reasons for stereotyping were the most interesting (although probably the hardest to answer).

JOURNALISTIC QUESTIONS

Who stereotypes Asian-Americans? Who suffers from this?

What is a stereotype? What exactly is an Asian? (Vietnamese, Chinese, Korean, Japanese, Indian?) What is an Asian-American? What is an American?

Why do people stereotype others? Why do they stereotype Asians? Why do people expect so much of Asians? Why do we ourselves accept these stereotypes? Why do we use them?

Where does most stereotyping occur? (In places where a lot of Asians live? In places where hardly any live?) Where do stereotypes appear? (In newspapers? On TV? In casual conversation?)

How has the stereotype of the "typical Asian" changed over the years? How are immigrants seen? How are their children seen? How do people see me? How are various kinds of Asians alike? How are they different?

IN-DEPTH QUESTIONS (EXCERPT)

What are some typical cases or examples of stereotyping of Asian-Americans? (suggests exemplification)

Asians are seen as good in math, science, engineering, and computers.
Everyone thinks I study all day.
People think my parents make me work hard.

What causes such stereotyping? (suggests cause and effect)

People don't understand other cultures. There are a lot of different kinds of people in the United States, so we have a lot of confusion and conflict.

4b Shaping Your Material

TOPIC TREE

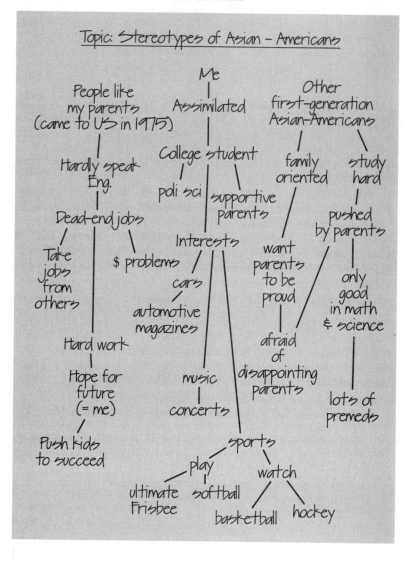

Topic: Stereotypes of Asian – Americans

Me
Assimilated

People like my parents (came to US in 1975)

Other first-generation Asian-Americans

Hardly speak Eng.

College student

poli sci

supportive parents

family oriented

study hard

Dead-end jobs

Interests

want parents to be proud

pushed by parents

Take jobs from others

$ problems

cars

automotive magazines

only good in math & science

Hard work

music

afraid of disappointing parents

Hope for future (= me)

concerts

lots of premeds

Push kids to succeed

sports

play

watch

ultimate Frisbee

softball

basketball

hockey

(1) Grouping Ideas: Making a Topic Tree

This diagram seemed at first to make things more complicated, but after I looked at it for a while I realized it showed some true ideas as well as some inaccurate stereotypes. Obviously, there are some things Asian-Americans have in common. In my paper I'll have to be careful to distinguish between stereotype and reality.

(2) Developing a Thesis

I tried some other ways to word my tentative thesis, but I wanted to make sure it included the most important ideas I was going to talk about-- that I'm Asian-American, that people stereotype me, and that this is a problem. This thesis seemed to do all that. It seemed to suggest I could include some examples of things that happened to me or things other people assume about me. And I could also dig into some causes and effects, explaining why this stereotyping has been a problem. This thesis was pretty specific and to the point, not too wordy or general. So, I thought I'd stick with it for the time being.

TENTATIVE THESIS STATEMENT

As an Asian-American, I am frequently a victim of ethnic stereotyping, and this has been a serious problem for me.

(3) Preparing an Informal Outline

My outline seemed kind of short, even after I added a category (Reality) that wasn't on my topic tree, but I thought I could follow it pretty easily as I wrote my rough draft, maybe getting a paragraph out of each section.

INFORMAL OUTLINE

Asian-American Stereotypes

Thesis statement: As an Asian-American, I am frequently a victim of ethnic stereotyping, and this has been a serious problem for me.

continued on the following page

59

continued from the previous page

Stereotypes of Asian immigrants
   –Poor English
   –Can't use skills and education here
   –Low-paid jobs
      –Sacrifice for children
      –Take from US citizens
Stereotypes of children of Asian immigrants
   –Hard workers
   –Study hard
      –Pushed by parents
   –Focus on math and science
      –Premed
Stereotypes applied to me
   –Science major
   –Forced to study all day
      –No social life
Reality
   –I have outside interests
   –I'm not premed
   –My parents don't push me

4c   Writing and Revising

(1)   Writing a Rough Draft

As I wrote my first draft, I tried to write quickly. Still, I checked my outline as I wrote, so I wouldn't wander too much.

ROUGH DRAFT

Asian-American Stereotypes

The United States prides itself on being the "melting pot" of the world. However, in reality, the abundance of different cultures in America often causes misunderstandings and even conflicts within the society.

continued on the following page

continued from the previous page

These misunderstandings and conflicts result from the society's lack of knowledge about other cultures. As an Asian-American, I am frequently a victim of ethnic stereotyping, and this has been a serious problem for me.

It has been within the last twenty years or so that the United States has seen a large rise in the number of Asian immigrants. First-generation immigrants are seen as an underclass of poor who struggle in low-paying jobs so their children will have a better future. Many accuse immigrants of accepting less pay for their work than the established majority is willing to accept, thus putting the established majority out of work. Although it is true that most newly arrived Asians do seek low-paying, low-skill jobs, they are just following the same trend that other immigrant groups followed when they first arrived in the United States. Because the first generation of Asian-Americans have poorly developed skills in English, they are forced into jobs that do not require those skills. Many Asians received degrees from institutions in their native countries or received advanced training of some kind but cannot use those skills in the United States.

Asian-American children are seen as hard workers who are pushed by their families to succeed. Asian children are seen as intelligent but only in scientific and technical knowledge. The media likes to point to the facts that most Asians succeed only in the math, science, and engineering fields and that there is an inordinate number of Asian college students who identify themselves as "premed."

continued on the following page

continued from the previous page

In my personal experience, in college, many of my friends assume that I am either a science or an engineering major and that my parents force me to study five to ten hours a day. They believe that I sacrifice all my free time and my social life in pursuit of a high grade point average.

In fact, I am a political science major. I also like to go to basketball games, listen to music, and read automotive magazines, just like other college students I know. My parents do encourage me to do well in school because they see that education is a stepping-stone to social class mobility; however, I am lucky because my parents do not push me in one direction or another, as some of my Asian friends' parents do. Many of my friends do not realize that just two or three generations ago, their parents and grandparents were going through the same process of social adjustment that all immigrants endure.

It is important to remember that not all Asians fit into the overachieving, success-oriented stereotype.

This first draft really only got me started writing. I wrote a short introduction to get into the subject and identify my problem, but I really didn't have a clear idea of where my paper was headed or how I was going to support my points. I thought I might like to compare my experiences with the experiences of other ethnic groups, particularly other minorities that are like Asians. I also saw that I had to revise my thesis statement to make it more focused on the problems that stereotyping causes.

(2)   Revising the Rough Draft

When I met with my collaborative revision group to discuss my draft, people said I had a good topic. They liked the idea that I was going to talk about stereotypes instead of more common problems like grades, money, or family. Also, they didn't know much about Asian-Americans, so they thought my paper could be pretty interesting. But they said what I had so far wasn't specific enough and wasn't really focused on my problem. I mostly talk about society in general or Asians in general. They said I should put in examples from my own experiences (which I was planning on doing anyway, but I forgot).

People in the group also talked about their own problems with being stereotyped. It's not just Asians--someone in my group said people always assume she's on a scholarship because she's African-American, but her parents own a business. A football player said his professors always assume he's dumb (which I admit I assumed too). I thought if I asked around, I could find other examples, and I thought I might be able to use some of them in my next draft.

ROUGH DRAFT WITH STUDENT'S REVISIONS

~~The unique characteristic of American culture, is its genuine desire to understand & embrace the wide range of traditions and values of its people.~~

The United States prides itself on being the "melting pot" of the
—a nation where diverse cultures intermingle
to form a unique and enlightened society.
world. However, in reality, the abundance of different cultures in America

often causes misunderstandings and even conflicts within the society.

These misunderstandings and conflicts result from the society's lack of
Still, as
knowledge about other cultures. As an Asian-American, I am frequently a
People keep trying to make me something I'm
not, and this is
victim of ethnic stereotyping, ~~and this has been~~ a serious problem for me.

It has been within the last twenty years or so that the United States

has seen a large rise in the number of Asian immigrants. First-generation
people
immigrants are seen as an underclass of poor who struggle in low-paying

jobs so that their children will have a better future. Many accuse
lower   other American citizens are
immigrants of accepting ~~less~~ pay for their work than ~~the established~~

~~majority is~~ willing to accept, thus putting the established majority out of

continued on the following page

continued from the previous page

work. Although it is true that most newly arrived Asians do seek low-paying,

low-skill jobs, they are just following the same ~~trend~~ *road* that other immigrant

groups followed when they first arrived in the United States. Because the
~~The Irish who escaped the potato famines came to the United States without
many advanced skills. To this day, many Latinos come to the United States,~~
first generation of Asian-Americans have poorly developed skills in
my parents included, *in search of a better life*
with little more than the
English, they are forced into jobs that do not require those skills. *shirts on
their backs.*

Many Asians received degrees from institutions in their native countries or

received advanced training of some kind but cannot use those skills in the
*Therefore, they have no choice but to accept whatever
low-paying job they can get--not to steal jobs from others,*
United States. *but to survive.*

Asian-American children are ~~seen as~~ hard workers who are pushed by
*Along with the view of the first-generation Asian-Americans as
low-skilled workers comes the notion that*
their families to succeed. Asian children are seen as intelligent, but only
terms of
in scientific and technical knowledge. The media likes to point *out* ~~to the facts~~

that most Asians succeed only in ~~the~~ math, science, and engineering ~~fields~~

a great
and that ~~there is an inordinate~~ number of Asian college students ~~who~~

identify themselves as "premed." *other immigrant groups also seem to prize*
What the media seems to forget is that
success above all else.

In my personal experience, in college, many of my friends assume

that I am either a science or an engineering major and that my parents

force me to study five to ten hours a day. They believe that I sacrifice all my

free time and my social life in pursuit of a high grade point average. *My
friends are quite surprised when I tell them that I take drawing classes and
that I am majoring in political science--not as a stepping-stone into law
school, but as a study of man & society.*

continued on the following page

continued from the previous page

∧ Add new ¶ here

In fact, I am a political science major. I also like to go to basketball games, listen to music, and read automotive magazines, just like other college students I know. My parents do encourage me to do well in school because they see that education is a stepping-stone to social class mobility; however, I am lucky because my parents do not push me in one direction or another, as many of my Asian friends' parents do. Many of my friends do not realize that just two or three generations ago, their parents and grandparents were going through the same process of social adjustment that all immigrants endure.

It is important to remember that ~~not all Asians~~ most people don't fit into ~~the~~ these cultural stereotypes. For example, not all Asians fit

overachieving, success-oriented stereotype. When any child comes from an economically disadvantaged background, many times they must sacrifice their academic pursuits in order to support their families. Also, as Asians, particularly the children, become more integrated into the society, the traditional Asian values of hard work & familial obligations will certainly clash with the American pursuits of recreation & individualism. The resolution of that conflict will add yet another facet to the complexity of America's society.

This practice of assuming that people of similar ethnic backgrounds share certain traits is certainly not limited to Asian-Americans. African-American students complain people expect them to be athletes, to like rap music, to be on scholarship, to be from single-parent families—even to be gang members. Athletes say people expect them to be dumb jocks, to drink a lot, and to mistreat their girlfriends. Latinos say people assume that their parents are immigrants and that they speak Spanish better than English. Business majors say people think they're politically conservative and not creative. Engineering students are expected to be dull & wear pocket protectors. Women are supposed to be weak in math & science. Overweight people are expected to be class clowns. In fact, my friends (of all ethnic groups) buy their clothes where I do, & we listen to the same music & laugh at the same jokes. But outsiders don't know this. They have different expectations for each of us, & these expectations are based on culture, not ability.

Revising this draft took a lot of time. I'd triple-spaced so I had room to write in ideas, but I think I might have gotten carried away, adding everything everyone suggested in class, plus every detail that occurred to me on my own. I'm kind of worried about handing it in--she's going to hate it.

(3)   Writing a Second Draft

Even though I had reservations about this draft, I typed in my changes, printed it out, and handed it in.

SECOND DRAFT WITH INSTRUCTOR'S COMMENTS

The Danger of Stereotypes

The United States prides itself on being the "melting pot" of the world--a nation where diverse cultures intermingle to form a unique and enlightened society. However, in reality, the abundance of different cultures in America often causes misunderstandings and even conflicts within the society. These misunderstandings result from the society's lack of knowledge about other cultures. The unique characteristic of American culture is its genuine desire to understand and embrace the wide range of traditions and values of its people. Still, as an Asian-American, I am a

Can you sharpen the thesis so it takes a stand?

victim of ethnic stereotyping: people keep trying to make me something

Why is stereotyping a problem?

I'm not, and this is a serious problem for me.

Wordy—see 13a

It has been within the last twenty years or so that the United States has seen a large rise in the number of Asian immigrants. First-generation immigrants are seen as an underclass of poor people who struggle in low-paying jobs so that their children will have a better future. Many are angry at immigrants, accusing them of accepting lower pay for their work than

continued on the following page

continued from the previous page

other American citizens are willing to accept, thus putting the established
Good background. But you might condense ¶s 2 & 3 a bit.
majority out of work.   *You're wandering from your topic.*

Although it is true that most newly arrived Asians do seek low-paid,

low-skill jobs, they are just following the same road that other immigrant

groups followed when they first arrived in the United States. The Irish who

escaped the potato famines came to the United States without many

advanced skills. To this day, many Latinos come to the United States in
cliché (See 20c4.) Also—you may be guilty of stereotyping here.
search of a better life <u>with little more than the shirts on their backs</u>.

Because the first generation of Asian-Americans, my parents included,

have poorly developed skills in English, they are forced into jobs that do

not require those skills. Many Asians received degrees from institutions in

their native countries or received advanced training of some kind but
pronoun ref.—see 24c
cannot use (those) skills in the United States. Therefore, they have no choice

but to accept whatever low-paying job they can get--not to steal jobs from

others, but to survive.

Along with the view of the first-generation Asian-Americans as low-

skilled workers comes the notion that Asian-American children are hard

workers who are pushed by their families to succeed. Asian children are

seen as intelligent, but only in terms of scientific and technical knowledge.

The media likes to point to the facts that most Asians succeed only in

math, science, and engineering and that a great number of Asian college
agreement—see 26a6
students identify themselves as "premed." What the media seems to
(Media = plural; medium = singular)
forget is that other immigrant groups also seem to prize success above

all else.

continued on the following page

continued from the previous page

Wordy—see 13a

In my personal experience, in college, many of my friends assume

that I am either a science or an engineering major and that my parents

force me to study five to ten hours a day. They believe that I sacrifice all my

free time and my social life in pursuit of a high grade point average. My

friends are really surprised when I tell them that I take drawing classes and

that I am majoring in political science--not as a stepping-stone into law

sexist language

school, but as a study of man and society.   *See 20f2*

This practice of assuming that people of similar ethnic backgrounds

share certain traits is certainly not limited to Asian-Americans. African-

American students complain people expect them to be athletes, to like rap

music, to be on scholarship, to be from single-parent families--even to be

gang members. Athletes say people expect them to be dumb jocks, to

drink a lot, and to mistreat their girlfriends. Latinos say people assume that

their parents are immigrants and that they speak Spanish better than

English. Business majors say people think they're politically conservative

Are you sure you need all this? Your focus in this paper is on

and not creative. Engineering students are expected to be dull and wear

ethnic (specifically Asian) stereotypes, remember?

pocket protectors. Women are supposed to be weak in math and science.

Overweight people are expected to be class clowns. In fact, my friends (of

all ethnic groups) buy their clothes where I do, and we listen to the same

music and laugh at the same jokes. But outsiders don't know this. They

have different expectations for each of us, and these expectations are

based on culture, not ability.

good point—but wordy (see 13a)

It is important to remember that most people do not fit these cultural

stereotypes. For example, not all Asians fit into the overachieving, success-

continued on the following page

continued from the previous page

oriented stereotype. When any ⟨child⟩ comes from an economically

agreement

disadvantaged background, many times ⟨they⟩ must sacrifice their academic

Are you sure this is what you   *see 26b*

pursuits in order to support their families. Also, as Asians, particularly the

want to leave your readers with?

children, become more integrated into the society, the traditional Asian

It doesn't really address your

values of hard work and familial obligations will certainly clash with the

essay's main point.

American pursuits of recreation and individualism. The resolution of that

conflict will add yet another facet to the complexity of America's society.

I like what you've done here, but something important is still missing. You really do need more examples from your own experience. Also, think about this question before our conference on Tuesday: Exactly why are the stereotypes you enumerate so harmful, so damaging? This idea needs to be developed in some detail (it's really the heart of your paper), and it should certainly be addressed in your thesis statement and conclusion as well.

When I reread my second draft before I handed it in, my two biggest worries were that it had too many ideas in it and that it didn't sound like me. Still, I liked it better than the rough draft--especially the material in paragraphs 5 and 6, which my collaborative revision group wanted me to add. Now I thought I might like to add something about how I've been limited by my own preconceptions. For example, I did start out as a premed student, although I'm now a political science major. Another idea I might want to look into is that many Asians, including some of my friends, are now reconsidering whether the drive for success is worth the price. I saw this as an interesting possibility, but I felt as if I was trying to do too much. Was I writing about a problem in US society or my own personal problem (the conflict between what people expect a good Asian boy to do vs. what I want to do)? Was I going to deal with all stereotypes? All ethnic stereotypes? Or only Asian-American stereotypes?

My conference with Professor Cross, and her comments on my draft, helped me solve some of my problems and get my assignment into focus. It also brought up some new problems. First, she reminded me that my paper was supposed to be only two to three pages long (something I was starting to forget), so I should stop looking for new material and start sorting through what I had. She said my knowledge of the Asian-American experience was my paper's biggest strength, but that I was going in too many directions at once. She thought all the stuff in paragraph 6 was interesting, but she said it didn't really fit if my paper was going to be on Asians and on the problems I face. I hate to take this paragraph out, but I guess she's right. She wants me to revise my thesis statement so it takes a stand about why and how stereotyping has been damaging to me (and, for the same reasons, to other people). Then, of course, I'll have to add support based on what I know firsthand.

This all makes sense, but it means I'll have to take out some of the background on immigrants in paragraphs 2 and 3 and cut most of paragraph 6. I won't have anything left! Now I'll have to list and explain *the problems I have, telling why they're problems, and I'll also have to redo my introduction and conclusion so they fit with the new ideas. It sounds like a lot of work.*

(4)   Revising the Second Draft

To move from this second draft to what I hoped would be my final draft, I had to get a clear sense of what to cross out, what to keep, and what to add. Professor Cross thought that making a formal outline of this draft could help me to see which ideas worked well together and which ones just floated.

I started by outlining my second draft, the one with all the problems, hoping that a topic outline would show me the relationships (if any) among my ideas and give me some idea about what to do next.

TOPIC OUTLINE

The Danger of Stereotypes
   Thesis statement: As an Asian-American, I am a victim of ethnic stereotyping: people keep trying to make me something I'm not, and this is a problem for me.

I.   Stereotypes of Asian immigrants
   A.   Underclass
      1.   Struggle in low-paying jobs
      2.   Hope children will do better
   B.   Displace Americans
      1.   Accept low pay
      2.   Put others out of work
II.   Reality
   A.   Similar to unskilled Irish immigrants
   B.   Similar to poor Latino immigrants
   C.   Limited
      1.   Poor English skills
      2.   Useless degrees

continued on the following page

---

continued from the previous page

III. Stereotypes of immigrants' children
    A. Work habits
        1. Work hard
        2. Pushed by parents
    B. Intelligence
        1. Highly intelligent
        2. Scientific and technical knowledge
            a. Math and science
            b. Premed
IV. My experience
    A. Stereotypes applied to me
        1. Science/engineering major
        2. Forced to study
            a. No free time
            b. No social life
    B. Reality
        1. Drawing classes
        2. Political science major
V. Other inaccurate stereotypes
    A. African-Americans
        1. Athletic
        2. Like rap music
        3. On scholarship
        4. From single-parent families
        5. Gang members
    B. Athletes
        1. Dumb
        2. Drinkers
        3. Mistreat girlfriends
    C. Latinos
        1. Immigrants
        2. Poor English
    D. Business majors
        1. Politically conservative
        2. Not creative
    E. Engineering students
        1. Dull
        2. Wear pocket protectors
    F. Women
    G. Overweight people

Outlining this draft showed me what Professor Cross had been trying to tell me: my paper was really unbalanced, with some areas underdeveloped and others overstuffed. (Most of the information, in fact, wasn't even about Asians.) After I finished the outline, I went through it again, indicating with x's and check marks what to keep and what to drop and making notes about what to add to my next draft.

Now I was finally ready to make an outline to guide my final draft. At this point, I thought the effort of a sentence outline would really pay off because I might be able to use sentences from my outline in my paper.

SENTENCE OUTLINE

My Problem: Escaping the Stereotype of the "Model Minority"
   Thesis statement: Such stereotypes are not only limiting to me, but also dangerous to the nation because they challenge the image of the United States as a place where people can be whatever they want to be.

I. Asian-Americans are stereotyped.
  A. First-generation immigrants are seen as a struggling underclass.
    1. They are viewed as poor and underpaid.
    2. They are viewed as hardworking.
    3. They are viewed as sacrificing for their children.
  B. Their children are seen as hard workers.
    1. They are viewed as driven.
      a. They need to succeed.
      b. They are pushed by their parents.
    2. They are viewed as intelligent.
      a. They excel only in scientific and technical fields.
      b. They are good only in math, science, and engineering.
      c. Many are premed.
  C. These traits are not limited to Asian-Americans.
    1. Other immigrant groups also value success.
    2. Everyone seeks the American Dream.
II. Because I am Asian-American I am unfairly stereotyped.
  A. I am viewed as a robot.
    1. People assume I am a science or engineering major.
    2. People assume my parents make me study.
    3. People assume I have no social life.
  B. Such stereotypes are inaccurate.
    1. I take drawing classes.
    2. I am a political science major.

continued on the following page

---

continued from the previous page

3. I am not quiet or shy.
4. I do not play a musical instrument.
5. I do not live in Chinatown.

III. These stereotypes have negative consequences for me.
   A. Teachers have unreasonable expectations for me.
      1. Teachers expect me to do well in certain areas.
         a. They have encouraged me to take AP math and science.
         b. They have encouraged me to try out for band.
         c. They have encouraged me to take an advanced computer seminar.
         d. They have encouraged me to join the chess club.
      2. Teachers do not expect me to do well in other areas.
         a. They don't expect me to be an athlete.
         b. They don't expect me to be a writer.
         c. They don't expect me to be a debater.
   B. I have conformed to their expectations.
IV. Similar stereotypes limit other groups' options.
   A. Stereotypes determine people's career paths.
      1. Teachers, bosses, and parents steer us in certain directions.
      2. We ourselves make choices based on stereotypes.
   B. Even in school, students are expected to follow certain predetermined paths.
V. Most people do not fit these cultural stereotypes.
   A. Stereotypes are invalid for Asians.
      1. Children of recent Asian immigrants do work and study hard.
      2. Even when they become assimilated, they retain Asian values.
         a. They work hard.
         b. They have obligations to their families.
      3. However, they also acquire the American drive for individuality.
   B. Stereotypes are invalid for other groups.

(5) Preparing a Final Draft

Even as I started to turn my paper into something I could hand in, I still worried that it didn't really sound like me. I didn't want to make my paper too informal, but I did want it to be a little less stiff. As I added information to my draft, though, I found that my style was becoming more relaxed and natural--maybe because the information was about me, not about people in general. The opening and closing paragraphs were still a little distant, but somehow that seemed to make sense, giving my personal problem some context.

Before I typed my final draft, I decided to change my title to something more specific, something that connected my paper to the assignment. After I finished printing out this final draft, I read it through one more time--and noticed a few typos. So I corrected them and printed it out again--and then I had a really final draft.

FINAL DRAFT

Dao 1

Nguyen Dao

Professor Cross

English 101

10 October 1997

My Problem:

Escaping the Stereotype of the "Model Minority"

The United States prides itself on being a nation where

diverse cultures intermingle to form a unique and enlightened

society. However, in reality, the existence of so many different

cultures in America often causes misunderstandings within the

society. These misunderstandings result from most people's lack

of knowledge about other cultures. The unique characteristic of

American culture is its genuine desire to understand and

embrace the wide range of traditions and values of its people.

Still, as an Asian-American, I am frequently confronted with

other people's ideas about who I am and how I should behave.

Such stereotypes are not only limiting to me, but also dangerous

to the nation because they challenge the image of the United

States as a place where people can be whatever they want to be.

Within the last twenty years, the United States has

experienced a sharp rise in the number of Asian immigrants, and

these immigrants, and their children, are stereotyped. First-

generation immigrants are seen as an underclass of poor people

who struggle in low-paying jobs, working long hours so that

Introductory paragraph presents basic background

Thesis statement

First body paragraph: Common stereotypes applied to Asian-Americans

Dao 2

their children will have a better future. Along with the view of the first-generation Asian-Americans as driven, low-skilled workers comes the notion that all Asian-American children are hard workers who are pushed by their families to succeed. Asian children are seen as intelligent, but only in terms of scientific and technical knowledge. The media like to point out that most Asians succeed only in math, science, and engineering and that a disproportionately large number of Asian college students identify themselves as premed. What the media seem to forget is that many other immigrant groups also value success. In a larger sense, America has always been seen as the land of opportunity, where everyone is in search of the American Dream.

Second body paragraph: Stereotype applied to student himself

Many of my college friends assume that I am some kind of robot. They think I must be either a science or an engineering major and that my parents force me to study many hours each day. They believe that I sacrifice all my free time and my social life in pursuit of a high grade point average. Naturally, these assumptions are incorrect. My friends are really surprised when I tell them that I take drawing classes and that I am majoring in political science--not as a stepping-stone into law school, but as a foundation for a liberal arts education. They are also surprised to find that I am not particularly quiet or shy, that I do not play a musical instrument, and that I do not live in Chinatown. (I don't know why this surprises people; I'm not even Chinese.)

I try to see these stereotypes as harmless, but they aren't. Even neutral or positive stereotypes can have negative consequences. For example, teachers have always had unreasonably high expectations for me, and these expectations have created pressure for academic success. And even though teachers expect me to do well, they expect me to excel only in certain areas. So, they have encouraged me to take AP math and science classes, try out for band, sign up for an advanced computer seminar, and join the chess club. No one has ever suggested that I (or any other Asian-American I know) pursue athletics, creative writing, or debating. I spent my high school years trying to be what other people wanted me to be, and I got to be pretty good at it.

Third body paragraph: Negative effects of stereotypes on student

I realize now, however, that I have been limited and that similar stereotypes also limit the options that other groups have. The law says we can choose our activities and choose our careers, but things do not always work out that way. Often, because of long-held stereotypes, we are gently steered (by peers, teachers, bosses, parents, and even by ourselves) in a certain direction, toward some options and away from others. We may have come a long way from the time when African-Americans were

Fourth body paragraph: Negative effects of stereotypes on society

Dao 4

expected to be domestics or blue-collar workers, Latinos to be migrant farmers or gardeners, and Asians to be restaurant workers. But at the college, high school, and even elementary school levels, students are expected to follow certain predetermined paths, and too often these expectations are based on culture, not on interests or abilities.

Conclusion   Most people do not fit these cultural stereotypes. For example, not all Asians fit into the overachieving, success-oriented mold. When children come from an economically disadvantaged background, as the children of some recent Asian immigrants do, they must work hard and study hard. But this situation is only temporary. As Asian children become more assimilated into American society, they do retain the traditional Asian values of hard work and family obligations--but they also acquire the American drive for individualism. I know from my own experience that the stereotypes applied to Asians are not accurate. In the same way, people of other ethnic groups know that the cultural stereotypes applied to them are not valid. My problem is not just <u>my</u> problem because ethnic and cultural stereotypes are never harmless. Whenever someone is stereotyped, that person has fewer choices. And freedom to choose our futures, to be whoever we want to be, is what living in the United States is supposed to be all about.

CHAPTER 5

ESSAY PATTERNS
AND PURPOSES

There are many options for arranging material within an essay. The pattern of development you choose is determined by your **purpose**, which in college writing is often stated in (or suggested by) your assignment. For example, if your purpose is to *analyze* the events that led to the Spanish-American War, you may use a **cause-and-effect** pattern; if your purpose is to *evaluate* the relative merits of two systems of government, you may use **comparison and contrast;** if your purpose is to *reflect* on an experience, you may use **narration** or **description;** and if your purpose is to *persuade* readers that a literary work's reputation is not deserved, you may use **exemplification.** In each case, of course, you have other options as well.

See
1b1

Writers do not generally decide in advance on a particular pattern of development and then write their essay accordingly. Rather, as they draft, they see the patterns into which their thoughts fall, and they are then able to rearrange information so that it conforms to the pattern that supports the thesis most effectively. (The same patterns used to structure essays can also be used as **patterns of paragraph development**.)

See
6e

 CLOSE-UP **COMBINING THE PATTERNS**

Many essays combine more than one pattern of development. After you have developed your writing skills, you may want to practice combining various patterns in a single essay.

5a Writing Narrative Essays

A **narrative** essay tells a story by presenting events in chronological (time) order. Sometimes a narrative begins in the middle of a story, or even at the end, and then moves back to the beginning. Most narrative essays, however, move in a logical, orderly sequence from beginning to end, from first event to last. Clear transitional words and phrases (*later, after that*) and time markers (*in 1990, two years earlier, the next day*) establish the chronological sequence and the relationship of each event to the others.

(1) Using Narration

You use narration in a variety of college writing situations—for example, when you review a novel's plot, when you write a case study, when you summarize your employment history in a letter of application for a job, when you present background on a history examination, when you recount personal experiences in a journal, or when you write an autobiographical essay.

Any assignment that asks you to *tell, trace, summarize the events, present the background,* or *outline* may call for narration. Some typical assignments that might suggest narrative writing include the following:

- *Trace* the events that led the Food and Drug Administration to ban thalidomide in this country. (Public health paper)
- *Summarize* the incidents that immediately preceded the French Revolution of 1789. (History exam)
- *Present some background* to show why nineteenth-century British workers were receptive to the ideas of social reformers like Robert Owen. (Political science exam)
- *Outline* the plot of Jane Austen's novel *Sense and Sensibility.* (English literature quiz)

(2) Student Essay: Narration

The following student essay was written by Gary McManus for a composition course. The instructor asked each student to interview a relative and to write a brief family history based on the interview.

Essay 5a

My Family History

On October 7 I interviewed my father, John McManus, about my family history. Although he knew more about his own ancestors than my mother's, he was able to give me valuable details about both sides of my family. The family history, as I have reconstructed it, shows me that although some of my relatives experienced the financial hardships and prejudice common to many other immigrants, many members of my family were lucky enough to achieve success.

My grandmother on my father's side was born in Newry, Ireland, in poverty caused by the potato famine. When she was a child, her father, a sea captain, took his family to Liverpool, England, so he could find work. While in England, my grandmother McManus was constantly teased by the English children because of her Irish-Catholic ancestry. When she was eighteen, she came alone to the United States to visit a distant cousin in Baltimore, Maryland. At the time she had no way of knowing that she would never return home. In Baltimore she met her future husband, and they were married a year later.

My grandfather McManus was born and raised in the Baltimore area and came from a well-to-do family. His uncle invented the bottle cap (before this, people used corks) and was president of the Crown Cork and Seal Bottle Company. One of my grandfather's aunts was a judge in juvenile court in Boston--no minor achievement for a woman in the late 1880s. Another of his uncles was an architect who designed several of Boston's churches. He had trouble getting other commissions, however, because of discrimination against the Irish. At that time, it was common in Boston to see signs in shop windows saying "Workers needed--N.I.N.A." (No Irish Need Apply). As an officer in the U.S. Army, my grandfather McManus fought in the

continued on the following page

Introduction (identifies subject; gives background)

Thesis statement

Events presented in sequence

continued from the previous page

Spanish-American War in the Philippines in the 1890s and later during the Boxer Rebellion in China. During his military career he served under both General Arthur MacArthur and his son Douglas MacArthur.

Narrative
continues

During World War I, from 1918 to 1919, a terrible influenza epidemic killed millions worldwide and hundreds of thousands in the United States. So many people died that there weren't enough gravediggers to bury the dead. Squads of men would go from house to house in many cities on the east coast, collecting the bodies of those who had died. Two of my grandparents' children died from influenza during the epidemic. One son only six years old died early one day just after sunrise, and later that evening their two-year-old daughter died in her sleep.

Shift to
mother's
family

My mother's family settled in Irish neighborhoods in Washington, DC, where my great-grandfather, John Howard, owned a livery stable. His son, my great-uncle Lee, was a U.S. attorney and judge who was known as one of the most influential Irish-American men in the District of Columbia. Because he had grown up poor and had to work to send himself through law school, he was sympathetic to the poor and often went to great lengths to find them employment.

My maternal grandfather, a builder, was among the first to attempt to organize his fellow workers. Eventually he became a union official for the AFL. He would have advanced much higher in the union if he had renounced Catholicism and joined the Masons, but he refused.

Conclusion

Many Irish immigrants in the late 1880s and early 1900s became priests, policemen, and blue-collar workers. That was as far as many of them could go because the anti-Irish prejudice that

continued on the following page

continued from the previous page

prevailed at this time severely limited their opportunities. In spite of some problems, however, many members of my family carved out good lives in this country.

EXERCISE 1

Write a narrative essay on one of the following topics.

• Interview an older relative or friend and write an account of his or her childhood.

• Retell a favorite short story or fairy tale from memory.

• Write the biography of a word. Look up a word in the *Oxford English Dictionary,* and write a narrative account of its development from its first use in English to its present meaning in modern usage.

5b Writing Descriptive Essays

A **descriptive** essay communicates to readers how something looks, sounds, smells, tastes, or feels. The most natural arrangement of details in a description reflects the way you actually look at a person, scene, or object: near to far, top to bottom, side to side, or front to back. This arrangement of details is made clear by transitions that identify precise spatial relationships: *next to, near, beside, under, above,* and so on.

NOTE: Sometimes a descriptive essay does not have an explicitly stated thesis statement. In such cases it is nevertheless unified by the **dominant impression** it conveys—the mood to which all the descriptive details contribute.

(1) Using Description

Description plays an important role in college writing. For example, technical reports, lab reports, case studies, and field notes all depend upon precise description. In addition, on a European history examination you might have to describe the scene of a famous battle, and in an American literature paper you might have to describe the setting of a play or novel. In other situations too description is necessary—for example, for presenting your reactions to a painting or a musical composition. The following assignments are typical of those you may encounter.

- Describe each of the structures you observed during your dissection of the reproductive system of the fetal pig. (Biology laboratory manual)
- Describe in detail the English political system at the time of the American Revolution. (European history midterm)
- Write an essay in which you describe one character in the novel *The Color Purple*. (American literature paper)
- In a short essay, describe Titian's use of color in his *Madonna with Members of the Pesaro Family*. (Art history final exam)

(2) Student Essay: Description

Barbara Quercetti, a student in a composition course, wrote this essay in response to an assignment asking her to describe a place that had made a strong impression on her. She based her descriptive essay largely on her own firsthand observations of her subject. (A few factual details were taken from an informational brochure that she picked up at the site.)

A Newport Mansion

Introduction (historical overview)

Located on Ochre Point Avenue in Newport, Rhode Island, The Breakers is a mansion presently owned by the Preservation Society of Newport County. The mansion was built in 1895 for Cornelius Vanderbilt, the financier who accumulated the renowned Vanderbilt fortune. This house, like other Newport mansions, was used only during the three summer months, when the Newport social season was at its peak. The architect, Richard Morris Hunt, modeled The Breakers after an Italian Renaissance Palace. Presently, The Breakers is one of Newport's most popular tourist attractions because its extravagant

Thesis statement

architecture and opulent appointments call up a time of lost elegance.

View of exterior

As you approach the grounds of the mansion, you see enormous black wrought iron gates that are thirty feet high at the

continued on the following page

continued from the previous page

center point and weigh seven tons. The arched top of the gates is decorated with elaborate rococo scroll work, and this arch motif is repeated throughout the exterior and interior of the mansion. To either side of the gates are two twenty-foot-high square posts, each with a black wrought iron lantern also decorated with scroll work. The buff Indian limestone that is used for the posts is also used for the facade of The Breakers.

Standing in front of the mansion, you see that although none of the faces of The Breakers is identical, each relates to the others. The first story of each exterior wall is made up of a series of arches, with the interior of each arch inlaid with ceramic tiles. Supporting the arches are round columns with Greek Ionic capitals. Each facade is three complete stories high, except for the east side, which has a terrace above the second-story level. This terrace is one of three that give a panoramic view of the Atlantic Ocean. The other two terraces are located on the north side of The Breakers. One, at the first-story level, extends out to the garden area. The other terrace is above the first-story level. The south face of the mansion has a semicircular protrusion that forms an open one-story foyer. The entire building is decorated with ornate figures sculpted by Karl Bitter.

View of exterior, continued

As you enter The Breakers, you see that the interior is as exquisite as the exterior. The first room that you encounter is the Great Hall or reception room, which is also decorated with intricately carved stone and marble. The Great Hall rises nearly fifty feet and is the largest room in any of the Newport mansions. Its ceiling is covered with geometric patterns of fourteen-karat gold gilding that run over the entire surface. There are eight chandeliers, each suspended by a single metal rod. The second story of the room is an

View of interior: Great Hall

continued on the following page

continued from the previous page

open balcony with a black wrought iron railing that repeats the scroll work motif of the entrance gates. The railing is divided into sections by two-story-high square stone columns with Ionic capitals. These Greek Ionic columns are similar to those used on the exterior of the mansion. The railing continues along the side of the royal red carpeted stairs to the first floor. Surrounding the room is a series of arches, each situated between two of the two-story-high columns. Floor-length royal red tie-back draperies hang inside the arches. The wood parquet floor is covered with Persian area rugs, and potted ferns at the base of each column add a touch of greenery to the room.

View of interior: dining room   Walking through the Great Hall, you come to an equally impressive dining room that is also two full stories high. Lavish decorations fill the room, which is lined with two-story-high columns with arches in between. The columns are red alabaster with bronze Corinthian capitals. As in the Great Hall, royal red tie-back draperies hang inside the arches. Above each arch is a gilded cornice around which is a ceiling arch containing life-sized sculptured figures. Four huge crystal chandeliers hang down the length of the room. On the west wall there is only one arch, and this outlines a blue carved Venetian marble fireplace. The room is richly furnished with antique European furniture, and the wood parquet floor is covered with Persian carpets. A solid oak dining table ten feet by ten feet square dominates the center of the room.

Conclusion   The Newport social season is now part of America's past, and so are the individuals who spent millions for a summer residence. But The Breakers remains one of the grandest mansions of the area. Now

Restatement of thesis   a tourist attraction, it retains its popularity because it stands as a

continued on the following page

continued from the previous page
reminder to us of a time when America was rapidly expanding and
life was a good deal more extravagant than it is today.

EXERCISE 2

Write a descriptive essay on one of the following topics.

- Describe a person, place, or object that has had a significant impact on you.
- Write a description of a room in your house or a place in your neighborhood.
- Visit a local museum or a site of historical interest, and describe one exhibit or section of it.

5c Writing Exemplification Essays

Exemplification essays support a thesis statement with a series of specific examples (or, sometimes, with a single extended example). These examples can be drawn from personal observation or experience or from the facts and opinions you gather through research. Within the essay, examples are linked to one another and to the thesis statement with clear transitional words and phrases: *the first example, another reason, in addition, finally,* and so on.

(1) Using Exemplification

Exemplification is basic to most college writing assignments. In fact, any time you are called upon to give a specific example of a more general principle, you use exemplification. The following assignments are typical of those you may encounter.

- Discuss three examples of *film noir.* (Film midterm)
- Write an essay in which you illustrate the following statement by the literary critic John Tytell: "Although the Beat movement lacked any shared platform such as the Imagist or surrealist manifestoes, it nonetheless cohered as a literary group." (Literature paper)
- In what ways does existentialism confront the problem of personal action in a universe devoid of purpose? (Philosophy final)

- Discuss four technological advances that took place during the Renaissance. (History of science paper)
- Identify and discuss three examples that Glazer and Moynihan give to support their thesis that in New York City and in much of the United States the melting pot does not exist. (Sociology midterm)

(2) Student Essay: Exemplification

The following paper on Walt Disney's early feature-length films was written for a film course by Brett Leonard. Brett, a film and video major with a special interest in animation, supports his analysis of Disney's work with three specific examples.

Disney's Early Feature-Length Films

Introduction   Walt Disney's climb to fame is a classic American success story: a tale of a poor boy from the Midwest who, with hard work and luck, gained international recognition and fame. He began as a maker of cartoon shorts and ended up as the head of a billion-dollar

Thesis statement   entertainment empire. Looking back at his film career, which began in the early 1920s and lasted until his death in 1966, one would think that his reputation rests on a forty-year body of work. However, much of his most memorable and ground-breaking work was done in three early feature-length works.

First example   By the early 1930s Disney had achieved commercial success with his short features. Mickey Mouse had caught on, and so had his Silly Symphony series. Disney wanted more, however, and by 1934 he started to plan the feature animated film <u>Snow White and the Seven Dwarfs</u>. An extension of the Silly Symphony concept, <u>Snow White</u> was first seen by Disney as a cartoon with musical accompaniment. Eventually, however, the project took a direction of its own and went well beyond his original conception. What made <u>Snow White</u> different from Disney's other films was its large cast of well-developed

continued on the following page

continued from the previous page

characters--the dwarfs, the wicked queen, and Snow White herself-- and the high quality of its animation. There were no nonessential elements in the film. Everything, including the film's music, contributed to the plot or to the development of the characters. When Snow White premiered in 1937, both audiences and film critics realized that they were seeing something new and gave it instant acceptance.

After the success of Snow White, Disney made what is probably his greatest film, Pinocchio, which makes expert use of music and sound but in addition uses visual images to stimulate the imagination. The first scene of the film illustrates this point. The camera, focusing on a star in the evening sky, slowly moves back to reveal a beautiful Italian village nestled in the hills. The camera gradually moves closer, stopping at Geppetto's window, showing the scene within. With this one sequence, Disney draws viewers from the everyday world into the world of the fairy tale. The music, especially the beautiful "When You Wish Upon a Star," reinforces the atmosphere of the film. Characters like Jiminy Cricket, the fox, Geppetto, and Pinocchio himself, along with the visual detail of the background scenes, reveal artistic possibilities previously unseen in animated cartoons. However, perhaps because of its somber mood or because World War II broke out one month before its release, Pinocchio never achieved the commercial success that Snow White did.

Second example

After his two classic fairy tales, Disney attempted to push the animated cartoon even further. He decided to make Fantasia, a film based on animated interpretations of seven musical pieces tied together by a narrator. For this film he hired Leopold Stokowski, conductor of the Philadelphia Orchestra, who along with Disney saw

Third example

continued on the following page

continued from the previous page

the possibility of using animation to bring classical music to the public. The film begins with a brief narrative sequence and then moves into Bach's <u>Toccata and Fugue in D Minor</u>, with the sound track itself acting as a character. Although certainly innovative, the animated interpretations of the music are quite uneven. For example, the <u>Nutcracker Suite</u> music is accompanied by abstract and romantic images that add to our enjoyment of the music, as does the animated "The Sorcerer's Apprentice" sequence. However, the animated accompaniments to the <u>Pastoral Symphony</u> and the <u>Dance of the Hours</u> have little to do with the music itself and are therefore distracting. Still, although it is somewhat uneven, <u>Fantasia</u> is a work that reveals a lot about the range and vision of which Disney was capable.

Conclusion Cinematically, <u>Snow White</u>, <u>Pinocchio</u>, and <u>Fantasia</u> were revolutionary. With these three films made during the 1930s and 1940s, Disney showed that he could make an animated feature-

Restatement of major points length film. More importantly, he showed that the animated cartoon was capable of communicating complex and subtle ideas.

EXERCISE 3

Write an exemplification essay on one of the following topics.

- Discuss the merits of television. Use specific examples from your own experience to support your thesis.
- Explain how several incidents at a family dinner or a neighborhood gathering revealed the social attitudes of the people who attended it.
- Discuss three things that you would like to change in your home, school, or job.

5d   Writing Process Essays

A **process** essay explains how to do something or how something works. It presents a series of steps in strict chronological order, using transitional words such as *first, then, next, after this,* and *finally* to link steps in the process.

Some process essays are **instructions,** providing all the specific information that enables readers to perform a procedure themselves. Instructions use commands and the present tense. Other process essays simply explain the process to readers, with no expectation that they will actually perform it. These process essays may use first or third person and past tense (for a process that has been completed) or present tense (for a process that occurs regularly).

(1)   Using Process

Academic situations frequently call for process explanations and sometimes for instructions. In scientific and technical writing you may describe how an apparatus works or how a procedure is carried out. Occasionally, you may even write a set of instructions telling your readers how to duplicate your procedure. In the humanities you might have to write a proposal for a research paper in which you explain how you plan to carry out your research. Here are some typical assignments that call for a process pattern of development.

- Explain how an amendment is added to the Constitution. (Political science quiz)
- Review the stages that each of the Old English long vowels went through during the Great Vowel Shift. (Examination in history of the English language)
- Outline the steps in the process of mitosis. (Biology lab quiz)
- Write a set of instructions that outlines a treatment plan for a patient complaining of lower back pain. (Physical therapy paper)

(2)   Student Essay: Process

Richard Patrone, a student in a course in animal biology, submitted the following laboratory report. In writing up his experiment, he was careful to provide an exact record of what he did in order to give readers the information they would need to understand his procedure.

Background

Introduction   Based on the postulation that pollen contains an anticarcinogenic principle that can be added to food, an experiment was set up in which female mice, fed with pollenized food, were checked for delays in the appearance of spontaneous mammary tumors. Mice used in the study were bred from a subline of the C_3H strain, which develops palpable tumors at between 18 and 25 weeks of age.

Procedure

Steps in the process   First, 10 mice were set aside as controls, to be fed only unpollenized food (Purina Laboratory Chow). Next, the pollen suspension was prepared: one gram of bee-gathered pollen was ground and then mixed with 50 ml of distilled water. Two different mixtures were then prepared using this pollen suspension. One mixture consisted of 6 lb of food with a 36 ml dosage of pollen suspension (1 part pollen per 3,800 parts food), and one consisted of 6 lb of lab chow with an 8 ml dosage of suspension (1 part pollen per 120,000 parts food). Each of these two mixtures was then fed to a different group of 10 mice. The mice were weighed weekly, and the amount of food eaten was recorded. As soon as estrus began, vaginal smears of each mouse were made daily and examined microscopically for the presence of cornified cells.

Results

Conclusion   The experimental results indicated that the development of mammary tumors in C_3H mice was delayed 10 to 12 weeks with the ingestion of pollenized food.

EXERCISE 4

Write a process essay on one of the following topics.

- Explain your typical writing process. Then, rewrite the explanation as a set of instructions.

- Write a detailed set of instructions for playing any computer game or board game whose rules you know well.

- Think about a time when you had to complete a complicated transaction that involved dealing with bureaucratic red tape—applying for a student loan, getting your driver's license, or withdrawing from a course, for instance. List the steps you went through, and then write an explanation of the process.

5e Writing Cause-and-Effect Essays

Cause-and-effect essays explore causes or predict or describe results; sometimes a single cause-and-effect essay does both. Because cause-and-effect relationships are often quite complex, clear, specific transitional words and phrases such as *one cause, another cause, a more important result, because,* and *as a result* are essential.

(1) Using Cause and Effect

Many of your course assignments call for writing that examines causes, predicts effects, or does both. Language like "How did X affect Y?" "What were the contributing factors?" "Describe some side effects," "What caused X?" "What were the results of X?" and "Why did X happen?" suggests cause-and-effect writing. Here are some typical assignments.

- Identify and explain some factors that contributed to the stock market crash of 1987. (Economics essay)

- Describe some of the possible side effects of dialysis. (Nursing exam)

- How have geologic changes affected the productivity of Pennsylvania soil? (Agronomy project)

- What factors led to the wave of eastern European immigration to this country at the end of the nineteenth century? (American history exam)

- How did Ernest Hemingway's experiences during World War I influence his writing? (American literature paper)

93

(2)   Student Essay: Cause and Effect

Michael Liebman wrote the essay that follows for a class in elementary education. The assignment was "Identify the causes of a social problem of concern to both parents and educators, and analyze the effects of this problem, making some recommendations about how the problem can be solved." Michael decided to examine the positive and negative effects on children of being left on their own after school.

The Latch-Key Children

Introduction (States primary cause: working parents)

In recent years, the inflationary economy and wider employment opportunities for women have combined to lead more and more mothers of school-aged children to return to work. In fact, more than half of the mothers of school-aged children are now employed, and the two-paycheck family has become the norm. As a result, hundreds of thousands--perhaps millions--of children are now left unsupervised between 3 and 6 p.m. every day. The lack of much-needed after-school programs has left many families in cities and suburbs alike with no other alternative but to leave the children on their own and

Thesis statement

hope for the best. Luckily, many of the children manage extraordinarily well.

Negative effects

The negative effects of the latch-key trend are fairly easily perceived. Many parents' firm rules--don't use the stove, don't open the door to anyone, don't let telephone callers know you are alone-- have made some children (especially those without siblings) fearful and jittery. These children may also become very lonely in an empty house or apartment. Because many working parents do not allow their children's friends to visit when no adult is present, their children may spend hours with no company but the television set. A lonely, frightened child turning to the TV for comfort and companionship is

continued on the following page

94

continued from the previous page

a common stereotype of the latch-key child. Fortunately, however, it is for the most part not an accurate one.

The latch-key phenomenon has the potential to have some even more disturbing effects on children. Parents and teachers have voiced fears that unattended children will be more vulnerable to violent crimes, especially sexual assaults and kidnapping. They also fear the children will be unable to protect themselves in case of fire or other disaster. Parents have been concerned as well that young adolescents left alone will be free to experiment with sex, drugs, and alcohol. But these fears have not been substantiated by statistical data.

Other possible negative effects

Surprisingly enough, in fact, many positive results have actually been observed--positive both for the children and parents involved and for our society as a whole. One such positive result has been the response of the many schools across the country that have instituted courses in "survival skills." In these courses, boys and girls as young as ten learn skills such as cleaning, cooking, and sewing; consumerism; safety and first aid; and how to care for younger siblings. The focus of the home economics courses in these schools has changed as the students' needs have, and the trend toward these "domestic survival courses" seems to be spreading.

First positive effect

Perhaps the most significant effect has been a rather subtle one: the emotional strengths so often observed in the latch-key children. As they learn to fend for themselves, and take pride in doing so, their self-esteem increases. Educators cite these children as more self-reliant, more mature, more confident; parents add that they are also more cooperative around the house. Of course it is still too early to tell whether the latch-key trend will produce a generation of more independent, self-reliant adults, but it is certainly a possibility.

Second positive effect

continued on the following page

continued from the previous page

Conclusion   Clearly, the latch-key syndrome has negative as well as positive results, but the answer is not to have parents leave the workforce. For the majority of working parents, especially in single-parent families, working is an economic necessity. Parents should be able to remain employed, and most of their children will benefit--though some, inevitably, will suffer. The best solution would be the continued development of government-sponsored programs to meet the needs of the latch-key child. Most important among these would be supervised after-school programs, perhaps utilizing school buildings and facilities. Communities and private industry can also contribute-- the former by establishing networks of "block parents" and information and referral services, the latter by offering "flextime" as an option for working parents. Most latch-key children are managing quite well, but their lives and their parents' lives can--and should--be made a lot easier.

EXERCISE 5

Write a cause-and-effect essay on one of the following topics.

- Discuss the likely effects on your present life of one of the following situations: losing your scholarship, loan, or job; becoming a parent; failing a course; inheriting ten thousand dollars.

- The rights of adopted children are under a good deal of scrutiny lately. Although adoptees have long been denied information about their parentage, many people think they should have the right to know the identities of their biological parents. Explore the possible effects of opening adoption files on *one* of the following groups: adoptive parents, foster parents, parents who give their children up for adoption, or adopted children.

- What led you to come to the school you now attend? For instance, were you influenced by the school's size, location, or course offerings? By your friends' choices? By your parents' wishes? By your financial situation?

5f   Writing Comparison-and-Contrast Essays

Comparison-and-contrast essays explain how two subjects are alike or different; sometimes a single comparison-and-contrast essay examines both similarities and differences. The two subjects being compared or contrasted must have a clear **basis of comparison.** That is, they must share qualities or elements in common that make the comparison or contrast logical. Similarities and differences are identified with appropriate transitional words and phrases, such as *similarly* and *likewise* for comparison and *however* and *in contrast* for contrast. These transitions can also signal movement from one subject to another.

(1)   Using Comparison and Contrast

Instructors often ask you to use comparison and contrast in answering examination questions.

- Compare and contrast the Neoclassic and Romantic views of nature. (Literature)
- Discuss the similarities and differences of the insanity defenses for murder under the M'Naghten test and the Durham rule. (Criminology)
- What are the advantages and disadvantages of load and no-load mutual funds? (Personal finance)
- Examine the benefits and liabilities of team-taught and individual teacher-centered classrooms. (Educational methods)
- How did Darwin and Lamarck differ on the subject of mutability of the species? (Biology)

Each of these assignments provides you with cues that tell you how to treat your material. Certain words and phrases—*compare and contrast, similarities and differences, advantages and disadvantages,* and *benefits and liabilities*—indicate that you should use comparison and contrast to structure your answer.

Many other situations also call for comparison and contrast. For example, if your supervisor on a work-study project asked you to write a report discussing the feasibility of two types of insulation, cellulose and urethane foam, you would use comparison and contrast to organize your ideas.

(2)   Student Essay: Comparison and Contrast

When asked by his composition instructor to compare any two subjects, Alan Escobero, a self-professed expert on arcade games, used a *point-by-point comparison* to present his ideas—that is, he alternated between subjects, making a point about one subject and then making a comparable point about the other subject. (A *subject-by-subject comparison* treats one subject in full and then moves on to discuss the other subject in full.)

Arcade Wars

Introduction   Long ago, in a time more innocent than ours, pinball aficionados were content to while away the hours watching silver balls bounce frenetically through a maze of bumpers and flashing lights. That, of course, was in the pre-Space Invader era, before solid-state technology revolutionized the coin-operated game industry and challenged pinball machines with computerized video games. Currently, pinball and video games are locked in deadly combat in arcades across the country for dominance of a multimillion-dollar

Thesis   market. How this battle will be won or lost depends, to a great
statement   extent, on how enthusiasts react to two entirely different game formats.

History   Pinball machines have a long history. They can be traced back to
(Pinball   a popular nineteenth-century game that was played on a table and
machines)   was similar to pool. The original pinball game, a board with a coin chute and variations on the placement of holes, went through a swift period of change. New machines had new scoring and play attraction features. Pinball games as we now know them got their start in the late 1930s and within a few years developed into the flippers, bumpers, and flashing lights we know today.

History (Video   Video games had their start in the solid-state technology that
games)   was a spinoff of the space program and computer research. The first video game, called Pong, appeared in 1972 and had a television screen and a few hand-held controls. This simple machine, which at
continued on the following page

Essay 5f

continued from the previous page
first was viewed by pinball manufacturers as a curiosity, eventually revolutionized the industry and prepared the way for the games that followed. Current video games combine intellectual strategies with elaborate visual effects.

Pinball games mainly attract young males. Players who talk about how they feel playing pinball say that they get great satisfaction from beating the machine. Some say that pinball challenges their skill and enables them to beat a machine on its own terms. Obviously the game provides a release of frustration, a challenge, and an opportunity to win--all very important. It also stimulates the senses with buzzers, gongs, and electronic sounds. One habitual player sums up the attraction of pinball games when he says, "When you play, nothing else counts. It's just you and the machine."

Players (Pinball machines)

Computerized video games attract a different type of player, as a trip to a downtown arcade any weekday at lunchtime will show. Standing beside the usual crowd of teenagers are groups of young executives. And no wonder, for video games draw you into a world that lets your imagination run wild. They can give a player the sense of piloting a starship or the thrill of maneuvering a tank through a realistic battle setting. The most popular--Hexen, Mace, and Street Fighter--allow you to work out your most violent and aggressive fantasies.

Players (Video games)

It is too soon to tell who will win the technological war that is presently being fought in arcades. The stakes are big, for a good machine can take in hundreds of dollars a week. Presently, both pinball and video game designers are planning new and spectacular games. But even the most eager pinball players believe that video

Restatement of thesis

continued on the following page

continued from the previous page

games will eventually triumph. Pinball is still a game of silver balls being bounced by flippers and bumpers, but video games are

Concluding
summary

constantly evolving as computer technology develops. Possibly the most important difference between the two is that when you play a pinball machine, you only push around a ball, but when you play a video game, you fight for a galaxy.

EXERCISE 6

Write a comparison-and-contrast essay on one of the following topics. (You may use a subject-by-subject or a point-by-point comparison.)

• Compare any two athletes, movie or TV stars, writers, or musicians.

• Write an essay about a disillusioning experience you have had. Contrast your original view of what you expected with your feelings after you were disillusioned.

• Try to account for the differences between the best and worst classes or teachers you have had in your academic career.

5g Writing Division-and-Classification Essays

A **division-and-classification** essay **divides** (breaks a subject into its component parts) and **classifies** (groups individual terms into categories). Division and classification are closely related processes. For example, when you *divide* the English language into three historical categories (Old English, Middle English, Modern English) you can then *classify* examples of specific linguistic characteristics by assigning them to the appropriate historical period. Transitional words and phrases help to distinguish categories from one another: *one kind, another group, a related category, the most important component.*

(1) Using Division and Classification

You divide and classify information every time you write an academic paper: you *divide* your subject into possible topics, you *classify* your notes into categories, and you *divide* your paper into paragraphs.

Division and classification are also called for in specific assignments. For example, when you study a laboratory animal, you may arrange your observations in categories that reflect the animal's systems: digestive, circulatory, nervous, and so on. When you write a book review, you may organize your information into sections devoted to plot, the author's previously published works, and your evaluation of the book you are reviewing. Assignments like the following are typical of the many that call for division and classification.

- The English language is constantly in the process of acquiring new words. Write an essay in which you classify some of the many examples of these coinages and adaptations into at least five distinct categories. (History of language midterm)
- Discuss recurrent themes in James Baldwin's novels, short stories, and essays. (American literature research paper)
- Analyze the workings of the federal court system, paying special attention to the relationship between the lower courts, the appellate courts, and the Supreme Court. (Take-home exam in American government)
- Write a detailed report analyzing the possible roles of each member of the management team during the proposed reorganization of the credit department. (Business management report)
- Explain in general terms how the most common orchestral instruments are classified, making sure you provide examples of instruments in each group. (Introduction to music quiz)

(2) Student Essay: Division and Classification

Robin Twery used division and classification to structure the following written version of a presentation she gave to her public speaking class. Before writing out her speech she made an informal outline that enabled her to establish categories and clarify the relationship of one category to another.

Classes of Rocks

To most people, rocks are distinguished from one another only by size: some are big; others are little. But actually, rocks are divided into three general classes: igneous rocks, sedimentary rocks, and metamorphic rocks.

Introduction
(Lists
categories)

continued on the following page

continued from the previous page

First category   Igneous rocks were once molten rock; now they have cooled down and solidified. Igneous rocks, like the one I'm holding up now, may be intrusive or extrusive. Intrusive igneous rocks, in their molten state, forced their way into other rocks and cooled and hardened there, sometimes forming very large masses called batholiths. These batholiths are frequently made up of granite, a crystalline rock. Some other intrusive igneous rocks can form between other rocks in the form of sills or dikes. Other igneous rocks are extrusive; that is, they are formed when molten rock is driven out onto the surface of the earth to cool and harden. The molten rock that flows along the earth's surface is lava. The bits of molten rock that are extruded into the air solidify in the air and fall to the ground in the form of volcanic ash and cinder.

Second category   Sedimentary rocks are formed when other rocks break apart. Pieces of rock, borne by water or wind, are deposited in the form of sediments. After a time, these particles are consolidated into rock. Sedimentary rocks may be classified according to the size of the grains of which they are composed, ranging from coarse gravel to finer sand, silt, or clay to fine lime and marl. As you can see in this picture, sedimentary rocks are usually deposited in layers (strata), with the oldest sediments on the bottom and the most recent on top.

Third category   The final category, metamorphic rock, has been subjected to great heat and pressure. Metamorphic rocks have been buried under other rocks so that their structures and their mineral components have been altered by the weight of the layers above and the high temperatures to which they are exposed under the earth. An example of a metamorphic rock is the crystalline rock called gneiss, which is now being passed around the room.

continued on the following page

continued from the previous page

The next time you take a walk, you can look for igneous, Conclusion

sedimentary, and metamorphic rocks. Now that you know that not all

rocks are alike, you will probably look at them in a different light.

EXERCISE 7

Write a division-and-classification essay on one of the following topics.

- Every social group is governed by a hierarchy, a system whereby individuals or groups of people are ranked at different levels according to their relative importance in the group. Choose one group you know well—your extended family, the population of your school, the people on your street, fellow members of a special interest group to which you belong, coworkers at your place of employment—and place individuals within the hierarchy. Explain why each person ranks where he or she does acccording to your scheme.

- Itemize the contents of your desk, the surface as well as the drawers, and classify the items into categories. Then, describe an ideal organization pattern for a college student's desk, adding any items you think are needed in each category.

5h Writing Definition Essays

A **formal definition** includes the term being defined, the class to which it belongs, and the details that distinguish it from the other members of its class.

(term)   (class)   (details)
Carbon is a nonmetallic element occurring as diamond, graphite, and charcoal.

A **definition** essay develops a formal definition with narration, description, exemplification, process, cause and effect, comparison and contrast, or division and classification—or any combination of these patterns. In addition, it may examine the origin of a term by using an **analogy** or by using negation (telling what a term is *not*).

See
6e6

(1) Using Definition

You must define your terms in academic writing to demonstrate to your audience that you know what you are talking about and to clarify crucial concepts or terms. Following are some typical assignments calling for definition.

- The WPA: History, Operation, and Contributions. (American history research paper)
- The Villanelle in French and American Poetry. (Comparative literature paper)
- Distinguish between the Organic and International schools of modern architecture. (Architecture exam)
- What is a colluvial soil? (Agronomy quiz)
- Define the school of painting known as Fauvism, paying particular attention to the early work of Matisse. (History of art midterm)
- Identify and define four of the following dysfunctions: anorexia, autism, schizophrenia, agoraphobia, paranoia, manic depression, dyssymbolia. (Psychology quiz)

(2) Student Essay: Definition

**See
Ch. 50**

In response to the **examination question** "Choose one early twentieth-century American social or political movement and briefly discuss its purpose, its leading supporters, and their social or political contribution," Suzanne Bohrer chose to write on the muckrakers. In defining the term *muckraker*, she decided to include a formal definition, provide a brief explanation of the term's origin, and expand the basic definition to discuss the movement's role in American social and political history.

Introduction
(Includes formal definition and origin of term)

Muckrakers were early twentieth-century reformers whose mission was to look for and uncover political and business corruption. The term muckraker, which referred to the "man with a muckrake" in John Bunyan's Pilgrim's Progress, was first used in a pejorative sense by Theodore Roosevelt, whose opinion of the muckrakers was that they were biased and overreacting. The movement began about

continued on the following page

continued from the previous page

1902 and died down by 1917. Despite its brief duration, however, it had a significant impact on the political, commercial, and even literary climate of the period.

Many popular magazines featured articles whose purpose was to expose corruption. Some of these muckraking periodicals included The Arena, Everybody's, The Independent, and McClure's. Lincoln Steffens, managing editor of McClure's (and later associate editor of American Magazine and Everybody's), was an important leader of the muckraking movement. Some of his exposés were collected in his 1904 book The Shame of the Cities and in two other volumes, and his 1931 autobiography also discusses the corruption he uncovered and the development of the muckraking movement. Ida Tarbell, another noted muckraker, wrote a number of articles for McClure's, some of which were gathered in her 1904 book The History of the Standard Oil Company.

Muckraking appeared in fiction as well. David Graham Phillips, who began his career as a newspaperman, went on to write muckraking magazine articles and eventually novels about contemporary economic, political, and social problems such as insurance scandals, state and municipal corruption, shady Wall Street dealings, slum life, and women's emancipation.

Perhaps the best-known muckraking novel was Upton Sinclair's The Jungle, the 1906 exposé of the Chicago meatpacking industry. The novel focuses on an immigrant family and sympathetically and realistically describes their struggles with loan sharks and others who take advantage of their innocence. More importantly, Sinclair graphically describes the brutal working conditions of those who find work in the stockyards. Sinclair's description of the main character's

Thesis statement

First point— movement's influence reflected in magazines

Second point— movement's influence reflected in fiction of D. G. Phillips

Third (and most important) point— movement's influence reflected in The Jungle

continued on the following page

105

continued from the previous page

work in the fertilizer plant is particularly gruesome; at the novel's end, this man turns to socialism.

Conclusion   With the muckrakers featured prominently in fiction, magazines, and newspapers--especially the New York <u>World</u> and the Kansas City <u>Star</u>--some results were forthcoming. Perhaps the most far-reaching was the pure-food legislation of 1906, supposedly a direct result of Roosevelt's reading of <u>The Jungle</u>. In any case, the muckrakers helped to nourish the growing tradition of social reform in America.

EXERCISE 8

Write a definition essay on one of the following topics.

- Select a term or concept that is central to an understanding of one of your courses other than English composition. Explain the term or concept to someone who has not yet taken the course.

- Choose a word or phrase that has a strong emotional meaning to almost everyone—*patriotism* or *family values*, for example—and interview five people from different age groups and backgrounds, asking each what the term means. Use their responses to write a definition essay developed with a series of examples.

✔ CHECKLIST: PATTERNS OF ESSAY DEVELOPMENT

✔ **Narration** Have you discussed enough events to enable readers to understand what occurred? Have you supported your thesis statement with specific details and dialogue?

✔ **Description** Have you supplied enough detail about what things look like, sound like, smell like, taste like, and feel like? Will your readers be able to visualize the person, object, or setting that your essay describes?

✔ **Exemplification** Have you presented enough individual examples to support your essay's thesis? If you have used a single extended example, will readers understand how it supports the essay's thesis?

continued on the following page

continued from the previous page

✔ **Process** Have you presented enough steps to enable readers to understand how the process is performed? Is the sequence of steps clear? If you are writing instructions, have you included enough explanation—including reminders and warnings—to enable readers to perform the process?

✔ **Cause and Effect** Have you identified enough causes (subtle as well as obvious, minor as well as major) to enable readers to understand why something occurred? Have you identified enough effects to show the significance of the causes and the impact they had?

✔ **Comparison and Contrast** Have you supplied a sufficient number of details to illustrate each of the subjects in the comparison? Have you presented a similar number of details for each subject?

✔ **Division and Classification** Have you presented enough information to enable readers to identify each category and distinguish one from another?

✔ **Definition** Have you presented enough detail (examples, analogies, and so on) to enable readers to understand the term you are defining and to distinguish it from others in its class?

CHAPTER 6

WRITING PARAGRAPHS

A **paragraph** is a group of related sentences, which may be complete in itself or part of a longer piece of writing. Paragraphs have three important functions:

- They join sentences together into units that support an essay's thesis. In a short essay, each paragraph may develop one part of the thesis. In a longer essay, a group of related paragraphs, called a **paragraph cluster,** may develop each point.
- They provide visual breaks in the text, enabling readers to pause and assimilate ideas.
- They indicate the progression of ideas in an essay.

WHEN TO PARAGRAPH

- **To signal a shift in focus** Begin a new paragraph whenever you move from one major point to another.
- **To signal a shift in time or place** Begin a new paragraph whenever you move your readers from one time period or location to another.
- **To clarify sequence** Begin a new paragraph every time you begin discussing a new step in a process or sequence.
- **To make ideas more emphatic** Underscore important ideas by isolating them in separate paragraphs.
- **To set off dialogue** Begin a new paragraph every time a new person speaks.
- **To set off introductions and conclusions** Begin a new paragraph to signal the end of your introduction and the beginning of your conclusion.

WRITING PARAGRAPHS

Although most paragraphs that you write will be part of an essay, some will stand alone. For example, you may write a **summary** or a **paraphrase**, a **response statement**, an **abstract**, or an **exam answer**.

See
41a1–2

See
47b1

See
49b1

See
50d

6a Charting Paragraph Structure

Charting a paragraph helps you see its underlying structure. By charting your paragraphs, you can make certain that each one is **unified**, **coherent**, and **well developed**.

See
6b–d

Begin charting by assigning the sentence that expresses the main idea of the paragraph to level 1. If no sentence in the paragraph expresses the main idea, compose a sentence that does. Then, read each sentence of the paragraph. Assign to level 1 sentences as important as the one containing the main idea. Indent and assign to level 2 more specific sentences, those that qualify or limit the main idea. Indent again and assign to level 3 any sentences that support level-2 sentences. Do this for every sentence in the paragraph, assigning increasingly higher numbers to more specific sentences.

Notice in the following paragraph how the first sentence (level 1) introduces the topic of the paragraph by stating the main idea. Each level-2 sentence restricts the topic by explaining this idea. Finally, the level-3 sentences illustrate the points made in the level-2 sentences.

1 My grandmother told me that fifty years ago life was not easy for a girl in rural Italy.
  2 At the age of six a girl was expected to help her mother with household chores.
    3 Girls of this age were no longer permitted to play games or to indulge in childish activities.
  2 At the age of twelve, a girl assumed most of the responsibilities of an adult.
    3 She worked in the fields, prepared meals, carried water, and took care of the younger children.
    3 It was an unusual family that allowed a girl to enroll in one of the few convent schools that took peasant children.

Keep in mind that a logically constructed paragraph has only one level-1 sentence. If your charting reveals more than one level-1 sentence, you need to revise your paragraph, perhaps dividing it into two paragraphs.

6b Writing Unified Paragraphs

A paragraph is **unified** when its sentences develop a single idea. You can create unified paragraphs by making sure that each paragraph has a **topic sentence** that states its main idea.

(1) Using Topic Sentences

Topic sentences can be placed at the beginning, in the middle, or at the end of a paragraph. In some cases, the paragraph's main idea is implied, and so there is no stated topic sentence.

Topic Sentence at the Beginning   Usually, you place a topic sentence at the beginning of a paragraph, where it tells readers what to expect and helps them to understand your paragraph's main idea immediately. Beginning with the topic sentence also helps you to stay focused on your subject.

I was a listening child, careful to hear the very different sounds of Spanish and English. Wide-eyed with hearing, I'd listen to sounds more than words. First, there were English *(gringo)* sounds. So many words were still unknown that when the butcher or the lady at the drugstore said something to me, exotic polysyllabic sounds would bloom in the midst of their sentences. Often the speech of people in public seemed to me very loud, booming with confidence. The man behind the counter would literally ask, "What can I do for you?" But by being so firm and so clear, the sound of his voice said that he was a *gringo;* he belonged in public society. (Richard Rodriguez, *Aria: A Memoir of a Bilingual Childhood*)

Topic Sentence in the Middle   You place a topic sentence in the middle of a paragraph when you want to lead up to the main idea gradually or give background information before you state and support your main idea.

African-American servicemen have played a role in the US military since revolutionary times. In the years before World War II, however, they were employed chiefly as truck drivers, quartermasters, bakers, and cooks. Then, in July 1941, a program was set up at

Alabama's Tuskegee Institute to train black fighter pilots. Eventually, nearly one thousand flyers—about half of whom fought overseas—were trained there; sixty-six of these men were killed in action. Ironically, even as African-American servicemen were fighting valiantly against fascism in Europe, they continued to experience discrimination in the US military. Black officers encountered hostility and even violence at officers' clubs. Enlisted men and women were frequently the target of bigoted remarks. Throughout the war, in fact, African-American servicemen were placed in separate, all-black units. This segregation was official army policy until 1948, when President Harry S. Truman signed an executive order to desegregate the military. (Student Writer)

Topic Sentence at the End   Occasionally, particularly if you are presenting a controversial idea, you may decide to place a topic sentence at the end of a paragraph. If you introduce an unusual, surprising, or hard-to-accept idea at the beginning of a paragraph, you risk alienating your audience. However, if you present a logical chain of reasoning and *then* state your conclusion in the topic sentence, you are more likely to convince readers that your conclusion is reasonable.

These sprays, dusts and aerosols are now applied almost universally to farms, gardens, forests, and homes—nonselective chemicals that have the power to kill every insect, the "good" and the "bad," to still the song of birds and the leaping of fish in the streams, to coat the leaves with a deadly film, and to linger on in soil—all this though the intended target may be only a few weeds or insects. Can anyone believe it is possible to lay down such a barrage of poisons on the surface without making it unfit for life? They should not be called "insecticides," but "biocides." (Rachel Carson, "The Obligation to Endure," *Silent Spring*)

Main Idea Implied   In some situations you may not need a topic sentence—for example, if the topic sentence is stated in the previous paragraph of a paragraph cluster or if an explicit topic sentence would seem forced or unnatural, as it might in some narrative or descriptive paragraphs. Even in such cases, your paragraph must have a central unifying idea, but this idea can be implied instead of stated in a topic sentence. In the following paragraph, for example, the author wants readers to conclude for themselves (as she did) that because she was female, she was considered inferior.

I am eight years old and a tomboy. I have a cowboy hat, cowboy boots, checkered shirt and pants, all red. My playmates are my brothers, two and four years older than I. Their colors are black and green, the only difference in the way we are dressed. On Saturday nights we all go to the picture show, even my mother; Westerns are her favorite kind of movie. Back home, "on the ranch," we pretend we are Tom Mix, Hopalong Cassidy, Lash LaRue (we've even named one of our dogs Lash LaRue); we chase each other for hours rustling cattle, being outlaws, delivering damsels from distress. Then my parents decide to buy my brothers guns. These are not "real" guns. They shoot "BBs," copper pellets my brothers say will kill birds. Because I am a girl, I do not get a gun. Instantly I am relegated to the position of Indian. Now there appears a great distance between us. They shoot and shoot at everything with their new guns. I try to keep up with my bow and arrows. (Alice Walker, "Beauty: When the Other Dancer Is the Self," *In Search of Our Mothers' Gardens*)

(2) Revising for Unity

Each sentence in a paragraph should support its main idea, whether that idea is stated or implied. When you reread your paragraphs, look carefully for sentences that do not support the main idea and revise or delete them to bring your paragraph into focus. The following paragraph is not unified because it includes sentences that do not support the main idea.

<u>One of the first problems that students have is learning to use a computer.</u> All students were required to buy a computer before school started. Throughout the first semester we took a special course to teach us to use a computer. My notebook computer has a large memory and can do word processing and spreadsheets. It has a hard drive and a modem. My parents were happy that I had a computer, but they were concerned about the price. Tuition was high, and when they added in the price of the computer, it was almost out of reach. To offset expenses, I got a part-time job in the school library. Now I am determined to overcome "computer anxiety" and to master my computer by the end of the semester. (Student Writer)

The lack of unity in the preceding paragraph becomes obvious when you **chart** its structure.

See
6a

1 One of the first problems that students have is learning to use a computer.
  2 All students were required to buy a computer before school started.
    3 Throughout the first semester we took a special course to teach us to use a computer.

1 My notebook computer has a large memory and can do word processing and spreadsheets.
2 It has a hard drive and a modem.
1 My parents were happy that I had a computer, but they were concerned about the price.
2 Tuition was high, and when they added in the price of the computer, it was almost out of reach.
3 To offset expenses, I arranged for a part-time job in the school library.
1 Now I am determined to overcome "computer anxiety" and to master my computer by the end of the semester.

Each level-1 sentence represents a topic that could be developed in its own paragraph; in other words, this paragraph has not one but four topic sentences. Instead of writing one unified paragraph, the writer has made a series of false starts.

Before revising this paragraph, the writer had to decide what his main idea actually was. Then he deleted the sentences about his parents' financial situation and the computer's characteristics, keeping only those details related to the main idea (expressed in the topic sentence below).

<u>One of the first problems that I had as a college student was learning to use my computer.</u> All first-year students were required to buy a computer before school started. Throughout the first semester, we took a special course to teach us to use the computer. In theory this system sounded fine, but in my case it was a disaster. In the first place, the closest I had ever come to a computer was the hand-held calculator I used in math class. In the second place, I could not type. And to make matters worse, many of the people in my computer orientation course already knew how to operate a computer. By the end of the first week I was convinced that I would never be able to work with my computer.

 WRITING UNIFIED PARAGRAPHS

The patterns you use to shape your ideas in essays **(see Chapter 5)**—narration, description, exemplification, process, cause and effect, comparison and contrast, division and classification, and definition—also give focus to paragraphs **(see 6e)**. Because readers recognize these patterns, they expect your discussion to proceed in certain ways. By fulfilling their expectations, you make it easy for readers to follow your ideas.

EXERCISE 1

Each of the following paragraphs is unified by one main idea, but that idea is not explicitly stated. Identify the main idea of each paragraph, write a topic sentence that expresses it, and decide where in the paragraph to place it.

A. The narrator in Ellison's novel leaves an all-black college in the South to seek his fortune—and his identity—in the North. Throughout the story he experiences bigotry in all forms. Blacks as well as whites, friends as well enemies, treat him according to their preconceived notions of what he should be, or how he can help to advance their causes. Clearly this is a book about racial prejudice. However, on another level, *Invisible Man* is more than the account of a young African-American's initiation into the harsh realities of life in the United States before the civil rights movement. The narrator calls himself invisible because others refuse to see him. He becomes so alienated from society—black and white—that he chooses to live in isolation. But, when he has learned to see himself clearly, he will emerge demanding that others see him too.

B. "Lite" can mean that a product has fewer calories, or less fat, or less sodium, or it can simply mean that the product has a "light" color, texture, or taste. It may also mean none of these. Food can be advertised as 86 percent fat free when it is actually 50 percent fat because the term "fat free" is based on weight, and fat is extremely light. Another misleading term is "no cholesterol," which is found on some products that never had any cholesterol in the first place. Peanut butter, for example, contains no cholesterol—a fact that manufacturers have recently made an issue—but it is very high in fat and so would not be a very good food for most dieters. Sodium labeling presents still another problem. The terms "sodium free," "very low sodium," "low sodium," "reduced sodium," and "no salt added" have very specific meanings, frequently not explained on the packages on which they appear.

6c Writing Coherent Paragraphs

A paragraph is **coherent** if its ideas flow logically from one sentence to another.

TECHNIQUES FOR ACHIEVING PARAGRAPH COHERENCE

- Arrange details according to an organizing principle.
- Use transitional words and phrases.
- Use pronouns.
- Use parallel structure.
- Repeat key words and phrases.

(1) Arranging Details

Even if its sentences are all about the same subject, a paragraph lacks coherence if the sentences are not arranged according to an organizing principle—*spatial, chronological,* or *logical.*

Spatial Order Paragraphs arranged in **spatial** order establish the perspective from which readers will view details. For example, an object or scene can be viewed from top to bottom or from near to far. Spatial order is central to paragraphs that use **description**. Notice how the following descriptive paragraph begins on top of a hill, moves down to a valley, follows a river through the valley into the distance, and then moves to a point behind the speaker, where Mount Adams stands.

See 6e2

East of us rose another hill like ours. Between the hills, far below, was the highway which threaded south into the valley. This was the Yakima valley; I had never seen it before. It is justly famous for its beauty, like every planted valley. It extended south into the horizon, a distant dream of a valley, a Shangri-la. All its hundreds of low, golden slopes bore orchards. Among the orchards were towns, and roads, and plowed and fallow fields. Through the valley wandered a thin, shining river; from the river extended fine, frozen irrigation ditches. Distance blurred and blued the sight, so that the whole valley looked like a thickness or sediment at the bottom of the sky. Directly behind us was more sky, and empty lowlands blued by distance, and Mount Adams. Mount Adams was an enormous, snow-covered volcanic cone rising flat, like so much scenery. (Annie Dillard, "Total Eclipse")

Chronological Order Paragraphs arranged in **chronological** order present details in sequence, using transitional words and phrases that establish the sequence of events—*at first, yesterday, later,* and so on. Chronological order is central to paragraphs that use **narration**. The following narrative paragraph gains coherence from the orderly sequence of events.

See 6e1

They married in February, 1921, and began farming. Their first baby, a daughter, was born in January, 1922, when my mother was 26 years old. The second baby, a son, was born in March, 1923. They were renting farms; my father, besides working his own fields, also was a hired man for two other farmers. They had no capital initially, and had to gain it slowly, working from dawn until midnight every day. My town-bred mother learned to set hens and raise chickens, feed pigs, milk cows, plant and harvest a garden, and can every fruit and vegetable she could scrounge. She carried water nearly a quarter of a mile from the well to fill her wash boilers in order to do her laundry on a scrub board. She learned to shuck grain, feed threshers, shuck and husk corn, feed corn pickers. In September, 1925, the third baby came, and in June, 1927, the fourth child—both daughters. In 1930, my parents had enough money to buy their own farm, and that March they moved all their livestock and belongings themselves, 55 miles over rutted, muddy roads. (Donna Smith-Yackel, "My Mother Never Worked")

See
6e4

Chronological order is also used to arrange details in **process** paragraphs, which explain how something works or how to carry out a procedure.

Logical Order   Paragraphs arranged in **logical** order present ideas in terms of their logical relationship to one another. For example, the ideas in a paragraph may move from *general to specific,* as in the conventional topic-sentence-at-the-beginning paragraph, or the ideas may progress from *specific to general,* as they do when the topic sentence appears at the end of the paragraph. A writer may also choose to begin with the *least important* idea and move to the *most important.* (In technical or business writing, writers often begin with the *most important* idea and move to the *least important.*)

The following paragraph moves from a *general* statement about the need to address the problem of the injury rate in boxing to *specific* solutions.

Several reforms would help solve the problem of the high injury rate in boxing. First, all boxers should wear protective equipment—head gear and kidney protectors, for example. This equipment is required in amateur boxing and should be required in professional boxing. Second, the object of boxing should be to score points, not to knock out opponents. An increased glove weight would make knockouts almost impossible. And finally, all fights should be limited to ten rounds. Studies show that most serious injuries occur in boxing between the eleventh and fifteenth rounds—when the boxers are tired and vulnerable. By limiting the number of rounds a boxer could fight, officials could substantially reduce the number of serious injuries. (Student Writer)

(2) Using Transitional Words and Phrases

Transitional words and phrases clarify the relationships among sentences in a paragraph by identifying spatial, chronological, and logical connections. (These words and phrases are also used to achieve **coherence between paragraphs** in an essay.) In the following paragraph, words and phrases such as *after, finally, once again,* and *in the end* identify the order in which events occurred.

See 6c6

Napoleon certainly made a change for the worse by leaving his small kingdom of Elba. <u>After Waterloo</u>, he went back to Paris, and he abdicated for a second time. <u>A hundred days after</u> his return from Elba, he fled to Rochfort in hope of escaping to America. <u>Finally</u>, he gave himself up to the English captain of the ship *Bellerophon*. <u>Once again</u>, he suggested that the Prince Regent grant him asylum, and <u>once again</u>, he was refused. <u>In the end</u>, all he saw of England was the Devon coast and Plymouth Sound as he passed on to the remote island of St. Helena. <u>After six years of exile</u>, he died on May 5, 1821, at the age of fifty-two. (Norman Mackenzie, *The Escape from Elba*)

USING TRANSITIONAL WORDS AND PHRASES

To Signal Sequence or Addition

again	furthermore
also	in addition
and	last
besides	next
finally	one . . . another
first . . . second . . . third	still
	too

To Signal Time

afterward	immediately
as soon as	in the meantime
at first	later
at length	meanwhile
at the same time	next
before	now
earlier	soon
eventually	subsequently
finally	then
	until

continued on the following page

---

continued from the previous page

To Signal Comparison

also	likewise
by the same token	similarly
in comparison	

To Signal Contrast

although	nevertheless
but	nonetheless
despite	on the contrary
even though	on the one hand . . .
however	on the other hand
in contrast	still
instead	whereas
meanwhile	yet

To Signal Examples

for example	specifically
for instance	thus
namely	

To Signal Narrowing of Focus

after all	in particular
indeed	specifically
in fact	that is
in other words	

To Signal Conclusions or Summaries

as a result	in summary
consequently	therefore
in conclusion	thus
in other words	to conclude

To Signal Concession

admittedly	naturally
certainly	of course
granted	

To Signal Causes or Effects

accordingly	since
as a result	so
because	then
consequently	therefore
hence	

(3) Using Pronouns

By referring to nouns or other pronouns, **pronouns** establish connections between sentences. Clear, well-placed **pronoun references**, such as those in the paragraph below, help to make a paragraph's ideas easier to follow.

See
24c

> Like Martin Luther, John Calvin wanted to return to the principles of early Christianity described in the New Testament. Martin Luther founded the evangelical churches in Germany and Scandinavia, and John Calvin founded a number of reformed churches in other countries. A third Protestant branch, episcopacy, developed in England. Its members rejected the word *Protestant* because they agreed with Roman Catholicism on most points. All these sects rejected the primacy of the pope. They accepted the Bible as the only source of revealed truth, and they held that faith, not good works, defined a person's relationship to God. (Student Writer)

(4) Using Parallel Structure

Parallelism—the use of similar grammatical constructions to reinforce similar ideas—can help to increase the coherence of a paragraph; the absence of parallelism can blur the relationships among ideas. Note in the following paragraph how parallel clauses (sentences that begin with "He was") link Thomas Jefferson's accomplishments and make the paragraph's emphasis clear.

See
12c;
18a

> Thomas Jefferson was born in 1743 and died at Monticello, Virginia, on July 4, 1826. During his eighty-four years he accomplished a number of things. Although best known for his draft of the Declaration of Independence, Jefferson was a man of many talents who had a wide intellectual range. He was a patriot who was one of the revolutionary founders of the United States. He was a reformer who, when he was governor of Virginia, drafted the Statute for Religious Freedom. He was an innovator who drafted an ordinance for governing the West and devised the first decimal monetary system. He was a president who abolished internal taxes, reduced the national debt, and made the Louisiana Purchase. And, finally, he was an architect who designed Monticello and the University of Virginia. (Student Writer)

(5) Using Key Words and Phrases

Repeating **key words and phrases**—those essential to meaning—throughout a paragraph increases coherence by connecting the sentences to one another and to the paragraph's main idea. The following paragraph repeats the key word *mercury* to help readers focus on the subject.

Mercury poisoning is a problem that has long been recognized. "Mad as a hatter" refers to the condition prevalent among nineteenth-century workers who were exposed to <u>mercury</u> during the manufacturing of felt hats. Workers in many other industries, such as mining, chemicals, and dentistry, were similarly affected. In the 1950s and 1960s there were cases of <u>mercury</u> poisoning in Minamata, Japan. Research showed that there were high levels of <u>mercury</u> pollution in streams and lakes surrounding the village. In the United States this problem came to light in 1969 when a New Mexico family got sick from eating food tainted with <u>mercury</u>. Since then pesticides containing <u>mercury</u> have been withdrawn from the market, and chemical wastes can no longer be dumped into the ocean. (Student Writer)

Notice that to avoid monotony the writer sometimes refers indirectly to the subject of the paragraph with phrases such as *similarly affected* and *this problem*.

(6) Achieving Coherence between Paragraphs

The strategies you use to establish coherence within paragraphs may also be used to link paragraphs in an essay. In addition to these strategies, you can use topic sentences to connect paragraphs. You can also use a transitional paragraph as a bridge between two paragraphs.

ACHIEVING COHERENCE BETWEEN PARAGRAPHS

- Arrange paragraphs within an essay according to an organizing principle. **(See 6c1.)**
- Use transitional words and phrases to connect paragraphs. **(See 6c2.)**
- Use pronouns to connect paragraphs. **(See 6c3.)**
- Use parallel structure to connect paragraphs. **(See 6c4.)**
- Connect paragraphs by repeating key words and phrases. **(See 6c5.)**
- Use topic sentences to connect paragraphs. **(See 6b1.)**
- Use transitional paragraphs to connect paragraphs. **(See 6f1.)**

The following **paragraph cluster** shows how some of the preceding strategies work together to create a tightly knit unit.

<u>A language may borrow a word directly or indirectly.</u> A direct borrowing means that the borrowed item is a native word in the language it is borrowed from. *Festa* was borrowed directly from

French and can be traced back to Latin *festa*. On the other hand, the word *algebra* was borrowed from Spanish, which in turn borrowed it from Arabic. Thus *algebra* was indirectly borrowed from Arabic, with Spanish as an intermediary.

Some languages are heavy borrowers. Albanian has borrowed so heavily that few native words are retained. On the other hand, most Native American languages have borrowed little from their neighbors.

English has borrowed extensively. Of the 20,000 or so words in common use, about three-fifths are borrowed. Of the 500 most frequently used words, however, only two-sevenths are borrowed, and because these "common" words are used over and over again in sentences, the actual frequency of appearance of native words is about 80 percent. Morphemes such as *and, be, have, it, of, the, to, will, you, on, that,* and *is* are all native to English. (Victoria Fromkin and Robert Rodman, *An Introduction to Language*, 4th ed.)

This paragraph cluster is arranged according to a logical organizing principle: it moves from the general concept of borrowing words to a specific discussion of English, which borrows extensively. In addition, each topic sentence contains a variation of the word group *A language may borrow*, repeating or echoing the key words *borrow* and *language*. Throughout the three paragraphs, some form of these key words (as well as *word* and the names of various languages) appears in almost every sentence.

EXERCISE 2

A. Read the following paragraph and determine how the author achieves coherence. Identify parallel elements, pronouns, repeated words, and transitional words and phrases that link sentences.

Some years ago the old elevated railway in Philadelphia was torn down and replaced by the subway system. This ancient El with its barnlike stations containing nut-vending machines and scattered food scraps had, for generations, been the favorite feeding ground of flocks of pigeons, generally one flock to a station along the route of the El. Hundreds of pigeons were dependent upon the system. They flapped in and out of its stanchions and steel work or gathered in watchful little audiences about the feet of anyone who rattled the peanut-vending machines. They even watched people who jingled change in their hands, and prospected for food under the feet of the crowds who gathered between trains. Probably very few among the waiting people who tossed a crumb to an eager pigeon realized that this El was like a food-bearing river, and that the life which haunted its banks was dependent upon the running of the trains with their human freight. (Loren Eiseley, *The Night Country*)

B. Revise the following paragraph to make it more coherent.

The theory of continental drift was first put forward by Alfred Wegener in 1912. The continents fit together like a gigantic jigsaw puzzle. The opposing Atlantic coasts, especially South America and Africa, seem to have been attached. He believed that at one time, probably 225 million years ago, there was one supercontinent. This continent broke into parts that drifted into their present positions. The theory stirred controversy during the 1920s and eventually was ridiculed by the scientific community. In 1954 the theory was revived. The theory of continental drift is accepted as a reasonable geological explanation of the continental system. (Student Writer)

EXERCISE 3

Read the following paragraph cluster. Then revise as necessary to increase coherence among paragraphs.

Leave It to Beaver and *Father Knows Best* were typical of the late 1950s and early 1960s. Both were popular during a time when middle-class mothers stayed home to raise their children while fathers went to "the office." The Beaver's mother, June Cleaver, always wore a dress and high heels, even when she vacuumed. So did Margaret Anderson, the mother on *Father Knows Best*. Wally and the Beaver lived a picture-perfect small-town life, and Betty, Bud, and Kathy never had a problem that father Jim Anderson couldn't solve.

The Brady Bunch featured six children and the typical Mom-at-home and Dad-at-work combination. Of course, Carol Brady did wear pants, and the Bradys were what today would be called a "blended family." Nevertheless, *The Brady Bunch* presented a hopelessly idealized picture of upper-middle-class suburban life. The Brady kids lived in a large split-level house, went on vacations, had two loving parents, and even had a live-in maid, the ever-faithful, wisecracking Alice. Everyone in town was heterosexual, employed, able-bodied, and white.

The Cosby Show was extremely popular. It featured two professional parents, a doctor and a lawyer. They lived in a townhouse with original art on the walls, and money never seemed to be a problem. In addition to warm relationships with their siblings, the Huxtable children also had close ties to their grandparents. *The Cosby Show* did introduce problems, such as son Theo's dyslexia, but in many ways it replicated the 1950s formula. Even in the 1980s, it seemed, father still knew best.

6d Writing Well-Developed Paragraphs

A paragraph is **well developed** when it includes all the support it needs to communicate its main idea. Support can consist of examples, statistics, anecdotes, or the opinions of experts. Without adequate development, a paragraph is just a series of generalizations that do little to persuade or enlighten readers.

TYPES OF SUPPORT

- **Examples**—Specific illustrations of a general point
- **Statistics**—Numerical summaries of a number of examples
- **Anecdotes**—Short narratives
- **Expert opinions**—Statements by those with experience in a particular field

---

Keep in mind that it is not the number of sentences or number of examples in a paragraph that determines whether or not the paragraph is well developed. The amount and kind of support you need depend on your audience, your main idea, and your purpose. If, for example, your purpose is to explain a complicated process or to describe an unfamiliar or unusual place, your paragraph will have to provide a good deal of detail. If, however, your main idea is one that your readers will have little difficulty understanding, you may need fewer details.

(1) Testing for Adequate Development

Just as **charting paragraph structure** can help you see whether a paragraph is unified, it can also help you determine whether the paragraph is well developed. At first glance, the following paragraph may seem adequately developed.

See 6a

> From Thanksgiving until Christmas, children and their parents are bombarded by ads for violent toys and games. Toy manufacturers persist in thinking that only toys that appeal to children's aggressiveness will sell. Despite claims that they (unlike action toys) have educational value, video games have escalated the level of violence. The real question is why parents continue to buy these violent toys and games for their children.

Charting the underlying structure of the paragraph, however, reveals a problem.

1 From Thanksgiving until Christmas, children and their parents
  are bombarded by ads for violent toys and games.
2 Toy manufacturers persist in thinking that only toys that appeal to children's aggressiveness will sell.
2 Despite claims that they (unlike action toys) have educational
  value, video games have escalated the level of violence.
2 The real question is why parents continue to buy these violent
  toys and games for their children.

Upon closer examination, we see that the paragraph does not contain
enough support to convince readers that children and parents are "bombarded by ads for violent toys." The first sentence of this paragraph, the
topic sentence, is a level-1 sentence. The level-2 sentences do qualify this
topic sentence, but the paragraph offers no level-3 sentences (specific examples). What kind of toys appeal to a child's aggressive tendencies?
What particular video games does the writer object to?

(2) Adding Support

You can improve undeveloped paragraphs like the one above by
adding specific examples that illustrate the statement made in the level-2
sentences.

From Thanksgiving until Christmas, children and their parents
are bombarded by ads for violent toys and games. Toy manufacturers persist in thinking that only toys that appeal to children's aggressiveness will sell. *One television commercial features a commando*
Examples → *team that attacks and captures a miniature enemy base. Toy soldiers*
wear realistic uniforms and carry automatic rifles, pistols, knives,
grenades, and ammunition. Another commercial shows laughing chil-
dren shooting one another with plastic rocket launchers and tanklike
vehicles. Despite claims that they (unlike action toys) have educational value, video games have escalated the level of violence. *The*
Examples → *most popular video games involve children in strikingly realistic com-*
bat simulations. One game lets children search out and destroy enemy
fighters on the ground and in the air. Other best-selling games graphi-
cally simulate hand-to-hand combat on city streets and feature dis-
membered bodies and the sound of breaking bones. The real question
is why parents continue to buy these violent toys and games for
their children.

You can use expert opinion and statistics to develop the paragraph
further.

From Thanksgiving to Christmas, children are bombarded by
ads for violent toys and games. Toy manufacturers persist in thinking that only toys that appeal to children's aggressiveness will sell.

The president of one large toy company recently observed that in spite   ← Expert
of what people may say, they buy action toys. This is why toy compa-   opinion
nies spend so much money on commercials that promote them (Wilson 54). One such television commercial features a commando team that attacks and captures a miniature enemy base. Toy soldiers wear realistic uniforms and carry automatic rifles, pistols, knives, grenades, and ammunition. Another commercial shows laughing children shooting one another with plastic rocket launchers and tanklike vehicles. Despite claims that (unlike action toys) they have educational value, video games have escalated the level of violence. *A parents' watchdog group has estimated that during the*   ← Statistic
past three years violent video games have increased sales by almost 20 percent ("Action Toys Sell" 17). The most popular video games involve children in strikingly realistic combat situations. One game lets children search out and destroy enemy fighters on the ground and in the air. Other best-selling games graphically simulate hand-to hand combat on city streets and feature dismembered bodies and chilling sound effects. The real question is why parents continue to buy these violent toys and games for their children.

This revised paragraph is effective because it does more than make a series of statements: it develops its points thoroughly, supporting statements with concrete details. Along with several specific examples, it includes an expert opinion—a statement by a toy manufacturer—and a statistic that shows the extent to which sales of violent video games have increased. (Notice that the writer documents both the expert opinion and the statistic because she got them from outside sources.)

The following paragraph is also not adequately developed.

> Hand-held calculators have made it impossible for people to think. People have lost their ability to solve simple problems in their minds without using a piece of equipment that does the work for them. Calculators have become too controlling over our intellect. Without calculators many people would be unable to function.

Once you chart the paragraph's structure, the problem becomes clear.

1   Hand-held calculators have made it difficult for many students to think independently.
1   People have lost their ability to think without using a piece of equipment that does the work for them.
1   Calculators have become too controlling over our intellect.
1   Without calculators most of us would be unable to function.

This paragraph contains only level-1 sentences. In other words, it keeps making the same general point over and over again. Because it never develops this point, the paragraph goes nowhere. By editing the first sentence into a topic sentence, editing the second sentence so it restricts the topic sentence, and adding supporting detail the writer expands the discussion and makes this paragraph much more convincing.

Anecdote →
Example →
Statistic →
Expert →
opinion

Hand-held calculators have made it difficult for many people to think independently. They have lost their ability to solve simple problems without using a piece of equipment that does the work for them. Recently, when my math instructor told our class to put away our calculators and take a test, some of the students were unable to solve the problems or to do simple calculations in their heads. Formal studies have shown similar results. In one college, for example, Domb reports that a number of students in physics, chemistry, and accounting classes were unable to do simple problems, even though they were able to use calculators to do complex tasks. Shockingly, 22 percent of the students had difficulty calculating 17 percent of $21 or estimating the yearly interest on a car loan. Domb concludes that the extensive use of calculators has made it unnecessary for students to master the basics of mathematics (43).

✔ CHECKLIST: PARAGRAPH DEVELOPMENT

✔ Chart your paragraph to assess the level of its support. How specific does the paragraph get? How specific should it get?
✔ Identify your audience. Will readers be familiar with your subject? Given the needs of your audience, is the paragraph adequately developed?
✔ Identify your purpose. Should the paragraph give readers a general overview of a topic, or should it present complex information? Given your purpose, is the paragraph adequately developed?
✔ Do you need to add an example, a statistic, an anecdote, or expert opinion?

EXERCISE 4

Write a paragraph for two of the following topic sentences. Make sure you include all the examples and other support necessary to develop the paragraph adequately. Assume that you are writing your paragraph for the members of your composition class.

1. First-year students can take specific steps to make sure that they are successful in college.
2. Setting up a first apartment can be quite a challenge.
3. Whenever I seem depressed, I think of _____, and I feel better.
4. The person I admire the most is _____.
5. If I won the lottery, I would do three things.

EXERCISE 5

Chart each of the paragraphs that you wrote for Exercise 4. If your charting indicates that you have not adequately developed a paragraph, revise it, adding the necessary detail.

6e Patterns of Paragraph Development

The pattern of a paragraph—narration, exemplification, and so on—like the **pattern of an essay**, reflects the way a writer arranges points to express ideas most effectively.

See Ch. 5

(1) Narration

Narrative paragraphs tell a story, usually (but not always) in chronological order. Transitional words and phrases move readers from one time period to the next.

My academic career almost ended as soon as it began when, three weeks after I arrived at college, I decided to pledge a fraternity. By midterms I was wearing a straw hat and saying "Yes sir" to every fraternity brother I met. When classes were over, I ran errands for the fraternity members, and after dinner I socialized and worked on projects with the other people in my pledge class. In between these activities I tried to study. Somehow I managed to write papers, take tests, and attend lectures. By the end of the semester, though, my grades had slipped, and I was exhausted. It was then that I began to ask myself some important questions. I realized that I wanted to be popular, but not at the expense of my grades and my future career. At the beginning of my second semester I dropped out of the fraternity and got a job in the biology lab. Looking back, I realize that it was then that I actually began to grow up. (Student Writer)

(2) Description

Descriptive paragraphs convey how something looks, sounds, smells, tastes, or feels. The arrangement of details is made clear by transitions that identify the spatial relationships.

> When you are inside the jungle, away from the river, the trees vault out of sight. It is hard to remember to look up the long trunks and see the fans, strips, fronds, and sprays of glossy leaves. Inside the jungle you are more likely to notice the snarl of climbers and creepers round the trees' boles, the flowering bromeliads and epiphytes in every bough's crook, and the fantastic silk-cotton tree trunks thirty or forty feet across, trunks buttressed in flanges of wood whose curves can make three high walls of a room—a shady, loamy-aired room where you would gladly live, or die. Butterflies, iridescent blue, striped, or clear-winged, thread the jungle paths at eye level. And at your feet is a swath of ants bearing triangular bits of green leaf. The ants with their leaves look like a wide fleet of sailing dinghies—but they don't quit. In either direction they wobble over the jungle floor as far as the eye can see. I followed them off the path as far as I dared, and never saw an end to ants or to those luffing chips of green they bore. (Annie Dillard, "In the Jungle," from *Teaching a Stone to Talk*, Harper, 1982)

(3) Exemplification

Exemplification paragraphs use specific illustrations to clarify a general statement. Some exemplification paragraphs, like the following, use several examples to support the topic sentence.

> Illiterates cannot travel freely. When they attempt to do so, they encounter risks that few of us can dream of. They cannot read traffic signs and, while they often learn to recognize and to decipher symbols, they cannot manage street names which they haven't seen before. The same is true for bus and subway stops. While ingenuity can sometimes help a man or woman to discern directions from familiar landmarks, buildings, cemeteries, churches, and the like, most illiterates are virtually immobilized. They seldom wander past the streets and neighborhoods they know. Geographical paralysis becomes a bitter metaphor for their entire existence. They are immobilized in almost every sense we can imagine. They can't move up. They can't move out. They cannot see beyond. Illiterates may take an oral test for drivers' permits in most sections of America. It is a questionable concession. Where will they go? How will they get there? How will they get home? Could it be that some of us might like it better if they stayed where they belong? (Jonathan Kozol, *Illiterate America*)

Other exemplification paragraphs develop a single extended example.

Let us imagine a country in which reading is a popular voluntary activity. There, parents read books for their own edification and pleasure, and are seen by their children at this silent and mysterious pastime. These parents also read to their children, give them books for presents, talk to them about books and underwrite, with their taxes, a public library system that is open all day, every day. In school—where an attractive library is invariably to be found—the children study certain books together but also have an active reading life of their own. Years later it may even be hard for them to remember if they read *Jane Eyre* at home and Judy Blume in class, or the other way around. In college young people continue to be assigned certain books, but far more important are the books they discover for themselves—browsing in the library, in bookstores, on the shelves of friends, one book leading to another, back and forth in history and across languages and cultures. After graduation they continue to read, and in the fullness of time produce a new generation of readers. Oh happy land! I wish we all lived there. (Katha Pollitt, "Canon to the Right of Me . . .")

(4) Process

Process paragraphs describe how something works, presenting a series of steps in strict chronological order. The topic sentence identifies the process, and the rest of the paragraph presents the steps involved.

Members of the court have disclosed, however, the general way the conference is conducted. It begins at ten A.M. and usually runs on until late afternoon. At the start each justice, when he enters the room, shakes hands with all others there (thirty-six handshakes altogether). The custom, dating back generations, is evidently designed to begin the meeting at a friendly level, no matter how heated the intellectual differences may be. The conference takes up, first, the applications for review—a few appeals, many more petitions for certiorari. Those on the Appellate Docket, the regular paid cases, are considered first, then the pauper's applications on the Miscellaneous Docket. (If any of these are granted, they are then transferred to the Appellate Docket.) After this the justices consider, and vote on, all the cases argued during the preceding Monday through Thursday. These are tentative votes, which may be and quite often are changed as the opinion is written and the problem thought through more deeply. There may be further discussion at later conferences before the opinion is handed down. (Anthony Lewis, *Gideon's Trumpet*)

When a process paragraph presents instructions to enable readers to actually perform the process, it is written in the present tense and in the imperative mood.

Take a variety of fabrics: velvet, satin, silk, cotton, muslin, linen, tweed, men's shirting; mix with a variety of notions: buttons, lace, grosgrain, or thick silk ribbon lithographed with city scenes, bits of drapery, appliqués of flora and fauna, honeymoon cottages, and clouds. Puff them up with: down, kapok, soft cotton, foam, old stockings. Lay between the back cloth a large expanse of cotton batting; stitch it all together with silk thread, embroidery thread, nylon thread. The stitches must be small, consistent, and reflect a design of their own. (Whitney Otto, *How to Make an American Quilt*)

(5) Cause and Effect

Cause-and-effect paragraphs explore why events occur and what happens as a result of them.
Some paragraphs examine causes.

The main reason that a young baby sucks his thumb seems to be that he hasn't had enough sucking at the breast or bottle to satisfy his sucking needs. Dr. David Levy pointed out that babies who are fed every 3 hours don't suck their thumbs as much as babies fed every 4 hours, and that babies who have cut down on nursing time from 20 minutes to 10 minutes . . . are more likely to suck their thumbs than babies who still have to work for 20 minutes. Dr. Levy fed a litter of puppies with a medicine dropper so that they had no chance to suck during their feedings. They acted just the same as babies who don't get enough chance to suck at feeding time. They sucked their own and each other's paws and skin so hard that the fur came off. (Benjamin Spock, *Baby and Child Care*)

Other paragraphs examine effects.

On December 8, 1941, the day after the Japanese attack on Pearl Harbor in Hawaii, my grandfather barricaded himself with his family—my grandmother, my teenage mother, her two sisters and two brothers—inside of his home in La'ie, a sugar plantation village on Oahu's North Shore. This was my maternal grandfather, a man most villagers called by his last name, Kubota. It could mean either "Wayside Field" or else "Broken Dreams," depending on which ideograms he used. Kubota ran La'ie's general store, and the previous night, after a long day of bad news on the radio, some locals had come by, pounded on the front door, and made threats. One was said to have brandished a machete. They were angry and shocked, as the whole nation was in the aftermath of the surprise attack. Kubota was one of the few Japanese Americans in the village and president of the local Japanese language school. He had become a target for their rage and suspicion. A wise man, he locked all his doors and windows and did not open his store the next day, but stayed closed and waited for news from some official. (Garrett Hongo, "Kubota")

(6) Comparison and Contrast

Comparison-and-contrast paragraphs examine the similarities and differences between two subjects. Comparison emphasizes similarities; contrast emphasizes differences.

Comparison-and-contrast paragraphs can be organized in one of two ways. In some comparison-and-contrast paragraphs, the subjects are compared **point by point:** the paragraph alternates points about one subject with comparable points about the other subject.

> There are two Americas. One is the America of Lincoln and Adlai Stevenson; the other is the America of Teddy Roosevelt and the modern superpatriots. One is generous and humane, the other narrowly egotistical; one is self-critical, the other self-righteous; one is sensible, the other romantic; one is good-humored, the other solemn; one is inquiring, the other pontificating; one is moderate, the other filled with passionate intensity; one is judicious and the other arrogant in the use of great power. (J. William Fulbright, *The Arrogance of Power*)

Other paragraphs, **subject-by-subject** comparisons, treat one subject completely and then move on to the other subject. In the following paragraph, notice how the writer shifts from one subject to the other with the transitional word *however*.

> First, it is important to note that men and women regard conversation quite differently. For women it is a passion, a sport, an activity even more important to life than eating because it doesn't involve weight gain. The first sign of closeness among women is when they find themselves engaging in endless, secretless rounds of conversation with one another. And as soon as a woman begins to relax and feel comfortable in a relationship with a man, she tries to have that type of conversation with him as well. However, the first sign that a man is feeling close to a woman is when he admits

that he'd rather she please quiet down so he can hear the TV. A man who feels truly intimate with a woman often reserves for her and her alone the precious gift of one-word answers. Everyone knows that the surest way to spot a successful long-term relationship is to look around a restaurant for the table where no one is talking. Ah . . . now *that's* real love. (Merrill Markoe, "Men, Women, and Conversation," *What the Dogs Have Taught Me*)

An **analogy** is a special kind of comparison that explains an unfamiliar concept or object by likening it to a familiar one. Here the writer uses the behavior of people to explain the behavior of ants.

Ants are so much like human beings as to be an embarrassment. They farm fungi, raise aphids as livestock, launch armies into wars, use chemical sprays to alarm and confuse enemies, capture slaves. The families of weaver ants engage in child labor, holding their larvae like shuttles to spin out the thread that sews the leaves together for their fungus gardens. They exchange information ceaselessly. They do everything but watch television. (Lewis Thomas, "On Societies as Organisms")

(7) Division and Classification

Division paragraphs take a single item and break it into its components.

The blood can be divided into four distinct components: plasma, red cells, white cells, and platelets. Plasma is 90 percent water and holds a great number of substances in suspension. It contains proteins, sugars, fat, and inorganic salts. Plasma also contains urea and other by-products from the breaking down of proteins, hormones, enzymes, and dissolved gases. In addition, plasma contains the red blood cells that give it color, the white cells, and the platelets. The red cells are most numerous; they get oxygen from the lungs and release it in the tissues. The less numerous white cells are part of the body's defense against invading organisms. The platelets, which occur in almost the same number as white cells, are responsible for clotting. (Student Writer)

Classification paragraphs take many separate items and group them into categories according to qualities or characteristics they share.

Charles Babbage, an English mathematician, reflecting in 1830 on what he saw as the decline of science at the time, distinguished among three major kinds of scientific fraud. He called the first "forging," by which he meant complete fabrication—the recording of observations that were never made. The second category he called "trimming"; this consists of manipulating the data to make them look better, or, as Babbage wrote, "in clipping off little bits here and there from those observations which differ most in *excess* from the mean and in sticking them on to those which are too small." His third category was data selection, which he called "cooking"—the choosing of those data that fitted the researcher's hypothesis and the discarding of those that did not. To this day, the serious discussion of scientific fraud has not improved on Babbage's typology. (Morton Hunt, *New York Times Magazine*)

(8) Definition

Definition paragraphs develop a definition with other patterns—for example, by telling a story (narration), by giving examples (exemplification), or by telling how something works (process).

A gadget is nearly always novel in design or concept and it often has no proper name. For example, the semaphore which signals the arrival of the mail in our rural mailbox certainly has no proper name. It is a contrivance consisting of a piece of shingle. Call it what you like, it saves us frequent frustrating trips to the mailbox in winter when you have to dress up and wade through snow to get there. That's a gadget! (*Smithsonian*)

EXERCISE 6

Determine one possible pattern of development for a paragraph on each of these topics. Then write a paragraph on one of the topics.

1. What success is (or is not)
2. How to write a résumé
3. The kinds of people who listen to radio talk shows
4. My worst date
5. American vs. Japanese education
6. The connection between stress and the immune system
7. Budgeting money wisely
8. Self-confidence
9. Preparing for the perfect vacation
10. Drinking and driving

EXERCISE 7

A. Read each of the following paragraphs, and then answer these questions: In general terms, how could each paragraph be developed further? What pattern of development might be used in each case?

B. Choose one paragraph, and rewrite it to develop it further.

1. Many new words and expressions have entered the English language in the last ten years or so. Some of them come from the world of computers. Others come from popular music. Still others have politics as their source. There are even some expressions that have their origins in films or television shows.

2. Making a good spaghetti sauce is not a particularly challenging task. First, assemble the basic ingredients: garlic, onion, mushrooms, green pepper, and ground beef. Sauté these ingredients in a large saucepan. Then, add canned tomatoes, tomato paste, and water, and stir. At this point, you are ready to add the spices: oregano, parsley, basil, and salt and pepper. Don't forget a bay leaf! Simmer for about two hours, and serve over spaghetti.

3. High school and college are not at all alike. Courses are a lot easier in high school, and the course load is lighter. In college, teachers expect more from students; they expect higher quality work, and they assign more of it. Assignments tend to be more difficult and more comprehensive, and deadlines are usually shorter. Finally, college students tend to be more focused on a particular course of study—even a particular career—than high school students are.

6f Writing Special Kinds of Paragraphs

So far this chapter has focused on **body paragraphs,** the paragraphs that carry the weight of your essay's discussion. Other kinds of paragraphs, however, have specialized functions in an essay.

 WRITING PARAGRAPHS

Body paragraphs present the information needed to support an essay's thesis. **(See 2b1; 6a–f.)**

Transitional paragraphs connect body paragraphs within an essay. **(See 6f1.)**

Introductory paragraphs introduce the essay's subject and give an overview of the essay's scope. **(See 6f2.)**

Concluding paragraphs reinforce the essay's key points. **(See 6f3.)**

(1) Transitional Paragraphs

A longer essay frequently includes one or more **transitional paragraphs** whose function is to connect one section of the essay to another.

At their simplest, transitional paragraphs can be single sentences that move readers from one point to the next.

Let us examine this point further.

This idea works better in theory than in practice.

We need to begin with a few examples.

More often, writers use a transitional paragraph to present a concise summary of what they have already said before moving on to a new point.

The following transitional paragraph uses a series of questions to sum up some of the ideas the writer has been discussing. In the next part of his essay, he goes on to answer these questions.

Can we bleed off the mass of humanity to other worlds? Right now the number of human beings on Earth is increasing by 80 million per year, and each year that number goes up by 1 and a fraction percent. Can we really suppose that we can send 80 million people per year to the Moon, Mars, and elsewhere, and engineer those worlds to support those people? And even so, nearly remain in the same place ourselves? (Isaac Asimov, "The Case Against Man")

(2) Introductory Paragraphs

An **introduction** prepares readers for the essay to follow. It draws readers into an essay, arousing their interest and making them want to read further. Introductions are often straightforward, concerned primarily with presenting information. They introduce the subject, narrow it down, and then state the essay's thesis.

Christine was just a girl in one of my classes. I never knew much about her except that she was strange. She didn't talk much. Her hair was dyed black and purple, and she wore heavy black boots and a black turtleneck sweater, even in the summer. She was attractive—in spite of the ring she wore through her left eyebrow—but she never seemed to care what the rest of us thought about her. Like the rest of my classmates, I didn't really want to get close to her. It was only when we were assigned to do our chemistry project together that I began to understand why Christine dressed the way she did. (Student Writer)

To arouse their audience's interest, writers may depart from this straightforward approach by using one of the following strategies.

135

STRATEGIES FOR EFFECTIVE INTRODUCTIONS

Quotation or Series of Quotations

When Mary Cassatt's father was told of her decision to become a painter, he said: "I would rather see you dead." When Edgar Degas saw a show of Cassatt's etchings, his response was: "I am not willing to admit that a woman can draw that well." When she returned to Philadelphia after twenty-eight years abroad, having achieved renown as an Impressionist painter and the esteem of Degas, Huysmans, Pissarro, and Berthe Morisot, the *Philadelphia Ledger* reported: "Mary Cassatt, sister of Mr. Cassatt, president of the Pennsylvania Railroad, returned from Europe yesterday. She has been studying painting in France and owns the smallest Pekingese dog in the world." (Mary Gordon, "Mary Cassatt," *Good Boys and Dead Girls*)

Question or Series of Questions

Of all the disputes agitating the American campus, the one that seems to me especially significant is that over "the canon." What should be taught in the humanities and social sciences, especially in introductory courses? What is the place of the classics? How shall we respond to those professors who attack "Eurocentrism" and advocate "multiculturalism"? This is not the sort of tedious quarrel that now and then flutters through the academy; it involves matters of public urgency. I propose to see this dispute, at first, through a narrow, even sectarian lens, with the hope that you will come to accept my reasons for doing so. (Irving Howe, "The Value of the Canon")

Definition

Moles are collections of cells that can appear on any part of the body. With occasional exceptions, moles are absent at birth. They first appear in the early years of life, between ages two and six. Frequently moles appear at puberty. New moles, however, can continue to appear throughout life. During pregnancy new moles may appear and old ones darken. There are three major designations of moles, each with its own unique distinguishing characteristics. (Student Writer)

Unusual Comparison

Once a long time ago, people had special little boxes called refrigerators in which milk, meat, and eggs could be

continued on the following page

continued from the previous page
kept cool. The grandchildren of these simple devices are large enough to store whole cows, and they reach temperatures comparable to those at the South Pole. Their operating costs increase each year, and they are so complicated that few home handymen attempt to repair them on their own. Why has this change in size and complexity occurred in America? It has not taken place in many areas of the technologically advanced world (the average West German refrigerator is about a yard high and less than a yard wide, yet refrigeration technology in Germany is quite advanced). Do we really need (or even want) all that space and cold? (Appletree Rodden, "Why Smaller Refrigerators Can Preserve the Human Race")

Controversial Statement
Something had to replace the threat of communism, and at last a workable substitute is at hand. "Multiculturalism," as the new menace is known, has been denounced in the media recently as the new McCarthyism, the new fundamentalism, even the new totalitarianism—take your choice. According to its critics, who include a flock of tenured conservative scholars, multiculturalism aims to toss out what it sees as the Eurocentric bias in education and replace Plato with Ntozake Shange and traditional math with the Yoruba number system. And that's just the beginning. The Jacobins of the multiculturalist movement, who are described derisively as P.C., or politically correct, are said to have launched a campus reign of terror against those who slip and innocently say "freshman" instead of "freshperson," "Indian" instead of "Native American" or, may the Goddess forgive them, "disabled" instead of "differently abled." (Barbara Ehrenreich, "Teach Diversity—with a Smile")

Your introduction should lead naturally into the body of your paper. It should also be consistent with the purpose, tone, and style of the rest of your essay. A serious, formal discussion should have a serious, formal introduction; if your discussion is relaxed and informal, your introduction should also be. Finally, you should avoid opening statements that do no more than announce your subject ("In my paper I will talk about Lady Macbeth") or that undercut your credibility ("I don't know much about alternative energy sources, but I would like to present my opinion about the subject").

✔ CHECKLIST: REVISING INTRODUCTIONS

✔ Does your introduction include your essay's thesis statement?
✔ Does it lead naturally into the body of your essay?
✔ Is it consistent with the purpose, tone, and style of the rest of your essay?
✔ Does it arouse your readers' interest?
✔ Does it avoid statements that simply announce your subject or that undercut your credibility?

(3) Concluding Paragraphs

A **conclusion** should be a complete paragraph that gives readers a sense of closure. Many conclusions begin with specifics—reviewing the essay's main points, for example—and then move to more general statements.

> As an Arab-American, I feel I have the best of two worlds. I'm proud to be part of the melting pot, proud to contribute to the tremendous diversity of cultures, customs and traditions that makes this country unique. But Arab-bashing—public acceptance of hatred and bigotry—is something no American can be proud of. (Ellen Mansoor Collier, "I Am Not a Terrorist")

Other conclusions, however, experiment with different techniques.

STRATEGIES FOR EFFECTIVE CONCLUSIONS

Prediction

　　Looking ahead, [we see that] prospects may not be quite as dismal as they seem. As a matter of fact, we are not doing so badly. It is something of a miracle that creatures who evolved as nomads in an intimate, small-band, wide-open-spaces context manage to get along at all villagers or surrounded by strangers in cubicle apartments. Considering that our genius as a species is adaptability, we may yet learn to live closer and closer to one another, if not in utter peace, then far more peacefully than we do today. (John Pheiffer, "Seeking Peace, Making War")

Opinion

　　A piece of writing is never finished. It is delivered to a deadline, torn out of the typewriter on demand, sent off

continued on the following page

---

continued from the previous page

with a sense of accomplishment and shame and pride and frustration. If only there were a couple more days, time for just another run at it, perhaps then. . . . (Donald Murray, "The Maker's Eye: Revising Your Own Manuscripts")

Quotation

When we let freedom ring, when we let it ring from every village and every hamlet, from every state and every city, we will be able to speed up that day when all of God's children, black men and white men, Jews and Gentiles, Protestants and Catholics, will be able to join hands and sing in the words of the old Negro spiritual, "Free at last! Free at last! Thank God almighty, we are free at last!" (Martin Luther King, Jr., "I Have a Dream")

Your conclusion should not introduce new points or go off in new directions. Because your conclusion is your last word, a confusing, weak, or uninteresting one detracts from an otherwise strong essay. Do not simply repeat your introduction in different words or apologize or in any way cast doubt on your concluding points ("I may not be an expert" or "At least this is my opinion"). If possible, try to end with a statement that readers will remember.

✔ CHECKLIST: REVISING CONCLUSIONS

✔ Is your conclusion a complete paragraph?
✔ Does your conclusion provide a sense of closure?
✔ Does it remind readers of the primary focus of your essay?
✔ Does it avoid digressions and new directions?
✔ Does it do more than repeat your introduction's points?
✔ Does it avoid apologies?
✔ Does it end memorably?

STUDENT WRITER AT WORK

Writing Body Paragraphs

The following draft of a student essay has weak body paragraphs. Rewrite these paragraphs so that they are unified, coherent, and well developed. You may want to chart these paragraphs to help you assess their effectiveness.

Oh, How Things Have Changed!

When my grandfather was supporting his family in 1950, a good job was easy to find. World War II was over, and the United States was experiencing an unprecedented economic boom. The American Dream was alive and well, and people thought they were living in a land of unlimited opportunity. Even though many people did not get past high school, they still got jobs that enabled them to marry and make a down payment on a house. Today, the situation is different. Education, even a college degree, no longer ensures a good job. Now, it takes two people working full-time to provide the lifestyle that people used to maintain with one salary. What has changed? Actually, a number of factors have helped to create the present job climate in the United States.

Currently, there are too many people who are qualified for jobs and not enough jobs to go around. In order to get a good job, a person must be the best. Even many qualified people are being laid off. Companies are now hiring young, inexperienced people because they work for less. High-paid positions are very hard to find.

The current corporate trend to downsize has also contributed to the decline in jobs. In order to cut expenses, many companies have laid off workers. Some companies have laid off thousands of workers, while others have laid off just a few. Whatever the number, the results are the same. People are out of work.

To keep their costs down, some companies have moved their operations to foreign countries where wages are a fraction of those in the United States. General Motors has plants in South America. Many national chains, such as The Gap, buy clothes from manufacturers who have relocated to Southeast Asia. Recently, I bought a pair of shoes and was

continued on the following page

continued from the previous page

surprised to see that they were made in China. American workers may have trouble getting manufacturing jobs as long as this situation exists.

Finally, companies no longer see their workers as valued employees. Too often, upper-level managers treat workers as if they were less than human. Workers are seen as numbers on a balance sheet and treated as if they had no feelings. Even workers who have been with a company for twenty years or more are not safe. They can lose their jobs as easily as someone who has been with the company for just a short time.

The employment situation that existed in the 1950s will never return. Too much has changed since then. Many businesses have become international and feel no loyalty to the United States or its workers. The result is that profit seems to be the only thing that motivates corporate executives. Certainly there are some executives who have supported their workers, but they are the exceptions. Unless our government does something to protect its workers, the United States not only will have a high unemployment rate, but also will be dependent on the rest of the world for its clothes, its appliances, and its transportation. This is a situation that neither the country nor its workers can afford.

Writing Introductions and Conclusions

The following draft of a student essay has an undeveloped introduction and conclusion. Rewrite the opening and closing paragraphs to increase their effectiveness.

Without a doubt, the best class I had during my time in high school was chemistry.

One thing that made the class great was the subject matter and the way it was presented. I can still remember the first day. We just dove right

continued on the following page

continued from the previous page

in, with no introduction at all! Maybe that was why I liked the class so much: there was no fooling around. Everything was presented clearly, and I ate it up. It was one of those classes that you take home with you and apply to everyday life. I used to tell my friends what I learned each day in chemistry. I also used to whine to them about how difficult the class was. Still, the challenge was one of the reasons I enjoyed the class. Chemistry was one of the first classes I worked diligently at, and it set the standard for the rest of my high school career.

Another reason I liked the class was, simply enough, the teacher. Mr. Karoulis was a large, bold, and outspoken man. At first, my classmates and I feared his boisterousness. Over time, though, we grew fond of the man. Because the class was "advanced," Mr. Karoulis gave us freedom. We were allowed to leave the class when we finished exams, and he let us voice our opinions and ask questions. Also, Mr. Karoulis did not just teach chemistry; he taught us many valuable lessons about life in general. If Mr. Karoulis thought something in the news was important, he would stop class and discuss the topic with us. Along the way, he taught me the importance of my heritage and the value of being an individual--a leader, and not a follower.

Of course, I also learned a lot about chemistry and about science in general. The things I learned in that class established the foundation for my later physics and chemistry classes. I still use the knowledge I gained in Mr. Karoulis's class and apply it to new concepts with which I am presented. Most important of all, Mr. Karoulis's class taught me that I could enjoy science and that I could do well in what I had always before seen as an impossibly difficult field.

That class laid the cornerstone upon which I have built my education and planned my future.

PART 2

THINKING CRITICALLY

CHAPTER 7

READING CRITICALLY AND WRITING CRITICAL RESPONSES

When you **read critically,** your goal should be not simply to get information, but also to assess the writer's credibility and to evaluate the soundness of his or her ideas. After all, the fact that something is printed in a book does not automatically establish it as free of bias or contradictions, let alone as meaningful, insightful, or even accurate. Keep in mind, though, that reading critically does not mean searching for flaws and inadequacies in a text. Rather, it means remaining open to new ideas while challenging and questioning what you read and how you react.

Questioning a writer's ideas is perfectly acceptable; in fact, scholars realize that challenging other writers' ideas helps to create new interpretations, perspectives, and theories. The questioning process contributes to an ongoing intellectual debate, a dialogue that helps to keep ideas current and fresh.

 CLOSE-UP READING CRITICALLY

Before you begin to read, you should agree to the following conditions.

- Keep an open mind.
- Withhold judgment.
- Acknowledge your own limitations and biases as a reader.
- Consider the possible reactions and questions of other readers—both to the text and to your ideas.

Once you begin to read, you must be willing to read the text several times. At first, you will simply *analyze* it, identifying its subject and emphasis; then you will *make connections,* comparing ideas so you can identify relationships and understand what the writer is saying. Eventually you will *evaluate* the text, making judgments about the writer's ideas so that you can begin to formulate a critical response.

7a   Reading Actively

Part of the process of becoming a critical reader is reading actively, with pen in hand, physically marking the text. As you do so, you distinguish important points from not-so-important ones; identify interesting parallels and significant relationships; and connect cause with effect, generalization with specific example. This process of **active reading** will help you to understand a text's ideas and prepare you to evaluate its arguments.

(1) Previewing

The first time you encounter a text, you should **preview** it—that is, skim it to gain a sense of the author's subject and emphasis.

When you preview a *book,* begin by looking at its table of contents, especially at the sections that pertain to your topic. A quick glance at the index will reveal the kind and amount of coverage the book gives to subjects that may be important to you. As you leaf through the chapters, look at pictures, graphs, or tables, reading the captions that appear under them.

When you preview a *magazine article,* scan the introductory and concluding paragraphs for summaries of the author's main points. (Journal articles in the sciences and social sciences often begin with summaries called **abstracts**. Read these as part of your previewing process.)

See
49b1

Thesis statements, topic sentences, repeated key terms, transitional words and phrases, and transitional paragraphs can also help you to understand a text's meaning and emphasis, thereby preparing you to react critically to its ideas. In addition, look for the visual cues that writers use to emphasize ideas.

VISUAL CUES

Headings	Color
Capital letters	Italics
Underlining	Lists—with items numbered or set off with
Boxes	bullets (•)
Boldface	

---

(2) Highlighting

When you **highlight** a text, you use symbols and underlining to identify important ideas. (If you are working with library material, photocopy the pages you need and then highlight them.)

✔ CHECKLIST: USING HIGHLIGHTING SYMBOLS

✔ Underline to indicate information you should read again.
✔ Box or circle key words or important phrases.
✔ Put a question mark next to confusing passages, unclear points, or words you need to look up.
✔ Draw lines or arrows to show connections between ideas.
✔ Number points that appear in sequence.
✔ Draw a vertical line in the margin to set off an important section of text.
✔ Star especially important ideas.

The student who highlighted the following passage used the symbols listed in the box above to help her isolate the author's key ideas and clarify the progression of ideas in the passage.

Public zoos came into existence at the beginning of the period ☆ which was to see the disappearance of animals from daily life. The zoo to which people go to meet animals, to observe them, to see them, is, in fact, a monument to the impossibility of such encoun- ☆ ters. Modern zoos are an epitaph to a relationship which was as old as man. They are not seen as such because the wrong questions have been addressed to zoos.

When they were founded—the London Zoo in 1828, the Jardin des Plantes in 1793, the Berlin Zoo in 1844—they brought consid- ①/ erable prestige to the national capitals. The prestige was not so different from that which had accrued to the private royal menageries. These menageries, along with gold plate, architecture, orchestras, players, furnishings, dwarfs, acrobats, uniforms, horses, art and food, had been demonstrations of an emperor's or king's power and wealth. Likewise in the 19th century, public zoos were an endorse- ②/ ment of modern colonial power. The capturing of the animals was a symbolic representation of the conquest of all distant and exotic lands. "Explorers" proved their patriotism by sending home a tiger or an elephant. The gift of an exotic animal to the metropolitan zoo became a token in subservient diplomatic relations.

Yet, like every other 19th century public institution, the zoo, however supportive of the ideology of imperialism, had to claim an independent and civic function. The claim was that it was another kind of museum, whose purpose was to further knowledge and

continued on the following page

147

continued from the previous page

public enlightenment. And so the first questions asked of zoos belonged to natural history; it was then thought possible to study the natural life of animals even in such unnatural conditions. A century

?? later, more sophisticated zoologists such as (Konrad Lorenz) asked (behavioristic) and (ethological) questions, the claimed purpose of which was to discover more about the springs of human action through the study of animals under experimental conditions. (John Berger, *About Looking*)

Notice how highlighting symbols helped the student understand the passage. In addition to underlining and starring the main idea and using arrows to show the relationship of one point to another, she circled and put a question mark next to unfamiliar words, phrases, and names that she needed to look up. Finally, she numbered the two reasons why impe-

See 7c

rial governments established public zoos. Once this student highlighted the passage, she went on to record her reactions to its ideas in the form of marginal **annotations**.

EXERCISE 1

Preview the following passage and then read it more carefully, highlighting it to help you understand the writer's ideas. Then, compare your highlighting with a classmate's. When you are satisfied that you have identified the most important ideas and that you both understand the passage, work together to answer the following questions:

What is the writer's subject?

What is the writer's most important point?

Which points are related?

What is their relationship to one another?

How does the writer make connections among related ideas clear?

My father loved to tell the story of how he got into college. It was 1947 and my father, poor, black and brilliant, was a 15-year-old high school senior in rural Sylvester, Ga. One day he was called into the principal's office to meet a visiting state education official, a white bureaucrat who had learned of my father's academic prowess. The state, the official said, had decided that it wanted to send "a nigra" to college. "You can go to any college in the state," the official told my father. "Except . . . for the University of Georgia, Georgia Tech, Georgia A & M, Emory . . ."

My father was happy and proud to attend Atlanta's Morehouse, perhaps the finest black college in America. But there was always a trace of bitterness when he told this story since his choice of college had, in effect, been made for him.

Times had changed when I applied to college in 1978. Thanks to my father's success as a financial consultant, I grew up in a solidly middle-class home in the Bronx, and, thanks largely to the social advances wrought by the civil rights movement, I was able to attend private school and get into Harvard.

I arrived in Cambridge just as the national backlash against affirmative action was gaining momentum. Many critics were suggesting that African-Americans were inherently inferior students, below the standards of the great universities. I found this argument fatuous, particularly when I encountered some of the less illustrious white students who had allegedly been accepted on "merit." There was, for example, the charming, wealthy young man I'll call "Ted." Intellectually incurious, struggling in most of his courses, Ted said he had been rejected by every college to which he had applied, except Harvard, the alma mater of his father and grandfather.

Ted was what is known as a "legacy." According to Harvard's dean of admissions, William Fitzsimmons, approximately 40 percent of alumni children who apply are admitted each year as against 14 percent of nonalumni applicants.

So Ted and I were beneficiaries of two different forms of affirmative action. He was accepted largely because his forebears had attended Harvard. I was accepted largely because my father had been denied the chance to apply to any predominantly white universities. Yet the type of affirmative action that benefited me is relentlessly assailed while the more venerable form of preferential treatment that Ted enjoyed goes virtually unchallenged.

Whether one is listening to Clarence Thomas's tortuous rationalizations about how he didn't really benefit from affirmative action, or George Bush's railing against racial quotas, which have never been widely supported by Americans, white or black, the underlying message is the same: were it not for affirmative action, America would function as a perfect meritocracy.

Of course there are people of all backgrounds who have succeeded solely through talent and perseverance. But at least as many have been assisted by personal connections, old-boy networks, family ties and the benefits traditionally accorded certain, primarily white, primarily male segments of the American population. Why, in the interminable debate over affirmative action, have these historic advantages generally been brushed aside?

I am not suggesting that most "legacies" or other beneficiaries of long-established de facto affirmative action programs are unqualified for the placements and positions they get. Most of the "legacies" I met at Harvard did just fine there, but so did the great majority of African-Americans. The difference was that the "legacies" were not stigmatized by their extra edge and the black students were. (Jake Lamar, "Whose Legacy Is It, Anyway?")

7b Reading Critically

Once you have a sense of what a writer is saying, you can begin to evaluate what you have read: to distinguish fact from opinion, assess the writer's support, and detect bias. At the same time, you should look for faulty reasoning, logical fallacies, and unfair appeals. As you begin to think critically about your text, you can also start to express your reactions in the form of written **annotations**.

See
7c

Thinking critically about what you read means more than just forming opinions about a writer's ideas. You must also allow what you read to call your own ideas into question, and you must seriously consider the merits of opposing points of view. As you read, remain open-minded; remember that a text may challenge your own accepted beliefs and expose your own biases.

(1) Distinguishing Fact from Opinion

As you read and react critically to a text, you should be evaluating how effectively the writer uses supporting evidence to back up his or her statements. This supporting evidence may be in the form of *fact* or *opinion.*

A **fact** is a verifiable statement that something is true or that something occurred. (Of course, facts may change as new information is uncovered and new discoveries are made. To most Europeans who lived during the late fifteenth century, it was a *fact* that there was no sea route to India. A few decades ago it was a *fact* that a person could not survive a heart transplant.)

An **opinion** is a conclusion or belief that is not substantiated by proof and is, therefore, debatable.

FACT: Measles is a potentially deadly disease.

OPINION: All children should be vaccinated against measles.

An opinion may be *supported* or *unsupported.*

UNSUPPORTED OPINION: All children should be vaccinated against measles.

SUPPORTED OPINION: Despite the fact that an effective measles vaccine is widely available, several unvaccinated Pennsylvania children have died of measles each year since 1992. States that have instituted immunization programs have had no deaths during the same time period. For this reason, all children in Pennsylvania should be vaccinated against measles.

As you read, be very careful to distinguish between fact and opinion as well as between unsupported opinion and opinion that is supported by evidence. Remember too that although offering support for an opinion makes a statement more convincing, it does not turn opinion into fact.

EXERCISE 2

Some of the following statements are facts; others are opinions. Identify each fact with the letter *F* and each opinion with the letter *O*. Then consider what kind of evidence, if any, could support each opinion.

1. The incidence of violent crime fell in the first six months of 1996.
2. New gun laws and more police officers led to a decrease in crime in early 1996.
3. The television rating system uses a system similar to the familiar movie rating codes to let parents know how appropriate a certain show might be for their children.
4. The new television rating system would be better if it gave specifics about the violence, sexual innuendo, and language content in rated television programs.
5. Affirmative action laws and policies have helped women and minority group members advance in the workplace.
6. Affirmative action policies have outlived their usefulness.
7. Women who work are better off today than they were twenty years ago.
8. The wage gap between men and women in similar jobs is smaller now than it was twenty years ago.
9. The Charles River and Boston Harbor currently test much lower for common pollutants than they did ten years ago.
10. We don't need to worry about environmental legislation anymore because we've made great advances in cleaning up our environment.

(2) Evaluating Supporting Evidence

The more reliable the supporting evidence, the more convincing a statement will be—and the more willing readers will be to accept it.

KINDS OF SUPPORTING EVIDENCE

Examples

The American Civil Liberties Union is an organization that has been unfairly characterized as left wing. It is true that it has opposed prayer in the public schools, defended conscientious objectors, and challenged police methods of conducting questioning and searches of suspects. However, it has also backed the antiabortion group Operation Rescue in a police brutality suit and presented a legal brief in support of a Republican politician accused of violating an ethics law.

Statistics

A recent National Institute of Mental Health study concludes that mentally ill people account for more than 30 percent of the homeless population. Because so many homeless people have psychiatric disabilities, the federal government should seriously consider expanding the state mental hospital system.

Expert Testimony

Clearly no young soldier ever really escapes the emotional consequences of war. As William Manchester, noted historian and World War II combat veteran, observes in his essay "Okinawa: The Bloodiest Battle of All," "the invisible wounds remain" (72).

No matter what kind of supporting evidence writers use, it must be *accurate, sufficient, representative,* and *relevant.*

Evidence must be accurate. Evidence is most likely to be accurate if it comes from a trustworthy source. Such a source will, for example, quote *exactly* and not present statements out of context. It will also present examples, statistics, and expert testimony fairly, drawing them from similarly reliable sources. For this reason, statistics published in a newspaper known for its balanced treatment of the issues should carry more weight than those published in one known for its support of a particular cause or political position.

Evidence must be sufficient. Evidence is sufficient if a writer presents an adequate amount of evidence. It is not enough, for instance, for a writer to cite just one example in an attempt to demonstrate that impoverished women are receiving high-quality prenatal care. Even though a single detailed case study might be quite convincing, this one example is not enough to support such a general statement. In addition, the statistical sample must be large enough to be meaningful. A recent article in the *Journal of the American Medical Association* noted that some researchers were publishing studies that included as few as ten participants. In many cases, the article pointed out, the results of such studies are misleading because a change in response by as few as two people can alter the results by 20 percent.

Moreover, a single expert, no matter how stellar his or her reputation or how compelling his or her testimony, may be disputed by other authorities. Look for the testimony of several experts, combined with other supporting evidence, when you evaluate a writer's evidence.

Evidence must be representative. Evidence is representative if it represents a fair range of facts and viewpoints. For example, if a writer is trying to convince readers that Asian immigrants as a group have had great success in achieving professional status in the United States, he or she must draw evidence from the experiences of a range of Asian immigrant groups—Vietnamese, Chinese, Japanese, Korean—and a representative sample of professions—law, medicine, teaching, and so on. No matter how accurate the information or how numerous the examples, a writer cannot draw a general conclusion about *all* Asian immigrants to the United States or *all* professions by citing a limited range of examples—Chinese in San Francisco becoming accountants or Indians in New Jersey becoming pharmacists, for example.

Evidence must be relevant. Evidence is relevant if it applies to the case being discussed. If a writer is arguing for US medical aid to developing nations, it is not relevant to present examples or statistics that support—however convincingly—US efforts to reform its own health-care system. Moreover, expert testimony is only as convincing as the expert. Not only should the authority whom a writer cites be a recognized expert in his or her field of study, but also that field of study should be relevant to the point that the expert is being called upon to support. Julia Child may be widely recognized as an authority on cooking and Spike Lee as a talented director; Lee's pronouncements on food or Child's on film, however, should carry no more weight than those of any other individual.

EXERCISE 3

Read the following student paragraph and evaluate its supporting evidence.

The United States is becoming more and more violent every day. I was talking to my friend Gayle, and she mentioned that a guy her roommate knows was attacked at dusk and had his skull crushed by the barrel of a gun. Later she heard that he was in the hospital with a blood clot in his brain. Two friends of mine were walking home from a party when they were attacked by armed men right outside the A-Plus Mini Market. These two examples make it very clear to me how violent our nation is becoming. My English professor, who is in his fifties, remembers a few similar violent incidents occurring when he was growing up, and he was even mugged in London last year. He believes that if London police carried guns, the city would be safer. Two of the twenty-five people in our class have been the victims of violent crime, and I feel lucky that I am not one of them.

(3) Detecting Bias

A **bias** is a predisposition to think a certain way. A writer is biased when he or she bases conclusions on preconceived ideas rather than on evidence. As a critical reader, you should be aware that bias may sometimes lead a writer to see only what he or she wants to see and to select evidence that supports one conclusion over all others. For this reason it is essential that you consider other points of view before drawing your own conclusions.

Some bias that you will encounter in your reading will be obvious and easy to detect.

- **A writer's stated beliefs.** In a recent article about the Middle East, a writer declared herself a strong supporter of the Palestinian position. This statement should tell readers that it is unlikely that she will present an unbiased view of Israel's policies in the West Bank. Such a bias does not automatically invalidate the writer's points. On the contrary, she may offer an interesting perspective. What she will probably *not* do, however, is present a *balanced* view of the subject.

- **Sexist or racist statements.** A writer who assumes that all engineers are male and that all nurses are female reflects a clear bias. A researcher who states that certain racial groups are intellectually superior to others is also presenting a biased view.

- **Slanted language.** Writers can use slanted language to influence readers' reactions. For example, saying "The politician presented an *impassioned* speech" gives one impression; saying "The politician delivered a *diatribe*" gives another. Similarly, describing a person as "a Wall Street type" is quite different from saying that he or she is successful in business.

- **Tone.** The tone of a piece of writing indicates a writer's attitude toward readers or toward his or her subject. As you read, ask yourself if the writer is being matter-of-fact, ironic, bitter, sarcastic, playful, tentative, angry, apologetic, or self-confident. In many cases, the tone of an essay can alert you to the possibility that the writer is slanting his or her case. An angry writer, for example, might not be able or willing to present an accurate summary of an opponent's position, and an apologetic writer might inadvertently dilute the strength of his or her case in an attempt to avoid offending readers.

See 7b2

- **Choice of evidence.** As you read, try to evaluate a writer's use of **evidence**. Frequently, the examples selected reveal the writer's biases—that is, a writer may include only examples that support a point and may leave out examples that might contradict it.

- **Choice of experts.** In order to support a point effectively, a writer must cite experts who represent a fair range of opinion. If, for instance, a writer assessing the president's economic policies toward Japan includes only statements by economists who advocate protectionism, he or she is presenting a biased case. The absence of statements by economists who advocate free trade should alert you to this bias.

Some bias is so subtle that it is extremely difficult to detect. For example, cultural biases creep into a text when a writer accepts one culture's ideas about material success, technology, personal freedom, and family values as universal, not realizing that they are limited to the culture in which he or she lives. Other biases can also affect a writer's thinking. Gender or social class, for instance, can determine how a writer sees the world and therefore influence his or her views about the status of women or about the welfare system.

Remember too that your *own* biases can also affect your reaction to a text—how you interpret a writer's ideas, whether you are convinced by what you read, and whether you react with sympathy or anger, for example. When you read, then, it is important to remain aware of your own values and beliefs and alert to how they may affect your reactions.

(4) Recognizing Faulty Reasoning

Faulty reasoning undermines a writer's credibility and confuses readers. As a critical reader, you should carefully scrutinize a writer's <u>reasoning</u>. The connection between evidence and conclusions should be clear, and the writer's inferences should be based on a logical chain of reasoning, with no missing links or unwarranted conclusions.

See
8a, b

(5) Recognizing Logical Fallacies

Writers who use <u>logical fallacies</u>—flawed arguments—cannot be trusted. A writer who uses these fallacies inadvertently is not thinking clearly or logically; a writer who uses them intentionally is trying to deceive readers. In either case, your identification of logical fallacies should lead you to challenge a writer's credibility.

See
8c

(6) Recognizing Unfair Appeals

Writers should make every effort to be <u>fair</u>. **Unfair appeals** are appeals to a reader's prejudices or fears. You should avoid these appeals in your own writing just as you would avoid faulty reasoning and logical fallacies.

See
9a8

155

✔ CHECKLIST: READING CRITICALLY

✔ What points is the writer making? What is stated? What is suggested?

✔ Do you agree with the writer's ideas?

✔ Are the writer's statements supported primarily by fact or by opinion? Does the writer present opinion as fact?

✔ Does the writer offer supporting evidence for his or her statements? What kind of evidence is provided? How convincing is it?

✔ Is the evidence accurate? Sufficient? Representative? Relevant?

✔ Does the writer display any bias? If so, is the bias revealed through language, tone, or choice of evidence?

✔ Does the writer present a balanced picture of the issue?

✔ Are any alternative viewpoints overlooked?

✔ Does the writer omit pertinent examples?

✔ Do your reactions reveal biases in your own thinking?

✔ Does the writer challenge your own values, beliefs, and assumptions?

✔ Does the writer use faulty reasoning?

✔ Does the writer use logical fallacies?

✔ Does the writer use unfair appeals, such as appeals to prejudice or fear?

✔ Does the writer make unsupported generalizations?

✔ Does the writer make reasonable inferences?

✔ Does the writer represent the ideas of others accurately? Fairly?

✔ Does the writer distort the ideas of others or present them out of context?

EXERCISE 4

Read the following excerpt from a statement on comparable worth, a method by which some people seek to balance inequities in jobs occupied primarily by women. First, identify the facts and opinions in the excerpt. Then, evaluate the quantity and quality of the writer's supporting evidence and try to determine what biases, if any, she has. Finally, evaluate the writer's reasoning, identifying logical fallacies and unfair appeals. Use the questions in the checklist above as a guide.

My name is Phyllis Schlafly, president of Eagle Forum, a national profamily organization. I am a lawyer, writer, and homemaker.

We oppose the concept called *comparable worth* for two principal reasons: (*a*) it's unfair to men and (*b*) it's unfair to women.

The comparable worth advocates are trying to freeze the wages of blue-collar men while forcing employers to raise the wages of *some* white- and pink-collar women above marketplace rates. According to the comparable worth rationale, blue-collar men are overpaid and their wages should be frozen until white- and pink-collar women have their wages artificially raised to the same level. The proof that this is really what the comparable worth debate is all about is in both their rhetoric and their statistics.

I've been debating feminists and listening to their arguments for more than a decade. It is impossible to overlook their rhetoric of envy. I've heard feminist leaders say hundreds of times, "It isn't fair that the man with a high school education earns more money than the woman who graduated from college or nursing or secretarial school." That complaint means that the feminists believe that truck drivers, electricians, plumbers, mechanics, highway workers, maintenance men, policemen, and firemen earn more money than feminists think they are worth. And how do the feminists judge "worth"? By paper credentials instead of by apprenticeship and hard work and by ignoring physical risk and unpleasant working conditions.

So the feminists have devised the slogan *comparable worth* to make the blue-collar man feel guilty for earning more money than women with paper credentials and to trick him into accepting a government-enforced wage freeze while all available funds are used to raise the wages of *some* women.

Statistical proof that the aim of comparable worth is to reduce the relative earning power of blue-collar men is abundantly available in the job evaluations commissioned and approved by the comparable worth advocates. You can prove this to yourself by making a job-by-job examination of *any* study or evaluation made with the approval of comparable worth advocates; it is always an elaborate scheme to devalue the blue-collar man.

For example, look at the Willis evaluation used in the famous case called *AFSCME v. State of Washington*. Willis determined that the electricians and truck drivers were overvalued by the state and that their "worth" was really far less than the "worth" of a registered nurse. More precisely, Willis produced an evaluation chart on which the registered nurse was worth 573 points, whereas the electrician was worth only 193 points (one-third of the nurse), while the truck driver was only worth 97 points (one-sixth of the nurse).

The federal court accepted the Willis evaluation as though it were some kind of divine law (refusing to listen to the Richard Jeanneret "PAQ" evaluation which produced very different estimates of "worth"). The federal court decision (unless it is overturned on appeal) means that the electricians and the truck drivers will probably have their salaries frozen until the state finds a way to pay the registered nurse three times and six times as much, respectively. [In a September 4, 1985, decision, the Ninth

US Circuit Court of Appeals overturned the decision.] (Phyllis
Schlafly, "Comparable Worth: Unfair to Men and Women")

7c Annotating the Text

As you read more critically, you should begin to make **annotations** in
the text, recording your reactions in the margins or between the lines.
This activity can help you to evaluate a text's ideas. At first you may write
down some relatively uncritical responses—for example, jot down definitions of new words, identify unfamiliar references, or write brief summaries. Eventually, however, you should start to include more critical
responses. For example, you may identify points that confirm (or challenge) your own thinking, question the appropriateness or accuracy of
the writer's support, uncover the writer's biases, identify slanted language or faulty reasoning, or even question the writer's conclusions.

The following passage illustrates a student's annotations of a section of
an article by Joseph Nocera about the decline of American public schools.

> One of the most compelling arguments about the Vietnam War
> is that it lasted as long as it did because of its "classist" nature. The
> central thesis is that because neither the decision makers in the gov-
> ernment *nor anyone they knew* had children fighting and dying in
> Vietnam, they had no personal incentive to bring the war to a halt.
> The government's generous college-deferment system, steeped as it
> was in class distinctions, allowed the white middle class to avoid the
> tragic consequences of the war. And the people who did the fighting
> and dying in place of the college-deferred were those whose voices
> were least heard in Washington: the poor and the disenfranchised.
>
> *Is this comparison valid? (seems forced)*
>
> I bring this up because I believe that the decline of the public
> schools is rooted in the same cause. Just as with the Vietnam War, as
> soon as the middle class no longer had a stake in the public schools,
> the surest pressure on school systems to provide a decent education
> instantly disappeared. Once the middle class was gone, no mayor was
> going to get booted out of office because the schools were bad. No in-
> competent teacher had to worry about angry parents calling for his or
> her head "downtown." No third-rate educationalist at the local teach-
> ers college had to fear having his or her methods criticized by anyone
> that mattered.
>
> *bias*

continued on the following page

continued from the previous page

The analogy to the Vietnam War can be extended even to the extent of the denial. It amuses me sometimes to hear people like myself decry the state of the public schools. We bemoan the lack of money, the decaying facilities, the absurd credentialism, the high foolishness of the school boards. We applaud the burgeoning reform movement. And everything we say is deeply, undeniably true. We can see every problem with the schools clearly except one: the fact that our deci-✳ sion to abandon the schools has helped create all the other problems. One small example: In the early 1980s, Massachusetts passed one of those tax cap measures, called Proposition 2 1/2, which has turned out to be a force for ⟨genuine evil⟩ in the public schools. Would Proposition 2 1/2 have passed had the middle class still had a stake in the schools? I wonder. I also wonder whether 20 years from now, in the next round of breast-beating memoirs, the exodus of the white middle class from the public schools will finally be seen for what it was. Individually, every parent's rationale made impeccable sense—"I can't deprive my children of a decent education"—but collectively, it was a deeply destructive act.

The main reason the white middle class fled, of course, is race, or more precisely, the complicated admixture of race and class and good intentions gone awry. ⟨The fundamental good intention⟩— which even today strikes one as both moral and right—was to integrate the public classroom, and in so doing, to equalize the resources available to all school children. In Boston, this was done through enforced busing. In Washington, it was done through a series of judicial edicts that attempted to spread the good teachers and resources throughout the system. In other big city districts, judges weren't involved; school committees, seeing the handwriting on the wall, tried to do it themselves.

However moral the intent, the result almost ⟨always⟩ was the same. The white middle class left. The historic parental vigilance I mentioned earlier had had a lot to do with creating the two-tiered system—one in which schools attended by the kids of the white middle class had better teachers, better equipment, better everything than those attended by the kids of the poor. This did not happen because the white middle-class parents were racists, necessarily; it happened because they knew how to manipulate the system and were willing to do so on behalf of their kids. Their neighborhood schools became little havens of decent education, and they didn't much care what happened in the other public schools.

Who are these people? Does he really represent them?

Is this "one small example" enough to support his claim? bias

Oversimplification—Do all parents have same motives?

Is this a valid assumption?

Why does he assume intent was "good" & "moral"? Is he right?

Interesting point—but is it true?

continued on the following page

continued from the previous page

Slanted
language
(over
emotional)
generalization?

In retrospect, this behavior, though perfectly understandable, was tragically short-sighted. When the judicial fiats made those safe havens untenable, the white middle class quickly discovered what the poor had always known: There weren't enough good teachers, decent equipment, and so forth to go around. For that matter, there weren't even enough good students to go around; along with everything else, middle-class parents had to start worrying about whether their kids were going to be mugged in school.

Either/or
fallacy? Were
there other
choices?

Faced with the grim fact that their children's education was quickly deteriorating, middle-class parents essentially had two choices: They could stay and pour the energy that had once gone into improving the neighborhood school into improving the entire school system—a frightening task, to be sure. Or they could leave. Invariably, they chose the latter.

Oversimpli-
fication? No
exceptions?

And it wasn't just the white middle class that fled. The black middle class, and even the black poor who were especially ambitious for their children, were getting out as fast as they could too, though not to the suburbs. They headed mainly for the parochial schools, which subsequently became integration's great success story, even as the public schools became integration's great failure. (Joseph Nocera, "How the Middle Class Has Helped Ruin the Public Schools")

As she read and reread the article, the student referred to the "Checklist: Reading Critically" on page 156 and expressed her reactions in the form of annotations. When she finished her annotations, the stu-dent was ready to draw her ideas together and write a **critical response** to the text.

See
7d

EXERCISE 5

Read the following short article, highlighting it as you read. Then, read the questions that follow the article. Reread the article, recording your reactions in the form of annotations. Finally, answer the questions.

"Go to Wall Street," my classmates said.
"Go to Wall Street," my professor advised.
"Go to Wall Street," my father threatened.
Whenever I tell people about my career indecisiveness, their answer is always the same: Get a blueprint for life and get one fast. Perhaps I'm simply too immature, but I think 20 is far too young to set my life in stone.

Nobody mentioned any award for being the first to have a white picket fence, 2.4 screaming kids and a spanking new Ford station wagon.

What's wrong with uncertainty, with exploring multiple options in multiple fields? What's wrong with writing, "Heck, I don't know" under the "objective" section of my résumé?

Parents, professors, recruiters and even other students seem to think there's a lot wrong with it. And they are all pressuring me to launch a career prematurely.

My sociology professor warns that my generation will be the first in American history not to be more successful than our parents' generation. This depressing thought drives college students to think of success as something that must be achieved at all costs as soon as possible.

My father wants me to emulate his success: Every family wants its children to improve the family fortune. I feel that desire myself, but I realize I don't need to do it by age 25.

This pressure to do better, to compete with the achievements of our parents in a rapidly changing world, has forced my generation to pursue definitive, lifelong career paths at far too young an age. Many of my friends who have graduated in recent years are already miserably unhappy.

My professors encourage such pre-professionalism. In upper level finance classes, the discussion is extremely career-oriented. "Learn to do this and you'll be paid more" is the theme of many a lecture. Never is there any talk of actually enjoying the exercise.

Nationwide, universities are finally taking steps in the right direction by a re-emphasizing the study of liberal arts and a return to the classics. If only job recruiters for Wall Street firms would do the same.

"Get your M.B.A. as soon as possible and you'll have a jump on the competition," said one overly zealous recruiter from Goldman Sachs. Learning for learning's sake was completely forgotten: Goldman Sachs refused to interview anybody without a high grade-point average, regardless of the courses composing that average.

In other interviews, it is expected that you know exactly what you want to do or you won't be hired. "Finance?" they say, "What kind of finance?"

A recruiter at Dean Witter Reynolds said investment banking demands 80 to 100 hours of work per week. I don't see how anyone will ever find time to enjoy the gobs of money they'll be making.

The worst news came from a partner at Salomon Brothers. He told me no one was happy there, and if they said they were, they're lying. He said you come in, make a lot of money and leave as fast as you can.

Two recent Wharton alumni, scarcely two years older than I, spoke at Donaldson, Lufkin & Jenrette's presentation. Their jokes about not having a life outside the office were only partially in jest.

Yet, students can't wait to play this corporate charade. They don ties and jackets and tote briefcases to class.

It is not just business students who are obsessed with their careers. The five other people who live in my house are not undergraduate business majors, but all five plan to attend graduate school next year. How is it possible that, without one iota of real work experience, these people are willing to commit themselves to years of intensive study in one narrow field?

Mom, dad, grandpa, recruiters, professors, fellow students: I implore you to leave me alone.

Now is my chance to explore, to spend time pursuing interests simply because they make me happy and not because they fill my wallet. I don't want to waste my youth toiling at a miserable job. I want to make the right decisions about my future.

Who knows, I may even end up on Wall Street. (Michael Finkel, "Undecided—and Proud of It")

1. What is the writer's main point? Do you agree with him?

2. How does he support this point?

3. Is his supporting evidence primarily fact or opinion? Does he support his opinions? Is the support convincing?

4. Where does the writer use expert testimony? How convincing are the experts he cites?

5. Should the writer have used other kinds of support? For example, should he have used statistics? If so, where? What kind of statistical evidence might have made his case more convincing?

6. Does the writer's choice of examples reveal any biases? What leads you to your conclusion?

7. The writer is a student at an Ivy League university. Do you think this status might give him a limited or unrealistic view of college students' professional options?

8. The writer is a college senior. Do his age and his lack of experience in the working world make his article less credible to you?

9. Do you have any biases against the writer based on your assessment of his economic status, social class, or educational level?

EXERCISE 6

Read, highlight, and annotate the short essay that follows. Then, draw a vertical line down the middle of a piece of paper. In the left-hand column, list the essay's main ideas. In the right-hand column, write down your reactions to each of these ideas in the form of complete sentences (statements or questions). You may explain or clarify, question or contradict, probe for further information, or relate the writer's ideas to ideas of your own or to ideas from other sources. Use the checklist on page 156 as a guide.

It happens in public, not behind a closed office door. There is no "he said/she said" dispute about the facts. Everybody can see what's going on. Friends, classmates, teachers.

A boy backs a girl up against her junior high locker. Day after day. A high school junior in the hallway grabs a boy's butt. A sophomore in the playground grabs a girl's blouse. An eighth-grade girl gets up to speak in class and the boys begin to "moo" at her. A ninth-grader finds out that her name and her "hot number" are posted in the boy's bathroom.

It's all quite normal, or at least it's become the norm. This aberrant behavior is now as much a part of the daily curriculum, the things children learn, as math or social studies. Or their worth in the world.

This is the searing message of another survey that came spilling out of the schoolhouse door last week. This one, commissioned by the American Association of University Women, confirmed the grim fact that four out of five public school students between grades 8 and 11—85 percent of the girls and 76 percent of the boys—have experienced sexual harassment.

That's if sexual harassment means—and it does—"unwanted and unwelcome sexual behavior which interferes with your life." That's if sexual harassment includes—and it does—sexual comments, touching, pinching, grabbing, and worse.

The girls in schools are the more frequent targets of the more serious verbal and physical assaults. They suffer more painful repercussions in their lives, their grades, their sense of well-being.

But the notion that "everybody does it" is not far off the mark. If some 81 percent of the students in the AAUW survey were targets, here's another figure to remember. Some 59 percent—66 percent of the boys and 52 percent of the girls—admitted that they had done unto others what was done to them.

In public spaces in public schools, nearly every student is then a target or a perpetrator or a bystander—or all three in turn. The vast majority have been up close and too personal with sexual harassment. Yet we are still grappling with how it happened and how to change the schoolhouse and hallway.

In Minnesota, the agent of change has been a fistful of lawsuits. In California, a new law was passed that allows expulsions.

Elsewhere, schools are looking for a magic bullet, a one-day work-shop, a 10-point program.

But cultural change requires more than a crash curriculum; there is no quick fix in the creeping court system. Indeed Mary Rowe of MIT, who has studied harassment for over a decade, has learned that the vast majority of students won't bring their stories to any formal grievance procedure, let alone a courtroom. They won't tattle tale.

For a host of reasons, she and others, like Nan Stein of Wellesley College, have come to believe that the schools need a wider range of choices to fill the space between doing nothing and suing. They need teachers who see and say no to harassment in class. They need designated adults in schools who can listen and help. They need to help students address each other directly and honestly. Indeed in one tactic, a student is encouraged to write a personal letter to the classmate who hurt her . . . maybe unwittingly.

A school culture of sexual harassment exists in a wide and troubling social context, but change ultimately rests in the hands of the students themselves. After all, not all boys will be boys. Not all girls follow the leader.

So, these days, when Nan Stein goes into a school, she says, "I talk a lot about courage." She thinks the role that everybody plays, the bystander, is pivotal. "Kids have to learn to speak out, to make moral judgments. I tell them not to be moral spectators."

Sexual harassment is, as Stein says, an older cousin to bullying. Students who understand the dividing line between teasing and bullying can learn the line between sexual play and harassment. They can draw that line.

The most powerful tool for the everyday garden-variety misery of name-calling, body-pinching and sexual bullying that turns a school hallway into a gauntlet may not be a lawsuit. It may be one high school senior walking by who says, "Don't do that, it's gross." It may be one group of buddies who don't laugh at the joke.

In our society, the courts are the last-ditch place for resolving conflicts. The schools must become the place for teaching basics. Like respect and courage. (Ellen Goodman, "Sexual Harassment in Schools: Nearly Everybody 'Is Doing It'")

7d   Writing a Critical Response

After you have read a text critically, you may want to draw your reactions together by writing a critical response.

In a **critical response** you express your evaluation of the text. As in any persuasive essay, your statements must be supported by specific examples. In addition, you must supply the logical and sequential links (transitions, topic sentences, and so on) that will help your readers follow the progression of your ideas.

Before you begin writing your critical response, review your annotations. Carefully reconsider your judgments and reactions to the text in light of any biases that you may have uncovered in your own thinking.

Begin your critical response by identifying your text and **summarizing** its position. Next, state your critical reaction to the text and present the support for your position: summarize and respond to the writer's key points one by one, carefully **paraphrasing** ideas and quoting key words and phrases where appropriate, supporting your judgments with the ideas that you wrote down as you annotated. Conclude by restating your critical reaction to the text. When you have finished, reread what you have written, making sure that it is as accurate, clear, and fair-minded as possible.

Following is a student's critical response to Joseph Nocera's "How the Middle Class Has Helped Ruin the Public Schools," an annotated section of which is reproduced on pages 158–160. In her remarks, the student uses her own knowledge, observations, and experiences to question and challenge Nocera's points.

See 41a1

See 41a2

In his article "How the Middle Class Has Helped Ruin the Public Schools," first published in the February 1989 issue of The Washington Monthly and later reprinted in the September/October 1990 Utne Reader, Joseph Nocera tries to have it both ways. He is confessing the guilt he feels for contributing to the decline of public education, and he is attacking those middle-class parents who have made the same choices he has made. What he seems to be asking his audience to do is to feel both sympathy and outrage toward parents in this situation. This is asking a lot.

Early in his essay Nocera tells readers that he moved to a small town because of its good public schools--which he attributes to "a large group of white middle-class parents deeply involved in the

Identification of text

Summary of text's position

Statement of critical reaction to the text

Support: summary and evaluation of writer's key points (¶2–4)

continued on the following page

continued from the previous page

public school system" (67). He cites the "outrages" of public schools in Boston, Washington, and New York and concludes that "The destruction of the large public school systems in America is one of the great tragedies of our time" (67). Then, he apologetically explains that he has chosen, for the sake of his children's education, "not to stand and fight" (68). After all, he argues, "Parents aren't willing to sacrifice their children on the altar of their social principles" (71). Throughout the essay, he seems to assume that his readers will agree with him simply because he is an ordinary middle-class parent.

Admitting that, as this typical middle-class parent, he has options that poor parents do not have, Nocera tries to justify his private decision despite the widespread public disaster that he admits it has helped to create. In doing so, he reveals his biases. At various points in his discussion he attacks the courts, unions, bureaucrats, and school committees. He talks about the nation's problems, but all his examples are drawn from the urban Northeast, particularly Boston. He also suggests that any middle-class parents who, unlike himself, keep their children in public schools are sacrificing their children's education for some abstract social principles. This conclusion ignores the fact that some parents may consider the understanding of such social principles to be a valuable part of their children's education. In addition, not all urban public schools provide an inferior education. Finally, he reveals a racial bias when he makes the assumption that white middle-class students (and parents) are the most valuable in a school system and that without these ingredients the system is doomed.

Nocera's reasoning is sometimes faulty. For instance, when he says, "Since the white middle class left, the system [in Boston] has simply fallen apart. Can this be sheer coincidence? I think not" (71),

continued on the following page

continued from the previous page

he is making a sweeping (and unsupported) generalization. He is also assuming that either white flight or coincidence--and no other factor--must have caused the schools' decline. Similarly, when he says the middle class could either try to improve the whole system or abandon it, he ignores the possibility of other options--such as working to improve one particular school in a system.

    Generalizations and oversimplifications like these reduce a complex issue to a simplistic, either-or situation. Given this limited perspective, it is not surprising that Nocera can offer no solution. Predictably, he believes that change should come not from people like him but rather from those outside the system. In his conclusion Nocera reveals that what he is really looking for is not a platform from which to effect change but an opportunity for confession and a plea for forgiveness.

Restatement of critical reaction to the text

✔ CHECKLIST: WRITING A CRITICAL RESPONSE

BEFORE WRITING:
- ✔ Review your annotations.
- ✔ Reconsider your judgments about the text in light of your own biases.

IN YOUR CRITICAL RESPONSE:
- ✔ Identify your text and summarize its position.
- ✔ State your critical reaction to the text.
- ✔ Summarize and evaluate the writer's key points, using paraphrase and quotation as needed.
- ✔ Restate your critical reaction to the text.
- ✔ Reread what you have written, checking for accuracy, clarity, and fair-mindedness.
- ✔ Document any words or ideas that you borrowed from a source.

EXERCISE 7

The following letter (*Utne Reader*, November/December 1990) was written by a Denver parent in response to Nocera's essay. Putting yourself in Nocera's place, write a brief critical response to the letter.

Multicultural Education

I believe Joseph Nocera's article is entirely accurate except for one major flaw. That flaw is the belief that sending your children to urban public schools is "sacrificing them." I believe it is in their best interest to do so.

I am a parent of four children in the Denver public school system. I have observed all of the rationalizations described in Nocera's article as dozens of good white liberals in our integrated neighborhood have fled to the suburbs and private schools. For years I tried to appeal to their altruism to support the schools. Then I realized that the reason I was sending my kids to the public schools was not "a sacrifice for my social principles" as Nocera would have us believe, but was actually because I knew it was in their own best interest, to help them learn how to relate and function within a multicultural, multiracial environment. Let me illustrate this point with personal anecdotes.

My son, who is a good fourth-grade student, asked why our friend's son was leaving our public school. I told him it was because "his parents didn't want him to be the only white boy in his class." Then I asked him, "Has that ever happened to you?" He pondered a moment and then said, "I don't think so. I can't remember." Actually, only the year before, he was the only white boy in his third-grade class, but he obviously had overcome any anxiety or prejudice or even awareness of this recent experience.

My daughter, who is a straight-A seventh grader, asked me, "What is an ethnic minority?" I explained that it was a small minority group like blacks. She said with a totally straight face, "Come on, Dad, blacks aren't a minority." In her world they aren't.

Duane Gall
Denver, CO

EXERCISE 8

Read this newspaper column and, after highlighting and annotating it carefully, write a brief critical response to the ideas that it discusses. Use the checklist on page 167 to guide you.

The thought police are busy this year. With all the best intentions in the world—because aren't their intentions always honorable, from preserving the sanctity of the family to promoting racial equality?—they have proffered petitions, organized boycotts, brought lawsuits. Last week they even had the capacity to surprise us. They came out of left field, and they were represented by those people who traditionally have been the quirky, the avant-garde, the antithesis of the thought police type.

That is, actors.

In Central Park this summer, Morgan Freeman, a gifted actor who is black, has played Petruchio in "The Taming of the Shrew," and Denzel Washington, a gifted actor who is black, is portraying Richard III.

This is the way I choose to describe them. I use sentence structure to make their race, in this context, descriptive, not definitive. The definitive reasons they were chosen are clear: craft and celebrity.

Actors' Equity, the union that represents them and others far less successful, believes that this is insufficient.

Last week Equity torpedoed a musical called "Miss Saigon," which includes parts for dozens of Asian actors. The celebrated actor Jonathan Pryce plays the Engineer in the London production, and was to do so on Broadway. Equity said it could not approve of Mr. Pryce playing the role, which he apparently does brilliantly, because the Engineer is Eurasian and Mr. Pryce is Caucasian.

That is, race as definition, not as description.

Let's be clear: this wish for politically correct casting goes only one way, the way designed to redress the injuries of centuries. When Pat Carroll, who is a woman, plays Falstaff, who is not, the casting is considered a stroke of brilliance. When Josette Simon, who is black, plays Maggie in "After the Fall" a part Arthur Miller patterned after Marilyn Monroe and which has traditionally been played, not by white women, but by blonde white women, it is hailed as a breakthrough.

But when the pendulum moves the other way, the actor's union balks. It is noted, quite correctly, that it is insufferable that roadshow companies of "The King and I" habitually use Causcasian men wearing eyeliner to play the King, rather than searching for suitable Asian actors. But the conclusion drawn from this is that a white man should never be permitted inside the skin of an Asian one, although all of acting is about getting inside someone else's skin, someone different, someone somehow foreign.

Anyone who has ever faced discrimination knows that bigotry begins when race, when gender, when ethnicity are applied as sole definition. The black man doesn't get into the country club; the savvy banker who is black might. The woman may not be a prime candidate for chief financial officer; the terrific numbers-cruncher who is a woman may get the job.

Actors are accustomed to this, too. How many of them have slunk off to coffee shops after a casting call, defeated and despondent after hearing "We're looking for a tall redhead."

Definitive can be limiting, reductive, making of a diverse group a collection of sameness.

Descriptive tries to force people to see us as individuals, with certain attributes, chief among them the proud one of race, the cherished one of gender, and the ineffable, unmistakable one of talent.

We women are familiar with what has become a tradition in the corporate culture. A woman is given an executive job, say vice president for human resources, and we all cheer. Except that, as the years go by, a woman is always vice president for human resources, but never anything else. Never controller. Never president. Vice president for human resources has become The Woman's Job. There is no need to worry about gender equity anymore.

Perhaps "Miss Saigon," if it ever comes to this country, will become the Asian show. An Asian actor will play the Engineer, and if he is seen as an Asian actor, he may never be offered Othello, or the Stage Manager in "Our Town," or the lead in a new John Guare play.

If he is seen as a brilliant actor who is Asian, it may be a different story.

It is dangerous to form a thought police force. Other people have been at it much longer; they have had months and months of fighting the ghost of Robert Mapplethorpe and trashing the righteous rage of Karen Finley. Who knows? One day one of them might run Actors' Equity.

And then perhaps Denzel Washington will not be playing Richard III. Perhaps there will be an open call for white male actors. Once you open certain doors, they swing both ways. (Anna Quindlen, "Error, Stage Left")

CHAPTER 8

THINKING LOGICALLY

The two most common methods of reasoning are *induction* and *deduction*. **Inductive reasoning** moves from specific facts, observations, or experiences to a general conclusion. **Deductive reasoning** moves from generalization believed to be true or self-evident to more specific conclusions. Quite often writers use a combination of inductive and deductive reasoning—relying both on conclusions drawn from evidence and on well-established beliefs.

8a Reasoning Inductively

(1) Moving from Observations to Conclusion

Writers use inductive reasoning whenever they draw a conclusion based on specific facts and observations. You can see how inductive reasoning operates by studying the following list of statements, which focuses on the relationship between SAT scores and admissions at one liberal arts college.

- The SAT is an admission requirement for all applicants.
- High school grades and rank in class are also examined.
- Nonacademic factors such as sports, activities, and interests are taken into account as well.
- Special attention is given to the applications of athletes, minorities, and children of alumni.
- Fewer than 52 percent of applicants for a recent class with SAT verbal scores between 600 and 700 were accepted.
- Fewer than 39 percent of applicants with similar math scores were accepted.
- Approximately 18 percent of applications with SAT verbal scores between 450 and 520 and about 19 percent of applicants with similar SAT math scores were admitted.

After reading the preceding statements, you can use inductive reasoning to draw the general conclusion that although important, SAT scores are not the single factor that determines whether a student is admitted.

(2) Making Inferences

No matter how much evidence is presented, inductive conclusions are never certain, only probable. They are arrived at by what is called an **inductive leap.** When we make an inductive leap, we are actually making an **inference,** a conclusion about the unknown based on the known. Naturally, the more observations we make, the narrower the gap between our observations and our conclusion and the better our chance of drawing an accurate conclusion. Even so, absolute certainty is not possible. At some point, writers must simply decide that they have enough evidence to present a convincing conclusion to their readers.

For example, suppose a student in a summer internship program is told to research a way of keeping her state free of the many soda bottles and cans that litter its towns and roadways. Her reading suggests a number of possible actions. The state could hire unemployed teenagers to pick up the litter. It could also place brightly colored refuse containers around the state to encourage people to dispose of bottles and cans properly. Finally, the state could require a deposit from all those who buy beverages in bottles or cans. Reviewing her reading, the student finds that the first two solutions have had no long-term effect on litter in states that tried them. However, mandatory deposit regulations, along with the outlawing of plastic beverage containers, have significantly decreased the number of bottles and cans in the two states that instituted such measures. Still, because the conditions in the student's state are not exactly the same as those in the states she studied, she must make a leap from the known—the states she studied—to the unknown—the situation in her state. By means of inductive reasoning, the student is able to infer that a mandatory deposit law could be a good solution to the problem.

EXERCISE 1

Read the following paragraphs and answer the questions that follow them.

A. The role—and reputation—of pawn shops seems to be changing. Once considered by many to be somewhat seedy, disreputable establishments with an equally suspect clientele, pawn shops are now becoming more socially acceptable. As many as one out of every ten adult Americans borrows money from a pawn shop each year. In the past five years, the number of pawn-shop licenses has increased by more than a third in some states. Many individuals who cannot get credit from banks or other lending institutions are able to do so at pawn shops. They can borrow modest amounts of cash at no interest simply by presenting identification, offering a piece of collateral, and signing an agreement. Although often criticized for being legalized usurers or receivers of stolen goods, pawn-shop owners insist that they legitimately fill a gap in the loan business. Pawn-shop owners are working diligently to improve their image and have begun to attract middle-class and even upper-middle-class borrowers.

Which of the following statements can be inferred from the paragraph?

1. More and more Americans are borrowing money.
2. Pawn shops are trying to improve their image by refusing to buy stolen goods.
3. Pawn shops are still not socially acceptable to some people.
4. Some states are trying to ban pawn shops because they are legalized usurers and receivers of stolen goods.
5. Pawn shops offer loans at no interest to qualified borrowers for any amount of money.

B. Americans are becoming more ecologically aware with each passing year, but their awareness may be limited. Most people know about the destruction of rain forests in South America, for example, or the vanishing African elephant, but few realize what is going on in their own backyards in the name of progress. Even people who are knowledgeable about such topics as the plight of the wild mustang, the dangers of toxic waste disposal, and acid rain frequently fail to realize either the existence or the importance of "smaller" ecological issues. The wetlands are a good case in point. In recent decades, more than 500,000 acres of wetlands a year have been filled, and it seems unlikely that the future will see any great change. What has happened in recent times is that United States wetlands are filled in in one area and "restored" in another area, a practice that is legal according to Section 404 of the Clean Water Act and one that does in fact result in "no net loss" of wetlands. Few see the problems with this. To most, wetlands are mere swamps, and getting rid of swamps is viewed as something positive. In addition, the wetlands typically contain few spectacular species—the sort of glamour animals, such as condors and grizzlies, that easily attract publicity and sympathy. Instead, they contain boring specimens of flora and fauna unlikely to generate great concern among the masses. Yet the delicate balance of the ecosystem *is* upset by the elimination or "rearrangement" of such marshy areas. True, cosmically speaking, it matters little if one organism (or many) is wiped out. But even obscure subspecies might provide some much-needed product or information in the future. We should not forget that penicillin was made from a lowly mold.

Which of the following statements can be inferred from the paragraph?

1. The loss of even a single species may be disastrous to the ecosystem of the wetlands.
2. Even though the wetlands are considered swamps, most people are very concerned about their fate.
3. Section 404 of the Clean Water Act is not sufficient to protect the wetlands.
4. Few Americans are concerned about environmental issues.
5. Most people would agree that the destruction of rain forests is worse than the destruction of the wetlands.

EXERCISE 2

Read this essay carefully, and answer the questions that follow.

As Deerfield Academy, following Lawrenceville, departs from its traditional mission of single-sex education for boys, I, like others involved in girls' schools, am saddened that few voices were apparently raised to defend a mission I cannot help comparing to our own.

Advocates of single-sex education for girls are enthusiastic defenders of the cause. We feel validated every day in our classrooms, dormitories, councils of student government, science and computer laboratories, and yearbook editing offices. We see growth, developing self-esteem, individuality, and leadership all around us.

It is not that good co-educational schools cannot offer girls these things; it is that girls' schools do so consistently. We are a fail-safe producer of first-class citizenship for girls in a world in which they are not guaranteed this opportunity elsewhere. We, like the women's colleges, provide not only "equal opportunity, but every opportunity," to quote Dr. Nannerl Keohane, the president of Wellesley College.

A colleague of mine described a vignette in her all-girls kindergarten class: A small girl surveyed the room, arms akimbo, and sized up the situation. "Thank heavens," she said. "No boys in the block corner." No, there aren't. She won't have to establish her right to build with blocks, just as later on she won't have to elbow her way to the computer terminals or perhaps feel out of place spending extra time in the physics lab.

Her voice will be heard in class, her opinion sought—on every topic—and taken seriously. Whatever the athletic facilities, they are for her alone. Moreover, leadership roles are more available: Girls get experience in managing radio stations, editing student newspapers and literary magazines, heading the debate and mathematics teams—all without having to fight for a place in the sun, because sex stereotyping does not complicate life in the school.

Since failure is less threatening, risk-taking becomes more bearable. For example, like many girls' schools we have a wonderful dance program, but our dancers don't have to care if they don't have figures like the models in *Seventeen* magazine—and few teenagers do. Like most people, they come in various shapes and sizes, yet they know no one will laugh at them or make disparaging remarks. So they learn to carry themselves with poise and grace, to be proud of their bodies—and stand a chance of becoming good dancers besides.

Relationships can flourish, both among peers and between students and adults. Communication with teachers and other adults is open and warm. Friendships grow strong and last long into adult life, as I have observed time and again by watching the alumnae of women's schools and colleges network and support each other in myriad ways. All this creates a learning and teaching atmosphere that is almost tangible: Our classrooms are lively, exciting places.

A graduate, finishing her sophomore year at a major New England (formerly all-male) college, visited Miss Porter's School last summer. She and I had known each other somewhat, had talked during her years with us but had never discussed the roles and expectations of women as such.

She and her friends were fighting for better health services for women at her college and were frustrated with their lack of progress. They were not being heard, she said. People were not taking them seriously. She talked about the climate of the classrooms, which she found alienating, and the effort she felt she must continually make to claim her equal place. The intensity and warmth of the conversation surprised me. "I wanted to talk to you," she said. "I knew you'd understand." That solidarity and that strength is what a women's single-sex school or college can provide.

We are sorry that Lawrenceville, and now Deerfield, did not feel that they could raise their voices in support of their historic educational environments. This is not a judgment—it is a sentiment—because women's schools, like women's colleges, find their mission constantly validated.

Ours is a co-educational world—no doubt about it—and single-sex education needs its defenders, promoters, believers and proselytizers. Yes, some people think girls' schools are anachronisms, but they succeed, better than most people realize, and remain necessary in a world where men and women still do not work equally together as professionals. (Rachel Phillips Belash, "Why Girls' Schools Remain Necessary")

1. What specific facts and observations does Belash include in her article?
2. Identify two examples of inductive reasoning.

3. At what point does Belash make an inductive leap?
4. What conclusion does Belash reach? Does this conclusion make sense in light of the facts and observations she presents?

8b Reasoning Deductively

See
Ch. 9   Writers use deductive reasoning (most often in argumentative essays) whenever they begin with a general or self-evident proposition and establish a chain of reasoning that leads to a specific conclusion. The process of deduction has traditionally been illustrated with a **syllogism,** a three-part set of statements or propositions that includes a *major premise,* a *minor premise,* and a *conclusion.*

MAJOR PREMISE: All books from that store are new.

MINOR PREMISE: These books are from that store.

CONCLUSION: Therefore, these books are new.

The major premise of a syllogism makes a general statement that the writer believes to be true. The minor premise presents a specific example of the belief that is stated in the major premise. If the reasoning is sound, the conclusion should follow from the two premises. (Note that these premises contain all the information expressed in the conclusion; that is, the conclusion introduces no terms that have not already appeared in the major and minor premises.)

You can use a syllogism when you plan an essay (to test the validity of your points), or you can use it as a revision strategy (to analyze your logic). In either case, the syllogism enables you to express your deductive argument in its most basic form and to see whether it makes sense.

(1) Constructing Valid Syllogisms

A syllogism is **valid** (or logical) when its conclusion follows from its premises. A syllogism is **true** when it makes accurate claims—that is, when the information it contains is consistent with the facts. To be **sound,** a syllogism must be both valid and true. However, a syllogism may be valid without being true or true without being valid. The following syllogism, for example, is valid but not true.

MAJOR PREMISE: All politicians are male.

MINOR PREMISE: Barbara Boxer is a politician.

CONCLUSION: Therefore, Barbara Boxer is male.

As odd as it may seem, this syllogism is valid. In the major premise, the phrase *all politicians* establishes that the entire class *politicians* is male. After Barbara Boxer is identified as a politician, the conclusion that she is male automatically follows—but, in fact, she is not. Because the major premise of this syllogism is not true, no conclusion based upon it can be true. For this reason, even though the logic of the syllogism is correct, its conclusion is not.

Just as a syllogism can be valid but not true, it can also be true but not valid. In each of the following situations, the structure of the syllogism undercuts its logic.

Syllogism with an Illogical Middle Term   A syllogism with an illogical middle term cannot have a valid conclusion. The **middle term** of a syllogism is the term that appears in both the major and minor premises but not in the conclusion. A rule of logic is that the middle term of a syllogism must refer to *all* members of the group. Consider the following syllogism.

INVALID SYLLOGISM

MAJOR PREMISE: All fathers are male.

MINOR PREMISE: Bill Cosby is a male.

CONCLUSION: Therefore, Bill Cosby is a father.

Even though the premises of this syllogism are true, the conlusion is illogical. *Males* is used as the middle term (that is, it appears in both the major and minor premises), but the term *male* does not refer to *all males*. Therefore, it cannot logically function as the middle term, and the conclusion—"Bill Cosby is a father"—is invalid.

Consider this version of the preceding syllogism.

VALID SYLLOGISM

MAJOR PREMISE: All fathers are male.

MINOR PREMISE: Bill Cosby is a father.

CONCLUSION: Therefore, Bill Cosby is a male.

Here the term *fathers* refers to all fathers; therefore, it can logically function as the middle term. Because the major premise establishes that *all* fathers are male, and the minor premise says that Bill Cosby is a father, the conclusion—*Bill Cosby is male*—logically follows.

Syllogism with a Term Whose Meaning Shifts   A syllogism in which the meaning of a key term shifts cannot have a valid conclusion.

INVALID SYLLOGISM

MAJOR PREMISE: Only man contemplates the future.

MINOR PREMISE: No woman is a man.

CONCLUSION: Therefore, no woman contemplates the future.

In the major premise, *man* is used to denote all human beings. In the minor premise, however, *man* denotes a person who is male. You can avoid this problem by making certain that the meaning of each key term in the major premise remains the same throughout the syllogism.

VALID SYLLOGISM

MAJOR PREMISE: Only human beings contemplate the future.

MINOR PREMISE: No dog is a human being.

CONCLUSION: Therefore, no dog contemplates the future.

Syllogism with Negative Premises   A syllogism in which *one* of the premises is negative can only have a negative conclusion.

INVALID SYLLOGISM

MAJOR PREMISE: No person may be denied employment because of a physical disability.

MINOR PREMISE: Deaf persons have a physical disability.

CONCLUSION: Therefore, a deaf person may be denied employment because of a physical disability.

Because the major premise of the preceding syllogism is negative (*"No person . . ."*), the only conclusion possible is a negative one. ("Therefore, *no* deaf person may be denied employment because of his or her disability.")

A syllogism in which *both* premises are negative cannot have a valid conclusion.

INVALID SYLLOGISM

MAJOR PREMISE: Injured workers may not be denied workers' compensation.

MINOR PREMISE: Frank is not an injured worker.

CONCLUSION: Therefore, Frank may not be denied workers' compensation.

In the preceding syllogism, both the major and minor premises are negative. As they now stand, the two premises do not establish a chain of reasoning. In fact, they cannot yield a valid conclusion. (How, for example, can Frank get workers' compensation if he is *not* an injured worker?)

If a syllogism is to yield a valid conclusion, only one of its premises may be negative.

VALID SYLLOGISM

MAJOR PREMISE: Injured workers may not be denied workers' compensation.

MINOR PREMISE: Frank is an injured worker.

CONCLUSION: Therefore, Frank may not be denied workers' compensation.

(2) Recognizing Enthymemes

An **enthymeme** is a syllogism in which one of the premises—often the major premise—is unstated. Enthymemes often occur as sentences containing words that signal conclusions—*therefore, consequently, for this reason, for, so, since,* or *because.*

Melissa is on the Dean's List; therefore, she is a good student.

The preceding sentence contains the minor premise and the conclusion of a syllogism. The reader must fill in the missing premise (in this case, the major premise) in order to complete the syllogism and see whether or not it is reasonable.

MAJOR PREMISE: All those on the Dean's List are good students.

MINOR PREMISE: Melissa is on the Dean's List.

CONCLUSION: Therefore, Melissa is a good student.

Some writers deliberately leave premises unstated in an attempt to influence an audience unfairly, keeping their basic assumptions ambiguous or pretending that assumptions are so self-evident that they need not be stated. Whenever you identify an enthymeme, whether in your own writing or in the writing of others, try to supply the missing premise and then determine whether or not the enthymeme is sound.

REVIEW: INDUCTIVE AND DEDUCTIVE REASONING

Inductive	Deductive
1. Begins with specific observations.	1. Begins with a general statement or proposition.
2. Moves from the specific to the general.	2. Moves from the general to the specific.
	continued on the following page

continued from the previous page

3. Conclusion is probable, never certain.
4. Progresses by means of inference.
5. Draws a conclusion about the unknown based on what is known.

3. Conclusion can be sound or unsound.
4. Progresses by means of the syllogism.
5. Draws a necessary conclu-sion about the known based on what is known.

(3) Using Toulmin Logic

The philosopher Stephen Toulmin has introduced another method for structuring arguments. **Toulmin logic** divides arguments into three parts: *the claim, the grounds,* and *the warrant.*

- **The claim** is the main point that the writer makes in the essay. Usually the writer states the claim, but in some arguments it may be implied.
- **The grounds** are the evidence and reasons on which the claim is based. They are the support that the writer uses to bolster the claim.
- **The warrant** is the assumption that links the claim to the data. It shows how the evidence supports the claim.

In its simplest terms, an argument following Toulmin's pattern would look like this.

Jane graduated from medical school. ——— Jane is a doctor.
(Grounds)   (Claim)
A person who graduates from medical
school is a doctor.
(Warrant)

Notice that the claim presents a specific situation, whereas the warrant is a general principle that can apply to a number of situations. In this sense the warrant is similar to the major premise of a syllogism and the claim is similar to the conclusion. (The grounds are the premises from which the claim is derived or the premises that make the claim probable or possible.)

In addition to suggesting a general way of structuring arguments, Toulmin logic offers a way of identifying and assessing an argument's assumptions.

- A warrant based on **authority** is based on the credibility of the person making the argument.

- A warrant based on **substance** is based on the reliability of the evidence.
- A warrant based on **motivation** is based on the values and beliefs of the writer and the readers.

Toulmin logic is an alternative method of constructing arguments. Far from replacing inductive and deductive logic, it provides another way of clarifying the major elements of an argument. Even so, it still relies on inductive and deductive reasoning: you arrive at your claim by moving *inductively* from your reading, and the relationship of your grounds and warrant to your claim is *deductive.*

EXERCISE 3

Read this essay carefully.

A nation succeeds only if the vast majority of its citizens succeed. It therefore stands to reason that with immigrants accounting for about 40 percent of our population growth, the future economic and social success of the United States is bound up with the success of these new Americans. Demography, in a word, is destiny.

This is an important principle to keep in mind as we try to come to grips with the problems and opportunities presented by the flood of legal and illegal immigrants from Mexico and other parts of South and Central America, who now constitute by far our largest immigrant group.

How are we doing in our efforts to assimilate these largely Hispanic newcomers and provide them with a bright future? Some signs are disturbing.

John Garcia, associate professor of political science at the University of Arizona, writing in *International Migration Review,* finds that the average rate of naturalization of Mexican immigrants is one-tenth that of other immigrant naturalization rates. The Select Commission on Immigration and Refugee Policy made a similar finding. Increasingly, immigrants are separated from everyone else by language, geography, ethnicity and class.

The future success of this country is closely linked to the ability of our immigrants to succeed. Yet 50 percent of our children of Hispanic background do not graduate from high school. Hispanic students score 100 points under the average student on Scholastic Aptitude Test scores. Hispanics have much higher rates of poverty, illiteracy and need for welfare than the national average. This engenders social crisis.

Not all the indicators of assimilation are pessimistic: the success of many Indochinese immigrants has been gratifying. But the warning signs of nonassimilation are increasing and ominous.

America must make sure the melting pot continues to melt: immigrants must become Americans. Seymour Martin Lipset, professor of political science and sociology at the Hoover Institution, Stanford University, observes: "The history of bilingual and bicultural societies that do not assimilate are histories of turmoil, tension and tragedy. Canada, Belgium, Malaysia, Lebanon—all face crises of national existence in which minorities press for autonomy, if not independence. Pakistan and Cyprus have divided. Nigeria suppressed an ethnic rebellion. France faces difficulties with its Basques, Bretons and Corsicans."

The United States is at a crossroads. If it does not consciously move toward greater integration, it will inevitably drift toward more fragmentation. It will either have to do better in assimilating all of the other peoples in its boundaries or it will witness increasing alienation and fragmentation. Cultural divisiveness is not a bedrock upon which a nation can be built. It is inherently unstable.

The nation faces a staggering social agenda. We have not adequately integrated blacks into our economy and society. Our education system is rightly described as "a rising tide of mediocrity." We have the most violent society in the industrial world; we have startlingly high rates of illiteracy, illegitimacy and welfare recipients.

It bespeaks a hubris to madly rush, with these unfinished social agendas, into accepting more immigrants and refugees than all of the rest of the world and then to still hope to keep a common agenda.

America can accept additional immigrants, but we must be sure that they become American. We can be a Joseph's coat of many nations, but we must be unified. One of the common glues that hold us together is language—the English language.

We should be color-blind but linguistically cohesive. We should be a rainbow but not a cacophony. We should welcome different peoples but not adopt different languages. We can teach English through bilingual education, but we should take great care not to become a bilingual society. (Richard D. Lamm, "English Comes First")

A. Answer the following questions about the essay.

1. Former Colorado governor Richard D. Lamm relies on a number of unstated premises about his subject that he expects his audience to share. What are some of these premises?

2. What kinds of information does Lamm use to support his position?

3. Where does Lamm state his conclusion? Restate the conclusion in your own words.

4. In paragraph 1 Lamm uses deductive reasoning. Express this reasoning as a syllogism.

5. Express the syllogism in paragraph 1 in terms of Toulmin logic.

B. Evaluate the reasoning in the following statements. (If the statement is in the form of an enthymeme, supply the missing term before evaluating it.)

1. All immigrants should speak English. If they do not, they are not real Americans.

2. Richard D. Lamm was born in the United States and grew up in an English-speaking household. Therefore, he has no credibility on the subject of bilingualism.

3. Spanish-speaking immigrants should be required by law to learn English. After all, most eastern European immigrants who came to this country early in the twentieth century learned English.

4. If immigrants do not care enough about our country to learn English, we should not allow them to become citizens.

5. Some immigrants have become financially successful even though they did not learn English. Obviously, then, learning English does not increase an immigrant's chances for success.

6. All Cuban immigrants speak Spanish. Former Secretary of Housing and Urban Development Henry Cisneros speaks Spanish, so he must be a Cuban immigrant.

7. As sociologist Seymour Martin Lipset points out, bilingual societies can be threatened by tension and political unrest. Therefore, it is important that immigrants not be bilingual.

8c Recognizing Logical Fallacies

Fallacies are flawed arguments. On the surface they may seem reasonable, but they are not. Unscrupulous writers often use logical fallacies to manipulate readers, appealing to prejudices and fears, for example, instead of to reason. But even when you write with the best of intentions and the greatest care, you may accidentally include fallacies. When readers detect fallacies, they may conclude that you are illogical—or even dishonest. It makes sense, then, to learn to recognize fallacies—to challenge them when you read and to avoid them when you write.

(1) Hasty Generalization

A **hasty generalization** draws a conclusion based on too little evidence. For example, one disappointing performance by an elected official is not enough to warrant the statement that you will never vote again. The number of examples you need depends on the statement you are supporting. A few examples could be enough to make the point that you and your former boyfriend or girlfriend were incompatible. Many more would be needed to support the statement that new writers have a difficult time getting their work published by American publishers.

(2) Sweeping Generalization

Sometimes confused with the hasty generalization, a **sweeping generalization** is a statement that cannot be adequately supported no matter how much evidence is supplied. **Absolute statements,** for example, are so sweeping that they allow for no exceptions.

Everyone should exercise.

Certainly, most people would agree that regular exercise promotes good health. This does not mean, however, that *all* people should exercise. For example, what if a person has a heart condition? To avoid making statements that cannot be supported, you should be careful to qualify your statements. For example, instead of saying, "Everyone should exercise," you might say, "Most people benefit from regular exercise." The easiest way to identify absolute statements is to examine each use of words such as *always, all, never,* and *everyone.* In many cases, a word such as *often, seldom, some,* or *most* will be more accurate.

Stereotypes are sweeping generalizations about the members of a race, religion, gender, nationality, or other group. Because such generalizations are rarely accurate, they undercut the credibility of those who make them.

(3) Equivocation

Equivocation occurs when the meaning of a key word or phrase shifts—often subtly—during an argument.

It is in the public interest for the government to provide for the welfare of those who cannot help themselves. The public's interest becomes aroused, however, when it hears of welfare recipients getting thousands of dollars by cheating or by fraud.

In the first sentence, *public interest* refers to social good and *welfare* to well-being. In the second sentence, *the public's interest* refers to self-interest and *welfare* to financial assistance provided by the government.

(4) The Either/Or Fallacy

The **either/or fallacy** occurs when a complex situation is presented as if it has only two sides. If you ask whether the policies of the United States toward Latin America are beneficial or harmful, you acknowledge only two possibilities, ruling out all others. In fact, the policies of the United States toward some Latin American countries may be beneficial, but US policies toward others may be harmful. Or, in a particular country they may be *both* beneficial and harmful. Avoid the either/or fallacy by acknowledging the complexity of an issue. Do not misrepresent issues by limiting them.

Of course, *some* either/or situations lead to valid conclusions. In biology lab, a test either will or will not indicate the presence of a certain enzyme. An either/or statement is valid as long as it encompasses *every* possible alternative.

(5) The *post hoc* Fallacy (*post hoc, ergo propter hoc*)

Post hoc, ergo propter hoc is Latin for "after this, therefore because of this." The *post hoc* fallacy occurs when you mistakenly infer that because one event follows another, the first event *caused* the second. For example, after the United States sold wheat to Russia, the price of wheat and wheat products rose dramatically. Many people blamed the wheat sale for this rapid increase. One event followed the other closely in time, so people falsely assumed that the first event caused the second. In fact, a complicated series of farm price controls that had been in effect for years was responsible for the increase in wheat prices.

Make certain that you identify the actual causes and effects of the events you discuss. Cause-and-effect relationships are difficult to prove, so you may have to rely on expert testimony to support your claim.

(6) Begging the Question

A writer **begs the question** when he or she states a debatable premise as if it were true. Often this fallacy occurs when a person incorrectly assumes that a proposition is so obvious that is needs no proof. Consider this example.

Sadistic experiments on animals should be stopped because they clearly constitute cruel and unusual punishment.

Certainly, sadistic experimentation is cruel. What has to be proven, however, is that the experiments on animals to which the writer refers actually are sadistic. By simply saying the same thing twice, the writer sidesteps this issue entirely.

(7) False Analogy

See
6e6

Analogies—extended comparisons—enable a writer to explain something unfamiliar by comparing it to something familiar. Skillfully used, an analogy can be quite effective, as when a student illustrates his frustration with the registration process at his college by comparing students to rats in a maze. In an argument, however, an analogy alone establishes nothing; it is no substitute for supporting evidence.

A **false analogy** (or faulty analogy) assumes that because issues or concepts are similar in some ways, they are similar in other ways. On a television talk show recently, a psychologist who was asked to explain why people commit crimes gave the following response.

> People commit crimes because they are weak and selfish. They are like pregnant women who know they shouldn't smoke but do anyway. They have a craving that they have to give in to. The answer is not to punish criminals, but to understand their behavior and to try to change it.

Admittedly, the analogy between criminals and pregnant women who smoke is convincing. However, it oversimplifies the issue. A pregnant woman does not intend to harm her unborn child by smoking; many criminals do intend to harm their victims. To undercut the psychologist's argument, you need only point out the shortcomings of his analogy.

(8) Red Herring

The **red herring** fallacy occurs when a writer changes the subject to distract the audience from the actual issue. Consider, for example, the statement, "This company may charge high prices, but it gives a great deal of money to charity each year." The latter observation has nothing to do with the former; still, it somehow manages to obscure the real issue.

(9) Argument to Ignorance (*argumentum ad ignorantiam*)

The **argument to ignorance** fallacy occurs when a writer says that something is true because it cannot be proved false or that something is false because it cannot be proved true. This fallacy occurred recently during a debate about a policy allowing children who have AIDS to attend public school. A parent asked a doctor, "How can you tell me to send my child to a school where there is a child with AIDS? After all, you doctors can't say for sure that my son won't catch AIDS from this child." In other words, the parent was saying, "My son could contract AIDS from another child in school because it has never been proven that he cannot." As persuasive as this line of reasoning can sometimes be, it is logically flawed: no evidence has been presented to support the speaker's conclusion.

(10)   The Bandwagon Fallacy

The **bandwagon** fallacy occurs when a writer tries to establish that something is true or worthwhile because everyone believes it is. For example, a recent newspaper editorial makes the statement, "Everyone knows that eating too much candy makes a child hyperactive." Instead of providing evidence to support this claim, the editorial relies on an appeal to numbers. A great number of people may believe that this statement is true, but that alone does not make it true.

(11)   Skewed Sample

A **skewed sample** occurs when a statistical sample is collected so that it will lead to one conclusion rather than another. To present accurate results, a statistical sample should be *representative;* that is, it should be typical of the broader population it represents. For example, a study of the spending habits of Americans would most likely be skewed in favor of relatively affluent individuals if all its respondents were luxury-car owners. Similarly, census questions asked only in English would skew results in favor of English-speaking respondents.

(12)   You Also (*tu quoque*)

The **you also** fallacy occurs when a writer argues that a point has no merit because the person making it does not follow his or her own advice. Such an argument is irrelevant because it focuses attention on the person rather than on the issue being debated.

How can government economists advise Americans to save? Look at how much money the government spent last year.

(13)   Argument to the Person (*ad hominem*)

Arguments *ad hominem* attack a person rather than an issue. By attacking an opponent, these arguments turn attention away from the real issues.

That woman has criticized the president's commitment to women's rights. But she believes in parapsychology. She thinks that she can communicate with the dead.

Congressman Rodriguez supports increases in the defense budget. What do you expect from a man who worked for a defense contractor before he ran for public office?

(14)   Argument to the People (*ad populum*)

Arguments *ad populum* appeal to people's prejudices. A senatorial candidate seeking support in a state whose textile industry has been hurt by foreign competition may allude to "foreigners who are attempting to overrun our shores." By exploiting the prejudices of the audience, the candidate is able to avoid the concrete issues of the campaign.

✔ CHECKLIST: LOGICAL FALLACIES

- ✔ **Hasty Generalization**   A conclusion based on too little evidence
- ✔ **Sweeping Generalization**   A statement that cannot be supported no matter how much evidence is supplied
- ✔ **Equivocation**   A shift in the meaning of a key word during an argument
- ✔ **Either/Or Fallacy**   A complex issue treated as if it has only two sides
- ✔ ***Post Hoc* Fallacy**   An unjustified link between cause and effect
- ✔ **Begging the Question**   A debatable premise stated as if it were true
- ✔ **False Analogy**   An assumption that because things are similar in some ways they are similar in other ways
- ✔ **Red Herring**   A change in subject to distract an audience
- ✔ **Argument to Ignorance**   A claim that something is true because it cannot be proved false, or vice versa
- ✔ **Bandwagon Fallacy**   An attempt to establish that something is true because everyone believes it is true
- ✔ **Skewed Sample**   A statistical sample that favors one population over another
- ✔ **You Also Fallacy**   A claim that a position is not valid because the person advocating it does not follow it
- ✔ **Argument to the Person**   An attack on the person and not the issue
- ✔ **Argument to the People**   An appeal to the prejudices of the people

EXERCISE 4

Identify the fallacies in the following statements. In each case, name the fallacy and rewrite the statement to correct the problem.

1. Membership in the Coalition against Pornography has more than quadrupled since the '80s. Convenience stores in many parts of the country have limited their selection of pornography and, in many cases, taken pornography off the shelves. In 1995, the defense appropriations bill included a ban on the sale of pornography on military installations. The American public clearly believes that pornography has a harmful effect on its audience.

2. With people like Larry Flynt and Hugh Hefner arguing that pornography is harmless, you know that pornography is causing its readers to live immoral lifestyles.

3. The Republican Party and conservative thinkers are all for the free market when the issue is environmental degradation, but they'll be the first ones to call for a limit to what can be shown on movies, television, and the Internet.

4. Television is out of control. There is more foul language, sex, and sexual innuendo on television than there has ever been before. The effects of this obscene and pornographic material have been clearly documented in studies that proved that serial killers and other criminals were much more likely to be regular consumers of pornographic materials.

5. We know that television causes children to be more violent. So what can we use to rein in television? The V-chip, television ratings, and more governmental control of television content will help us reduce violence.

6. Study after study has been completed, and none of the researchers has presented incontrovertible evidence that rap music causes an increase in violent behavior among its listeners.

7. A boy in Idaho set fire to his family's home after watching an episode of *Beavis and Butt-head.* From this incident, we can see that television has a negative influence on children's behavior.

8. We want our children to grow up in safe neighborhoods. We'd like to see less violence in the schools and on the playgrounds. We'd like to be less fearful when we have to go out at night. If we stop polluting our culture with violent images from television and popular music, we can reclaim our communities and our children.

9. Ted Bundy and Richard Ramirez, two of the most violent serial killers ever caught, both used pornography regularly. Pornography caused them to kill women.

10. Some people believe that violence on television affects children and want the government to find ways to limit violence. Others believe

that children are unaffected by the violence they see on television. I don't think violence on television causes children to become violent.

EXERCISE 5

Read the following excerpt. Identify as many logical fallacies as you can. Then, write a letter to the author pointing out the fallacies and explaining how they weaken his argument.

Hunting and eating a free-roaming wild deer is one thing; slaughtering and eating a [wounded] deer is another.

The point . . . is that—despite what our enemies are saying— hunters are just as compassionate as the next fellow. It hurts us to see an animal suffer, and when we can help an animal in need, we go out of our way to do whatever we can.

A case in point is the story . . . about SCI Alaska vice president Dave Campbell's efforts to help a cow moose. That animal had carried a poorly shot arrow in its body for weeks until Campbell saw it and made certain it got help.

Despite how some media handled that story, there is no irony in hunters coming to the rescue of the same species we hunt.

We do it all the time.

A story of hunters showing compassion for an animal is something you'll never see in *The Bunny Huggers' Gazette* (yes, there *is* such a publication. It's a bimonthly magazine produced on newsprint. According to the publisher's statement, it provides information about vegetarianism, and "organizations, protests, boycotts or legislation on behalf of animal liberation . . .").

Among the protests announced in the June issue of *BHG* are boycotts against the countries of Ireland and Spain, the states and provinces of the Yukon Territory, Alberta, British Columbia, Pennsylvania and Alaska, the companies of American Express, Anheuser-Busch, Bausch & Lomb, Bloomingdale's, Coca-Cola Products, Coors, Gillette, Hartz, L'Oreal, McDonald's, Mellon Bank, Northwest Airlines, Pocono Mountain resorts and a host of others.

Interestingly, *BHG* tells how a subscribing group, Life Net of Montezuma, New Mexico, has petitioned the US Forest Service to close portions of the San Juan and Rio Grande National Forests between April and November to all entry "to provide as much protection as possible" for grizzly bears that may still exist there. Another subscriber, Predator Project of Bozeman, Montana, is asking that the entire North Cascades region be closed to coyote hunting because gray wolves might be killed by "sportsmen (who) may not be able to tell the difference between a coyote and a wolf."

Although it's not a new idea, another subscriber, Prairie Dog Rescue, is urging persons who are opposed to hunting to apply for limited quota hunting permits because "one permit in peaceful hands means one less opportunity for a hunter to kill."

And if you ever doubted that the vegetarian/animal rights herd is a wacko bunch, then consider the magazine's review of *Human Tissue, A Neglected Experimental Resource.* According to the review, the 24-page essay encourages using human tissues to test "medicines and other substances, any of which would save animals' lives." (Bill Roberts, "The World of Hunting")

EXERCISE 6

The following statements provide the claim and the grounds for an argument. Identify the claim and the grounds. Then supply the warrant.

EXAMPLE: Cigarette smoking should be illegal because it isn't healthful.
CLAIM: Cigarette smoking should be illegal.
GROUNDS: Cigarette smoking isn't healthful.
WARRANT: Things that aren't healthful should be illegal.

1. Buy this car because it has a powerful engine.
2. Karate is good for overactive kids because it teaches them to control their bodies.
3. Legal immigrants contribute to the economy by paying taxes, so they should be allowed to receive welfare and Medicare benefits.
4. Sports figures shouldn't be paid so much because their work doesn't contribute to the betterment of society.
5. Because it takes a long time to complete the income tax forms required by the IRS, we should change the current tax system to a flat tax system.

CHAPTER 9

WRITING AN ARGUMENTATIVE ESSAY

See
Pt. 1
For many people, the true test of their critical thinking skills comes when they write an argumentative essay. When you write an argumentative essay, you follow the same process you use when you write any **essay**. The special demands of argument, though, require you to employ some additional strategies to make your ideas convincing to readers.

 ARGUMENT AND PERSUASION

Many people use the terms *argument* and *persuasion* as if they meant the same thing. Strictly speaking, however, there is a distinction between the two. *Persuasion* is a general term that refers to the various ways that writers can encourage readers to accept their positions—appealing to the emotions, for example. *Argument* usually refers to the use of logic and evidence to convince readers.

 Planning an Argumentative Essay

(1) Choosing a Debatable Topic

An argumentative essay attempts to change the way readers think and act. For this reason, it must focus on a **debatable topic,** one about which reasonable people disagree. Factual statements—those about which reasonable people do not disagree—are, therefore, not suitable for argument.

FACT: Many countries hold political prisoners.

DEBATABLE TOPIC: The United States *should not* trade with countries that hold political prisoners.

FACT: First-year students are not required to purchase a meal plan from the university.

DEBATABLE TOPIC: First-year students *should* be required to purchase a meal plan from the university.

In addition to being debatable, your topic should be one about which you know something. The more evidence you can provide, the more likely you are to influence your audience. General knowledge is seldom convincing by itself, however, so you will probably have to do some **research**. See Ch. 39

It helps if you care about your topic, but that is not an absolute requirement. In fact, when you feel very strongly about an issue, you may not be able to view it clearly. If this is the case, consider another topic or try writing an argument in support of a position other than the one you hold. (Dr. Samuel Johnson, the eighteenth-century lexicographer and critic, said that he preferred to argue on what he called the "wrong" side of an issue because all the interesting things were to be said there.)

You should also make sure your topic is narrow enough so that you can write about it within the page limit you have been given. After all, in your argumentative essay you will have to develop your own ideas and present supporting evidence, while also pointing out the strengths and weaknesses of opposing arguments. If your topic is too broad, you will not be able to cover it in enough detail.

Finally, keep in mind that some topics—such as "The Need for Gun Control" or "The Effectiveness of the Death Penalty"—have been discussed and written about so often that you will probably not be able to say anything new or interesting about them. Such topics usually inspire tired, uninteresting essays that add little or nothing to a reader's understanding of an issue. Instead of relying on an overused topic, choose one that enables you to contribute something new to the debate.

(2) Developing an Argumentative Thesis

After you have chosen a topic, your next step is to state your position in an **argumentative thesis,** one that asserts or denies something about your topic. Properly worded, this thesis statement lays the foundation for the rest of your argument.

Because the purpose of an argumentative essay is to convince readers to accept your position, your thesis statement must take a strong stand.

One way to make sure that your thesis statement actually does take a stand is to formulate an **antithesis,** a statement that takes an arguable position opposite from yours. If you can create an antithesis, your thesis statement takes a stand. If you cannot, your statement needs further revision to make it argumentative.

THESIS STATEMENT: Term limits would improve government by bringing people with fresh ideas into office every few years.

ANTITHESIS: Term limits would harm government because elected officials would always be inexperienced.

Whenever possible, test a tentative thesis statement on classmates—either informally in classroom conversations or formally in collaborative work. You may also want to talk to your instructor, do some reading about your topic, or do research in the **library** or on the **Internet**. Your goal should be to get a grasp of your topic so you can make an informed statement about it. Before you feel ready to do this, however, you may want to review your annotations, your journal entries, and any notes you made when you were choosing your topic. If you still have trouble formulating a thesis statement, you may want to try some of the techniques for **getting started** discussed in Chapter 1.

See 39b

See Ch. 40

See 1c

(3) Defining Your Terms

Be sure to define any potentially ambiguous terms you use in your argument; after all, the soundness of an entire argument may hinge on the definition of a word that may mean one thing to one person and another thing to someone else. In the United States, *democratic* elections involve the selection of government officials by popular vote. In other countries rulers have used the same term to describe elections in which only one candidate has run or in which several candidates—all from the same party—have run. For this reason, when you use a term such as *democratic,* you should make sure that your readers know exactly what you mean. The same is true for other potentially slippery terms, such as *freedom of speech, cruel and unusual punishment,* and *assisted suicide.*

In some cases you may want to use a formal definition in your essay. Instead of quoting from a dictionary, however, you may want to develop an extended **definition** that includes examples from your own experience or reading. Not only can it be tailored to the specific issue you are writing about but it also can provide much more specific information than a dictionary definition.

See 6e8

DEFINING YOUR TERMS

Be particularly careful to use precise terms in your thesis statement, avoiding vague and judgmental words such as *wrong, bad, good, right,* and *immoral.*

VAGUE: Censorship of the Internet would be wrong.

CLEARER: Censorship of the Internet would unfairly limit free speech.

(4) Considering Your Audience

As you plan your essay, keep a specific **audience** in mind. Are your readers unbiased observers or people deeply concerned about the issue you plan to discuss? Can they be cast in a specific role—concerned parents, victims of discrimination, irate consumers—or are they so diverse that they cannot be categorized? If you cannot be certain who your readers are, you will have to direct your arguments to a general audience.

See 1b2

Always assume a skeptical audience. Even if your readers are sympathetic to your position, you cannot assume that they will accept your ideas without question. At times—especially if your topic is highly controversial or emotionally charged—you may even have to assume that your readers are hostile. The strategies you use to convince your readers will vary according to your relationship with them. Sympathetic readers may need to see only that your argument is logical and that your evidence is solid. Skeptical readers may need a good deal of reassurance that you understand their concerns and that you concede some of their points. However, you may never be able to convince hostile readers that your conclusion is valid. The best you can hope for is that these readers will acknowledge the strength of your argument.

(5) Refuting Opposing Arguments

As you develop your argument, you must **refute**—that is, disprove—opposing arguments by showing that they are untrue, unfair, illogical, unimportant, or irrelevant. In the following paragraph, a student refutes an argument against her position.

> Of course, some will say that Sea World wants to capture only a few whales, as George Will points out in his commentary in *Newsweek.* Unfortunately, Will downplays the fact that Sea World

195

wants to capture a hundred whales, not just "a few." And, after releasing ninety of these whales, Sea World intends to keep ten for "further work." At hearings in Seattle last week, several noted marine biologists went on record as condemning Sea World's research program.

When an opponent's position is so strong that it cannot be refuted, concede the point and then, if possible, discuss its limitations. Martin Luther King, Jr., uses this tactic in his "Letter from Birmingham Jail."

> You express a great deal of anxiety over our willingness to break laws. This is certainly a legitimate concern. Since we so diligently urge people to obey the Supreme Court's decision of 1954 outlawing segregation in the public schools, at first glance it may seem rather paradoxical for us consciously to break laws. One may well ask: "How can you advocate breaking some laws and obeying others?" The answer lies in the fact that there are two types of laws: just and unjust. I would be the first to advocate obeying just laws. Conversely, one has a moral responsibility to disobey unjust laws. I would agree with St. Augustine that "an unjust law is no law at all."

When you acknowledge an opposing view, as King does in the second sentence of the preceding paragraph, do not distort it or present it as ridiculously weak. This tactic, called creating a **straw man,** could seriously undermine your credibility.

EXERCISE 1

Make two columns by drawing a line down the center of a piece of paper. Choose one of the following five statements, and list the arguments in favor of it in one column and the arguments against it in the other column. Then, choose one position and write a paragraph or two supporting it. Be sure to refute the arguments against your position.

1. Public school students should have to wear school uniforms.
2. The federal government should limit the amount of violence shown on television.
3. All health-care workers should be required to take a yearly AIDS test.
4. Retirees making more than $50,000 a year should not be eligible for Social Security benefits.
5. Colleges and universities should provide free child care for students with children.

(6) Presenting Support

See
7b2

Most arguments are built on **assertions**—claims that you make about a debatable topic—backed by <u>supporting evidence</u>—information, in the form of examples, statistics, or expert opinion—that reinforces your argument. You could, for instance, assert that law-enforcement officials are beginning to win the war against violent crime. You could then support this assertion by referring to a government report stating that violent crime in several of the largest US cities has decreased during the last few years. This report would be one piece of persuasive evidence.

Certain assertions need no proof: statements that are *self-evident* ("All human beings are mortal"), statements that are true by *definition* (2 + 2 = 4), and *statements of fact* that you can expect the average person to know ("The Atlantic Ocean separates England and the United States"). All other kinds of assertions require support.

 ## PRESENTING SUPPORT

Remember that an argumentative essay never proves a thesis conclusively—if it did, there would be no argument. The best you can do is to provide enough support to establish a high probability that your thesis is correct or establish that it is reasonable.

(7) Establishing Credibility

Clear reasoning, compelling evidence, and pointed refutations go a long way toward making an argument solid. But these elements are not sufficient in themselves to create a convincing argument. In order to sway readers, you have to satisfy them that you are someone they should listen to—in other words, that you have **credibility.**

Certain individuals, of course, bring credibility with them every time they speak. When a Nobel Prize winner in physics makes a speech about the need to control proliferation of nuclear weapons, we assume that he or she speaks with authority. But most people do not have this kind of credibility and thus must work to establish it—by *finding common ground, demonstrating knowledge,* and *maintaining a reasonable tone.*

Finding Common Ground When you write an argument, it is tempting to go on the attack, emphasizing the differences between your position and those of your opponents. In argument, as in foreign policy and labor negotiations, however, lack of agreement can cause animosity, mistrust, and eventually a total breakdown of communications. Writers of effective arguments know they can avoid this breakdown by establishing common ground between their opponents and themselves.

One way to avoid a confrontational stance, and thereby increase your credibility, is to use the techniques of **Rogerian argument,** based on the work of the psychologist Carl Rogers. According to Rogers, you should think of the members of your audience as colleagues with whom you must collaborate to find solutions to problems. Instead of verbally assaulting them, you should emphasize points of agreement. In this way, you establish common ground and work toward a resolution of the issue you are discussing. For example, you could begin an essay in which you argue against the establishment of speech codes (policies that prohibit speech calculated to hurt, intimidate, or demean others) on your campus by asserting that all Americans are interested in protecting First Amendment rights. Once you and your readers occupy this common ground, you will more easily convince them of the dangers of speech codes.

Demonstrating Knowledge   Including relevant personal experiences in your argumentative essay can show readers that you know a lot about your subject and thus can give you authority. Describing your observations at a National Rifle Association conference, for example, can give you authority in an essay arguing for (or against) gun control. Similarly, a discussion of your experiences as an employee of a landscaping company can give you credibility when you argue for (or against) banning certain lawn-care products.

You can also establish credibility by showing you have done research into a subject. By mentioning important research sources you have consulted and documenting the information you got from them, you show readers that you have done the necessary background work. Including references to several sources—not just one—suggests to readers that you have a balanced knowledge of your subject. If you use sources other than your own knowledge and experience, make certain that you **document** them carefully.

See
Ch. 43

Questionable sources, inaccurate documentation, and factual errors can undermine an argument. For many readers, an undocumented quotation or even an incorrect date can call an entire argument into question.

Maintaining a Reasonable Tone   The tone you adopt is almost as important as the information you convey. Avoid sounding high-handed or pedantic. Talk *to* your readers, not *at* them. If you lecture your readers or appear to talk down to them, you will alienate them. Remember that readers are more likely to respond to a writer who is conciliatory than to one who is insulting.

As you write your essay, be sure to use moderate language. Words and phrases such as *never, all,* and *in every case* can make your claims seem exaggerated and unrealistic. Learn to qualify **sweeping generalizations** so that they seem reasonable. The statement "Euthanasia is never acceptable," for example, leaves you no room for compromise. A more conciliatory statement might be "In cases of extreme suffering one can understand a patient's desire for death, but in most cases the moral, social, and legal implications of

See
8c2

euthanasia make it unacceptable." By qualifying your position, you demonstrate that you are making every effort to adopt a reasonable point of view.

✔ CHECKLIST: ESTABLISHING YOUR CREDIBILITY

FIND COMMON GROUND
✔ Identify the various sides of the issue.
✔ Identify the points on which you and your readers agree.
✔ Work these areas of agreement into your argument.

DEMONSTRATE KNOWLEDGE
✔ Include relevant personal experiences.
✔ Include relevant special knowledge of your subject.
✔ Refer to research sources.

MAINTAIN A REASONABLE TONE
✔ Avoid talking down to your readers.
✔ Use moderate language, and avoid sweeping generalizations.

---

(8) Being Fair

The line between being persuasive and being unfair is sometimes a fine one, and no clear-cut rules exist to help you make this distinction. Writers of effective and sometimes brilliant argumentative essays are often less than fair to their opponents. We could hardly call Jonathan Swift "fair" when, in "A Modest Proposal," he implies that the English are cannibals. Similarly a supporter of King George III would argue that Thomas Jefferson and the other writers of the Declaration of Independence were less than fair when they criticized British policies in the American colonies. Of course, "A Modest Proposal" is bitter satire, and Swift employs overstatement to express his rage at social conditions. Similarly, in justifying their break with England, the writers of the Declaration of Independence did not intend to be fair to the king.

Argument promotes one point of view, so it is seldom objective. For better or worse, however, college writing requires that you stay within the bounds of fairness. To be sure that the support for your argument is not misleading or distorted, you should take the following steps.

Avoid Distorting Evidence Distortion is misrepresentation. Writers sometimes intentionally misrepresent their opponents' views by exaggerating them and then attacking this extreme position. For example, a governor of a northeastern state proposed requiring unmarried mothers receiving welfare to identify their children's fathers and supply information about them. A critic attacked him with the following statements.

What is the governor's next idea in his headlong rush to embrace the extreme right-wing position? A program of tattoos for welfare mothers? A badge sewn on to their clothing identifying them as welfare recipients? Creation of colonies, similar to leper colonies, where welfare recipients would be forced to live? How about an involuntary relocation program into camps?

The governor made a controversial proposal, and his critic could certainly have challenged it on its own merits. Instead, by distorting the governor's position, his critic attacked it unfairly.

Avoid Quoting Out of Context　　A writer or speaker quotes out of context by taking someone's words from their original setting and using them in another. When you select certain statements and ignore others, you can change the meaning of what someone has said or implied. Consider the following example.

MR. N, TOWNSHIP RESIDENT: I don't know why you are opposing the new highway. According to your own statements the highway will increase land values and bring more business into the area.

MS. L, TOWNSHIP SUPERVISOR: I think you should look at my statements more carefully. I have a copy of the paper that printed my interview, and what I said was [*reading*]: "The highway will increase land values a bit and bring some business to the area. But at what cost? One hundred and fifty families will be displaced, and the highway will divide our township in half." My comments were not meant to support the new highway but to underscore the problems that its construction will cause.

By repeating only some of Ms. L's remarks, Mr. N altered her meaning to suit his purpose. In context, Ms. L's words indicate that although she concedes the highway's few benefits, she believes that its drawbacks outweigh them.

Avoid Slanting Support　　When you select information that supports your case and ignore information that does not—for example, if you support your position that smoking should not be prohibited in public places by choosing only evidence provided by the American Tobacco Institute—you are guilty of slanting supporting information. Inflammatory language is another form of slanting that creates bias in your writing. A national magazine slanted its information, to say the least, when it described an accused felon as "a hulk of a man who looks as if he could burn out somebody's eyes with a propane torch." Although one-sided presentations frequently appear in newspapers and magazines, you should avoid such distortions in your argumentative essays.

Avoid Using Unfair Appeals　　Traditionally, writers of arguments use three kinds of appeals to influence readers. The **logical appeal** addresses an audience's sense of reason. Using the principles of inductive and deductive reasoning discussed in Chapter 8, the logical appeal moves from evidence to conclusions. The **emotional appeal** plays on the emotions of a reader, and the **ethical appeal** calls the reader's attention to the credibility of the writer. Problems arise when these appeals are used unfairly. For example, writers can use <u>fallacies</u> to fool readers into thinking that a conclusion is logical when it is not. Writers can also employ inappropriate emotional appeals—to prejudice or fear, for example—to influence readers. And finally, writers can use their credentials in one area of expertise to bolster their stature in another area that they are not qualified to discuss. Not only are these techniques misleading and dishonest, but they also frequently backfire. Readers will frequently dismiss even the most compelling argument if they begin to doubt a writer's integrity.

See
8c

9b   Organizing an Argumentative Essay

In its simplest form, an argument consists of a thesis statement and supporting evidence. However, argumentative essays frequently include additional elements calculated to win audience approval and overcome potential opposition.

ELEMENTS OF AN ARGUMENTATIVE ESSAY

Introduction
The <u>introduction</u> of your argumentative essay orients readers to your subject. Here you can show how your subject concerns your audience, explain why it is important, or perhaps discuss how it has been misunderstood.

See
6f2

Background
In this section you briefly present a narrative of past events, a summary of others' opinions on your subject, or a review of basic facts.

Thesis Statement
Your thesis statement can appear anywhere in your argumentative essay. Frequently, you present your thesis after you have given your readers an overview of your subject. However, in highly controversial arguments—those to which you believe your readers might react negatively—you may postpone stating your thesis until later in your essay, after you have made your arguments in its support.

continued on the following page

---

continued from the previous page

Arguments in Support of Your Thesis

See
8a, b

This section contains the **inductive and deductive** arguments that support your thesis. Here you present your points and the evidence you have gathered to convince readers to accept them.

Most often, you begin with your weakest argument and work up to your strongest. If all your arguments are equally strong, you might want to begin with those points with which your readers are already familiar (and which they are therefore likely to accept) and then move on to relatively unfamiliar points.

Refutation of Opposing Arguments

In an argumentative essay, you must summarize and refute the arguments against your thesis. If you do not confront these opposing arguments, doubts about your case will remain in the minds of your readers. If the opposing arguments are relatively weak, refute them after you have made your case. However, if the opposing arguments are strong, concede their strengths and refute them *before* you present your own points.

Conclusion

See
6f3

Most often, the conclusion restates in general terms the major arguments you have marshaled in support of your thesis. Your **conclusion** can also summarize key points, restate your thesis, remind readers of the weaknesses of opposing arguments, or underscore the logic of your position. Many writers like to end their arguments with a strong last sentence, one calculated to stay in the minds of their readers. An apt quotation, for example, can crystallize the sentiments or capture the intensity of your argument.

 9c Writing and Revising an Argumentative Essay

(1) Writing an Argumentative Essay

See
Ch. 39;
Ch. 40

The following student essay includes many of the elements discussed in the preceding box. The student, Samantha Masterton, was asked by her instructor to write an argument, drawing her supporting evidence from her own experience as well as from her **research**.

Masterton 1

Samantha Masterton

Professor Wade

English 102

15 March 1996

The Returning Student:

Older Is Definitely Better

After graduating from high school, young people must   Introduction

decide what they want to do with the rest of their lives. Many

graduates (often without much thought) decide to continue

their education uninterrupted, and they go on to college. This

group of teenagers makes up what many see as the typical

first-year college student. Recently, however, this stereotype

has been challenged by an influx of older students into

American colleges and universities. Not only do these students

make a valuable contribution to the schools they attend, but

they also present an alternative to young people who go to

college simply because it is the thing to do. A few years off

between high school and college can give many--perhaps   Thesis
                                                          statement
most--students the life experience they need to appreciate the

value of higher education.

The college experience of an eighteen-year-old is quite   Background
                                                           statement
different from that of an older student. The typical teenager is

often concerned with things other than cracking books--going

to parties, dating, and testing personal limits, for example.

Masterton 2

Although the maturation process from teenager to adult is something we all must go through, college is not necessarily the appropriate place for this to occur. My experience as an adult enrolled in a university has convinced me that many students would benefit from delaying entry into college. I almost never see older students cutting lectures or not studying. Most have saved for tuition and want to get their money's worth, just as I do. Many are also balancing the demands of home and work to attend classes, so they know how important it is to do well.

Argument in support of thesis

Generally, young people just out of high school have not been challenged by real-world situations that include meeting deadlines and setting priorities. Younger college students often find themselves hopelessly behind or scrambling at the last minute simply because they have not learned how to budget their time. Although success in college depends on the ability to set realistic goals and organize time and materials, college itself does little to help students develop these skills. On the contrary, the workplace--where reward and punishment are usually immediate and tangible--is the best place to learn such lessons. Working teaches the basics that college takes for granted: the value of punctuality and attendance, the importance of respect for superiors and

Masterton 3

colleagues, and the need for establishing priorities and

meeting deadlines.

The adult student who has gained experience in the

workplace has advantages over the teenaged freshman. In

general, the older student enrolls in college with a definite

course of study in mind. As Laura Mansnerus reports in her

article "A Milieu Apart," for the older student, "college is no

longer a stage of life but a place to do work" (17). For the

adult student, then, college becomes an extension of work

rather than a place to discover what work will be. This greater

sense of purpose is not lost on college instructors. Dr. Laurin

Porter, Assistant Professor of English at the University of Texas

at Arlington, echoes the sentiments of many of her colleagues

when she says, "Returning older students, by and large, seem

more focused, more sure of their goals, and more highly

motivated."

Given their age and greater experience, older students

bring more into the classroom than younger students do.

Eighteen-year-olds have been driving for only a year or two;

they have just earned the right to vote; and they usually have

not lived on their own. They cannot be expected to have

formulated definite goals or developed firm ideas about

themselves or about the world in which they live. In contrast,

Argument in support of thesis

Argument in support of thesis

Masterton 4

older students have generally had a variety of real-life experiences. Most have worked for several years; many have started families. Their years in the "real world" have helped them to become more focused and more responsible than they were when they graduated from high school. As a result, they are better prepared for college. Thus, they not only bring more into the classroom, but also take more out of it.

Refutation of opposing argument

Of course, postponing college for a few years is not for everyone. There are certainly some teenagers who have a definite sense of purpose and a maturity well beyond their years, and these individuals might benefit from an early college experience, so that they can get a head start on their careers. Charles Woodward, a law librarian, went to college directly after high school, and for him the experience was positive. "I was serious about learning, and I loved my subject," he said. "I felt fortunate that I knew what I wanted from college and from life." For the most part, though, students are not like Woodward; they graduate from high school without any clear sense of purpose. For this reason, it makes sense for most students to stay away from college until they are mature enough to benefit from the experience.

Refutation of opposing argument

Granted, some older students do have difficulties when they return to college. Because these students have been out

Masterton 5

of school for so long, they may have difficulty studying and adapting to the routines of academic life. Some older students may even feel ill at ease because they are in class with students who are many years younger than they are and because they are too busy to participate in extracurricular activities. As I have seen, though, these problems soon disappear. After a few weeks, older students get into the swing of things and adapt to college. They make friends, get used to studying, and even begin to participate in campus life.

All things considered, higher education is wasted on the young, who are either too immature or too unfocused to take advantage of it. Taking a few years off between college and high school would give these students the breathing room they need to make the most of a college education. The increasing numbers of older students returning to college would seem to indicate that many students are taking this path. According to one study, 45 percent of the students enrolled in American colleges in 1987 were twenty-five years of age or older (Aslanian 57). Older students such as these have taken time off to serve in the military, to get a job, or to raise a family. Many have traveled, engaged in informal study, and taken the time to grow up. By the time they get to college they have defined their goals and made a commitment

Conclusion

Masterton 6

to achieve them. It is clear that postponing college for a few

years can result in a better educational experience for both

students and teachers. As Dr. Porter says, when the older

student brings more life experience into the classroom,

"everyone benefits."

Masterton 7

Works Cited

Aslanian, Carol B. "The Changing Face of American

Works Cited
list begins
new page

Campuses." USA Today Magazine May 1991: 57–59.

Mansnerus, Laura. "A Milieu Apart." New York Times 4 Aug.

1991, late ed.: A7.

Porter, Laurin. Personal interview. 23 Feb. 1996.

Woodward, Charles B. Personal interview. 25 Feb. 1996.

(2) Revising an Argumentative Essay

See
3c

    When you **revise** your argumentative essay, you use the same strate-
gies you use for any essay. In addition, you concentrate on some specific
concerns that are listed in the following checklist.

✔ CHECKLIST: ARGUMENTATIVE ESSAYS

  ✔ Is your topic debatable?
  ✔ Does your essay include an argumentative thesis?

continued on the following page

continued from the previous page

✔ Have you adequately defined the terms you use in your argument?
✔ Have you considered the opinions, attitudes, and values of your audience?
✔ Have you identified and refuted opposing arguments?
✔ Have you supported your assertions with evidence?
✔ Have you established your credibility?
✔ Have you documented any information that is not your own?
✔ Have you been fair?
✔ Have you constructed your arguments logically?
✔ Have you avoided logical fallacies?
✔ Have you provided your readers with enough background information?
✔ Have you presented your points clearly and organized them logically?
✔ Does your essay have an interesting introduction and a strong conclusion?

CLOSE-UP USING TRANSITIONS IN ARGUMENTATIVE ESSAYS

Argumentative essays should include transitional words and phrases to indicate which paragraphs are *arguments in support of the thesis,* which are *refutations* of arguments that oppose the thesis, and which are *conclusions.*

Arguments in support of thesis	Accordingly, because, for example, for instance, in general, given, generally, since
Refutations	Although, admittedly, certainly, despite, granted, in all fairness, naturally, nonetheless, of course
Conclusions	All things considered, as a result, in conclusion, in summary, therefore, thus

EXERCISE 2

Samantha Masterton deleted the following paragraph from her essay "The Returning Student: Older Is Definitely Better." Was Samantha right to delete it? Is it relevant? Logical? If it belongs in the essay, where would it go? Does it need any revision?

The dedication of adult students is evident in the varied roles they must play. Many of the adults who return to school are seeking to increase their earning power. They have established themselves in the working world, only to find they cannot advance without more education or a graduate degree. The dual-income family structure enables many of these adults to return to school, but it is unrealistic for them to put their well-established lives on hold while they pursue their education. In addition to the rigors of college, older students are often juggling homes, families, and jobs. However, adult students make up in determination what they lack in time. In contrast, younger students often lack the essential motivation to succeed in school. Teenagers in college often have no clear idea of why they are there and, lacking this sense of purpose, may do poorly even though they have comparatively few outside distractions.

STUDENT WRITER AT WORK

Writing an Argumentative Essay

Revise the following draft of an argumentative essay, paying particular attention to the essay's logic, its use of support, and the writer's efforts to establish credibility. Be prepared to identify the changes you made and to explain how they make the essay more convincing. If necessary, revise further to strengthen coherence, unity, and style.

Television Violence: Let Us Exercise Our Choice

Television began as what many people thought was a fad. Now, over fifty years later, it is the subject of arguments and controversy. There are even some activist groups who spend all their time protesting television's role in society. The weirdest of these groups is definitely the one that attacks television for being too violent. As far as I am concerned, these people should find better things to do with their time. There is nothing wrong with American television that a little bit of parental supervision wouldn't fix.

The best argument against these protest groups is that television gives people what they want. I am not an expert on the subject, but I do know that the broadcasting industry is a business, a very serious business.

continued on the following page

continued from the previous page

Television programming has to give people what they want, or else they won't watch it. This is a fact that many of the so-called experts forget. If the television networks followed the advice of the protestors, they would be out of business within a year.

Another argument against the protest groups is that the First Amendment of the US Constitution guarantees all citizens the right of free speech. I am a citizen, so I should be able to watch whatever I want to. If these protestors do not want to watch violent programs, let them change the channel or turn off their sets. The Founding Fathers realized that an informed citizenry is the best defense against tyranny. Look at some of the countries that control the programs that citizens are able to watch. In Iran and in China, for example, people see only what the government wants them to see. A citizen can be put into prison if he or she is caught watching an illegal program. Is this where our country is heading?

Certainly, American society is too violent. No one can deny this fact, but we cannot blame all the problems of American society on television violence. As far as I know, there is absolutely no proof that the violence that people see on television causes them to act violently. Violence in society is probably caused by a number of things--drugs, the proliferation of guns, and increased unemployment, for example. Before focusing on violence on television, the protestors should address these things. Protestors should also remember that movies don't kill people; people kill people. Obviously the protestors are forgetting this fact.

All things considered, the solution to violence on television is simple: parents should monitor what their children watch. If they don't like what their children are watching, they should change the channel or turn off the television. There is no reason why the majority of television watchers--who are for the most part law-abiding people--should have to stop watching

continued on the following page

continued from the previous page
programs they like. I for one do not want some protestor telling me what I can or cannot watch, and if, by chance, these protestors do succeed in eliminating all violence, the result will be television programming that is boring, and television, the vast wasteland, will suddenly be turned into the <u>dull</u> wasteland.

PART 3

COMPOSING SENTENCES

CHAPTER 10

BUILDING SIMPLE SENTENCES

A **sentence** is an independent grammatical unit that contains a <u>subject</u> and a <u>predicate</u> and expresses a complete thought.

<u>The quick brown fox</u> <u>jumped over the lazy dog</u>.

<u>It</u> <u>came from outer space</u>.

A **simple subject** is a noun or noun substitute (*fox, it*) that tells who or what the sentence is about. A **simple predicate** is a verb or verb phrase (*jumped, came*) that tells or asks something about the subject. The **complete subject** of a sentence includes the simple subject plus all its modifiers (*the quick brown fox*). The **complete predicate** includes the verb or verb phrase as well as all the words associated with it—such as modifiers, objects, and complements (*jumped over the lazy dog, came from outer space*).

10a Constructing Simple Sentences

A **simple sentence** is a single independent clause. Simple sentences may conform to one of five basic patterns.

(1) Subject + Intransitive Verb (s + v)

The most basic simple sentence consists of just a subject and a verb or **verb phrase** (the <u>main verb</u> plus all its <u>auxiliary verbs</u>).

See
23c1

$$\overset{\text{s}}{\underline{\text{The price of gold}}} \quad \overset{\text{v}}{\underline{\text{rose}}}.$$

$$\overset{\text{s}}{\underline{\text{Stock prices}}} \quad \overset{\text{v}}{\underline{\text{may fall}}}.$$

Here the verbs *rose* and *may fall* are **intransitive**—that is, they do not need an object to complete their meaning.

215

(2) Subject + Transitive Verb + Direct Object (s + v + do)

Another kind of simple sentence consists of the subject, a transitive verb, and a direct object.

<pre>
         s   v   do
Van Gogh created The Starry Night.
</pre>

<pre>
        s   v   do
Caroline saved Jake.
</pre>

Here the verbs *created* and *saved* are **transitive**—each requires an object to complete its meaning in the sentence. In each sentence the **direct object** indicates where the verb's action is directed and *who* or *what* is affected by it.

(3) Subject + Transitive Verb + Direct Object + Object Complement (s + v + do + oc)

This pattern includes an **object complement,** which renames or describes the direct object.

<pre>
       s   v   do   oc
The class elected Bridget treasurer.
</pre>
(Object complement *treasurer* renames direct object *Bridget.*)

<pre>
s   v   do   oc
I found the exam easy.
</pre>
(Object complement *easy* describes direct object *exam.*)

(4) Subject + Linking Verb + Subject Complement (s + v + sc)

See
23c1

Another kind of simple sentence consists of a subject, a <u>linking verb</u> (a verb that connects a subject to its complement), and the **subject complement** (the word or phrase that describes or renames the subject).

<pre>
         s   v   sc
The injection was painless.
</pre>

<pre>
    s   v   sc
Tony Blair became prime minister.
</pre>

Note that the linking verb is like an equal sign, equating the subject with its complement (*Tony Blair = prime minister*).

(5) Subject + Transitive Verb + Indirect Object + Direct Object (s + v + io + do)

In this sentence pattern the **indirect object** indicates to whom or for whom the verb's action was done.

s   v   io   do
<u>Cyrano</u> <u>wrote</u> Roxanne a poem. (Cyrano wrote a poem for Roxanne.)

s   v   io   do
<u>The officer</u> <u>handed</u> Frank a ticket. (The officer handed a ticket to Frank.)

SIMPLE SENTENCE PATTERNS

1. Subject + intransitive verb

           s   v
      <u>The bell</u> <u>rang</u>.

2. Subject + transitive verb + direct object

           s   v
      <u>Toni Morrison</u> <u>won</u> the 1993
      do
      <u>Nobel Prize</u>.

3. Subject + transitive verb + direct object + object complement

           s   v   do
      <u>Artists and writers</u> <u>found</u> Paris
      oc
      <u>exciting</u>.

4. Subject + linking verb + subject complement

           s   v
      <u>The cowardly lion</u> <u>looked</u>
      sc
      <u>frightened</u>.

5. Subject + transitive verb + indirect object + direct object

           s
      <u>The 1882 Chinese Exclusion</u>
      v   io
      <u>Act</u> <u>denied</u> a specific ethnic
      do
      <u>group citizenship</u>. (The act
      denied citizenship to a specific
      ethnic group.)

EXERCISE 1

In each of the following sentences underline the subject once and the predicate twice. Then label direct objects, indirect objects, subject complements, and object complements.

                              sc
EXAMPLE: <u>Isaac Asimov</u> <u>was</u> a science fiction writer.

1. Isaac Asimov first saw science fiction stories in the newsstand of his parents' Brooklyn candy store.
2. He practiced writing by telling his schoolmates stories.
3. Asimov published his first story in *Astounding Science Fiction*.

4. The magazine's editor, John W. Campbell, encouraged Asimov to continue writing.
5. The young writer researched scientific principles to make his stories better.
6. Asimov's "Foundation" series of novels is a "future history."
7. The World Science Fiction Convention awarded the series a Hugo Award.
8. Sometimes Asimov used "Paul French" as a pseudonym.
9. *Biochemistry and Human Metabolism* was Asimov's first nonfiction book.
10. Asimov coined the term *robotics*.

10b Identifying Phrases and Clauses

Individual words may be combined into *phrases* and *clauses*.

(1) Identifying Phrases

A **phrase** is a grammatically ordered group of related words that lacks a subject or predicate or both and functions as a single part of speech. It cannot stand alone as a sentence.

• A **verb phrase** consists of a main verb and all its auxiliary verbs.

Time <u>is flying</u>.

• A **noun phrase** includes a noun or pronoun plus all related modifiers.

I'll climb <u>the highest mountain</u>.

• A **prepositional phrase** consists of a preposition, its object, and any modifiers of that object.

They discussed the ethical implications <u>of the animal studies</u>.

He was last seen heading <u>into the sunset</u>.

• A **verbal phrase** consists of a <u>verbal</u> and its related objects, modifiers, or complements. A verbal phrase may be a **participial phrase,** a **gerund phrase,** or an **infinitive phrase.**

<u>Encouraged by the voter turnout</u>, the candidate predicted a victory. (participial phrase)

<u>Taking it easy</u> always makes sense. (gerund phrase)

The jury recessed <u>to evaluate the evidence</u>. (infinitive phrase)

- An **absolute phrase** usually consists of a noun or pronoun and a participle, accompanied by modifiers. It modifies an entire independent clause rather than a particular word or phrase.

  See
  10c5

<u>Their toes tapping</u>, they watched the auditions.

(2) Identifying Clauses

A **clause** is a group of related words that includes a subject and a predicate. An **independent** (main) **clause** may stand alone as a sentence, but a **dependent** (subordinate) **clause** must always be accompanied by an independent clause.

[Lucretia Mott was an abolitionist.] [She was also a pioneer for women's rights.] (two independent clauses)

[Lucretia Mott was an abolitionist] [who was also a pioneer for women's rights.] (independent clause, dependent clause)

[Although Lucretia Mott was most widely known for her support of women's rights,] [she was also a prominent abolitionist.] (dependent clause, independent clause)

Depending on how they function in a sentence, dependent clauses may be classified as *adjective, adverb,* or *noun* clauses.

- **Adjective clauses,** sometimes called **relative clauses,** modify nouns or pronouns and always follow the nouns or pronouns they modify. They are introduced by relative pronouns—*that, what, whatever, which, who, whose, whom, whoever,* or *whomever.* The adverbs *where* and *when* function as relative pronouns when the adjective clause modifies a place or time.

The television series *M*A*S*H,* <u>which depicted life in an army hospital in Korea during the Korean War,</u> ran for eleven years. (Adjective clause modifies the noun *M*A*S*H.*)

William Styron's novel *Sophie's Choice* is set in Brooklyn, <u>where the narrator lives in a house painted pink.</u> (Adjective clause modifies the noun *Brooklyn.*)

NOTE: Some adjective clauses, called **elliptical clauses,** are grammatically incomplete but nevertheless can be easily understood from the context of the sentence. Typically, a part of the subject or predicate or the entire subject or predicate is missing.

<u>Although</u> [they were] <u>full</u>, they could not resist dessert.

Matt has never been able to read maps <u>as well as Jay</u> [can read maps].

- **Adverb clauses** modify single words (verbs, adjectives, or adverbs), entire phrases, or independent clauses. They are always introduced by subordinating conjunctions. Adverb clauses provide information to answer the questions *how? where? when? why?* and *to what extent?*

Exhausted <u>after the match was over,</u> Kim decided to take a long nap. (Adverb clause modifies *exhausted*, telling *when* Kim was exhausted.)

Mark will go <u>wherever there's a party.</u> (Adverb clause modifies *will go*, telling *where* Mark will go.)

<u>Because 75 percent of its exports are fish products,</u> Iceland's economy is heavily dependent on the fishing industry. (Adverb clause modifies independent clause, telling *why* the fishing industry is so important.)

- **Noun clauses** do not act as modifiers; they function in a sentence as nouns (as subjects, direct objects, indirect objects, or complements). A noun clause may be introduced by a relative pronoun or by *whether, when, where, why,* or *how.*

<u>Whatever happens to us</u> will be for the best. (Noun clause serves as subject of sentence.)

They finally decided <u>which candidate was most qualified.</u> (Noun clause serves as direct object of verb *decided.*)

EXERCISE 2

Which of the following groups of words are independent clauses? Which are dependent clauses? Which are phrases? Label each word group *IC, DC,* or *P.*

EXAMPLE: Coming through the rye. (P)

1. Beauty is truth.	6. Whenever you're near.
2. When knights were bold.	7. The clock struck ten.
3. In a galaxy far away.	8. The red planet.
4. He saw stars.	9. Slowly I turned.
5. I hear a symphony.	10. For the longest time.

10c Expanding Simple Sentences

A simple sentence can consist of just a subject and a verb.

Jessica fell.

A brief simple sentence like this one gives basic information, but more detailed and more varied sentences can make your emphasis clearer and your writing more interesting. Simple sentences can be quite elaborate, expanded and enriched with additional words and phrases.

Jessica fell in love with Henry Goodyear. (prepositional phrases)

Both Jessica and her sister fell in love with Henry Goodyear. (compound construction)

Both Jessica and her younger sister Victoria almost immediately fell hopelessly in love with the very mysterious Henry Goodyear. (adjectives and adverbs)

Rebounding from unhappy love affairs, both Jessica and her younger sister Victoria almost immediately fell hopelessly in love with the very mysterious Henry Goodyear. (verbal phrase)

Rebounding from unhappy love affairs, both Jessica and her younger sister Victoria almost immediately fell hopelessly in love with the very mysterious Henry Goodyear, an unfortunate condition for both. (absolute phrase)

When they are joined with other clauses, simple sentences can also be expanded into **compound and complex sentences**.

See Ch. 11

(1) Expanding Simple Sentences with Adjectives and Adverbs

Descriptive **adjectives and adverbs** can expand a simple sentence. Read this sentence again:

See 27a

Jessica and her younger sister Victoria almost immediately fell hopelessly in love with the very mysterious Henry Goodyear.

Here two adjectives describe nouns.

Adjective	Noun
younger	sister
mysterious	Henry Goodyear

Four adverbs describe the action of verbs or modify adjectives or other adverbs.

Adverb

almost	immediately (adverb)
immediately	fell (verb)
hopelessly	fell (verb)
very	mysterious (adjective)

EXERCISE 3

Label all descriptive adjectives and adverbs in the following sentences.

                             adv   adj   adj
EXAMPLE: Marge listened secretly to the quiet conversation at the next table.

1. John swallowed the last of his cold coffee and gently set the thermos down. (Sherman Alexie, *Indian Killer*)
2. Each year I watched the field across from the Store turn caterpillar green, then gradually frosty white. (Maya Angelou, *I Know Why the Caged Bird Sings*)
3. He gingerly held the box and studied the old, familiar pictures. (Alan Lightman, *Good Benito*)
4. Stealthy and alert, he hunkers down like a predator and sneaks right up behind the seal, climbs decisively onto its back, and grips its cheeks in both hands. (Diane Ackerman, *The Rarest of the Rare*)
5. In late mammal times, the body evidently added a third brain. (Robert Bly, *The Sibling Society*)

EXERCISE 4

Using the following sentences as models, write five original simple sentences. Use adverbs and adjectives where the model sentences use them, and then underline and label these modifiers.

                       adv   adj
EXAMPLE: Manek gazed <u>shyly</u> at the <u>beautiful</u> girl.

                       adv   adv
The cat ran <u>wildly</u> around the <u>empty</u> house.

1. Walkways from the Washington Monument to the Lincoln Memorial quickly filled.
2. People, shrugging off their winter coats, seemed to step more lightly around the mall.
3. Some sat on benches in carefully pressed white shirts with half-eaten sandwiches in pale hands.

4. Others spun wildly by on bikes or Rollerblades wearing shiny spandex and torn T-shirts, sweatily celebrating the first days of spring.
5. Finally, the cherry blossoms burst into flower.

(2) Expanding Simple Sentences with Nouns and Verbals

Nouns and verbals can help you build richer simple sentences.

Nouns   Nouns can act as adjectives modifying other nouns.

He needed two <u>cake</u> pans for the <u>layer</u> cake.

Verbals   **Verbals**, which include participles, infinitives, and gerunds, may act as modifiers or as nouns.

See 23c2

All the <u>living</u> former presidents attended the funeral. (Present participle serves as adjective.)

The Grand Canyon is the attraction <u>to visit</u>. (Infinitive serves as adjective.)

The puzzle was impossible <u>to solve</u>. (Infinitive serves as adverb.)

When the <u>going</u> gets tough, the tough get going. (Gerund serves as noun.)

<u>To err</u> is human. (Infinitive serves as noun.)

It took me an entire three-hour lab period to identify my <u>unknown</u>. (Past participle serves as noun.)

EXERCISE 5

1. List ten nouns that can be used as modifiers.

   EXAMPLES: <u>word</u> processor, <u>truck</u> stop, <u>peanut</u> butter

2. List ten participles that can be used as modifiers.

   EXAMPLES: crushed, ringing

3. Choosing words from your lists, write five original sentences, each of which includes both a noun and a participle used as modifiers.

   EXAMPLE: The <u>word</u> processor was a <u>crushed</u> mass of metal and plastic.

4. Then add adjectives and adverbs to enrich the sentence further.

EXAMPLE: The <u>new</u> word processor was a <u>gruesomely</u> crushed mass of metal and plastic.

EXERCISE 6

For additional practice in building simple sentences with individual words, combine each of the following groups of sentences into one simple sentence that contains several modifiers. You will have to add, delete, or reorder words.

EXAMPLE: The night was cold. The night was wet. The night scared them. They were terribly scared.

REVISED: The cold, wet night scared them terribly.

1. The ship landed. The ship was from space. The ship was tremendous. It landed silently.
2. It landed in a field. The field was grassy. The field was deserted.
3. A dog appeared. The dog was tiny. The dog was abandoned. The dog was a stray.
4. The dog was brave. The dog was curious. He approached the spacecraft. The spacecraft was burning. He approached it carefully.
5. A creature emerged from the spaceship. The creature was smiling. He was purple. He emerged slowly.
6. The dog and the alien stared at each other. The dog was little. The alien was purple. They stared meaningfully.
7. The dog and the alien walked. They walked silently. They walked carefully. They walked toward each other.
8. The dog barked. He barked tentatively. He barked questioningly. The dog was uneasy.
9. The alien extended his hand. The alien was grinning. He extended it slowly. The hand was hairy.
10. In his hand was a bag. The bag was made of canvas. The bag was green. The bag was for laundry.

See
10b1

You can also expand a simple sentence with phrases. Because a <u>phrase</u> lacks a subject or predicate (or both), it cannot stand alone as a sentence. Within a sentence, however, phrases add information and provide connections between ideas.

(3) Expanding Simple Sentences with Prepositional Phrases

See
23f

A <u>preposition</u> indicates the relationship between a noun or noun substitute and other words in a sentence. A **prepositional phrase** consists of the preposition, its object (the noun or noun substitute), and any modifiers of that object. Prepositional phrases can function in a sentence as *adjectives* or as *adverbs*.

prep   obj
Carry Nation was a crusader for temperance. (Prepositional phrase functions as adjective modifying the noun *crusader*.)

prep   mod   obj
The Madeira River flows into the mighty Amazon. (Prepositional phrase functions as adverb modifying the verb *flows*.)

In these examples the prepositions come *before* their objects. In informal speech, however, the preposition often appears *after* the object.

obj   prep
I see the person you're looking for.

EXERCISE 7

Read the following sentences. Underline each prepositional phrase, and then connect it with an arrow to the word it modifies. Finally, tell whether each phrase functions as an adjective or an adverb.

                               adj   adv
EXAMPLE: The porch of her grandmother's house wraps around all three sides.

1. Carol sat on the front porch and rocked in her grandmother's chair.
2. Age had surprised her in the middle of her life, crept up behind her in the mirror, and attacked her at the joints of her knees and hips.
3. Now she sat on the porch—Juliet's balcony in her memories—and felt that it too creaked in the joints.
4. Inside the house, her grandmother slept in a narrow bed under a worn chenille spread, the mattress sagging and spilling over the edges of the frame.
5. The slow rocking of the chair soothed the worries from the edges of Carol's eyes.

EXERCISE 8

For additional practice in using prepositional phrases, combine each pair of sentences to create one simple sentence that includes a prepositional phrase. You may add, delete, or reorder words. Some sentences may have more than one possible correct version.

EXAMPLE: America's drinking water is being contaminated. Toxic substances are contaminating it.

REVISED: America's drinking water is being contaminated by toxic substances.

1. Toxic waste disposal presents a serious problem. Americans have this problem.

2. Hazardous chemicals pose a threat. People are threatened.
3. Some towns, like Times Beach, Missouri, have been completely abandoned. Their residents have abandoned them.
4. Dioxin is one chemical. It has serious toxic effects.
5. Dioxin is highly toxic. The toxicity affects animals and humans.
6. Toxic chemical wastes like dioxin may be found. Over fifty thousand dumps have them.
7. Industrial parks contain toxic wastes. Open pits, ponds, and lagoons are where the toxic substances are.
8. Toxic wastes pose dangers. The land, water, and air are endangered.
9. In addition, toxic substances are a threat. They threaten our public health and our economy.
10. Immediate toxic waste cleanup would be a tremendous benefit. Americans are the ones who would benefit.

(4) Expanding Simple Sentences with Verbal Phrases

A **verbal phrase** consists of a **verbal** (participle, gerund, or infinitive) and its related objects, modifiers, or complements.

Some verbal phrases act as nouns. **Gerund phrases,** for example, like gerunds themselves, are always used as nouns. **Infinitive phrases** may also be used as nouns.

Making a living isn't always easy. (Gerund phrase serves as sentence's subject.)

Wendy appreciated Tom's being honest. (Gerund phrase serves as object of verb *appreciated.*)

The entire town was shocked by their breaking up. (Gerund phrase is object of preposition *by.*)

To know him is to love him. (Infinitive phrase *to know him* serves as sentence's subject; infinitive phrase *to love him* is subject complement.)

Other verbal phrases act as modifiers. **Participial phrases** are always used to modify nouns or pronouns, and **infinitive phrases** may function as adjectives or as adverbs.

Fascinated by Scheherazade's story, they waited anxiously for the next installment. (Participial phrase modifies pronoun *they.*)

The next morning young Goodman Brown came slowly into the street of Salem Village, staring around him like a bewildered man. (Nathaniel Hawthorne, "Young Goodman Brown") (Participial phrase modifies noun *Goodman Brown.*)

It wasn't the ideal time <u>to do homework</u>. (Infinitive phrase modifies noun *time*.)

Henry M. Stanley went to Africa <u>to find Dr. Livingstone</u>. (Infinitive phrase modifies verb *went*.)

CLOSE-UP — EXPANDING SIMPLE SENTENCES

When you use verbal phrases as modifiers, be especially careful not to create **misplaced modifiers** or **dangling modifiers**.

See
17a2;
17b1

EXERCISE 9

For practice in using verbal phrases, combine each of these sentence pairs to create one simple sentence that contains a participial phrase, a gerund phrase, or an infinitive phrase. Underline and label the verbal phrase in your sentence. You will have to add, delete, or reorder words, and you may find more than one way to combine each pair.

EXAMPLE: The American labor movement has helped millions of workers. It has won them higher wages and better working conditions.

REVISED: The American labor movement has helped millions of
                              participial phrase
workers, <u>winning them higher wages and better working conditions</u>.

1. In 1912 the textile workers of Lawrence, Massachusetts, went on strike. They were demonstrating for "Bread and Roses, too."
2. The workers wanted higher wages and better working conditions. They felt trapped in their miserable jobs.
3. Mill workers toiled six days a week. They earned about $1.50 for this.
4. Most of the workers were women and children. They worked up to sixteen hours a day.
5. The mills were dangerous. They were filled with hazards.
6. Many mill workers joined unions. They did this to fight exploitation by their employers.
7. They wanted to improve their lives. This was their goal.
8. Finally, twenty-five thousand workers walked off their jobs. They knew they were risking everything.
9. The police and the state militia were called in. Attacking the strikers was their mission.

10. After sixty-three days, the American Woolen Company surrendered. This ended the strike with a victory for the workers.

(Adapted from William Cahn, *Lawrence 1912: The Bread and Roses Strike*)

(5) Expanding Simple Sentences with Absolute Phrases

An **absolute phrase** usually consists of a noun or pronoun and a past or present participle, along with its modifiers.

<u>All things considered</u>, I prefer Maine's cold winters to California's smog.

Sometimes, however, an infinitive phrase functions as an absolute phrase.

<u>To make a long story short</u>, our team lost.

Absolute phrases act as modifiers, but they are not connected grammatically to any particular word or phrase in a sentence. Instead, an absolute phrase modifies the whole independent clause to which it is linked.

EXERCISE 10

For practice in using absolute phrases, combine each group of sentences to create one simple sentence that includes an absolute phrase. You will have to change, add, delete, or reorder some words.

EXAMPLE: Paris was beautiful. Its streets looked exceptionally clean.

REVISED: Paris was beautiful, its streets [looking] exceptionally clean.

1. Notre Dame stood majestically.
   Its rose window glowed in the darkness.
2. We took a boat ride down the Seine.
   Our feet were throbbing.
3. The Louvre is open six days a week.
   Its doors are closed on Tuesdays.
4. The Jeu de Paume displays Impressionist paintings. Its exhibits showcase Manet, Degas, Renoir, and van Gogh.
5. We were forced to cut our vacation short.
   Our francs were spent.

(6) Expanding Simple Sentences with Appositives

An **appositive** is a noun or a noun phrase that identifies an adjacent noun or pronoun by defining or renaming it.

Trigger, <u>a golden palomino</u>, was featured in several movies. (Appositive *a golden palomino* identifies noun *Trigger*.)

Farrington hated his boss, <u>a real tyrant</u>. (Appositive *a real tyrant* identifies noun *boss*.)

<u>A barrier island off the coast of New Jersey</u>, Long Beach Island is a popular vacation spot. (Appositive *A barrier island off the coast of New Jersey* identifies noun *Long Beach Island*.)

NOTE: Appositives are sometimes introduced by the phrases *such as, or, that is, for example,* or *in other words.*

A regional airline, <u>such as Southwest</u>, frequently accounts for more than half the departures at so-called second-tier airports.

Rabies, <u>or hydrophobia</u>, was nearly always fatal until Pasteur's work.

For information on punctuating sentences that include appositives, see **29d1.**

EXERCISE 11

For practice in using appositives when you write, build five new simple sentences by combining each of the following pairs, turning one sentence in each pair into an appositive. (Note that each pair can be combined in a variety of different ways and that the appositive can precede or follow the noun it modifies.) You may need to delete or reorder words in some cases.

> **EXAMPLE:** René Descartes was a noted French philosopher. Descartes is best known for his famous declaration, "I think, therefore I am."
>
> **REVISED:** René Descartes, <u>a noted French philosopher</u>, is best known for his famous declaration, "I think, therefore I am."

1. *I Know Why the Caged Bird Sings* is the first book in Maya Angelou's autobiography. It deals primarily with her life as a young girl in Stamps, Arkansas.
2. Catgut is a tough cord generally made from the intestines of sheep. Catgut is used for tennis rackets, for violin strings, and for surgical stitching.
3. Hermes was the messenger of the Greek gods. He is usually portrayed as an athletic youth wearing a cap and winged sandals.
4. Emiliano Zapata was a hero of the Mexican Revolution. He is credited with effecting land reform in his home state of Morelos.
5. Pulsars are celestial objects that emit regular pulses of radiation. Pulsars were discovered in 1967.

(7) Expanding Simple Sentences with Compound Constructions

Compound constructions consist of two or more grammatically equivalent items, parallel in importance. Within simple sentences, compound words or phrases—subjects, predicates, complements, or modifiers—may be joined in one of three ways.

- With commas:

  He took one <u>long,</u> <u>loving</u> look at his '57 Chevy.

See 11a1

- With a **coordinating conjunction**:

  They <u>reeled,</u> <u>whirled,</u> <u>flounced,</u> <u>capered,</u> <u>gamboled,</u> <u>and</u> <u>spun.</u> (Kurt Vonnegut, Jr., "Harrison Bergeron")

- With a pair of **correlative conjunctions** (*both/and, not only/but also, either/or, neither/nor, whether/or*):

  <u>Both milk and carrots</u> contain Vitamin A.

  <u>Neither the twentieth-century poet Sylvia Plath nor the nineteenth-century poet Emily Dickinson</u> achieved recognition during her lifetime.

 EXPANDING SIMPLE SENTENCES

See 18a

Be sure to use **parallelism** when you join two or more grammatically equivalent words or phrases in a compound construction.

EXERCISE 12

A. Expand each of the following sentences by using compound subjects and/or predicates.

EXAMPLE: Bill played guitar.

REVISED: Bill and Juan played guitar and sang.

B. Then expand your simple sentence with modifying words and phrases, using compound constructions whenever possible.

EXAMPLE: Despite butterflies in their stomachs and a restless audience, Bill and Juan played guitar and sang.

1. Cortés explored the New World.
2. Virginia Woolf wrote novels.
3. Edison invented the phonograph.
4. PBS airs educational television programming.
5. Thomas Jefferson signed the Declaration of Independence.

EXERCISE 13

To practice building sentences with compound subjects, predicates, and modifiers, combine the following groups of sentences into one.

> **EXAMPLE:** Marion studied. Frank studied. They studied quietly. They studied diligently.
>
> **REVISED:** Marion and Frank studied quietly and diligently.

1. Robert Ludlum writes best-selling spy thrillers. Tom Clancy writes best-selling spy thrillers. John le Carré writes best-selling spy thrillers.
2. Smoking can cause heart disease. A high-fat, high-cholesterol diet can cause heart disease. Stress can cause heart disease.
3. Walter Mosley and Sue Grafton write detective novels. They both write about tough, "hard-boiled" detectives.
4. Successful rock bands give concerts. They record albums. They make videos. They license merchandise bearing their names and likenesses.
5. Sports superstars like Tiger Woods and Michael Jordan earn additional income by making personal appearances. They earn money by endorsing products.

CHAPTER 11

BUILDING COMPOUND AND COMPLEX SENTENCES

 Building Compound Sentences

A **compound sentence** consists of two or more independent clauses connected with *coordinating conjunctions, transitional words or phrases, correlative conjunctions, semicolons,* or *colons.*

USE COMPOUND SENTENCES

- to show addition (*and, in addition, not only . . . but also,* semicolon)
- to show contrast (*but, however*)
- to show cause and effect (*so, therefore, consequently*)
- to present a choice of alternatives (*or, either . . . or*)

---

(1) Using Coordinating Conjunctions

See
30a

You can join two <u>independent clauses</u> with a **coordinating conjunction**—*and, or, nor, but, for, so,* or *yet*—preceded by a comma.

> [The cowboy is a workingman], <u>yet</u> [he has little in common with the urban blue-collar worker]. (John R. Erickson, *The Modern Cowboy*)

> [In the fall the war was always there], <u>but</u> [we did not go to it any more]. (Ernest Hemingway, "In Another Country")

> [She carried a thin, small cane made from an umbrella], <u>and</u> [with this she kept tapping the frozen earth in front of her]. (Eudora Welty, "A Worn Path")

Sent 11a

(2) Using Transitional Words and Phrases

You can join two independent clauses with a **transitional word or phrase,** preceded by a semicolon (and followed by a comma).

[Aerobic exercise can help lower blood pressure]; <u>however</u>, [those with high blood pressure should still limit salt intake].

[The saxophone does not belong to the brass family]; <u>in fact</u>, [it is a member of the woodwind family].

Commonly used <u>**transitional words and phrases**</u> include **conjunctive adverbs** like *however, therefore, nevertheless, consequently, finally, still,* and *thus* and expressions like *for example, in fact, on the other hand,* and *for instance.*

See 6c2

(3) Using Correlative Conjunctions

You can use <u>**correlative conjunctions**</u> to join two independent clauses into a compound sentence.

See 23g

Sharon <u>not only</u> passed the exam, <u>but</u> she <u>also</u> received the highest grade in the class.

<u>Either</u> he left his coat in his locker, <u>or</u> he left it on the bus.

(4) Using Semicolons

A **semicolon** can link two closely related independent clauses.

[Alaska is the largest state]; [Rhode Island is the smallest].

[Theodore Roosevelt was president after the Spanish-American War]; [Andrew Johnson was president after the Civil War].

(5) Using Colons

A <u>colon</u> can link two independent clauses.

See 33a

He got his orders: he was to leave for France on Sunday.

They thought they knew the outcome: Truman would lose to Dewey.

EXERCISE 1

Bracket the independent clauses in these compound sentences.

EXAMPLE: Before joining Pancho Villa's forces in the Mexican Revolution, [writer Mariano Azuela practiced medicine]; [his novel *The Underdogs* describes the suffering he saw in the war].

1. The paddlefish has an enormous paddle-shaped snout, and it feeds by straining planktonic organisms from the water.

2. The BBC was first established as a private company, but it now relies on government revenue from television licenses rather than from advertising.

3. The Chimera was a mythical Greek monster with a lion's head, a goat's body, and a serpent's tail; the name is applied now to any fantastic imaginary creation.

4. Golda Meir was born in Russia, but she immigrated to Palestine in 1921.

5. Albert Einstein is best known for a single formula: $E = mc^2$.

EXERCISE 2

After reading the following paragraph, use coordination to build as many compound sentences as you think your readers need to understand the links between ideas. When you have finished, bracket the independent clauses and underline the coordinating conjunctions, correlative conjunctions, or punctuation marks that link clauses.

Paolo Soleri came to the United States from Italy. He came as an apprentice to Frank Lloyd Wright. Frank Lloyd Wright's designs celebrate the suburban lifestyle, with stand-alone homes meant for single families. Soleri's Utopian designs celebrate the city. Soleri believes that suburban lifestyles separate people from true nature. He also believes that our lifestyle separates us from the energy of the city. His first theoretical design was called Mesa City. It proposed to house two million people. Soleri is currently building one of his dream cities, Arcosanti, in the desert outside of Scottsdale, Arizona. This project is funded privately by Soleri. He teaches design and building classes to students who help build the city. The students' tuition helps pay for construction. He also makes wind bells and chimes. He sells these all over the world. The profits further finance Arcosanti. The design for Arcosanti evokes images of colonies erected on space stations. It also resembles the hillside towns in Soleri's home country, Italy. The problems with our current city structures grow each year. People are looking for ways to revitalize the city. Some are looking at Soleri's Arcosanti as a model for sustainable urban development and renewal.

EXERCISE 3

Add appropriate coordinating conjunctions, conjunctive adverbs, or correlative conjunctions as indicated to combine each pair of sentences into one well-constructed compound sentence that retains the meaning of the original pair. Be sure to use correct punctuation.

EXAMPLE: The American population is aging. People seem to be increasingly concerned about what they eat. (coordinating conjunction)

REVISED: The American population is aging, so people seem to be increasingly concerned about what they eat.

1. The average American consumes 128 pounds of sugar each year. Most of us eat much more sugar than any other food additive, including salt. (conjunctive adverb)
2. Many of us are determined to reduce our sugar intake. We have consciously eliminated sweets from our diets. (conjunctive adverb)
3. Unfortunately, sugar is not found only in sweets. It is also found in many processed foods. (correlative conjunction)
4. Processed foods like puddings and cake contain sugar. Foods like ketchup and spaghetti sauce do too. (coordinating conjunction)
5. We are trying to cut down on sugar. We find limiting sugar intake extremely difficult. (coordinating conjunction)
6. Processors may use sugar in foods for taste. They may also use it to help prevent foods from spoiling and to improve the texture and appearance of food. (correlative conjunction)
7. Sugar comes in many different forms. It is easy to overlook on a package label. (coordinating conjunction)
8. Sugar may be called sucrose or fructose. It may also be called corn syrup, corn sugar, brown sugar, honey, or molasses. (coordinating conjunction)
9. No sugar is more nourishing than the others. It really doesn't matter which is consumed. (conjunctive adverb)
10. Sugars contain empty calories. Whenever possible, they should be avoided. (conjunctive adverb)

(Adapted from *Jane Brody's Nutrition Book*)

11b　Building Complex Sentences

A **complex sentence** consists of one **independent clause** and at least one **dependent clause.**

A dependent clause cannot stand alone; it must be combined with an independent clause to form a sentence. A **subordinating conjunction** or **relative pronoun** links the independent and dependent clauses and indicates the relationship between them.

dependent clause   independent clause
[After the town was evacuated], [the hurricane began].

independent clause   dependent clause
[Officials watched the storm], [which threatened to destroy the town].

Sometimes a dependent clause may be embedded within an independent clause.

dependent clause
Town officials, [who were very concerned], watched the storm.

Dependent clauses may function in a sentence either as adverb clauses or as adjective clauses. Adverb clauses are introduced by subordinating conjunctions, and adjective clauses are introduced by relative pronouns.

BUILDING COMPLEX SENTENCES

Frequently Used Subordinating Conjunctions

after	in order that	unless
although	now that	until
as	once	when
as if	rather than	whenever
as though	since	where
because	so that	whereas
before	that	wherever
even though	though	while
if		

Relative Pronouns

that	whatever	who (whose, whom)
what	which	whoever (whomever)

EXERCISE 4

Bracket the independent and dependent clauses in the following complex sentences. Then, using these sentences as models, create two new complex sentences in imitation of each. For each set of new sentences, use the same subordinating conjunction or relative pronoun that appears in the original.

1. I said what I meant.
2. Isadora Duncan is the dancer who best exemplifies the phrase "poetry in motion."

3. Because she was considered a heretic, Joan of Arc was burned at the stake.
4. The oracle at Delphi predicted that Oedipus would murder his father and marry his mother.
5. The ghost vanished before Hamlet could question him further.

EXERCISE 5

Use a subordinating conjunction or relative pronoun to combine each of the following pairs of sentences into one well-constructed complex sentence. The connecting word you select must clarify the relationship between the two sentences. You will have to change or reorder words, and in most cases you will have a choice of connecting words.

EXAMPLE: Some colleges are tightening admissions requirements. The pool of students is growing smaller.

REVISED: Although the pool of students is growing smaller, some colleges are tightening admissions requirements.

1. Millions of people are currently out of work. They need new skills for new careers.
2. Talented high school students are usually encouraged to go to college. Some high school graduates are now starting to see that a college education may not guarantee them a job.
3. A college education can cost a student more than $100,000. Vocational education is becoming increasingly important.
4. Vocational students complete their work in less than four years. They can enter the job market more quickly.
5. Nurses' aides, paralegals, travel agents, and computer technicians do not need college degrees. They have little trouble finding work.
6. Some four-year colleges are experiencing growth. Public community colleges and private trade schools are growing much more rapidly.
7. The best vocational schools are responsive to the needs of local businesses. They train students for jobs that actually exist.
8. For instance, a school in Detroit might offer advanced automotive design. A school in New York City might focus on fashion design.
9. Other schools offer courses in horticulture, respiratory therapy, and computer programming. They are able to place their graduates easily.
10. Laid-off workers, returning housewives, recent high school graduates, and even college graduates are reexamining vocational education. They all hope to find rewarding careers.

11c Building Compound-Complex Sentences

A **compound-complex sentence** consists of two or more independent clauses and at least one dependent clause.

dependent clause
[When small foreign imports began dominating the US automobile
independent clause   independent clause
industry], [consumers were very responsive], but [American auto workers were dismayed].

EXERCISE 6

In each of these sentences, identify subjects and verbs; bracket and label dependent and independent clauses; and identify each sentence as simple, compound, complex, or compound-complex.

1. Use of the telephone involves personal risk because it involves exposure; for some, to be "hung up on" is among the worst fears; others dream of a ringing telephone and wake up with a pounding heart. (John Brooks, *Telephone: The First Hundred Years*)

2. This nation is even more litigious than religious, and the school prayer issue has prompted more, and more sophisticated, arguments about constitutional law than about the nature of prayer. (George F. Will, *Newsweek*)

3. The first time I ever went naked in mixed company was at the house of a girl whose father had a bad back and had built himself a sauna in the corner of the basement. (Garrison Keillor, *New Yorker*)

4. I am the son of Mexican-American parents, who speak a blend of Spanish and English, but who read neither language easily. (Richard Rodriguez, *Aria: A Memoir of a Bilingual Childhood*)

5. The most alarming of all man's assaults upon the environment is the contamination of air, earth, rivers, and sea with dangerous and even lethal materials. (Rachel Carson, *Silent Spring*)

EXERCISE 7

Write an original sentence in imitation of each sentence in Exercise 6.

238

STUDENT WRITER AT WORK

Building Sentences

A student in a freshman composition class was assigned to interview a grandparent and write a short paper about his or her life. When she set out to turn her grandmother's words into a paper, the student faced a set of choppy notes—words, phrases, and simple sentences—that she had jotted down as her grandmother spoke. She needed to combine these fragments and short sentences into varied, interesting sentences that would establish the relationships among her ideas.

Read the following notes, turn them into complete sentences when necessary, and combine sentences wherever it seems appropriate. Your goal is to build simple, compound, and complex sentences enriched by modifiers—without adding any information. When you have finished, revise further to strengthen coherence, unity, and style.

Notes

67 years old. Born in Lykens, PA (old coal-mining town). Got her first paying job at 13. Her parents lied about her age. Working age was 14. Parents couldn't afford all the mouths they had to feed. Before that, she helped with the housework. At work, she was a maid. Got paid only about a dollar a week. Most of that went to her parents. Ate her meals on job. Worked in house where 3 generations of men lived. They all worked in the mines. Had to get up at 4 a.m. First chore was to make lunch for the men. She'd scrub the metal canteens. Then she'd fill them with water. Then she'd make biscuits and broth. Then she'd start breakfast. Mrs. Muller would help. Cooking for 6 hungry men was a real job. Then she did the breakfast dishes. Then she did the chores. The house had 3 stories. She had to scrub floors, dust, and sweep. It wasn't easy. Then Mrs. Muller would need help patching and darning. She had just enough time to get dinner started. Grabbed her meals after the family finished eating. Had no spare time. When not working she had chores to do at home. In spring and summer she would grow vegetables. Canned vegetables for her family. What was left over, she sold. Got married at 16.

CHAPTER 12

WRITING EMPHATIC SENTENCES

In speech, you emphasize certain ideas and deemphasize others with facial expressions, with gestures, and by raising or lowering your voice. In writing, you convey your **emphasis**—the relative importance of your ideas—through the selection and arrangement of words.

12a Conveying Emphasis through Word Order

Where you place words, phrases, and clauses within a sentence conveys your emphasis to readers. Readers tend to focus on the *beginning* and the *end* of a sentence, expecting to find key information there.

(1) Beginning with Important Ideas

Placing key ideas at the beginning of a sentence stresses their importance. The following sentence places emphasis on the study, not on those who conducted it or those who participated in it.

In a landmark study of alcoholism, Dr. George Vaillant of Harvard followed two hundred Harvard graduates and four hundred inner-city working-class men from the Boston area.

Rephrasing focuses attention on the researcher, not on the study.

Dr. George Vaillant of Harvard, in a landmark study of alcoholism, followed two hundred Harvard graduates and four hundred inner-city working-class men from the Boston area.

Situations that demand a straightforward presentation—laboratory reports, memos, technical papers, business correspondence, and the like—call for sentences that present vital information first and qualify ideas later.

Treating cancer with interferon has been the subject of a good deal of research. (emphasizes the treatment, not the research)

Dividends will be paid if the stockholders agree. (emphasizes the dividends, not the stockholders)

 WRITING EMPHATIC SENTENCES

An empty phrase, such as *there is* or *there are,* at the beginning of a sentence generally weakens the sentence.

UNEMPHATIC: There is heavy emphasis placed on the development of computational skills at MIT.

EMPHATIC: Heavy emphasis is placed on the development of computational skills at MIT.

or

MIT places heavy emphasis on the development of computational skills.

---

(2) Ending with Important Ideas

Placing key elements at the end of a sentence is another way to convey their importance.

Using a Colon or a Dash   A colon or a dash can add emphasis by isolating an important word or phrase at the end of a sentence.

Beth had always dreamed of owning one special car: a 1953 Corvette.

The elderly need a good deal of special attention—and they deserve that attention.

 WRITING EMPHATIC SENTENCES

At the end of a sentence, qualifiers such as conjunctive adverbs or other transitional expressions lose their power to indicate the

continued on the following page

continued from the previous page
relationship between ideas. Place transitional words and phrases earlier, where they can fulfill their purpose and also add emphasis.

LESS EMPHATIC: Smokers do have rights; they should not try to impose their habit on others, however. (conjunctive adverb at end of clause)

MORE EMPHATIC: Smokers do have rights; however, they should not try to impose their habit on others. (conjunctive adverb at beginning of clause)

Using Climactic Word Order   **Climactic word order** is the arrangement of a series of items from the least to the most important. When you use climactic word order, the momentum of the sentence places emphasis on the key idea at the end.

The nation's most prominent orchestras all boast large annual budgets, locations in important cities, and the most talented musicians and conductors. (*Talent* is the key idea.)

EXERCISE 1

Underline the most important ideas in each sentence of the following paragraph. Then identify the strategy that the writer used to emphasize those ideas. Are the key ideas placed at the beginning or the end of a sentence? Does the writer use climactic order?

Listening to diatribes by angry callers or ranting about today's news, the talk radio host spreads ideas over the air waves. Every day at the same time, the political talk show host discusses national events and policies, the failures of the opposite view, and the foibles of the individuals who espouse those opposite views. Listening for hours a day, some callers become recognizable contributors to many different talk radio programs. Other listeners are less devoted, tuning in only when they're in the car and never calling to voice their opinions. Political radio hosts usually structure their programs around a specific agenda, espousing the party line and ridiculing the opponent's position. With a style of presentation aimed both at entertainment and information, the host's ideas become caricatures of party positions. Sometimes, in order to keep the information lively and interesting, a host may either state the issues too simply or deliberately mislead the audience. A host can excuse these errors by insisting that the show is harmless: it's for entertainment, not information. Many are concerned about how the political process will be affected by this misinformation.

(3) Experimenting with Word Order

In English sentences, the most common word order is subject-verb-object (or complement). When you depart from this expected word order, you call attention to the word, phrase, or clause that you have relocated. You may even call attention to the entire sentence.

> More modest and less inventive than Turner's paintings are John Constable's landscapes.

Here the writer calls special attention to the modifying phrase *more modest and less inventive than Turner's paintings* by placing the complement and the verb before the subject.

EXERCISE 2

Revise the following sentences to make them more emphatic. For each, decide which ideas should be highlighted and group key ideas at sentence beginnings or endings. Use climactic order or depart from conventional word order where appropriate.

1. Police want to upgrade their firepower because criminals are better armed than ever before.
2. A few years ago felons used so-called Saturday night specials, small-caliber six-shot revolvers.
3. Now semiautomatic pistols capable of firing fifteen to twenty rounds, along with paramilitary weapons like the AK-47, have replaced these weapons.
4. Police are adopting such weapons as new fast-firing shotguns and 9mm automatic pistols in order to gain an equal footing with their adversaries.
5. Faster reloading and a hair trigger are among the numerous advantages that automatic pistols, the weapons of choice among law-enforcement officers, have over the traditional .38-caliber police revolver.

12b Conveying Emphasis through Sentence Structure

As you write, you can construct sentences that emphasize more important ideas and deemphasize less important ones.

(1) Using Cumulative Sentences

A **cumulative sentence** begins with an independent clause, followed by additional words, phrases, or clauses that expand or develop it.

> She holds me in strong arms, arms that have chopped cotton, dismembered trees, scattered corn for chickens, cradled infants, shaken the daylights out of half-grown upstart teenagers. (Rebecca Hill, *Blue Rise*)

Because it presents its main idea first, a cumulative sentence tends to be clear and straightforward. (Most English sentences are cumulative.)

(2) Using Periodic Sentences

A **periodic sentence** places the main idea at the end of the sentence. It moves from supporting details, expressed in modifying phrases and dependent clauses, to the main idea, which is placed in the independent clause.

> Unlike World Wars I and II, which ended decisively with the unconditional surrender of the United States's enemies, the war in Vietnam did not end when American troops withdrew.

In the preceding sentence, the writer adds emphasis to his main idea not only by placing it in the independent clause but also by keeping readers waiting for it.

NOTE: In some periodic sentences the modifying phrase or dependent clause comes between subject and predicate.

> Columbus, after several discouraging and unsuccessful voyages, finally reached America.

 CLOSE-UP WRITING EMPHATIC SENTENCES

Periodic sentences are generally more emphatic than cumulative sentences, but the most emphatic sentence is not always the best choice. Because the periodic structure forces readers to wait—or even to search—for the delayed main idea, periodic sentences tend not to be as straightforward as cumulative ones.

EXERCISE 3

A. Bracket the independent clause(s) in each sentence and underline each modifying phrase and dependent clause. Label each sentence cumulative or periodic.

B. Relocate the supporting details to make cumulative sentences periodic and periodic sentences cumulative, adding words or rephrasing to make your meaning clear.

C. Be prepared to explain how your revision changes the emphasis of the original sentence.

EXAMPLE: Feeling isolated, sad, and frightened, [the small child sat alone in the train depot.] (periodic)

REVISED: The small child sat alone in the train depot, feeling isolated, sad, and frightened. (cumulative)

1. However different in their educational opportunities, both Jefferson and Lincoln as young men became known to their contemporaries as "hard students." (Douglas L. Wilson, "What Jefferson and Lincoln Read," *Atlantic Monthly*)

2. The road came into being slowly, league by league, river crossing by river crossing. (Stephen Harrigan, "Highway 1," *Texas Monthly*)

3. Without willing it, I had gone from being ignorant of being ignorant to being aware of being aware. (Maya Angelou, *I Know Why the Caged Bird Sings*)

4. To those of us who remain committed mainly to the exploration of moral distinctions and ambiguities, the feminist analysis may have seemed a particularly narrow and cracked determinism. (Joan Didion, "The Women's Movement")

5. [Henry] Moore's personal history is as familiar in outline as are his sculptures: his birth in 1898 as the seventh child of a Yorkshire coal-mining family; his early skill at carving; a conservative artistic education at the Royal College of Art, in London. (Kay Larson, *New York Magazine*)

EXERCISE 4

A. Combine each of the following sentence groups into one cumulative sentence, subordinating supporting details to main ideas.

B. Then combine each group into one periodic sentence. Each group can be combined in a variety of ways, and you may have to add, delete, change, or reorder words.

C. How do the two versions of the sentence differ in emphasis?

EXAMPLE: More women than ever before are running for office. They are encouraged by the success of other female candidates.

CUMULATIVE: More women than ever before are running for office, encouraged by the success of other female candidates.

PERIODIC: Encouraged by the success of other female candidates, more women than ever before are running for office.

1. Many politicians opposed the MX missile. They believed it was too expensive. They felt that a smaller, single-warhead missile was preferable.

2. Smoking poses a real danger. It is associated with various cancers. It is linked to heart disease and stroke. It threatens even non-smokers.

3. Infertile couples who want children sometimes go through a series of difficult processes. They may try adoption. They may also try artificial insemination or in vitro fertilization. They may even seek out surrogate mothers.

4. The Thames is a river that meanders through southern England. It has been the inspiration for literary works such as *Alice's Adventures in Wonderland* and *The Wind in the Willows*. It was also captured in paintings by Constable, Turner, and Whistler.

5. Black-footed ferrets are rare North American mammals. They prey on prairie dogs. They are primarily nocturnal. They have black feet and black-tipped tails. Their faces have raccoonlike masks.

EXERCISE 5

Combine each of the following sentence groups into one sentence in which you subordinate supporting details to the main idea. In each case, create either a periodic or a cumulative sentence, depending on which structure you think will best convey the sentence's emphasis. Add, delete, change, or reorder words when necessary.

EXAMPLE: The fears of today's college students are based on reality. They are afraid there are too many students and too few jobs.

REVISED: The fears of today's college students—that there are too many students and too few jobs—are based on reality. (periodic)

1. Today's college students are under a good deal of stress. Job prospects in some fields are not very good. Financial aid is not as easy to come by as it was in the past.

2. Education has grown very expensive. The job market has become tighter. Pressure to get into graduate and professional schools has increased.

3. Family ties seem to be weakening. Students aren't always able to count on family support.

4. College students have always had problems. Now college counseling centers report more—and more serious—problems.

5. The term *student shock* was coined several years ago. This term describes a syndrome that may include depression, anxiety, headaches, and eating and sleeping disorders.

6. Many students are overwhelmed by the vast array of courses and majors offered at their colleges. They tend to be less decisive. They take longer to choose a major and to complete school.

7. Many drop out of school for brief (or extended) periods or switch majors several times. Many take five years or longer to complete their college education.

8. Some colleges are responding to the pressures that students feel. They hold stress-management workshops and suicide-prevention courses. They advertise the services of their counseling centers. They train students as peer counselors. They improve their vocational counseling services.

12c Conveying Emphasis through Parallelism and Balance

By highlighting corresponding grammatical elements, **parallelism** helps writers convey information clearly, quickly, and emphatically.

See 18a

> We seek an individual <u>who is</u> a self-starter, <u>who owns</u> a late-model automobile, and <u>who is</u> willing to work evenings. (classified advertisement)

> <u>Do not pass</u> Go; <u>do not collect</u> $200. (instructions)

> The Faust legend is central in <u>Benét's *The Devil and Daniel Webster,*</u> in Goethe's *Faust,* and in Marlowe's *Dr. Faustus.* (examination answer)

A **balanced sentence** is neatly divided between two parallel structures—for example, two independent clauses in a compound sentence. The symmetrical structure of a balanced sentence highlights correspondences or contrasts between clauses.

> In the 1950s, the electronic miracle was the television; in the 1980s, the electronic miracle was the computer.

> Alive, the elephant was worth at least a hundred pounds; dead, he would only be worth the value of his tusks, five pounds, possibly. (George Orwell, "Shooting an Elephant")

12d Conveying Emphasis through Repetition

See
13b **Unnecessary repetition** makes sentences dull and monotonous as well as wordy.

He had a good arm and <u>also</u> could field well, and he was <u>also</u> a fast runner.

We got three estimates, and <u>the one we got from</u> the Johnson Brothers seemed more reasonable than <u>the one we got from</u> Country Carpenters.

Effective repetition, however, can place emphasis on key words or ideas.

They decided to begin again: <u>to begin</u> hoping, <u>to begin</u> trying to change, <u>to begin</u> working toward a goal.

During those years when I was just learning to speak, my mother and father addressed me only <u>in Spanish; in Spanish</u> I learned to reply. (Richard Rodriguez, *Aria: A Memoir of a Bilingual Childhood*)

If ever <u>two groups</u> were opposed, surely those <u>two groups</u> are runners and smokers. (Joseph Epstein, *Familiar Territory*)

See
6c6 Words may be effectively repeated within a sentence or within a paragraph—or even **between paragraphs** in a paragraph cluster. In the following group of sentences, the parallel structure and repetition of *still* add emphasis, stressing how hard the author's mother worked.

<u>Still</u> she sewed—dresses and jackets for the children, housedresses and aprons for herself, weekly patching of jeans, overalls, and denim shirts. She <u>still</u> made pillows, using the feathers she had plucked, and quilts every year—intricate patterns as well as patchwork, stitched as well as tied—all necessary bedding for her family. Every scrap of cloth too small to be used in quilts was carefully saved and painstakingly sewed together in strips to make rugs. She <u>still</u> went out in the fields to help with the haying whenever there was a threat of rain. (Donna Smith-Yackel, "My Mother Never Worked")

EXERCISE 6

Revise the sentences in this paragraph, using parallelism and balance whenever possible to highlight corresponding elements and using repetition of key words and phrases to add emphasis. (To achieve repetition, you must change some synonyms.) You may combine sentences and add, delete, or reorder words.

Many readers distrust newspapers. They also distrust what they read in magazines. They do not trust what they hear on the radio and what television shows them, either. Of these media, newspapers have been the most responsive to audience criticism. Some newspapers even have ombudsmen. They are supposed to listen to reader complaints. They are also charged with acting on these grievances. One complaint that many people have is that newspapers are inaccurate. Newspapers' disregard for people's privacy is another of many readers' criticisms. Reporters are seen as arrogant, and readers feel that journalists can be unfair. They feel that reporters tend to glorify criminals, and they believe there is a tendency to place too much emphasis on bizarre or offbeat stories. Finally, readers complain about poor writing and editing. Polls show that despite its efforts to respond to reader criticism, the press continues to face hostility. (Adapted from *Newsweek*)

12e Conveying Emphasis through Active Voice

Active voice is generally more emphatic—and more concise—than passive voice.

PASSIVE: The prediction that oil prices will rise is being made by economists.

ACTIVE: Economists now predict that oil prices will rise.

The passive voice tends to focus your readers' attention on the action or on its receiver rather than on who is performing it. The receiver of the action is the subject of a passive sentence, so the actor fades into the background (*by economists*) or is omitted (*the prediction is now being made*).

Sometimes, of course, you *want* to stress the action rather than the actor. If so, it makes sense to use the **passive** voice. Compare these two sentences.

See
25k

PASSIVE: The West was explored by Lewis and Clark. (stresses the exploration of the West, not who explored it)

ACTIVE: Lewis and Clark explored the West. (stresses the contribution of the explorers)

You also use passive voice when the identity of the person performing the action is irrelevant or unknown.

The course was canceled.

Littering is prohibited.

See
Ch. 49

For this reason, the passive voice is frequently used in **scientific** and technical writing.

EXERCISE 7

Revise this paragraph to eliminate awkward or excessive use of passive constructions.

Jack Dempsey, the heavyweight champion between 1919 and 1926, had an interesting but uneven career. He was considered one of the greatest boxers of all time. Dempsey began fighting as "Kid Blackie," but his career didn't take off until 1919, when Jack "Doc" Kearns became his manager. Dempsey won the championship when Jess Willard was defeated by him in Toledo, Ohio, in 1919. Dempsey immediately became a popular sports figure; Franklin Delano Roosevelt was one of his biggest fans. Influential friends were made by Jack Dempsey. Boxing lessons were given by him to the actor Rudolph Valentino. He made friends with Douglas Fairbanks, Sr., Damon Runyon, and J. Paul Getty. Hollywood serials were made by Dempsey, but the title was lost by him to Gene Tunney, and Dempsey failed to regain it the following year. Meanwhile, his life was marred by unpleasant developments such as bitter legal battle with his manager and his 1920 indictment for draft evasion. In subsequent years, after his boxing career declined, a restaurant was opened by Dempsey, and many major sporting events were attended by him. This exposure kept him in the public eye until he lost his restaurant. Jack Dempsey died in 1983.

STUDENT WRITER AT WORK

Writing Emphatic Sentences

Identify the strategies that a freshman composition student has used in this draft to convey his emphasis to readers. Revise the draft to make his emphasis clearer, and then revise again if necessary to strengthen coherence, unity, and style.

"Fight, Fight, Fight for the Home Team"

It is pathetic for an athlete being paid millions of dollars to get into a fight for something so ridiculous as a bad call by a referee or an accidental push by a player. Players have to be tough in order to win. This shouldn't mean they have to be violent, however. The amount of violence increases every day in the world of sports. It is a national embarrassment that this situation exists.

It is a disgrace to see professional athletes getting into fights. This situation occurs in nearly every game. If a fight breaks out at an event, the game is disrupted, the players involved in the altercation are fined, and spectators are disappointed or angry. What does a fight solve, therefore? Nothing. Things are only made worse by fights.

In hockey, there are always fights that break out. These fights aren't even stopped by the referees. The players are allowed to continue beating each other to a pulp instead. The crowd gets into the hitting and checking, and a fight erupts in the stands before you know it. A family can seldom go to a peaceful game without witnessing a fight between players or a riot in the stands.

America's pastime, baseball, can be a beautiful sport to watch. Imagine the crack of the bat, the smell (in some ballparks) of fresh-cut grass, the cheers for a home run, and the sounds of both teams rushing out of the dugouts to the mound to demolish the other team. Fighting shouldn't be part of the game, obviously, but often it seems it is. A batter should just walk it off on the way to first base if he gets hit by a pitch. Usually, he runs after the pitcher, though. Within seconds, the dugouts are empty, and fists are flying on the mound.

Violence is even more obvious in sports like football, lacrosse, boxing, and rugby. It is becoming harder and harder to go to a sporting event and

continued on the following page

continued from the previous page
have a plain old-fashioned good time because of all the violence on the field or court. A player can be "bad" or "hungry," but this shouldn't mean getting into violent fights. What ever happened to the spirit of "Buy me some peanuts and Cracker Jack, I don't care if I never get back"?

CHAPTER 13

WRITING CONCISE SENTENCES

A **concise sentence** contains exactly the number of words necessary to make its point. Because it is free of unnecessary words and convoluted constructions, a concise sentence is also clear and emphatic.

 13a Eliminating Nonessential Words

One way to find out which words are essential to the meaning of a sentence is to underline the key words. Then, look carefully at the remaining words so that you can see which are unnecessary and delete them.

> It seems to me that it doesn't make sense to allow any <u>bail</u> to be <u>granted</u> to <u>anyone</u> who has ever been <u>convicted</u> of a <u>violent crime</u>.

The following revision includes just the words necessary to convey the key ideas.

> Bail should not be granted to anyone who has ever been convicted of a violent crime.

Nonessential words fall into three categories: *deadwood, utility words,* and *circumlocution.*

(1) Deleting Deadwood

Deadwood denotes unnecessary phrases that add nothing to meaning.

WORDY: The main reason <u>as to why</u> Tom left home was to find adventure.

CONCISE: The main reason Tom left home was to find adventure.

WORDY: Sometimes <u>there would be an accumulation of</u> water on the roof.

CONCISE: Sometimes water accumulated on the roof.

WORDY: The two plots are <u>both</u> similar in <u>the way</u> that they trace the characters' increasing rage.

CONCISE: The two plots are similar in that they trace the characters' increasing rage.

WORDY: Shoppers <u>who are</u> looking for bargains often patronize outlets.

CONCISE: Shoppers looking for bargains often patronize outlets.

WORDY: They played a racquetball game <u>which was</u> exhausting.

CONCISE: They played an exhausting racquetball game.

WORDY: <u>In</u> this article <u>it</u> discusses lead poisoning.

CONCISE: This article discusses lead poisoning.

Many familiar expressions—such as *as the case may be, I feel, it seems to me, all things considered, without a doubt, in conclusion,* and *by way of explanation*—are also deadwood. You may think they balance or fill out a sentence or make your writing sound more authoritative, but they are more likely to distract or annoy your readers than to impress them.

WORDY: <u>In my opinion,</u> I disagree with Thomas's position.

CONCISE: I disagree with Thomas's position.

WORDY: <u>As far as this course is concerned,</u> it looks interesting.

CONCISE: This course looks interesting.

WORDY: <u>For all intents and purposes,</u> the two brands are alike.

CONCISE: The two brands are essentially alike.

WORDY: <u>As compared to</u> those two universities, my school is different.

CONCISE: My school is different from those two universities.

WORDY: <u>It is important to note that</u> the results were identical in both clinical trials.

CONCISE: The results were identical in both clinical trials.

(2) Deleting or Replacing Utility Words

Utility words are simply fillers; they contribute nothing to a sentence. Utility words include nouns with imprecise meanings (*factor, kind, type, quality, aspect, thing, sort, field, area, situation,* and so on); adjectives so general that they are almost meaningless (*good, nice, bad, fine, important, significant*); and common adverbs denoting degree (*basically, completely, actually, very, definitely, quite*).

WORDY: The registration <u>situation</u> was disorganized.

CONCISE: Registration was disorganized.

WORDY: The scholarship offered Fran a <u>good</u> opportunity to study Spanish.

CONCISE: The scholarship offered Fran an opportunity to study Spanish.

WORDY: It was <u>actually</u> a worthwhile book, but I didn't <u>completely</u> finish it.

CONCISE: It was a worthwhile book, but I didn't finish it.

If you cannot simply delete a utility word, replace it with a more specific word.

(3) Avoiding Circumlocution

Taking a roundabout way to say something (using ten words when five will do) is called **circumlocution.** Instead of using complicated phrases and rambling constructions, you should use concrete, specific words and phrases and come right to the point.

WORDY: The experience that changed Andy most <u>would have to be</u> the hunting trip.

CONCISE: The experience that changed Andy most was the hunting trip.

WORDY: The curriculum was <u>of a unique nature</u>.

CONCISE: The curriculum was unique.

WORDY: <u>It is not unlikely that</u> the trend toward smaller cars will continue.

CONCISE: The trend toward smaller cars will probably continue.

WORDY: Joel was in the army <u>during the same time that</u> I was in college.

CONCISE: Joel was in the army while I was in college.

WORDY: <u>It is entirely possible that</u> the lake is frozen.

CONCISE: The lake may be frozen.

 REVISING WORDY PHRASES

Wordy phrases can almost always be revised. If you cannot edit a wordy construction, delete it and substitute a more concise, more direct term.

continued on the following page

continued from the previous page

Wordy	Concise
at the present time	now
at this point in time	now
for the purpose of	for
due to the fact that	because
on account of the fact that	because
until such time as	until
in the event that	if
by means of	by
in the vicinity of	near
have the ability to	be able to

EXERCISE 1

Revise the following paragraph to eliminate deadwood, utility words, and circumlocution. When a word or phrase seems superfluous, delete it or replace it with a more concise expression.

For all intents and purposes, the shopping mall is no longer an important factor in the American cultural scene. In the '80s, shopping malls became gathering places where teenagers met, walkers came to get in a few miles, and shoppers who were looking for a wide selection and weren't concerned about value went to shop. There are several factors that have worked to undermine the mall's popularity. First, due to the fact that today's shoppers are more likely to be interested in value, many of them have headed to the discount stores. Today's shopper is now more likely to shop in discount stores or bulk-buying warehouse stores than in the small, expensive specialty shops in the large shopping malls. Add to this a resurgence of the values of community, and you can see how malls would have to be less attractive than shopping at local stores. Many malls actually have up to 20 percent empty storefronts, and some have had to close down altogether. Others have met the challenge by expanding their roles from shopping centers into community centers. They've added playgrounds for the kids and more amusements and restaurants for the adults. They've also appealed to the growing sense of value shopping by giving gift certificates and discounts to shoppers who spend money in their stores. In the early '90s, it seemed as if the huge shopping malls that had become familiar cultural icons were dying out. Now, it looks as if some of those icons just might make it by meeting the challenges and continue to survive as more than just places to shop.

13b Eliminating Unnecessary Repetition

__Repetition__ can add emphasis to your writing, but unnecessary repetition obscures your meaning. Repeated words and **redundant** word groups (words or phrases that say the same thing) are the chief problems.

See 12d

You can correct unnecessary repetition by using one of the following strategies.

(1) Deleting Repeated Words

WORDY: The childhood <u>disease</u> chicken pox occasionally leads to dangerous complications, such as the <u>disease</u> known as Reye's syndrome.

CONCISE: The childhood disease chicken pox occasionally leads to dangerous complications, such as Reye's syndrome. (Repeated word is deleted.)

(2) Substituting a Pronoun

WORDY: Agatha Christie's <u>Miss Marple</u> solves many difficult cases. *The Murder at the Vicarage* was one of <u>Miss Marple's</u> most challenging puzzles.

CONCISE: Agatha Christie's Miss Marple solves many difficult cases. *The Murder at the Vicarage* was one of her most challenging puzzles. (The pronoun *her* is substituted for *Miss Marple.*)

(3) Using Elliptical Clauses

WORDY: Quincy Market <u>is a popular tourist attraction</u> in Boston; the White House <u>is a popular tourist attraction</u> in Washington, DC; and the Statue of Liberty <u>is a popular tourist attraction</u> in New York City.

CONCISE: Quincy Market is a popular tourist attraction in Boston; the White House, in Washington, DC; and the Statue of Liberty, in New York City. (**Elliptical clauses** eliminate unnecessary repetition.)

See 10b2

(4) Creating Appositives

WORDY: Red Barber <u>was</u> a sportscaster. He <u>was</u> known for his colorful expressions.

CONCISE: Red Barber, a sportscaster, was known for his colorful expressions. (**Appositive** eliminates unnecessary repetition.)

See 10c6

(5)   Creating Compounds

WORDY: Wendy <u>found the exam difficult</u>, and Karen <u>also found it hard</u>. Ken <u>thought it was tough too</u>.

CONCISE: Wendy, Karen, and Ken all found the exam difficult. (Compound subject eliminates unnecessary repetition.)

WORDY: *Huckleberry Finn* <u>is</u> an adventure story. <u>It is also</u> a sad account of an abused, neglected child.

CONCISE: *Huckleberry Finn* is both an adventure story and a sad account of an abused, neglected child. (Compound complement eliminates unnecessary repetition.)

WORDY: In 1964 Ted Briggs was discharged from the Air Force. <u>He</u> then got a job with Maxwell Data Processing. <u>He</u> married Susan Thompson that same year.

CONCISE: In 1964 Ted Briggs was discharged from the Air Force, got a job with Maxwell Data Processing, and married Susan Thompson. (Compound predicate eliminates unnecessary repetition.)

(6)   Creating Complex Sentences

WORDY: Americans value <u>freedom of speech</u>. <u>Freedom of speech</u> is guaranteed by the First Amendment.

CONCISE: Americans value freedom of speech, which is guaranteed by the First Amendment. (Creating a compound sentence eliminates needless repetition.)

EXERCISE 2

Eliminate any unnecessary repetition of words or ideas in this paragraph. Also revise to eliminate deadwood, utility words, or circumlocution.

For a wide variety of different reasons, more and more people today are choosing a vegetarian diet. There are three kinds of vegetarians: strict vegetarians eat no animal foods at all; lactovegetarians eat dairy products, but they do not eat meat, fish, poultry, or eggs; and ovolactovegetarians eat eggs and dairy products, but they do not eat meat, fish, or poultry. Famous vegetarians include such well-known people as George Bernard Shaw, Leonardo da Vinci, Ralph Waldo Emerson, Henry David Thoreau, and Mahatma Gandhi. Like these well-known vegetarians, the vegetarians of today have good reasons for becoming vegetarians. For instance, some religions recommend a vegetarian diet. Some of these religions are Buddhism, Brahmanism, and Hinduism. Other people turn to vegetarianism for reasons of health or for reasons of hygiene. These people believe that meat is a source of potentially harmful chemicals, and they believe meat contains infectious organisms. Some people feel meat may cause digestive problems and may lead to other difficulties as well. Other vegetarians adhere to a vegetarian diet because they feel it is ecologically wasteful to kill animals after we feed plants to them. These vegetarians believe *we* should eat the plants. Finally, there are facts and evidence to suggest that a vegetarian diet may possibly help people live longer lives. A vegetarian diet may do this by reducing the incidence of heart disease and lessening the incidence of some cancers. (Adapted from *Jane Brody's Nutrition Book*)

13c Revising Rambling Sentences

Nonessential words, unnecessary repetition, and complicated syntax create rambling sentences. Making such sentences concise involves more than crossing out a word or two. In fact, revising rambling sentences can require extensive editing.

(1) Eliminating Excessive Coordination

Excessive coordination, stringing a series of clauses together with coordinating conjunctions, often creates a rambling, unfocused **compound sentence**. Such excessive coordination presents all your ideas as if they have equal weight when they do not. To revise such sentences, identify the main idea, state that idea in the independent clause, and then subordinate the supporting details to the main idea.

See
14c

WORDY: Puerto Rico is the fourth largest island in the Caribbean, and it is predominantly mountainous, and it has steep slopes, and they fall to gentle coastal plains.

CONCISE: Fourth largest island in the Caribbean, Puerto Rico is predominantly mountainous, with steep slopes falling to gentle coastal plains. (*National Geographic*) (Puerto Rico's mountainous terrain is the sentence's main idea.)

(2) Eliminating Adjective Clauses

To write clearer, more direct sentences, substitute more concise modifying words or phrases for a series of adjective clauses.

WORDY: *Moby-Dick,* which is a novel about a white whale, was written by Herman Melville, who was friendly with Nathaniel Hawthorne, who encouraged him to revise the first draft.

CONCISE: *Moby-Dick,* a novel about a white whale, was written by Herman Melville, who revised the first draft at the urging of his friend Nathaniel Hawthorne.

(3) Eliminating Passive Constructions

Use active voice, which is usually more concise than passive voice, whenever possible.

WORDY: The sense of being safe inside an airplane is no longer felt by many people.

CONCISE: Many people no longer feel safe inside an airplane.

WORDY: Water rights are being fought for in court by Indian tribes like the Papago in Arizona and the Pyramid Lake Paiute in Nevada.

CONCISE: Indian tribes like the Papago in Arizona and the Pyramid Lake Paiute in Nevada are fighting in court for water rights.

(4) Eliminating Wordy Prepositional Phrases

When you revise, substitute single adjectives or adverbs for wordy prepositional phrases.

WORDY: The trip was one of danger but also one of excitement.

CONCISE: The trip was dangerous but exciting. (Adjectives replace prepositional phrases.)

WORDY: He spoke in a confident manner and with a lot of authority.

CONCISE: He spoke confidently and authoritatively. (Adverbs replace prepositional phrases.)

(5) Eliminating Wordy Noun Constructions

Substitute strong verbs for wordy noun phrases.

WORDY: The normalization of commercial relations between the United States and China in 1979 led to an increase in trade between the two countries.

CONCISE: When the United States and China normalized commercial relations in 1979, trade between the two countries increased.

WORDY: We have made the decision to postpone the meeting until after the appearance of all the board members.

CONCISE: We have decided to postpone the meeting until all the board members appear.

EXERCISE 3

Revise the rambling sentences in this paragraph by eliminating excessive coordination, unnecessary use of the passive voice, and overuse of adjective clauses, wordy prepositional phrases, and noun constructions. As you revise, make your sentences more concise by deleting nonessential words and superfluous repetition.

Some colleges that have been in support of fraternities for a number of years are at this time in the process of conducting a reevaluation of the position of those fraternities on campus. In opposition to the fraternities are a fair number of students, faculty members, and administrators who claim fraternities are inherently sexist, which they say makes it impossible for the groups to exist in a coeducational institution, which is supposed to offer equal opportunities for members of both sexes. More and more members of the college community also see fraternities as elitist as well as sexist and favor their abolition. In addition, many point out that fraternities are associated with dangerous practices, such as hazing and alcohol abuse. The problems that are presented by fraternities have already been dealt with at some colleges. For instance, Williams College made a decision in favor of the abolition of single-sex fraternities in 1968. Colby College banned fraternities in 1984. At Wesleyan University a decision was made by officials to sever formal ties to all-male fraternities. This was done because of the university's inability to persuade the fraternities to consider the acceptance of women. At Middlebury College in Vermont, the banning of single-sex fraternities and sororities took place in 1990. Now the fraternities (which are now called "houses") must now offer membership to women as well as men.

In 1997, the administration at Bowdoin College, which is located in Maine, told all fraternities that they would have to disband by the year 2000 and that they would be replaced at that time by a "house system." To address problems associated with intake of alcohol in fraternities, Select 2000, a pilot program to ban alcohol completely in fraternities, has been started at five schools, which are Villanova, Florida Southern, Southern Illinois, Northern Colorado, and the Rochester Institute of Technology. In some cases, however, students, faculty, and administration remain wholeheartedly in support of traditional fraternities, which they believe are responsible for helping students make the acquaintance of people and learn the leadership skills which they believe will be of assistance to them in their future lives as adults. (In fact, underground fraternities thrive at many institutions of higher learning at which traditional fraternities have been outlawed.) Supporters of fraternities believe students should retain the right to make their own social decisions and that joining a fraternity is one of those decisions, and they also believe fraternities are responsible for providing valuable services. Some of these are tutoring, raising money for charity, and running campus escort services. Therefore, these individuals are not of the opinion that the abolition of traditional fraternities makes sense.

STUDENT WRITER AT WORK

Writing Concise Sentences

Revise this excerpt from an essay examination in American literature to make it more concise. After you have done so, revise further if necessary to strengthen coherence, unity, and style.

Oftentimes in the course of a literary work, characters may find themselves misfits in the sense that they do not seem to be a real part of the society in which they find themselves. This problem often leads to a series of genuinely serious and severe problems, conflicts either between the misfits and their own identities or possibly between them and that society into which they so poorly fit.

In "The Minister's Black Veil" Reverend Hooper all of a sudden gives to the townspeople and members of his parish a surprise: a piece of black material that he has wrapped over his face, which causes readers to be as completely and thoroughly confused as the townspeople about the possible reason for the minister's decision to hide his face, until readers learn, in his sermon, that he is covering his face (from God, his fellow man, and himself) to atone for the sins of mankind. As far as readers can tell, they are never quite sure exactly why he is in possession of the notion that this act must be carried out by him, and they are never completely sure whether Reverend Hooper feels this guilt for some sin that may exist in his own past or for those sins that may have been committed by mankind in general, but in any case it is clear that he feels it is his duty to place himself in isolation from

continued on the following page

continued from the previous page
the world at large around him. To the reverend, there is no solution to his problem, and he lives his whole entire life wearing the veil. Even after his death he insists that the veil remain covering his features, for it is said by the reverend that his face must not be revealed on earth.

For Reverend Hooper, a terrible conflict exists within himself, and so Reverend Hooper voluntarily makes himself a misfit even at the expense of losing everything, even his true love Elizabeth.

CHAPTER 14

WRITING VARIED SENTENCES

Writing varied sentences can help you make your writing lively and interesting. This strategy can also help you emphasize an important idea.

14a Varying Sentence Length

A mixture of long and short sentences not only gives a pleasing rhythm to your writing but also keeps readers interested.

(1) Mixing Long and Short Sentences

A paragraph consisting entirely of short sentences (or entirely of long ones) can be dull.

> Drag racing began in California in the 1940s. It was an alternative to street racing, which was illegal and dangerous. It flourished in the 1950s and 1960s. Eventually, it became almost a rite of passage. Then, during the 1970s, almost one-third of America's racetracks closed. Today, however, drag racing is making a comeback.

Combining some short sentences creates sentence variety.

> Drag racing began in California in the 1940s as an alternative to street racing, which was illegal and dangerous. It flourished in the 1950s and 1960s, eventually becoming almost a rite of passage. Then, during the 1970s, almost one-third of America's racetracks closed. Today, however, drag racing is making a comeback.

(2) Following a Long Sentence with a Short One

Using a short sentence after one or more long ones immediately attracts reader attention. The following passages illustrate how this shifting of gears emphasizes the short sentence and its content while adding interest.

There are two social purposes for family dinners—the regular exchange of news and ideas and the opportunity to teach small children not to eat like pigs. These are by no means mutually exclusive. (Judith Martin, "Miss Manners")

Over the years, vitamin boosters say, a misconception has grown that as long as there are no signs or symptoms of, say, scurvy, then we have all of the vitamin C we need. Although we know how much of a particular vitamin or mineral will prevent clinical disease, we have practically no information on how much is necessary for peak health. In short, we know how sick is sick, but we don't know how well is well. (*Philadelphia Magazine*)

EXERCISE 1

Combine each of the following sentence groups into one long sentence. Then, compose a relatively short sentence to follow each long one. Finally, combine all the sentences into a paragraph, adding a topic sentence and any transitions necessary for coherence. Proofread your paragraph to be sure the sentences are varied in length.

1. Chocolate is composed of more than three hundred compounds. Phenylethylamine is one such compound. Its presence in the brain may be linked to the emotion of falling in love.

2. Americans now consume a good deal of chocolate. On average, they eat more than nine pounds of chocolate per person per year. The typical Belgian, however, consumes almost fifteen pounds per year.

3. In recent years, Americans have begun a serious love affair with chocolate. Elegant chocolate boutiques sell exquisite bonbons by the piece. At least one hotel offers a "chocolate binge" vacation. The bimonthly *Chocolate News* for connoisseurs is flourishing.

(Adapted from *Newsweek*)

14b Combining Choppy Simple Sentences

Strings of short simple sentences can be tedious, as the following paragraph illustrates.

John Peter Zenger was a newspaper editor. He waged and won an important battle for freedom of the press in America. He criticized the policies of the British governor. He was charged with criminal libel as a result. Zenger's lawyers were disbarred by the governor. Andrew Hamilton defended him. Hamilton convinced the jury that Zenger's criticisms were true. Therefore, the statements were not libelous.

You can revise choppy sentences like these by combining them with adjacent sentences, using *coordination, subordination,* or *embedding.*

(1) Using Coordination

Coordination pairs similar elements—words, phrases, or clauses— giving equal weight to each. The following revision links two of the original paragraph's choppy simple sentences with *and* to create a compound sentence.

John Peter Zenger was a newspaper editor. He waged and won an important battle for freedom of the press in America. <u>He criticized the policies of the British governor, and as a result, he was charged with criminal libel.</u> Zenger's lawyers were disbarred by the governor. Andrew Hamilton defended him. Hamilton convinced the jury that Zenger's criticisms were true. Therefore, the statements were not libelous.

(2) Using Subordination

Subordination clarifies the relationships among ideas. You use subordination when you want to indicate that one idea is less important than another. You do this by placing the more important idea in the independent clause and the less important idea in the dependent clause. The following revision of the paragraph above uses subordination to change two simple sentences into dependent clauses, creating two **complex sentences**.

See
11b

John Peter Zenger was a newspaper editor <u>who waged and won an important battle for freedom of the press in America.</u> He criticized the policies of the British governor, and as a result, he was charged with criminal libel. <u>When Zenger's lawyers were disbarred by the governor, Andrew Hamilton defended him.</u> Hamilton convinced the jury that Zenger's criticisms were true. Therefore, the statements were not libelous.

(3) Using Embedding

Embedding—working additional words and phrases into sentences—is another strategy for varying sentence structure. In the following revision, the sentence *Hamilton convinced the jury . . .* has been reworded to create a phrase (*convincing the jury*) that modifies the independent clause *Andrew Hamilton defended him.*

John Peter Zenger was a newspaper editor who waged and won an important battle for freedom of the press in America. He criticized the policies of the British governor, and as a result, he was charged with criminal libel. When Zenger's lawyers were disbarred by the governor, Andrew Hamilton defended him, convincing the jury that Zenger's criticisms were true. Therefore, the statements were not libelous.

The final revision of the original string of choppy sentences is a varied, readable paragraph that uses coordination, subordination, and embedding to vary sentence length. (It retains the final short simple sentence for emphasis.)

EXERCISE 2

Using coordination, subordination, and embedding, revise this string of choppy simple sentences into a more varied and interesting paragraph.

The first modern miniature golf course was built in New York in 1925. It was an indoor course with 18 holes. Entrepreneurs Drake Delanoy and John Ledbetter built 150 more indoor and outdoor courses. Garnet Carter made miniature golf a worldwide fad. Carter built an elaborate miniature golf course. He later joined with Delanoy and Ledbetter. Together they built more miniature golf courses. They abbreviated playing distances. They highlighted the game's hazards at the expense of skill. This made the game much more popular. By 1930 there were 25,000 miniature golf courses in the United States. Courses grew more elaborate. Hazards grew more bizarre. The craze spread to London and Hong Kong. The expansion of miniature golf grew out of control. Then, interest in the game declined. By 1931 most miniature golf courses were out of business. The game was revived in the early 1950s. Today there are between eight and ten thousand miniature golf courses. The architecture of miniature golf remains an enduring form of American folk art. (Adapted from *Games*)

14c Breaking Up Strings of Compound Sentences

An unbroken series of compound sentences can be dull. Moreover, when you connect clauses only with coordinating conjunctions, you do not indicate exactly how ideas are related or which is most important.

ALL COMPOUND SENTENCES: A volcano that is erupting is considered *active,* but one that may erupt is designated *dormant,* and one that has not erupted for a long time is called *extinct.* Most active volcanoes are located in "The Ring of Fire," a belt that circles the Pacific Ocean, and they can be extremely destructive. Italy's Vesuvius erupted in AD 79, and it destroyed the town of Pompeii. In 1883 Krakatoa, located between the Indonesian islands of Java and Sumatra, erupted, and it caused a tidal wave, and more than 36,000 people were killed. Martinique's Mont Pelée erupted in 1902, and its hot gas and ash killed 30,000 people, and this completely wiped out the town of St. Pierre.

VARIED SENTENCES: A volcano that is erupting is considered *active.* [**simple sentence**] One that may erupt is designated *dormant,* and one that has not erupted for a long time is called *extinct.* [**compound sentence**] Most active volcanoes are located in "The Ring of Fire," a belt that circles the Pacific Ocean. [**simple sentence with modifier**] Active volcanoes can be extremely destructive. [**simple sentence**] Erupting in AD 79, Italy's Vesuvius destroyed the town of Pompeii. [**simple sentence with modifier**] When Krakatoa, located between the Indonesian islands of Java and Sumatra, erupted in 1883, it caused a tidal wave that killed 36,000 people. [**compound-complex sentence with modifier**] The eruption of Martinique's Mont Pelée in 1902 produced hot gas and ash that killed 30,000 people, completely wiping out the town of St. Pierre. [**complex sentence with modifier**]

EXERCISE 3

Revise the compound sentences in this passage so the sentence structure is varied. Be sure that the writer's emphasis and the relationships between ideas are clear.

Dr. Alice I. Baumgartner and her colleagues at the Institute for Equality in Education at the University of Colorado surveyed two thousand Colorado schoolchildren, and they found some startling results. They asked, "If you woke up tomorrow and discovered that you were a (boy) (girl), how would your life be different?" and the answers were sad and shocking. The researchers assumed they would find that boys and girls would see advantages in being either male or female, but instead they found that both boys and girls had a fundamental contempt for females. Many elementary schoolboys titled their answers "The Disaster" or "Doomsday," and they described the terrible lives they would lead as girls, but the girls seemed to feel they would be better off as boys, and they expressed feelings that they would be able to do more and have easier lives.

Boys and girls alike realized that girls are judged by their looks more than boys, and both felt girls have to pay more attention to their looks, so all children perceived boys as having an advantage. In addition, boys and girls both valued boys' activities more highly, and boys and girls agreed that "women's work" is less valuable and less valued than "men's work." Both boys and girls also felt that boys are expected to behave differently, and they felt that boys could get away with more and be more active, but girls did have one advantage and that was that they could express their feelings openly.

Finally, both boys and girls agreed that boys are treated better and respected more than girls, so in other words there is a prejudice against females among both boys and girls, and this sex stereotyping is a psychological handicap for both men and women. (Adapted from *Redbook*)

14d Varying Sentence Types

You can mix **declarative sentences** (statements) with occasional **imperative sentences** (commands or requests), **exclamations,** and **rhetorical questions** (questions that readers are not expected to answer). The following paragraph does just this.

Local television newscasts seem to be delivering less and less news. Although we stay awake for the late news hoping to be updated on local, national, and world events, only about 30 percent of most newscasts is devoted to news. Up to 25 percent of the typical program—even more during "sweeps weeks"—can be devoted to feature stories, with another 25 percent reserved for advertising. The remaining time is spent on weather, sports, and casual conversation between anchors. Given this focus on "soft" material, what options do those of us wishing to find out what happened in the world have? [**rhetorical question**] Critics of local television have a few suggestions. First, write to your local station's management voicing your concern and threatening to boycott the news if changes are not made; then, try to get others who feel the way you do to sign a petition. [**imperatives**] If changes are not made, try turning off your television and reading the newspaper! [**exclamation**]

Other options for varying sentence types include mixing simple, compound, and complex sentences **(see 14b and c)**; mixing cumulative and periodic sentences **(see 12b)**; and using balanced sentences **(see 12c).**

EXERCISE 4

The following paragraph is composed entirely of declarative sentences. To make it more varied, add three sentences—one exclamation, one rhetorical question, and one imperative—anywhere in the paragraph. Be sure the new sentences are consistent with the paragraph's purpose and tone.

> When the Fourth of July comes around, the nation explodes with patriotism. Everywhere we look we see parades and picnics, firecrackers and fireworks. An outsider might wonder what all the fuss is about. We could explain that this is America's birthday party, and all the candles are being lit at once. There is no reason for us to hold back our enthusiasm—or to limit the noise that celebrates it. The Fourth of July is watermelon and corn on the cob, American flags and sparklers, brass bands and more. Everyone looks forward to this celebration, and everyone has a good time.

14e Varying Sentence Openings

Rather than begin every sentence with the subject, try beginning with a modifying word, phrase, or clause.

(1) Beginning with an Adjective, Adverb, or Dependent Clause

<u>Proud</u> and <u>relieved</u>, they watched their daughter receive her diploma. (adjectives)

<u>Hungrily</u>, he devoured his lunch. (adverb)

<u>After Woodrow Wilson was incapacitated by a stroke</u>, his wife unofficially performed many presidential duties. (dependent clause)

(2) Beginning with a Prepositional Phrase, Participial Phrase, or Absolute Phrase

<u>For better or worse</u>, credit cards are now readily available to college students. (prepositional phrase)

<u>Located on the west coast of Great Britain</u>, Wales is part of the United Kingdom. (participial phrase)

<u>His interests widening</u>, Picasso designed ballet sets and illustrated books. (absolute phrase)

(3) Beginning with a Coordinating Conjunction or a Transitional Word or Phrase

The Big Bang may be the beginning of the universe, or it may be a discontinuity in which information about the earlier history of the universe was destroyed. <u>But</u> it is certainly the earliest event about which we have any record. (Carl Sagan, *The Dragons of Eden*) (coordinating conjunction)

Pantomime was first performed in ancient Rome. <u>However</u>, it remains a popular dramatic form today. (transitional word)

 CLOSE-UP VARYING SENTENCE OPENINGS

If you begin a sentence with a coordinating conjunction, be sure that it is a complete sentence and not a **fragment**.

See
Ch. 15

(4) Beginning with an Appositive

<u>Famous for having discovered penicillin</u>, Alexander Fleming was a British scientist. (appositive)

EXERCISE 5

Each of these sentences begins with the subject. Revise each so that it has a different opening, and then identify the opening strategy that you used.

EXAMPLE: N. Scott Momaday, the prominent Native American writer, tells the story of his first fourteen years in *The Names*.

REVISED: Prominent Native American writer N. Scott Momaday tells the story of his first fourteen years in *The Names*. (appositive)

1. Momaday was taken as a very young child to Devil's Tower, the geological formation in Wyoming that is called Tsoai (Bear Tree) in Kiowa, and there he was given the name Tsoai-talee (Bear Tree Boy).
2. The Kiowa myth of the origin of Tsoai is about a boy who playfully chases his seven sisters up a tree, which rises into the air as the boy is transformed into a bear.
3. The boy-bear becomes increasingly ferocious and claws the bark of the tree, which becomes a great rock with a flat top and deeply scored sides.
4. The sisters climb higher and higher to escape their brother's wrath, and eventually they become the seven stars of the Big Dipper.

5. This story, from which Momaday received one of his names, appears as a constant in his works *The Way to Rainy Mountain, House Made of Dawn,* and *The Ancient Child.*

14f Varying Standard Word Order

You can vary standard subject-verb-object (or complement) word order either by intentionally inverting this usual order or by placing words between subject and verb.

(1) Inverting Word Order

Sometimes you can place the complement or direct object *before* the verb instead of in its conventional position after the verb, or place the verb *before* the subject instead of after it. These strategies draw attention to the word or word group that appears in an unexpected place.

> (subject)
> Nature I loved and, next to Nature, Art. (Walter Savage Landor)
> (object) (verb)

> (complement)
> The book was extremely helpful; especially useful was its index.
> (verb) (subject)

NOTE: Be careful to use inverted word order in moderation; when overused, inversion loses its force and can sound pretentious.

(2) Separating Subject from Verb

You can also place words or phrases between subject and verb—but be sure that the word group does not obscure the connection between subject and verb or create an **agreement** error.

See
26a

> Many <u>states</u> <u>require</u> that infants and young children ride in government-approved child safety seats because they hope this will reduce needless fatalities. (subject and verb together)

> Many <u>states</u>, hoping to reduce needless fatalities, <u>require</u> that infants and young children ride in government-approved child safety seats. (subject and verb separated)

EXERCISE 6

The following sentences use conventional word order. Revise each in one of two ways: either invert the sentence, or vary the word order by placing words between subject and verb. After you have completed your revisions, create a varied five-sentence paragraph by linking the sentences together.

EXAMPLE: Dada was an artistic and literary rebellion that defied the conventional values of the early twentieth century.

REVISION: Dada, an artistic and literary rebellion, defied the conventional values of the early twentieth century.

1. The Dada movement first appeared in 1915 and effectively ended in 1925 with the rise of Surrealism.

2. The name *Dada*, French for "hobby horse," was selected at random from a dictionary and was meant to symbolize the antirational, antiaesthetic stance taken by its practitioners, who were in part rebelling against the militarism of World War I.

3. The Dadaists abandoned their original antimilitarist protest, and they ultimately rejected all traditional values, especially of culture, which was seen as symptomatic of the falseness and hypocrisy of society, and their goal became to destroy art as an aesthetic cult and replace it with "antiart" and "nonart."

4. The Dadaists rejected the artifact as art, and they substituted the nonsense poem, the ready-made object, and the collage, all of which depended more on the arbitrary and the accidental than on conscious artistry for the crafted design.

5. The most notorious example of Dada art is the sculpture *Fountain* (1917), which was a urinal Marcel Duchamp found and signed *R. Mutt* and entered into a gallery exhibit.

STUDENT WRITER AT WORK

Writing Varied Sentences

Read this draft of a student essay carefully. Then, revise it to achieve greater sentence variety by varying the length, type, openings, and word order of the sentences. After you have done so, revise further if necessary to strengthen coherence, unity, and style.

The American Dream

Although I was only seven at the time, I can vividly recall my family's escape from Vietnam to America. My mother, brother, and I came to America together. My father had fought against the communists during

continued on the following page

continued from the previous page
the war. As a result, my brother and I were forbidden from obtaining any education beyond the high school level. Also, Vietnam was an impoverished nation. It seemed as if we had no choice but to leave.

The boat we left in was small. It held only fifty-two people. We left at two o'clock in the morning. At that time passage by boat cost a sum equal to fifteen hundred American dollars for each child and three thousand dollars for each adult. This was a great deal of money, and very few families could afford to escape. My family was fairly well off in Vietnam. Still, this was a lot of money for us.

Unlike other "boat people," we were fortunate to be rescued by a Norwegian liner only three days after we left Vietnam. When we saw this ship, all the men in our boat hid. They told the women and children to sit up and stay in the ship's view. They hoped the crew would feel sorry for the women and children and rescue us. This is exactly what happened. When we first boarded the ship, the crew asked us if we wanted anything. We cupped our hands and brought them to our lips. This showed them we were thirsty.

The Norwegian ship left us in Japan at a United Nations refugee camp. We stayed there nearly a year. Then, United Nations staff came to pick up people who had sponsors in other countries. My father had come to the United States two years earlier, so he was our sponsor.

When my mother, brother, and I arrived in America, we stayed for two months in a boardinghouse with my father. Then we all moved into an apartment of our own. My mother found a job as a housekeeper in a hospital. This was hard for her at first because she could not speak or understand English. It was frustrating to her when she was accused of not doing her work. She couldn't defend herself. My brother and I were more fortunate. At our school there were many people to help us adjust to

continued on the following page

continued from the previous page

American life. When we came home from school, however, we had to fend for ourselves. Both of our parents worked until 6 p.m.

Before they arrived in America, my parents expected life to be much easier in America than it was in Vietnam. They were surprised to find out just how hard life could be here. Because of the limited education my parents had, they cannot expect a life much better than what they currently have. However, they do expect more for their children. We left Vietnam so my brother and I could have a better education and a better life. Now we are in America. The rest is up to us.

PART 4

SOLVING COMMON SENTENCE PROBLEMS

CHAPTER 15

REVISING SENTENCE FRAGMENTS

A **sentence fragment** is an incomplete sentence—a phrase or clause punctuated as if it were a complete sentence. A sentence may be incomplete for any of the following reasons:

- **It lacks a subject.**

  Many astrophysicists now believe that galaxies are distributed in clusters. And even form supercluster complexes.

- **It lacks a verb.**

  Three key events defined my generation. The Gulf War, the Oklahoma City bombing, and the Rodney King verdict.

- **It lacks both a subject and a verb.**

  Researchers are engaged in a variety of studies. Suggesting a link between alcoholism and heredity. (*Suggesting* is a **verbal,** which cannot serve as a sentence's main verb.)

- **It is a dependent clause.**

  Bishop Desmond Tutu was awarded the 1984 Nobel Peace Prize. Because he struggled to end apartheid.

When readers cannot see where sentences begin and end, they have difficulty understanding what you have written. For instance, it is impossible to tell to which independent clause the fragment in each of the following sequences belongs.

The course requirements were changed last year. Because a new professor was hired at the very end of the spring semester. I was unable to find out about this change until after preregistration.

In *The Ox-Bow Incident* the crowd is convinced that the men are guilty. Even though the men insist they are innocent and Davies pleads for their lives. They are hanged.

✔ CHECKLIST: REVISING SENTENCE FRAGMENTS

To determine whether or not a sentence is complete, ask these three questions.

✔ Does the word group have a subject?
✔ Does the word group have a verb?
✔ Does the word group consist of an independent clause? (A sentence cannot consist of a single clause that begins with a subordinating conjunction or with a relative pronoun like *that;* moreover, unless it is a question, it cannot consist of a single clause beginning with *when, where, who, which, what, why,* or *how.*)

If you cannot answer yes to all three questions, the word group is a fragment, and you will need to use one or more of the following strategies to revise it.

✔ Attach the fragment to an adjacent independent clause.

FRAGMENT: According to German legend, Lohengrin is the son of Parzival. And a knight of the Holy Grail.

REVISED: According to German legend, Lohengrin is the son of Parzival and a knight of the Holy Grail.

✔ Supply the missing subject and/or verb.

FRAGMENT: Lancaster County, Pennsylvania, is home to many Pennsylvania Dutch. Descended from eighteenth-century settlers from southwest Germany.

REVISED: Lancaster County, Pennsylvania, is home to many Pennsylvania Dutch. They are descended from eighteenth-century settlers from southwest Germany.

✔ Delete the subordinating conjunction or relative pronoun.

FRAGMENT: Property taxes rose sharply. Although city services showed no improvement.

REVISED: Property taxes rose sharply. City services showed no improvement.

The following sections identify the grammatical structures most likely to appear as fragments and illustrate the most effective ways of revising each.

15a Revising Dependent Clauses

A **dependent clause** contains a subject and a verb, but it cannot stand alone as a sentence. Because it needs an independent clause to complete its meaning, a **dependent clause** (also called a *subordinate clause*) must always be attached to at least one independent clause to form a complete sentence. You can recognize a dependent clause because it is always introduced by a **subordinating conjunction** or a **relative pronoun**.

See
11b

To correct a dependent clause fragment, either join the dependent clause to a neighboring independent clause, or delete the subordinating conjunction or relative pronoun, creating a complete sentence with a subject and a verb. (You may have to replace the relative pronoun with another word that can serve as the subject.)

FRAGMENT: The United States declared war. Because the Japanese bombed Pearl Harbor. (Dependent clause is incorrectly punctuated as a sentence.)

REVISED: The United States declared war because the Japanese bombed Pearl Harbor. (Dependent clause has been attached to an independent clause to create a complete sentence.)

REVISED: The Japanese bombed Pearl Harbor. The United States declared war. (Subordinating conjunction *because* has been deleted; the result is a complete sentence.)

FRAGMENT: The battery is dead. Which means the car won't start. (Dependent clause is incorrectly punctuated as a sentence.)

REVISED: The battery is dead, which means the car won't start. (Dependent clause has been attached to an independent clause to create a complete sentence.)

REVISED: The battery is dead. This means the car won't start. (Relative pronoun *which* has been replaced by *this*, an acceptable subject, to create a complete sentence.)

EXERCISE 1

Identify the sentence fragments in the following paragraph and correct each, either by attaching the fragment to an independent clause or by deleting the subordinating conjunction or relative pronoun to create a sentence that can stand alone. In some cases you will have to replace a relative pronoun with another word that can serve as the subject.

The drive-in movie came into being just after World War II. When both movies and cars were central to the lives of many Americans. Drive-ins were especially popular with teenagers and young families during the 1950s. When cars and gas were relatively inexpensive. Theaters charged by the carload. Which meant that a group of teenagers or a family with several children could spend an evening at the movies for a few dollars. In 1958, when the fad peaked, there were over four thousand drive-ins in the United States. While today there are fewer than three thousand. Many of these are in the Sunbelt, with most in California. Although many Sunbelt drive-ins continue to thrive because of the year-round warm weather. Many northern drive-ins are in financial trouble. Because land is so expensive. Some drive-in owners break even only by operating flea markets or swap meets in daylight hours. While others, unable to attract customers, are selling their theaters to land developers. Soon drive-ins may be a part of our nostalgic past. Which will be a great loss for many who enjoy them.

15b Revising Phrases

A **phrase** works as part of a sentence, providing information—description, examples, and so on—about other words or word groups in the sentence. However, a phrase cannot stand alone. Many fragments are created when a phrase is incorrectly punctuated as a sentence.

(1) Prepositional Phrases

See
10c3

A **prepositional phrase** consists of a preposition, its object, and any modifiers of the object.

To correct a prepositional phrase fragment, attach it to the independent clause that contains the word or word group modified by the prepositional phrase.

FRAGMENT: President Lyndon Johnson decided not to seek reelection. For a number of reasons. (Prepositional phrase is incorrectly punctuated as a sentence.)

REVISED: President Lyndon Johnson decided not to seek reelection for a number of reasons. (Prepositional phrase has been attached to an independent clause.)

FRAGMENT: He ran sixty yards for a touchdown. In the final minutes of the game. (Prepositional phrase is incorrectly punctuated as a sentence.)

Revised: He ran sixty yards for a touchdown in the final minutes of the game. (Prepositional phrase has been attached to an independent clause.)

EXERCISE 2

Read the following passage and identify the sentence fragments. Then correct each one by attaching it to the independent clause that contains the word or word group it modifies.

Most college athletes are caught in a conflict. Between their athletic and academic careers. Sometimes college athletes' responsibilities on the playing field make it hard for them to be good students. Often athletes must make a choice. Between sports and a degree. Some athletes would not be able to afford college. Without athletic scholarships. But, ironically, their commitments (training, exercise, practice, and travel to out-of-town games, for example) deprive athletes. Of valuable classroom time. The role of college athletes is constantly being questioned. Critics suggest that athletes exist only to participate in and promote college athletics. Because of the importance of this role to academic institutions, scandals occasionally develop. With coaches and even faculty members arranging to inflate athletes' grades to help them remain eligible. For participation in sports. Some universities even lower admissions standards. To help remedy this and other inequities. The controversial Proposition 48, passed at the NCAA convention in 1982, established minimum College Board scores and grade standards for college students. But many people feel that the NCAA remains overly concerned. With profits rather than with education. As a result, college athletic competition is increasingly coming to resemble pro sports. From the coaches' pressure on the players to win to the network television exposure to the wagers on the games' outcomes.

(2) Verbal Phrases

A **verbal phrase** consists of a **verbal**—a present participle (*walking*), past participle (*walked*), infinitive (*to walk*), or gerund—plus related objects and modifiers (*walking along the lonely beach*). Because a verbal cannot serve as a sentence's main verb, a verbal phrase is not a complete sentence and should not be punctuated as one.

See 10c4

To correct a verbal phrase fragment, either attach the verbal phrase to a related independent clause or change the verbal to a verb and add a subject.

Fragment: In 1948 India became independent. Divided into the nations of India and Pakistan. (Verbal phrase is incorrectly punctuated as a sentence.)

REVISED: Divided into the nations of India and Pakistan, India became independent in 1948. (Verbal phrase has been attached to the related independent clause to create a complete sentence.)

REVISED: In 1948 India became independent. It was divided into the nations of India and Pakistan. (Verbal *divided* has been changed to verb *was divided,* and subject *it* has been added; the result is a new independent clause.)

FRAGMENT: The pilot changed course. <u>Realizing the weather was worsening.</u> (Verbal phrase is incorrectly punctuated as a sentence.)

REVISED: The pilot changed course, realizing the weather was worsening. (Verbal phrase has been attached to the related independent clause to create a complete sentence.)

REVISED: The pilot changed course. She realized the weather was worsening. (Verb *realized* has been substituted for verbal *realizing,* and subject *she* has been added; the result is a new independent clause.)

EXERCISE 3

Identify the sentence fragments in the following paragraph and correct each. Either attach the fragment to a related independent clause or add a subject and a verb to create a new independent clause.

Many food products have well-known trademarks. Identified by familiar faces on product labels. Some of these symbols have remained the same, while others have changed considerably. Products like Sun-Maid Raisins, Betty Crocker potato mixes, Quaker Oats, and Uncle Ben's Rice use faces. To create a sense of quality and tradition and to encourage shopper recognition of the products. Many of the portraits have been updated several times. To reflect changes in society. Betty Crocker's portrait, for instance, has changed five times since its creation in 1936. Symbolizing women's changing roles. The original Chef Boy-ar-dee has also changed. Turning from the young Italian chef Hector Boiardi into a white-haired senior citizen. Miss Sunbeam, trademark of Sunbeam Bread, has had her hairdo modified several times since her first appearance in 1942; the Blue Bonnet girl, also created in 1942, now has a more modern look, and Aunt Jemima has also been changed. Slimmed down a bit in 1965. Similarly, the Campbell's Soup kids are less chubby now than in the 1920s when they first appeared. But the Quaker on Quaker Oats remains as round as he was when he first adorned the product label in 1877. The Morton Salt girl has evolved gradually. Changing several times from blonde to brunette and from straight- to curly-haired. But manufacturers are very careful about selecting a trademark or modifying an existing one.

Typically spending a good deal of time and money on research before a change is made. After all, a trademark of long standing can help a product's sales. Giving shoppers the sense that they are using products purchased and preferred by their parents and grandparents.

(3) Appositives

An **appositive**—a noun or noun phrase that identifies or renames a noun or pronoun that precedes it—cannot stand alone as a sentence.

To correct an appositive fragment, attach the appositive to the independent clause that contains the word or word group the appositive renames.

FRAGMENT: Piero della Francesca was a leader of the Umbrian school of painting. A school that remained close to the traditions of Gothic art. (Appositive, a fragment that identifies *the Umbrian school of painting*, is incorrectly punctuated as a complete sentence.)

REVISED: Piero della Francesca was a leader of the Umbrian school of painting, a school that remained close to the traditions of Gothic art. (Appositive has been attached to the word group it identifies.)

Sometimes an appositive fragment takes the form of a list. To correct this kind of fragment, add a colon to connect the list to the sentence that introduces it.

FRAGMENT: Tourists often outnumber residents in four European cities. Venice, Florence, Canterbury, and Bath. (List is incorrectly punctuated as a sentence.)

REVISED: Tourists often outnumber residents in four European cities: Venice, Florence, Canterbury, and Bath. (List has been attached with a colon to the sentence that introduces it.)

Appositives are also sometimes introduced by a word or phrase like *that is, for example, for instance, namely*, or *such as*. Even with those introductory phrases, appositives still cannot stand alone as sentences. To correct this kind of fragment, attach the appositive to the preceding independent clause.

FRAGMENT: Fairy tales are full of damsels in distress. Such as Snow White, Cinderella, and Rapunzel. (Appositive, a phrase that identifies *damsels in distress*, is incorrectly punctuated as a sentence.)

REVISED: Fairy tales are full of damsels in distress, such as Snow White, Cinderella, and Rapunzel. (Appositive has been attached to the word group it identifies.)

See
10c6

285

REVISING APPOSITIVES

You can also correct an appositive fragment by embedding the appositive within the related independent clause.

FRAGMENT: Some popular novelists are highly respected by later generations. For example, Mark Twain and Charles Dickens. (Appositive, a phrase that identifies *some popular novelists*, is incorrectly punctuated as a sentence.)

REVISED: Some popular novelists—for example, Mark Twain and Charles Dickens—are highly respected by later generations. (Appositive has been embedded within the related independent clause, directly following the word group it identifies.)

See
29d1

Note that a **nonrestrictive** appositive is set off by commas but that a **restrictive** appositive takes no commas.

EXERCISE 4

Identify the fragments in this paragraph and correct them by attaching each to the independent clause containing the word or word group the appositive modifies.

Until the early 1900s communities in West Virginia, Tennessee, and Kentucky were isolated by the mountains that surrounded them. The great chain of the Appalachian Mountains. Set apart from the emerging culture of a growing America and American language, these communities retained a language rich with the dialect of Elizabethan English. Sprinkled with hints of a Scotch-Irish influence. In 1910s and '20s the communities in these mountains began to long for a better future for their children. The key to that future, as they saw it, was education. In some communities that education took the form of Settlement Schools. Schools led by the new rash of idealistic young graduates of eastern women's colleges. These teachers taught the basic academic subjects. Such as reading, writing, and mathematics. They also schooled their students in the culture of the mountains. For example, the crafts, music, and folklore of the Appalachians. In addition, they taught them skills that would help them survive when the coal market began to decline. The Settlement Schools attracted artisans from around the world. Quilters, luthiers, weavers, basketmakers, and carpenters. Some criticize the schools for exerting outside influence on the traditional

Appalachian crafts. Others praise the Settlement Schools for teaching new skills while respecting the traditional mountain style and even respecting the traditional culture and linguistic history of the mountains. Still, the schools did open the mountains to the world and thus caused the Elizabethan dialect to fade.

15c Revising Compounds

The last part of a **compound predicate, compound object,** or **compound complement** cannot stand alone as a sentence.

To correct this kind of fragment, connect the detached part of the compound to the rest of the sentence.

FRAGMENT: People with dyslexia have trouble reading. <u>And may also find it difficult to write.</u> (Fragment, part of the compound predicate *have . . . and may also find,* is incorrectly punctuated as a sentence.)

REVISED: People with dyslexia have trouble reading and may also find it difficult to write. (Detached part of the compound predicate has been connected to the rest of the sentence.)

FRAGMENT: They took only a compass and a canteen of water. <u>And some trail mix.</u> (Fragment, part of the compound object *compass . . . canteen . . . trail mix,* is incorrectly punctuated as a sentence.)

REVISED: They took only a compass, a canteen of water, and some trail mix. (Detached part of the compound object has been connected to the rest of the sentence.)

FRAGMENT: When their supplies ran out, they were surprised. <u>And hungry.</u> (Fragment, part of the compound complement *surprised and hungry,* is incorrectly punctuated as a sentence.)

REVISED: When their supplies ran out, they were surprised and hungry. (Detached part of the compound complement has been connected to the rest of the sentence.)

EXERCISE 5

Identify the sentence fragments in this passage and correct them by attaching each detached compound to the rest of the sentence.

As more and more Americans discover the pleasures of the wilderness, our national parks are feeling the stress. Wanting to get away for a weekend or a week, hikers and backpackers stream from the cities into nearby state and national parks. They bring with them a hunger for wilderness. But very little knowledge about how to behave ethically in the wild. They also don't know how to keep themselves safe. Some of them think of the national parks as inexpensive amusement parks. Without proper camping supplies and lacking enough food and water for their trip, they are putting at risk their lives and the lives of those who will be called on to save them. One family went for a hike up a desert canyon with an eight-month-old infant. And their seventy-eight-year-old grandmother. Although the terrain was difficult, they weren't wearing the proper shoes. Or good socks. Nor did they carry a first aid kit. Or a map or compass. They were on an unmarked trail in a little-used section of Bureau of Land Management lands. And following vague directions from a friend. They were soon lost. They hadn't brought water or food. Or even rain gear or warm clothes. Luckily for them, they had brought a cellular phone. They called for help. By the time they called, however, it was getting dark and a storm was building. The rescue helicopters had to attempt a rescue because of the infant and the likelihood of flash floods, even though conditions would have normally precluded flying. The pilot and his crew safely located the family. And rescued them. Still, a little planning before they hiked in an inhospitable area, and a little awareness and preparedness for the terrain they were traveling in, would have saved this family much worry. And the taxpayers a lot of money.

 SENTENCE FRAGMENTS

In some special situations, sentence fragments may be acceptable. For example, we commonly use fragments in speech and in informal writing.

| See you later. | No sweat. | In a minute. |
| Back soon. | Could be trouble. | Not now. |

In advertising, journalism, and creative writing, fragments may be used to achieve special effects—for instance, to represent casual conversation or to convey disconnected thinking.

Finally. Vegetables with no salt added.

Then the curtains breathing out of the dark upon my face, leaving the breathing upon my face. A quarter hour yet.

continued on the following page

continued from the previous page
And then I'll not be. <u>The peacefullest words</u>. (William Faulkner,
The Sound and the Fury)

Keep in mind, however, that in most college writing situations,
sentence fragments are not acceptable.

EXERCISE 6

Contemporary essayists and fiction writers often use fragments for effect. Find a paragraph from a magazine or novel that uses sentence fragments. Why did the writer choose to use fragments? What effect do they
have on you? Is the use of sentence fragments successful or not?

STUDENT WRITER AT WORK

Revising Sentence Fragments

Carefully read this excerpt from a draft of a student essay. Identify all
the sentence fragments and determine why each is a fragment. Correct
each sentence fragment by adding, deleting, or modifying words to create a sentence or by attaching the fragment to a neighboring independent clause. Finally, go over the draft again and, if necessary, revise
further to strengthen coherence, unity, and style.

Ab Snopes: A Trapped Man

Abner (Ab) Snopes, the father in William Faulkner's story "Barn
Burning," is trapped in a hopeless situation. Disgusted with his lack of
status yet unable to do much to remedy his dissatisfaction. He has little
control over his life, but he still struggles. Fighting his useless battle as best
he can.

Ab is a family man. Responsible for a wife, children, and his wife's
sister. Unfortunately, he is unable to meet his responsibilities. Such as
providing a stable home for his family. Evicted because of Ab's "barn
burnings," the family constantly moves from town to town. With all its
continued on the following page

continued from the previous page
belongings piled on a wagon. Still, Ab continues to burn barns. Because he hopes that these acts will give him power as well as revenge.

To the rich landowners he works for, Ab is of little significance. Poor, uneducated, uncultured. There are many men just like him. Who can work the land. Ab understands this situation. But is unwilling to accept his inferior status. Consequently, he approaches new employers with arrogance, and his actions and manner soon causing trouble. This behavior, of course, ensures his eventual dismissal. Ab feels that because he can never gain their respect. He should not even bother behaving in a civilized manner. So he insists on playing the role. Of a belligerent, raging man.

Ab's behavior sets in motion a self-fulfilling prophecy. Each time Ab's actions cause an employer to ask him to leave, his prophecy that he will be mistreated is fulfilled. He pretends that the failure is his employer's, not his own. And vents his frustration. By destroying the employer's property with fire. He also feels that such actions will earn him respect. People will be frightened of him, and he will create a name for himself. Only Ab's son, Sarty, sees the truth. That Ab is to his employers "no more . . . than a buzzing wasp."

CHAPTER 16

REVISING COMMA SPLICES AND FUSED SENTENCES

A **comma splice** occurs when two independent clauses are joined by a comma alone. A **fused sentence** occurs when two independent clauses are joined with no punctuation.

COMMA SPLICE: Charles Dickens created the character of Mr. Micawber, he also created Uriah Heep.

FUSED SENTENCE: Charles Dickens created the character of Mr. Micawber he also created Uriah Heep.

REVISED: Charles Dickens created the character of Mr. Micawber. He also created Uriah Heep.

✔ CHECKLIST: REVISING COMMA SPLICES AND FUSED SENTENCES

To determine whether you have created a comma splice or fused sentence, ask these two questions.

✔ Does your sentence join two independent clauses with a comma alone? If so, it is a comma splice.
✔ Does your sentence join two independent clauses with no punctuation? If so, it is a fused sentence.

If you identify a comma splice or fused sentence in your writing, you can use one of the following strategies to revise it.

✔ Use a period to separate the clauses, creating two sentences.
✔ Use a semicolon between the clauses, creating a compound sentence.
✔ Add an appropriate coordinating conjunction (and a comma if necessary) between the clauses, creating a compound sentence.
✔ Use a subordinating conjunction or relative pronoun to link the clauses, creating a complex sentence.

16a Revising with Periods

Use a period to separate independent clauses, creating two sentences when the clauses are of equal importance but are not related closely enough to be joined in one sentence.

COMMA SPLICE: In 1894 Alfred Dreyfus, a Jewish captain in the French army, was falsely convicted of treason, his struggle for justice pitted the army and the Catholic establishment against the civil libertarians.

FUSED SENTENCE: In 1894 Alfred Dreyfus, a Jewish captain in the French army, was falsely convicted of treason his struggle for justice pitted the army and the Catholic establishment against the civil libertarians.

REVISED: In 1894 Alfred Dreyfus, a Jewish captain in the French army, was falsely convicted of treason. His struggle for justice pitted the army and the Catholic establishment against the civil libertarians.

CLOSE-UP COMMA SPLICES AND FUSED SENTENCES

Use a period—not a comma—to punctuate an interrupted quotation that consists of two complete sentences.

COMMA SPLICE: "This is a good course," Eric said, "in fact, I wish I'd taken it sooner."

REVISED: "This is a good course," Eric said. "In fact, I wish I'd taken it sooner."

 ## 16b Revising with Semicolons

See
30a

Use a semicolon between two **independent clauses** that are closely related, especially if you want to emphasize that relationship.

COMMA SPLICE: Chippendale chairs have straight legs, Queen Anne chairs have curved legs.

FUSED SENTENCE: Chippendale chairs have straight legs Queen Anne chairs have curved legs.

REVISED: Chippendale chairs have straight legs; Queen Anne chairs have curved legs.

COMMA SPLICE: In pre-World War II western Europe only a small elite had access to a university education, this situation changed dramatically after the war.

FUSED SENTENCE: In pre-World War II western Europe only a small elite had access to a university education this situation changed dramatically after the war.

REVISED: In pre-World War II western Europe only a small elite had access to a university education; this situation changed dramatically after the war.

 COMMA SPLICES AND FUSED SENTENCES

You cannot correct a comma splice or fused sentence simply by adding a **transitional word or phrase** (*however, nevertheless, therefore, for example, in fact, on the other hand,* and so on) between the independent clauses. You will still have a comma splice or fused sentence unless you also add a semicolon or period before the transitional word or phrase.

See 30b

COMMA SPLICE: The international date line is drawn north and south through the Pacific Ocean, largely at the 180th meridian, thus, it separates Wake and Midway islands.

FUSED SENTENCE: The international date line is drawn north and south through the Pacific Ocean, largely at the 180th meridian thus, it separates Wake and Midway islands.

REVISED: The international date line is drawn north and south through the Pacific Ocean, largely at the 180th meridian; thus, it separates Wake and Midway islands. (Semicolon is added before transitional word.)

REVISED: The international date line is drawn north and south through the Pacific Ocean, largely at the 180th meridian. Thus, it separates Wake and Midway islands. (Period is added before transitional word.)

16c Revising with Coordinating Conjunctions

See
23g

If two closely related clauses are of equal importance, you can join them into one compound sentence, using a **coordinating conjunction** to indicate whether the clauses are linked by addition (*and*), contrast (*but, yet*), causality (*for, so*), or a choice of alternatives (*or, nor*).

COMMA SPLICE: Elias Howe invented the sewing machine, Julia Ward Howe was a poet and social reformer.

FUSED SENTENCE: Elias Howe invented the sewing machine Julia Ward Howe was a poet and social reformer.

REVISED: Elias Howe invented the sewing machine, but Julia Ward Howe was a poet and social reformer. (Coordinating conjunction *but* shows that emphasis is on contrast.)

16d Revising with Subordinating Conjunctions or Relative Pronouns

See
11b

When the ideas in two clauses are not of equal importance, correct the comma splice or fused sentence by creating a **complex sentence**, placing the less important idea in a dependent clause. The subordinating conjunction or relative pronoun establishes the nature of the relationship between the clauses.

COMMA SPLICE: Stravinsky's ballet *The Rite of Spring* shocked Parisians in 1913, its rhythms and the dancers' movements seemed erotic.

FUSED SENTENCE: Stravinsky's ballet *The Rite of Spring* shocked Parisians in 1913 its rhythms and the dancers' movements seemed erotic.

REVISED: Because its rhythms and the dancers' movements seemed erotic, Stravinsky's ballet *The Rite of Spring* shocked Parisians in 1913. (Subordinating conjunction *because* has been added to make the second clause subordinate to the first; the result is one complex sentence.)

COMMA SPLICE: Lady Mary Wortley Montagu had suffered from smallpox herself, she helped spread the practice of inoculation against the disease in eighteenth-century England.

Fused Sentence: Lady Mary Wortley Montagu had suffered from smallpox herself she helped spread the practice of inoculation against the disease in eighteenth-century England.

Revised: Lady Mary Wortley Montagu, who had suffered from smallpox herself, helped spread the practice of inoculation against the disease in eighteenth-century England. (Relative pronoun *who* has been added to make the first clause subordinate to the second; the result is a complex sentence.)

CLOSE-UP COMMA SPLICES AND FUSED SENTENCES

In a few special cases comma splices may be acceptable. For instance, a comma is used in dialogue between a statement and a tag question, even though each is a separate independent clause.

This is Ron's house, isn't it?

I'm not late, am I?

In addition, commas may connect two short balanced independent clauses or two or more short parallel independent clauses, especially when one clause contradicts the other.

Commencement isn't the end, it's the beginning.

EXERCISE 1

Find the comma splices and fused sentences in the following paragraph. Correct each in *two* of the four possible ways listed on page 291. If a sentence is correct, leave it alone.

Example: The fans rose in their seats, the game was almost over.

The fans rose in their seats; the game was almost over.

The fans rose in their seats, for the game was almost over.

Entrepreneurship is the study of small businesses, college students are embracing it enthusiastically. Many schools offer one or more courses in entrepreneurship these courses teach the theory and practice of starting a small business. Students are signing up for courses, moreover, they are starting their own businesses. One student started with a car-waxing business, now he sells condominiums. Other students are setting up catering services they supply everything from waiters to bartenders. One student has a thriving cake-decorating business, in fact, she employs fifteen students to deliver the cakes. All over the country, student businesses are selling everything from tennis balls to bagels, the student owners are making impressive profits. Formal courses at the graduate as well as undergraduate level are attracting more business students than ever, several business schools (such as Baylor University, the University of Southern California, and Babson College) even offer degree programs in entrepreneurship. Many business school students are no longer planning to be corporate executives instead, they plan to become entrepreneurs.

EXERCISE 2

Combine each of the following sentence pairs into one sentence without creating comma splices or fused sentences. In each case, connect the clauses into a compound sentence with a semicolon or with a comma and a coordinating conjunction. Use each method at least twice. You may have to add, delete, reorder, or change words or punctuation.

> EXAMPLE: People think of spring when they see crocuses blooming and robins hopping along on their lawns. I have less traditional methods for telling when spring is imminent.

> REVISED: People think of spring when they see crocuses blooming and robins hopping along on their lawns, but I have less traditional methods for telling when spring is imminent.

1. Tiny fragments of broken egg shells are one sign. Dog hair clumping in the corners of my rooms is another.
2. I know it's time to break out the light-blocking shades in mid-March. I move my bed across the room, away from the window.
3. The sound of geese retreating is another clue. The woodpeckers begin searching for termites again in the sides of my wood-shingled house.
4. The baby mice start to rustle around in the old newspapers in the garage. I have to hide the sugar bowl from the ants.
5. I think T. S. Eliot was right. April is the cruelest month.

EXERCISE 3

Combine each of the following sentence pairs into one sentence without creating comma-splice or fused-sentence errors. In each case, subordinate one clause to the other to create a complex sentence. You may have to add, delete, reorder, or change words or punctuation.

> EXAMPLE: I grew up on the beach in Florida. People think I'm lucky.

> REVISED: Because I grew up on the beach in Florida, people think I'm lucky.

1. Other beach rats know better than to envy me. Inlanders romanticize life by the ocean.

2. The sound of the waves is comforting. The sand gets into everything.
3. In the summer, tourists clog the roads. In the winter, many of the locals are out of work.
4. Beach towns have a difficult time attracting any stable industry. Taxes are often prohibitive.
5. After a while, going to the beach in the summer loses its charm. The beach in winter, empty of other people, is a beautiful sight.

EXERCISE 4

Combine each of the following sentence pairs into one sentence without creating comma splices or fused sentences. In each case, either connect the clauses into a compound sentence with a semicolon or with a comma and a coordinating conjunction, or subordinate one clause to the other to create a complex sentence. You may have to add, delete, reorder, or change words or punctuation.

1. Several recent studies indicate that many American high school students have a poor sense of history. This is affecting our future as a democratic nation and as individuals.
2. Surveys show that nearly one-third of American seventeen-year-olds cannot identify the countries the United States fought against in World War II. One-third think Columbus reached the New World after 1750.
3. Several reasons have been given for this decline in historical literacy. The main reason is the way history is taught.
4. This problem is bad news. The good news is that there is increasing agreement among educators about what is wrong with current methods of teaching history.
5. History can be exciting and engaging. Too often it is presented in a boring manner.
6. Students are typically expected to memorize dates, facts, and names. History as adventure—as a "good story"—is frequently neglected.
7. One way to avoid this problem is to use good textbooks. Texts should be accurate, lively, and focused.
8. Another way to create student interest in historical events is to use primary sources instead of so-called comprehensive textbooks. Autobiographies, journals, and diaries can give students insight into larger issues.
9. Students can also be challenged to think about history by taking sides in a debate. They can learn more about connections among historical events by writing essays than by taking multiple-choice tests.
10. Finally, history teachers should be less concerned about specific historical details. They should be more concerned about conveying the wonder of history.

Revising Comma Splices and Fused Sentences

Read the following answer to an economics examination question that asked students to discuss the provisions of the 1935 Social Security Act; then, correct all comma splices and fused sentences. After you have corrected the errors, go over the answer again and, if necessary, revise further to strengthen coherence, unity, and style.

In June of 1934 Franklin D. Roosevelt selected Frances Perkins to head the new Committee on Economic Security, its report was the basis of our current Social Security program. The committee formulated two policies, one dealt with the employable the other with the unemployable. Roosevelt insisted that these programs be self-financing, as a result both employer insurance and employee social insurance were required. In 1935 the Social Security Act was passed it attempted to categorize the poor and provided for federal sharing of the cost, but under local control. (The Social Security Act did not include a public works program, this feature of the New Deal was eliminated.)

Unemployment insurance was one major part of the act. Funds were to be payable through public employment offices, also the money was to be paid into a trust fund. It was to be used solely for benefits an individual could not be denied funds even if work were available. The program provided for payroll taxes, in addition separate records were to be kept by each state. Old Age Survivor Insurance, another major provision of the act, was for individuals over sixty-five it was amended in 1939 to cover dependents. One-quarter of the recipients were disabled. Public Assistance was the third major part of the act this program was designed to help children left alone by the death or absence of the parents and children with mental or physical disabilities. General assistance covered everything not included under the Public Assistance Program this coverage varied from state to state.

continued on the following page

continued from the previous page

The Social Security Act stressed public administration of federal emergency relief assistance thus, it forced reorganization of public assistance. These efforts differed from previous efforts earlier there were no clear guidelines defining which individuals should get aid and why. The Social Security Act attempted to eliminate gaps and overlaps in services.

CHAPTER 17

REVISING FAULTY MODIFICATION

A **modifier** is a word, phrase, or clause that acts as an adjective or an adverb—that is, describes, limits, or qualifies another word or word group in the sentence. A modifier is generally placed close to its **headword,** the word or word group it modifies, and readers expect to find it there.

Wendy watched the storm, <u>dark and threatening</u>.

Faulty modification, the awkward or confusing placement of modifiers or the modification of nonexistent words, takes two forms: *misplaced modifiers* and *dangling modifiers.*

17a Revising Misplaced Modifiers

A **misplaced modifier** is a word or word group whose placement indicates that it modifies one word or phrase when it is intended to modify another.

<u>Faster than a speeding bullet</u>, the citizens of Metropolis saw Superman flying overhead.

This introductory phrase appears to modify *citizens* when it should logically modify *Superman.* Here is a corrected version.

The citizens of Metropolis saw Superman flying overhead, <u>faster than a speeding bullet</u>.

When writing and revising, take care to put modifying words, phrases, and clauses in a position that clearly identifies the headword and that does not awkwardly interrupt a sentence.

Modify 17a

(1) Placing Modifying Words with Care

Certain modifiers—such as *almost, only, even, hardly, merely, nearly, exactly, scarcely, just,* and *simply*—should always immediately precede the words they modify. Different placements of these modifiers change the meaning of a sentence.

Nick *just* set up camp at the edge of the burned-out town. (He set up camp just now.)

Just Nick set up camp at the edge of the burned-out town. (He set up camp alone.)

Nick set up camp *just* at the edge of the burned-out town. (His camp was precisely at the edge.)

The imprecise placement of modifiers like these sometimes produces a **squinting modifier,** one that could modify either a word before it or one after it, conveying a different meaning in each case. To avoid ambiguity, place the modifier so it clearly modifies its headword.

SQUINTING:
The life that everyone thought would fulfill her <u>totally</u> bored her. (Was she supposed to be totally fulfilled, or is she totally bored?)

REVISED:
The life that everyone thought would <u>totally</u> fulfill her bored her. (Everyone expected her to be totally fulfilled.)

REVISED:
The life that everyone thought would fulfill her bored her <u>totally</u>. (She was totally bored.)

EXERCISE 1

In the following sentence pairs, the modifier in each sentence points to a different headword. Underline the modifier and draw an arrow to the word it modifies. Then explain the meaning of each sentence.

EXAMPLE: She <u>just</u> came in wearing a hat. (She just now entered.)

She came in wearing <u>just</u> a hat. (She wore only a hat.)

1. He wore his almost new jeans.
   He almost wore his new jeans.
2. He had only three dollars in his pocket.
   Only he had three dollars in his pocket.
3. I don't even like freshwater fish.
   I don't like even freshwater fish.

4. I go only to the beach on Saturdays.
   I go to the beach only on Saturdays.
5. He simply hated living.
   He hated simply living.

(2) Relocating Misplaced Phrases

Placing a modifying verbal or prepositional phrase incorrectly can change the meaning of a sentence or create an unclear or confusing sentence.

See 10c4

Misplaced Verbal Phrases A **verbal phrase** that acts as a modifier should be placed directly *before* or directly *after* the nouns or pronoun it modifies. The incorrect placement of a verbal phrase can make a sentence convey an entirely different meaning or make no sense at all.

MISPLACED: Jane watched the boats roller-skating along the shore. (Were the boats roller-skating?)

REVISED: Roller-skating along the shore, Jane watched the boats.

MISPLACED: Rolling down the hill, she watched the car. (Was she rolling down the hill?)

REVISED: She watched the car rolling down the hill.

See 10c3

Misplaced Prepositional Phrases A **prepositional phrase** used as an adjective nearly always directly *follows* the word it modifies.

This is a Dresden figurine from Germany.

Created by a famous artist, *Venus de Milo* is a statue with no arms.

Incorrect placement of such modifiers can give rise to confusion or even unintended humor.

Venus de Milo is a statue created by a famous artist with no arms.
   (Did the artist have no arms?)

A prepositional phrase used as an adverb also usually *follows* its headword.

Cassandra looked into the future.

Be careful to avoid ambiguous placement of prepositional phrases that serve as adverbs.

MISPLACED: She saw the house she built <u>in her mind</u>. (Did she build the house in her mind?)

REVISED: <u>In her mind</u>, she saw the house she built.

REVISED: She saw <u>in her mind</u> the house she built.

As long as the meaning of the sentence is clear, however, and as long as the headword is clearly identified, you can place an adverbial modifier in other positions.

He had been waiting anxiously at the bus stop <u>for a long time</u>.

EXERCISE 2

Underline the modifying verbal phrases or prepositional phrases in each sentence and draw arrows to their headwords.

> **EXAMPLE:** Calvin is the democrat <u>running for town council</u>.

1. The bridge across the river swayed in the wind.
2. The spectators on the shore were involved in the action.
3. Mesmerized by the spectacle, they watched the drama unfold.
4. The spectators were afraid of a disaster.
5. Within the hour, the state police arrived to save the day.
6. They closed off the area with roadblocks.
7. Drivers approaching the bridge were asked to stop.
8. Meanwhile, on the bridge, the scene was chaos.
9. Motorists in their cars were paralyzed with fear.
10. Struggling against the weather, the police managed to rescue everyone.

EXERCISE 3

Use the word or phrase that follows each sentence as a modifier in that sentence. Then draw an arrow to indicate its headword.

> **EXAMPLE:** He approached the lion. (timid)
>
> <u>Timidly</u>, he approached the lion.

1. The lion paced up and down in his cage, ignoring the crowd. (watching Jack)
2. Jack stared back at the lion. (nervous yet curious)
3. The crowd around them grew. (anxious to see what would happen)
4. Suddenly Jack heard a growl from deep in the lion's throat. (terrifying)
5. Jack ran from the zoo, leaving the lion behind. (scared to death)

(3) Revising Misplaced Dependent Clauses

A dependent clause that serves as a modifier must be clearly related to its headword. An adjective clause usually appears immediately *after* the word it modifies.

During the Civil War Lincoln was the president who governed the United States.

An adverb clause can appear in any of several positions, as long as the relationship to the word or word group it modifies is clear and as long as its position conveys the intended emphasis.

During the Civil War Lincoln was president.

Lincoln was president during the Civil War.

Correct misplaced dependent clauses by making the relationship between modifier and headword clear.

MISPLACED ADJECTIVE CLAUSE: This diet program will limit the consumption of possible carcinogens, which will benefit everyone. (Will carcinogens benefit everyone?)

REVISED: This diet program, which will benefit everyone, will limit the consumption of possible carcinogens.

MISPLACED ADVERB CLAUSE: The parents checked to see that the children were sleeping after they had a glass of wine. (Did the children drink the wine?)

REVISED: After they had a glass of wine, the parents checked to see that the children were sleeping.

EXERCISE 4

Relocate the misplaced verbal phrases, prepositional phrases, or dependent clauses so that they clearly point to the words or word groups they modify.

EXAMPLE: *Silent Running* is a film about a scientist left alone in space with Bruce Dern.

Silent Running is a film with Bruce Dern about a scientist left alone in space.

1. She realized that she had married the wrong man after the wedding.
2. *The Prince and the Pauper* is a novel about an exchange of identities by Mark Twain.

3. The energy was used up in the ten-kilometer race that he was saving for the marathon.
4. He loaded the bottles and cans into his new Porsche, which he planned to leave at the recycling center.
5. The manager explained the sales figures to the board members using a graph.

(4) Revising Intrusive Modifiers

An **intrusive modifier** interrupts a sentence, making it difficult to understand.

Interrupted Verb Phrases   Revise when a long modifying phrase comes between an auxiliary verb and a main verb.

AWKWARD: She <u>had</u>, without giving it a second thought or considering the consequences, <u>planned</u> to reenlist.

REVISED: Without giving it a second thought or considering the consequences, she <u>had planned</u> to reenlist.

AWKWARD: He <u>will</u>, if he ever gets his act together, <u>be</u> ready to leave on Friday.

REVISED: If he ever gets his act together, he <u>will</u> be ready to leave on Friday.

A brief modifier, however, can usually interrupt a verb phrase.

She <u>had</u> always <u>planned</u> to reenlist.

He <u>will</u>, therefore, <u>be</u> ready to leave on Friday.

Split Infinitives   Revise when modifiers awkwardly interrupt an **infinitive** (*to* plus the base form of the verb).

AWKWARD: He hoped <u>to</u> quickly and easily <u>defeat</u> his opponent.

REVISED: He hoped <u>to defeat</u> his opponent quickly and easily.

SPLIT INFINITIVES

Although at one time the general rule was never to split an infinitive, this is no longer the case. When the intervening modifier is short, and when the alternative is awkward or ambiguous, a split

continued on the following page

continued from the previous page

infinitive is acceptable. In the following sentence, for example, readers would have no trouble connecting the parts of the infinitive.

ACCEPTABLE: She expected <u>to</u> not quite <u>beat</u> her previous record.

Interrupted Subjects and Verbs or Verbs and Objects or Complements
It is standard practice to place a complex or lengthy adjective phrase or clause between a subject and a verb or between a verb and its object or complement.

ACCEPTABLE: Major <u>films</u> that were financially successful in the 1930s <u>include</u> *Gone with the Wind* and *The Wizard of Oz*. (Adjective clause between subject and verb does not obscure sentence's meaning.)

An adverb phrase or clause in this position, however, may not be clear or sound natural. Revise if you have any doubts about letting a modifier stand between subject and verb or between verb and object or complement.

CONFUSING: The <u>election</u>, because officials discovered that some people voted twice, <u>was</u> contested. (Adverb clause intrudes between subject and verb.)

REVISED: Because officials discovered that some people voted twice, the <u>election was</u> contested. (Subject and verb are no longer separated.)

CONFUSING: A. A. Milne <u>wrote</u>, when his son Christopher Robin was a child, <u>*Winnie the Pooh*</u>. (Adverb clause intrudes between verb and object.)

REVISED: When his son Christopher Robin was a child, A. A. Milne <u>wrote *Winnie the Pooh*</u>. (Verb and object are no longer separated.)

EXERCISE 5

Revise these sentences so that the modifying phrases or clauses do not interrupt the parts of a verb phrase or infinitive or separate a subject from a verb or a verb from its object or complement.

EXAMPLE: A play can sometimes be, despite the playwright's best efforts, mystifying to the audience.

Despite the playwright's best efforts, a play can sometimes be mystifying to the audience.

1. The people in the audience, when they saw the play was about to begin and realized the orchestra had finished tuning up and had begun the overture, finally quieted down.
2. They settled into their seats, expecting to very much enjoy the first act.
3. However, most people were, even after watching and listening for twenty minutes and paying close attention to the drama, completely baffled.
4. In fact, the play, because it had nameless characters, no scenery, and a rambling plot that didn't seem to be heading anywhere, puzzled even the drama critics.
5. Finally one of the three major characters explained, speaking directly to the audience, what the play was really about.

17b Revising Dangling Modifiers

A **dangling modifier** is a word or phrase that cannot logically describe, limit, or qualify any word or word group in the sentence. In fact, its true headword does not appear in the sentence. In the following sentence, *using this drug* is a dangling modifier.

Using this drug, many undesirable side effects are experienced.

Using this drug appears to modify *side effects,* but this interpretation makes no sense. Because its true headword does not appear in the sentence, the modifier dangles.

There are two ways to correct this dangling modifier. The first way is to *create a new subject* by supplying a word or word group that it can logically modify.

REVISED: Using this drug, patients experience many undesirable side effects.

The second way to correct the dangling modifier is to reword it to *create a dependent clause.*

REVISED: Many undesirable side effects are experienced when this drug is used.

These two options for correcting dangling modifiers are further explained and illustrated on page 308.

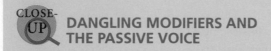

CLOSE-UP   DANGLING MODIFIERS AND THE PASSIVE VOICE

Most sentences that include dangling modifiers are in the passive voice and therefore do not include a headword. Changing the **passive voice** to **active voice** corrects the dangling modifier by changing the subject of the sentence's main clause to a word that the dangling modifier can logically modify.

Sometimes, however, passive voice is a desirable stylistic option. If you wish to retain the passive voice, you can correct the dangling modifier by supplying a subject.

REVISED: Many undesirable side effects are experienced by patients using this drug.

(1) Creating a New Subject

DANGLING: Using a pair of forceps, the skin of the rat's abdomen was lifted, and a small cut was made into the body with scissors. (Modifier cannot logically modify *skin.*)

REVISED: Using a pair of forceps, the technician lifted the skin of the rat's abdomen and made a small cut into the body with scissors. (Subject of main clause has been changed from *the skin* to *the technician,* a logical headword.)

DANGLING: With fifty pages left to read, *War and Peace* was absorbing. (Modifier cannot logically modify *War and Peace.*)

REVISED: With fifty pages left to read, Meg found *War and Peace* absorbing. (Subject of main clause has been changed from *War and Peace* to *Meg,* a logical headword.)

(2) Creating a Dependent Clause

DANGLING PHRASE: To implement a plus/minus grading system, all students were polled. (Modifier cannot logically modify *students.*)

REVISED: Before a plus/minus grading system was implemented, all students were polled. (Modifying phrase is now a dependent clause.)

DANGLING: On the newsstands only an hour, its sales surprised everyone. (Modifier cannot logically modify *sales*.)

REVISED: Because the magazine had been on the newsstands only an hour, its sales surprised everyone. (Modifying phrase is now a dependent clause.)

 REVISING DANGLING ELLIPTICAL CLAUSES

Elliptical clauses are incomplete constructions. Typically, the writer has intentionally omitted part of the subject or predicate (or the entire subject or predicate) from a dependent clause in order to create a more concise sentence. When such a clause cannot logically modify the subject of the sentence's main clause, it dangles. To revise a dangling elliptical clause, either create a new subject or create a complete dependent clause.

See
10b2

DANGLING: While still in the Buchner funnel, you should press the crystals with a clear stopper to eliminate any residual solvent. (Elliptical clause cannot logically modify *you*.)

REVISED: While still in the Buchner funnel, the crystals should be pressed with a clear stopper to eliminate any residual solvent. (Subject of main clause has been changed from *you* to *crystals*, a word the elliptical clause can logically modify.)

DANGLING: Though a high-pressure field, I find great personal satisfaction in nursing. (Elliptical clause cannot logically modify *I*.)

REVISED: Though it is a high-pressure field, I find great personal satisfaction in nursing. (Elliptical clause has been expanded into a complete dependent clause.)

EXERCISE 6

Eliminate the dangling modifier from each of the following sentences. Either supply a word or word group the dangling modifier can logically modify or change the dangling modifier into a dependent clause.

EXAMPLE: Skiing down the mountain, the restaurant seemed warm and inviting. (dangling modifier)

Skiing down the mountain, I thought the restaurant seemed warm and inviting. (logical headword added)

As I skied down the mountain, the restaurant seemed warm and inviting. (dependent clause)

1. Although architecturally unusual, most people agree that Buckminster Fuller's geodesic dome is well designed.
2. Writing for eight hours every day, her lengthy books are published every year or so.
3. As an out-of-state student without a car, it was difficult to get to off-campus cultural events.
4. To build a campfire, kindling is necessary.
5. Researched carefully by a staff of three, she wants everything in her books to be realistic and correct.
6. With every step upward, the trees became sparser.
7. Being an amateur tennis player, my backhand is weaker than my forehand.
8. To make her books more interesting, all the scenes are researched on location.
9. When exiting the train, the station will be on your right.
10. Driving through the Mojave, the bleak landscape was oppressive.
11. Written for a broad audience, she has enjoyed popular success.
12. By requiring auto manufacturers to further improve emission-control devices, the air quality will get better.
13. Using a piece of filter paper, the ball of sodium is dried as much as possible and placed in a test tube.
14. Having missed work for seven days straight, my job was in jeopardy.
15. Waiting for her next book to come out, libraries can't purchase enough copies.

STUDENT WRITER AT WORK

Revising Faulty Modification

Read this draft of a student's technical writing exercise, a description of a 10-cc syringe. Correct misplaced and dangling modifiers and revise again if necessary to strengthen coherence, unity, and style.

Designed to inject liquids into, or withdraw them from, any vessel or cavity, the function of a syringe is often to inject drugs into the body or

continued on the following page

continued from the previous page

withdraw blood from it. Syringes are also used to precisely measure amounts of drugs or electrolytes that must be added to intravenous solutions.

There are available on the market today many different types of syringes, but the one most commonly used in hospitals is the 10-cubic centimeter (cc) disposable syringe. Approximately 5 inches long, the primary composition of this particular syringe is transparent polyethylene plastic. The 10-cc syringe and the majority of other syringes all have a round plunger or piston within a barrel.

The barrel of a syringe is a round hollow cylinder about 4 1/2" long with a diameter of 3/8". The bottom end of the barrel has two extensions on its opposite sides, which are perpendicular to the cylinder. With a width equal to the diameter of the barrel, the length of these extensions is about 1/2". The purpose of these extensions is to enable one to hold with the index finger and middle finger the barrel of the syringe while depressing the plunger with the thumb.

The barrel of the syringe is calibrated on the side in black ink subdivided into gradations of 2cc. At the top of the syringe the barrel abruptly narrows to a very small cylinder, 1/8" in diameter and 1/4" in length. This small cylinder is surrounded by another hollow cylinder with a slightly larger diameter. The inside wall of the outer cylinder is threaded like a corkscrew. The purpose of this thread is to keep the needle in place.

The other major part of the syringe is the plunger. The plunger is a solid round cylinder that fits snugly into the barrel made of plastic. At the bottom of the plunger is a plastic ring the size of a dime, which provides something to grasp while withdrawing the plunger. The body of the plunger connects the bottom rim with the tip of the plunger, which is made of black rubber.

CHAPTER 18

REVISING FAULTY PARALLELISM

Parallelism is the use of corresponding grammatical elements—words, phrases, or clauses—or sentence structures to express equivalent ideas.

 Using Parallelism

Effective parallelism makes sentences clear and easy to follow and emphasizes relationships among equivalent ideas. It helps readers keep track of ideas and makes your emphasis clear.

(1) With Items in a Series

Coordinate elements—words, phrases, or clauses—in a series should be presented in parallel form. (For information on punctuating elements in a series, see **29b** and **30c.**)

Eat, drink, and be merry.

I came; I saw; I conquered.

Baby food consumption, toy production, and marijuana use are likely to decline as the US population grows older.

Three factors influenced his decision to seek new employment: his desire to relocate, his need for greater responsibility, and his dissatisfaction with his current job.

(2) With Paired Items

Paired points or ideas (words, phrases, or clauses) should be presented in parallel terms. Parallelism emphasizes their equivalence and relates the two ideas to each other.

The thank-you note was short but sweet.

Roosevelt represented the United States, and Churchill represented
Great Britain.

The research focused on muscle tissue and nerve cells.

Ask not what your country can do for you; ask what you can do for
your country. (John F. Kennedy, "Inaugural Address")

Paired items are frequently linked by **correlative conjunctions** (such
as *not only/but also, both/and, either/or, neither/nor,* and *whether/or*).
Items introduced by correlative conjunctions are always presented in
parallel form.

The design team paid close attention not only to color but also to
texture.

Either repeat physics or take calculus.

Both cable television and videocassette recorders continue to
threaten the dominance of the major television networks.

Parallelism is also used with paired elements linked by *than.* In such
cases, parallel structure stresses the contrast between the paired elements.

Richard Wright and James Baldwin chose to live in Paris rather than
to remain in the United States.

(3) In Lists and Outlines

Elements in a list should be expressed in parallel terms.

The Irish potato famine had four major causes:
1. The establishment of the landlord-tenant system
2. The failure of the potato crop
3. The reluctance of England to offer adequate financial assistance
4. The passage of the Corn Laws

Elements in a **formal outline** also should be parallel.

See
3c3

EXERCISE 1

Identify the parallel elements in these sentences by underlining parallel
words and bracketing parallel phrases and clauses.

EXAMPLE: Manek spent six years in America [going to school] and
[working for a computer company].

1. Manek returned to India after he completed his engineering degree to
visit his large extended family and to find a wife.
2. Unfamiliar with marriage practices in India and accustomed to
American notions of marriage for love, Manek's American friends
frowned on his plans.

3. Not only Manek but also his parents wanted an arranged marriage.
4. He didn't believe that either you married for love or you had a loveless marriage.
5. His parents' marriage, an arranged one, continued happily; his aunt's marriage, also arranged, has lasted thirty years.

EXERCISE 2

Combine each of the following sentence pairs or sentence groups into one sentence that uses parallel structure. Be sure all parallel words, phrases, and clauses are expressed in parallel terms.

1. Originally, there were five performing Marx Brothers. One was nicknamed Groucho. The others were called Chico, Harpo, Gummo, and Zeppo.
2. Groucho was very well known. So were Chico and Harpo. Gummo soon dropped out of the act. And later Zeppo did too.
3. They began in vaudeville. That was before World War I. Their first show was called *I'll Say She Is*. It opened in New York in 1924.
4. The Marx Brothers' first movie was *The Coconuts*. The next was *Animal Crackers*. And this was followed by *Monkey Business, Horsefeathers,* and *Duck Soup.* Then came *A Night at the Opera.*
5. In each of these movies, the Marx Brothers make people laugh. They also exhibit a unique, zany comic style.
6. In their movies, each brother has a set of familiar trademarks. Groucho has a mustache and a long coat. He wiggles his eyebrows and smokes a cigar. There is a funny hat that Chico always wears. And he affects a phony Italian accent. Harpo never speaks.
7. Groucho is always cast as a sly operator. He always tries to cheat people out of their money. He always tries to charm women.
8. In *The Coconuts* he plays Mr. Hammer, proprietor of the run-down Coconut Manor, a Florida hotel. In *Horsefeathers* his character is named Professor Quincy Adams Wagstaff. Wagstaff is president of Huxley College. Huxley also has financial problems.
9. In *Duck Soup* Groucho plays Rufus T. Firefly, president of the country of Fredonia. Fredonia was formerly ruled by the late husband of a Mrs. Teasdale. Fredonia is now at war with the country of Sylvania.
10. Margaret Dumont is often Groucho's leading lady. She plays Mrs. Teasdale in *Duck Soup.* In *A Night at the Opera* she plays Mrs. Claypool. Her character in *The Coconuts* is named Mrs. Potter.

18b Revising Faulty Parallelism

Faulty parallelism occurs when equivalent ideas in a sentence are not presented in corresponding grammatical terms. When a sentence is flawed by faulty parallelism, the ideas it equates are difficult to identify.

FAULTY PARALLELISM: Many people in developing countries suffer because the countries lack sufficient housing to accommodate them, sufficient food to feed them, and their health-care facilities are inadequate.

Because the three reasons in the sentence above are presented in a series, readers expect them to be expressed in parallel terms. The first two elements satisfy this expectation.

- sufficient housing to accommodate them
- sufficient food to feed them

The third item in the series, however, breaks this pattern.

- their health-care facilities are inadequate

To correct the faulty parallelism and create a clear, emphatic sentence, all three elements must be presented in the same terms.

Many people in developing countries suffer because the countries lack <u>sufficient housing to accommodate them</u>, <u>sufficient food</u> to <u>feed them</u>, and <u>sufficient health-care facilities to serve them</u>.

(1) Using Parallel Elements

To create parallelism, match nouns with nouns, verbs with verbs, and phrases and clauses with similarly constructed phrases and clauses.

FAULTY PARALLELISM:	REVISED:
Popular exercises for men and women include aerobic dancing, weight lifters, and jogging.	Popular exercises for men and women include aerobic <u>dancing</u>, <u>weight lifting</u>, and <u>jogging</u>.
Some of the side effects are skin irritation and eye irritation, and mucous membrane irritation may also develop.	Some of the side effects that may develop are <u>skin</u>, <u>eye</u>, and <u>mucous membrane</u> irritation.

315

FAULTY PARALLELISM:	REVISED:
I look forward to hearing from you and to have an opportunity to tell you more about myself.	I look forward to <u>hearing from you</u> and to <u>having an opportunity</u> to tell you more about myself.

(2) Repeating Signals of Parallelism

Faulty parallelism also occurs when a writer does not repeat words that signal parallelism: prepositions, articles, the *to* that is part of the infinitive, or the word that introduces a phrase or clause. Although the use of similar grammatical structures may sometimes be enough to convey parallelism, sentences are even clearer and more emphatic if other key words in parallel constructions are also parallel.

FAULTY PARALLELISM:	REVISED:
Computerization has helped industry by not allowing labor costs to skyrocket, increasing the speed of production, and improving efficiency. (Does *not* apply to all three phrases, or only the first?)	Computerization has helped industry <u>by not allowing labor costs to skyrocket</u>, <u>by increasing the speed of production</u>, and <u>by improving efficiency</u>. (Preposition *by* is repeated to clarify the boundaries of the three parallel phrases.)

(3) Repeating Relative Pronouns

Like correlative conjunctions, *who . . . and who, whom . . . and whom,* and *which . . . and which* are always paired and always introduce parallel clauses. If you omit the first part of the expression, you throw readers off balance.

INCORRECT: *The Thing,* directed by Howard Hawks, and which was released in 1951, featured James Arness as the monster.

REVISED: *The Thing,* <u>which</u> was directed by Howard Hawks <u>and</u> <u>which</u> was released in 1951, featured James Arness as the monster.

NOTE: In some cases both relative pronouns can be eliminated: *The Thing,* directed by Howard Hawks and released in 1951, featured James Arness as the monster.

EXERCISE 3

Identify and correct faulty parallelism in these sentences. Then underline the parallel elements—words, phrases, and clauses—in your corrected sentences. If a sentence is already correct, mark it with a *C* and underline the parallel elements.

EXAMPLE: Alfred Hitchcock's films include *North by Northwest, Vertigo, Psycho,* and he also directed *Notorious* and *Saboteur.*

REVISED: Films directed by Alfred Hitchcock include *North by Northwest, Vertigo, Psycho, Notorious,* and *Saboteur.*

1. The world is divided between those with galoshes on and those who discover continents.
2. Soviet leaders, members of Congress, and the American Catholic bishops all pressed the president to limit the arms race.
3. A national task force on education recommended improving public education by making the school day longer, higher teachers' salaries, and integrating more technology into the curriculum.
4. The fast-food industry is expanding to include many kinds of restaurants: those that serve pizza, fried-chicken chains, some offering Mexican-style menus, and hamburger franchises.
5. The consumption of Scotch in the United States is declining because of high prices, tastes are changing, and increased health awareness has led many whiskey drinkers to switch to wine or beer.

STUDENT WRITER AT WORK

Revising Faulty Parallelism

In the following section of a draft of a paper written for a class in public health, a student discusses factors that must be taken into account by medical practitioners at the Indian Health Service. Correct the faulty parallelism and revise again if necessary to strengthen coherence, unity, and style.

The average life span of Native Americans is considerably lower than that of the general population. Not only is their infant mortality rate four times higher than that of the general population, but they also have a suicide rate that is twice as high as that of other races. Moreover, Native Americans both die in homicides more often than people of other races do and there are more alcohol-related deaths among Native Americans than

continued on the following page

continued from the previous page
among people of other races. Medical care available for them does not meet their needs and is presenting a challenge for the health professionals who serve them.

The Indian Health Service (IHS), a branch of the US Public Health Service, is responsible for providing medical care to Native Americans who live on reservations. The IHS has been criticized for its inability to deal with cultural differences between health professionals and Native Americans-- cultural differences that interfere with adequate medical care. In order to diagnose disease states, for prescribing drug therapy, and to counsel patients, health professionals need to acquire an understanding of Native American culture. They must gain a working knowledge of Native Americans' ideas and feelings toward health and also God, relationships, and death. Only then can health professionals communicate their goals, provide quality medical care, and in addition they will be able to achieve patient compliance.

There are many obstacles to effective communication: hostility to white authority and whites' structured, organized society; language is another obvious barrier to communication; Native Americans' view of sickness, which may be different from Anglos'; and some Indian cultures' concept of time is also different from that of the Anglo health workers. Other problems are more basic: a physician cannot expect a patient to refrigerate medication if no refrigerators are available or dilute dosage forms at home or be changing wet dressings several times a day if clean water is not readily available nor quart/pint measuring devices to dilute stock solutions.

The problems in Native American health care cannot be completely solved by the improvement of communication channels or making these channels stronger. But the health professionals' communication with the

continued on the following page

continued from the previous page
Native American patient can be effective enough so that medical staff can acquire an adequate medical history, monitor drug use, be alert for possible drug interactions, and to provide useful discharge counseling. If health professionals can communicate understanding and respect for Native American culture and concern for their welfare, they may be able to meet the needs of their Native American patients more effectively.

CHAPTER 19

REVISING AWKWARD OR CONFUSING SENTENCES

Confusing, hard-to-understand sentences are most often caused by unwarranted shifts, mixed constructions, faulty predication, or illogical comparisons.

19a Shifts in Tense

See 25f

Verb tenses in a sentence or in a related group of sentences should shift only with good reason—to indicate changes of time, for example.

The Wizard of Oz <u>is</u> a film that has enchanted audiences since it <u>was made</u> in 1939. (acceptable shift from present to past)

Unwarranted shifts can mislead readers and obscure your meaning.

FAULTY: The prisoner <u>told</u> the parole board that he <u>promises</u> to stay out of trouble. (unwarranted shift from past to present)

REVISED: The prisoner <u>told</u> the parole board that he <u>promised</u> to stay out of trouble. (both verbs in past tense)

FAULTY: On the Road <u>is</u> a novel about friends who <u>drove</u> across the United States in the 1950s. (unwarranted shift from present to past)

See 51c

REVISED: On the Road <u>is</u> a novel about friends who <u>drive</u> across the United States in the 1950s. (<u>literary work</u> discussed in both clauses; both verbs in present tense)

FAULTY: Medical researchers <u>know</u> that asbestos <u>caused</u> cancer. (unwarranted shift from present to past tense)

Revised: Medical researchers <u>know</u> that asbestos <u>causes</u> cancer. (general truth stated in both clauses; both verbs in **present tense**)

See
25c1

Faulty: I <u>registered</u> for Media and Society because it sounded interesting. After the first week, however, I <u>start</u> having trouble understanding the lectures, so I <u>go</u> to the instructor, and he <u>tells</u> me I should be attending the recitations. (unwarranted shift from past to present)

Revised: I <u>registered</u> for Media and Society because it sounded interesting. After the first week, however, I <u>started</u> having trouble understanding the lectures, so I <u>went</u> to the instructor, and he <u>told</u> me I should be attending the recitations. (all verbs in past tense)

19b Shifts in Voice

Unwarranted shifts from active to passive voice (or from passive to active) can confuse and mislead readers. In the following sentence, for instance, the shift from active (*wrote*) to passive (*was written*) creates ambiguity.

Faulty: F. Scott Fitzgerald <u>wrote</u> *This Side of Paradise,* and later *The Great Gatsby* <u>was written</u>. (Who wrote *The Great Gatsby?*)

Revised: F. Scott Fitzgerald wrote *This Side of Paradise* and later wrote *The Great Gatsby.* (consistent use of active voice)

 SHIFTS IN VOICE

Sometimes a shift from active to passive voice may be necessary to give a sentence proper emphasis.

Even though consumers protested, the gasoline tax was increased.

Here the shift from active (*protested*) to passive (*was increased*) enables the writer to keep the focus on consumer groups and the issue they protested. To say *the state legislature increased the gasoline tax* would shift readers' attention to the legislature.

19c Shifts in Mood

See
25g, h

Unnecessary shifts in **mood** can also be confusing and annoying.

FAULTY: It is important that each student buy a dictionary and uses it. (shift from subjunctive to indicative mood)

REVISED: It is important that each student buy a dictionary and use it. (both verbs in subjunctive mood)

FAULTY: Next, heat the mixture in a test tube, and you should make sure it does not boil. (shift from imperative to indicative mood)

REVISED: Next, heat the mixture in a test tube and be sure it does not boil. (both verbs in imperative mood)

19d Shifts in Person and Number

Person indicates who is speaking (first person—*I, we*), who is spoken to (second person—*you*), and who is spoken about (third person—*he, she, it,* and *they*).

Unwarranted shifts between second- and third-person pronouns cause most errors.

FAULTY: When one looks for a car loan, you compare the interest rates of several banks. (shift from third to second person)

REVISED: When you look for a car loan, you compare the interest rates of several banks. (consistent use of second person)

REVISED: When people look for car loans, they compare the interest rates of several banks. (consistent use of third person)

See
26b

Number indicates one (singular—*novel, it*) or more than one (plural—*novels, they, them*). Singular **pronouns** should refer to singular antecedents and plural pronouns to plural antecedents.

FAULTY: If a person does not study regularly, they will have a difficult time passing organic chemistry. (shift from singular to plural)

REVISED: If a person does not study regularly, he or she will have a difficult time passing organic chemistry. (Singular pronouns refer to singular antecedent.)

REVISED: If <u>students</u> do not study regularly, <u>they</u> will have a difficult time passing organic chemistry. (Plural pronoun refers to plural antecedent.)

SHIFTS IN PERSON AND NUMBER

Although college writing follows standard conventions of pronoun-antecedent agreement, use of a plural pronoun referring to a singular antecedent is increasingly common in speech and in informal writing, when such use enables the speaker or writer to avoid **sexist language**.

Buddy Holly and Janis Joplin <u>each</u> made a significant contribution with <u>their</u> music.

See
20f2

EXERCISE 1

Read the following sentences and eliminate any shifts in tense, voice, mood, person, or number. Some sentences are correct, and some can be revised in more than one way.

EXAMPLE: When one looks at the history of the women's movement, you see that it had many different beginnings.

REVISED: When you look at the history of the women's movement, you see that it had many different beginnings.

1. Some historians see World War II and women's work in the factories as the beginning of the push toward equal rights for women.

2. Women went to work in the fabric mills of Lowell, Massachusetts, in the late 1800s, and her efforts at reforming the workplace are seen by many as the beginning of the equal rights movement.

3. Farm girls from New Hampshire, Vermont, and western Massachusetts came to Lowell to make money for their trousseaus, and they wanted to experience life in the city.

4. The factories promised the girls decent wages, and parents were promised that their daughters would live in a safe, wholesome environment.

5. Dormitories were built by the factory owners; they are supposed to ensure a safe environment for the girls.

6. First, visit the loom rooms at the Boot Mills Factory, and then you should tour a replica of a dormitory.
7. When one visits the working loom room at the factory, you are overcome with a sense of the risks and dangers the girls faced in the mills.
8. For a mill girl, moving to the city meant freedom and an escape from the drudgery of farm life; it also meant they had to face many new social situations for which they weren't always prepared.
9. Harriet Robinson wrote *Loom and Spindle*, the story of her life as a mill girl, and then a book of poems was published.
10. When you look at the lives of the loom girls, one can see that their work laid part of the foundation for women's later demands for equal rights.

19e Shifts from Direct to Indirect Discourse

Direct discourse quotes the exact words of a speaker or writer. The words are always enclosed in quotation marks and often accompanied by an **identifying tag** (*he says, she asked*). **Indirect discourse** summarizes the words of a speaker or writer. Because words are not quoted directly, no quotation marks are used; the identifying tag is often followed by the word *that* (or, in the case of questions, with *who, what, why, whether, how,* or *if*).

DIRECT DISCOURSE: My instructor said, "<u>I want</u> your paper by this Friday."

INDIRECT DISCOURSE: My instructor said that <u>he wanted</u> my paper by this Friday.

NOTE: Direct and indirect discourse use different verb tenses.

Statements and questions that shift between indirect and direct discourse are often confusing to readers.

FAULTY: During the trial, John Brown repeatedly defended his actions and said that <u>I am not guilty</u>. (shift from indirect to direct discourse)

REVISED: During the trial, John Brown repeatedly defended his actions and said, " <u>I am not guilty</u>." (consistent use of direct discourse)

REVISED: During the trial, John Brown repeatedly defended his actions and said <u>that he was not guilty</u>. (consistent use of indirect discourse)

FAULTY: My mother asked <u>was I ever going to get a job</u>. (question is neither direct nor indirect discourse)

REVISED: My mother asked <u>whether I was ever going to get a job.</u> (consistent use of indirect discourse)

REVISED: My mother asked, "<u>Are you ever going to get a job?</u>" (consistent use of direct discourse)

EXERCISE 2

Change the direct discourse in the following sentences to indirect discourse. Remember to use the present tense when discussing general truths or literary works.

EXAMPLE: Anna Quindlen explained why she kept her maiden name when she married: "It was a political decision, a simple statement that I was somebody and not an adjunct of anybody, especially a husband."

Anna Quindlen explained that she made a decision to keep her maiden name when she married because it was a simple political statement that she was somebody and not an adjunct to anybody, especially not to a husband.

1. In cases of possible sexual harassment, Ellen Goodman suggests a "reasonable woman standard" be applied: "How would a reasonable woman interpret this? How would a reasonable woman behave?"

2. Sally Thane Christensen, advocating the use of an endangered species of tree, the yew, as a treatment for cancer, asked, "Is a tree worth a life?"

3. Stephen Nathanson, considering the morality of the death penalty, asked, "What if the death penalty did save lives?"

4. Martin Luther King, Jr., said, "I have a dream that one day this nation will rise up and live out the true meaning of its creed."

5. Mohandas K. Gandhi wrote, "Complete civil disobedience is a state of peaceful rebellion—a refusal to obey every single State-made law."

6. Benjamin Franklin once stated, "The older I grow, the more apt I am to doubt my own judgment of others."

7. Speaking of the theater of the absurd in 1962, Edward Albee asked, "Is it, as it has been accused of being, obscure, sordid, destructive, anti-theater, perverse, and absurd (in the sense of foolish)?"

8. Thoreau said, "The finest qualities of our nature, like the bloom on fruits, can be preserved only by the most delicate handling."

9. In *Death Knocks,* Death asks Nat, "Who should I look like?"

10. In *Death of a Salesman,* Linda stands by her husband's grave after his funeral and asks, "Why didn't anybody come?"

19f Mixed Constructions

A **mixed construction** occurs when a sentence begins with one grammatical strategy and then abruptly shifts to another. Typically, this occurs when a prepositional phrase or a dependent or independent clause is illogically used as the subject of a sentence.

MIXED: Because she studies every day explains why she gets good grades.

Here the sentence begins with a dependent clause (*Because she studies every day*), which should logically be followed by an independent clause. Instead, the dependent clause is incorrectly used as the subject of the sentence. Deleting *explains why* creates a correct sentence.

REVISED: Because she studies every day, she gets good grades.

The following groups of sentences illustrate the three most common kinds of mixed constructions and present some options for revision.

MIXED: By calling for information is the way to learn more about the benefits of ROTC. (Prepositional phrase cannot logically serve as subject.)

REVISED: By calling for information you can learn more about the benefits of ROTC. (Subject *you* is provided.)

REVISED: Calling for information is one way to learn more about the benefits of ROTC. (Prepositional phrase has been changed to gerund phrase, which can serve as a sentence's subject.)

MIXED: Even though he published a paper on the subject does not mean he should get credit for the discovery. (Dependent clause cannot logically serve as subject.)

REVISED: Even though he published a paper on the subject, he should not get credit for the discovery. (Subject *he* is provided.)

REVISED: Publishing a paper on the subject does not necessarily mean he should get credit for the discovery. (Dependent clause has been changed to a gerund phrase, which can serve as a sentence's subject.)

MIXED: He was late was what made him miss Act 1. (Independent clause cannot logically serve as subject.)

REVISED: Being late made him miss Act 1. (Independent clause has been changed to a gerund phrase, which can serve as a sentence's subject.)

REVISED: Because he was late, he missed Act 1. (Independent clause has been changed to a dependent clause, creating a complex sentence.)

EXERCISE 3

Revise the following mixed constructions so their parts fit together both grammatically and logically.

> EXAMPLE: By investing in commodities made her rich.
>
> Investing in commodities made her rich.

1. In implementing the "motor voter" bill has made it easier for people to register to vote.
2. She sank the basket was the reason they won the game.
3. Just because situations change, doesn't change the characters' hopes and dreams.
4. By dropping the course would be his only chance to avoid a low GPA.
5. Even though she works for a tobacco company does not mean that she should be against laws prohibiting smoking in restaurants.

19g Faulty Predication

Faulty predication (sometimes called *illogical predication*) occurs when a sentence's predicate does not logically complete its subject.

(1) Incorrect Use of *Be*

Faulty predication is especially common in sentences that contain a *linking verb*—a form of the verb *be*, for example—and a subject complement.

FAULTY: Mounting costs and decreasing revenues <u>were the downfall</u> of the hospital.

This sentence incorrectly states that mounting costs and decreasing revenues were the *downfall* of the hospital when, in fact, they were the *reasons* for its downfall. You can correct this problem by providing a subject complement that relates logically to the subject.

REVISED: Mounting costs and decreasing revenues <u>were the reasons</u> for the downfall of the hospital.

(2) Intervening Words

Faulty predication can also occur when intervening words obscure the connection between the subject and the verb. When you revise, be sure the connection between subject and verb is logical.

FAULTY: The <u>purpose</u> of Hitler's campaign <u>failed</u> because of the severity of the Russian winter. (Intervening words obscure the relationship between the subject, *purpose,* and the verb, *failed.*)

REVISED: <u>Hitler's campaign failed</u> because of the severity of the Russian winter. (*Hitler's campaign* is now the sentence's subject.)

REVISED: The <u>purpose</u> of Hitler's campaign <u>was thwarted</u> by the severity of the Russian winter. (The verb is now consistent with the subject.)

(3) *Is When* or *Is Where*

Another kind of faulty predication occurs when sentences that present a definition contain constructions like *is where* or *is when*. Keep in mind that a definition must have a noun or noun phrase on <u>both</u> sides of *is.*

FAULTY: <u>Taxidermy</u> is <u>where you construct</u> a lifelike representation of an animal from its preserved skin. (In a definition, the form of the verb *be* must be preceded and followed by nouns or noun phrases.)

REVISED: <u>Taxidermy</u> is <u>the construction</u> of a lifelike representation of an animal from its preserved skin. (The subject complement is now a noun phrase.)

(4) *The Reason . . . Is Because*

A similar type of faulty predication occurs when the phrase *the reason is* precedes *because.* (*Because,* which means "for the reason that," is redundant and can be deleted.)

FAULTY: <u>The reason</u> we drive <u>is because</u> we are afraid to fly.

REVISED: <u>The reason</u> we drive <u>is that</u> we are afraid to fly.

REVISED: We drive because we are afraid to fly.

(5) Faulty Appositive

A **faulty appositive** is a type of faulty predication in which an appositive is equated with a noun or pronoun it cannot logically modify.

FAULTY: The salaries are high in <u>professional athletics, such as baseball players.</u> (*Professional athletics* is not the same as *baseball players.*)

REVISED: The salaries are high for <u>professional athletes, such as baseball players.</u> (*baseball players = professional athletes*)

EXERCISE 4

Revise the following sentences to eliminate faulty predication. Keep in mind that each sentence may be revised in more than one way.

EXAMPLE: The reason traffic jams occur at 9 a.m. and 5 p.m. is because too many people work traditional rather than staggered hours.

REVISED: Traffic jams occur at 9 a.m. and 5 p.m. because too many people work traditional rather than staggered hours.

1. Inflation is when the purchasing power of currency declines.
2. Hypertension is where the blood pressure is elevated.
3. Computers have become part of our everyday lives, such as instant cash machines.
4. Some people say the reason for the increasing violence in American cities is because guns are too easily available.
5. The reason for all the congestion in American cities is because too many people live too close together.

19h Incomplete or Illogical Comparisons

A comparison tells how two things are alike or unlike. When you make a comparison, be sure it is *complete* (that readers can tell what two items are being compared) and *logical* (that it equates two comparable items).

INCOMPLETE: My communications course is harder. (What two things are being compared?)

COMPLETE: My communications course is harder <u>than Craig's</u>. (Comparison is now complete.)

ILLOGICAL: The intelligence of a pig is greater than a dog. (illogically compares the intelligence of a pig to a dog)

LOGICAL: The intelligence of a pig is greater than <u>that of</u> a dog.

EXERCISE 5

Revise the following sentences to correct any incomplete or illogical comparisons.

INCOMPLETE: Technology-based industries are concerned about inflation as much as service industries.

COMPLETE: Technology-based industries are concerned about inflation as much as service industries are.

1. Opportunities in technical writing are more promising than business writing.

329

2. Technical writing is more challenging.
3. In some ways, technical writing requires more attention to detail and is, therefore, more difficult.
4. Business writers are concerned about clarity as much as technical writers.
5. Technology-based industries may one day create more writing opportunities than any industry.

STUDENT WRITER AT WORK

Revising Awkward or Confusing Sentences

Following is an excerpt from a draft of a student's research paper on immigrant factory workers in New York City in the early twentieth century. In this section of her paper, the student focuses on a devastating fire that eventually contributed to the creation of stricter fire safety codes. Read the paragraphs and correct any mixed constructions, faulty predication, unwarranted grammatical shifts, or incomplete or illogical comparisons. If necessary, revise further to strengthen coherence, unity, and style.

In one particularly compelling section of <u>World of Our Fathers</u>, Irving Howe describes the devastating 1911 fire at the Triangle Shirtwaist Company (304–6). By quoting an eyewitness account and contemporary reactions and by reproducing graphic photographs is how he added drama to his account of an already dramatic event. For instance, Howe quotes labor activist Rose Schneiderman, who said this is not the first time girls have been burned alive in this city, and "The life of men and women is so cheap and property is so sacred" (305).

In his book <u>The Triangle Fire</u>, Leon Stein suggests that the fire, in the ten-story Asch Building near Washington Square in New York City, probably began with a cigarette or spark in a rag bin. Some people in the building apparently tried dousing the flames, but because of rotted hoses and rusted water valves made their efforts useless (15).

The announcement of the many causes of the fire deaths was obvious. According to the investigating committee, the one fire escape

continued on the following page

continued from the previous page

visible from Greene Street collapsed after fewer than twenty people escaped. In addition, although sprinkler systems had been invented in 1895 did not mean any were present in the Asch Building. They were considered more expensive. Records show that six months before the fire, the building was cited as a firetrap by the city. The owners failed to make alterations was what the report identified as a cause of the fire. Failure to have regular fire drills and a lack of clearly marked exits also contributed to the high death toll (Stein 117–19).

Because it was 4:30 p.m. on a Saturday--a work day--when the fire broke out meant that there were 650 workers in the building. The majority of these were young Jewish and Italian women, and there was no common language spoken by them. By not sharing a common language was one reason for the chaos among the workers (Stein 14–15). When those on the ninth floor found the fire exit doors locked, their panic peaked. With their exit blocked forced everyone to jump from the windows to avoid the intense fire that swept through the building. Although it took firefighters only eighteen minutes to bring the fire under control, 146 workers died.

PART 5

USING WORDS EFFECTIVELY

CHAPTER 20

CHOOSING WORDS

20a Choosing an Appropriate Level of Diction

Diction, which comes from the Latin word meaning "say," denotes the choice and use of words. Different audiences and situations call for different levels of diction. When you know who your readers are and what they expect, you can determine the level of diction you should use.

(1) Formal Diction

Formal diction is grammatically correct and uses words familiar to an educated audience. For example, a writer using formal diction may choose *impoverished* rather than *poor, wealthy* or *affluent* rather than *rich, intelligent* rather than *smart,* and *automobile* rather than *car.* A writer who is using formal diction may also maintain emotional distance from the audience by using the impersonal *one.* In addition, the tone of the writing—as created by word choice and sentence structure—is dignified and objective. Academics frequently use formal diction in journal articles and books aimed at a learned audience.

> We learn to perceive in the sense that we learn to respond to things in particular ways because of the contingencies of which they are a part. We may perceive the sun, for example, simply because it is an extremely powerful stimulus, but it has been a permanent part of the environment of the species throughout its evolution, and more specific behavior with respect to it could have been selected by contingencies of survival (as it has been in many other species). (B. F. Skinner, *Beyond Freedom and Dignity*)

(2) Informal Diction

Informal diction is the language people use in conversation. Although you will encounter informal diction in your reading, you should use it in your college writing only to reproduce speech or dialect.

Colloquialisms **Colloquial diction,** the language of everyday speech, is perfectly acceptable in informal situations. Contractions—*isn't, won't, I'm, he'd*—are typical colloquialisms, as are **clipped forms**—**abbreviations** like *phone* for *telephone, TV* for *television, dorm* for *dormitory.* Other colloquialisms include placeholders like *you know, sort of, kind of,* and *I mean* and **utility words** like *nice, funny,* and *great.* Colloquial English also includes the use of *fun* as an adjective ("Rollerblading is a fun sport") and the use of *way* instead of *much* or *far* ("Costs are way too high"; "This school has way too many rules") as well as verb forms like *get across* for *communicate, come up with* for *find,* and *check out* for *investigate.*

See 28a2

See 13a2

Slang **Slang** is a vivid and forceful use of language that is often restricted to a single group—urban teenagers, rock musicians, or computer users, for example. Slang words are extremely informal. Whether they are newly coined phrases or existing words redefined, they add spice to spoken language and create group cohesion. For example, words like *uptight, hippie,* and *groovy* emerged in the 1960s. During the 1970s, technology, music, politics, and feminism influenced slang, giving us expressions like *hacker, disco, stonewalling,* and *macho.* The 1980s contributed *sound bite, yuppie,* and *chocoholic.* Slang in the 1990s includes expressions such as *clueless, wonk, hip hop,* and *downsize.*

Regionalisms **Regionalisms** are words, expressions, and idiomatic forms commonly used in particular geographical areas; such expressions may not be understood by or sound natural to a general audience. Regionalisms include words like *overshoe, fried cake,* and *angledog* and expressions like *take sick* and *come down with a cold.* In eastern Tennessee, for example, a paper bag is a *poke,* and empty soda bottles are *dope bottles.* In the Ozarks *I suspicioned* is used to mean *I suspected.* In Lancaster, Pennsylvania, which has a large Amish population, it is not unusual to hear an elderly person saying *darest* for *dare not* or *daresome* for *adventurous.* Similarly, New Yorkers stand *on* line for a movie, whereas people in most other parts of the country stand *in* line.

Nonstandard Diction **Nonstandard** diction refers to words and expressions not generally considered a part of standard English diction—words like *ain't, nohow, anywheres, nowheres, hisself, theirselves,* and *wait on* (instead of *wait for*).

No absolute rules distinguish standard from nonstandard usage. (In fact, this issue is currently the subject of much debate. Some linguists reject the idea of nonstandard usage altogether, arguing that this designation serves only to relegate both the language and those who use it to second-class status.) Compilers of **dictionaries** and handbooks set standards by observing and describing the norms of language. Still, in the end, you will have to supplement the guidelines these books provide with your own assessment of what is appropriate usage in a particular writing situation.

See
21a-d

(3) College Writing

The level of diction appropriate for college writing depends on your assignment and your audience. A personal experience essay calls for a natural, informal style, but a research paper, an examination, or a report requires a more formal vocabulary and a detached tone. In general, most college writing falls somewhere between formal and informal English, using a conversational tone but maintaining grammatical correctness. (Keep in mind that colloquial expressions are almost always inappropriate in your college writing, as are slang, regionalisms, and other nonstandard usages.)

EXERCISE 1

The diction of this paragraph, from Toni Cade Bambara's short story "The Hammer Man," is informal. In order to represent the speech of a young girl, the writer includes slang expressions and grammatical inaccuracies. Underline the words that identify the diction of this paragraph as informal. Then rewrite the paragraph, using standard diction.

Manny was supposed to be crazy. That was his story. To say you were bad put some people off. But to say you were crazy, well, you were officially not to be messed with. So that was his story. On the other hand, after I called him what I called him and said a few choice things about his mother, his face did go through some piercing changes. And I did kind of wonder if maybe he sure was nuts. I didn't wait to find out. I got in the wind. And then he waited for me on my stoop all day and all night, not hardly speaking to the people going in and out. And he was there all day Saturday, with his sister bringing him peanut-butter sandwiches and cream sodas. He must've gone to the bathroom right there cause every time I looked out the kitchen window, there he was. And Sunday, too. I got to thinking the boy was mad.

EXERCISE 2

After reading the following paragraphs, underline the words and phrases that identify each as formal diction. Then choose one paragraph and rewrite it using the level of diction that you would use in your college writing. Use a dictionary if necessary.

1. In looking at many small points of difference between species, which, as far as our ignorance permits us to judge, seem quite unimportant, we must not forget that climate, food, etc., have no doubt produced some direct effect. It is also necessary to bear in mind that owing to the law of correlation, when one part varies and the variations are accumulated through natural selection, other modifications, often of the most unexpected nature, will ensue. (Charles Darwin, *The Origin of Species*)

2. I hope you are able to see the distinction I am trying to point out. In no sense do I advocate evading or defying the law, as would the rabid segregationist. That would lead to anarchy. One who breaks an unjust law must do so openly, lovingly, and with a willingness to accept penalty. I submit that an individual who breaks a law that conscience tells him is unjust, and who willingly accepts the penalty of imprisonment in order to arouse the conscience of the community over its injustice, is in reality expressing the highest respect for law. (Martin Luther King, Jr., "Letter from Birmingham Jail")

20b | Choosing the Right Word

According to Mark Twain, the difference between the right word and almost the right word is the difference between the lightning and the lightning bug. If you use the wrong word—or even *almost* the right one—you run the risk of understating or misrepresenting your feelings and ideas.

(1) Denotation and Connotation

A word's **denotation** is its literal meaning, what it stands for apart from its emotional associations. A word's **connotations** are the emotional, social, and political associations it has in addition to its denotative meaning.

Word	Denotation	Connotation
Politician	Someone who holds a political office	Opportunist; wheeler-dealer

You would think that determining the denotative meaning of a word would present few problems, but this is not so. Words can have different denotations for different people. Moreover, words can have similar but not identical denotations, and this too can cause confusion. For example, you make an error in denotation when you say *molecule* when you mean *atom* or when you say *compound* when you mean *mixture*.

Selecting a word with the appropriate connotation can be even more of a challenge than choosing one with the accurate denotative meaning. For example, the word *pushy* has negative connotations, whereas *assertive* is neutral, and *dynamic* and *determined* are positive. Moreover, some closely related words—such as *mentally ill, insane, neurotic, crazy, psychopathic,* and *disturbed*—have different social and political connotations that affect the way people respond. If you use such terms without considering their connotations, you run the risk of undercutting your credibility, to say nothing of confusing and possibly alienating your readers.

EXERCISE 3

The following words have negative connotations. For each, list one word with a similar meaning whose connotation is neutral and another whose connotation is favorable.

EXAMPLE: *Negative*   skinny
Neutral   thin
Favorable   slender

1. deceive
2. antiquated
3. egghead
4. pathetic
5. cheap
6. blunder
7. weird
8. politician
9. shack
10. stench

EXERCISE 4

Think of a trip you took. First, write a one-paragraph description that would discourage anyone from taking the same trip. Next, rewrite your paragraph, describing your trip favorably. Finally, rewrite your paragraph again, using neutral words that convey no judgments. In each version of your paragraph, underline the words that helped you to convey your impression to your readers.

(2) Euphemisms

A **euphemism** is a term used in place of a blunt or impolite term that describes a subject society considers disagreeable, frightening, or offensive. Many people are uncomfortable discussing certain subjects, such as bodily functions, death, and some social problems. Therefore, they avoid direct language and use euphemisms. For example, toilets are called *lounges, bathrooms,* or *powder rooms;* we say that the dead have *passed on,* *gone to their reward,* or *departed,* and we call graveyards *resting places* or *memorial parks.* We refer to divorce as *marital dissolution,* adultery as an *affair,* the poor as *deprived* or *disadvantaged,* and mentally retarded children as *developmentally delayed.*

College writing is no place for euphemisms. Say what you mean— *pregnant,* not *expecting; died,* not *passed away; strike,* not *work stoppage; drunk,* not *inebriated;* and *used car,* not *preowned automobile.*

(3) Specific and General Words

Specific words refer to particular persons, items, or events; **general** words signify an entire class or group. *Queen Elizabeth II,* for example, is more specific than *monarch; jeans* is more specific than *clothing;* and *Jeep* is more specific than *automobile.* The use of general words may be necessary—for example, to describe entire classes of items or events. But you must also include specific words to clarify such generalizations. The more specific your choice of words, the more vivid your writing will be.

Whether a word is general or specific is determined by its relationship to other words. The following word chains move from most general (on the left) to most specific (on the right). The word farthest to the left denotes a general category or class, and the one farthest to the right names a specific, tangible member of that class.

history—American history—Civil War history—History 263

apparel—accessory—tie—my Three Stooges tie

human being—official—president—Bill Clinton

reading matter—book—novel—*The Bluest Eye*

machine—vehicle—train—*Orient Express*

(4) Abstract and Concrete Words

Abstract words—*beauty, truth, justice,* and so on—refer to ideas, qualities, or conditions that cannot be perceived by the senses. **Concrete** words, on the other hand, convey a vivid picture by naming things that readers can *see, hear, taste, smell,* or *touch.* Of course, we need abstract words to discuss concepts. The works of many great writers examine abstractions such as *truth, faith,* and *beauty,* but these writers know they must go on to describe abstractions with concrete details. As with general and specific words, whether a word is abstract or concrete is relative. The more concrete your words and phrases, the more vivid the image you evoke in the reader.

ABSTRACT: The night I stayed too late I was spellbound by the beautiful sights.

CONCRETE: The night I stayed too late I was hunched on the log staring spellbound at spreading, reflected stains of lilac on the water. A cloud in the sky suddenly lighted as if turned on by a switch; its reflection just as suddenly materialized on the water upstream, flat and floating, so that I couldn't see the creek bottom, or life in the water under the cloud. Downstream, away from the cloud on the water, water turtles smooth as beans were gliding down with the current in a series of easy, weightless pushoffs, as men bound on the moon. (Annie Dillard, *Pilgrim at Tinker Creek*)

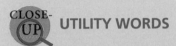

UTILITY WORDS

Avoid abstract terms such as *nice, great,* and *terrific* that say nothing and could be used in almost any sentence. These <u>utility words</u> convey only enthusiasm, not precise meanings. Replace them with more specific words.

See
13a2

VAGUE: The book was good.

BETTER: The book was <u>a complex and suspensefully plotted mystery.</u>

EXERCISE 5

Effective writing usually mixes specific and general words and abstract and concrete words. Read the following passage and underline words that are relatively specific and concrete. How do they make the paragraph more effective? Are any very general or abstract words used? What is their function? What impression does the writer want to convey?

I grew up slowly beside the tides and marshes of Colleton; my arms were tawny and strong from working long days on the shrimp boat in the blazing South Carolina heat. Because I was a Wingo, I worked as soon as I could walk; I could pick a blue crab clean when I was five. I had killed my first deer by the age of seven, and at nine was regularly putting meat on my family's table. I was born and raised on a Carolina sea island and I carried the sunshine of the low-country, inked in dark gold, on my back and shoulders. As a boy I was happy above the channels, navigating a small boat between the sandbars with their quiet nation of oysters exposed on the brown flats at the low watermark. I knew every shrimper by name, and they knew me and sounded their horns when they passed me fishing in the river. (Pat Conroy, *The Prince of Tides*)

EXERCISE 6

Revise the following paragraph from a job application letter by substituting specific, concrete language for general or abstract words and phrases.

I have had several part-time jobs lately. Some of them would qualify me for the position you advertised. In my most recent job, I sold products in a store. My supervisor said I was a good worker who possessed a number of valuable qualities. I am used to dealing with different types of people in various kinds of settings. I feel that my qualifications would make me a good candidate for your job opening.

20c Avoiding Unoriginal Language

(1) Jargon

Jargon refers to the specialized or technical vocabulary of a trade, profession, or academic discipline when it is used outside the field for which it was developed. Within a particular field a term may be easily understood, but outside that field it is often imprecise and confusing. For example, a medical doctor may say that a procedure is *contraindicated* or that he or she is going to carry out a *differential diagnosis*. A business executive may want departments to *interface* effectively, and a sociologist may identify the need for *perspectivistic thinking* to achieve organizational goals. If they are addressing other professionals in their respective fields, the use of these terms is perfectly appropriate. If, however, they are addressing a lay audience, the terms become jargon.

Jargon is often accompanied by overly formal diction, the passive voice, and wordy constructions.

ORIGINAL: Procedures were instituted to implement changes in the parameters used to evaluate all aspects of the process.

TRANSLATION: We began using different criteria to judge the process.

Although many people deliberately use jargon to impress their audience, its effect is usually just the opposite. When you write for a general college audience, use a vocabulary that is appropriate for your readers and your purpose.

(2) Neologisms

Neologisms are newly coined words that are not part of standard English. New situations call for new words, and frequently such words become a part of the language—*E-mail, carjack,* and *outsource,* for example.

Some coined words, however, may never be considered part of standard English. For example, questionable neologisms are created when the suffix *-wise* is added to existing words—creating new words like *weatherwise, sportswise, timewise,* and *productwise.*

If you are not sure whether to use a word, look it up in a current college dictionary. If it is not there, you probably should not use it.

(3) Pretentious Diction

Pretentious diction is language that is inappropriately elevated and wordy. In an effort to impress readers, some writers elevate their style, overusing adjectives and adverbs, polysyllabic words, complex sentences, and poetic devices.

PRETENTIOUS DICTION: The expectations of offspring may be appreciably different from their parents'.

REVISED: Children's goals may be different from those of their parents.

PRETENTIOUS DICTION: As I fell into slumber, I cogitated about my day ambling through the splendor of the Appalachian Mountains.

REVISED: As I fell asleep, I thought about my day hiking through the Appalachian Mountains.

Pretentious diction is not formal diction used in an inappropriate situation; it is always out of place. By calling attention to itself, it gets in the way of communication and draws readers away from the point you are making. Good writing is clear writing, and pompous or flowery language is no substitute for clarity.

(4) Clichés

Clichés are trite expressions that have lost their impact because they have been so overused. Familiar sayings like "rush to judgment," "what goes around comes around," and "a penny for your thoughts," for example, do little to enhance your writing.

The purpose of college writing is always to convey information clearly; clichés do just the opposite. Take the time to think of fresh expressions.

EXERCISE 7

Rewrite the following passage, eliminating jargon, neologisms, pretentious diction, and clichés. Feel free to add words and phrases and to reorganize sentences to make their meaning clear. If you are not certain about the meaning or status of a word, consult a dictionary.

At a given point in time there coexisted a hare and a tortoise. The aforementioned rabbit was overheard by the tortoise to be blowing his horn about the degree of speed he could attain. The latter quadruped thereupon put forth a challenge to the former by advancing the suggestion that they interact in a running competition. The hare acquiesced, laughing to himself. The animals concurred in the decision to acquire the services of a certain fox to act in the capacity of judicial referee. This particular fox was in agreement, and consequently implementation of the plan was facilitated. In a relatively small amount of time the hare had considerably outdistanced the tortoise and, after ascertaining that he himself was in a more optimized position distancewise than the tortoise, he arrived at the unilateral decision to avail himself of a respite. He made the implicit assumption in so doing that he would anticipate no difficulty in overtaking the tortoise when his suspension of activity ceased. An unfortunate development racewise occurred when the hare's somnolent state endured for a longer-than-anticipated time frame, facilitating the tortoise's victory in the contest and affirming the concept of unhurriedness and firmness triumphing in competitive situations. Thus, the hare was unable to snatch victory out of the jaws of defeat. Years later he was still ruminating about the exigencies of the situation.

EXERCISE 8

Go through a newspaper or magazine and list the jargon, neologisms, pretentious diction, or clichés you find. Then substitute more original words for the ones you identified. Be prepared to discuss your interpretation of each word and of the word you chose to put in its place.

20d Using Figurative Language

Language that conforms to the standard meaning of words is called **literal language.** But writers often use **figurative language**—language that departs from the literal meaning or order of words—in order to achieve unusual effects or convey special meanings. Although you should not overuse figurative language, you should experiment with it to help you add interest to your writing.

TYPES OF FIGURATIVE LANGUAGE

A **simile** is a comparison between two essentially unlike things on the basis of a shared quality. A simile is introduced by *like* and *as*.

Like travelers with exotic destinations on their minds, the graduates were remarkably forgetful. (Maya Angelou, *I Know Why the Caged Bird Sings*)

NOTE: A simile must compare two *dissimilar* things. For that reason, "My dog is like your dog" is not a simile.

A **metaphor** also compares two essentially dissimilar things, but instead of saying that one thing is *like* another, it *equates* them.

Perhaps it is easy for those who have never felt the stings and darts of segregation to say, "Wait." (Martin Luther King, Jr., "Letter from Birmingham Jail")

An **analogy** explains an unfamiliar object or idea by comparing it to a more familiar one.

According to Robert Frost, writing free verse is like playing tennis without a net.

Personification gives an idea or inanimate object human attributes, feelings, or powers.

Truth strikes us from behind, and in the dark, as well as from before in broad daylight. (Henry David Thoreau, *Journals*)

A **hyperbole** (or overstatement) is an intentional exaggeration for emphasis. For example, Jonathan Swift uses hyperbole in his essay "A Modest Proposal" when he suggests that eating Irish babies would help the English solve their food shortage.

Understatement intentionally downplays a situation or sentiment by saying less than is really meant.

According to Mao Tse-tung, a revolution is not a tea party.

NOTE: Experienced writers use overstatement and understatement to achieve irony or to add humor. Carelessly used, however, overstatement can make your ideas seem inappropriately exaggerated and understatement can make them appear trivial.

EXERCISE 9

Read the following paragraph from Mark Twain's *Life on the Mississippi* and identify as many figures of speech as you can.

Now when I had mastered the language of this water, and had come to know every trifling feature that bordered the great river as familiarly as I knew the letters of the alphabet, I had made a valuable acquisition. But I had lost something, too. I had lost something which could never be restored to me while I lived. All the grace, the beauty, the poetry, had gone out of the majestic river! I still keep in mind a certain wonderful sunset which I witnessed when steamboating was new to me. A broad expanse of the river was turned to blood; in the middle distance the red hue brightened into gold, through which a solitary log came floating black and conspicuous; in one place a long, slanting mark lay sparkling upon the water; in another the surface was broken by boiling, tumbling rings, that were as many-tinted as an opal; where the ruddy flush was faintest, was a smooth spot that was covered with graceful circles and radiating lines, ever so delicately traced; the shore on our left was densely wooded, and the somber shadow that fell from this forest was broken in one place by a long, ruffled trail that shone like silver; and high above the forest wall a clean-stemmed dead tree waved a single leafy bough that glowed like a flame in the unobstructed splendor that was flowing from the sun. There were graceful curves, reflected images, woody heights, soft distances; and over the whole scene, far and near, the dissolving lights drifted steadily, enriching it every passing moment with new marvels of coloring.

20e Avoiding Ineffective Figures of Speech

Effective figures of speech enrich your diction; ineffective figures of speech weaken it.

(1) Dead Metaphors and Similes

Metaphors and similes stimulate thought by calling up vivid images in a reader's mind. A **dead metaphor** or **simile,** however, has been so overused it has become a pat, meaningless expression that evokes no particular visual image. Here are some examples.

off the beaten path   happy as a clam
sit on the fence   a shot in the arm
free as a bird   smooth sailing

spread like wildfire   fit like a glove
Herculean efforts   fighting like cats and dogs

Avoid dead metaphors and similes; instead, take the time to think of images that make your writing fresher and more vivid.

(2) Mixed Metaphors

A **mixed metaphor** results when you combine two or more incompatible images. The result is a meaningless sentence. Always revise mixed metaphors to make your imagery consistent.

MIXED: Management <u>extended an olive branch</u> in an attempt <u>to break some of the ice</u> between the company and the striking workers.

REVISED: Management extended an olive branch with the hope that the striking workers would pick it up.

EXERCISE 10

Rewrite the following sentences, adding one of the types of figurative language discussed in the preceding pages to each sentence to make the ideas more vivid and exciting. Identify each figure of speech you use. Be careful to avoid ineffective figures of speech.

EXAMPLE: The room was cool and still.

The room was cool and still like the inside of a cathedral. (simile)

1. The last of the marathon runners limped toward the finish line.
2. The breeze gently stirred the wind chimes.
3. Jeremy has shoulder-length hair and a high forehead and wears small, wire-framed glasses.
4. The computer classroom was quiet.
5. The demolition crew worked slowly but efficiently.
6. Interstate highways often make for tedious driving.
7. Diego found calculus hard.
8. Music is essentially mathematical.
9. Katrina claims her dog is far more intelligent than her brother.
10. Emotions are curious.

20f   Avoiding Offensive Language

The language we use not only expresses ideas but also shapes our thinking. For this reason we all should be aware of the influence of language on our perceptions as well as the way what we see affects what we say. Although we may not be able to change the language, we can avoid using words that insult or degrade others.

(1) Racial, Ethnic, and Other Stereotypes

When referring to any racial, ethnic, or religious group, use words with neutral connotations or words that the group uses in *formal* speech or writing to refer to itself. This is not always an easy task because the preferred names for specific groups change over time. For example, *African-American* is now preferred by many Americans of African ancestry over *black*, which itself replaced *Negro* in the 1960s. People from East Asia—once called *Orientals*—now generally refer to themselves as *Asian, Asian-American*, or by their country of origin (*Korean*, for example). Many of America's native peoples prefer *Native American*, although some call themselves *Indian*, and others identify themselves as members of a particular tribe—for example, *Kiowa* or *Navajo*. Native Americans in Canada and Alaska, who consider *Eskimo* demeaning, have adopted *Inuit*. The preferences of people of Spanish descent vary according to their national origin. *Hispanic*—a term coined by the US Bureau of the Census—is often used to refer to anyone of Spanish descent, as are *Latino* and *Latina*. But many individuals prefer other designations—for example, *Chicano* and *Chicana* for people from Mexico. A large number of Americans of Spanish descent, however, prefer to use names that emphasize their dual heritages—*Cuban-American, Mexican-American, Dominican-American*, and so on.

In addition to conveying racial, ethnic, and religious stereotypes, words that label particular groups of people can convey insulting stereotypes based on other factors.

Age Unwarranted assumptions based on age can offend readers. Do not assume, for example, that all people over a certain age are forgetful, sickly, or inactive. Also, do not express surprise or shock at the ability of an older person to do something that would be perfectly natural for someone younger to do. Many older people like to call themselves "senior citizens" or "seniors," and these terms are commonly used by the media and the government. Keep in mind, however, that some older people may feel stereotyped by these terms or may see them as euphemisms for the more direct *older people* or *elderly*.

Class Your readers may not share your background or your assumptions about particular groups of people. Do not demean certain jobs because they are low paying or praise others because they have impressive titles. Similarly, do not use words—*hick, cracker, redneck, white trash*, or *WASP*, for example—that denigrate people based on their class.

Geographical Area Avoid making unwarranted assumptions about people based on where they live. People who live on the East Coast are not all loud and pushy, just as people who live in the Midwest are not all soft-spoken and polite. Not all Californians eat health food and join cults, and not all Texans wear cowboy boots and carry sixshooters. Also remember that *American* can refer to anyone living in the Western Hemisphere—not just to someone living in the United States.

Physical Ability There is a real difference between saying someone has a physical disability ("Frank has epilepsy") and describing someone as a disabled person ("Frank is an epileptic"). In the first case, the disability is just part of how a person is characterized, but in the second, the focus is totally on the disability. In general, you should not even mention a person's disability unless it is relevant to the discussion. If it is relevant, use the preferred term—*disability, not handicap,* for example.

Sexual Orientation You should not mention an individual's sexual orientation unless it is pertinent to your subject. For example, the sexual orientation of a retired army colonel who made her lesbian lifestyle public would be relevant if you were writing an essay about gays in the military, but not if you were writing an article about women in the military.

(2) Sexist Language

Insulting to both men and women, sexist language entails much more than the use of derogatory words such as *broad, hunk, chick,* and *bimbo.* Assuming that some professions are exclusive to one gender—for instance, that *nurse* denotes only women and *engineer* denotes only men—is also sexist. So is the use of job titles such as *postman* for *letter carrier, fireman* for *firefighter,* and *stewardess* for *flight attendant.*

Sexist language also occurs when a writer fails to use the same terminology when referring to both men and women. For example, you should refer to two scientists with PhDs not as Dr. Sagan and Mrs. Yallow, but as Dr. Sagan and Dr. Yallow. You should refer to two writers as James and Wharton, or Henry James and Edith Wharton, not Henry James and Mrs. Wharton.

In your writing, always use *women*—not *girls*—when referring to adult females. Use *Ms.* as the form of address when a woman's marital status is unknown or irrelevant. (If the woman you are addressing refers to herself as *Mrs.* or *Miss,* however, use the form of address she prefers.) Finally, avoid using the generic *he* or *him* when your subject could be either male or female. Use the third-person plural or the phrase *he or she* (not *he/she*).

TRADITIONAL: Before boarding, each passenger should make certain that <u>he</u> has <u>his</u> ticket.

REVISED: Before boarding, <u>passengers</u> should make certain that <u>they</u> have <u>their</u> tickets.

REVISED: Before boarding, each <u>passenger</u> should make certain that <u>he or she</u> has a ticket.

Remember, however, not to overuse *his or her* or *he or she* constructions, which can make your writing repetitious and wordy.

 SEXIST LANGUAGE

When trying to avoid sexist use of *he* and *him,* be careful not to create ungrammatical constructions such as the following.

UNGRAMMATICAL: Before the publication of Richard Wright's novel *Native Son,* any unknown African-American <u>writer</u> had trouble getting <u>their</u> work published.

Although many speakers do use *they* and *their* in cases such as the one above, in your college writing you should avoid using a plural pronoun to refer to a singular noun.

REVISED: Before the publication of Richard Wright's novel *Native Son,* unknown African-American <u>writers</u> had trouble getting <u>their</u> work published.

REVISING SEXIST LANGUAGE

Sexist Usage	Possible Revisions
1. Equality is a desirable goal for <u>all men.</u>	Equality is a desirable goal for <u>everyone.</u>
2. Mankind	People, human beings
Man's accomplishments	Human accomplishments
Man-made	Synthetic
3. Female doctor (lawyer, mechanic, etc.), male nurse	Doctor (lawyer, mechanic, etc.), nurse

continued on the following page

---

continued from the previous page

4. Policeman/woman	Police officer
Salesman/woman/girl	Salesperson/representative
Businessman/woman	Businessperson/executive
5. Everyone should complete his application by Tuesday.	Everyone should complete his or her application by Tuesday; All students should complete their applications by Tuesday.
6. Who's teaching composition? I hope he's good.	Who's teaching composition? I hope it's someone good.

EXERCISE 11

Identify the stereotypes in the following sentences.

1. Max wasn't surprised to find the driver of the car that rear-ended his new BMW was a woman.
2. Every new medical student knows that he faces several years of hard work.
3. California has a large Oriental population.
4. She couldn't wait to leave her hometown because it was populated with rednecks and hicks.
5. Phyllis Knable, wife of Dr. Peter Knable, is an outstanding surgeon.
6. I was surprised to notice that my hairdresser wears a wedding ring.
7. My roommate is from New York, but she is surprisingly friendly.
8. Next Tuesday is her day to have the girls over for bridge.

EXERCISE 12

Suggest alternative forms for any of the following constructions you consider sexist. In each case, comment on the advantages and disadvantages of the alternative you recommend. If you feel that a particular term is not sexist, explain why.

forefathers	(to) man the battle stations
man-eating shark	Girl Friday
manpower	point man
workman's compensation	stock boy
men at work	cowboy
copy boy	man overboard
bus boy	fisherman
first baseman	foreman
corpsman	manned space program

congressman
advance man
manhunt
longshoreman
committeeman

gentleman's agreement
no-man's-land
spinster
old maid
old wives' tale

EXERCISE 13

These terms denote professions that have traditionally been associated with a particular gender. Now that the professions are open to both sexes, are any new terms needed? If so, suggest possible terms. If not, explain why not.

miner   farmer
mechanic   barber
soldier   rabbi
sailor   minister
rancher   bartender

EXERCISE 14

The following terms have emerged in the last few years as possible alternatives for older gender-specific words. Which usages do you believe are likely to become part of the English language? Which do you expect to disappear? Explain.

Coinage   *Older Form*
• waitperson   waiter or waitress
  server
• househusband   housewife
  homemaker
• weather forecaster   weatherman, weathergirl
• chair   chairman
  chairwoman
  chairperson
• spokesperson   spokesman

EXERCISE 15

Each of the following pairs of terms includes a feminine form that was at one time in wide use; all are still used to some extent. Which do you think are likely to remain in our language for some time, and which do you think will disappear? Explain your reasoning.

heir/heiress   author/authoress
benefactor/benefactress   poet/poetess
murderer/murderess   tailor/seamstress
actor/actress   comedian/comedienne

hero/heroine	villain/villainess
host/hostess	prince/princess
aviator/aviatrix	widow/widower
executor/executrix	

EXERCISE 16

In recent years the word *parenting* has been introduced as a gender-free equivalent of *mothering*. How do the connotations of *parenting* differ from those associated with *mothering?* With *fathering?* Given those differences, what is your prediction about the continued use of *parenting* in years to come?

STUDENT WRITER AT WORK

Choosing Words

The following excerpt is from a draft written for a communications class. Underline any words and phrases you think are not appropriate, accurate, or fresh. Then revise the essay, changing words and sentences as you see fit. If necessary, revise again to strengthen coherence, unity, and style.

Saying It with a Smile

Our first impressions of a local television news program come from the newscasters, those smiling people who converse with us every evening. Undoubtedly, there are many qualifications local reporters must have, including a superlative educational background and some experience in broadcasting. They should also be sharp and have a keen interest in exposing the real truth. Above all, however, broadcasters must have a pleasing appearance.

Using familiar faces has become an effective marketing strategy for the news . A number of station managers have seen their market share increase and their negatives decrease when they slotted a newscaster with whom the audience identified. Market research has shown that viewers like to visualize the newscaster as if he were one of the family. Therefore, people chosen for the job must look nice--just like the boy or girl next

continued on the following page

353

continued from the previous page

door. Promos for the local news reinforce this squeaky clean image. In one spot we see a newsman walking through a deteriorating urban neighborhood playing ball with lower-class kids and shaking hands with their moms and dads. In another, we see a female anchor bringing her son and some schoolmates to the station. Their eyes are as big as saucers as they look around. These kids are in seventh grade, and they use words like "cool" and "awesome" as they talk about the evening news. Clearly, this rather blatant tactic is calculated to present the reporters to the viewers as everyday people.

Just as tranquilizers calm someone's nerves, these newscasters lull us into not caring and then feed us empty calories. We are so conditioned to identify with the reporters that we never think about the actual content of the news. Beyond a shadow of a doubt we are inclined to remember those stories that consume the most time in the half-hour broadcast. Except for national emergencies, the "big" stories are happy talk about local issues. Many of these have almost no news value--a rock concert, ice skating at a pond, and a pizza-eating contest, for example. This is obviously what we want to know and why we tune in. It must be, for ratings have never been higher. There is no mention of the unsolved hit-and-run murder of a young boy in my neighborhood. This is outrageous! But what the heck, that's what we expect anyhow. Tomorrow night we will ritualistically tune in and hear our favorite newsman tell us the big story: "Beer drinking banned at the baseball stadium."

CHAPTER 21

USING THE DICTIONARY AND BUILDING A VOCABULARY

21a Exploring the Parts of a Dictionary

A dictionary is usually divided into three parts: the *front matter,* the *alphabetical listing,* and the *back matter.*

The **front matter** generally contains a preface explaining how the dictionary is set up and guides for pronunciation and abbreviations. Some dictionaries include special material in the front matter—articles focusing on the history of the language, for example.

The **alphabetical listing** is the largest section of every dictionary. Entries tell how a word is spelled, pronounced, and used.

The **back matter** in some dictionaries may contain a list of weights and measures; in others, it may include an essay on punctuation or a glossary of foreign words.

21b Understanding a Dictionary Entry

Dictionary entries typically include all or most of the following items.

(1) Entry Word

The **entry word,** which appears in boldface at the beginning of the entry, gives the spelling of the word and any variant spellings.

col · or n. Also chiefly British **col · our**

(2) Guide to Pronunciation

A guide to the pronunciation of the word appears in parentheses or between slashes after the main entry. Dictionaries use symbols to represent sounds, and an explanation of these symbols usually appears at the bottom of each page or across the bottom of facing pages throughout the alphabetical listing.

(3) Part-of-Speech Labels

Dictionaries use abbreviations to indicate parts of speech and grammatical forms. For example, if a verb is irregular, the part-of-speech label indicates the principal parts of the verb.

with · draw ... v. -drew; -drawn; -drawing

See
10b1-2

In addition, the label indicates whether a verb is **transitive** (*tr.*), **intransitive** (*intr.*), or both.
Part-of-speech labels also indicate the plural forms of irregular nouns.

child ... n. pl. children

moth · er-in-law ... n. pl. moth · ers-in-law

When the plural form is regular, it is not shown.
Finally, part-of-speech labels usually indicate the comparative and superlative forms of both regular and irregular adjectives and adverbs.

red ... adj. redder; reddest

bad ... adv. worse; worst

EXERCISE 1

Use your college dictionary to help you answer the following questions about grammatical forms.

1. What are the principal parts of the following verbs: *drink, deify, carol, draw,* and *ring?*
2. Which of the following nouns can be used as verbs: *canter, minister, council, command, magistrate, mother,* and *lord?*
3. What are the plural forms of these nouns: *silo, sheep, seed, scissors, genetics,* and *alchemy?*
4. What are the comparative and superlative forms of the following adverbs and adjectives: *fast, airy, good, mere, homey,* and *unlucky?*
5. Are the following verbs transitive, intransitive, or both: *bias, halt, dissatisfy, die,* and *turn?* Copy from the dictionary the phrase or sentence that illustrates the use of each verb.

(4) Etymology

Many dictionaries include information about the **etymology** of a word—its history over the years. This information, which appears in brackets either before or after the list of meanings, traces a word back to its roots and shows its form when it entered English. For instance, *The American Heritage Dictionary* (see Figure 1) shows that *couple* came into Middle English (ME) from Old French (OFr.) and into Old French from Latin (Lat.).

Figure 1 ENTRY FROM *THE AMERICAN HERITAGE DICTIONARY*

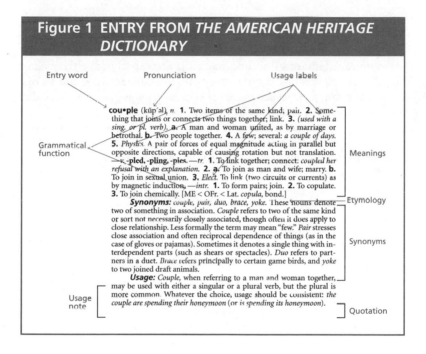

(5) Meanings

Some dictionaries give the most common meaning first and then list less common ones. Others begin with the oldest meaning and move to the most current one. Check the front matter of your dictionary to find out how its meanings are arranged.

Remember that if a word is in the process of acquiring new meanings, the dictionary may not yet include them. Also remember that a dictionary meaning is primarily a record of the **denotations**, or exact meanings, of a word. A word's emotional associations, or **connotations**, are not always listed.

See 20b1

(6) Synonyms and Antonyms

A dictionary entry often lists synonyms and occasionally antonyms in addition to definitions. **Synonyms** are words that have similar meanings, such as *well* and *healthy.* **Antonyms** are words that have opposite meanings, such as *courage* and *cowardice.* When you go beyond your dictionary to consult a **thesaurus,** a book or computer program that lists synonyms, remember that no two words have exactly the same meanings. Therefore, you should use synonyms carefully, making certain that the connotations of the synonym are as close as possible to those of the original word.

(7) Idioms

Dictionary entries often show how certain words are used in set expressions called **idioms.** This information is necessary because the meaning of such expressions cannot always be determined from the words alone. For example, what are **speakers of other languages** to make of the expressions "catch a cold," "shut the light," and "blow your top"?

See App. B

Dictionaries also indicate the idiomatic use of prepositions. This information tells us, for example, that we do not say that we *abide with* a decision or that we *interfere on* an election; we say that we *abide by* and *interfere with.*

(8) Labels

Dictionaries use **labels** to indicate restrictions on word usage. Where such labels involve value judgments, dictionaries differ.

LABELS

Status	Definition	Example
Nonstandard	A word in wide use but not considered standard usage	*ain't*
Informal/ Colloquial	A word used in conversation and acceptable in informal writing	*I've* for *I have* *sure* for *surely* *prof* for *professor*
Slang	A word appropriate only in extremely informal situations	*rip off*

continued on the following page

---

continued from the previous page

Dialect	Definition	Example
Regional	A word or meaning of a word limited to a certain geographical region	*arroyo* (used in the Southwest), meaning "deep gully"
Temporal		
Obsolete	A word no longer in use	*egal*, meaning "equal"
Archaic/Rare	A once-common word or meaning that is now seldom used	*affright*, meaning "to arouse fear or terror" (archaic)
Poetic	A word used commonly only in poetry	*eve* for *evening* *o'er* for *over*
Subject		
Biology/Physics/Military/etc.	A word or meaning of a word limited to a particular field or discipline	*couple* (in electricity), meaning "to link by magnetic induction"

EXERCISE 2

Use your college dictionary to find the restrictions on the use of the following words.

1. irregardless
2. apse
3. flunk
4. lorry
5. kirk
6. gofer
7. whilst
8. sine
9. bannock
10. blowhard

(9) General Information

When no other reference works are handy, dictionaries can be excellent sources of general information. If you want to find out the year in which John Glenn orbited the earth, you can look up the entry *Glenn, John*. If you need to find out for whom the Davis Cup is named, you can look up *Davis Cup*.

EXERCISE 3

To test the research capability of your dictionary, use it to answer the following questions.

1. What is the ninth month in the Muslim calendar?
2. In what year did William Faulkner win the Nobel Prize in literature?
3. When was Sandra Day O'Connor appointed to the Supreme Court?
4. What is Dadaism?
5. From which language is Yiddish primarily derived?
6. When was the King James Version of the Bible published?
7. What was novelist George Eliot's given name?
8. What does the abbreviation *FRB* stand for?
9. What two oceans border the continent of Africa?
10. When did Desmond Tutu win the Nobel Peace Prize?

21c Surveying Abridged Dictionaries

An **abridged dictionary** is one that is condensed from a more complete collection of words and meanings. A good hardback abridged dictionary will contain about 1,500 pages and about 150,000 entries. Paperback dictionaries usually contain fewer entries, treated in less detail. A paperback dictionary is adequate for checking spelling, but for reference, you should consult one of the following hardback abridged dictionaries.

The American Heritage College Dictionary. This extensively illustrated dictionary contains more than 180,000 entries. Within the alphabetical listing the principal and most current meaning appears first, with other meanings following. Throughout the dictionary, the editors have provided usage notes and short essays on word history. Synonyms (and sometimes antonyms) are also listed.

The Concise Oxford Dictionary of Current English. This no-nonsense dictionary contains no illustrations and gives little guidance on usage. It lists meanings according to the most common usage, includes illustrative quotations, and gives British as well as American spellings. Front and back matter is sparse.

The Random House College Dictionary. This is an abridged version of the larger unabridged *Random House Dictionary of the English Language.* It lists meanings according to frequency of use and indicates informal and slang usage. It also gives synonyms and antonyms as well as geographical and biographical names. Back matter includes a manual of style.

Merriam-Webster's Collegiate Dictionary. Like *The Random House College Dictionary,* this illustrated dictionary is an abridged version of a larger unabridged dictionary. Words are defined by their current usage rather than their original definitions. Many entries are followed by usage notes.

The front matter of this dictionary contains a detailed essay on the English language. Foreign words and phrases as well as biographical and geographical names appear in separate sections in the back matter.

Webster's New World College Dictionary. This good basic dictionary presents meanings in historical order. Foreign terms and geographical and biographical names are included in the alphabetical listing.

NOTE: The name *Webster,* referring to the great lexicographer Noah Webster, is in the public domain. Because it cannot be copyrighted, it appears in the titles of many dictionaries of varying quality.

 CD-ROM DICTIONARIES

A number of dictionaries are available on CD-ROM or as networked databases. These include *The American Heritage Dictionary, The Random House College Dictionary,* and *The Oxford English Dictionary.* These dictionaries contain special features. For example, *The American Heritage Dictionary* includes a thesaurus and has a function that enables you to find all the words that correspond to a particular definition.

21d Surveying Unabridged Dictionaries

In some situations you may need more information than your college dictionary offers. When you are looking for a detailed history of a word or when you want to look up an especially rare usage, you need to consult an unabridged dictionary in the reference section of your library. An **unabridged dictionary** attempts to present a comprehensive survey of all words in a language. Consequently, it gives a wider and more detailed treatment of entries than an abridged dictionary does, and its listings may extend over several volumes.

The Random House Unabridged Dictionary. This short unabridged dictionary contains about 315,000 entries. In the process of updating this dictionary since its first (1966) edition, the editors have added many new words and new definitions of old words.

Webster's Third New International Dictionary of the English Language.
This unabridged dictionary contains over 450,000 entries along with illustrations, some in color. Meanings appear in chronological order and
are extensively illustrated with quotations. This dictionary does not,
however, give much guidance on usage.

The Oxford English Dictionary. Consisting of twenty volumes plus four
supplements, *The Oxford English Dictionary* offers over 500,000 definitions, chronologically arranged, and more than two million supporting
quotations. The quotations begin with the earliest recorded use of a word
and progress through each century either until the word becomes obsolete
or until its latest meaning is listed. For this reason, many scholars consider
The Oxford English Dictionary the best place to find the history of a word
or to locate illustrations of its usage. However, *The Oxford English Dictionary* emphasizes British usage and does not treat American usage fully.
Figure 2 illustrates the in-depth coverage offered by an unabridged dictionary.

Figure 2   EXCERPT FROM *THE OXFORD ENGLISH DICTIONARY* ENTRY

courage ('kʌridʒ), *sb.* Forms: 4-7 corage,
curage, (4-6 corrage, 5 curag, coreage, 6
currage, courra(d)ge, 7 corege), 5- courage.
[ME. *corage*, a. OF. *corage, curage,* later *courage*
= Pr. and Cat. *coratge,* Sp. *corage,* It. *coraggio,*
a Common Romanic word, answering to a L.
type *corāticum,* f. *cor* heart. Cf. the parallel
ætāticum from *ætāt-em* (AGE); and see -AGE.]
  †1. The heart as the seat of feeling, thought,
etc.; spirit, mind, disposition, nature. *Obs.*
  c 1300 K. *Alis.* 3559 Archelaus, of proud
corage. c 1386 CHAUCER *Prol.* 11 Smale
fowles maken melodie . . So priketh hem
nature in here corages. c 1430 *Pilgr. Lyf
Manhode* 1. xxxiii. (1869) 20 What thinkest
in thi corage? c 1430 *Stans Puer* 5 To all
norture thi corage to enclyne. c 1500 *Knt.
Curtesy* 407 in Ritson *Met. Rom.* III. 213 in
his courage he was full sad. 1593 SHAKS. 3

Hen. VI, II. ii. 57 This soft courage makes
your Followers faint. 1638 DRUMM. OF
HAWTH. *Irene* Wks. (1711) 163 Men's
courages were growing hot, their hatred
kindled. 1659 B. HARRIS *Parival's Iron Age* 41
The Spaniards . . attacked it with all the force
and maistry the greatest courages were able
to invent.
  †b. *transf.* Of a plant. *Obs.* (Cf. 'To bring a
thing into *good heart.*')
  c 1420 *Palladius on Husb.* XI. 90 In this
courage Hem forto graffe is goode.
  †c. Applied to a person: of. *spirit. Obs.*
  1561 T. Hoby tr. *Castiglione's Courtyer*
(1577) V j b, The prowes of those diuine
courages [viz. Marquesse of Mantua, etc.].
1647 W. BROWNE *Polex.* II 197 These two
great courages being met, and followed by a
small companie of the most resolute pirates.

21e Building a Better Vocabulary

A good vocabulary strengthens your performance on written examinations, in papers, and in oral presentations; it also increases your ability
to understand reading material and your instructors' statements in class.
Without an extensive vocabulary, your ability to learn is limited.

Learning new words takes work and, at first, a good deal of time. The following steps, however, can make your task easier.

(1) Become a Reader

Focusing on words as you read is one of the best ways of learning new words. Seeing words in context, remembering the sentences in which they appear and the ideas with which they are associated, helps you remember their meanings.

(2) Learn the Histories of Words

Many of the words you encounter have interesting histories, or etymologies. Knowing the etymology of a word can help you remember its definition. For example, *cliché*, meaning a worn-out expression, is a French word that refers to a plate used for printing. This meaning suggests the idea of being cast in metal from a mold. Hence a *cliché* is a fixed form of expression.

EXERCISE 4

Look up the histories of the following words in your college dictionary. How does the history of each word help you remember its definition?

1. mountebank
2. pyrrhic
3. pittance
4. protean
5. gargantuan
6. cicerone
7. fathom
8. gossamer
9. rigmarole
10. maudlin

(3) Become Familiar with Roots, Prefixes, and Suffixes

The words you encounter in your college studies are sometimes long and complex. Usually, however, these words can be broken down into smaller units that give you clues to their meanings.

Roots   A **root** is a word from which other words are formed. Both *hypodermic* and *dermatologist,* for example, come from the Greek root *derma,* meaning "skin." *Manual* means "working by hand," *manuscript* refers to a handwritten draft of a book, and *manufacture* literally means "making a product by hand." All these words derive from the Latin root *manus,* meaning "hand." When you come across words that contain these roots, you already know half their meaning.

Prefixes   A **prefix** is a letter or group of letters placed before a root or word to add to or modify the word. The prefix *anti-,* for example, means "against." When combined with other words, it forms new words—*anti-aircraft, antibiotic,* and *anticoagulant,* for example.

 BUILDING A VOCABULARY

Be careful when making generalizations based on roots, prefixes, and suffixes. Some words appear to have the same root but do not—for instance, *homosexual* (from the Greek *homos,* meaning "same") and *homo sapiens* (from the Latin *homo,* meaning "man").

Here is a list of prefixes that, combined with different roots, form thousands of words.

PREFIXES INDICATING NUMBER

Prefix	Meaning	Example	Definition
uni-	one	unify	To make into a unit
bi-	two	bimonthly	Every two months
duo-	two	duotone	Printed in two tones of the same color
tri-	three	triad	A group of three
quadri-	four	quadruped	A four-footed animal
tetra-	four	tetrachloride	A chemical with four chlorine atoms
quint-	five	quintuplets	Five offspring born in a single birth
pent-	five	pentagon	A five-sided figure
multi-	many	multilateral	Having many sides
mono-	one	monogamy	Having one spouse
poly-	many	polygamy	Having many spouses
omni-	all	omnivore	Eating all kinds of food

PREFIXES INDICATING SMALLNESS

Prefix	Meaning	Example	Definition
micro-	small	microscope	An instrument for observing small things
mini-	small	minibus	A small bus

PREFIXES INDICATING SEQUENCE AND SPACE

Prefix	Meaning	Example	Definition
ante-	before	antebellum	Before the war
pre-	before	prehistory	Before history
intro-	within	introspective	Looking into oneself
post-	after	postscript	A message written after the body of the letter
re-	back, again	review	To look at again
sub-	under	submarine	An underwater ship
super-	above	supervise	To look over the performance of others
inter-	between	international	Between nations
intra-	within	intramural	Within the bounds of an institution
in-	in, into	incorporate	To form into a body
ex-	out, from	exhale	To breathe out
circum-	around	circumnavigate	To sail or fly around (the earth, an island, etc.)
con-	with, together	congregate	To come or bring together

PREFIXES INDICATING NEGATION

Prefix	Meaning	Example	Definition
non-	not	nonpartisan	Not affiliated
in-	not	inactive	Not active
un-	not, the opposite of, against	unequal	Not equal
anti-	against	antiseptic	Free from germs
counter-	opposing	countermand	To revoke an order with another order
contra-	against	contradict	To speak against
dis-	not, the opposite of	dislike	To not like
mis-	wrong, ill	mislead	To give bad advice
mal-	bad, wrong, ill	malformed	Incorrectly shaped
pseudo-	false	pseudonym	A false name

Suffixes   **Suffixes,** syllables added to the end of a word or root, change the word's part of speech. For example, suffixes added to the verb *believe* form two nouns, an adjective, and an adverb.

believe	(verb)
believ<u>er</u>	(noun)
believ<u>ability</u>	(noun)
believ<u>able</u>	(adjective)
believ<u>ably</u>	(adverb)

VERB SUFFIXES

Suffix	Meaning	Example
-en	to cause to or become	cheapen, redden
-ate	to cause to be	activate, animate
-ify, -fy	to make or cause to be	fortify, magnify
-ize	to make, to give, to practice	memorize, modernize

ADVERB SUFFIXES

The only regular suffix for adverbs is *-ly,* as in *slowly, wisely,* and *casually.*

ADJECTIVE SUFFIXES

Suffix	Meaning	Example
-al	capable of, suitable for	comical
-ial	pertaining to	managerial
-ic	pertaining to	democratic
-ly	resembling	sisterly
-ly	at specific intervals	hourly
-ful	abounding in	colorful
-ous, -ose	full of	porous, verbose
-ive	quality of	creative, adaptive
-less	lack of, free of	toothless
-ish	having the qualities of, preoccupied with	childish, bookish

NOUN SUFFIXES

Suffix	Meaning	Example
-ance, -ence	quality or state of	insurance, competence
-acy	quality or state of	piracy, privacy
-or	one who performs an action	actor
-arium, -orium	place for	aquarium, auditorium
-ary	place for, pertaining to	dictionary
-cide	kill	suicide, homicide
-icle, -cle	a diminutive ending	icicle, corpuscle
-hood	state or condition of	childhood
-ism	quality or doctrine of	Marxism, conservatism
-ity	quality or state of	acidity
-itis	inflammation of	appendicitis
-ics	the science or art of	economics
-ment	act or condition of	resentment
-mony	resulting condition	testimony
-ology	the study of	biology, psychology

(4) Learn Words According to a System

Learning related words according to a system is far more effective than memorizing words at random. You can, for example, study **homophones** or other <u>commonly confused words</u> together.

See
22c4

imminent   about to occur
eminent   prominent

ascent   a rise
assent   agreement

You can also study words that are confusing because they look somewhat alike.

marital   referring to marriage
martial   referring to war

descent   a downward movement
decent   characterized by good taste or morality

Finally, you can study words that are confusing because their meanings are so closely associated with each other.

| imply | to suggest |
| infer | to conclude |

| explicit | stated outright |
| implicit | implied, unsaid |

CHAPTER 22

IMPROVING SPELLING

If spelling has always given you trouble, you probably will not become a good speller overnight. But the situation is not hopeless. Most people can spell even difficult words "almost" correctly; usually only a letter or two are wrong. For this reason, memorizing a few simple rules and their exceptions and learning the correct spelling of the most commonly misspelled words can make a big difference.

22a Understanding Spelling and Pronunciation

Sound alone does not necessarily indicate a word's spelling. For instance, *gh* is silent in *light* but pronounced *f* in *cough;* the *ō* sound is spelled differently in *mow, toe, though, sew,* and *beau.* Problems are created by these and other inconsistencies between sound and spelling.

(1) Vowels in Unstressed Positions

Many unstressed vowels sound exactly alike when we say them. For instance, it is hard to tell from pronunciation alone that the *i* in *terrible* is not an *a.* In addition, the unstressed vowels *a, e,* and *i* are impossible to distinguish in the suffixes **-able and -ible**, *-ance* and *-ence,* and *-ant* and *-ent.* Because their pronunciation gives no clues to spelling, you must memorize the spellings of such words.

See 22b7

comfort*able*	brilli*ance*	serv*ant*
compat*ible*	excell*ence*	independ*ent*

(2) Silent Letters

Some English words contain silent letters. The *b* in *climb* is silent, as is the *t* in *mortgage.* Silent letters at the beginning of a word are especially bothersome: you cannot look up the spelling of *gnu* (pronounced *new*) in a dictionary if you do not already know that it begins with a *g*. The spelling of words with silent letters follows no rules, so you have to memorize such words as you encounter them.

ai̠sle	dum̠b̠	p̠neumonia
condem̠n̠	k̠nife	sil̠houette
depo̠t̠	k̠nig̠ht	sovereig̠n

(3) Words That Are Often Pronounced Carelessly

Most people pronounce words rather carelessly in everyday speech. Consequently, when spelling, they leave out, add, or transpose letters. The following words are often misspelled because they are pronounced incorrectly.

Febr̠uary	recog̠nize	proba̠b̠ly
candi̠date	nuc̠lear	s̠pecific
libr̠ary	environ̠ment	sur̠prise
govern̠ment	hundr̠ed	supposed̠ to
quanti̠ty	lightn̠ing	used̠ to

(4) Variant Forms of the Same Word

Spelling problems can occur when the verb and noun forms of a word are spelled differently.

advise (v)	advice (n)
describe (v)	description (n)
omit (v)	omission (n)

In addition, some words are spelled one way in the United States and another way in Great Britain and the Commonwealth nations.

American	*British*
color	colour
defense	defence
honor	honour
judgment	judgement
theater	theatre
traveled	travelled

(5) Homophones

See
22c4

Homophones are words—such as *accept* and *except*—that are pronounced alike but spelled differently.

| accept | to receive |
| except | other than |

| affect | to have an influence on (*verb*); an emotional response (*noun*) |
| effect | result (*noun*); to cause (*verb*) |

| its | possessive of *it* |
| it's | contraction of *it is* |

| principal | most important (*adjective*); head of a school (*noun*) |
| principle | a basic truth; rule of conduct |

 SPELLING: ONE WORD OR TWO?

Some words may be written as one word or two. The form you use is determined by meaning.

any way vs. *anyway*
It began to rain, but the game continued *anyway.*
The early pioneers made the trip West *any way* they could.

every day vs. *everyday*
Every day brings new opportunities.
John thought of himself as an *everyday* type of person.

Other words may be misspelled because you don't know whether they are one word or two.

a lot	even though
all right	as well
already	classroom
no one	overweight

Consult a dictionary if you have any doubts about whether to write one word or two.

22b Learning Spelling Rules

The few reliable rules that govern English spelling can help you overcome the general inconsistency between pronunciation and spelling.

(1) The *ie/ei* Combinations

The old rule still stands: use *i* before *e* except after *c* (or when pronounced *ay*, as in *neighbor*).

i *before* e	ei *after* c	ei *pronounced* ay
belief	ceiling	neighbor
chief	conceit	weigh
field	deceit	freight
niece	receive	eight
piece	perceive	
friend		

Exceptions: *either, neither, foreign, leisure, weird, seize.* In addition, if the *ie* combination is not pronounced as a unit, the rule does not apply: *atheist, science.*

EXERCISE 1

Fill in the blanks with the proper *ie* or *ei* combination. After completing the exercise, use your dictionary or spell checker to check your answers.

EXAMPLE: conc__ei__ve

1. rec_____pt
2. var_____ty
3. caff_____ne
4. ach_____ve
5. kal_____doscope
6. misch_____f
7. effic_____nt
8. v_____n
9. spec_____s
10. suffic_____nt

(2) Doubling Final Consonants

The only words that double their consonants before a suffix that begins with a vowel (*-ed, -ing*) are those that pass the following three tests.

1. They have one syllable or are stressed on the last syllable.
2. They contain only one vowel in the last syllable.
3. They end in a single consonant.

The word *tap* satisfies all three conditions: it has only one syllable, it contains only one vowel (*a*), and it ends in a single consonant (*p*). Therefore, the final consonant doubles before a suffix beginning with a vowel (*tapped, tapping*). The word *relent* passes two of the tests (it is stressed on the last syllable, and it has one vowel in the last syllable), but it does not end in a single consonant. Therefore, its final consonant is not doubled (*relented, relenting*).

(3) Prefixes

The addition of a prefix never affects the spelling of the root (*mis* + *spell* = *misspell*). Some prefixes can cause spelling problems, however, because they are pronounced alike although they are not spelled alike. Be especially careful of the prefixes *ante-/anti-, en-/in-, per-/pre-,* and *de-/di-*.

antebellum	antiaircraft
encircle	integrate
perceive	prescribe
deduct	direct

(4) Silent *e* before a Suffix

When a suffix that starts with a consonant is added to a word that ends in silent *e*, the *e* is generally kept: *hope/hopeful; lame/lamely; bore/boredom*. **Exceptions:** *argument, truly, ninth, judgment,* and *abridgment*.

When a suffix that starts with a vowel is added to a word that ends in silent *e*, the *e* is generally dropped: *hope/hoping; trace/traced; grieve/grievance; love/lovable*. **Exceptions:** *changeable, noticeable, courageous*. (In these cases the *e* is kept so that the *c* or *g* will be pronounced like the initial consonants in *cease* or *gem* and not like the initial consonants in *come* or *game*.)

EXERCISE 2

Combine the following words with the suffixes in parentheses. Keep or drop the silent *e* as you see fit; be prepared to explain your choices.

EXAMPLE: fate (al)
fatal

1. surprise (ing)
2. sure (ly)
3. force (ible)
4. manage (able)
5. due (ly)

6. outrage (ous)
7. service (able)
8. awe (ful)
9. shame (ing)
10. shame (less)

(5) *y* before a Suffix

When a word ends in a consonant plus *y*, the *y* generally changes to an *i* when a suffix is added (*beauty* + *ful* = *beautiful*). The *y* is retained, however, when the suffix *-ing* is added (*tally* + *ing* = *tallying*). It is also retained when the *y* ends a proper name (*McCarthy* + *ite* = *McCarthyite*) and in some one-syllable words (*dry* + *ness* = *dryness*). **Exception:** *city* + *scape* = *cityscape*.

When a word ends in a vowel plus *y*, the *y* is retained (*joy* + *ful* = *joyful; employ* + *er* = *employer*). **Exception:** *day* + *ly* = *daily.*

EXERCISE 3

Add the endings in parentheses to the following words. Change or keep the final *y* as you see fit; be prepared to explain your choices.

EXAMPLE: party (ing)

partying

1. journey (ing)
2. study (ed)
3. carry (ing)
4. shy (ly)
5. study (ing)

6. sturdy (ness)
7. merry (ment)
8. likely (hood)
9. plenty (ful)
10. supply (er)

(6) *seed* Endings

Endings with the sound *seed* are nearly always spelled *cede*, as in *precede, intercede, concede*, and so on. **Exceptions:** *supersede, exceed, proceed, succeed.*

(7) *-able, -ible*

If the root of a word is itself an independent word, the suffix *-able* is most commonly used. If the stem of a word is not an independent word, the suffix *-ible* is most often used.

comfort<u>able</u>
agree<u>able</u>
dry<u>able</u>

compat<u>ible</u>
incred<u>ible</u>
plaus<u>ible</u>

(8) Plurals

Most nouns form plurals by adding *s*.

savage/savages
girl/girls
boat/boats

tortilla/tortillas
gnu/gnus
taxi/taxis

There are, however, a number of exceptions.

Words Ending in f *or* fe   Some words ending in *f* or *fe* form plurals by changing the *f* to *v* and adding *es* or *s: life/lives, self/selves.* Others add just *s: belief/beliefs, safe/safes.* Words ending in double *f* take *s* to form plurals: *tariff/tariffs.*

Words Ending in y   Most words that end in a consonant followed by *y* form plurals by changing the *y* to *i* and adding *es: baby/babies.* **Exceptions:** proper nouns such as the *Kennedys* (never the *Kennedies*).
Words that end in a vowel followed by a *y* form plurals by adding *s: day/days, monkey/monkeys.*

Words Ending in o   Words that end in a vowel followed by *o* form the plural by adding *s: radio/radios, stereo/stereos, zoo/zoos.* Most English words that end in a consonant followed by *o* add *es* to form the plural: *tomato/tomatoes, hero/heroes.* **Exceptions:** *silo/silos, piano/pianos, memo/memos, photo/photos, soprano/sopranos, typo/typos.*

Words Ending in s, ss, sh, ch, x, *and* z   These words form plurals by adding *es: Jones/Joneses, mass/masses, rash/rashes, lunch/lunches, box/boxes, buzz/buzzes.*

NOTE: Some one-syllable words that end in *s* or *z* double their final consonants when forming plurals: *quiz/quizzes.*

Compound Nouns   Compound nouns—nouns formed from two or more words—usually conform to the rules governing the last word in the compound construction: *welfare state/welfare states; snowball/snowballs.* However, where the first element of the compound noun is more important than the others, the plural is formed with the first element: *sister-in-law/sisters-in-law, point of view/points of view.*

Foreign Plurals   Some words, especially those borrowed from Latin or Greek, keep their foreign plurals. Look up their plural forms in a dictionary if you do not know them.

Singular	*Plural*
basis	bases
criterion	criteria
datum	data
larva	larvae
medium	media
memorandum	memoranda
stimulus	stimuli

22c Developing Spelling Skills

In addition to studying the rules outlined above, you can take some additional steps to help yourself become a better speller.

USING A SPELL CHECKER

If you use a spell checker, remember that it will not identify a word spelled correctly but used incorrectly—homophones or near-homophones like *then* for *than* or *its* for *it's,* for example—or a typo that creates another word, such as *form* for *from* or *work* for *word.* For this reason you must always proofread even after you have run a spell check.

(1) Make Your Own Spelling List

Keep a list of your own problem words. When you read through your first draft, circle any words whose spellings you are unsure of. Then, look them up in your dictionary as you revise, and add them all (even those you have spelled correctly) to your list. When your instructor returns a paper, record any words you have misspelled. In addition, record problem words that you encounter when reading, including those from class notes and textbooks.

(2) Uncover Patterns of Misspelling

Do you consistently have a problem with plurals or with *ible/able* endings? If so, review the spelling rules that apply to these particular problems. By using this strategy, you can eliminate the need to memorize single words.

(3) Fix Each Word in Your Mind

Think of associations that will help fix the correct spellings in your mind. For example, you can remember the correct spelling of *definite* (often misspelled *definate*) by remembering that it contains the word *finite,* which suggests the concept of limit, as does *definite.* You can recall the *a* in *brilliance* (often misspelled *brillience*) by remembering that brilliant people often get *A's* in their classes.

The best way to fix words in your mind is to write them down. When you review your spelling list, don't just *read* the words on it; *write* them.

(4) Learn to Distinguish Commonly Confused Words

Following is a list of commonly confused **homophones** (words that sound exactly alike but have different spellings and meanings, such as *night* and *knight*) and near-homophones (words that sound similar, such as *accept* and *except*).

accept	to receive
except	other than
advice	recommendation
advise	to recommend
affect	to have an influence on (*verb*); an emotional response (*noun*)
effect	result (*noun*); to cause (*verb*)
all ready	prepared
already	by or before this or that time
allude	to refer to indirectly
elude	to avoid
allusion	indirect reference
illusion	false belief or perception
ascent	movement upward
assent	agreement
bare	uncovered
bear	to carry (*verb*); an animal (*noun*)
board	a wooden plank (*noun*); to get on an airplane, etc. (*verb*)
bored	uninterested
born	brought into life
borne	carried
brake	device for stopping
break	destroy, smash
buy	purchase
by	next to; near
capital	the seat of government; monetary assets
capitol	government building
Capitol	the building in Washington, DC, where the US Congress meets
cite	to quote, refer to
sight	the ability to see
site	a place

377

coarse	rough
course	path; class
complement	to complete or add to (*verb*); something that completes (*noun*)
compliment	praise
conscience	sense of right and wrong
conscious	mentally awake
council	governing body
counsel	advice (*noun*); to give advice (*verb*)
descent	downward movement
dissent	disagreement
desert	to abandon
dessert	sweet course at the end of a meal
device	an implement; a plan
devise	to invent
die	to lose life
dye	to change the color of something
discreet	reserved
discrete	individual, distinct
elicit	to draw out, evoke
illicit	unlawful; forbidden
eminent	prominent
immanent	inherent
imminent	about to happen
fair	equitable; light-complected
fare	a fee for transportation
forth	forward
fourth	referring to the number 4
gorilla	the animal
guerrilla	a type of soldier or warfare
hear	to perceive by ear
here	in this place
heard	past tense of *hear*
herd	group of animals

hole	an opening
whole	complete
its	possessive of *it*
it's	contraction of *it is*
later	after a time
latter	the last in a series
lead	to guide or direct (*verb*); a metal (*noun*)
led	past tense of *lead*
lessen	to reduce
lesson	something learned
loose	not tight; unbound
lose	to misplace
maybe	perhaps
may be	might be
meat	flesh
meet	encounter
no	negative
know	to be certain
passed	past tense of *pass*
past	a previous time; a time gone by
patience	forbearance
patients	persons receiving medical care
peace	the absence of war; quiet
piece	a portion of something
persecute	to harass or worry
prosecute	to institute criminal proceedings against
personal	private; one's own
personnel	employees
plain	unadorned
plane	an aircraft; a carpenter's tool
precede	to come before
proceed	to continue
principal	most important (*adjective*); head of a school (*noun*)
principle	a basic truth; rule of conduct

quiet	silent
quite	very

rain	precipitation
reign	to rule
rein	a strap (e.g., for a horse's bridle)

raise	to build up
raze	to tear down

right	correct
rite	a ritual
write	to put words on paper

road	street, highway
rode	past tense of *ride*

scene	place of action; section of a play
seen	viewed

sense	perception, understanding
since	from a time in the past up to the present

stationary	standing still
stationery	writing paper

straight	unbending
strait	a water passageway

than	as compared with
then	at that time; next

their	possessive of *they*
there	in that place
they're	contraction of *they are*

through	finished; into and out of
threw	past tense of *throw*
thorough	complete

to	toward
too	also; more than sufficient
two	the number

waist	the middle of the body
waste	discarded material (*noun*); to squander (*verb*)

weak	not strong
week	seven days

weather	atmospheric conditions
whether	in either case
which	one of a group
witch	female sorcerer
who's	contraction of *who is*
whose	possessive of *who*
your	possessive of *you*
you're	contraction of *you are*

PART 6

UNDERSTANDING GRAMMAR

CHAPTER 23

PARTS OF SPEECH

The building blocks for all English sentences are the eight basic parts of speech: *nouns, pronouns, verbs, adjectives, adverbs, prepositions, conjunctions,* and *interjections.* The part of speech to which a word belongs is determined by its function in a sentence.

23a Nouns

Nouns name people, places, things, ideas, actions, or qualities.

A **common noun** names any one of a class of people, places, or things: *artist, judge, building, event, city.*

A **proper noun,** always **capitalized**, refers to a particular person, place, or thing: *Mary Cassatt, Learned Hand, World Trade Center, Crimean War, St. Louis.*

A **count noun** names something that can be counted: five *dogs,* two dozen *grapes.*

A **noncount noun** names a quantity that is not countable: *time, dust, work, gold.* Noncount nouns are generally treated as singular.

A **collective noun** designates a group of people, places, or things thought of as a unit: *committee, class, navy, band, family.* **Collective nouns** are generally singular unless the members of the group are referred to as individuals.

An **abstract noun** refers to an intangible idea or quality: *love, hate, justice, anger, fear, prejudice.*

See
34b

See
26a5

23b Pronouns

Pronouns are words used in place of nouns. The noun for which a pronoun stands is called its **antecedent.**

If you use a quotation in your paper, you must document it. (Pronoun *it* refers to antecedent *quotation*.)

Although different types of pronouns may have exactly the same forms, they are distinguished from one another by their functions in a sentence.

A **personal pronoun** stands for a person or thing. Personal pronouns include *I, me, we, us, my, mine, our, ours, you, your, yours, he, she, it, its, him, his, her, hers, they, them, their,* and *theirs*.

They made her an offer she couldn't refuse.

An **indefinite pronoun** functions as a noun, but it does not refer to any particular person or thing. For this reason, indefinite pronouns do not require antecedents. Indefinite pronouns include *another, any, each, few, many, some, nothing, one, anyone, everyone, everybody, everything, someone, something, either,* and *neither*.

Many are called, but few are chosen.

A **reflexive pronoun** ends with *-self* and refers to a recipient of the action that is the same as the actor. The reflexive pronouns are *myself, yourself, himself, herself, itself, oneself, themselves, ourselves,* and *yourselves*.

They found themselves in downtown Pittsburgh.

Intensive pronouns have the same form as reflexive pronouns; an intensive pronoun emphasizes a preceding noun or pronoun.

Darrow himself was sure his client was innocent.

A **relative pronoun** introduces an adjective or noun clause in a sentence. Relative pronouns include *which, who, whom, that, what, whose, whatever, whoever, whomever,* and *whichever*.

Gandhi was the charismatic man who helped lead India to independence. (introduces adjective clause)

Whatever happens will be a surprise. (introduces noun clause)

An **interrogative pronoun** introduces a question. Interrogative pronouns include *who, which, what, whom, whose, whoever, whatever,* and *whichever*.

Who was that masked man?

A **demonstrative pronoun** points to a particular thing or group of things. *This, that, these,* and *those* are demonstrative pronouns.

This is one of Shakespeare's early plays.

A **reciprocal pronoun** denotes a mutual relationship. The reciprocal pronouns are *each other* and *one another.*

Each other generally indicates a relationship between two individuals; *one another* generally denotes a relationship among more than two.

Romeo and Juliet declared their love for <u>each other</u>.

Concertgoers jostled <u>one another</u> in the ticket line.

23c Verbs

(1) Recognizing Verbs

A verb may express either action or a state of being.

He <u>ran</u> for the train. (action)

Elizabeth II <u>became</u> queen after the death of her father, George VI. (state of being)

Verbs can be classified into two groups: *main verbs* and *auxiliary verbs.*

Main Verbs   **Main verbs** carry most of the meaning in the sentences or clauses in which they appear. Some main verbs are action verbs.

Bulfinch's *Mythology* <u>contains</u> a discussion of Greek mythology.

Emily Dickinson <u>anticipated</u> much of twentieth-century poetry.

Other main verbs function as linking verbs. A **linking verb** does not show any physical or emotional action. Its function is to link the sentence's subject to a **subject complement,** a word or phrase that renames or describes the subject.

Carbon disulfide <u>smells</u> bad.

FREQUENTLY USED LINKING VERBS

appear	believe	look	seem	taste
be	feel	prove	smell	turn
become	grow	remain	sound	

Auxiliary Verbs **Auxiliary verbs** (also called **helping verbs**), such as *be* and *have*, combine with main verbs to form **verb phrases.** Auxiliary verbs indicate tense, voice, or mood.

[auxiliary] [main verb] [auxiliary] [main verb]

The train has started. We are leaving soon.

[verb phrase]   [verb phrase]

Certain auxiliary verbs, known as **modal auxiliaries,** indicate necessity, possibility, willingness, obligation, or ability.

In the near future farmers <u>might</u> cultivate seaweed as a food crop.

Coal mining <u>would</u> be safer if dust were controlled in the mines.

MODAL AUXILIARIES

can	might	ought [to]	will
could	must	shall	would
may	need [to]	should	

---

(2) Recognizing Verbals

Verbals, such as *known* or *swimming* or *to go*, are verb forms that act as adjectives, adverbs, or nouns. A verbal can never serve as a sentence's main verb unless it is used with one or more auxiliary verbs (*has known, should be swimming*). Verbals include *participles, infinitives,* and *gerunds.*

Participles Virtually every verb has a **present participle,** which ends in *ing* (*loving, learning, going, writing*), and a **past participle,** which usually ends in *d* or *ed* (*agreed, learned*). Some verbs have <u>irregular</u> past participles (*gone, begun, written*). Participles may function in a sentence as adjectives or as nouns.

See
25a2

Twenty brands of <u>running</u> shoes were displayed at the exhibition. (Present participle *running* serves as adjective modifying noun *shoes.*)

The <u>crowded</u> bus went right by those waiting at the corner. (Past participle *crowded* serves as adjective modifying noun *bus.*)

The <u>wounded</u> were given emergency first aid. (Past participle *wounded* serves as a noun, the sentence's subject.)

Infinitives An **infinitive**—*to* plus the base form of the verb—may function as an adjective, an adverb, or a noun.

Ann Arbor was clearly the place <u>to be</u>. (Infinitive *to be* serves as adjective modifying noun *place.*)

They say that breaking up is hard <u>to do</u>. (Infinitive *to do* serves as adverb modifying adjective *hard.*)

Carla went outside <u>to think</u>. (Infinitive *to think* serves as adverb modifying verb *went.*)

<u>To win</u> was everything. (Infinitive *to win* serves as a noun, the sentence's subject.)

Gerunds **Gerunds,** special forms of verbs ending in *ing,* are always used as nouns.

<u>Seeing</u> is <u>believing</u>. (Gerund *seeing* serves as sentence's subject; gerund *believing* serves as subject complement.)

He worried about <u>interrupting</u>. (Gerund *interrupting* is object of preposition *about.*)

Andrew loves <u>skiing</u>. (Gerund *skiing* is direct object of verb *loves.*)

NOTE: When the *-ing* form of a verb is used as a noun, it is considered a *gerund;* when it is used as a modifier, it is a *present participle.*

23d Adjectives

Adjectives are words that describe, limit, qualify, or in any other way modify nouns or pronouns.

(1) Descriptive Adjectives

Descriptive adjectives, the largest class of adjectives, name a quality of the noun or pronoun they modify.

After the game, they were <u>exhausted</u>.

They ordered a <u>chocolate</u> soda and a <u>butterscotch</u> sundae.

Some descriptive adjectives are formed from common nouns or from verbs (*friend/friendly, agree/agreeable*). Others, called **proper adjectives,** are formed from proper nouns.

Eubie Blake was a talented <u>American</u> musician who died in 1983.

The Shakespearean or English sonnet consists of an octave and a sestet.

See
36b1

Two or more words may be joined, with or without a hyphen, to form a **compound adjective** (*foreign born, well-read*).

(2) Determiners

Determiners are words that function as adjectives to limit or qualify nouns. Determiners include *articles, possessive nouns, certain pronouns,* and *numbers*.

Articles (*a, an, the*)

The boy found a four-leaf clover.

Possessive nouns

Lesley's mother lives in New Jersey.

Possessive pronouns (the personal pronouns *my, your, his, her, its, our, their*)

Their lives depended on my skill.

Demonstrative pronouns (*this, these, that, those*)

This song reminds me of that song we heard yesterday.

Interrogative pronouns (*what, which, whose*)

Whose book is this?

Indefinite pronouns (*another, each, both, many, any, some,* and so on)

Both candidates agreed to return another day.

Relative pronouns (*what, whatever, which, whichever, whose, whosever*)

I forgot whatever reasons I had for leaving.

Numbers (*one, two, first, second,* and so on)

The first time I played I got only one hit.

23e Adverbs

Adverbs describe the action of verbs or modify adjectives, other adverbs, or complete phrases, clauses, or sentences. They answer the questions

"How?" "Why?" "Where?" "When?" "Under what conditions?" and "To what extent?"

> He walked <u>rather hesitently</u> toward the front of the room. (walked *how?*)
>
> Let's meet <u>tomorrow</u> for coffee. (meet *when?*)

Adverbs that modify other adverbs or adjectives limit or qualify the words they modify.

> He pitched an <u>almost</u> perfect game.

Interrogative adverbs—the words *how, when, why,* and *where*—introduce questions.

> <u>Why</u> did the compound darken?

Conjunctive adverbs act as transitional words, joining and relating independent clauses.

Conjunctive adverbs may appear in any of several positions in a sentence.

> Jason forgot to register for chemistry. <u>However</u>, he managed to sign up during the drop/add period. (conjunctive adverb at beginning of sentence)
>
> Jason forgot to register for chemistry; <u>however</u>, he managed to sign up during the drop/add period. (conjunctive adverb at beginning of clause)
>
> Jason forgot to register for chemistry. He managed, <u>however</u>, to sign up during the drop/add period. (conjunctive adverb within sentence)
>
> Jason forgot to register for chemistry. He managed to sign up during the drop/add period, <u>however</u>. (conjunctive adverb at end of sentence)

FREQUENTLY USED CONJUNCTIVE ADVERBS

accordingly	furthermore	meanwhile	similarly
also	hence	moreover	still
anyway	however	nevertheless	then
besides	incidentally	next	thereafter
certainly	indeed	nonetheless	therefore
consequently	instead	now	thus
finally	likewise	otherwise	undoubtedly

23f Prepositions

A **preposition** introduces a noun or pronoun (or a phrase or clause functioning in the sentence as a noun), linking it to other words in the sentence. The word or word group the preposition introduces is called its **object.**

prep obj   prep   obj prep obj

They received a postcard <u>from</u> Bobby telling <u>about</u> his trip <u>to</u> Canada.

FREQUENTLY USED PREPOSITIONS

about	beneath	inside	since
above	beside	into	through
across	between	like	throughout
after	beyond	near	to
against	by	of	toward
along	concerning	off	under
among	despite	on	underneath
around	down	onto	until
as	during	out	up
at	except	outside	upon
before	for	over	with
behind	from	past	within
below	in	regarding	without

23g Conjunctions

Conjunctions connect words, phrases, clauses, or sentences. Different conjunctions establish different relationships between the items they connect.

Coordinating conjunctions (*and, or, but, nor, for, so, yet*) connect words, phrases, or clauses that are grammatically equivalent.

We could choose pheasant <u>or</u> venison. (*Or* links two nouns.)

... of the people, by the people, <u>and</u> for the people. (*And* links three prepositional phrases.)

Thoreau wrote *Walden* in 1854, <u>and</u> he died in 1862. (*And* links two independent clauses.)

Correlative conjunctions, always used in pairs, also link grammatically equivalent items.

See
11a3

FREQUENTLY USED CORRELATIVE CONJUNCTIONS

both . . . and	neither . . . nor
either . . . or	not only . . . but also
just as . . . so	whether . . . or

<u>Both</u> Hancock <u>and</u> Jefferson signed the Declaration of Independence. (Correlative conjunctions link two nouns.)

<u>Either</u> I will renew my lease, <u>or</u> I will move. (Correlative conjunctions link two independent clauses.)

Subordinating conjunctions include *since, because, although, if, after, when, while, before, unless,* and so on. A subordinating conjunction introduces a dependent (subordinate) clause, connecting it to the sentence's independent (main) clause to form a **complex sentence**. The subordinating conjunction indicates the relationship between the clauses.

See
11b

<u>Although</u> drug use is a serious concern for parents, many parents are afraid to discuss it with their children.

It is best to diagram your garden <u>before</u> you start to plant it.

Conjunctive adverbs, also known as *adverbial conjunctions,* are discussed in **23e.**

23h Interjections

Interjections are words used as exclamations: *Oh! Ouch! Wow! Alas! Hey!* These words, which express emotion, are grammatically independent; that is, they do not have a grammatical function in a sentence. Interjections may be set off in a sentence by commas.

The message, alas, arrived too late.

For greater emphasis, interjections can be punctuated as independent units, set off with an exclamation point.

Alas! The message arrived too late.

Other kinds of words may also be used in isolation. These include *yes, no, hello, good-bye, please,* and *thank you.* All such words, including interjections, are collectively referred to as **isolates.**

CHAPTER 24

NOUNS AND PRONOUNS

24a Case

Pronouns change **case** to indicate their function in a sentence. English has three cases: *subjective, objective,* and *possessive.*

Nouns change form only in the possessive case: the *cat's* eyes, *Molly's* book. Pronouns, however, have many case forms.

PRONOUN CASE FORMS

Subjective

I	he, she	it	we	you	they	who
						whoever

Objective

me	him, her	it	us	you	them	whom
						whomever

Possessive

my	his, her	its	our	your	their	whose
mine	hers		ours	yours	theirs	

---

(1) Using the Subjective Case

SUBJECT OF A VERB: I bought a mountain bike. (*I* is the subject of the verb *bought.*)

SUBJECT COMPLEMENT: It was he for whom the men were looking. (*He* is the subject complement.)

APPOSITIVE IDENTIFYING SUBJECT: Both scientists, <u>Oppenheimer and he</u>, worked on the atomic bomb. (*Oppenheimer and he* is an appositive identifying the subject *both scientists.*)

395

PRONOUN CASE

Most people feel silly saying "It is I" or "It is he," so they use the colloquial constructions "It's me" or "It's him" in speech or informal writing. In college writing, however, you should be careful to use the correct pronoun case.

(2) Using the Objective Case

DIRECT OBJECT: My sociology teacher likes <u>me</u>. (*Me* is the direct object of the verb *likes.*)

INDIRECT OBJECT: During the 1950s the Kinsey report gave <u>them</u> quite a shock. (*Them* is the indirect object of the verb *gave.*)

OBJECT OF A PREPOSITION: In 1502 Leonardo da Vinci designed the fortifications of the city for <u>him</u>. (*Him* is the object of the preposition *for.*)

APPOSITIVE IDENTIFYING AN OBJECT: Rachel discussed both authors, <u>Hannah Arendt and her</u>. (*Hannah Arendt and her* is an appositive identifying the object *authors.*)

 PRONOUN CASE

I is not necessarily more appropriate than *me* in every context. In compound constructions like the following, for example, *me* is correct.

He told <u>Jason and me</u> [not *I*] to put our dog on a leash. (*Jason and me* is the indirect object of the verb *told.*)

Between <u>you and me</u> [not *I*] we own ten shares of stock. (*You and me* is the object of the preposition *between.*)

Let's <u>you and me</u> [not *I*] go to the art museum. (*You and me* is an appositive identifying *us,* direct object of the verb *let.*)

(3) Using the Possessive Case

A pronoun takes the **possessive case** when it indicates ownership (*our* car, *your* book). Remember to use the possessive, not the objective, case before a gerund.

Napoleon approved of <u>their</u> [not *them*] ruling Naples. (*Ruling* is a gerund.)

NOTE: Be sure to distinguish **gerunds**, which always function as nouns, from **present participles** functioning as adjectives.

See
23c2

 NOUNS AND PRONOUN CASE

Remember the distinction between the possessive pronoun *its* and the contraction *it's: its* designates ownership (*its* leg), whereas *it's* is the contraction of *it is* (*"It's* a nice day") or *it has* (*"It's* been a long day").

EXERCISE 1

Choose the correct form of the pronoun within the parentheses. Be prepared to explain why you chose each form.

EXAMPLE: Toni Morrison, Alice Walker, and (<u>she</u>, her) are perhaps the most widely recognized African-American women writing today.

1. Both Walt Whitman and (he, him) wrote a great deal of poetry about nature.
2. Randall Jarrell, Wilfred Owen, and (he, him) wrote about their war experiences.
3. Both (she, her) and the Pulitzer Prize–winning poet Gwendolyn Brooks were born in Kansas but moved early in life to Chicago's South Side.
4. Our instructor gave Matthew and (me, I) an excellent idea for our project.
5. The philosophy class made (we, us) more aware of how we form our values.
6. The sales clerk objected to (me, my) returning the sweater.
7. (We, Us) students have the opportunity to attend the concert free of charge.
8. Ezra Pound, Sylvia Plath, and (he, him) were plagued with bouts of mental illness.
9. I understand (you, your) being unavailable to work tonight.
10. The waiter asked Michael and (me, I) to move to another table.

24b Determining Pronoun Case in Special Situations

(1) Implied Comparisons with *Than* or *As*

When a sentence containing an implied comparison ends with a pronoun, your meaning determines your choice of pronoun.

Darcy likes John more than I. (*more than I like John*)

Darcy likes John more than me. (*more than she likes me*)

Alex helps Dr. Elliott as much as I. (*as much as I help Dr. Elliott*)

Alex helps Dr. Elliott as much as me. (*as much as he helps me*)

(2) *Who* and *Whom*

The case of the pronouns *who* and *whom* depends on their function *within their own clause*. When a pronoun serves as the subject of a clause, use *who* or *whoever;* when it functions as an object, use *whom* or *whomever.*

Shortly after leaving Oklahoma the Joads were reminded who they were. (*Who* is the subject of the dependent clause *who they were.*)

The Salvation Army gives food and shelter to whoever is in need. (*Whoever* is the subject of the dependent clause *whoever is in need.*)

I wonder whom jazz musician Miles Davis influenced. (*Whom* is the object of *influenced* in the dependent clause *whom jazz musician Miles Davis influenced.*)

Whomever Stieglitz photographed, he revealed. (*Whomever* is the object of *photographed* in the dependent clause *Whomever Stieglitz photographed.*)

 PRONOUN CASE

To determine the case of *who* at the beginning of a question, use a personal pronoun to answer the question. The case of *who* should be the same as the case of the personal pronoun.

continued on the following page

---

continued from the previous page

<u>Who</u> wrote *The Age of Innocence?* <u>She</u> wrote it. (subject)

<u>Whom</u> do you support for mayor? I support <u>her</u>. (object)

To <u>whom</u> is the letter addressed? It is addressed to <u>them</u>. (object of a preposition)

NOTE: In all but the most formal situations, current usage accepts *who* at the beginning of questions (<u>Who</u> do you support for mayor?).

EXERCISE 2

Using the word in parentheses, combine each pair of sentences into a single sentence. You may change word order and add or delete words.

> EXAMPLE: Even after he left the band The Police, bass player Sting's musical career continued to thrive. He once taught middle school English. (who)
>
> REVISED: Even after he left the band The Police, bass player Sting, who once taught middle school English, continued to have a thriving musical career.

1. The photographs of Herb Ritts of world leaders, leading artistic figures in dance and drama, and a vanishing African tribe are technically beautiful and emotionally compelling. He got his start by taking photographs of Hollywood stars. (who)
2. Tim Green has written several novels about a fictional football team. He played for the Atlanta Hawks and has a degree in law. (who)
3. Some say Carl Sagan did more to further science education in America than any other person. He wrote many books on science and narrated many popular television shows. (who)
4. Jodie Foster has won two Academy Awards for her acting. She was a child star. (who)
5. Sylvia Plath met the poet Ted Hughes at Cambridge University in England. She later married him. (whom)

(3) *We* and *Us* before a Noun

When a first-person plural pronoun precedes a noun, the case of the pronoun depends on the way the noun functions in the sentence.

> <u>We</u> women must stick together. (*Women* is the subject of the sentence; the pronoun *we* must be in the subjective case.)

Teachers make learning easy for us students. (*Students* is the object of the preposition *for;* the pronoun *us* must be in the objective case.)

24c Pronoun Reference

An **antecedent** is the word or word group to which a pronoun refers. Pronoun reference is clear when readers can easily identify the pronoun's antecedent. In the following passage, notice how each of the underlined pronouns clearly refers to the noun *warts*.

Warts are wonderful structures. They can appear overnight on any part of the skin, like mushrooms on a damp lawn, full grown and splendid in the complexity of their architecture. Viewed in stained sections under a microscope, they are the most specialized of cellular arrangements, constructed as though for a purpose. They sit there like turreted mounds of dense impenetrable horn, impregnable, designed for defense against the world outside. (Lewis Thomas, *The Medusa and the Snail*)

Pronoun reference is not clear, however, when a pronoun's antecedent is *ambiguous, remote,* or *nonexistent.*

(1) Ambiguous Antecedents

Pronoun reference is ambiguous if the pronoun appears to refer to more than one antecedent. The pronouns *this, that, which,* and *it* are most likely to invite this kind of confusion.

AMBIGUOUS: The accountant took out his calculator and completed the tax return. Then, he put it in his briefcase. (The pronoun *it* can refer either to *calculator* or to *tax return.*)

CLEAR: The accountant took out his calculator and completed the tax return. Then, he put the calculator in his briefcase.

AMBIGUOUS: Some one-celled organisms contain chlorophyll yet are considered animals. This illustrates the difficulty of classifying single-celled organisms as either animals or plants. (Exactly what does *this* refer to?)

CLEAR: Some one-celled organisms contain chlorophyll yet are considered animals. This paradox illustrates the difficulty of classifying single-celled organisms as either animals or plants.

(2) Remote Antecedents

When a pronoun is far from its antecedent, readers have difficulty making a connection between them. As a result, they may not understand the sentence.

UNCLEAR: Rumors of gold, letters from friends and relatives, and newspaper articles praising democracy persuaded many Czechs to come to America. By 1860, about twenty thousand Czechs had left their country. By 1900, thirteen thousand Czech immigrants were coming to <u>its</u> shores each year. (The pronoun *its* in the last sentence is so far removed from its antecedent, *America,* that the reference cannot easily be understood.)

CLEAR: By 1900, thirteen thousand Czech immigrants were coming to <u>America's</u> shores each year.

(3) Nonexistent Antecedents

When a pronoun refers to a nonexistent antecedent, readers may be confused.

UNCLEAR: Our township has decided to build a computer lab in the elementary school. <u>They</u> feel that children should learn to use computers in fourth grade. (*They* refers to an antecedent that the writer has neglected to mention.)

CLEAR: Our township has decided to build a computer lab in the elementary school. <u>Teachers</u> feel that children should learn to use computers in fourth grade.

 PRONOUN REFERENCE

References such as *"It* says in the paper" and *"They* said on the news" refer to unidentified antecedents and therefore are not acceptable in college writing. To clarify such a reference, substitute an appropriate noun for the pronoun: *"The article* in the paper says. . . ." and "On the news, *Cokie Roberts* said. . . ."

(4) *Who, Which,* and *That*

In general, the pronoun *who* refers to people or to animals that have names. The pronouns *which* and *that* usually refer to objects, events, or unnamed animals and sometimes to groups of people. In speech and informal writing, however, *that* is often used to refer to people.

David Henry Hwang, <u>who</u> wrote the Tony Award–winning play *M. Butterfly,* also wrote *Family Devotions* and *FOB.*

The spotted owl, <u>which</u> lives in old-growth forests, is in danger of extinction.

Houses <u>that</u> are built today are more energy efficient than those built twenty years ago.

Kevin is the student <u>that</u> got the best grade. (Informal)

See
29d1

NOTE: Make certain that you use *which* in nonrestrictive clauses, which are always set off with commas. In most cases, use *that* in restrictive clauses. *Who* may be used in both **restrictive and nonrestrictive clauses**.

EXERCISE 3

Analyze the pronoun errors in each of the following sentences. After doing so, revise each sentence by substituting an appropriate noun or noun phrase for the underlined pronoun.

> **EXAMPLE:** Jefferson asked Lewis to head the expedition, and Lewis selected <u>him</u> as his associate.
>
> **ANALYSIS:** *Him* refers to a nonexistent antecedent.
>
> **REVISION:** Jefferson asked Lewis to head the expedition, and Lewis selected Clark as his associate.

1. The purpose of the expedition was to search out a land route to the Pacific and to gather information about the West. The Louisiana Purchase increased the need for <u>it</u>.
2. The expedition was going to be difficult. <u>They</u> trained the men in Illinois, the starting point.
3. Clark and most of the men who descended the Yellowstone River camped on the bank. <u>It</u> was beautiful and wild.
4. Both Jefferson and Lewis had faith that <u>he</u> would be successful in this transcontinental journey.
5. The expedition was efficient, and only one man was lost. <u>This</u> was extraordinary.

STUDENT WRITER AT WORK

Nouns and Pronouns

Following is part of a draft of a student essay about John Updike. This section of the essay gives a plot summary of Updike's short story "A & P." Read the draft and revise it to correct errors in case and to eliminate inexact pronoun reference. After you have corrected the errors, go over the draft again and, if necessary, revise further to strengthen coherence, unity, and style.

John Updike's "A & P," a short story that appears in the collection Pigeon Feathers and Other Stories, takes place in a small town similar to Updike's hometown. The character which has the significant role in "A & P" is Sammy, a cashier at the supermarket. Sammy is a nineteen-year-old boy that is just out of high school. He analyzes everyone who comes to the A & P to shop. It is him who is the narrator of the story.

The story takes place on a Thursday afternoon when three girls in bathing suits walk into the store. They are different from the other shoppers. Their manner and the way they walk make them different from them. Sammy notices that one of the girls, who he calls Queenie, leads the other girls. This appeals to him. He identifies with her because he feels that he too is a leader.

When the girls come to his check-out counter, he rings up their purchase. Suddenly the store manager, Lengel, begins scolding the girls for coming into the store in bathing suits. Sammy feels sorry for them, and in a gesture of defiance he quits. Sammy feels that him quitting is a rejection of him and all that he stands for. To Sammy, Lengel is a person that represents the narrow morality of the town.

Sammy's quitting is the climax of the story. Sammy chooses to follow his conscience and in doing so pays the price. He feels that not following his ideals would be bad. Because he is young, however, he does not realize the significance of the act which he commits. For a moment Lengel and Sammy face each other, but he does not change his mind. Sammy feels that he has won his freedom. His confidence is short-lived, though. When he walks out into the parking lot, the girls are gone, and he is alone. It is then he realizes that the world is going to be hard for him from this point on.

CHAPTER 25

VERBS

VERBS: KEY TERMS

Form The spelling of a verb that conveys tense, person, number, and so on.

Tense The form a verb takes to indicate when an action occurs or when a condition exists—*present, past, future,* and so on.

Person The form a verb takes to indicate whether someone is speaking (*first person*), is spoken to (*second person*), or is spoken about (*third person*).

Number The form a verb takes to indicate whether the verb is singular (The child *writes*) or plural (The children *write*).

Mood The form a verb takes to indicate the writer's attitude—for example, whether he or she is making a statement, giving a command, or making a recommendation (I *read* the book; *Read* the book!; I suggest you *read* the book).

Voice The form a verb takes to indicate whether the subject acts or is acted upon (He *wrote* the book; The book *was written* by him).

25a Verb Forms

Every verb has four **principal parts:** a **base form** (the form of the verb used with *I, we, you,* and *they* in the present tense),* a **present participle,** a **past tense form,** and a **past participle.**

---

*The verb *be* is so irregular that it is the one exception to this definition; its base form is *be.*

(1)   Principal Parts of Regular Verbs

Most verbs in English are **regular** and form their principal parts with *ing* and *ed* or *d* added to the base form. Consult a dictionary whenever you are uncertain about the form of a verb. (If the dictionary lists only the base form, the verb is regular.)

PRINCIPAL PARTS OF REGULAR VERBS

Base Form	Present Participle	Past Tense Form	Past Participle
smile	smiling	smiled	smiled
talk	talking	talked	talked
jump	jumping	jumped	jumped

(2)   Principal Parts of Irregular Verbs

Irregular verbs are those that do not form their principal parts as regular verbs do. If a verb is irregular, the dictionary lists its principal parts, three if the past tense and past participle are different and two if the past tense and past participle are the same.

hide, v (past hid, pp hidden)

make, v (made)

The following chart lists the principal parts of the most frequently used irregular verbs.

FREQUENTLY USED IRREGULAR VERBS

Base Form	Present Participle	Past Tense Form	Past Participle
arise	arising	arose	arisen
awake	awaking	awoke, awaked	awoke, awaked
be	being	was/were	been
beat	beating	beat	beaten
begin	beginning	began	begun
bend	bending	bent	bent
bet	betting	bet, betted	bet

continued on the following page

405

continued from the previous page

Base Form	Present Participle	Past Tense Form	Past Participle
bite	biting	bit	bitten
blow	blowing	blew	blown
break	breaking	broke	broken
bring	bringing	brought	brought
build	building	built	built
burst	bursting	burst	burst
buy	buying	bought	bought
catch	catching	caught	caught
choose	choosing	chose	chosen
cling	clinging	clung	clung
come	coming	came	come
deal	dealing	dealt	dealt
dig	digging	dug	dug
dive	diving	dived, dove	dived
do	doing	did	done
drag	dragging	dragged	dragged
draw	drawing	drew	drawn
dream	dreaming	dreamed, dreamt	dreamed, dreamt
drink	drinking	drank	drunk
drive	driving	drove	driven
eat	eating	ate	eaten
fall	falling	fell	fallen
feel	feeling	felt	felt
fight	fighting	fought	fought
find	finding	found	found
fly	flying	flew	flown
forget	forgetting	forgot	forgotten, forgot
forsake	forsaking	forsook	forsaken
freeze	freezing	froze	frozen
get	getting	got	gotten
give	giving	gave	given
go	going	went	gone
grow	growing	grew	grown
hand (suspend)	hanging	hung	hung
hang (execute)	hanging	hanged	hanged

continued on the following page

continued from the previous page

Base Form	Present Participle	Past Tense Form	Past Participle
have	having	had	had
hear	hearing	heard	heard
keep	keeping	kept	kept
know	knowing	knew	known
lay	laying	laid	laid
lead	leading	led	led
lend	lending	lent	lent
let	letting	let	let
lie (recline)	lying	lay	lain
lie (tell an untruth)	lying	lied	lied
make	making	made	made
plead	pleading	pleaded, pled	pleaded, pled
prove	proving	proved	proved, proven
read	reading	read	read
ride	riding	rode	ridden
ring	ringing	rang	rung
rise	rising	rose	risen
run	running	ran	run
say	saying	said	said
see	seeing	saw	seen
set	setting	set	set
shake	shaking	shook	shaken
shrink	shrinking	shrank, shrunk	shrunk, shrunken
sing	singing	sang	sung
sink	sinking	sank	sunk
sit	sitting	sat	sat
sneak	sneaking	sneaked, snuck	sneaked, snuck
speak	speaking	spoke	spoken
speed	speeding	sped, speeded	sped, speeded
spin	spinning	spun	spun
spring	springing	sprang	sprung
stand	standing	stood	stood
steal	stealing	stole	stolen

continued on the following page

continued from the previous page

Base Form	Present Participle	Past Tense Form	Past Participle
strike	striking	struck	struck, stricken
swear	swearing	swore	sworn
swim	swimming	swam	swum
swing	swinging	swung	swung
take	taking	took	taken
teach	teaching	taught	taught
throw	throwing	threw	thrown
wake	waking	woke, waked	waked, woken
wear	wearing	wore	worn
write	writing	wrote	written

 CLOSE-UP *LIE* AND *LAY, SIT* AND *SET*

The irregular verbs *lie* and *lay* and *sit* and *set* frequently give writers trouble because each pair of verbs has similar-sounding forms with similar meanings.

Lie means "to recline" and does not take an object (He likes to *lie* on the floor); *lay* means "to place" or "to put" and does take an object (He wants to *lay* a rug on the floor).

Base Form	Present Participle	Past Tense Form	Past Participle
lie	lying	lay	lain
lay	laying	laid	laid

Sit means "to assume a seated position" and does not take an object (She wants to *sit* on the table); *set* means "to place" or "to put" and usually takes an object (She wants to *set* a vase on the table).

Base Form	Present Participle	Past Tense Form	Past Participle
sit	sitting	sat	sat
set	setting	set	set

EXERCISE 1

Complete the sentences in the following paragraph with an appropriate form of the verbs in parentheses.

> EXAMPLE: An air of mystery surrounds many of those who have
> _____ (sing) and played the blues.
>
> An air of mystery surrounds many of those who have <u>sung</u> and played the blues.

The legendary bluesman Robert Johnson supposedly _____ (sell) his soul to the devil in order to become a guitar virtuoso. Myth has it that the young Johnson could barely chord his instrument and annoyed other musicians by trying to sit in at clubs, where he _____ (sneak) onto the band stand to play every chance he got. He disappeared for a short time, the story goes, and when he returned he was a phenomenal guitarist, having _____ (swear) a Faustian oath to Satan. Johnson's song "Crossroads Blues"—rearranged and recorded by the sixties supergroup Cream as simply "Crossroads"—supposedly recounts this exchange, telling how Johnson _____ (deal) with the devil. Some of his other songs, such as "Hellhound on My Trail," are allegedly about the torment he suffered as he _____ (plead) for his soul.

EXERCISE 2

Complete the following sentences with appropriate forms of the verbs in parentheses.

> EXAMPLE: Mary Cassatt _____ down her paintbrush. (lie, lay)
>
> Mary Cassatt <u>lay</u> down her paintbrush.

1. Impressionist artists of the nineteenth century preferred everyday subjects and used to _____ fruit on a table to paint. (sit, set)
2. They were known for their technique of _____ dabs of paint quickly on canvas, giving an "impression" of a scene, not extensive detail. (lying, laying)
3. Claude Monet's *Women in the Garden* featured one woman in the foreground who _____ on the grass in a garden. (sat, set)
4. In Pierre Auguste Renoir's *Nymphs* two nude figures talk while _____ on flowers in a garden. (lying, laying)
5. Paul Cézanne liked to _____ in front of his subject as he painted and often completed paintings out of doors rather than in a studio. (sit, set)

25b Tense

Tense is the form a verb takes to indicate when an action occurs or when a condition exists. However, tense is not the same as time. The present tense, for example, indicates present time, but it can also indicate future time or a generally held belief.

ENGLISH VERB TENSES

Simple Tenses
Present (I finish; she or he finishes)
Past (I finished)
Future (I will finish)

Perfect Tenses
Present perfect (I have finished; she or he has finished)
Past perfect (I had finished)
Future perfect (I will have finished)

Progressive Tenses
Present progressive (I am finishing; she or he is finishing)
Past progressive (I was finishing)
Future progressive (I will be finishing)
Present perfect progressive (I have been finishing)
Past perfect progressive (I had been finishing)
Future perfect progressive (I will have been finishing)

25c Using the Simple Tenses

The **simple tenses** include *present, past,* and *future.*

(1) Present Tense

The **present tense** usually indicates an action taking place at the time it is expressed in speech or writing (I *smile;* she *smiles*).

In addition to expressing an action that takes place in the present, the present tense has some special uses.

SPECIAL USES OF THE PRESENT TENSE

The rector <u>opens</u> the chapel every morning at six o'clock. (indicates that something occurs regularly)

The grades <u>arrive</u> next Thursday. (indicates future time)

Studying <u>pays</u> off. (states a generally held belief)

An object at rest <u>tends</u> to stay at rest. (states a scientific truth)

In *Family Installments* Edward Rivera <u>tells</u> the story of a family's journey from Puerto Rico to New York City. (discusses a literary work)

Note that words like *every* and *next* sometimes help to indicate time.

---

(2) Past Tense

The **past tense** indicates that an action has already taken place.

John Glenn <u>orbited</u> the earth three times on February 20, 1962. (indicates an action completed in the past)

When he <u>was</u> young, Mark Twain <u>traveled</u> through the mining towns of the Southwest. (indicates actions that recurred in the past but did not extend into the present)

(3) Future Tense

The **future tense** indicates that an action will take place. The future tense is formed with the auxiliaries *will* or *shall* plus the present tense. The future tense has several uses.

Halley's Comet <u>will reappear</u> in 2061. (indicates a future action that will definitely occur)

The dean has announced that the college <u>will require</u> all entering students to buy computers. (indicates intention)

The land boom in Nevada <u>will</u> most likely <u>continue</u>. (indicates probability)

 VERB TENSE

At one time *will* was used exclusively for the second- and third-person future tense of a verb, and *shall* was used for the first person. Except in formal usage, however, *shall* is now rare.

411

25d Using the Perfect Tenses

The **perfect tenses** designate actions that were or will be completed before other actions or conditions. The perfect tenses are formed with the appropriate tense form of the auxiliary verb *have* plus the past participle.

(1) Present Perfect Tense

The **present perfect** tense can indicate either of two types of continuing action beginning in the past.

Dr. Kim <u>has finished</u> studying the effects of BHA on rats. (indicates an action that began in the past and is finished at the present time)

My mother <u>has invested</u> her money wisely. (indicates an action that began in the past and extends into the present)

(2) Past Perfect Tense

The **past perfect** tense has two uses.

By 1946 engineers <u>had built</u> the first electronic digital computer. (indicates an action occurring before a certain time in the past)

We <u>had hoped</u> to visit Disney World on our trip to Florida. (indicates an unfulfilled desire in the past)

(3) Future Perfect Tense

The **future perfect** tense has two uses.

By Tuesday the transit authority <u>will have run</u> out of money. (indicates that an action will be finished by a certain future time)

By the time a commercial fusion reactor is developed, the government <u>will have spent</u> billions of dollars on research. (indicates that one action will be finished before another occurs in the future)

25e Using the Progressive Tenses

The **progressive tenses** express continuing action. They consist of the appropriate tense of the verb *be* plus the present participle.

(1) Present Progressive Tense

The **present progressive** tense has two uses.

The volcano is erupting, and lava is flowing toward the town. (indicates that something is happening at the time it is expressed in speech or writing)

Law is becoming an overcrowded profession. (indicates that an action is happening even though it may not be taking place at the time it is expressed in speech or writing)

(2) Past Progressive Tense

The **past progressive** tense has two uses.

Roderick Usher's actions were becoming increasingly bizarre. (indicates a continuing action in the past)

The French revolutionary Jean-Paul Marat was stabbed to death while he was bathing. (indicates an action occurring at the same time in the past as another action)

(3) Future Progressive Tense

The **future progressive** tense has two uses.

The secretary of the treasury will be carefully monitoring the money supply. (indicates a continuing action in the future)

Next month NATO forces will be holding military exercises. (indicates a continuing action at a specific future time)

(4) Present Perfect Progressive Tense

The **present perfect progressive** tense has only one use.

The number of women in the military has been increasing steadily. (indicates action continuing from the past into the present and possibly into the future)

(5) Past Perfect Progressive Tense

The **past perfect progressive** tense has only one use.

Before President Kennedy was assassinated, he had been working on civil rights legislation. (indicates that one past action went on until a second occurred)

(6) Future Perfect Progressive Tense

The **future perfect progressive** tense has only one use.

By eleven o'clock <u>we will have been driving</u> for seven hours. (indicates that an action will continue until a certain future time)

EXERCISE 3

A verb is missing from each of the following sentences. Fill in the form of the verb indicated in parentheses after each sentence.

EXAMPLE: The Outer Banks _____ (stretch: present) along the North Carolina coast for more than 175 miles.

The Outer Banks <u>stretch</u> along the North Carolina coast for more than 175 miles.

1. Many portions of the Outer Banks of North Carolina _____ (give: present) the visitor a sense of history and timelessness.

2. Many students of history _____ (read: present perfect) about the Outer Banks and its mysteries.

3. It was on Roanoke Island in the 1580s that English colonists _____ (establish: past) the first settlement in the New World.

4. That colony vanished soon after it was settled, _____ (become: present participle) known as the famous "lost colony."

5. By 1718 the pirate Blackbeard _____ (made: past perfect) the Outer Banks a hiding place for his treasures.

6. It was at Ocracoke, in fact, that Blackbeard _____ (meet: past) his death.

7. Even today, fortune hunters _____ (search: present progressive) the Outer Banks for Blackbeard's hidden treasures.

8. The Outer Banks are also famous for Kitty Hawk and Kill Devil Hills; even as technology has advanced into the space age, the number of tourists flocking to the site of the Wright brothers' epic flight _____. (grow: present perfect progressive)

9. Long before that famous flight occurred, however, the Outer Banks _____ (claim: past perfect) countless ships along its ever-shifting shores, resulting in its nickname—the "Graveyard of the Atlantic."

10. If the Outer Banks continue to be protected from the ravages of overdevelopment and commercialization, visitors _____ (enjoy: future progressive) the mysteries of this tiny finger of land for years to come.

25f Using Verb Tenses in a Sentence

When a single sentence contains several verbs describing actions that occur at different times, the tenses of the verbs must be different. Which tense to use depends both on the sentence's meaning and on the nature of the clauses in which the verbs occur.

(1) Verbs in Independent Clauses

Verbs that appear in adjacent independent clauses can have different tenses as long as the relationships of the verbs to their subjects and to each other are clear.

> The debate <u>was</u> impressive, but the election <u>will determine</u> the winner.

(2) Verbs in Dependent Clauses

When a verb appears in a dependent clause, its tense depends on the tense of the main verb in the independent clause. When the main verb is in the past tense, the verb in the dependent clause is usually in the past or past perfect tense. When the main verb is in the past perfect, the verb in the dependent clause is usually in the past tense.

MAIN VERB	VERB IN DEPENDENT CLAUSE
George Hepplewhite <u>was</u> (past) an English cabinetmaker	who <u>designed</u> (past) distinctive chair backs.
The battle <u>had ended</u> (past perfect)	by the time reinforcements <u>arrived</u> (past).

When the main verb in the independent clause is in any tense except the past or past perfect, the verb in the dependent clause may be in any tense needed to convey meaning.

MAIN VERB	VERB IN DEPENDENT CLAUSE
Ryan <u>knows</u> (present)	that the Beatles <u>appeared</u> (past) in three movies.
Senator Mikulski <u>will explain</u> (future)	why she <u>changed</u> (past) her position.

415

(3) Infinitives in Verbal Phrases

When an infinitive appears in a verbal phrase, the tense it expresses depends on the tense of the sentence's main verb. The *present infinitive* (*to* plus the base form of the verb) indicates an action happening at the same time as or later than the main verb. The *perfect infinitive* (*to have* plus the past participle) indicates action happening earlier than the main verb.

MAIN VERB	INFINITIVE
I <u>went</u>	<u>to see</u> the Rangers play last week. (The going and the seeing occurred at the same time.)
I <u>want</u>	<u>to see</u> the Rangers play tomorrow (Wanting occurs in the present, and seeing occurs in the future.)
I would <u>like</u>	<u>to have seen</u> the Rangers play. (Liking occurs in the present, and seeing would have occurred in the past.)

(4) Participles in Verbal Phrases

When a participle appears in a verbal phrase, its tense depends on the tense of the sentence's main verb. The *present participle* indicates action happening at the same time as the action of the main verb. The *past participle* or the *present perfect participle* indicates action occurring before the action of the main verb.

PARTICIPLE	MAIN VERB
<u>Addressing</u> the 1896 Democratic Convention,	William Jennings Bryan <u>delivered</u> his "Cross of Gold" speech. (The addressing and the delivery occurred at the same time.)
<u>Having written</u> her term paper,	Camille <u>studied</u> for her history final. (The writing occurred before the studying.)

EXERCISE 4

From inside each set of parentheses, choose the correct verb form. Make certain you use the correct sequence of verb tenses.

EXAMPLE: Sophocles _____ (won, had won) his first victory in the Athenian spring drama competition in 468 BC.

Sophocles <u>won</u> his first victory in the Athenian spring drama competition in 468 BC.

1. In Sophocles's famous tragedy *Oedipus Rex*, Oedipus _____ (declares, declared) that the murderer of King Laios, his predecessor to the throne, will be found and removed from the city of Thebes.

2. His declaration comes after he _____ (learned, has learned) that the presence of the murderer has caused the plague on the city.

3. Sophocles _____ (was, is) one of the three great ancient Greek writers of tragedy; in keeping with the characteristics of tragedy, he portrayed Oedipus as a character with a tragic flaw.

4. By the time Oedipus learns of the presence of the murderer in the city, the citizens _____ (gave, have given) up hope of restoring the city to its former glory.

5. Oedipus comes to the city just after King Laios's death, and when he solves the riddle of the Sphinx, he _____ (becomes, became) the new king.

6. Having been widowed as a result of the king's death, Queen Iocaste _____ (has married, married) Oedipus.

7. When the blind prophet Tiresias says that Oedipus is the murderer being sought, Oedipus _____ (accused, accuses) Tiresias of being involved in a plot against him.

8. In spite of his protestations, Oedipus _____ (learned, learns) that he is indeed the murderer and, worse, the son of his wife.

25g Mood

Mood is the form a verb takes to indicate whether a writer is making a statement or asking a question (indicative), giving a command (imperative), or expressing a wish or a contrary-to-fact statement (subjunctive).

The **indicative** mood expresses an opinion, states a fact, or asks a question.

Jackie Robinson <u>had</u> a significant impact on professional baseball.

<u>Did</u> Margaret Mead <u>say</u> that behavioral differences are rooted in culture?

The **imperative** mood is used in commands and direct requests; usually the imperative uses only the base form of the verb without a subject. Writers including themselves in a command use *let's* or *let us* before the base form of the verb.

<u>Use</u> a dictionary.

<u>Let us examine</u> Machiavelli's view of human nature.

25h Using the Subjunctive Mood

The **subjunctive** mood is used in certain *that* clauses, in contrary-to-fact statements, and in certain idiomatic expressions.

The *present subjunctive* uses the base form of the verb, regardless of the subject. The *past subjunctive* has the same form as the past tense of the verb. (The auxiliary verb *be,* however, takes the form *were* regardless of the number or person of the subject.) The *past perfect subjunctive* has the same form as the past perfect.

Dr. Gorman suggested that I <u>study</u> the Cambrian period. (present subjunctive)

I wish I <u>were</u> going to Europe. (past subjunctive)

I wish I <u>had gone</u> to the review session. (past perfect subjunctive)

(1) *That* Clauses

Use the subjunctive in *that* clauses after words such as *ask, suggest, require, recommend,* and *demand.*

The report <u>recommended that</u> juveniles <u>be</u> given mandatory counseling.

Captain Ahab <u>insisted that</u> his crew <u>hunt</u> the white whale.

(2) Conditional Statements

Use the subjunctive in **conditional statements** (statements beginning with *if* that are contrary to fact, including statements that express a wish).

If the condition is impossible or **contrary to fact,** use the subjunctive mood for the verb in the *if* clause.

If John <u>were</u> there, he would have seen Marsha. (John was not there.)

I wish I <u>were</u> more organized. (I am not very organized.)

NOTE: A conditional clause beginning with *as if* is contrary to fact and should be in the subjunctive mood.

> The father acted as if he <u>were</u> having the baby. (The father wasn't having the baby.)

 CONDITIONAL STATEMENTS

If an *if* clause expresses a condition that is even remotely possible, use the indicative mood (not the subjunctive) for the verb in the *if* clause.

If a peace treaty <u>is</u> signed, the world will be safer. (A peace treaty is possible.)

(3) Idiomatic Expressions

The subjunctive is used in some idiomatic expressions.

If need <u>be</u>, we will stay up all night to finish the report.

<u>Come</u> what may, they will increase their steel production.

Far <u>be</u> it for me to correct an expert.

Special interest groups have, as it <u>were</u>, shifted the balance of power.

EXERCISE 5

Complete the sentences in the following paragraph by inserting the appropriate form (indicative, imperative, or subjunctive) of the verb in parentheses. Be prepared to explain your choices.

Harry Houdini was a famous escape artist. He _____ (perform) escapes from every type of bond imaginable: handcuffs, locks, straitjackets, ropes, sacks, and sealed chests underwater. In Germany workers _____ (challenge) Houdini to escape from a packing box. If he _____ (be) to escape, they would admit that he _____ (be) the best escape artist in the world. Houdini accepted. Before getting into the box he asked that the observers _____ (give) it a thorough examination. He then asked that a worker _____ (nail) him into the box. "_____ (place) a screen around the box," he ordered after he had been sealed inside. In a few minutes Houdini _____ (step) from behind the screen. When the workers demanded that they _____ (see) the box, Houdini pulled down the screen. To their surprise they saw the box with the lid still nailed tightly in place.

25i Voice

Voice is the form a verb takes to indicate whether its subject acts or is acted upon. When the subject of a verb does something—that is, acts—the verb is in the **active voice.** When the subject of a verb receives the action—that is, is acted upon—the verb is in the **passive voice.**

ACTIVE VOICE: <u>Hart Crane wrote</u> *The Bridge.*

PASSIVE VOICE: *The Bridge* <u>was written</u> by Hart Crane.

 **VOICE**

Because the active voice emphasizes the person or thing performing an action, it is usually briefer, clearer, and more emphatic than the passive voice. For this reason, you should use active constructions in your college writing. Some situations, however, require use of the passive voice. For example, you should use passive constructions when the actor is unknown or unimportant or when the recipient of an action should logically receive the emphasis.

DDT <u>was found</u> in soil samples. (Passive voice emphasizes finding DDT; who found it is not important.)

Grits <u>are eaten</u> throughout the South. (Passive voice emphasizes fact that grits are eaten, not those who eat them.)

EXERCISE 6

Read the following paragraph and determine which verbs are active and which are passive. Comment if you can on why the author used the passive voice in each case.

By the beginning of the seventeenth century, European fireworks technicians could create elaborate flares that exploded into historic scenes and figures of famous people. This type of costly and lavish entertainment that was popular at the French royal palace at Versailles. For eight centuries, though, the colors of fireworks explosions were limited mainly to yellows and reddish amber. It was not until 1830 that chemists produced metallic zinc powders that yield a greenish-blue flare. Within the next decade, combinations of chemicals were discovered that gave starlike explosions in first pure white, then bright red, and later a pale whitish blue. The last and most challenging basic color to be added to the fireworks palette, in 1845, was a brilliant pure blue. By mid-century, all the colors we enjoy today had arrived.

25j Changing from Passive to Active Voice

You can change a verb from passive to active voice by making the subject of the passive verb the object of the active verb. The person or thing performing the action then becomes the subject of the new sentence.

PASSIVE: The novel *Frankenstein* <u>was written</u> by Mary Shelley.

ACTIVE: Mary Shelley <u>wrote</u> the novel *Frankenstein*.

If a passive verb has no object, you must supply one that will become the subject of the active verb.

PASSIVE: Baby elephants are taught to avoid humans. (By whom are baby elephants taught?)

ACTIVE: <u>Adult elephants</u> teach baby elephants to avoid humans.

EXERCISE 7

Determine which verbs in the following paragraph should be changed from the passive to the active voice. Rewrite the sentences containing these verbs.

Rockets were invented by the Chinese about AD 1000. Gunpowder was packed into bamboo tubes and ignited by means of a fuse. These rockets were fired by soldiers at enemy armies and usually caused panic. In thirteenth-century England an improved form of gunpowder was introduced by Roger Bacon. As a result, rockets were used in battles and were a common—although unreliable—weapon. In the early eighteenth century a twenty-pound rocket that traveled almost two miles was constructed by William Congreve, an English artillery expert. By the late nineteenth century thought was given to supersonic speeds by the physicist Ernst Mach. The sonic boom was predicted by him. The first liquid-fuel rocket was launched by the American Robert Goddard in 1926. A pamphlet written by him anticipated almost all future rocket developments. As a result of his pioneering work, he is called the father of modern rocketry.

25k Changing from Active to Passive Voice

You can change a verb from active to passive voice by making the object of the active verb the subject of the passive verb. The subject of the active verb then becomes the object of the passive verb.

ACTIVE: Sir James Murray compiled *The Oxford English Dictionary.*

PASSIVE: *The Oxford English Dictionary* was compiled by Sir James Murray.

Remember that an active verb must have an object or else it cannot be put into the passive voice. If an active verb has no object, supply one. This will become the subject of the passive sentence.

ACTIVE: Jacques Cousteau invented.
Cousteau invented _____?_____.

PASSIVE: _____?_____ was invented by Jacques Cousteau.
The scuba was invented by Jacques Cousteau.

EXERCISE 8

Determine which sentences in the following paragraph would be more effective in the passive voice. Rewrite those sentences, making sure that you can explain the reasons for your choices.

The Regent Diamond is one of the world's most famous and coveted jewels. A slave discovered the 410-carat diamond in 1701 in an Indian mine. Over the years, people stole and sold the diamond several times. In 1717, the regent of France bought the diamond for an enormous sum, but during the French Revolution, it disappeared again. Someone later found it in a ditch in Paris. Eventually, Napoleon had the diamond set into his ceremonial sword. At last, when the French monarch fell, the government placed the Regent Diamond in the Louvre, where it still remains to be enjoyed by all.

STUDENT WRITER AT WORK

Verbs

This is a draft of a paper written for a technical writing class. The student was told to write an essay in which she explained a basic scientific principle to readers who had little or no understanding of science. As you read, look for inaccuracies or inconsistencies in verb form, tense, and mood; in addition, make sure the writer has made effective use of both passive and active voice. You may add and delete words and phrases as well as rearrange sentences. After you have corrected this draft, go over it again and, if necessary, revise further for coherence, unity, and style.

How Fast Did That Piece of Paper Fall?

Most people who never studied physics assume that heavier objects fall faster than light objects will. This assumption was also made by Aristotle, the brilliant philosopher of ancient Greece. He believed that heavy objects naturally tended to be closer to the ground than light objects. For this reason, they must have fell faster than light objects. This explanation was assumed by Aristotle to conform to common sense. Was it true that heavier bodies fell faster than lighter ones did?

In the seventeenth century, Galileo Galilei, an Italian scientist, laid the groundwork for modern physics. It was recognized by him that heavier objects did not always fall faster than lighter objects. As a result of Galileo's analysis of falling bodies, it is now known by students that in the absence of air resistance, all objects fall at the same rate.

By repeating his experiments in the classroom, you can test Galileo's principle. At the same time you prove the validity of Galileo's ideas, Aristotle's assumptions can be disproved. When you raise two objects--a stone and a flat piece of paper--that were laying on a table to equal distances above the ground and let go, you should see the heavier object reach the ground first. This experiment would seem to confirm Aristotle's belief that heavier objects fall faster than light ones. Repeat the experiment,

continued on the following page

continued from the previous page
this time crumpling the flat piece of paper into a wad. Now the two objects should reach the ground at almost the same time. How is this difference explained?

The key to explaining the difference lies in Galileo's principle. The paper, whose weight was the same whether it was flat or crumpled up, falls faster when it is in a wad because it has a smaller cross-sectional area. It is the cross-sectional area of an object that determines the rate at which it will drop: the larger the area, the more air resistance the object encountered and the slower it will have dropped. If the flat piece of paper was dropped in a vacuum--where there is no air resistance--it would have dropped as fast as the heavy object. This, then, is why the phrase "in the absence of air resistance" is added to Galileo's principle.

CHAPTER 26

AGREEMENT

Agreement is the correspondence between words in number, gender, or person. Subjects and verbs must agree in **number** (singular or plural) and **person** (first, second, or third); pronouns and their antecedents must agree in number, person, and **gender** (masculine, feminine, or neuter).

26a Subject-Verb Agreement

Singular subjects take singular verbs, and plural subjects take plural verbs.

SINGULAR: <u>Hydrogen peroxide</u> <u>is</u> an unstable compound.

PLURAL: <u>Characters</u> <u>are</u> not well developed in O. Henry's short stories.

Present tense verbs, except *be* and *have*, add *s* or *es* when the subject is third-person singular. (Third-person singular subjects include nouns; the personal pronouns *he, she, it,* and *one;* and many indefinite pronouns.)

The <u>president</u> <u>has</u> the power to veto congressional legislation.

<u>She</u> frequently <u>cites</u> statistics to support her assertions.

In every group <u>somebody</u> <u>emerges</u> as a natural leader.

Present tense verbs do not add *s* or *es* when the subject is first-person singular (*I*), first-person plural (*we*), second-person singular or plural (*you*), or third-person plural (*they*).

<u>I</u> <u>recommend</u> that dieters avoid processed meat because of its high salt content.

In our Bill of Rights, <u>we</u> <u>guarantee</u> all defendants the right to a speedy trial.

At this stratum, <u>you</u> <u>see</u> rocks dating back fifteen million years.

<u>They</u> <u>say</u> that some wealthy people have defaulted on their student loans.

Subject-verb agreement is generally straightforward, but some situations can be troublesome.

(1) Words between Subject and Verb

If a modifying phrase comes between subject and verb, the verb should agree with the subject, not with a word in the intervening phrase.

The <u>sound</u> of the drumbeats <u>builds</u> in intensity in *The Emperor Jones.*

The <u>games</u> won by the intramural team <u>are</u> usually few and far between.

When phrases introduced by *along with, as well as, in addition to, including,* and *together with* come between subject and verb, the verb should still agree with the sentence's subject.

Heavy <u>rain</u>, together with high winds, <u>causes</u> hazardous driving conditions along the Santa Monica Freeway.

(2) Compound Subjects Joined by *And*

Compound subjects joined by *and* usually take plural verbs.

<u>Air bags and antilock brakes</u> <u>are</u> available on all new models.

However, when compound subjects joined by *and* stand for a single idea or person, they should be treated as a unit and used with singular verbs.

<u>Rhythm and blues</u> <u>is</u> a forerunner of rock and roll.

When *each* or *every* precedes a compound subject joined by *and,* the subject also takes a singular verb.

<u>Every desk and file cabinet</u> <u>was</u> searched before the letter was found.

(3) Compound Subjects Joined by *Or*

Compound subjects joined by *or* or by *either . . . or* or *neither . . . nor* may take singular or plural verbs.

If both subjects are singular, use a singular verb; if both subjects are plural, use a plural verb.

<u>Either radiation or chemotherapy</u> <u>is</u> combined with surgery for the most effective results. (Both parts of the compound subject, *radiation* and *chemotherapy*, are singular, so the verb is singular.)

<u>Either radiation treatments or chemotherapy sessions</u> <u>are</u> combined with surgery for the most effective results. (Both parts of the compound subject, *treatments* and *sessions*, are plural, so the verb is plural.)

When a singular and a plural subject are linked by *or*, or by *either . . . or, neither . . . nor*, or *not only . . . but also*, the verb agrees with the subject that is nearer to it.

<u>Either radiation treatments or chemotherapy</u> <u>is</u> combined with surgery for the most effective results. (Singular verb agrees with *chemotherapy*, the part of the compound subject closer to it.)

<u>Either chemotherapy or radiation treatments</u> <u>are</u> combined with surgery for the most effective results. (Plural verb agrees with *treatments*, the part of the compound subject closer to it.)

CLOSE-UP SUBJECT-VERB AGREEMENT WITH COMPOUND SUBJECTS

When a compound subject is made up of nouns and pronouns that differ in person, the verb should agree in both person and number with the nearest element of the compound subject.

<u>Neither my running mate nor</u> I <u>wish</u> to contest the election. (first-person singular)

<u>Neither I nor my running mate</u> <u>wishes</u> to contest the election. (third-person singular)

(4)   Indefinite Pronouns

Some **indefinite pronouns**—*both, many, few, several, others*—are always plural and take plural verbs. Most others—*another, anyone, everyone, one, each, either, neither, anything, everything, something, nothing, nobody,* and *somebody*—are always singular and take singular verbs.

427

Anyone <u>is</u> welcome to apply for this grant.

<u>Each</u> of the chapters <u>includes</u> a review exercise.

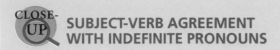

SUBJECT-VERB AGREEMENT WITH INDEFINITE PRONOUNS

A few indefinite pronouns—*some, all, any, more, most,* and *none*—can be singular or plural. In these cases the noun to which the pronoun refers determines whether the verb form should be singular or plural.

Of course, <u>some</u> of this trouble <u>is</u> to be expected. (*Some* refers to *trouble;* therefore, the verb is singular.)

<u>Some</u> of the spectators <u>are</u> getting restless. (*Some* refers to *spectators;* therefore, the verb is plural.)

(5) Collective Nouns

A **collective noun** names a group of persons or things—for instance, *navy, union, association, band.* A collective noun is always singular in form. When it refers to a group as a unit, as it usually does, a collective noun takes a singular verb; when it refers to the individuals or items that make up the group, it takes a plural verb.

To many people <u>the royal family</u> <u>symbolizes</u> Great Britain. (The family, as a unit, is the symbol.)

<u>The family</u> all <u>eat</u> at different times. (Each member eats separately.)

If a plural verb sounds awkward with a collective noun, reword the sentence.

<u>The family members</u> all <u>eat</u> at different times.

Phrases that name a fixed amount—*three-quarters, twenty dollars, the majority*—are treated like collective nouns. When the amount denotes a unit, it takes a singular verb; when it denotes part of the whole, it takes a plural verb.

<u>Three-quarters</u> of his usual salary <u>is</u> not enough. (*Three-quarters* denotes a unit.)

<u>Three-quarters</u> of workshop participants <u>improve</u> dramatically.
(*Three-quarters* denotes part of the group.)

SUBJECT-VERB AGREEMENT WITH COLLECTIVE NOUNS

The number is always singular, and *a number* is always plural.

<u>The number</u> of voters <u>has</u> declined.

<u>A number</u> of students <u>have</u> missed the opportunity to prereg-ister.

(6) Singular Subjects with Plural Forms

Be sure to use a singular verb with a singular subject, even if the form of the subject is plural.

<u>Politics</u> <u>makes</u> strange bedfellows.

<u>Statistics</u> <u>deals</u> with the collection, classification, analysis, and in-terpretation of data.

When such words have plural meanings, however, use a plural verb.

<u>Her politics</u> <u>are</u> too radical for her parents. (*Politics* refers not to the science of political government but rather to political prin-ciples or opinions.)

<u>The statistics</u> <u>prove</u> him wrong. (*Statistics* denotes not a body of knowledge but the numerical facts or data themselves.)

Be sure that the title of an individual work takes a singular verb even if the title's form is plural.

<u>The Grapes of Wrath</u> <u>describes</u> the journey of migrant workers and their families from the Dust Bowl to California.

A word referred to as a word also takes a singular verb even if the form of the word is plural.

<u>Good vibes</u> <u>is</u> a 1960s slang term meaning "positive feelings."

429

SUBJECT-VERB AGREEMENT WITH FOREIGN PLURALS

See
22b8

Some words retain their Latin **plural** forms, which do not look like English plural forms. Be particularly careful to use the correct verbs with such words.

criterion is	criteria are
medium is	media are

(7) Inverted Subject-Verb Order

Be sure that a verb agrees with its subject even when the verb comes before the subject, as it does in questions and sentences beginning with *there is* or *there are.*

<u>Is</u> <u>either</u> answer correct?

There <u>is</u> a <u>monument</u> to Emiliano Zapata in Mexico City.

There <u>are</u> currently twelve <u>circuit courts</u> of appeals in the federal court system.

(8) Linking Verbs

See
23c1

Be sure that a **linking verb** agrees with its subject, not with the subject complement.

The <u>problem</u> <u>was</u> termites.

Here the verb *was* correctly agrees with the subject *problem,* not with the subject complement *termites.* If *termites* were the subject, the verb would be plural.

<u>Termites</u> <u>were</u> the problem.

(9) Relative Pronouns

When you use a **relative pronoun** (*who, which, that,* and so on) to introduce a dependent clause, the verb in that clause should agree in number with the pronoun's **antecedent** (the word to which the pronoun refers).

The farmer is among the <u>ones</u> who <u>suffer</u> during a grain embargo.

Here the verb *suffer* agrees with the antecedent (*ones*) of the relative pronoun *who*. Compare the following sentence.

The farmer is the only <u>one</u> who <u>suffers</u> during the grain embargo.

Now the verb agrees with the antecedent *one,* which is singular.

EXERCISE 1

Each of these ten correct sentences illustrates one of the conventions just explained. Read the sentences carefully and explain why each verb form is used in each case.

> EXAMPLE: *Harold and Maude* is a popular cult film. (The verb is singular because the subject *Harold and Maude* is the title of an individual work, even though it is plural in form.)

1. Jack Kerouac, along with Allen Ginsberg and William S. Burroughs, was a major figure in the "beat" movement.
2. Every American boy and girl needs to learn basic computational skills.
3. Aesthetics is not an exact science.
4. The audience was restless.
5. The Beatles' *Sergeant Pepper* album is one of those albums that remain popular long after the time they are issued.
6. All is quiet.
7. The subject was roses.
8. When he was young, Benjamin Franklin's primary concern was books.
9. Fifty dollars is too much to spend on one concert ticket.
10. "There are more things in heaven and earth, Horatio, than are dreamt of in your philosophy."

EXERCISE 2

Some of the following sentences are correct, but others illustrate common errors in subject-verb agreement. If a sentence is correct, mark it with a *C;* if it has an error, correct it.

1. *I Love Lucy* is one of those television shows that almost all Americans have seen at least once.
2. The committee presented its findings to the president.
3. Neither Western novels nor science fiction appeal to me.
4. Stage presence and musical ability makes a rock performer successful today.
5. *It's a Wonderful Life,* like many old Christmas movies, seems to be shown on television every year.

6. Hearts are my grandmother's favorite card game.
7. The best part of B. B. King's songs are the guitar solos.
8. Time and tide waits for no man.
9. Sports are my main pastime.
10. *Vincent and Theo* is Robert Altman's movie about the French Impressionist painter Van Gogh and his brother.

26b Pronoun-Antecedent Agreement

See
23b

A <u>pronoun</u> must agree with its **antecedent**—the word or word group to which the pronoun refers. Singular pronouns—such as *he, him, she, her, it, me, myself,* and *oneself*—should refer to singular antecedents. Plural pronouns—such as *we, us, they, them,* and *their*—should refer to plural antecedents.

(1) Compound Antecedents

In most cases, use a plural pronoun to refer to a **compound antecedent** (two or more antecedents connected by *and*) even if one or more of the antecedents are singular.

<u>Mormonism and Christian Science</u> were influenced in <u>their</u> beginnings by Shaker doctrines.

However, if a compound antecedent denotes a single unit—one person, thing, or idea—use a singular pronoun to refer to the compound antecedent.

In 1904 <u>the husband and father</u> brought <u>his</u> family from Germany to the United States.

When a compound antecedent is preceded by *each* or *every,* use a singular pronoun.

<u>Every programming language and software package</u> has <u>its</u> limitations.

Use a singular pronoun to refer to two or more singular antecedents linked by *or* or *nor.*

<u>Neither Thoreau nor Whitman</u> lived to see <u>his</u> work read widely.

When one part of a compound antecedent is singular and one part is plural, the pronoun agrees in person and number with the closer antecedent.

Neither Great Britain nor the Benelux nations have experienced
changes in their borders in recent years.

(2) Collective Noun Antecedents

If the meaning of the collective noun antecedent is singular (as it will
be in most cases), use a singular pronoun. If the meaning is plural, use a
plural pronoun.

The teachers' union was ready to strike for the new contract its members had been promised. (All the members act as one.)

When the whistle blew, the team left their seats and moved toward the
court. (Each member acts individually.)

 PRONOUN-ANTECEDENT AGREEMENT

Within any one sentence a collective noun should be treated
consistently as either singular or plural. When a single collective
noun serves as both the subject of a verb and the antecedent of a
pronoun, both verb and pronoun must agree with the noun.

CORRECT: The teachers' union, ready to strike for the new
contract its members had been promised, was still willing to
negotiate.

(3) Indefinite Pronoun Antecedents

Most **indefinite pronouns**—*each, either, neither, one, anyone,* and the
like—are singular and require singular pronouns. (Others may be plural
and require plural pronouns.)

See
26a4

Neither of these men had his proposal ready by the deadline.

Each of these neighborhoods is like a separate nation, with its own
traditions and values.

433

PRONOUN-ANTECEDENT AGREEMENT

See
20f2

Because indefinite pronouns like *no one, someone, everyone, everybody, somebody,* and *nobody* do not specify gender, convention has dictated that they be referred to by the pronoun *his.* But indefinite pronouns really denote members of both genders, so *his* is clearly inaccurate as well as **sexist language**. In journalistic writing, it is common to see the plural pronouns *they* or *their* with indefinite pronouns that refer to people.

Everyone will get instruction in the foreign language of their choice.

In college writing, however, using a plural pronoun with a singular subject is generally not acceptable. Instead, you can use both masculine and feminine pronouns.

Everyone will get instruction in the foreign language of his or her choice.

You can also change the sentence's subject and use a plural pronoun.

All students will get instruction in the foreign language of their choice.

EXERCISE 3

Find and correct any errors in subject-verb and/or pronoun-antecedent agreement.

1. The core of a computer is a collection of electronic circuits that are called the central processing unit.

2. Computers, because of advanced technology that allows the central processing unit to be placed on a chip, a thin square of semiconducting material about one-quarter of an inch on each side, has been greatly reduced in size.

3. Computers can "talk" to each other over phone lines through a modem, an acronym for *modulator-demodulator.*

4. Pressing of keys on keyboards resembling typewriter keyboards generate electronic signals that are input for the computer.

5. Computers have built-in memory storage, and equipment such as disks or tapes provide external memory.

6. RAM (random-access memory), the erasable and reusable computer memory, hold the computer program, the computations executed by the program, and the results.

7. After computer programs are "read" from a disk or tape, the computer uses the instructions as needed to execute the program.

8. ROM (read-only memory), the permanent memory that is "read" by the computer but cannot be changed, are used to store programs that are needed frequently.

9. A number of arcade-style video games with sound and color is available for home computers.

10. Although some computer users write their own programs, most buy ready-made software programs such as the ones that allows a computer to be used as a word processor.

EXERCISE 4

The following ten sentences illustrate correct subject-verb and pronoun-antecedent agreement. After following the instructions in parentheses after each sentence, revise each so its verbs and pronouns agree with the newly created subject.

> EXAMPLE: One child in ten suffers from a learning disability. (Change *one child in ten* to *ten percent of all children.*)
>
> Ten percent of all children suffer from a learning disability.

1. The governess is seemingly pursued by evil as she tries to protect Miles and Flora from those she feels seek to possess the children's souls. (Change *The governess* to *The governess and the cook.*)

2. Insulin-dependent diabetics are now able to take advantage of new technology that can help alleviate their symptoms. (Change *diabetics* to *the diabetic.*)

3. All homeowners in shore regions worry about the possible effects of a hurricane on their property. (Change *All homeowners* to *Every homeowner.*)

4. Federally funded job-training programs offer unskilled workers an opportunity to acquire skills they can use to secure employment. (Change *workers* to *the worker.*)

5. Foreign imports pose a major challenge to the American automobile market. (Change *Foreign imports* to *The foreign import.*)

6. *Brideshead Revisited* tells how one family and its devotion to its Catholic faith affect Charles Ryder. (Delete *and its devotion to its Catholic faith.*)

7. *Writer's Digest* and *The Writer* are designed to aid writers as they seek markets for their work. (Change *writers* to *the writer.*)

8. Most American families have access to television; in fact, more have televisions that have indoor plumbing. (Change *Most American families* to *Almost every American family.*)

9. In Montana it seems as though every town's elevation is higher than its population. (Change *every town's elevation* to *all the towns' elevations.*)

10. A woman without a man is like a fish without a bicycle. (Change *A woman/a man* to *Women/men.*)

STUDENT WRITER AT WORK

Agreement

Read the following draft of an English composition essay carefully, correcting all errors in subject-verb and pronoun-antecedent agreement. After you have corrected the errors, go over the draft again and, if necessary, revise further to strengthen coherence, unity, and style.

Marriage in the Ashanti Tribe

The Ashanti tribe is the largest in the small West African country of Ghana. The language of the Ashantis, Akan, is the most widely spoken in the country. The unity in the Ashanti tribe is derived from a golden stool that the Ashantis believe descended from the skies at the command of their chief priest. This unity has encouraged the Ashantis to create a system in which the family is so strong that the tribe has little need for formal support services. For instance, the tribe need few institutions to care for their orphans or homeless people. Among the Ashanti people, home and family means plenty of relatives, living and working and playing and worrying as well-knit units who live in single or neighboring households. Marriage among members of the Ashanti tribe is therefore a union of two families as well as of two individuals.

In Ashanti, marriage is less an agreement entered into by two individuals before God or the justice of the peace than it is a social contract between two families, each of which are represented by a partner

continued on the following page

continued from the previous page
to the marriage. Because a marriage binds two families together, it is not to be entered into hurriedly. In fact, everyone in the tribe fear the social consequences of an ill-conceived union. The families of both of the young people are active counselors during the courtship, and its wholehearted approval and endorsement is essential to the success of the marriage. The family seek the answers to many questions. For instance, are the bride and bridegroom of similar age? Have either been married before? If so, why did the previous marriage fail? What is the history of the family? Is the family in debt? Most importantly, of what clan is the family?

When all the questions have been answered satisfactorily, the man and the woman are married. The respective troths--for bride and groom, for bride's family and groom's family--are plighted in a quiet ceremony without benefit of either clergy or justice of the peace. The crucial part of the ceremony is the giving of a small sum of money and various gifts and drinks by the family of the groom to that of the bride. The actual value of such payments are often small, amounting to about fifty dollars. (A royal family gives more and receives more.) This money is sometimes referred to as "bridewealth." It constitutes only a token of the agreement reached between bride and groom and between their families. In the giving and receiving of the gifts the young people and their families mutually pledge their faithfulness and support. When this transaction has been witnessed by both families, the man and woman are joined together as husband and wife. For better or for worse, they are married.

CHAPTER 27

ADJECTIVES AND ADVERBS

27a Understanding Adjectives and Adverbs

Adjectives modify nouns and pronouns. **Adverbs** modify verbs; adjectives; other adverbs; or entire phrases, clauses, or sentences. Both adjectives and adverbs describe, limit, or qualify other words, phrases, or clauses.

 CLOSE-UP ADJECTIVES AND ADVERBS

The *function* of a word, not its *form*, determines whether it is classified as an adjective or an adverb. Although many adverbs (like *immediately* and *hopelessly*) end in *ly*, others (such as *almost* and *very*) do not. Moreover, some adjectives (such as *lively*) end in *ly*. Only by locating the modified word and determining what part of speech it is can you identify a modifier as an adjective or an adverb.

27b Using Adjectives

See 23d

See 23c1

Be sure to use an **adjective**—not an adverb—as a subject complement. A **subject complement** is a word that follows a **linking verb** and modifies the sentence's subject, not its verb. Because a subject complement modifies the subject—a noun or pronoun—it must be an adjective.

Michelle seemed <u>brave</u>. (*Seemed* shows no action and is therefore a linking verb. Because *brave* is a subject complement that modifies the noun *Michelle,* the adjective form is used.)

Michelle smiled <u>bravely</u>. (*Smiled* shows action, so it is not a linking verb. *Bravely* modifies *smiled*, so it takes the adverb form.)

NOTE: Sometimes the same verb can either serve as a linking verb or convey action.

He remained <u>stubborn</u>. (He was still stubborn.); He remained <u>stubbornly</u>. (He remained, in a stubborn manner.)

Also be sure to use an adjective as an **object complement,** a word that follows a sentence's direct object and modifies that object and not the verb. Objects are nouns or pronouns, so their modifiers must be adjectives.

Most people called him <u>timid</u>. (People consider him to be timid; here *timid* modifies *him,* the sentence's direct object, so the adjective form is correct.)

Most people called him <u>timidly</u>. (People were timid when they called him; here *timidly* modifies the verb *called*—not the object—so the adverb form is correct.)

PLACEMENT OF ADJECTIVES

Adjectives are generally placed close to the nouns or pronouns they modify. They most often appear immediately *before* nouns and directly *after* linking verbs, direct objects, and indefinite pronouns.

They bought <u>two</u> shrubs for the yard. (before noun)

The name seemed <u>familiar</u>. (after linking verb)

The coach ran them <u>ragged</u>. (after direct object)

Anything <u>sad</u> makes me cry. (after indefinite pronoun)

27c | Using Adverbs

Be sure to use an <u>**adverb**</u>—not an adjective—to modify verbs; adjectives; other adverbs; or entire phrases, clauses, or sentences.

See
23e

FAULTY: Most students did <u>great</u> on the midterm. (adjective form used to modify verb)

REVISED: Most students did <u>well</u> (or <u>very well</u>) on the midterm.

FAULTY: My parents dress a lot more <u>conservative</u> than my friends do. (adjective form used to modify verb)

REVISED: My parents dress a lot more <u>conservatively</u> than my friends do.

PLACEMENT OF ADVERBS

Adverbs, like adjectives, are usually located close to the words they modify. However, they may appear in a greater variety of positions.

He walked <u>slowly</u> across the room.

<u>Slowly</u> he walked across the room.

He <u>slowly</u> walked across the room.

He walked across the room <u>slowly</u>.

 CLOSE-UP ADJECTIVES AND ADVERBS

In informal speech adjective forms such as *good, bad, sure, real, slow, quick,* and *loud* are often used to modify verbs, adjectives, and adverbs. Avoid these informal modifiers in college writing; instead, use adverbs to modify verbs, adjectives, and other adverbs.

INFORMAL: The program ran <u>good</u> the first time we tried it, but the new system performed <u>bad</u>.

REVISED: The program ran <u>well</u> the first time we tried it, but the new system performed <u>badly</u>.

EXERCISE 1

Revise each of the incorrect sentences in the following paragraph so that only adjectives modify nouns and pronouns and only adverbs modify verbs, adjectives, or other adverbs. Be sure to eliminate informal forms.

The most popular self-help trend in the United States today is sub-liminal tapes. These tapes, with titles like "How to Attract Love," "Freedom from Acne," and "I Am a Genius," are intended to solve every problem known to modern society—quick and easy. The tapes are said to work because their "hidden messages" bypass conscious defense mechanisms. The listener hears only music or relaxing sounds, like waves rolling slow and steady. At decibel levels perceived only subconsciously, positive words and phrases are embedded, usu-ally by someone who speaks deep and rhythmic. The top-selling cas-settes are those to help you lose weight or quit smoking. The popularity of such tapes is not hard to understand. They promise easy solutions to complex problems. But the main benefit of these tapes appears to be for the sellers, who are accumulating profits real fast.

EXERCISE 2

Being careful to use adjectives—not adverbs—as subject complements and object complements, write five sentences in imitation of each of the following sentences. Consult the list of linking verbs in **23c1,** and use a different linking verb in each of your sentences.

1. Julie looked worried.
2. Dan considers his collection valuable.

27d Using Comparatives and Superlatives

COMPARATIVE AND SUPERLATIVE FORMS

Form	Function	Example
Positive	Describes a quality; indicates no comparison	big
Comparative	Indicates comparison between *two* qualities (greater or lesser)	bigger
Superlative	Indicates comparison among *more than two* qualities (greatest or least)	biggest

NOTE: Some adverbs, particularly those indicating time, place, and degree (*almost, very, here, yesterday,* and *immediately*), do not have comparative or superlative forms.

---

(1) Comparative Forms

Comparative forms indicate a greater or lesser degree.

Adjectives To indicate a *greater* degree, all one-syllable adjectives and many two-syllable adjectives (particularly those that end in *y, ly, le, er,* and *ow*) add *er:* slow<u>er</u>, funn<u>ier</u>.

NOTE: A final *y* becomes *i* before *er* is added.

Other two-syllable adjectives and all long adjectives indicate a greater degree with *more:* <u>more</u> famous, <u>more</u> incredible.

NOTE: Many two-syllable adjectives can indicate a greater degree with either *more* or *er*—for example, *more lovely* or *lovelier.*

All adjectives indicate a lesser degree with *less:* <u>less</u> lovely, <u>less</u> famous.

Adverbs Adverbs ending in *ly* indicate a greater degree with *more:* <u>more</u> slowly.
Other adverbs use the *er* ending to indicate a greater degree: soon<u>er</u>.
All adverbs indicate a lesser degree with *less:* <u>less</u> slowly, <u>less</u> soon.

NOTE: Never use both *more* and *er* to form the comparative degree.

FAULTY: Nothing could have been <u>more easier</u>.

REVISED: Nothing could have been <u>easier</u>.

(2) Superlative Forms

Superlative forms indicate the greatest or least degree.

Adjectives Adjectives that form the comparative (a greater degree) with *er* add *est* to form the superlative: nic<u>est</u>, funni<u>est</u>.
Adjectives that indicate the comparative with *more* use *most* to indicate the superlative: <u>most</u> famous, <u>most</u> challenging.
All adjectives indicate the least degree with *least:* <u>least</u> interesting, <u>least</u> enjoyable.

Adverbs Most adverbs use *most* to indicate the greatest degree: <u>most</u> quickly, <u>most</u> helpfully, <u>most</u> efficiently.
Others use the *est* ending to indicate the greatest degree: soon<u>est</u>.
All adverbs use *least* to indicate the least degree: <u>least</u> willingly, <u>least</u> fashionably.

NOTE: Never use both *most* and *est* to form the superlative degree.

FAULTY: Jack is the <u>most meanest</u> person in town.

REVISED: Jack is the <u>meanest</u> person in town.

ADJECTIVES AND ADVERBS

Never use the superlative when you are comparing only two items.

FAULTY: Stacy is the tallest of the two sisters.

REVISED: Stacy is the taller of the two sisters.

(3) Irregular Comparatives and Superlatives

Some adjectives and adverbs have irregular comparative and superlative forms. Instead of adding a word or an ending to the positive form, they use different words to indicate the comparative and the superlative.

IRREGULAR COMPARATIVES AND SUPERLATIVES

	Positive	Comparative	Superlative
Adjectives	good	better	best
	bad	worse	worst
	a little	less	least
	many, some, much	more	most
Adverbs	well	better	best
	badly	worse	worst

(4) Illogical Comparisons

Many adjectives and adverbs have absolute meanings—that is, they can logically exist only in the positive degree. For this reason, words like *perfect, unique, excellent, impossible,* and *dead* can never be used in the comparative or superlative degree.

FAULTY: The vase is the <u>most unique</u> piece in her collection.

REVISED: The vase in her collection is <u>unique</u>. (It is one of a kind.)

These words can, however, be modified by words that suggest approaching the absolute state—*nearly* or *almost,* for example.

He revised until his draft was <u>almost perfect</u>.

443

EXERCISE 3

Supply the correct comparative and superlative forms for each of the following adjectives or adverbs. Then use each form in a sentence.

> **EXAMPLE:** strange   stranger   strangest
>
> The story had a *strange* ending.
> The explanation sounded *stranger* each time I heard it.
> This is the *strangest* gadget I have ever seen.

1. many	6. softly
2. eccentric	7. embarrassing
3. confusing	8. well
4. bad	9. often
5. mysterious	10. tiny

27e   Avoiding Double Negatives

Be careful not to create a **double negative** by combining two negative modifiers (such as *no, not, never, nearly, barely, hardly,* or *scarcely*) or by using a negative modifier with another negative word, such as *none* or *nothing.*

> **DOUBLE NEGATIVE:** Old dogs can<u>not</u> learn <u>no</u> new tricks.
>
> **REVISED:** Old dogs cannot learn new tricks.

See 31c1

NOTE: Remember that many **contractions** include the negative word *not.*

> **DOUBLE NEGATIVE:** The instructor <u>doesn't</u> give <u>no</u> partial credit.
>
> **REVISED:** The instructor doesn't give partial credit.

27f   Using Nouns as Adjectives

Nouns can function as adjectives in a sentence.

> He made a sandwich of <u>turkey</u> bologna, <u>egg</u> salad, and <u>tomato</u> slices on <u>wheat</u> bread.

Many familiar phrases, such as *space station, art history,* and *amusement park,* consist of one noun modifying another. In such cases using a noun as a modifier saves words. Overusing nouns as modifiers, however, can create clumsy—even incoherent—sentences.

> CONFUSING: The Chestnut Hill Fathers' Club Pony League beginners spring baseball clinic will be held Saturday.

To revise such cluttered sentences, restructure to break up a long series of nouns. You can also substitute equivalent adjective forms, where such forms exist, or possessives for some of the nouns used as modifiers.

> IMPROVED: The Chestnut Hill Fathers' Club's spring baseball clinic for beginning Pony League players will be held Saturday.

Eliminating the passive voice would make this sentence even clearer.

> IMPROVED: On Saturday, the Chestnut Hill Fathers' Club will hold its spring baseball clinic for beginning Pony League players.

EXERCISE 4

Identify every noun used as a modifier in the following passage. Then revise where necessary to eliminate clumsy or unclear phrasing created by overuse of nouns as modifiers. Try substituting adjective or possessive forms, and rearrange word order where you feel it is indicated.

The student government business management trainee program is extremely popular on campus. The student government donated some of the seed money to begin this management trainee program, which is one of the most successful the university business school has ever offered to undergraduate students. Three core courses must be taken before the student intern can actually begin work. First, a management theory course is given every spring semester in conjunction with the business school. Then, the following fall semester, students in the trainee program are required to take a course in personnel practices, including employee benefits. Finally, they take a business elective.

During the summer, the student interns are placed in junior management positions in large electronics, manufacturing, or public utility companies. This job experience is considered the most valuable part of the program because it gives students a taste of the work world.

STUDENT WRITER AT WORK

Adjectives and Adverbs

Read this draft of an essay and correct errors in the use of adjectives and adverbs. Check to be sure adjectives modify nouns or pronouns and adverbs modify verbs, adjectives, or other adverbs; make sure the correct comparative and superlative forms are used; and eliminate any double negatives and any overuse of nouns as modifiers. After you have corrected the errors, go over the draft again and, if necessary, revise further to strengthen coherence, unity, and style.

Working

My attitude toward work was shaped by my grandfather when I was real young, around the age of four. He did everything he could to encourage me to choose a job where I would use my brain, not my hands or my back. He tried hard to make his feelings real clearly to me. Still, it took a long time before I realized what he was telling me. Eventually, I learned that I had two choices: I could take it easy and drift into a job, or I could work hard and train for a career. I chose the most difficult of the two alternatives.

Every morning, my mother would drop me off at my grandparents' house real early, on her way to work. I would eat breakfast, and my grandfather would tell me stories about his life in the mines. He would tell me about his three friends who were crushed by a cave-in and about a terrifying gas explosion incident that nearly took his life. His most commonest stories were about the long, hard hours he had spent in the mines working for minimum wage, which was just a couple of cents an hour at that time. He didn't tell me none of these stories to scare me, but to make me think hard about the kind of job I might get when I grew up.

Years later, around the time of my sixteenth birthday, I needed money quick. I needed spending money when I went out with my friends, and I had to start saving regular for college. I decided to get a job, and I soon

continued on the following page

continued from the previous page

found one at Insalaco's supermarket. There I hauled heavy boxes of canned goods and unpacked them, stocked shelves, and labeled cans and boxes. This work was monotonous, and as time went on it grew more and more tediously. At the end of each day, I really felt very badly. In fact, every bone in my body ached. This was without a doubt the worse job I could imagine.

Everyone in my family had always considered me intelligently, and they thought I should go to college. To me, the thought of studying and doing homework for four more years after high school hadn't never been very appealing. After working at Insalaco's, however, I knew my family was right, and I understood what my grandfather had been trying to tell me.

PART 7

UNDERSTANDING PUNCTUATION AND MECHANICS

OVERVIEW OF SENTENCE PUNCTUATION: COMMAS, SEMICOLONS, COLONS, DASHES, PARENTHESES

(Further explanations and examples are located in the sections listed in parentheses after each example.)

SEPARATING INDEPENDENT CLAUSES

With a Comma and a Coordinating Conjunction
The year was 2081, and everybody was finally equal. (Kurt Vonnegut, Jr., "Harrison Bergeron") **(29a)**

With a Semicolon
Paul Revere's *The Boston Massacre* is traditional American protest art; Edward Hicks's paintings are socially conscious art with a religious strain. **(30a)**

With a Semicolon and a Coordinating Conjunction
If such a world government is not established by a process of agreement among nations, I believe it will come anyway, and in a much more dangerous form; for war or wars can only result in one power being supreme and dominating the rest of the world by its overwhelming military supremacy. (Albert Einstein, *Einstein on Peace*) **(30a)**

With a Semicolon and a Transitional Word or Phrase
Thomas Jefferson brought two hundred vanilla beans and a recipe for vanilla ice cream back from France; thus, he gave America its all-time favorite ice-cream flavor. **(30b)**

SEPARATING ITEMS IN A SERIES

With Commas
Chipmunk, raccoon, and *Mugwump* are Native American words. **(29b)**

With Semicolons
As ballooning became established, a series of firsts ensued: The first balloonist in the United States was 13-year-old Edward Warren, 1784; the first woman aeronaut was a Madame Thible who,

depending on your source, either recited poetry or sang as she lifted off; the first airmail letter, written by Ben Franklin's grandson, was carried by balloon; and the first bird's-eye photograph of Paris was taken from a balloon. (Elaine B. Steiner, *Games*) **(30c)**

SETTING OFF EXAMPLES, EXPLANATIONS, OR SUMMARIES

With a Colon
Each camper should bring the following: a sleeping bag, a mess kit, a flashlight, and plenty of insect repellent. **(33a1)**

With a Dash
Walking to school by myself, spending the night at a friend's house, getting my ears pierced, and starting to wear makeup—these were some of the milestones of my childhood and adolescence. **(33b2)**

SETTING OFF NONESSENTIAL MATERIAL

With a Single Comma
His fear increasing, he waited to enter the haunted house. **(29d4)**

With a Pair of Commas
It was Roger Maris, not Mickey Mantle, who broke Babe Ruth's home run record. **(29d3)**

With a Pair of Dashes
Although we are by all odds the most social of all social animals—more interdependent, more attached to each other, more inseparable in our behavior than bees—we do not often feel our conjoined intelligence. (Lewis Thomas, *Lives of a Cell*) **(33b1)**

With a Single Dash
They could not afford to jump to conclusions—any conclusions. (Michael Crichton, *The Andromeda Strain*) **(33b1)**

With Parentheses
It took Gilbert Fairchild two years at Harvard College (two academic years, from September, 1955, to June, 1957) to learn everything he needed to know. (Judith Martin, *Gilbert: A Comedy of Manners*) **(33c1)**

CHAPTER 28

END PUNCTUATION

USING END PUNCTUATION

Use a Period . . .
- To end a sentence (**28a1**)
- To mark an abbreviation (**28a2**)
- To mark divisions in dramatic, poetic, and biblical references (**28a3**)
- To mark divisions in electronic addresses (**28a4**)

Use a Question Mark . . .
- To mark the end of a direct question (**28b1**)
- To mark questionable dates and numbers (**28b2**)

Use an Exclamation Point . . .
- To mark emphasis (**28c1**)

28a Using Periods

Use **periods** to end declarative sentences (statements), mild commands, polite requests, and indirect questions. Also use periods in most abbreviations and in dramatic and poetic references and electronic addresses.

(1) Ending a Sentence

Periods signal the end of a statement, a mild command or polite request, or an indirect question.

Something is rotten in Denmark. (statement)

Be sure to have the oil checked before you start out. (mild command)

When the bell rings, please exit in an orderly fashion. (polite request)

They wondered whether it was safe to go back in the water. (indirect question)

(2) Marking an Abbreviation

Periods are used in most abbreviations.

Mr. Spock	221B Baker St.	9 p.m.
Dr. Who	Aug.	etc.

If the abbreviation falls at the end of a sentence, do not add another period.

FAULTY: He promised to be there at 6 a.m..

REVISED: He promised to be there at 6 a.m.

However, add a question mark after the abbreviation's final period if the sentence is a question.

Did he arrive at 6 p.m.?

If the abbreviation falls within a sentence, use normal punctuation after the abbreviation's final period.

FAULTY: He promised to be there at 6 p.m. but he forgot.

REVISED: He promised to be there at 6 p.m., but he forgot.

 ABBREVIATIONS WITHOUT PERIODS

All-capital-letter abbreviations do not usually require periods unless they are the initials of people's names (E. B. White).

Familiar capital-letter abbreviations, such as MD, RN, BC, and AD, and abbreviations of names of corporations, associations, or government agencies and scientific and technical terms do not require periods.

CIA	NAACP	GPO	URL	HIV
EPA	IBM	UCLA	FAQ	WWW
MGM	DNA	WCAU-FM	FTP	GE
MLA	HBO	USA	ATM	CD-ROM
APA	FBI	UFO	VCR	GM

continued on the following page

continued from the previous page

Acronyms (new words formed from the initial letters or first few letters of a series of words) do not include periods.

radar	scuba	NAFTA
AIDS	CAT scan	hazmats

Fannie Mae (Federal National Mortgage Association)
Gestapo (Geheime Staats Polizei)
modem (modulator-demodulator)
Soweto (Southwest townships)
FedEx (Federal Express)

Clipped forms (commonly accepted shortened forms of words) do not include periods.

gym   dorm   math   gas   decaf   Net (Internet)   fax (facsimile)

Postal abbreviations do not include periods.

NY   CA   MS   FL   TX

(3) Marking Divisions in Dramatic, Poetic, and Biblical References

Periods separate act, scene, and line numbers in plays; book and line numbers in long poems; and chapter and verse numbers in biblical references. (Do not space between the periods and the elements they separate.)

DRAMATIC REFERENCE: *Hamlet* 2.2.1–5

POETIC REFERENCE: *Paradise Lost* 7.163–67

BIBLICAL REFERENCE: Judges 4.14

(4) Marking Divisions in Electronic Addresses

Periods, along with other punctuation marks (such as slashes and colons), are frequently used in electronic addresses.

g.mckay@smu.edu

http://www.nwu.org/nwu

NOTE: When you type an electronic address, do not end it with a period or add spaces after periods within the address.

EXERCISE 1

Correct these sentences by adding missing periods and deleting unnecessary ones. If a sentence is correct, mark it with a *C*.

EXAMPLE: Their mission changed the war
          Their mission changed the war.

1. Julius Caesar was killed in 44 B.C.
2. Dr. McLaughlin worked hard to earn his Ph.D..
3. Carmen was supposed to be at A.F.L.-C.I.O. headquarters by 2 p.m.; however, she didn't get there until 10 p.m.
4. After she studied the fall lineup proposed by N.B.C., she decided to work for C.B.S.
5. Representatives from the U.M.W. began collective bargaining after an unsuccessful meeting with Mr. L Pritchard, the coal company's representative.

28b Using Question Marks

Use **question marks** at the end of direct questions or to indicate questionable dates or numbers.

(1) Marking the End of a Direct Question

Use a question mark to signal the end of a direct question.

Who was that masked man? (direct question)

"Is this a silver bullet?" they asked. (declarative sentence opening with a direct question)

They asked, "Could he have been the Lone Ranger?" (declarative sentence closing with a direct question)

Who was it who asked, "Who was that masked man"? (question within a question)

Did he say where he came from, who his companion was, or where they were headed? (series of direct questions)

Did he say where he came from? Who his companion was? Where they were headed? (series of direct questions with each question asked separately)

Dashes or parentheses are used around a direct question within a declarative sentence.

Someone—a disgruntled office seeker?—is sabotaging the campaign.

Part of the shipment (three dozen cases?) was delayed.

(2) Marking Questionable Dates or Numbers

Use a question mark in parentheses to indicate that a date or number is uncertain.

Aristophanes, the Greek playwright, was born in 448 (?) BC and died in 380 (?) BC.

The clock struck five (?) and stopped.

(3) Editing Misused or Overused Question Marks

Do not use question marks in the following situations.

After an Indirect Question   Use a period, not a question mark, with an **indirect question** (a question that is not quoted directly).

FAULTY: The personnel officer asked whether he knew how to type?

REVISED: The personnel officer asked whether he knew how to type.

With Other Punctuation   Do not use other punctuation marks along with question marks.

FAULTY: "Can it be true?," he asked.

REVISED: "Can it be true?" he asked.

FAULTY: Can you believe this run of good luck?!

REVISED: Can you believe this run of good luck?

With Another Question Mark   Do not end a sentence with more than one question mark.

FAULTY: You did what?? Are you crazy??

REVISED: You did what? Are you crazy?

As an Indication of Attitude   Do not use question marks to convey sarcasm. Instead, suggest your attitude through word choice.

FAULTY: I refused his generous (?) offer.

REVISED: I refused his not-very-generous offer.

In an Exclamation   Do not use a question mark after an exclamation phrased as a question.

FAULTY: Will you please stop that at once?

REVISED: Will you please stop that at once!

EXERCISE 2

Correct the use of question marks and other punctuation in the following sentences.

> **EXAMPLE:** She asked whether Freud's theories were accepted during his lifetime?
>
> She asked whether Freud's theories were accepted during his lifetime.

1. He wondered whether he should take a nine o'clock class?
2. The instructor asked, "Was the Spanish-American War a victory for America?"?
3. Are they really going to China??!!
4. He took a modest (?) portion of dessert—half a pie.
5. "Is *data* the plural of *datum*?," he inquired.

28c Using Exclamation Points

Use an **exclamation point** to convey strong feeling, such as astonishment or shock.

(1) Marking Emphasis

Use an exclamation point to signal the end of an emotional or emphatic statement, an emphatic interjection, or a forceful command.

> Remember the *Maine*!
>
> No! Don't leave!
>
> Finish this job at once!

NOTE: An exclamation point can follow a complete sentence ("What big teeth you have!") or a phrase ("What big teeth!").

(2) Editing Misused or Overused Exclamation Points

Do not use exclamation points in the following situations.

With Mild Statements   Do not use exclamation points with mildly emphatic statements or with mild interjections or commands.

Please close the door behind you.

Stand by your man.

With Another Exclamation Point   Do not end a sentence with more than one exclamation point.

FAULTY: I could hardly believe my eyes!!!

REVISED: I could hardly believe my eyes!

With Other Punctuation   Do not use other punctuation marks along with exclamation points.

FAULTY: "Fire!," he shouted.

REVISED: "Fire!" he shouted.

FAULTY: You can't be serious?!

REVISED: You can't be serious!

As an Indication of Attitude   Do not use an exclamation point to suggest sarcasm or humor. Use word choice and sentence structure instead.

FAULTY: The team's record was a near-perfect (!) 0 and 12.

REVISED: The team's record was a far-from-perfect 0 and 12.

 USING EXCLAMATION POINTS

Unless you are recording dialogue, do not use exclamation points in college writing. Even in informal writing, use exclamation points sparingly; too many exclamation points give readers the impression that you are overwrought, even hysterical.

EXERCISE 3

Correct the use of exclamation points and other punctuation in these sentences.

EXAMPLE: "My God," she cried. "I've been shot!!!"

         "My God," she cried. "I've been shot!"

1. Are you kidding?! I never said that.
2. When the cell divided, each of the daughter cells had an extra chromosome!

3. This is fantastic. I can't believe you bought this for me.
4. Wow!! Just what I always wanted!! A pink Cadillac!!
5. "Eureka!," cried Archimedes as he sprang from his bathtub.

EXERCISE 4

Add appropriate punctuation to this passage.

Dr Craig and his group of divers paused at the shore, staring respectfully at the enormous lake Who could imagine what terrors lay beneath its surface Which of them might not emerge alive from this adventure Would it be Col Cathcart Capt Wilks, the MD from the naval base Her husband, P L Fox Or would they all survive the task ahead Dr Craig decided some encouraging remarks were in order

"Attention divers," he said in a loud, forceful voice "May I please have your attention The project which we are about to undertake—"

"Oh, no" screamed Mr Fox suddenly "Look out It's the Loch Ness Monster"

"Quick" shouted Dr Craig "Move away from the shore" But his warning came too late

CHAPTER 29

THE COMMA

USE COMMAS . . .

- To set off independent clauses (**29a**)
- To set off items in a series (**29b**)
- To set off introductory elements (**29c**)
- To set off nonessential elements (**29d**)
- In other conventional contexts (**29e**)
- To prevent misreading (**29f**)

29a Setting Off Independent Clauses

Use a comma when you link two independent clauses with a **coordinating conjunction** (*and, but, or, nor, for, yet, so*).

> The year was 2081, and everybody was finally equal. (Kurt Vonnegut, Jr., "Harrison Bergeron")

> The bride was not young, nor was she very pretty. (Stephen Crane, "The Bride Comes to Yellow Sky")

Use a comma before each coordinating conjunction, no matter how many independent clauses a compound sentence has.

> She had bonny children, yet she felt they had been thrust upon her, and she could not love them. (D. H. Lawrence, "The Rocking-Horse Winner")

NOTE: You may omit the comma if two clauses connected by a coordinating conjunction are very short.

> Seek and ye shall find.

> Love it or leave it.

**See
23g**

Use a comma after the first clause when pairs of **correlative conjunctions** link two independent clauses.

Just as it's fascinating to find out where your barber gets his hair cut or what the top chef eats, so it can be worthwhile to find out how top brokers invest their own money. (*Money*)

CLOSE-UP SEPARATING INDEPENDENT CLAUSES

**See
30b**

For clarity, you may use a semicolon—not a comma—to separate two **independent clauses** linked by a coordinating conjunction when one clause already contains one or more commas.

The tourists visited Melbourne, the capital of Australia, for three days; and they toured Wellington, New Zealand, for two.

EXERCISE 1

Combine each of the following sentence pairs into one compound sentence, adding commas where necessary.

EXAMPLE: Emergency medicine became an approved medical specialty in 1979. Now pediatric emergency medicine is become increasingly important. (and)

Emergency medicine became an approved medical specialty in 1979, and now pediatric emergency medicine is becoming increasingly important.

1. The Pope did not hesitate to visit his native Poland. He did not hesitate to meet with Solidarity leader Lech Walesa. (nor)
2. Agents place brand-name products in prominent positions in films. The products will be seen and recognized by large audiences. (so)
3. Unisex insurance rates may have some drawbacks for women. These rates may be very beneficial. (or)
4. Cigarette advertising no longer appears on television. It does appear in print media. (but)
5. Dorothy Day founded the Catholic Worker movement more than fifty years ago. Today her followers still dispense free food, medical care, and legal advice to the needy. (and)

29b Setting Off Items in a Series

(1) Coordinate Elements

Use commas with three or more coordinate elements (words, phrases, or clauses) in a series.

Chipmunk, *raccoon*, and *Mugwump* are Native American words. (series of words)

She is a child of her age, of depression, of war, of fear. (Tillie Olsen, "I Stand Here Ironing") (series of phrases)

Brazilians speak Portuguese, Colombians speak Spanish, and Haitians speak French and Creole. (series of clauses)

Do not use a comma to introduce or to close a series.

FAULTY: Three important criteria are, fat content, salt content, and taste.

REVISED: Three important criteria are fat content, salt content, and taste.

FAULTY: Quebec, Ontario, and Alberta, are Canadian provinces.

REVISED: Quebec, Ontario, and Alberta are Canadian provinces.

If phrases or clauses in a **series** already contain commas, use semicolons to separate the items.

See
30c

 USING COMMAS WITH ITEMS IN A SERIES

Journalists usually omit the comma that separates the last two items in a series. In your college writing, however, you should always use a comma before the coordinating conjunction because the final comma eliminates the possibility of ambiguity.

AMBIGUOUS: The party was made special by the company, the light from the hundreds of twinkling candles and the excellent hors d'oeuvres. (Did the hors d'oeuvres give off light?)

REVISED: The party was made special by the company, the light from the hundreds of twinkling candles, and the excellent hors d'oeuvres.

(2)   Coordinate Adjectives

Use a comma between two or more **coordinate adjectives**—adjectives that modify the same word or word group—unless they are joined by a conjunction.

She brushed her <u>long</u>, <u>shining</u> hair.

The fruit was <u>crisp</u>, <u>tart</u>, <u>mellow</u>—in short, good enough to eat.

The baby was <u>tired</u> and <u>cranky</u> and <u>wet</u>. (adjectives joined by conjunctions; no commas required)

Sometimes several adjectives will all seem to be coordinate when they are not. In the sentence *Ten red balloons fell from the ceiling,* for instance, the adjective *red* modifies the noun *balloons,* but the adjective *ten* modifies the word group *red balloons.* In this case, only one adjective modifies the noun; the adjectives are not coordinate, so no comma is required.

✔ CHECKLIST: PUNCTUATING ADJECTIVES IN A SERIES

✔ **If you can reverse the order of the adjectives, the adjectives are coordinate, and you should use a comma.**

She brushed her shining, long hair.
She brushed her long, shining hair.

If you cannot, the adjectives are not coordinate, and you should not use a comma.

Red ten balloons fell from the ceiling.
Ten red balloons fell from the ceiling.

✔ **If you can insert *and* between the adjectives without changing the meaning of the sentence, the adjectives are coordinate, and you should use a comma.**

She brushed her long [and] shining hair.
She brushed her long, shining hair.

If you cannot, the adjectives are not coordinate, and you should not use a comma.

Ten [and] red balloons fell from the ceiling.
Ten red balloons fell from the ceiling.

(Numbers—such as *ten* in the preceding example—are not coordinate with other adjectives.)

EXERCISE 2

Correct the use of commas in the following sentences, adding or deleting commas where necessary. If a sentence is punctuated correctly, mark it with a *C*.

EXAMPLE: Neither dogs snakes bees nor dragons frighten her.

Neither dogs, snakes, bees, nor dragons frighten her.

1. Seals, whales, dogs, lions, and horses, all are mammals.
2. Mammals are warm-blooded vertebrates that bear live young, nurse them, and usually have fur.
3. Seals are mammals but lizards, and snakes, and iguanas are reptiles, and newts and salamanders are amphibians.
4. Amphibians also include frogs, and toads.
5. Eagles geese ostriches turkeys chickens and ducks are classified as birds.

EXERCISE 3

Add two coordinate adjectives to modify each of the following combinations, inserting commas where required.

EXAMPLE: classical music

strong, beautiful classical music

1. distant thunder
2. silver spoon
3. New York Yankees
4. miniature golf
5. Rolling Stones
6. loving couple
7. computer science
8. wheat bread
9. art museum
10. new math

29c Setting Off Introductory Elements

Use a comma to separate most introductory elements from the rest of the sentence.

(1) Introductory Adverb Clauses

Introductory adverb clauses, including **elliptical clauses**, are generally set off from the rest of the sentence by commas.

See 10b2

Although the CIA used to call undercover agents *penetration agents*, they now routinely refer to them as *moles*.

When war came to Beirut and Londonderry and Saigon, the victims were the children.

While working in the mines, Paul longed for a better life.

If the adverb clause is short, you may omit the comma—provided the sentence will be clear without it.

When I exercise I drink plenty of water.

See 29g7 NOTE: An **adverb clause** at the *end* of a sentence is not set off by a comma.

(2) Introductory Phrases

An introductory phrase is usually set off from the rest of the sentence by a comma.

Thinking that this might be his last chance, Scott struggled toward the Pole.

To succeed in a male-dominated field, women engineers must work extremely hard.

During the worst days of the Depression, movie attendance rose dramatically.

If the introductory phrase is short and no ambiguity is possible, you may omit the comma.

For the first time Clint felt truly happy.

After the exam I took a four-hour nap.

 USING COMMAS

See 10b1 **Gerund phrases** and **infinitive phrases** that serve as subjects are not set off by commas.

FAULTY (GERUND PHRASE): Laughing out loud, can release tension.

REVISED: Laughing out loud can release tension.

FAULTY (INFINITIVE PHRASE): To know him, is to love him.

REVISED: To know him is to love him.

(3) Introductory Transitional Words and Phrases

When a **transitional word or phrase** begins a sentence, it is usually set off from the rest of the sentence with a comma.

See 6c2

Certainly, any plan that is enacted must be fair.

In other words, we cannot act hastily.

Therefore, let us reconsider our options.

EXERCISE 4

Add commas in the following paragraph where needed to set off introductory elements from the rest of the sentence.

While childhood is shrinking adolescence is expanding. Whatever the reason girls are maturing earlier. The average onset of puberty is now two years earlier than it was only forty years ago. What's more both boys and girls are staying in the nest longer. Today it isn't unusual for children to stay in their parents' home until they're twenty or twenty-one, delaying adulthood and extending adolescence. To some who study the culture this increase in adolescence portends dire consequences. With teenage hormones running amuck for longer the problems of teenage pregnancy and sexually transmitted diseases loom large. Young boys' spending long periods of their lives without responsibilities is also a recipe for disaster. Others see this "youthing" of American culture in a more positive light. Without a doubt adolescents are creative, lively, more willing to take risks. If we channel their energies carefully they could contribute, even in their extended adolescence, to American culture and technology.

29d Setting Off Nonessential Material from the Rest of the Sentence

Sometimes certain modifying words, phrases, or clauses, although they may *contribute* to the meaning of the sentence, are not *essential* to its meaning. That is, deleting the material would not substantially change the sentence's meaning or emphasis. Commas should set off such nonessential material.

Designer jeans are a contradiction in terms, like educational television. (Fran Lebowitz)

There is no place I know of, other than the bathtub, where people should not have to worry about manners. (Judith Martin)

(1) Nonrestrictive Modifiers

Modifying phrases or clauses may be *restrictive* or *nonrestrictive*. **Restrictive modifiers** supply essential information—they narrow the meaning of the word or word group they modify—and are *not* separated from it by commas. **Nonrestrictive modifiers,** which do not restrict or particularize the word or word group they modify (and are therefore not essential to the sentence's meaning), *are* set off by commas.

Compare these two sentences.

Actors who have big egos are often insecure.

Actors , who have big egos , are often insecure.

At first glance, the two sentences above seem to mean exactly the same thing. Upon closer examination, however, you can see that they convey different meanings. Look at the first sentence again.

Actors <u>who have big egos</u> are often insecure.

In this sentence, *who have big egos* is **restrictive;** the writer's intention is to limit the noun *actors* only to those who have big egos. The sentence suggests that only those actors with big egos—not all actors—are insecure. The modifying phrase restricts the meaning of *actors,* the noun it modifies, and therefore it is not set off by commas.

Now look at the second sentence again.

Actors , <u>who have big egos</u> , are often insecure.

In this sentence, the modifying phrase *who have big egos* is nonrestrictive because it suggests that *all* actors have big egos. Because the modifying phrase does not restrict the meaning of the noun *actors,* it is set off by commas.

As the following examples illustrate, commas set off only nonrestrictive modifiers—those whose elimination would not change the sentence's meaning—never restrictive modifiers, which supply essential information.

Adjective Clauses

The artist <u>who created Zap Comix during the 1960s</u> has also had artwork displayed at the Whitney Museum of American Art. (restrictive; no commas used)

Robert Crumb , <u>who created Zap Comix during the 1960s</u> , is credited with popularizing the slogan "Keep on Truckin'." (nonrestrictive; commas used)

Speaking in public is something <u>that most people fear</u>. (restrictive; no comma used)

He ran for the bus , which was late as usual. (nonrestrictive; comma used)

Prepositional Phrases

The man with the gun demanded their money. (restrictive; no commas used)

The surgical team , with smiles on their faces , pronounced the operation a success. (nonrestrictive; commas used)

Verbal Phrases

The candidates running for mayor have agreed to a debate. (restrictive; no commas used)

The marathoner , running as fast as he could , beat his previous time by several seconds. (nonrestrictive; commas used)

Appositives

Orson Welles's film *Citizen Kane* has received great critical acclaim. (restrictive; no commas used)

Maya Angelou , a native of Arkansas , read an original poem at President Clinton's 1992 inauguration. (nonrestrictive; commas used)

✔ CHECKLIST: DISTINGUISHING RESTRICTIVE MODIFIERS FROM NONRESTRICTIVE MODIFIERS

To determine whether a modifier is restrictive or nonrestrictive, ask these four questions.

✔ Does the modifier restrict the meaning of the noun it modifies (*The artist who created Zap Comix*, not just any artist; *the man with the gun*, not just any man)? If so, it is restrictive and does not take commas. If not, commas should set off the modifier.

✔ Is the modifier introduced by *that* (*something that most people fear*)? If so, it is restrictive. *That* cannot introduce a nonrestrictive clause.

✔ Can you delete the relative pronoun without causing ambiguity or confusion (*something [that] most people fear*)? If so, the clause is restrictive and requires no commas.

✔ Is the appositive more specific than the noun that precedes it (*Orson Welles's film Citizen Kane*)? If so, it is restrictive and should not be set off by commas.

CLOSE-UP   *THAT* AND *WHICH*

That is used to introduce only restrictive clauses.

I bought a used car <u>that</u> cost $2,000.

Although *which* can be used to introduce both restrictive and non-restrictive clauses, many writers prefer to use *which* only to introduce nonrestrictive clauses.

RESTRICTIVE: I bought a used car <u>which</u> cost $2,000.

NONRESTRICTIVE: The used car I bought, <u>which</u> cost $2,000, broke down after a week.

NOTE: When *which* introduces a nonrestrictive clause, it is preceded by a comma.

EXERCISE 5

Insert commas where necessary to set off nonrestrictive modifiers.

The Statue of Liberty which was dedicated in 1886 has undergone extensive renovation. Its supporting structure whose designer was the French engineer Alexandre Gustave Eiffel is made of iron. The Statue of Liberty created over a period of nine years by sculptor Frédéric-Auguste Bartholdi stands 151 feet tall. The people of France who were grateful for American help in the French Revolution raised the money to pay the sculptor who created the statue. The people of the United States contributing over $100,000 raised the money for the pedestal on which the statue stands.

(2) Transitional Words and Phrases

<u>Transitional words and phrases</u>—which include **conjunctive adverbs** like *however, therefore, thus,* and *nevertheless* as well as expressions like *for example* and *on the other hand*—qualify, clarify, and make connections explicit, but they are not essential to meaning. For this reason, they are set off by commas.

When a transitional word or phrase interrupts a clause, it is set off by a pair of commas.

See 6c2

The House Ethics Committee recommended reprimanding two members of Congress. The House, however, overruled the recommendation and voted to censure them.

A transitional word or phrase at the *end* of a clause is separated from the rest of the sentence by a single comma.

Some things were easier after school started. Other things were a lot harder, however.

A transitional word or phrase at the *beginning* of a clause is also usually set off by commas.

Some wilderness programs are dangerous. However, the Outward Bound program is extremely safe.

 USING COMMAS

When a conjunctive adverb or other transitional expression separates two **independent clauses**, it is preceded by a semicolon or a period and followed by a comma.

See 30b

Laughter is the best medicine; of course, penicillin also comes in handy sometimes.

(3) Alternative or Contrasting Phrases

A phrase that expresses an alternative or a contrast is usually set off by commas.

It was a special, even magical, evening.

This medication should be taken after a meal, never on an empty stomach.

It was Roger Maris, not Mickey Mantle, who broke Babe Ruth's home run record.

(4) Absolute Phrases

An **absolute phrase**, which usually consists of a noun plus a participle, is always set off by commas from the sentence it modifies.

See 10c5

His fear increasing, he waited to enter the haunted house.

The Roanoke colonists vanished in 1591, their bodies never recovered.

(5) Miscellaneous Nonessential Elements

Certain nonessential elements are separated from the rest of the sentence by commas no matter where they are placed in a sentence.

Tag Questions (Auxiliary Verb + Pronoun Added to a Statement)

This is your first day on the job **,** isn't it?

It seems possible **,** does it not **,** that carrots may provide some protection against cancer?

Names in Direct Address

I wonder **,** Mr. Honeywell **,** whether Mr. Albright deserves a raise.

Doctor **,** what's your opinion?

What do you think **,** Your Honor?

Yes and No

Yes **,** we have no bananas.

No **,** we're all out of lemons.

Mild Interjections

See
28c1

Well **,** it's about time.

NOTE: Stronger interjections may be set off by **exclamation points**.

 EXERCISE 6

Set off the nonessential elements in these sentences with commas. If a sentence is correct, mark it with a *C*.

EXAMPLE: Piranhas like sharks will attack and eat almost anything if the opportunity arises.

Piranhas **,** like sharks **,** will attack and eat almost anything if the opportunity arises.

1. Kermit the Frog is a Muppet a cross between a marionette and a puppet.
2. The common cold a virus is frequently spread by hand contact not by mouth.
3. The account in the Bible of Noah's Ark and the forty-day flood may be based on an actual deluge.
4. Many US welfare recipients, such as children, the aged, and the severely disabled, have legitimate reasons for not working.
5. The submarine *Nautilus* was the first to cross under the North Pole wasn't it?

6. The 1958 Ford Edsel was advertised with the slogan "Once you've seen it, you'll never forget it."
7. Superman was called Kal-El on the planet Krypton; on earth however he was known as Clark Kent not Kal-El.
8. Its sales topping any of his previous singles "Heartbreak Hotel" was Elvis Presley's first million-seller.
9. Two companies Nash and Hudson joined in 1954 to form American Motors.
10. A firefly is a beetle not a fly and a prairie dog is a rodent not a dog.

29e Using Commas in Other Conventional Contexts

(1) Around Direct Quotations

In most cases, use commas to set off a direct quotation from the **identifying tag**—the phrase that identifies the speaker (*he said, she answered*).

Emerson said to Thoreau , "I greet you at the beginning of a great career."

"I greet you at the beginning of a great career ," Emerson said to Thoreau.

"I greet you ," Emerson said to Thoreau , "at the beginning of a great career."

When the identifying tag comes between two complete sentences, however, the tag is introduced by a comma but followed by a period.

"Winning isn't everything ," Vince Lombardi said . "It's the only thing."

If the first sentence of an interrupted quotation ends with a question mark or exclamation point, do not use commas.

"Should we hold the front page?" she asked. "After all, it's a slow news day."

"Hold the front page!" he cried. "This is the biggest story of the decade."

(2) Between Names and Titles or Degrees

Use commas to set off a degree or title that follows a name.

C. Everett Koop , MD , served as surgeon general.

No movie has been made about Martin Luther King, Jr.

Hamlet, prince of Denmark, is Shakespeare's most famous character.

If the title or degree precedes the name, however, no comma is required: Dr. Koop, Prince Hamlet.

No comma is used between a name and *II, III,* and so on.

King George III

(3) In Dates and Addresses

Use commas to separate items in dates and addresses.

The space shuttle *Challenger* was launched on August 30, 1983, from Cape Canaveral. (30 August 1983—without commas—is also acceptable.)

Her address is 600 West End Avenue, New York, NY 10024.

NOTE: Commas are not used to separate the day from the month or the month from the year when the day is omitted (May 1968). Do not use a comma to separate the street number from the street or the state name from the ZIP code. Within a sentence, a comma follows the last element of a date or address.

(4) In Salutations and Closings

Use commas in informal correspondence following salutations and closings and following the complimentary close in personal or business correspondence.

Dear John,   Love,
Dear Aunt Sophie,   Sincerely,

See 52a

In **business letters**, always use a colon, not a comma, after the salutation.

(5) In Long Numbers

For a number of four digits or more, place a comma before every third digit, counting from the right.

    1,200
    12,000
    120,000
    1,200,000

NOTE: Commas are not required in long numbers used in page and line numbers, addresses, telephone numbers, ZIP codes, or four-digit year numbers.

EXERCISE 7

Add commas where necessary to set off quotations, names, dates, addresses, and numbers.

1. India became independent on August 15 1947.
2. The UAW has more than 1500000 dues-paying members.
3. Nikita Khrushchev, former Soviet premier, said "We will bury you!"
4. Mount St. Helens, northeast of Portland Oregon, began erupting on March 27 1980 and eventually killed at least thirty people.
5. Located at 1600 Pennsylvania Avenue Washington DC, the White House is a popular tourist attraction.
6. In 1956, playing before a crowd of 64519 fans in Yankee Stadium in New York New York, Don Larsen pitched the first perfect game in World Series history.
7. Lewis Thomas MD was born in Flushing New York and attended Harvard Medical School in Cambridge Massachusetts.
8. In 1967 2000000 people worldwide died of smallpox, but in 1977 only about twenty died.
9. "The reports of my death" Mark Twain remarked "have been greatly exaggerated."
10. The French explorer Jean Nicolet landed at Green Bay Wisconsin in 1634, and in 1848 Wisconsin became the thirtieth state; it has 10355 lakes and a population of more than 4700000.

29f　Using Commas to Prevent Misreading

(1) To Clarify Meaning

Use a comma to avoid ambiguity.

Those who can , sprint the final lap.

Without the comma, *can* appears to be an auxiliary verb ("Those who can sprint. . . .") and the sentence seems incomplete. The comma clarifies the sentence's meaning.

(2) To Indicate an Omission

Use a comma to acknowledge the omission of a repeated word, usually a verb.

Pam carried the box; Tim, the suitcase.

Edwina went first; Marco, second.

(3) To Separate Repeated Words

Use a comma to separate words repeated consecutively within a sentence.

Everything bad that could have happened, happened.

EXERCISE 8

Add commas where necessary to prevent misreading.

> EXAMPLE: Whatever will be will be.
>
> Whatever will be, will be.

1. According to Bob Frank's computer has three disk drives.
2. Da Gama explored Florida; Pizarro Peru.
3. By Monday evening students must begin preregistration for fall classes.
4. Whatever they built they built with care.
5. When batting practice carefully.
6. Brunch includes warm muffins topped with whipped butter and freshly brewed coffee.
7. Students go to school to learn not to play sports.
8. Technology has made what once seemed impossible possible.

EXERCISE 9

Add commas to the following sentences where needed, and be prepared to explain why each is necessary. If a sentence is correct, mark it with a *C*.

> EXAMPLE: Once again Congress is looking to make changes in immigration law.
>
> REVISED: Once again, Congress is looking to make changes in immigration law.

1. In 1996 the Welfare Reform Act not only limited benefits for citizens born in the United States but also mandated refusal of benefits for all immigrants legal or illegal.
2. While Congress removed benefits the Immigration and Naturalization Service (INS) reduced its backlog of applications for citizenship.
3. The INS naturalized almost a million new citizens in 1996 double the number of citizens naturalized in 1995.
4. According to some critics the test which new citizens must take before they are naturalized is simple and shallow.

5. Others claim that making the test more difficult would be unfair because many graduates of American high schools can't answer the basic civics questions about the design of the American flag the structure of the US government and the events of American political history required by the test.

6. Some fear that too many new citizens from foreign countries will undermine core American values but others argue that those values came from earlier immigrants and that change is not necessarily bad.

7. Fear of immigrants while seemingly unfounded is not new.

8. In the 1940s the American government forced immigrants from Japan and their American-born children into internment camps after the Japanese bombed Pearl Harbor initiating America's involvement in World War II.

9. Not surprisingly there are some who still fear excessive immigration.

10. Some say that the movement toward a declaration of English as the official language is one product of that fear but others note that it just makes good sense to limit government dealings to English because of the money saved in printing and translation services.

29g Editing Misused or Overused Commas

DO NOT USE COMMAS ...

- To join two independent clauses (**29g1**)
- Around restrictive elements (**29g2**)
- Between inseparable grammatical constructions (**29g3**)
- To set off an indirect quotation or indirect question (**29g4**)
- Between phrases that contain correlative conjunctions (**29g5**)
- Between certain paired elements (**29g6**)
- Before an adverb clause that falls at the end of a sentence (**29g7**)

---

(1) To Join Two Independent Clauses

A comma alone cannot join two independent clauses; it must be preceded by a coordinating conjunction. Using just a comma to connect two independent clauses creates a **comma splice**.

See
Ch. 16

FAULTY: The season was unusually cool, nevertheless the orange crop was not seriously harmed.

REVISED: The season was unusually cool; nevertheless, the orange crop was not seriously harmed.

REVISED: The season was unusually cool. Nevertheless, the orange crop was not seriously harmed.

REVISED: The season was unusually cool, but the orange crop was not seriously harmed.

REVISED: Although the season was unusually cool, the orange crop was not seriously harmed.

(2) To Set Off Restrictive Modifiers

See
29d1

Commas are not used to set off **restrictive modifiers**.

FAULTY: Women, who seek to be equal to men, lack ambition.

REVISED: Women who seek to be equal to men lack ambition.

FAULTY: The film, *Malcolm X,* was directed by Spike Lee.

REVISED: The film *Malcolm X* was directed by Spike Lee.

(3) Between Inseparable Grammatical Constructions

A comma should not be placed between a subject and its predicate; a verb and its complement or direct object; a preposition and its object; or an adjective and the noun, pronoun, or noun phrase it modifies.

FAULTY (COMMA BETWEEN SUBJECT AND PREDICATE): We think that anyone who can walk a straight line out of the office before lunch, ought to be able to travel the same route on the way back. (Spirits Council of the United States)

REVISED: We think that anyone who can walk a straight line out of the office before lunch ought to be able to travel the same route on the way back.

FAULTY (COMMA BETWEEN VERB AND OBJECT): Louis Braille developed, an alphabet of raised dots for the blind.

REVISED: Louis Braille developed an alphabet of raised dots for the blind.

FAULTY (COMMA BETWEEN PREPOSITION AND OBJECT): They relaxed somewhat during, the last part of the obstacle course.

REVISED: They relaxed somewhat during the last part of the obstacle course.

FAULTY (COMMA BETWEEN ADJECTIVE AND WORDS IT MODIFIES): Wind-dispersed weeds include the well-known and plentiful, dandelions, milkweed, and thistle.

REVISED: Wind-dispersed weeds include the well-known and plentiful dandelions, milkweed, and thistle.

(4) To Set Off an Indirect Quotation or Indirect Question

Commas are not used to set off indirect quotations or indirect questions.

FAULTY: Humorist Art Buchwald once said, that the problem with television news is that it has no second page.

REVISED: Humorist Art Buchwald once said that the problem with television news is that it has no second page.

FAULTY: The landlord asked, whether we would be willing to sign a two-year lease.

REVISED: The landlord asked whether we would be willing to sign a two-year lease.

(5) Between Phrases Linked by Correlative Conjunctions

Commas are not used to separate phrases linked by **correlative conjunctions.**

See 23g

FAULTY: Thirty years ago, most college students had access to neither photocopiers, nor pocket calculators.

REVISED: Thirty years ago, most college students had access to neither photocopiers nor pocket calculators.

FAULTY: Both typewriters, and tape recorders were generally available, however.

REVISED: Both typewriters and tape recorders were generally available, however.

(6) Between Certain Paired Elements

Commas are not used between two elements of a compound subject, predicate, object, complement, or auxiliary verb.

FAULTY (COMMA INTERRUPTS COMPOUND SUBJECT.): Plagues, and pestilence were common during the Middle Ages.

REVISED: Plagues and pestilence were common during the Middle Ages.

FAULTY (COMMA INTERRUPTS COMPOUND PREDICATE.): Many women thirty-five and older are returning to college, and tend to be good students.

REVISED: Many women thirty-five and older are returning to college and tend to be good students.

FAULTY (COMMA INTERRUPTS COMPOUND OBJECT.): Mattel has marketed a doctor's lab coat, and an astronaut suit for its Barbie doll.

REVISED: Mattel has marketed a doctor's lab coat and an astronaut suit for its Barbie doll.

FAULTY (COMMA INTERRUPTS COMPOUND COMPLEMENT.): People buy bottled water because it is pure, and fashionable.

REVISED: People buy bottled water because it is pure and fashionable.

FAULTY (COMMA INTERRUPTS COMPOUND AUXILIARY VERB.): She can, and will be ready to run in the primary.

REVISED: She can and will be ready to run in the primary.

REVISED: She can, and will, be ready to run in the primary.

(7) Before an Adverb Clause that Falls at the End of a Sentence

Commas are generally not used before an adverb clause that falls at the end of a sentence.

FAULTY: Jane Addams founded Hull House, because she wanted to help Chicago's poor.

REVISED: Jane Addams founded Hull House because she wanted to help Chicago's poor.

EXERCISE 10

Unnecessary commas have been intentionally added to some of the sentences that follow. Delete any unnecessary commas. If a sentence is correct, mark it with a C.

EXAMPLE: Spring fever, is a common ailment.

Spring fever is a common ailment.

1. A book is like a garden, carried in the pocket. (Arab proverb)
2. Like the iodine content of kelp, air freight, is something most Americans have never pondered. (*Time*)
3. Charles Rolls, and Frederick Royce manufactured the first Rolls-Royce Silver Ghost, in 1907.

4. The hills ahead of him were rounded domes of grey granite, smooth as a bald man's pate, and completely free of vegetation. (Wilbur Smith, *Flight of the Falcon*)

5. Food here is scarce, and cafeteria food is vile, but the great advantage to Russian raw materials, when one can get hold of them, is that they are always fresh and untampered with. (Andrea Lee, *Russian Journal*)

EXERCISE 11

In the following passage, punctuation errors have been deliberately introduced. Delete excess commas and add any necessary ones. Be prepared to justify your revisions.

What I learned first of all was the intense delight of flying an open plane. I'm not sure that I can explain why it is so different from a closed cockpit but, it must come from the intimate presence of the air, itself, the medium that you fly in streaming past and around you. You can thrust your whole arm out into the slipstream and press back against the flow of air; you can lean to the side and the air will force tears from your eyes, and rush into your lungs. And you can look straight into space down to the earth and up to the sky with nothing, between you and the whole world. The plane is not a protective shell as an automobile is but an extension, of your body moving as you move and your head is the brain of the whole stretched and vibrating organism. Flying alone in an open plane, is the purest experience of flight possible. (Samuel Hynes, "The Feeling of Flying")

CHAPTER 30

THE SEMICOLON

A **semicolon** is weaker than a period but stronger than a comma. Semicolons are used only between items of equal grammatical rank: two independent clauses, two phrases, and so on.

USE SEMICOLONS...

- To separate independent clauses **(30a)**
- To separate clauses introduced by transitional words and phrases **(30b)**
- To separate items in a series **(30c)**

30a Separating Independent Clauses

Use a semicolon between independent clauses that are closely related in meaning but not joined by a coordinating conjunction.

Paul Revere's *The Boston Massacre* is traditional American protest art; Edward Hicks's paintings are socially conscious art with a religious strain. (clauses related by contrast)

In the preceding example, the semicolon emphasizes the close relationship between the clauses.

NOTE: You may use a semicolon instead of a comma between two clauses even if they are already separated by a coordinating conjunction if one clause contains internal punctuation or is long or complex.

If such a world government is not established by a process of agreement among nations, I believe it will come anyway, and in a much more dangerous form; for war or wars can only result in one power being supreme and dominating the rest of the world by its overwhelming military supremacy. (Albert Einstein, *Einstein on Peace*)

USING SEMICOLONS BETWEEN INDEPENDENT CLAUSES

If you use only a comma or no punctuation at all between independent clauses, you will create **a comma splice or a fused sentence**.

See Ch. 16

EXERCISE 1

Add semicolons, periods, or commas plus coordinating conjunctions where necessary to separate independent clauses. Then, reread the paragraph to make certain no comma splices or fused sentences remain.

EXAMPLE: *Birth of a Nation* was one of the earliest epic movies it was based on the book *The Klansman*.

Birth of a Nation was one of the earliest epic movies; it was based on the book *The Klansman*.

During the 1950s movie attendance declined because of the increasing popularity of television. As a result, numerous gimmicks were introduced to draw audiences into theaters. One of the first of these was Cinerama, in this technique three pictures were shot side by side and projected onto a curved screen. Next came 3-D, complete with special glasses, *Bwana Devil* and *The Creature from the Black Lagoon* were two early 3-D ventures. *The Robe* was the first picture filmed in Cinemascope in this technique a shrunken image was projected on a screen twice as wide as it was tall. Smell-O-Vision (or Aroma-rama) was a short-lived gimmick that enabled audiences to smell what they were viewing problems developed when it became impossible to get one odor out of the theater in time for the next smell to be introduced. William Castle's *Thirteen Ghosts* introduced special glasses for cowardly viewers who wanted to be able to control what they saw, the red part of the glasses was the "ghost viewer" and the green part was the "ghost remover." Perhaps the ultimate in movie gimmicks accompanied the film *The Tingler* when this film was shown seats in the theater were wired to generate mild electric shocks. Unfortunately, the shocks set off a chain reaction that led to hysteria in the theater. During the 1960s such gimmicks all but disappeared, viewers were able once again to simply sit back and enjoy a movie. In 1997 *Mr. Payback,* a short interactive film that contained elements of a videogame, brought back the gimmick, it allowed viewers to vote on how they wanted the plot to unfold.

EXERCISE 2

Combine each of the following sentence groups into one sentence that contains only two independent clauses. Use a semicolon to join the two clauses. You will need to add, delete, relocate, or change some words; keep experimenting until you find the arrangement that best conveys the sentence's meaning.

EXAMPLE: The Congo River Rapids is a ride at the Dark Continent in Tampa, Florida. Riders raft down the river. They glide alongside jungle plants and animals.

The Congo River Rapids is a ride at the Dark Continent in Tampa, Florida; riders raft down the river, gliding alongside jungle plants and animals.

1. Theme parks offer exciting rides. They are thrill packed. They flirt with danger.
2. Free Fall is located in Atlanta's Six Flags over Georgia. In this ride, riders travel up a 128-foot-tall tower. They plunge down at fifty-five miles per hour.
3. In the Sky Whirl riders go 115 feet up in the air and circle about seventy-five times. This ride is located in Great America. Great America parks are in Gurnee, Illinois, and Santa Clara, California.
4. The Kamikaze Slide can be found at the Wet 'n Wild parks in Arlington, Texas, and Orlando, Florida. This ride is a slide three hundred feet long. It extends sixty feet in the air.
5. Viper is an exciting ride. It is found at Six Flags Great Adventure in Jackson, New Jersey. Its outside loop has a 360-degree spiral.
6. Astroworld in Houston, Texas, boasts Greezed Lightnin'. This ride is an eighty-foot-high loop. The ride goes from zero to sixty miles per hour in four seconds and moves forward and backward.
7. The Beast is at Kings Island near Cincinnati, Ohio. The Beast is a wooden roller coaster. It has a 7,400-foot track and goes seventy miles per hour.
8. Busch Gardens in Williamsburg, Virginia, features Escape from Pompeii. This is a water ride. It allows riders to explore ruins and see Mount Vesuvius.

9. Wild Arctic is at Sea World in Orlando, Florida. This ride includes a simulated helicopter flight. The flight goes to Base Station Wild Arctic. The ride also goes to a wrecked ship.

10. At Busch Gardens Tampa Bay in Tampa, Florida, Egypt is a thrill-packed attraction. It features an inverted roller coaster with cars hanging from the top. A replica of King Tut's tomb is also featured.

30b Separating Independent Clauses Introduced by Transitional Words and Phrases

Use a semicolon between two closely related independent clauses when the second clause is introduced by a **transitional word or phrase**.

See 6c2

Thomas Jefferson brought two hundred vanilla beans and a recipe for vanilla ice cream back from France; thus, he gave America its all-time favorite ice-cream flavor.

EXERCISE 3

Combine each of the following sentence groups into one sentence that contains only two independent clauses. Use a semicolon and the transitional word or phrase in parentheses to join the two clauses, adding commas within clauses where necessary. You will need to add, delete, relocate, or change some words. There is no one correct version; keep experimenting until you find the arrangement you feel is most effective.

EXAMPLE: The Aleutian Islands are located off the west coast of Alaska. They are an extremely remote chain of islands. They are sometimes called America's Siberia. (in fact)

The Aleutian Islands, located off the west coast of Alaska, are an extremely remote chain of islands; in fact, they are sometimes called America's Siberia.

1. The Aleutians lie between the North Pacific Ocean and the Bering Sea. The weather there is harsh. Dense fog, 100-mph winds, and even tidal waves and earthquakes are not uncommon. (for example)

2. These islands constitute North America's largest network of active volcanoes. The Aleutians boast some beautiful scenery. The islands are relatively unexplored. (still)

3. The Aleutians are home to a wide variety of birds. Numerous animals, such as fur seals and whales, are found there. These islands may house the largest concentration of marine animals in the world. (in fact)

4. During World War II, thousands of American soldiers were stationed on Attu Island. They were stationed on Adak Island. The Japanese eventually occupied both Attu and Adak islands. (however)

5. The islands' original population of native Aleuts was drastically reduced in the eighteenth century by Russian fur traders. Today the total population is only about 8,500. US military employees comprise more than half of this. (consequently)

(Adapted from *National Geographic*)

30c Separating Items in a Series

Use semicolons between items in a series when one or more of those items include commas. Without semicolons it is difficult to distinguish the individual elements in the series.

Three papers are posted on the bulletin board outside the building: a description of the exams; a list of appeal procedures for students who fail; and an employment ad from an automobile factory, addressed specifically to candidates whose appeals are turned down. (Andrea Lee, *Russian Journal*)

As ballooning became established, a series of firsts ensued: The first balloonist in the United States was 13-year-old Edward Warren, 1784; the first woman aeronaut was a Madame Thible who, depending on your source, either recited poetry or sang as she lifted off; the first airmail letter, written by Ben Franklin's grandson, was carried by balloon; and the first bird's-eye photograph of Paris was taken from a balloon. (Elaine B. Steiner, *Games*)

CLOSE-UP USING SEMICOLONS WITH OTHER PUNCTUATION

Even when items in a series are brief, semicolons are needed for clarity if any element in the series contains commas or other internal punctuation.

Laramie, Wyoming; Wyoming, Delaware; and Delaware, Ohio, were the first three places they visited.

EXERCISE 4

Replace commas with semicolons where necessary to separate internally punctuated items in a series. (For information on use of semicolons with quotation marks, **see 32e2.**)

> EXAMPLE: Luxury automobiles have some strong selling points: they are status symbols, some, such as the Corvette, appreciate in value, and they are usually comfortable and well appointed.
>
> Luxury automobiles have some strong selling points: they are status symbols; some, such as the Corvette, appreciate in value; and they are usually comfortable and well appointed.

1. The history of modern art seems at times to be a collection of "isms": Impressionism, a term that applies to a variety of painters who attempted to depict contemporary life in a new objective manner by reproducing an "impression" of what the eye sees, Abstract Expressionism, which applies to a wide-ranging group of artists who stress emotion and the unconscious in their nonrepresentational works, and, more recently, Minimalism, which applies to a group of painters and sculptors whose work reasserts the physical reality of the object.

2. Although the term *Internet* is widely used to refer only to the World Wide Web and E-mail, the Internet consists of a variety of discrete elements, including network news, which allows users to post and receive messages dealing with an unbelievably broad range of topics, Gopher, *Archie,* and WAIS, which allow users to track and retrieve information from a variety of sources in different ways, and FTP, which lets users download material from remote computers.

3. Three of rock and roll's best-known guitar heroes played with the "British Invasion" group The Yardbirds: Eric Clapton, the group's first lead guitarist, went on to play with John Mayall's Bluesbreakers, Cream, and Blind Faith, and still enjoys popularity as a solo act, Jeff Beck, the group's second guitarist, though not as visible as Clapton, made rock history with the Jeff Beck Group and inventive solo albums, and Jimmy Page, the group's third and final guitarist, transformed the remnants of the original group into the premier heavy metal band, Led Zeppelin.

4. Some of the most commonly confused words in English are *aggravate,* which means "to worsen," and *irritate,* which means "to annoy," *continual,* which means "recurring at intervals," and *continuous,* which means "an action occurring without interruption," *imply,* which means "to hint, suggest," and *infer,* which means "to conclude

from," and *compliment*, which means "to praise," and *complement*, which means "to complete or add to."

5. Tennessee Williams wrote *The Glass Menagerie*, which is about Laura Wingfield, a disabled young woman, and her family, *A Streetcar Named Desire*, which starred Marlon Brando, and *Cat on a Hot Tin Roof*, which won a Pulitzer Prize.

EXERCISE 5

Combine each of the following sentence groups into one sentence that includes a series of items separated by semicolons. You will need to add, delete, relocate, or change words. Try several versions of each sentence until you find the most effective arrangement.

> EXAMPLE: Collecting baseball cards is a worthwhile hobby. It helps children learn how to bargain and trade. It also encourages them to assimilate, evaluate, and compare data about major league ball players. Perhaps most important, it encourages them to find role models in the athletes whose cards they collect.
>
> Collecting baseball cards is a worthwhile hobby because it helps children learn how to bargain and trade; encourages them to assimilate, evaluate, and compare data about major league ball players; and, perhaps most important, encourages them to find role models in the athletes whose cards they collect.

1. A good dictionary offers definitions of words, including some obsolete and nonstandard words. It provides information about synonyms, usage, and word origins. It also offers information on pronunciation and syllabication.

2. The flags of the Scandinavian countries all depict a cross on a solid background. Denmark's flag is red with a white cross. Norway's flag is also red, but its cross is blue, outlined in white. Sweden's flag is blue with a yellow cross.

3. Over one hundred international collectors' clubs are thriving today. One of these associations is the Cola Clan, whose members buy, sell, and trade Coca-Cola memorabilia. Another is the Citrus Label Society. There is also a Cookie Cutter Collectors' Club.

4. Listening to the radio special, we heard "Shuffle Off to Buffalo" and "Moon over Miami," both of which are about eastern cities. We heard "By the Time I Get to Phoenix" and "I Left My Heart in San Francisco," which mention western cities. Finally, we heard "The Star-Spangled Banner," which seemed to be an appropriate finale.

5. There are three principal types of contact lenses. Hard contact lenses, also called "conventional lenses," are easy to clean and handle and quite sturdy. Soft lenses, which are easily contaminated and must be cleaned and disinfected daily, are less durable. Gas-permeable lenses, sometimes advertised as "semihard" or "semisoft" lenses, look and feel like hard lenses but are more easily contaminated and less durable.

30d Editing Misused or Overused Semicolons

Do not use semicolons in the following situations.

(1) Between Items of Unequal Grammatical Rank

Do not use a semicolon between a dependent and an independent clause or between a phrase and a clause.

FAULTY (SEMICOLON INCORRECTLY USED BETWEEN DEPENDENT AND INDEPENDENT CLAUSE): Because new drugs can now suppress the body's immune reaction; fewer organ transplants are rejected by the body.

REVISED: Because new drugs can now suppress the body's immune reaction, fewer organ transplants are rejected by the body.

FAULTY (SEMICOLON INCORRECTLY USED BETWEEN PHRASE AND CLAUSE): Increasing rapidly; computer crime poses a challenge for government, financial, and military agencies.

REVISED: Increasing rapidly, computer crime poses a challenge for government, financial, and military agencies.

(2) To Introduce a List

Use a colon, not a semicolon, to introduce a **list**.

See 33a1

FAULTY: The evening news is a battleground for the three major television networks; CBS, NBC, and ABC.

REVISED: The evening news is a battleground for the three major television networks: CBS, NBC, and ABC.

(3) To Introduce a Direct Quotation

See 32a

Do not use a semicolon to introduce a **direct quotation**.

FAULTY: Marie Antoinette may not have said; "Let them eat cake."

REVISED: Marie Antoinette may not have said, "Let them eat cake."

EXERCISE 6

Read the following paragraph carefully. Then add semicolons where necessary and delete excess or incorrectly used ones, substituting other punctuation where necessary.

Barnstormers were aviators; who toured the country after World War I, giving people short airplane rides and exhibitions of stunt flying, in fact, the name *barnstormer* was derived from the use of barns as airplane hangars. Americans' interest in airplanes had all but disappeared after the war; planes had served their function in battle, but when the war ended, most people saw no future in aviation. The barnstormers helped popularize flying; especially in rural areas. Some of them were pilots who had flown in the war; others were just young men with a thirst for adventure. They gave people rides in airplanes; sometimes charging a dollar a minute. For most passengers, this was their first ride in an airplane, in fact, sometimes it was their first sight of one. In the early 1920s, people grew bored with what the barnstormers had to offer; so groups of pilots began to stage spectacular—but often dangerous—stunt shows. Then, after Lindbergh's 1927 flight across the Atlantic; Americans suddenly needed no encouragement to embrace aviation. The barnstormers had outlived their usefulness; and an era ended. (Adapted from William Goldman, *Adventures in the Screen Trade*)

CHAPTER 31

THE APOSTROPHE

USE AN APOSTROPHE

- To form the possessive case (**31a**)
- To indicate omissions in contractions (**31c**)
- To form plurals (**31d**)

31a Forming the Possessive Case

The possessive case indicates ownership. In English the possessive case of nouns and indefinite pronouns is indicated either with a phrase that includes the word *of* (the hands *of* the clock) or with an apostrophe and, in most cases, an *s* (the clock's hands). Personal pronouns do not use apostrophes to indicate the possessive case; instead, special forms are used to indicate the possessive.

(1) Singular Nouns and Indefinite Pronouns

To form the possessive case of singular nouns and indefinite pronouns, add *'s*.

"The Monk's Tale" is one of Chaucer's *Canterbury Tales*.

When we would arrive was anyone's guess.

(2) Singular Nouns Ending in *s*

To form the possessive case of singular nouns that end in *s*, add *'s* in most cases.

Reading Henry James's *The Ambassadors* was not Maris's idea of fun.

The class's time was changed to 8 a.m.

NOTE: Because pronouncing the possessive ending as a separate syllable can sound awkward, some people prefer to use just an apostrophe.

> For goodness' sake—are we really required to read both Aristophanes' *Lysistrata* and Thucydides' *History of the Peloponnesian War?*

An apostrophe is not used to form the possessive case of a title that already contains an *'s* ending; use a phrase instead.

> FAULTY: *A Midsummer Night's Dream's* staging
>
> REVISED: the staging of *A Midsummer Night's Dream*

(3) Plural Nouns Ending in *s*

To form the possessive case of regular plural nouns (those that end in *s* or *es*), add only an apostrophe.

> *The Readers' Guide to Periodical Literature* is available online.
>
> Two weeks' severance pay and three months' medical benefits were available to some workers.
>
> The Lopezes' three children are identical triplets.

(4) Irregular Plural Nouns

To form the possessive case of nouns that have irregular plurals, add *'s.*

> Long after they were gone, the geese's honking could still be heard.
>
> *The Children's Hour* is a play by Lillian Hellman; *The Women's Room* is a novel by Marilyn French.
>
> The two oxen's yokes were securely attached to the cart.

(5) Compound Nouns or Word Groups

To form the possessive case of compound nouns or of word groups, add *'s* to the last word.

> The editor-in-chief's position is open.
>
> He accepted the secretary of state's resignation under protest.
>
> This is someone else's responsibility.

(6) Two or More Items

To indicate individual ownership of two or more items, add *'s* to each item. To indicate joint ownership, add *'s* only to the last item.

INDIVIDUAL OWNERSHIP: Ernest Hemingway's and Gertrude Stein's writing styles have some similarities. (Hemingway and Stein have two separate writing styles.)

JOINT OWNERSHIP: Gilbert and Sullivan's operettas include *The Pirates of Penzance* and *The Mikado.* (Gilbert and Sullivan collaborated on both operettas.)

EXERCISE 1

Change the modifying phrases that follow the nouns to possessive forms that precede the nouns.

> **EXAMPLE:** the pen belonging to my aunt
>
> my aunt's pen

1. the songs recorded by Ray Charles
2. the red glare of the rockets
3. the idea Warren had
4. the housekeeper Rick and Leslie hired
5. the first choice of everyone
6. the dinner given by Harris
7. furniture designed by William Morris
8. the climate of the Virgin Islands
9. the sport the Russells play
10. the role created by the French actress

EXERCISE 2

Change each word or phrase in parentheses to its possessive form. In some cases you may have to use a phrase to indicate the possessive.

> **EXAMPLE:** The (children) toys were scattered all over their (parents) bedroom.
>
> The children's toys were scattered all over their parents' bedroom.

1. Jane (Addams) settlement house was called Hull House.
2. (*A Room of One's Own*) popularity increased with the rise of feminism.
3. The (chief petty officer) responsibilities are varied.
4. Vietnamese (restaurants) numbers have grown dramatically in ten (years) time.
5. (Charles Dickens) and (Mark Twain) works have sold millions of copies.

31b Avoiding Apostrophes with Plural Nouns and Personal Pronouns

Do not use apostrophes with plural nouns that are not possessive or to form the possessive case of personal pronouns.

FAULTY (APOSTROPHES WITH PLURAL NOUNS THAT ARE NOT POSSESSIVE):	REVISED:
The Thompson's are not at home.	The Thompsons are not at home.
The down vest's are very warm.	The down vests are very warm.
The Philadelphia Seventy Sixer's sometimes play well.	The Philadelphia Seventy Sixers sometimes play well.

FAULTY (APOSTROPHES WITH PERSONAL PRONOUNS):	REVISED:
This ticket must be your's or her's.	This ticket must be yours or hers.
The next turn is their's.	The next turn is theirs.
The doll had lost it's right eye.	The doll had lost its right eye.
The next great moment in history is our's.	The next great moment in history is ours.

See
31c1
Be especially careful not to confuse the possessive forms of personal pronouns with **contractions**.

EXERCISE 3

In the following sentences, correct any errors in the use of apostrophes to form noun plurals or the possessive case of personal pronouns. If a sentence is correct, mark it with a *C*.

    EXAMPLE: Dr. Sampson's lecture's were more interesting than her's.

                Dr. Sampson's lectures were more interesting than hers.

1. The Schaefer's seats are right next to our's.
2. Most of the college's in the area offer computer courses open to outsider's as well as to their own students.
3. The network completely revamped its daytime programming.
4. Is the responsibility for the hot dog concession Cynthia's or your's?
5. Romantic poets are his favorite's.

6. Debbie returned the books to the library, forgetting they were her's.
7. Cultural revolution's do not occur very often, but when they do they bring sweeping change's.
8. Roll-top desk's are eagerly sought by antique dealer's.
9. A flexible schedule is one of their priorities, but it isn't one of our's.
10. Is yours the red house or the brown one?

31c Indicating Omissions

Apostrophes are used to mark the omission of letters or numbers.

(1) Omitted Letters

Apostrophes replace omitted letters in **contractions.**

FREQUENTLY USED CONTRACTIONS

it's (it is)	let's (let us)
he's (he is)	we've (we have)
who's (who is)	they're (they are)
isn't (is not)	we'll (we will)
wouldn't (would not)	I'm (I am)
couldn't (could not)	we're (we are)
don't (do not)	you'd (you would)
won't (will not)	we'd (we would)

NOTE: Although common in speech and informal writing, contractions are not acceptable in college writing except to reproduce dialogue or to deliberately create an informal tone.

 CLOSE-UP USING APOSTROPHES

Be careful not to confuse contractions (which always include apostrophes) with the possessive forms of personal pronouns (which never include apostrophes).

continued on the following page

continued from the previous page

Contractions	Possessive Forms
Who's on first?	Whose book is this?
They're playing our song.	Their team is winning.
It's raining.	Its paws were muddy.
You're a real pal.	Your résumé is very impressive.

(2) Omitted Numbers

In informal writing an apostrophe may be used to represent the century in a year.

Crash of '29   class of '97   '57 Chevy

In college writing, however, write out the year in full: *the Crash of 1929, the class of 1997, a 1957 Chevrolet.*

EXERCISE 4

In the following sentences correct any errors in the use of standard contractions or personal pronouns. If a sentence is correct, mark it with a *C*.

EXAMPLE: Who's troops were sent to Korea?

Whose troops were sent to Korea?

1. Its never easy to choose a major; whatever you decide, your bound to have second thoughts.
2. Olive Oyl asked, "Whose that knocking at my door?"
3. Their watching too much television; in fact, they're eyes are glazed.
4. Whose coming along on the backpacking trip?
5. The horse had been badly treated; it's spirit was broken.
6. Your correct in assuming its a challenging course.
7. Sometimes even you're best friends won't tell you your boring.
8. They're training had not prepared them for the hardships they faced.
9. It's too early to make a positive diagnosis.
10. Robert Frost wrote the poem that begins, "Who's woods these are I think I know."

31d Forming Plurals

The apostrophe plus *s* is used to form plurals of letters and plurals of words referred to as words.

FORMING PLURALS WITH APOSTROPHES

Plurals of Letters
The Italian language has no *j*'s or *k*'s.

NOTE: Do not use apostrophes to form plurals of numbers (1970s, not 1970's) or plurals of abbreviations (URLs, not URL's; SATs, not SAT's).

Plurals of Words Referred to as Words
The supervisor would accept no *if* 's, *and* 's, or *but* 's.
His first sentence contained three *therefore* 's.

NOTE: Letters and words spoken of as themselves are usually underlined in manuscript but italicized in a printed work; the plural ending, however, is never underlined or italicized.

EXERCISE 5

In the following sentences, form correct plurals for the letters and words in parentheses. Underline to indicate italics where necessary.

> EXAMPLE: The word *bubbles* contains three (b).
> The word *bubbles* contains three *b*'s.

1. She closed her letter with a row of (x) and (o) to indicate kisses and hugs.
2. The three (R) are reading, writing, and 'rithmetic.
3. The report included far too many (maybe) and too few (definitely).
4. The word bookkeeper contains two (o), two (k), and three (e).
5. His letter included many (please) and (thank you).

CHAPTER 32

QUOTATION MARKS

USE QUOTATION MARKS . . .

- To set off direct quotations (**32a**)
- To set off titles (**32b**)
- To set off words used in a special sense (**32c**)
- To set off dialogue, prose passages, and poetry (**32d**)

32a Setting Off Direct Quotations

Use quotation marks with **direct quotations**—someone's exact written or spoken words. Enclose the borrowed material in a pair of quotation marks.

> Gloria Steinem observed, "We are becoming the men we once hoped to marry."

Do not use quotation marks with **indirect quotations**—when you report someone else's written or spoken words without quoting the words exactly.

> Gloria Steinem observed that many women were becoming the men they had once hoped to marry.

Punctuation problems can occur when quoted material must be set off from **identifying tags,** phrases (such as *he said*) that identify the material's source. The following guidelines cover the most common situations.

QUOTATIONS WITHIN QUOTATIONS

Use single quotation marks to enclose a **quotation within a quotation.**

> Claire noted, "It was Liberace who first said, 'I cried all the way to the bank.'"

Use double quotation marks to quote material within a <u>long passage of quoted prose</u>.

See 32d2

(1) An Identifying Tag in the Middle of a Passage

Use a pair of commas to set off the identifying tag that interrupts a passage.

> "In the future," pop artist Andy Warhol once said, "everyone will be world-famous for 15 minutes."

If the identifying tag follows a completed sentence but the quoted passage continues, use a period after the tag, and begin the new sentence with a capital letter.

> "Be careful," Erin warned. "Reptiles can be tricky."

(2) An Identifying Tag at the Beginning

Use a comma after an identifying tag that introduces quoted speech or writing.

> The Raven repeated, "Nevermore."

If no identifying tag introduces the quotation, no comma is necessary.

> The meteorologist said he expected March to be "unpredictable."

Use a colon instead of a comma before a quotation if it is introduced by a complete sentence.

> She gave her final answer: "No."

Also use a colon—not a comma—to introduce a long prose quotation (a quoted passage of more than four typed lines).

(3) An Identifying Tag at the End

Use a comma to separate a quotation from an identifying tag that follows it.

"Be careful out there," the sergeant warned.

If the quotation ends with a question mark or an exclamation point, use that punctuation mark instead of the comma. In this situation, the tag begins with a lowercase letter even though it follows end punctuation.

"Is Ankara the capital of Turkey?" she asked.

"Oh boy!" he cried.

NOTE: Commas and periods are always placed *inside* quotation marks. For information on placement of other punctuation marks with quotation marks, **see 32e**.

EXERCISE 1

Add single and double quotation marks to these sentences where necessary to set off direct quotations from identifying tags. If a sentence is correct, mark it with a *C*.

> EXAMPLE: Wordsworth's phrase splendour in the grass was used as the title of a movie about young lovers.
>
> Wordsworth's phrase "splendour in the grass" was used as the title of a movie about young lovers.

1. Mr. Fox noted, Few people can explain what Descartes's words I think, therefore I am actually mean.
2. Gertrude Stein said, You are all a lost generation.
3. Freedom of speech does not guarantee anyone the right to yell fire in a crowded theater, she explained.
4. Dorothy kept insisting that there was no place quite like home.
5. If everyone will sit down the teacher announced the exam will begin.

32b Setting Off Titles

See 35a

Titles of short works and titles of parts of long works are enclosed in quotation marks (other titles are set in **italics**).

NOTE: Titles of your own papers should not be enclosed in quotation marks or italicized.

TITLES REQUIRING QUOTATION MARKS

Articles in Magazines, Newspapers, and Professional Journals
"Why Johnny Can't Write"

Essays
"Fenimore Cooper's Literary Offenses"

Short Stories
"Flying Home"

Short Poems (Those not Divided into Numbered Sections)
"The New Colossus"

Songs
"The Star-Spangled Banner"

Chapters or Sections of Books
"Miss Sharp Begins to Make Friends" (Chapter 10 of *Vanity Fair*)

Speeches
"How to Tell a Story"

Episodes of Radio or Television Series
"Lucy Goes to the Hospital" (*I Love Lucy*)

TITLES WITHIN QUOTATIONS

When a title that is normally enclosed in quotation marks appears within a quotation, set the title off in *single* quotation marks.

I think what she said was, "Play it, Sam. Play 'As Time Goes By.'"

If you use such a title in the title of one of your own papers, enclose it in double quotation marks: Imagery in Emily Dickinson's "Wild Nights—Wild Nights."

EXERCISE 2

Add quotation marks to the following sentences where necessary to set off titles. If italics are incorrectly used, substitute quotation marks.

> EXAMPLE: Canadian author Margaret Atwood has written stories, such as *Rape Fantasies;* poems, such as You Fit Into Me; and novels, such as *Alias Grace.*
>
> Canadian author Margaret Atwood has written stories, such as "Rape Fantasies"; poems, such as "You Fit Into Me"; and novels, such as *Alias Grace.*

1. One of the essays from her new book *Good Bones and Simple Murder* was originally published in *Harper's* magazine.
2. Her latest collection of poems *Morning in the Burned House* contains the moving poem *In the Secular Night.*
3. You may have seen the movie *The Handmaid's Tale,* starring Robert Duvall, based on her best-selling novel.
4. *Surfacing* was the first book of hers I read, but my favorite work of hers is the short story Hair Ball.
5. I wasn't surprised to find her poems The Animals in the Country and This Is a Photograph of Me in our English textbook last year.

32c Setting Off Words Used in Special Ways

A word used in a special or unusual way, or purposely misused for effect, is enclosed in quotation marks.

> It was clear that adults approved of children who were "readers," but it was not at all clear why this was so. (Annie Dillard, *New York Times Magazine*)
>
> It is often remarked that words are tricky—and that we were all prone to be deceived by "fast talkers," such as high-pressure salesmen, skillful propagandists, politicians or lawyers. (S. I. Hayakawa, "How Words Change Our Lives")

NOTE: If you use the expression *so-called* before an unusual usage, do not use quotation marks as well.

A **coinage**—an invented word—also takes quotation marks.

> After the twins were born, the station wagon became a "baby-mobile."

When a word is referred to as a word, however, it is italicized.

How do you pronounce *trough?*

Compose and *comprise* should not be used interchangeably.

 USING QUOTATION MARKS WITH DEFINITIONS

When you quote a dictionary definition, put the word you are defining in italics and the definition in quotation marks.

To *infer* means "to draw a conclusion"; to *imply* means "to suggest."

EXERCISE 3

Add quotation marks to the following sentences where necessary to set off words used in special ways. If italics are incorrectly used, delete them or substitute quotation marks.

> EXAMPLE: After the *power suits* of the 1980s, American businesses have seemingly loosened their *dress codes.*
>
> After the "power suits" of the 1980s, American businesses have seemingly loosened their dress codes.

1. In many places in the 1990s corporate America has decreed, "Wear what you like"—on Fridays, anyway.
2. This policy of *dressing down* was started in order to give workers an additional benefit—not having to buy business clothes for Fridays—and to allow people to express themselves.
3. In reality, workers have found that *casual day* really means they need a third wardrobe.
4. Although *casual* means informal or relaxed, there is nothing relaxed about dressing for casual day.
5. Their *play* clothes are too casual; their *work* clothes are too stuffy.
6. Not surprisingly, clothing retailers have stepped in to solve this *dilemma* by developing clothing lines that are casual yet professional, and now workers find themselves having to buy a third wardrobe for so-called casual days.

32d Setting Off Dialogue, Prose Passages, and Poetry

(1) Dialogue

When you record dialogue, begin a new paragraph each time you introduce a new speaker. Be sure to enclose the quoted words in quotation marks.

"Sharp on time as usual," Davis said with his habitual guilty grin.

"My watch is always a little fast," Castle said, apologizing for the criticism which he had not expressed. "An anxiety complex, I suppose." (Graham Greene, *The Human Factor*)

Notice that the identifying tags (*Davis said, Castle said*) appear in the same paragraph as the speaker's words.

 USING QUOTATION MARKS

When you are quoting several paragraphs of dialogue by one speaker, begin each new paragraph with quotation marks. However, use closing quotation marks only at the end of the *entire quoted passage*, not at the end of each paragraph.

EXERCISE 4

Add appropriate quotation marks to the dialogue in this passage, beginning a new paragraph whenever a new speaker is introduced.

First Corinthians pulled her fingers through her hair. It was long, lightweight hair, the color of wet sand. Are you going anyplace special, or are we just driving around? She kept her eyes on the street, watching the men and women walking by. Careful, Macon. You always take the wrong turn here. Ruth spoke softly from the right side of the car. Do you want to drive? Macon asked her. You know I don't drive, she answered. Then let me do it. All right but don't blame me if . . . Macon pulled smoothly into the left fork of the road that led through downtown and into a residential area. Daddy? Are we going any special place? Honoré, Macon said. . . . Lena pushed her stocking further down her legs. On the lake? What's out there? There's nothing out there, nobody. There's a beach community out there, Lena. Your father wants to look at it. Ruth reasserted herself into the conversation. What for? Those are white people's houses, said Lena. All of it's not white people's houses. Some of it's nothing. Just land. Way over on the other side. It could be a nice summer place for colored people. Beach houses. You understand what I mean? Macon glanced at his daughter through the rear view mirror. Who's going to live in them? There's no colored people who can afford to have two houses, Lena said. Reverend Coles can, and Dr. Singleton, Corinthians corrected her. (Toni Morrison, *Song of Solomon*)

(2) Long Prose Passages

When you quote a prose passage of no more than four typed lines, run it into the text and set it off in quotation marks.

Galsworthy describes Aunt Juley as "prostrated by the blow" (329).

However, do not enclose a prose passage of more than four typed lines in quotation marks. Instead, set it off by indenting it ten spaces (or one inch) from the left-hand margin. Double-space above and below the quotation, and double-space between lines within it. Introduce the passage with a colon. (For special emphasis, shorter passages may also be set off in this way.)

The following portrait of Aunt Juley illustrates several of the devices Galsworthy uses throughout The Forsyte Saga, such as a journalistic detachment that is almost cruel in its scrutiny, a subtle sense of the grotesque, and an ironic stance:

> Aunt Juley stayed in her room, prostrated by the blow. Her face, discoloured by tears, was divided into compartments by the little ridges of pouting flesh which had swollen with emotion. . . . At fixed intervals she went to her drawer, and took from beneath the lavender bags a fresh pocket-handkerchief. Her warm heart could not bear the thought that Ann was lying there so cold. (329)

Similar characterizations appear throughout the book. . . .

CLOSE UP   QUOTING LONG PROSE PASSAGES

When a prose passage longer than four lines is a single paragraph or less, do not indent the first line. When quoting two or more paragraphs, indent the first line of each paragraph, including the first, three additional spaces (or one-quarter inch). If the first sentence does not begin a paragraph, do not indent it. Indent only the second and subsequent paragraphs.

If the passage you are quoting already includes material quoted by the author, enclose those words in double quotation marks.

(3) Poetry

One line of poetry is treated like a short prose passage: enclosed in quotation marks and run into the text.

> One of John Donne's best-known poems begins with the line, "Go and catch a falling star."

Two or three lines of poetry are run into the text and separated by **slashes** (/).

See 33e2

> Alexander Pope writes, "True Ease in Writing comes from Art, not Chance, / As those move easiest who have learned to dance."

See 32d2

More than three lines of poetry should be set off like a **long prose passage**. (For special emphasis, fewer lines may also be set off in this manner.) Punctuation, spelling, capitalization, and indentation are reproduced *exactly*.

> Wilfred Owen, a poet who was killed in action in World War I,
>
> expressed the horrors of war with vivid imagery:
>
> > Bent double, like old beggars under sacks.
> >
> > Knock-kneed, coughing like hags, we cursed through sludge.
> >
> > Till on the haunting flares we turned our backs
> >
> > And towards our distant rest began to trudge. (1–4)

32e Using Quotation Marks with Other Punctuation

Quotation marks frequently occur along with other punctuation marks. At the end of a quotation, other punctuation is sometimes placed inside quotation marks and sometimes placed outside them.

(1) With Final Commas or Periods

Commas and periods are always placed *inside* quotation marks.

Many, like Frost, think about "the road not taken ," but not many have taken "the one less traveled by ."

(2) With Final Semicolons or Colons

Semicolons and colons are always placed *outside* quotation marks.

Students who do not pass the functional-literacy test receive "certificates of completion "; those who pass are awarded diplomas.

Taxpayers were pleased with the first of the candidate's promised "sweeping new reforms ": a balanced budget.

(3) With Question Marks, Exclamation Points, and Dashes

A question mark, exclamation point, or dash that occurs at the end of a quotation may be placed inside or outside the quotation marks, depending on whether or not the punctuation mark is part of the quotation.

If a question mark, exclamation point, or dash is part of the quotation, place the quotation marks *after* the punctuation.

"Who's there ?" she demanded.

"Stop !" he cried.

"Should we leave now, or —" Vicki paused, unable to continue.

If a question mark, exclamation point, or dash is *not* part of the quotation, place the quotation marks *before* the punctuation.

Did you finish reading "The Black Cat "?

Whatever you do, don't yell "Uncle "!

The first essay—George Orwell's "Politics and the English Language "—made quite an impression on the class.

If both the quotation and the sentence are questions or exclamations, place the quotation marks *before* the punctuation.

Who asked, "Is Paris burning"?

32f Editing Misused or Overused Quotation Marks

Quotation marks should not be used in the following situations.

(1) To Convey Emphasis

FAULTY: William Randolph Hearst's "fabulous" home is a castle called San Simeon.

REVISED: William Randolph Hearst's fabulous home is a castle called San Simeon.

(2) To Set Off Nicknames or Slang

FAULTY: The former "Lady Di" became the Princess of Wales when she married Prince Charles.

REVISED: The former Lady Diana Spencer became the Princess of Wales when she married Prince Charles.

FAULTY: Dawn is "into" running.

REVISED: Dawn is very involved in running.

 USING QUOTATION MARKS

Quotation marks do not make nonstandard or slang terms acceptable in college writing. Avoid substituting nicknames for full names or slang for standard diction.

(3) To Enclose Titles of Long Works

FAULTY: "War and Peace" is even longer than "Paradise Lost."

REVISED: *War and Peace* is even longer than *Paradise Lost.*

See
35a

NOTE: Titles of long works are italicized.

(4) To Set Off Terms Being Defined

FAULTY: The word "tintinnabulation," meaning the ringing sound of bells, was used by Poe in his poem "The Bells."

REVISED: The word *tintinnabulation,* meaning the ringing sound of bells, was used by Poe in his poem "The Bells."

NOTE: Words that are being **defined** are italicized.

See
35c

(5) To Set Off Technical Terms

FAULTY: "Biofeedback" is sometimes used to treat migraine headaches.

REVISED: Biofeedback is sometimes used to treat migraine headaches.

(6) To Set Off Indirect Quotations

FAULTY: Freud wondered "what a woman wanted."

REVISED: Freud wondered what a woman wanted.

REVISED: Freud wondered, "What does a woman want?"

EXERCISE 5

In the following paragraph, correct the use of single and double quotation marks to set off direct quotations, titles, and words used in special ways. Supply the appropriate quotation marks where required and delete those not required, substituting italics where necessary.

In her essay 'The Obligation to Endure' from the book "Silent Spring," Rachel Carson writes: As Albert Schweitzer has said, 'Man can hardly even recognize the devils of his own creation.' Carson goes on to point out that many chemicals have been used to kill insects and other organisms which, she writes, are "described in the modern vernacular as pests." Carson believes such "advanced" chemicals, by contaminating our environment, do more harm than good. In addition to "Silent Spring," Carson is also the author of the book "The Sea Around Us." This work, divided into three sections (Mother Sea, The Restless Sea, and Man and the Sea About Him) was published in 1951.

EXERCISE 6

Correct the use of quotation marks in the following sentences, making sure that the use and placement of any accompanying punctuation marks are consistent with accepted conventions. If a sentence is correct, mark it with a C.

EXAMPLE: The "Watergate" incident brought many new expressions
into the English language.

The Watergate incident brought many new expressions
into the English language.

1. Kilroy was here and Women and children first are two expressions
   Bartlett's Familiar Quotations attributes to "Anon."
2. Neil Armstrong said he was making a small step for man but a giant
   leap for mankind.
3. "The answer, my friend", Bob Dylan sang, "is blowin' in the wind".
4. The novel was a real "thriller," complete with spies and counterspies,
   mysterious women, and exotic international chases.
5. The sign said, Road liable to subsidence; it meant that we should
   look out for potholes.
6. One of William Blake's best-known lines—To see a world in a grain
   of sand—opens his poem Auguries of Innocence.
7. In James Thurber's short story The Catbird Seat, Mrs. Barrows an-
   noys Mr. Martin by asking him silly questions like Are you tearing
   up the pea patch? Are you scraping around the bottom of the pickle
   barrel? and Are you lifting the oxcart out of the ditch?
8. I'll make him an offer he can't refuse, promised "the godfather" in
   Mario Puzo's novel.
9. What did Timothy Leary mean by "Turn on, tune in, drop out?"
10. George, the protagonist of Bernard Malamud's short story, A Sum-
    mer's Reading, is something of an "underachiever."

CHAPTER 33

OTHER PUNCTUATION MARKS

USING OTHER PUNCTUATION MARKS

Use a Colon ...
- To introduce lists or series (**33a1**)
- To introduce explanatory material (**33a2**)
- To introduce quotations (**33a3**)
- In other conventional situations (**33a4**)

Use Dashes ...
- To set off nonessential material (**33b1**)
- To introduce a summary (**33b2**)
- To indicate an interruption (**33b3**)

Use Parentheses ...
- To set off nonessential material (**33c1**)
- In other conventional situations (**33c2**)

Use Brackets ...
- To set off comments within quotations (**33d1**)
- In place of parentheses within parentheses (**33d2**)

Use a Slash ...
- To separate one option from another (**33e1**)
- To separate lines of poetry run into the text (**33e2**)
- To separate the numerator from the denominator in fractions (**33e3**)

Use Ellipses ...
- To indicate an omission in a quotation (**33f1**)
- To indicate an omission in quoted poetry (**33f2**)
- To indicate unfinished statements (**33f1**)

33a Using Colons

The **colon** is a strong punctuation mark that points ahead to the rest of the sentence, linking the words that follow it to the words that precede it.

Use colons in the following situations.

(1) To Introduce Lists or Series

Colons set off lists or series, including those introduced by phrases like *the following* or *as follows.*

> He looked like whatever his beholder imagined him to be: a bank clerk, a high school teacher, a public employee, a librarian, a fussy custodian, an office manager. (Norman Katkov, *Blood and Orchids*)

> Like croup and whooping cough, it was treated with remedies Ida Rebecca compounded from ancient folk-medicine recipes: reeking mustard plasters, herbal broths, dosings of onion syrup mixed with sugar. (Russell Baker, *Growing Up*)

CLOSE-UP   USING COLONS TO INTRODUCE LISTS OR SERIES

When it introduces a list or series, a colon must be preceded by a complete sentence.

FAULTY: Each camper should be equipped with: a sleeping bag, a mess kit, a flashlight, and plenty of insect repellent. (*Each camper should be equipped with* is not a complete sentence.)

REVISED: Each camper should bring the following: a sleeping bag, a mess kit, a flashlight, and plenty of insect repellent.

(2) To Introduce Explanatory Material

Colons often introduce material that explains, details, exemplifies, clarifies, or summarizes. Frequently this material is presented in the form of an **appositive**, a construction that identifies or renames a noun, pronoun, or noun phrase that precedes it.

See
10c6

Diego Rivera painted a controversial mural: the one commissioned for Rockefeller Center in the 1930s.

Her hair was the longest and strangest Mrs. Miller had ever seen: absolutely silver-white, like an albino's. (Truman Capote, "Miriam")

Sometimes a colon separates two independent clauses: one general clause and a subsequent, more specific one that illustrates or clarifies the first.

A *US News & World Report* survey has revealed a surprising fact: Americans spend more time at shopping malls than anywhere else except at home and at work.

 USING COLONS

In most cases, when a complete sentence follows a colon, that sentence begins with a lowercase letter (unless the first word is a proper noun). However, if the sentence introduced by a colon is a quotation, its first word is always capitalized, unless it was not capitalized in the source.

(3) To Introduce Quotations

A colon is used to set off a quotation introduced by a complete sentence.

The French Declaration of the Rights of Man includes these words: "Liberty consists in being able to do anything that does not harm another person."

Bartleby repeated the words once again: "I prefer not to."

A **long prose quotation** is always introduced by a colon.

See
32d2

(4) In Other Conventional Situations

CONVENTIONAL USES OF COLONS

To Separate Titles from Subtitles
Family Installments: Memories of Growing Up Hispanic

continued on the following page

continued from the previous page
To Separate Minutes from Hours in Numerical Expressions of Time
    6:15 a.m.   3:30 p.m.

To Separate Place of Publication from Name of Publisher in a Works Cited list
    Fort Worth: Harcourt, 1998.

See
43a2

After Salutations in Business Letters
    Dear Dr. Evans:

See
52a

(5) Editing Misused or Overused Colons

Do not use colons in these situations.

After Such As, For Example, and Similar Expressions   Colons are not used after expressions like *such as, namely, for example,* or *that is.* Remember that a colon introduces a list or series only after a complete sentence.

FAULTY: The Eye Institute treats patients with a wide variety of conditions, such as: myopia, glaucoma, and cataracts.

REVISED: The Eye Institute treats patients with a wide variety of conditions, such as myopia, glaucoma, and cataracts.

In Verb and Prepositional Constructions   Colons should not be placed between verbs and their objects or complements or between prepositions and their objects.

FAULTY: James A. Michener wrote: *Hawaii, Centennial, Space,* and *Poland.*

REVISED: James A. Michener wrote *Hawaii, Centennial, Space,* and *Poland.*

FAULTY: Hitler's armies marched through: the Netherlands, Belgium, and France.

REVISED: Hitler's armies marched through the Netherlands, Belgium, and France.

EXERCISE 1

Add colons where required in the following sentences. If necessary, delete excess colons.

EXAMPLE: There was one thing he really hated getting up at 700 every morning.

There was one thing he really hated: getting up at 7:00 every morning.

1. Books about the late John F. Kennedy include the following A Hero for Our Time; Johnny, We Hardly Knew Ye; One Brief Shining Moment; and JFK: Reckless Youth.
2. Only one task remained to tell his boss he was quitting.
3. The story closed with a familiar phrase "And they all lived happily ever after."
4. The sergeant requested: reinforcements, medical supplies, and more ammunition.
5. She kept only four souvenirs a photograph, a matchbook, a theater program, and a daisy pressed between the pages of William Shakespeare The Complete Works.

33b Using Dashes

Commas are the mark of punctuation most often used to set off **nonessential material**, but dashes and parentheses also serve this function. While parentheses deemphasize the enclosed words, **dashes** call attention to the material they set off.

See 29d

Use dashes in the following situations.

(1) To Set Off Nonessential Material

Explanations, qualifications, examples, definitions, and appositives that interrupt a sentence may be set off by dashes for emphasis or clarity. Use a pair of dashes to set off material within a sentence.

Although we are by all odds the most social of all social animals— more interdependent, more attached to each other, more inseparable in our behavior than bees—we do not often feel our conjoined intelligence. (Lewis Thomas, *Lives of a Cell*)

Use a single dash to set off material at the end of a sentence.

Most of the best-sellers are cookbooks and diet books—how not to eat it after you've cooked it. (Andy Rooney, *New Yorker*)

(2) To Introduce a Summary

Use a dash to introduce a statement that summarizes a list or series before it.

> Walking to school alone, spending the night at a friend's house, getting my ears pierced, and starting to wear makeup—these were some of the milestones of my childhood and adolescence.

> "Study hard," "Respect your elders," "Don't talk with your mouth full"—Sharon had often heard her parents say these things.

(3) To Indicate an Interruption

A dash is sometimes used in dialogue to mark a sudden interruption—for example, a correction, a hesitation, or a sudden shift in tone.

> Groucho told the steward, "I'll have three hard-boiled eggs—make that four hard-boiled eggs."

> "I think—no, I know—this is the worst day of my life," Julie sighed.

(4) Editing Misused or Overused Dashes

Too many dashes can make a passage seem choppy and out of control. For this reason, dashes should not be overused (they should not, for example, be used in place of periods or commas). In general, use only one dash (or one pair of dashes) per sentence.

FAULTY (OVERUSE OF DASHES): Registration was a nightmare—most of the courses I wanted to take—geology and conversational Spanish, for instance—met at inconvenient times—or were closed by the time I tried to sign up for them—it was really depressing—even for registration.

REVISED (MODERATE USE OF DASHES): Registration was a nightmare. Most of the courses I wanted to take—geology and conversational Spanish, for instance—met at inconvenient times or were closed by the time I tried to sign up for them. It was really depressing—even for registration.

 CLOSE-UP **USING DASHES**

When typing, indicate a dash with two unspaced hyphens (some word-processing programs have a dash function that you can use instead of two unspaced hyphens); when writing, form a dash with an unbroken line about as long as two hyphens.

EXERCISE 2

Add dashes where needed in the following sentences. If a sentence is correct, mark it with a *C*.

> EXAMPLE: World War I called "the war to end all wars" was, unfortunately, no such thing.
>
> World War I—called "the war to end all wars"—was, unfortunately, no such thing.

1. Tulips, daffodils, hyacinths, lilies all of these flowers grow from bulbs.
2. St. Kitts and Nevis two tiny island nations are now independent after 360 years of British rule.
3. "But it's not" She paused and reconsidered her next words.
4. He considered several different majors history, English, political science, and business before deciding on journalism.
5. The two words added to the Pledge of Allegiance in the 1950s "under God" remain part of the Pledge today.

33c Using Parentheses

Like commas and dashes, **parentheses** may be used to set off interruptions within a sentence. Parentheses, however, indicate that the enclosed material is less important than the rest of the sentence.

Use parentheses in the following situations.

(1) To Set Off Nonessential Material

Parentheses may be used to set off nonessential material that expands, clarifies, defines, illustrates, or supplements an idea.

> A compound may be used in any grammatical function: as noun (*wishbone*), adjective (*foolproof*), adverb (*overhead*), verb (*gainsay*), or preposition (*without*). (Thomas Pyles, *The Origin and Development of the English Language*)

> It took Gilbert Fairchild two years at Harvard College (two academic years, from September, 1955, to June, 1957) to learn everything he needed to know. (Judith Martin, *Gilbert: A Comedy of Manners*)

When a complete sentence set off by parentheses falls within another sentence, it should not begin with a capital letter or end with a period.

Born in 1893, four years before Queen Victoria's Diamond Jubilee, at Cathedral Choir School, Oxford, where her father was headmaster, Sayers became a first-rate medievalist (she translated Dante) and a theologian (her miracle play, *The Man Born to Be King*, outsold her mystery novels in her lifetime); she died in 1957. (Barbara Grizzuti Harrison, *Off Center*)

If the parenthetical sentence does not fall within another sentence, it must begin with a capital letter and end with a period, question mark, or exclamation point placed inside the closing parenthesis.

A few days later he called and asked me to come in and bring anything else I had written. (The only thing I had was a notebook full of isolated sentences like "She walked across the room wearing her wedding ring like a shield.") (Jeremy Bernstein, *New York Times Book Review*)

USING PARENTHESES WITH OTHER PUNCTUATION

When parentheses fall within a sentence, punctuation never precedes the opening parenthesis. Punctuation may follow the closing parenthesis, however.

INCORRECT: George Orwell's *1984*, (1949), which focuses on the dangers of a totalitarian society, is required reading.

REVISED: George Orwell's *1984* (1949), which focuses on the dangers of a totalitarian society, is required reading.

(2) Where Convention Requires Their Use

Parentheses are used to set off letters and numbers that identify points on a list and around dates, cross-references, and documentation.

All reports must include the following components: (1) an opening summary; (2) a background statement; and (3) a list of conclusions and recommendations.

Russia defeated Sweden in the Great Northern War (1700–1721).

Other historians also make this point (see p. 54).

One critic has called the novel "puerile" (Arvin 72).

EXERCISE 3

Add parentheses where necessary in the following sentences. If a sentence is correct, mark it with a *C*.

> EXAMPLE: The greatest battle of the War of 1812 the Battle of New Orleans was fought after the war was declared over.
>
> The greatest battle of the War of 1812 (the Battle of New Orleans) was fought after the war was declared over.

1. During the Great War 1914–1918, Britain censored letters written from the front lines.
2. Those who lived in towns on the southern coast like Dover could often hear the mortar shells across the channel in France.
3. Wilfred Owen wrote his most famous poem "Dulce et Decorum Est" in the trenches in France.
4. The British uniforms with bright red tabs right at the neck were responsible for many British deaths.
5. It was difficult for the War Poets as they are now called to return to writing about subjects other than the horrors of war.

33d Using Brackets

Brackets are used in two situations.

(1) To Set Off Comments Within Quotations

Brackets are used within quotations to tell readers that the enclosed words are yours and not those of your source. You can bracket an explanation, a clarification, a correction, or an opinion.

> "Dues are being raised $1 per week [to $5]," the treasurer announced.
>
> "The use of caricature by Dickens is reminiscent of the satiric sketches done by [Joseph] Addison and [Richard] Steele [in *The Spectator*]."
>
> "Even as a student at Princeton he [F. Scott Fitzgerald] felt like an outsider."
>
> "The miles of excellent trails are perfect for [cross-country] skiing."

If a quotation contains an error, indicate that the error is not yours by following the error with the italicized Latin word *sic* ("thus") in brackets.

> "The octopuss [*sic*] is a cephalopod mollusk with eight arms."

519

USING BRACKETS TO EDIT QUOTATIONS

See
41b1

When you quote a source in a paper, use brackets to enclose changes you make to tailor the **quotation** so that it fits stylistically and logically into your sentence.

(2) In Place of Parentheses Within Parentheses

When one set of parentheses falls within another, use brackets in place of the inner set.

> In her study of American education between 1945 and 1960 (*The Trouble Crusade* [New York: Basic, 1963]), Diane Ravitch addresses issues like progressive education, race, educational reforms, and campus unrest.

33e Using Slashes

The **slash** is used in three situations.

(1) To Separate One Option from Another

> The either/or fallacy assumes that a given question has only two possible answers.

> Will pass/fail courses be accepted for transfer credit?

> The producer/director attracted more attention at the film festival than the actors.

NOTE: When you use a slash to separate one option from another, do not leave a space before or after the slash.

(2) To Separate Lines of Poetry Run into the Text

> The poet James Schevill writes, "I study my defects / And learn how to perfect them."

See
32d3

NOTE: When you use a slash to separate lines of **poetry**, leave a space both before and after the slash.

(3) To Separate the Numerator from the Denominator in Fractions

7/8

1 4/5

33f Using Ellipses

Use ellipses in the following situations.

(1) To Indicate an Omission in Quoted Prose

Use an **ellipsis**—three *spaced* periods—to indicate words or entire sentences omitted from a quotation. When deleting material, be careful not to change the meaning of the original passage.

ORIGINAL: "When I was a young man, being anxious to distinguish myself, I was perpetually starting new propositions. But I soon gave this over; for I found that generally what was new was false." (Samuel Johnson)

WITH OMISSIONS: "When I was a young man, ... I was perpetually starting new propositions. But I soon ... found that generally what was new was false." (Three spaced periods indicate omissions.)

NOTE: When you delete words immediately after an internal punctuation mark, such as a comma, you retain the punctuation mark before the ellipsis.

 USING ELLIPSES

Never begin a quoted passage with an ellipsis.

FAULTY: Barzun notes that Dickens "... might just as well have been the common schoolboy. ..."

REVISED: Barzun notes that Dickens "might just as well have been the common schoolboy. ..."

Do not end a quotation with an ellipsis unless you have deleted words at the end of the quoted sentence.

Deleting Words at the Beginning of a Sentence   When you delete words at the beginning of a sentence that falls within a quoted passage, retain the previous sentence's end punctuation, followed by an ellipsis.

> In the final paragraph, Jaynes poses—and answers—her central question: "What is power? . . . the option not only of saying *no* but also of saying *yes.*"

Deleting Words at the End of a Sentence   When you delete words at the end of a sentence that ends a quoted passage, retain the sentence's end punctuation, followed by an ellipsis.

> According to humorist Dave Barry, "From outer space Europe appears to be shaped like a large ketchup stain. . . ."

> The play ends with George sadly crooning, "Who's afraid of Virginia Woolf, Virginia Woolf, Virginia Woolf? . . ."

NOTE: An ellipsis can also indicate an interrupted statement.

> "If only. . . ." He sighed and turned away.

This use is generally not appropriate in college writing unless you are reproducing dialogue.

Deleting One or More Complete Sentences   If you omit one or more complete sentences from a quoted passage, retain the previous sentence's end punctuation, followed by an ellipsis.

> According to Donald Hall, "Everywhere one meets the idea that reading is an activity desirable in itself. . . . People surround the idea of reading with piety and do not take into account the purpose of reading. . . ."

NOTE: A period plus an ellipsis at the end of a sentence can indicate not just an omitted sentence or two but also a whole paragraph or more.

 USING ELLIPSES

If a quotation ending with an ellipsis is followed by parenthetical documentation, the end punctuation follows the documentation.

> As Jarman argues, "There was no willingness to compromise . . ." (161).

(2) To Indicate an Omission in Quoted Poetry

When you omit one or more lines of poetry (or a paragraph or more of prose), use a complete line of spaced periods.

ORIGINAL: Stitch! Stitch! Stitch!
> In poverty, hunger, and dirt,
> And still with a voice of dolorous pitch,
> Would that its tone could reach the Rich,
> She sang this "Song of the Shirt!"
>   —Thomas Hood

WITH OMISSION: Stitch! Stitch! Stitch!
> In poverty, hunger, and dirt,
>
> . . . .
> She sang this "Song of the Shirt!"

EXERCISE 4

Read the following paragraph and follow the instructions below it, taking care in each case not to delete essential information.

> The most important thing about research is to know when to stop. How does one recognize the moment? When I was eighteen or thereabouts, my mother told me that when out with a young man I should always leave a half-hour before I wanted to. Although I was not sure how this might be accomplished, I recognized the advice as sound, and exactly the same rule applies to research. One must stop *before* one has finished; otherwise, one will never stop and never finish. (Barbara Tuchman, *Practicing History*)

1. Delete a phrase from the middle of one sentence and mark the omission with ellipses.
2. Delete words at the beginning of any sentence and mark the omission with ellipses.
3. Delete words at the end of any sentence and mark the omission with ellipses.
4. Delete one complete sentence from the middle of the passage and mark the omission with ellipses.

EXERCISE 5

Add appropriate punctuation—colons, dashes, parentheses, brackets, or slashes—to the following sentences. If a sentence is correct, mark it with a *C*.

EXAMPLE: There was one thing she was sure of if she did well at the interview, the job would be hers.

There was one thing she was sure of: if she did well at the interview, the job would be hers.

1. Mark Twain Samuel L. Clemens made the following statement "I can live for two months on a good compliment."
2. Liza Minnelli, the actress singer who starred in several films, is the daughter of Judy Garland.
3. Saudi Arabia, Oman, Yemen, Qatar, and the United Arab Emirates all these are located on the Arabian Peninsula.
4. John Adams 1735–1826 was the second president of the United States; John Quincy Adams 1767–1848 was the sixth.
5. The sign said "No tresspassing *sic.*"
6. *Checkmate* a term derived from the Persian phrase meaning "the king is dead" announces victory in chess.
7. The following people were present at the meeting the president of the board of trustees, three trustees, and twenty reporters.
8. Before the introduction of the potato in Europe, the parsnip was a major source of carbohydrates in fact, it was a dietary staple.
9. In this well-researched book (*Crime Movies* New York Norton, 1980), Carlos Clarens studies the gangster genre in film.
10. I remember reading though I can't remember where that Upton Sinclair sold plots to Jack London.

STUDENT WRITER AT WORK

Punctuation

Review Chapters 28–33; then, read this student essay. Commas, semicolons, quotation marks, apostrophes, parentheses, and dashes have been intentionally deleted; only the end punctuation has been retained. When you have read the essay carefully, add all appropriate punctuation marks.

The dry pine needles crunched like eggshells under our thick boots.

Wont the noise scare them away Dad?

He smiled knowingly and said No deer rely mostly on smell and sight.

I thought That must be why were wearing fluorescent orange jumpsuits but I didn't feel like arguing the point.

continued on the following page

continued from the previous page

It was a perfect day for my first hunting experience. The biting winds were caught by the thick bushy arms of the tall pines and I could feel a numbing redness in my face. Now I realized why Dad always grew that ugly gray beard that made him look ten years older. A few sunbeams managed to carve their way through the layers of branches and leaves creating pools of white light on the dark earth.

How far have we come? I asked.

Oh only a couple of miles. We should be meeting Joe up ahead.

Joe was one of Dads hunting buddies. He always managed to go off on his own for a few hours and come back with at least a four-pointer. Dad was envious of Joe and liked to tell people what he called the real story.

You know Joe paid a fortune for that buck at the checking station hed tell his friends. Dad was sure that this would be his lucky year.

We trudged up a densely wooded hill for what seemed like hours. The sharp-needled branches whipped my bare face as I followed close behind my father occasionally I wiped my cheeks to discover a new cut in my frozen flesh.

All this for a deer I thought.

The still pine air was suddenly shattered by four rapid gunshots echoing across the vast green valley below us.

Joes got another one. Come on! Dad yelled. It seemed as if I were following a young kid as I watched my father take leaping strides down the path we had just ascended. I had never seen him so enthusiastic before. I plodded breathlessly along trying to keep up with my father.

Suddenly out of the corner of my eye I caught sight of an object that didnt fit in with the monotony of trunks and branches and leaves and needles. I froze and observed the largest most majestic buck I had ever seen. It too stood motionless apparently grazing on some leaves or berries.

continued on the following page

continued from the previous page

Its coloring was beautiful with alternating patches of tan brown and snow-white fur. The massive antlers towered proudly above its head as it looked up and took notice of me. What struck me most were the tearful brown eyes almost feminine in their gaze.

Once again the silence was smashed this time by my fathers thundering call and I watched as the huge deer scampered gracefully off through the trees. I turned and scurried down the path after my father. I decided not to mention a word of my encounter to him. I hoped the deer was far away by now.

Finally I reached the clearing from where the shots had rung out. There stood Dad and Joe smiling over a fallen six-point buck. The purple-red blood dripped from the wounds to form a puddle in the dirt. The bucks sad brown eyes gleamed in the sun but no longer smiled and blinked.

Where have you been? asked Dad. Before I could answer he continued Do you believe this guy? Every year he bags the biggest deer in the whole state!

While they laughed and talked I sat on a tree stump to rest my aching legs. Maybe now we can go home I thought.

But before long I heard Dad say Come on Bob I know theres one out there for us.

We headed right back up that same path and sure enough that same big beautiful buck was grazing in that same spot on the same berry bush. The only difference was that this time Dad saw him.

This is our lucky day he whispered.

I froze as Dad lifted the barrel of his rifle and took careful aim at the silently grazing deer. I closed my eyes as he squeezed the trigger but instead of the deadly gun blast I heard only a harmless click. His rifle had jammed.

continued on the following page

continued from the previous page
Use your rifle quick he whispered.

As I took aim through my scope the deer looked up at me. Its soulful brown eyes were magnified in my sight like two glassy bulls-eyes. My finger froze on the trigger.

Shoot him! Shoot him!

But instead I aimed for the clouds and fired. The deer vanished along with my fathers dreams. Dad never understood why this was the proudest moment of my life.

CHAPTER 34

CAPITALIZATION

 Capitalize the First Word of a Sentence or of a Line of Poetry

Capitalize the first word of a sentence, including a sentence of quoted speech or writing.

> The square of the hypotenuse is equal to the sum of the squares of the other two sides.

> As Shakespeare wrote, "Who steals my purse steals trash."

Do not capitalize the first word of a sentence set off within another sentence by dashes or parentheses.

FAULTY: Finding the store closed—It was a holiday—they went home.

REVISED: Finding the store closed—it was a holiday—they went home.

FAULTY: The candidates are Frank Lester and Jane Lester (They are not related).

REVISED: The candidates are Frank Lester and Jane Lester (they are not related).

NOTE: When a complete sentence is introduced by a colon, it is generally not capitalized.

 USING CAPITAL LETTERS IN POETRY

When you quote poetry, remember that the first word of a line of poetry is generally capitalized. If the poet uses a lowercase letter to begin a line, however, you should too when you quote the line.

34b Capitalize Proper Nouns, Titles Accompanying Them, and Adjectives Formed from Them

Capitalize **proper nouns**—the names of specific persons, places, or things (Diana Ross, Madras, the Enoch Pratt Free Library)—and adjectives formed from proper nouns (Shakespearean, Elizabethan).

(1) Specific People's Names

Eleanor Roosevelt	Elvis Presley
Jackie Robinson	William the Conqueror

When a title precedes a person's name or is used instead of the name, it too is capitalized.

Dad	Pope John XXIII
Count Dracula	Justice Ruth Bader Ginsburg

Titles that *follow* names or those that refer to a general position, not the particular person who holds it, are usually not capitalized. A title denoting a family relationship is never capitalized when it follows an article or a possessive pronoun.

CAPITALIZE:	DO NOT CAPITALIZE:
Grandma	my grandmother
Private Hargrove	Mr. Hargrove, a private in the army
Queen Mother Elizabeth	a popular queen mother
Sen. Barbara Boxer	Barbara Boxer, the senator from California
Uncle Harry	my uncle
Gen. Patton	a four-star general

Titles or abbreviations that designate academic degrees are always capitalized, even when they follow a name.

Perry Mason, Attorney-at-Law	Michelle Russo, PhD
Benjamin Spock, MD	

Titles that indicate high-ranking positions may be capitalized even when they are used alone or when they follow a name.

the Pope

William Jefferson Clinton, President of the United States

(2) Names of Particular Structures, Special Events, Monuments, Vehicles, and So On

the *Titanic*   the Taj Mahal
the Brooklyn Bridge   Mount Rushmore
the World Series   the Eiffel Tower

NOTE: When a common noun such as *bridge, river, county,* or *lake* is part of a proper noun, it too is capitalized (Lake Erie, Kings County).

(3) Places, Geographical Regions, and Directions

Saturn   the Straits of Magellan
Budapest   the Western Hemisphere
Walden Pond   the Fiji Islands

North, east, south, and *west* are capitalized when they denote particular geographical regions, but not when they designate directions.

The Midwest seemed like a wasteland to F. Scott Fitzgerald's Nick Carraway, so he decided to come East. (Capital letters necessary because *Midwest* and *East* refer to specific regions.)

Turn west at the corner of Broad Street and continue north until you reach Market. (No capitals used because *west* and *north* refer to directions, not specific regions.)

(4) Days of the Week, Months of the Year, and Holidays

Saturday   Ash Wednesday
January   Rosh Hashanah
Veterans Day   Kwanza

(5) Historical Periods, Events, and Documents; Names of Legal Cases and Awards

the Battle of Gettysburg   the Treaty of Versailles
the Industrial Revolution   the Voting Rights Act
the Reformation   *Brown v. Board of Education*

NOTE: Names of court cases are underlined or italicized in the text of your papers but not in bibliographic entries.

(6) Philosophic, Literary, and Artistic Movements

Naturalism   Dadaism
Romanticism   Fauvism
Neoclassicism   Expressionism

(7) Races, Ethnic Groups, Nationalities, and Languages

African-American   Korean
Latino   Dutch
Caucasian   Turkish

NOTE: When the words *black* and *white* refer to races, they have traditionally not been capitalized. Current usage is divided on whether or not to capitalize *black*.

(8) Religions and Their Followers; Sacred Books and Figures

Muslims   the Talmud   Buddha
Jews   the Koran   the Virgin Mary
Islam   God   the Messiah
Judaism   the Lord   the Scriptures

NOTE: It is not necessary to capitalize pronouns referring to God (although some people do so as a sign of respect).

(9) Political, Social, Athletic, Civic, and Other Groups and Their Members

the New York Yankees
the Democratic Party
the International Brotherhood of Electrical Workers
the American Civil Liberties Union
the National Council of Teachers of English
Pearl Jam

NOTE: When the name of a group or institution is abbreviated, the abbreviation uses capital letters in place of the capitalized words.

See
37b

IBEW   ACLU   NCTE

(10) Businesses; Government Agencies; and Medical, Educational, and Other Institutions

Congress   Lincoln High School
Environmental Protection Agency   the University of Maryland

(11) Trade Names and Words Formed from Them

Velcro   Coke   Post-it   Rollerblades

NOTE: Trade names that have been used so often and for so long that they have become synonymous with the product—for example, *aspirin* and *nylon*—are no longer capitalized.

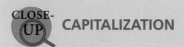 **CAPITALIZATION**

In general, use generic references, not brand names, in college writing—*photocopy*, not *Xerox*, for example.

(12) Specific Academic Courses

Sociology 201   English 101

NOTE: Do not capitalize a general subject area unless it is the name of a language.

FAULTY: He had a double major in English and Accounting.

REVISED: He had a double major in English and accounting.

(13) Adjectives Formed from Proper Nouns

Freudian slip   Elizabethan era
Platonic ideal   Shakespearean sonnet
Aristotelian logic   Marxist ideology

When words derived from proper nouns have lost their original associations, do not capitalize them.

The <u>china</u> pattern was very elaborate.

We need a 75-<u>watt</u> bulb.

34c Capitalize Important Words in Titles

In general, capitalize all words in titles of books, articles, essays, films, and the like—including your own papers—with the exception of articles (*a, an,* and *the*), prepositions, coordinating conjunctions, and the *to* in infinitives. (If an article, preposition, or conjunction is the *first* or *last* word in the title, however, it is capitalized.)

"Dover Beach"
The Declaration of Independence
Across the River and into the Trees

On the Waterfront
The Skin of Our Teeth
Of Human Bondage

34d Capitalize the Pronoun *I* and the Interjection *O*

Capitalize the pronoun *I* even if it is part of a contraction (*I'm*, *I'll*, *I've*).

Sam and I finally went to the Grand Canyon, and I'm glad we did.

The interjection *O* is also always capitalized.

Give us peace in our time, O Lord.

Capitalize the interjection *oh* only when it begins a sentence.

NOTE: Many other single letters are capitalized in certain usages: U-boat, D-Day, Model T, Vitamin B, an *A* in history, C major.

34e Capitalize Salutations and Closings of Letters

Always capitalize the first word of the salutation of a personal or **business letter**.

Dear Fred,   Dear Mr. Reynolds:

Always capitalize the first word of the complimentary close.

Sincerely,   Very truly yours,

See 52a

34f Editing Misused or Overused Capitals

Do not capitalize names in the following cases.

(1) Seasons

Do not capitalize the names of the seasons—summer, fall, winter, spring—unless they are personified, as in *Old Man Winter.*

533

(2) Centuries and Loosely Defined Historical Periods

Do not capitalize the names of centuries or general historical periods.

seventeenth-century poetry   the automobile age

Do, however, capitalize names of specific historical, anthropological, and geological periods.

Iron Age   Paleozoic Era

(3) Diseases and Other Medical Terms

Do not capitalize names of diseases or medical tests or conditions unless a proper noun is part of the name or unless the disease is an **acronym.**

See 28a2

polio	Apgar test	AIDS
Reye's syndrome	mumps	SIDS

EXERCISE

Capitalize words where necessary in these sentences.

EXAMPLE: John F. Kennedy won the pulitzer prize for his book *profiles in courage.*

John F. Kennedy won the Pulitzer Prize for his book *Profiles in Courage.*

1. Two of the brontë sisters wrote *jane eyre* and *wuthering heights,* nineteenth-century novels that are required reading in many english classes that study victorian literature.
2. It was a beautiful day in the spring—it was april 15, to be exact—but all Ted could think about was the check he had to write to the internal revenue service and the bills he had to pay by friday.
3. Traveling north, they hiked through british columbia, planning a leisurely return on the cruise ship *canadian princess.*
4. Alice liked her mom's apple pie better than aunt nellie's rhubarb pie; but she liked grandpa's punch best of all.
5. A new elective, political science 30, covers the vietnam war from the gulf of tonkin to the fall of saigon, including the roles of ho chi minh, the viet cong, and the buddhist monks; the positions of presidents johnson and nixon; and the influence of groups like the student mobilization committee and vietnam veterans against the war.
6. When the central high school drama club put on a production of shaw's *pygmalion,* the director xeroxed extra copies of the parts for

eliza doolittle and professor henry higgins so he could give them to the understudies.

7. Shaking all over, Bill admitted, "driving on the los angeles freeway is a frightening experience for a kid from the bronx, even in a bmw."

8. The new united federation of teachers contract guarantees teachers many paid holidays, including columbus day, veterans day, and washington's birthday; a week each at christmas and easter; and two full months (july and august) in the summer.

9. The sociology syllabus included the books *beyond the best interests of the child, regulating the poor,* and *a welfare mother;* in anthropology we were to begin by studying the stone age; and in geology we were to focus on the mesozoic era.

10. Winners of the nobel peace prize include lech walesa, former leader of the polish trade union solidarity; the reverend dr. martin luther king, jr., founder of the southern christian leadership conference; and bishop desmond tutu of south africa.

CHAPTER 35

ITALICS

35a Setting Off Titles and Names

The titles of books, newspapers, magazines, and journals; pamphlets; films; television and radio programs; software programs; long poems; plays; long musical works; and paintings and sculpture are set in italic type. The names of ships, trains, aircraft, and spacecraft are also italicized. All other **titles** are enclosed in quotation marks.

See
32b

NOTE: In research papers and manuscripts submitted for publication, indicate italics by underlining. If your instructor gives you permission, you may use an italic font.

 USING ITALICS

Titles of your own essays, typed at the top of the first page or on a title page, are neither italicized nor enclosed in quotation marks. Names of sacred books, such as the Bible, and laws, acts, or similar documents—such as the Constitution, the Declaration of Independence, and the Voting Rights Act—are also neither italicized nor placed within quotation marks.

TITLES AND NAMES SET IN ITALICS

Books
David Copperfield   *The Bluest Eye*

continued on the following page

continued from the previous page

Newspapers

the *Washington Post*   *The Philadelphia Inquirer*

Articles and names of cities are italicized only when they are part of the title.

Magazines

Rolling Stone   *Scientific American*   *Wired*

Journals

New England Journal of Medicine
American Sociological Review

Pamphlets

Common Sense

Films

Casablanca   *Who's Afraid of Virginia Woolf?*

Punctuation is italicized when it is part of a title.

Television Programs

Sesame Street   *Seinfeld*   *The X-Files*

Radio Programs

All Things Considered   *Prairie Home Companion*

Software Programs

Excel   *Word*

Long Poems

John Brown's Body   *The Faerie Queen*

Plays

Macbeth   *A Raisin in the Sun*   *Rent*

Operas and Symphonies

La Bohème   *Eroica*

Paintings and Sculpture

Guërnica   *Pietà*

Ships

Lusitania   USS *Saratoga*

SS and USS are not italicized when they precede the name of a ship.

continued on the following page

continued from the previous page
Trains
> *City of New Orleans*   *Orient Express*

Aircraft
> the *Hindenburg*   *Enola Gay*

Only particular aircraft, not makes or types such as Boeing 747, are italicized.

Spacecraft
> *Sputnik*   *Enterprise*

35b Setting Off Foreign Words and Phrases

Thousands of foreign words and phrases are now considered part of the English language. These words receive no special treatment.

> naive   lasso
> chaperon   catharsis

Foreign words and phrases that have not been assimilated into the English language, however, are italicized.

> *"C'est la vie,"* Madeline said when she saw that the show was sold out.

> *Spirochaeta plicatilis, Treponema pallidum,* and *Spirilbum minus* all are bacteria with corkscrew-like shapes.

If you are not sure whether a foreign word has been assimilated into English, consult a dictionary.

NOTE: Foreign proper nouns, such as the Bastille and the Taj Mahal, are not italicized.

35c Setting Off Elements Spoken of as Themselves and Terms Being Defined

Letters, numerals, words, and phrases are italicized when they are referred to as themselves.

> Is that a *p* or a *g*?

I forget the exact address, but I know it has a *3* in it.

Does *through* rhyme with *cough*?

His pronunciation of the phrase *Mary was contrary* told us he was from the Midwest.

Italicize to set off words and phrases that you go on to define.

A *closet drama* is a play meant to be read, not performed.

35d Using Italics for Clarity

Occasionally, it is necessary to italicize a word to avoid confusion or ambiguity when a sentence may have more than one meaning.

This time Jill forgot the *key.* (Last time Jill forgot something else.)

This time *Jill* forgot the key. (Last time someone else forgot the key.)

 USING ITALICS

Because italics place strong emphasis on a word or phrase, they should be used in moderation. Overuse of italics can be distracting, and it can interfere with the tone and even the meaning of what you write. Whenever possible, then, indicate emphasis with word choice and sentence structure.

FAULTY: The first semester was hard, but the second semester was *really* hard.

REVISED: The first semester was hard, but the second semester was even harder.

 EXERCISE

Underline to indicate italics where necessary, and delete any italics that are incorrectly used. If a sentence is correct, mark it with a *C.*

EXAMPLE: However is a conjunctive adverb, not a coordinating conjunction.

<u>However</u> is a conjunctive adverb, not a coordinating conjunction.

1. I said Carol, not Darryl.
2. A *deus ex machina,* an improbable device used to resolve the plot of a fictional work, is used in Charles Dickens's novel Oliver Twist.
3. He dotted every i and crossed every t.
4. The Metropolitan Opera's production of Carmen was a tour de force for the principal performers.
5. *Laissez-faire* is a doctrine holding that government should not interfere with trade.
6. Antidote and anecdote are often confused because their pronunciations are similar.
7. Hawthorne's novels include Fanshawe, The House of the Seven Gables, The Blithedale Romance, and The Scarlet Letter.
8. Words like mailman, policeman, and fireman have been replaced by nonsexist terms like letter carrier, police officer, and firefighter.
9. A classic black tuxedo was considered de rigueur at the charity ball, but Jason preferred to wear his *dashiki.*
10. Thomas Mann's novel Buddenbrooks is a bildungsroman.

CHAPTER 36

HYPHENS

Hyphens have two conventional uses: to break a word at the end of a typed or handwritten line and to link words in certain compounds.

36a Breaking a Word at the End of a Line

Whenever possible, avoid breaking a word at the end of a line; if you must do so, divide a word only between syllables. (Consult a dictionary if necessary to determine correct syllabication.) When you can, divide a word between prefix and root (sus • pending) or between root and suffix (develop • ment). Divide a word that contains doubled consonants between the doubled letters (let • ter) unless the doubled letters are part of the root (cross • ing) or unless the doubled letters do not break into two syllables (ex • pelled). Do not end two consecutive lines with hyphens, and never divide a word at the end of a page.

NOTE: If you use a computer, you do not have to make decisions about how to hyphenate at the end of a line. Unless you tell it to, a computer does not hyphenate; instead, it brings the entire word down to the next line.

DIVIDING ELECTRONIC ADDRESSES

Do not use a hyphen when dividing a long electronic address at the end of a line. (A hyphen at this point could confuse readers, making them think it is part of the address.) Instead, simply break the address in a logical place—before or after a slash or a period,

continued on the following page

continued from the previous page
for example—or avoid the problem entirely by putting the entire address on one line.

> Weiser, Jay. "The Tyranny of Informality." New Republic 26 Feb.
>
> 1996. 1 Mar. 1996 <http://www.enews.com/magazines/
>
> tnr/current/022696.3.html>.

Additional guidelines for determining how words should be divided are listed below.

(1) One-Syllable Words

Never hyphenate a one-syllable word. Keep a one-syllable word intact even if it is relatively long (*thought, laughed*). If you cannot fit the whole word at the end of the line, move it to the next line.

FAULTY: Mark Twain's novel *The Prin-*
ce and the Pauper considers the
effects of environment on personality.

REVISED: Mark Twain's novel *The Prince and the Pauper* considers
the effects of environment on personality.

(2) Short Syllables

Never leave a single letter at the end of a line or carry one or two letters to the beginning of a new line. One-letter prefixes (like the *a-* in *away*) or short suffixes (like *-y, -ly, -er,* and *-ed*) should not be separated from the rest of the word. The suffixes *-able* and *-ible* should not be broken into two syllables.

FAULTY: Nadia walked very slowly a-
long the balance beam.

REVISED: Nadia walked very slowly along
the balance beam.

FAULTY: Amy's parents wondered whether the terrible twos would ever end.

REVISED: Amy's parents wondered whether the terrible twos would ever end.

(3) Compound Words

If you must hyphenate a **compound word**, put the hyphen between the elements of the compound.

See 36b

FAULTY: Environmentalists believe snowmo-
               biles produce air and noise pollution.

REVISED: Environmentalists believe snow-
               mobiles produce air and noise pollution.

If the compound already contains a hyphen, divide it at the existing hyphen.

FAULTY: She met her hus-
               band-to be on a blind date.

REVISED: She met her husband-
               to-be on a blind date.

(4) Illogical or Confusing Hyphenation

Some words contain letter combinations that look like other words. To avoid confusing readers, do not isolate a part of a word that can be read as a separate word.

CONFUSING: The supervisor did not appreciate the face-
                tious remark.

REVISED: The supervisor did not appreciate the
                facetious remark.

(5) Numerals, Contractions, and Abbreviations

Numerals, contractions, and abbreviations (including acronyms) should not be divided. Do not use a hyphen between a numeral and an abbreviation.

FAULTY: The special program on child abuse was presented to over 23,-
               000 schoolchildren.

REVISED: The special program on child abuse was presented to over
               23,000 schoolchildren.

FAULTY: Whether or not the meeting began on time was-
               n't important.

REVISED: Whether or not the meeting began on time
               wasn't important.

FAULTY: During the 1960s, participation in RO-
               TC declined on many college campuses.

543

REVISED: During the 1960s, participation in ROTC declined on many college campuses.

FAULTY: The balloon was launched at precisely 8-p.m.

REVISED: The balloon was launched at precisely 8 p.m.

EXERCISE 1

Divide each of these words into syllables, consulting a dictionary if necessary; then, indicate with a hyphen where you would divide each word at the end of a line.

EXAMPLE: underground
un • der • ground
under-ground

1. transcendentalism
2. calliope
3. martyr
4. longitude
5. bookkeeper
6. side-splitting
7. markedly
8. amazing
9. unlikely
10. thorough

36b Dividing Compound Words

A **compound word** is composed of two or more words. Some familiar compound words are hyphenated.

no-hitter   helter-skelter

Other compounds are written as one word.

fireplace   peacetime   sunset

Finally, some compounds are written as two separate words.

medical doctor   hard drive   bunk bed

Your dictionary can tell you whether a particular compound requires a hyphen: *snow job*, for instance, is two unhyphenated words; *snowsuit* is one word; and *snow-white* is hyphenated. Usage changes, however, and different dictionaries may divide compound words differently.

Although hyphenation of compound words is not uniform, a few reliable rules do apply.

(1) Hyphenating Compound Adjectives

A **compound adjective** consists of two or more words combined into a single grammatical unit that modifies a noun. When a compound adjective *precedes* the noun it modifies, its elements are joined by hyphens.

> He stayed tuned to his favorite listener-supported radio station, waiting for a hard-hitting editorial.

> The research team tried to use nineteenth-century technology to design a space-age project.

However, when a compound adjective *follows* the noun it modifies, it does not include a hyphen.

> The three government-operated programs were run smoothly, but the one that was not government operated was short of funds.

Use **suspended hyphens**—hyphens followed by space or by the appropriate punctuation and space—in a series of compounds that have the same principal elements.

> The three-, four-, and five-year-old children take daily naps.

 COMPOUND ADJECTIVES

> Compound adjectives that contain adverbs ending in *ly* are not hyphenated, even when they precede the noun.

> Many upwardly mobile families consider items like home computers, microwave ovens, and videocassette recorders to be necessities.

(2) Hyphenating with Certain Prefixes and Suffixes

Use a hyphen between a prefix and a proper noun or an adjective formed from a proper noun.

> mid-July   pre-Columbian

Use a hyphen to connect the prefixes *all-, ex-, half-, quarter-, quasi-,* and *self-* and the suffixes *-elect* and *-odd* to a noun.

all-pro	quasi-serious
ex-senator	self-centered
half-pint	president-elect
quarter-moon	thirty-odd

NOTE: The words *selfhood, selfish,* and *selfless* do not include hyphens. In these cases *self* is the root, not a prefix.

(3) Hyphenating for Clarity

Hyphenate to prevent misreading one word for another.

In order to <u>reform</u> criminals, we must <u>re-form</u> our ideas about prisons.

Hyphenate to avoid combinations that are hard to read, such as two *i*'s (*semi-illiterate*) or more than two of the same consonant (*shell-less*).

Hyphenate in most cases between a capital initial and a word when the two combine to form a compound.

A-frame   T-shirt

But check your dictionary; some letter- or numeral-plus-word compounds do not require hyphens.

B flat   C major

(4) Hyphenating Compound Numerals and Fractions

Hyphenate compounds that represent numbers below one hundred, even if they are part of a large number.

the <u>twenty-first</u> century   three hundred <u>sixty-five</u> days

Compounds that denote numbers over ninety-nine (*two thousand, thirty million, two hundred fifty*) are not hyphenated. Therefore, in the expression *three hundred sixty-five days,* the compound *sixty-five* is hyphenated because it denotes a number below one hundred, but no hyphens connect *three* to *hundred.*

Hyphenate the written form of a fraction when it modifies a noun.

a <u>two-thirds</u> share of the business

a <u>three-fourths</u> majority

Hyphens are not required in other cases, but most writers do use them.

546

PREFERRED: seven-eighths of the circle

ACCEPTABLE: seven eighths of the circle

(5) Hyphenating Coined Compounds

A **coined compound,** one that uses a new combination of words as a unit, requires hyphens.

He looked up with a <u>who-do-you-think-you-are</u> expression on his face.

EXERCISE 2

Form compound adjectives from the following word groups, inserting hyphens where necessary.

EXAMPLE: A contract for three years

a three-year contract

1. a relative who has long been lost
2. someone who is addicted to video games
3. a salesperson who goes from door to door
4. a display calculated to catch the eye
5. friends who are dearly beloved
6. a household that is centered on a child
7. a line of reasoning that is hard to follow
8. the border between New York and New Jersey
9. a candidate who is thirty-two years old
10. a computer that is friendly to its users

EXERCISE 3

Add hyphens to the compounds in these sentences wherever they are required. Consult a dictionary if necessary.

EXAMPLE: Alaska was the forty ninth state to join the United States.

Alaska was the forty-ninth state to join the United States.

1. One of the restaurant's blue plate specials is chicken fried steak.
2. Virginia and Texas are both right to work states.
3. He stood on tiptoe to see the near perfect statue, which was well hidden by the security fence.
4. The five and ten cent store had a self service makeup counter and stocked many up to the minute gadgets.
5. The so called Saturday night special is opposed by pro gun control groups.
6. He ordered two all beef patties with special sauce, lettuce, cheese, pickles, and onions on a sesame seed bun.

7. The material was extremely thought provoking, but it hardly presented any earth shattering conclusions.
8. The Dodgers Phillies game was rained out, so the long suffering fans left for home.
9. Bone marrow transplants carry the risk of what is known as a graft versus host reaction.
10. The state funded child care program was considered a highly desirable alternative to family day care.

CHAPTER 37

ABBREVIATIONS

Abbreviations communicate meaning quickly and efficiently—but only when they are familiar to your readers.

Many abbreviations are acceptable only in informal writing and are not appropriate in college writing. Others are acceptable in scientific, technical, or business writing, or only in a particular discipline, such as computer science. If you are unsure whether to use a particular **abbreviation**, check a style manual in your field.

See
43f

37a Abbreviating Titles

Titles before and after proper names are usually abbreviated.

Mr. Homer Simpson	Dr. Mathilde Krim
Henry Kissinger, PhD	St. Jude
Rep. Chaka Fattah	Prof. Elie Weisel
Gen. George Patton	Sen. Ben Nighthorse Campbell

Do not, however, use an abbreviated title without a name.

FAULTY: The Dr. diagnosed hepatitis.

REVISED: The doctor diagnosed hepatitis.

37b Abbreviating Organization Names and Technical Terms

Many abbreviations frequently used in speech and in college writing to designate familiar organizations, groups, and scientific or technical terms are composed of capitalized initials. These abbreviations fall into

See
28a2

two categories: those in which the initials are pronounced as separate units (MTV) and **acronyms**, in which the initials are pronounced as a word (NATO).

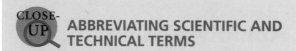

CLOSE-UP ABBREVIATING SCIENTIFIC AND TECHNICAL TERMS

If you use abbreviations for terms that are not well known, spell out the full term the first time you mention it, followed by the abbreviation in parentheses.

Citrus farmers have been injecting ethylene dibromide (EDB), a chemical pesticide, into the soil for more than twenty years. Now, however, EDB has seeped into wells and contaminated water supplies, and it is a suspected carcinogen.

37c Abbreviating Dates, Times of Day, Temperatures, and Numbers

50 BC (*BC* follows the date.)	AD 432 (*AD* precedes the date.)
525 BCE	730 CE
6 a.m.	3:03 p.m.
20° C (Centigrade or Celsius)	180° F (Fahrenheit)

Always capitalize *BC* and *AD*. (The more neutral alternatives *BCE*, for "before the common era," and *CE*, for "common era," are also capitalized.) Use lowercase letters for *a.m.* and *p.m.* These abbreviations are used only when they are accompanied by numbers.

FAULTY: We will see you in the a.m.

REVISED: We will see you in the morning.

REVISED: We will see you at 8 a.m.

Avoid the abbreviation *no.* (written either *no.* or *No.*), except in technical writing, and then use it only before a numeral.

FAULTY: The no. on the label of the unidentified substance wasn't clear.

REVISED: The unidentified substance was labeled no. 52.

37d Editing Misused or Overused Abbreviations

In college writing abbreviations are not used in the following cases.

(1) Familiar Latin Expressions

Abbreviations of the common Latin phrases *i.e.* ("that is"), *e.g.* ("for example"), and *etc.* ("and so forth") are sometimes appropriate for informal writing, and they may occasionally be acceptable in a parenthetical note. In most college writing, however, they are not appropriate, and an equivalent phrase should be written out in full.

INFORMAL: Poe wrote "The Gold Bug," "The Tell-Tale Heart," etc.

PREFERABLE: Poe wrote "The Gold Bug," "The Tell-Tale Heart," and other stories.

INFORMAL: Other musicians (e.g., Bruce Springsteen) have been influenced by Dylan.

PREFERABLE: Other musicians (for example, Bruce Springsteen) have been influenced by Dylan.

NOTE: The Latin abbreviations *et al.* ("and others") and *cf.* ("compare") are used only in parenthetical documentation, footnotes, and bibliographic entries.

Davidson, Harley, et al. You and Your Motorcycle. New York: Ten

Speed, 1968.

(2) The Names of Days, Months, or Holidays

FAULTY: Sat., Aug. 9, was the hottest day of the year.

REVISED: Saturday, August 9, was the hottest day of the year.

FAULTY: Only twenty-three shopping days remain until Xmas.

REVISED: Only twenty-three shopping days remain until Christmas.

(3) Units of Measurement

In informal or technical writing, some units of measurement are abbreviated when preceded by a numeral.

The hurricane had winds of 35 mph.

One Honda gets over 50 mpg.

In college writing, however, write out such expressions, and spell out words such as *inches, feet, years, miles, pints, quarts,* and *gallons.*

NOTE: Even in informal or technical writing, abbreviations for units of measurement are not used in the absence of a numeral.

> FAULTY: The laboratory equipment included pt. and qt. measures and a beaker that could hold a gal. of liquid.

> REVISED: The laboratory equipment included pint and quart measures and a beaker that could hold a gallon of liquid.

(4) Names of Streets and Places

Abbreviations of names of streets, cities, states, countries, and geographical regions are common in informal writing and in correspondence. In college writing, however, these words should be spelled out.

FAULTY:	REVISED:
B'way	Broadway
Riverside Dr.	Riverside Drive
Phila.	Philadelphia
Catskill Mts.	Catskill Mountains

EXCEPTIONS: The abbreviation *US* is often acceptable (US Coast Guard), as is *DC* in *Washington, DC.* It is also permissible to use the abbreviation *Mt.* before the name of a mountain (*Mt. Etna*) and *St.* in a place name (*St. Albans*).

(5) Names of Academic Subjects

Names of academic subjects are not abbreviated.

> FAULTY: Psych., soc., and English lit. are required courses.

> REVISED: Psychology, sociology, and English literature are required courses.

(6) Parts of Books

Abbreviations that designate parts of written works (*pt. 2, ch. 3*) should not be used within the body of a paper except in parenthetical documentation.

(7) People's Names

> FAULTY: Mr. Harris's five children were named Robt., Eliz., Jas., Chas., and Wm.

Revised: Mr. Harris's five children were named Robert, Elizabeth, James, Charles, and William.

(8) Company Names

The abbreviations *Inc., Bros., Co.,* or *Corp.* and the **ampersand** *(&)* are not used unless they are part of a firm's official name.

Company names are written exactly as the firms themselves write them.

Western Union Telegraph Company   AT&T
Santini Bros.   Charles Schwab & Co., Inc.

NOTE: **MLA documentation format** requires abbreviations of publishers' company names—for example, *Harcourt* for *Harcourt Brace College Publishers.*

Abbreviations for *company, corporation,* and the like are not used in the absence of a company name.

Faulty: The corp. merged with a small co. in Pittsburgh.

Revised: The corporation merged with a small company in Pittsburgh.

The ampersand is used in college writing only in the name of a company that requires it or in citations that follow APA documentation style.

(9) Symbols

The symbols %, =, +, #, and ¢ are acceptable in technical and scientific writing but not in other college writing.

Faulty: The price of admission has increased 50%.

Revised: The price of admission has increased fifty percent.

The symbol *$* is acceptable before specific numbers, but not as a substitute for the words *money* or *dollars.*

Correct: The book of poetry cost only $4.25.

Faulty: The value of the $ has declined steadily in the last two decades.

Revised: The value of the dollar has declined steadily in the last two decades.

EXERCISE

Correct any incorrectly used abbreviations in the following sentences, assuming that all are intended for a college audience. If a sentence is correct, mark it with a *C*.

EXAMPLE: *Romeo & Juliet* is a play by Wm. Shakespeare.

Romeo and Juliet is a play by William Shakespeare.

1. The committee meeting, attended by representatives from Action for Children's Television (ACT) and NOW, Sen. Putnam, & the pres. of ABC, convened at 8 A.M. on Mon. Feb. 24 at the YWCA on Germantown Ave.

2. An econ. prof. was suspended after he encouraged his students to speculate on securities issued by a corp. under investigation by the SEC.

3. Benjamin Spock, the MD who wrote *Baby and Child Care,* is a respected dr. known throughout the USA.

4. The FDA banned the use of Red Dye no. 2 in food in 1976, but other food additives are still in use.

5. The Rev. Dr. Martin Luther King, Jr., leader of the SCLC, led the famous Selma, Ala., march.

6. Wm. Golding, a novelist from the U.K., won the Nobel Prize in lit.

7. The adult education center, financed by a major computer corp., offers courses in basic subjects like introductory bio. and tech. writing as well as teaching programming languages, such as PASCAL.

8. All the bros. in the fraternity agreed to write to Pres. Dexter appealing their disciplinary probation under Ch. 4, Sec. 3, of the IFC constitution.

9. A 4 qt. (i.e., 1 gal.) container is needed to hold the salt solution.

10. According to Prof. Morrison, all those taking the exam should bring two sharpened no. 2 pencils to the St. Joseph's University auditorium on Sat.

CHAPTER 38

NUMBERS

In some disciplines, such as the social sciences and engineering, the rule is to spell out all numbers less than ten and to use numerals for ten and above. The conventions that follow apply to papers in the humanities. For information on conventions that apply to another discipline, consult the appropriate **style manual**.

See
43e

38a Spelling Out Numbers That Begin Sentences

Never begin a sentence with a numeral. If a number begins a sentence, spell out the number.

FAULTY: 250 students are currently enrolled in English composition courses.

REVISED: Two hundred fifty students are currently enrolled in English composition courses.

You may also reword the sentence.

Current enrollment in English composition courses is 250 students.

38b Spelling Out Numbers Expressed in One or Two Words

Unless a number falls into one of the categories listed in **38d,** spell it out if you can do so in one or two words.

The Hawaiian alphabet has only twelve letters.

Class size stabilized at twenty-eight students.

Approximate numbers can often be expressed in one or two words.

Guards turned away more than ten thousand disappointed fans.

The subsidies are expected to total about two million dollars.

 USING NUMBERS

Use a hyphen when you spell out compound numbers from twenty-one to ninety-nine.

38c Using Numerals for Numbers Expressed in More Than Two Words

Use numerals to represent numbers that would be expressed in more than two words.

The pollster interviewed 3,250 voters before the election.

The dietitian prepared 125 sample menus.

When Levittown, Pennsylvania, was built in the early 1950s, the builders' purchases included 300,000 doorknobs, 153,000 faucets, 53,600 ice cube trays, and 4,000 manhole covers.

NOTE: Numerals and spelled-out forms denoting the same kind of item should not be mixed in the same passage. For consistency, then, the number 4,000 in the last example sentence above is expressed in figures even though it could be written in only two words.

38d Using Numerals Where Convention Requires Their Use

(1) Addresses

1600 Pennsylvania Avenue

10 Downing Street

111 Fifth Avenue, New York, NY 10003

(2) Dates

January 15, 1929   62 BC
November 22, 1963   1914–1919

(3) Exact Times

9:16   10 a.m.   6:50

EXCEPTIONS: Spell out times of day when they are used with *o'clock:* *eleven o'clock,* not *11 o'clock.* Also spell out times expressed as round numbers: *They were in bed by ten.*

(4) Exact Sums of Money

$25.11

$6,752

$25.5 million (or $25,500,000)

EXCEPTION: You may write out a round sum of money if the number can be expressed in one or two words.

five dollars   two thousand dollars
fifty-three cents   six hundred dollars

(5) Pages and Divisions of Written Works

Use arabic (not roman) numerals for chapter and volume numbers; acts, scenes, and lines of plays; chapters and verses of the Bible; and line numbers of long poems.

The "Out, out brief candle" speech appears in Act 5, scene 5, of *Macbeth* (lines 17–28); in Kittredge's *Complete Works of Shakespeare* it appears on page 1142.

(6) Measurements

When a measurement is expressed by a number accompanied by a symbol or an abbreviation, use numerals.

55 mph   12"
32°   15 cc

(7) Numbers Containing Percentages, Decimals, or Fractions

80% (or 80 percent)   6 3/4
98.6   3.14

(8) Ratios, Scores, and Statistics

Children preferred Crispy Crunchies over Total Bran by a ratio of 20 to 1.

The Knicks defeated the Bullets 92 to 84.

The median age of the voters was 42; the mean age was 40.

(9) Identification Numbers

Route 66   Track 8   Channel 12

38e Using Numerals with Spelled-Out Numbers

Even when all the numbers in a passage are short enough to be spelled out, numerals are sometimes used along with spelled-out numbers to distinguish one number from another.

CONFUSING: The team was divided into twenty two-person squads.

CLEAR: The team was divided into twenty 2-person squads.

EXERCISE

Revise the use of numbers in these sentences, making sure usage is correct and consistent. If a sentence uses numbers correctly, mark it with a *C*.

> EXAMPLE: The Empire State Building is one hundred and two stories high.
>
> The Empire State Building is 102 stories high.

1. *1984*, a novel by George Orwell, is set in a totalitarian society.
2. The English placement examination included a 30-minute personal-experience essay, a 45-minute expository essay, and a 150-item objective test of grammar and usage.
3. In a control group of two hundred forty-seven patients, almost three out of four suffered serious adverse reactions to the new drug.
4. Before the Thirteenth Amendment to the Constitution, slaves were counted as 3/5 of a person.
5. The intensive membership drive netted 2,608 new members and additional dues of over 5 thousand dollars.
6. They had only 2 choices: either they could take the yacht at Pier Fourteen, or they could return home to the penthouse at Twenty-seven Harbor View Drive.

7. The atomic number of lithium is three.

8. Approximately 3 hundred thousand schoolchildren in District 6 were given hearing and vision examinations between May third and June 26.

9. The United States was drawn into the war by the Japanese attack on Pearl Harbor on December seventh, 1941.

10. An upper-middle-class family can spend over 250,000 dollars to raise each child up to age 18.

PART 8

WRITING WITH SOURCES

CHAPTER 39

RESEARCH FOR WRITING

Research is the study and investigation of a topic outside your own experience and knowledge. When you do research you move from what you know about a topic to what you do not know. As your research becomes more focused, so do your ideas.

39a Mapping Out a Search Strategy

When you do research, you should follow a **search strategy,** a systematic process of collecting and evaluating source material. You begin by doing **exploratory research,** looking at general reference works that give you a broad overview of your topic and its possibilities. Once you have finished your exploratory research, you do **focused research**—returning to the library with more narrowly focused objectives and making use of specialized reference works, books, articles, electronic resources, and special library services.

The diagram on page 564 presents an overview of a possible search strategy. Although you will not go through every stage each time you do research, you will follow the same general order, moving from exploratory to focused research. As you map out your plans, though, you should remain flexible and willing to modify your search strategy as your research progresses.

 CLOSE-UP **USING THE INTERNET FOR RESEARCH**

You can use the **Internet** as a resource at any stage of your research. During exploratory research you can browse electronically

See Ch. 40

continued on page 565

SEARCH STRATEGY

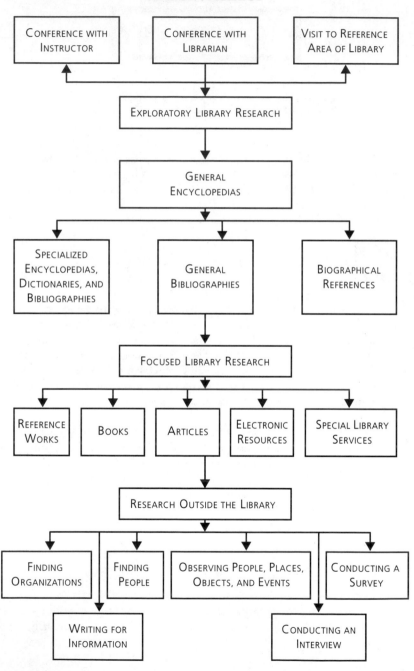

continued from page 563

to discover issues that could lead you to a research question, or you can look through online encyclopedias to get a general sense of your subject. Later, during focused research, you can use the Internet to help you identify promising sources, and you can sometimes even download full texts of articles.

39b Doing Library Research

STRATEGIES FOR DOING LIBRARY RESEARCH

Before You Start:
- Know your library's physical layout. (Take a tour of the library if one is offered.)
- Familiarize yourself with the library's holdings.
- Find out if your college library has a printed guide to its resources.
- Meet with a reference librarian or your instructor if necessary.
- Be aware of the library's hours.

As You Do Research:
- Copy down or print out the complete publication information—author, title, volume number, date of publication, and page numbers—that you will need to locate a particular source.
- Remember how to distinguish between a book and a periodical citation: a periodical citation includes an article title set in quotation marks as well as the underlined periodical title.
- Get a copy of any material that your library provides to explain how to use its electronic resources. Attend an orientation session if your library offers one.

NOTE: Doing library research may mean visiting the library to look through print sources or **electronic resources**. It may also mean accessing your library's holdings through your own computer at home or in your dorm or from a computer terminal on your campus.

See
39b5

(1) Exploratory Research

See
44b

During exploratory research your goal is to find a **research question** that your paper can answer. By looking through reference works that provide useful overviews and that are not too specialized, you familiarize yourself with key terms, people, and events relevant to your topic. The following reference works, many of which are available in electronic form as well as in print, are useful for exploratory research.

General Encyclopedias   General multivolume encyclopedias, such as *Encyclopedia Americana, Collier's Encyclopedia,* and *The New Encyclopedia Britannica* (also available on CD-ROM), are a good place to begin your exploratory research.

To get a quick overview of your topic, use a one-volume general encyclopedia such as *The New Columbia Encyclopedia* or *The Random House Encyclopedia.* Remember, though, that one-volume encyclopedias do not contain the cross-references and in-depth bibliographical information provided by multivolume encyclopedias.

 CLOSE-UP

USING ENCYCLOPEDIAS

Articles in encyclopedias aimed at general readers are usually not up to date or detailed enough for a college-level research paper. Articles in specialized encyclopedias, dictionaries, and bibliographies, however, are aimed at a more advanced audience. For this reason, they are more likely to be appropriate for your research.

See
Pt. 9

Specialized Encyclopedias, Dictionaries, and Bibliographies   These specialized reference works contain in-depth articles focusing on a single **academic discipline** or subject area. Specialized reference works are listed in Robert Balay's *Guide to Reference Books,* available at the reference desk in most libraries.

General Bibliographies   General bibliographies list books available in a wide variety of fields.

Books in Print. A helpful index of authors and titles of every book in print in the United States. *The Subject Guide to Books in Print* indexes books according to subject area.

The Bibliographic Index. A tool for locating bibliographies.

Biographical References   Biographical reference books provide valuable information about people's lives and times as well as bibliographic listings. The *Biography and Genealogy Master Index* is a good place to begin when you know very little about a person's life.

Living Persons

Who's Who in America. Gives very brief biographical data and addresses of prominent living Americans.

Who's Who. Collects concise biographical facts about notable living British men and women.

Current Biography. Includes informal articles on living people of many nationalities.

Deceased Persons

Dictionary of American Biography. Considered the best of American biographical dictionaries. Includes articles on over thirteen thousand deceased Americans.

Dictionary of National Biography. The most important reference work for British biography.

Webster's Biographical Dictionary. Perhaps the most widely used biographical reference work. Includes people from all periods and places.

Who Was When? A Dictionary of Contemporaries. A reference source for historical biography; covers 500 BC through the early 1970s.

Who Was Who in America. Consists of eleven volumes covering 1607 to 1985, a historical volume covering 1607 to 1896, and an index volume.

(2)   Focused Research: Locating Reference Works

When you do **focused research**, you keep your research question in mind as you look for information, using reference works to help you fill in specific details—facts, examples, statistics, definitions, quotations—to support your ideas. The following reference works—many of which are

See
44e

available on CD-ROM or online as well as in print versions—are most useful for focused research.

See
21d

Unabridged Dictionaries **Unabridged dictionaries**, such as *The Oxford English Dictionary,* are comprehensive works that give detailed information about words.

Special Dictionaries These dictionaries focus on topics such as usage, synonyms, slang and idioms, etymologies, and foreign terms. Some specialized dictionaries focus on specific **disciplines**.

See
Pt. 9

Yearbooks and Almanacs A **yearbook** is an annual publication that updates factual and statistical information already published in a reference source. An **almanac** provides lists, charts, and statistics about a wide variety of subjects.

> *World Almanac.* Includes statistics about government, population, sports, and many other subjects. Includes a chronology of events of the previous year. Published annually since 1868.
>
> *Information Please Almanac.* Could be used to supplement the *World Almanac* (each work includes information unavailable in the other). Published annually since 1947.
>
> *Facts on File.* Covering 1940 to the present, this work offers digests of important news stories from metropolitan newspapers.
>
> *Editorials on Files.* Reprints important editorials from American and Canadian newspapers. Editorials represent both sides of controversial issues.
>
> *Statistical Abstract of the United States.* Summarizes the innumerable statistics gathered by the US government. Published annually.

Atlases An **atlas** contains maps and charts and often a wealth of supplementary historical, cultural, political, and economic information.

> National Geographic Society. *National Geographic Atlas of the World.* The most up-to-date atlas available.
>
> *Rand McNally Cosmopolitan World Atlas.* A modern and extremely legible medium-sized atlas.
>
> *Times,* London. *The Times Atlas of the World* (5 vols.). Considered one of the best large world atlases.

We the People: An Atlas of America's Ethnic Diversity. Presents information about specific ethnic groups, including immigration, relocation history, economic status, and employment patterns. Maps show immigration routes and settlement patterns.

Shepherd, William Robert. *Historical Atlas,* 9th ed. Covers period from 2000 BC to 1955. Excellent maps showing war campaigns and development of commerce.

Quotation Books A **quotation book** contains numerous quotations on a wide variety of subjects. Such quotations can be especially useful for your paper's introductory and concluding paragraphs.

Bartlett's Familiar Quotations. Quotations are arranged chronologically by author.

The Home Book of Quotations. Quotations are arranged by subject. An author index and a key-word index are also included.

(3) Focused Research: Locating Books

Some libraries list their holdings by author, title, and subject in print form on cards arranged in drawers of **card catalogs.** Most libraries now have **online catalogs,** computerized systems that allow students to call up catalog entries by author, title, or subject on video terminals. Figure 1 is an entry from an online catalog.

Figure 1 ONLINE CATALOG ENTRY

Subject Search: College Sports--Economic Aspects--United States

Call Number: 796.06073D

Author: Dealy, Francis X.

Title: Winning at any cost: the sell out of college athletics

Publisher: Carol	Publication Date: 1990
Edition: First edition	Type/Language: Book/English
ISBN/ISSN: 1-55972-052-2	Description: 230 pages, illustrated

ONLINE CATALOGS

Because the online catalogs of various libraries differ, the techniques you use to retrieve information from one online catalog will not necessarily work with another. As with any technical task, however, the more you use the online catalog, the more adept you will get. In addition, most college libraries have printed instructions designed to help you use their online catalog.

Locate a book by its **call number,** which refers you to the area of the library that houses books on your subject. (The same call number that appears in the catalog is written on the spine of the book.) When you find a book you need, look through the books shelved nearby. In itself, browsing is not an effective research technique, but as part of a focused search strategy, it can sometimes yield good results. Also keep in mind that catalog entries may include cross-references that can help you identify additional books related to your subject.

If you cannot find a book on the shelf, go to the circulation desk for help. The book may be out, on reserve, or shelved in a different section of the library.

✔ CHECKLIST: TRACKING DOWN A MISSING SOURCE

PROBLEM	POSSIBLE SOLUTION
✔ Book has been checked out of library.	Consult person at circulation desk.
✔ Book is not in library's collection.	Check other nearby libraries. Ask instructor if he or she owns a copy. Arrange for interlibrary loan (if time permits).
✔ Journal is not in library's collection/article is ripped out of journal.	Arrange for interlibrary copy (if time permits). Check to see whether article is available in a full-text database. Ask librarian whether article has been reprinted as part of a collection.

(4) Focused Research: Locating Articles

Periodicals are magazines, newspapers, or scholarly journals that are published regularly throughout the year. A **magazine** is a serial publication—such as *Time, MacUser,* or *National Geographic*—aimed at general readers. A **journal** is a serial publication—such as *Nature, American Anthropologist,* or *College English*—written for specialists in a particular field.

Periodical indexes list articles from a selected group of magazines, newspapers, or scholarly journals. These indexes may be available in bound volumes, on microfilm or microfiche, on CD-ROM, or in a database that you can access with a computer. Consult a librarian to determine the best way to access the indexes you need. Figure 2 illustrates the information usually contained in a citation from a bound periodical index.

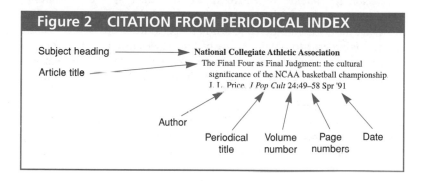

Figure 2   CITATION FROM PERIODICAL INDEX

Subject heading ⟶ National Collegiate Athletic Association
Article title ⟶ The Final Four as Final Judgment: the cultural significance of the NCAA basketball championship
J. J. Price *J Pop Cult* 24:49–58 Spr '91

Author
Periodical title Volume number Page numbers Date

There are three levels of periodical indexes: *general indexes, specialized indexes,* and *abstracting services.*

General Indexes   General indexes lead you to articles in newspapers and popular magazines.

> *Readers' Guide to Periodical Literature.* This index, which you have probably used before, lists articles that appear in more than 150 magazines for general readers. Articles in the *Readers' Guide* are listed and cross-referenced under subject headings. Keep in mind, however, that the *Readers' Guide* indexes only popular periodicals. Because these articles may sometimes oversimplify complex issues, you should ask your instructor or your librarian about the reliability of your source.

> *InfoTrac.* Widely used in college libraries, InfoTrac **databases** are available on CD-ROM or from a commercial information

See
39b5

service. *Expanded Academic ASAP* is an InfoTrac database that lists entries for more than a thousand general interest and scholarly periodicals; some entries include the full text of articles. Other InfoTrac databases cover business, technical, health, computer, and other periodicals.

New York Times Index. The *New York Times Index* lists major articles and features of the *Times* since 1851 by year. Articles are listed alphabetically by subject with short summaries. Supplements are published every two weeks. If your library subscribes to the *New York Times* microfilm service, you have access to every issue of the *Times* back to 1851. Indexing of the *New York Times* and four other major newspapers is also available on InfoTrac's *National Newspaper Index.* (Articles from current issues of the *New York Times* are available on the Internet.)

Specialized Indexes Specialized indexes, such as the *Humanities Index,* lead you to articles in professional and scholarly journals. The most commonly used indexes to scholarly periodicals are largely American and fairly easy to obtain. Many of the articles listed in such indexes assume expert knowledge, but some are accessible to general readers. For information on specialized indexes used in specific disciplines, **see Part 9.**

Abstracting Services Abstracting services have a wider scope than general or specialized indexes, with comprehensive, often international, listings of published articles in a discipline. In addition to providing citations for journal articles, abstracting services also include **abstracts,** brief summaries of the articles' major points. For information on abstracting services used in specific disciplines, **see Part 9.**

(5) Focused Research: Using the Library's Electronic Resources

You can also use the electronic resources of the library to access databases online, on CD-ROM, or on microfilm or microfiche. Often, the information about a single periodical article will be available in more than one of these formats as well as in print. Information can, therefore, be retrieved in a number of ways, some of which are considerably faster and more flexible than others. In many cases, for example, bibliographic information about periodical articles (and in some cases, the articles themselves) may be available in a **database**—a compilation of related information that you access with your computer or with special scanners or readers. Computer terminals and printers located at designated areas in the library enable you to print out citations, abstracts, and even the full text of articles. In some cases, you may be able to download information onto one of your own disks. Consult a librarian to determine the most accessible format for the indexes you need.

Online Databases The fastest way to locate material is to use the library's computer terminals to access a commercial online service. (Many college libraries offer students access to this service at no cost.) Some colleges may make the same databases available to students via the library Web page, though a password may be required. A number of useful databases are available online, including *Lexis* (law) and *Nexis* (business). Your library may also offer WILSONLINE or DIALOG, online services that contain databases that enable you to access thousands of sources in the humanities, social sciences, sciences, engineering, business, and education. For example, DIALOG contains ERIC (education), PsychINFO (psychology), *MLA International Bibliography* (literature), NewsBank (periodicals), and the *Government Printing Office Monthly Catalog*. See Figure 3 for an excerpt from an online database.

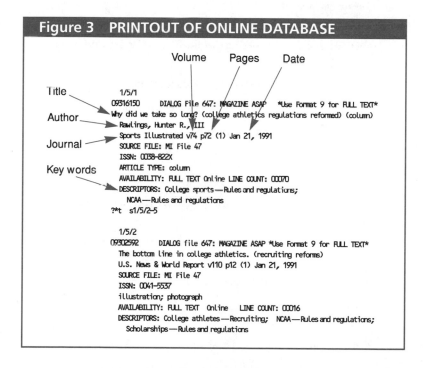

Figure 3 PRINTOUT OF ONLINE DATABASE

CD-ROM *(Compact Disk—Read-Only Memory) Databases* Many of the same databases that are available online are also available on CDs similar to the ones on which music is recorded. One CD can contain an entire database, such as the *Readers' Guide* or InfoTrac. In some cases, the library subscribes to a CD service the same way it does to a journal and receives updated disks periodically. In other cases, books and encyclopedias that are available in print are also published as CDs—for example, *The Oxford English Dictionary* and *The Encyclopaedia Britannica.*

Microfilm and Microfiche   Extremely small images of pages of a periodical may be stored on microfilm. (You need a microfilm scanner to read or photocopy the pages.) Microfiche is similar to microfilm, but images are on a 5- by 7-inch sheet of film and are scanned with a microfiche reader.

CLOSE-UP   USING THE LIBRARY'S ELECTRONIC RESOURCES

Online Databases
Advantages:

• Information is current because online databases are updated frequently.

• You can search several years of databases at once.

• A great number of specific databases are available.

• Selected information can be printed out.

Disadvantages:

• Access may be limited by the library.

• Some databases may not be user-friendly; you may need an orientation session.

• If not subsidized by the college, database searching, which charges by the minute, is expensive for students.

• The large number of databases can be overwhelming.

CD-ROM Databases
Advantages:

• CD-ROMs are portable and easy to use.

• Because the library owns or holds the CD-ROMs, there is no charge for use.

continued on the following page

continued from the previous page
- Students can access specific databases without wading through a confusing menu of options.

- Selected information usually can be printed out.

Disadvantages:

- Databases are not as current as those available online.

- CD-ROMs can be expensive, so some libraries may not have a wide variety.

- Smaller libraries may not have CD-ROM readers.

   Microfilm and Microfiche
Advantages:

- Microfilm and microfiche store a great amount of information, especially copies of periodicals, in a small amount of space.

- You can see original pages, not just text of periodicals.

Disadvantages:

- Special readers or scanners are required.

- Users must scroll through information, so retrieval is cumbersome.

✔ CHECKLIST: CARRYING OUT A KEY-WORD SEARCH

The following general guidelines will help you retrieve information from online databases and CD-ROMs.

✔ **Choose appropriate databases.** Not all databases are equally useful. Some may be geared toward a particular discipline, while others may be too advanced. Consult your librarian to decide which is appropriate for your research.

✔ **Narrow your topic to key words.** In order to find information from an electronic source, you must narrow your topic to one or more **key words,** or **descriptors.** The computer will call up articles that contain these words in their titles or their abstracts. The more precise your key words, the more specific and useful the information you get will be. For example, the key words *college sports* or *college athletics* might yield hundreds of entries. The narrower

continued on the following page

continued from the previous page

college sports and *rules and regulations,* however, will yield a more manageable number. When you enter the key words, the computer will indicate the number of citations that have been found. You can then decide whether you want to narrow or widen your search.

✔ **Select the format for your citations.** With many databases, you can view just the bibliographic citation or an abstract; with others you can access the full text of an article.

✔ **Print out citations.** You can print out all the citations that the key words found or just the ones that seem most useful. (Sometimes you can also print out an abstract or the full text of an article.) Once you have printed out the citations, you can locate the articles in your college library, or you can use your library's Interlibrary Loan Service to obtain photocopies.

(6) Focused Research: Using Special Library Services

Your most valuable resource is your librarian, a trained professional whose business is knowing how to locate information. Before you begin any complicated research project, you should ask your librarian about any of the following special services you plan to use.

Interlibrary Loans If you need a book or periodical the library does not own, you can ask your librarian to arrange an **interlibrary loan.** Because interlibrary loans may take a few days to several weeks, you may not be able to take advantage of this service unless you initiate the loan early in your research.

Special Collections Your library may house **special collections** of books, manuscripts, or documents. In addition, churches, ethnic societies, historical trusts, and museums sometimes have materials you cannot find anywhere else, and your librarian may be able to get you permission to use these.

Government Documents Federal, state, and local governments publish a variety of print and electronic materials, ranging from consumer information to detailed statistical reports. A large university library may have a separate government documents area with its own catalog or index. The *Monthly Catalog of US Government Publications,* an index of many, but not all, publications of the federal government, may be located either there or among the indexes in the reference room. It is often available in electronic format as well as in print.

Vertical File   The **vertical file** contains pamphlets from a variety of organizations and interest groups, some requested by your library and others unsolicited. The file may also include newspaper clippings and other material collected by your librarians because of its relevance to the research interests of your college's population.

EXERCISE 1

Which library research sources would you consult to find the following information?

1. A discussion of Maxine Hong Kingston's *China Men* (1980)
2. Biographical information about the American anthropologist Margaret Mead
3. Books about Margaret Mead and her work
4. Information about the theories of Albert Einstein
5. Whether your college library has *The Human Use of Human Beings* by Norbert Wiener
6. How many pages there are in *On Death and Dying* by Elisabeth Kübler-Ross and how long the bibliography is
7. Where you could find other books on death and dying
8. Where you could find other books by Elisabeth Kübler-Ross
9. Articles about Walt Whitman's *Leaves of Grass*
10. Whether *Leaves of Grass* is presently available in a Norton Critical Edition

EXERCISE 2

Use the resources of your library to help you answer the following questions. Cite the source or sources of your answers.

1. Which government publication could give you information about how to heat your home with solar energy?
2. Which government agency could you contact to find out what is being done to help the aging receive proper nutrition?
3. At what address could you contact Bruce Evans, an American artist?
4. At what university does the physicist Stephen Hawking teach?
5. Which organizations could you contact to find out what is being done to prevent the killing of wolves in North America?
6. How could you get current information about the tobacco lobby?
7. Which government agency could tell you what government services are available to resident aliens?
8. At what address could you contact Harold Bloom, a scholar who does work on nineteenth-century English literature?
9. Is there a government pamphlet that gives information about buying a new car?
10. How could you get current information about the Job Corps?

39c   Gathering Information Outside the Library

In addition to accessing material through the library's resources, you can find valuable information through direct contact with individuals and organizations.

(1)   Finding Organizations

Numerous organizations offer literature, often free of charge, to interested parties. Your instructor or reference librarian may suggest the most appropriate organizations for you to contact, and local businesses, chambers of commerce, corporate public information departments, and government offices or publications may also refer you to helpful groups. The most useful source of information, however, is the *Encyclopedia of Associations,* which lists thousands of organizations by subject area. (If you have access to the Internet, check to see if an organization has a site on the **World Wide Web**.)

See
40c

(2)   Writing for Information

See
52a

Once you have identified an organization that may be able to supply useful information, your next step is to contact it directly and ask for its help. If the organization is local or has a toll-free number, call to request information. If not, you may want to write a **letter** (if you have enough time to wait for an answer). Whether you call or write, be sure you are prepared with the following information.

- The name of the person or department to contact
- The specific information you would like
- Why you want the information
- When you need it

(3)   Finding People

An important step in your research is locating people who can suggest reliable and up-to-date sources of information—or even provide you with some of that information. A meeting with your instructor may be all that you need to get started, or your instructor may refer you to someone else more familiar with your topic. Just one or two good contacts can help you establish a **research network:** your first contact suggests another, who in turn suggests two more.

Many excellent guides to experts in various fields are available in the reference section of your library. The following guides are among the most useful: *Who's Who among Black Americans, Who's Who and Where in Women's Studies, Who's Who in American Education, Who's Who in American Politics, Biographical Directory of the American Psychological Association,* and *Directory of the Modern Language Association.*

Remember too that your own college or university is likely to have a number of experts in particular subjects on its faculty. Your instructor or librarian can identify such experts for you. If you have access to the Internet, check to see if there is a **newsgroup** or **Listserv** where you can communicate with experts and others interested in your topic. Keep in mind, however, that not everyone online *is* an expert.

See
40b2-3

EXERCISE 3

You are beginning to gather information for the research projects outlined below. Where in your college or your community might you turn if you wanted to establish a research network? Write five questions that you would ask each person.

1. A paper for a biology course examining new developments in DNA recombinant research
2. A short paper for a history course in which you examine the usefulness of slave narratives for historical research
3. A research paper for a composition course in which you explore the possible future uses of virtual reality
4. A paper for a political science course about issues in a local election

(4) Observing People, Places, Objects, and Events

Your own observations can be a useful source of information. For example, an art or music paper may be enriched by information gathered during a visit to a museum or a concert; an education paper may include a report of a classroom observation; and a psychology or sociology paper may include observations of an individual's behavior or of group dynamics.

✔ CHECKLIST: MAKING OBSERVATIONS

✔ Determine in advance what information you hope to gain from your observations.
✔ Decide exactly what you want to observe and where you are going to observe it.
✔ Bring a small notepad or tape recorder so you can keep a record of your observations.

continued on the following page

continued from the previous page
✔ Bring any additional materials you may need—a camera, video-cassette recorder, or stopwatch, for example.
✔ Copy your observations onto note cards. Include the date, place, and time of your observations.

(5) Conducting an Interview

Interviews often give you material that you cannot get by any other means—for instance, biographical information, a firsthand account of an event, or the views of an expert on a particular subject.

The kinds of questions you ask in an interview depend on the information you are seeking. **Open-ended questions**—those intended to elicit general information—allow a respondent great flexibility in answering.

Do you think students today are motivated? Why or why not?

If you could change something in your life, what would it be?

Closed-ended questions—those designed to elicit specific information—enable you to zero in on a particular aspect of a subject.

Has your family become more or less religious over the past ten years? How do you account for this?

How much money did the government's cost-cutting programs actually save?

Can you give some examples of cost-effective measures?

Your interview questions should elicit detailed, useful responses. **Leading questions**—those phrased to elicit a certain answer—tend to make people defensive, and **vague questions**—those too general to elicit useful responses—can be confusing. **Dead-end questions**—questions that call for yes or no answers—yield limited information and therefore should always be accompanied by more specific follow-up questions.

The city intends to spend two billion dollars over the next ten years to rehabilitate the port area. What is your opinion of this plan? (good question)

Why should anyone favor the city's shortsighted plans to rehabilitate the port area? (leading question)

How do you feel about the port area? (vague question)

Do you think the port area should be developed? (dead-end question)

✔ CHECKLIST: CONDUCTING AN INTERVIEW

✔ Always make an appointment.
✔ Prepare a list of specific questions tailored to the subject matter and time limit of your interview.
✔ Do background reading about your topic. Be sure you do not ask for information you can easily find elsewhere.
✔ Have a pen and paper with you. If you want to tape the interview, get the respondent's permission in advance.
✔ Allow the person you are interviewing to complete an answer before you ask another question.
✔ Take notes, but continue to pay attention as you do so. Maintain eye contact, and occasionally nod or make comments to show you are interested and to encourage the respondent to continue.
✔ Pay attention to reactions of the respondent.
✔ Be willing to depart from your list of questions to ask follow-up questions.
✔ At the end of the interview, thank the respondent for his or her time and cooperation.
✔ Send a brief note of thanks.

 ## CONDUCTING AN E-MAIL INTERVIEW

Using E-mail to conduct an interview can save you a great deal of time. Before you send an E-mail message, however, make sure the person you want to contact is willing to cooperate. If the person agrees to be interviewed, send a short list of questions you would like the person to answer. After you have received the answers, send a message thanking the person for his or her cooperation.

(6) Conducting a Survey

If you are examining a contemporary social, psychological, or economic issue—the level of racism on your college campus, for instance—a **survey** of attitudes or opinions could be valuable.

Begin by identifying the group of people you will poll. This group can be a **convenient sample**—for example, people in your chemistry lecture—

or a **random sample**—names chosen from a telephone directory, for instance. When you choose a sample, your goal is to designate a population that is *representative*. You do not want, for example, a sample composed of all sophomores, all females, or all business majors—unless, of course, the goal of your survey is to poll only these groups.

You must have enough respondents to convince readers that your sample is *significant*. If you poll ten people in your French class about an issue of college policy, and your university has ten thousand students, you cannot expect your readers to be convinced by your results.

You should also be sure your questions are worded clearly and specifically designed to elicit the information you wish to get. Short-answer or multiple-choice questions, whose responses can be quantified, are much easier to classify than questions that call for paragraph-length answers.

If your population is your fellow students, you can slip questionnaires under their doors in the residence hall, or you can distribute them in class (with the instructor's permission). If your questionnaire is brief, allow respondents a specific amount of time to fill it out, and collect the forms yourself. If filling out forms on the spot will be too time consuming, request responses be returned to you—placed in a box set up in a central location, for instance.

 ## CONDUCTING AN E-MAIL SURVEY

If the students in a particular class have computers and E-mail accounts, you can distribute questionnaires electronically. Students can then send their completed questionnaires back to you by E-mail.

If you have a manageable number of questions and responses, you should be able to sort them yourself. If your questionnaire is complex, get a friend to help you with this step. Determining exactly what the results tell you is challenging and sometimes unpredictable. For example, the fact that only 20 percent of your respondents think there are not enough daytime activities on your campus may seem insignificant, but if that 20 percent includes nearly all of those who identified themselves as commuters, it *would* be significant.

✔ CHECKLIST: CONDUCTING A SURVEY

✔ Determine what you want to know.
✔ Select your sample.
✔ Design your questions.
✔ Type and photocopy the questionnaire.
✔ Distribute the questionnaires.
✔ Collect the questionnaires.
✔ Analyze your responses.
✔ Decide how to use the results in your paper.

CHAPTER 40

USING THE INTERNET FOR RESEARCH

40a Understanding the Internet

The **Internet** is a vast system of networks linking millions of computers. Because of its size and diversity, the Internet enables people from all over the world to share information and to communicate with one another. The Internet is an enormous research resource. On the Internet you will find newsgroups and Listservs, and you can communicate with your instructor and classmates via electronic mail or search the online catalogs of other libraries. You will also be able to connect to the World Wide Web, which contains text as well as pictures and sound. The Internet gives you access to a world of information—business, associations, research organizations, colleges and universities, the US government, community organizations, and even individuals—that you can use in your research and in your daily life.

 INFORMATION AVAILABLE ON THE INTERNET

- Timely data, including pending legislation, stock market quotes, research study findings, and other current information
- Information disseminated by individuals, institutions, and corporations that is not published by traditional media
- Online editions of newspapers and magazines

continued on the following page

continued from the previous page
- Internet-only publications about a wide variety of topics, including the Internet itself
- Catalogs and indexes for libraries and periodicals, which can help you locate print resources
- Reference material, including many encyclopedias and almanacs

40b Using the Internet

Before you can do research on the Internet, you should have a sense of the many tools that you can use to get information. Each of the tools described in this section has been developed to make the job of accessing a specific type of information easier.

(1) E-Mail

E-mail is a way of sending a message from one computer to another. It enables you to send messages to people all over the world quickly and economically. In addition, you can send a single message to many people as easily as you can to an individual.

You can use E-mail to talk to friends at different colleges or to relatives at home. You can communicate with professors, conduct interviews with experts in the field you are researching, or even transfer entire files from one computer to another.

NOTE: The information you get via E-mail is only as good as the person who is sending it to you. You must evaluate this type of information just as you would that from any other source.

 ACCESSING E-MAIL

All you need to send E-mail is the E-mail address of the person with whom you want to communicate and access to a communication network.

(2) Newsgroups

Newsgroups are discussion groups that are part of a network called the USENET system. Currently, thousands of newsgroups enable people from all over the world to carry on discussions about subjects from anthropology to stand-up comedy. These groups function like gigantic bulletin boards where users post messages that others read and respond to. Newsgroups are organized by topics and subtopics. For example, under the topic *science* are subtopics like *research methods, organic chemistry,* and *numeric analysis.*

You can use newsgroups to get specific information—facts, statistics, and opinions. (In fact, many postings on newsgroups are simply requests for information.) You can also use newsgroups to get a sense of how others will respond to your ideas before you use them in your paper.

At best, newsgroups provide a wealth of interesting and current information about a wide variety of subjects. At worst, newsgroups supply a daunting amount of information that users find difficult to evaluate. The best advice about newsgroups is to choose your material carefully, remembering to check the reliability of your sources in the same way you would check the reliability of any other source.

 ACCESSING NEWSGROUPS

You need a newsreader program to gain access to newsgroups. Most of the software that enables you to access the World Wide Web also includes a newsreader program.

(3) Listservs

Listservs are similar to newsgroups. Like newsgroups, they enable you to communicate with people who are interested in a topic, but unlike newsgroups, Listservs use E-mail (instead of a newsreader) to send and receive messages. There are two types of Listservs—*moderated* and *unmoderated*. In **moderated** groups, the Listserv selects information and sends it to subscribers in the form of an electronic digest. In **unmoderated** groups, all material, regardless of quality, is routed to subscribers as soon as it is received.

Like newsgroups, Listservs offer a tremendous amount of information about many topics, and subscribers can ask questions and join in conversations that interest them. However, members of Listservs can be overwhelmed with information. Once you subscribe to an unmoderated group, the host computer automatically sends you all the E-mail it receives. For this reason, you must be especially careful to check the accuracy of the information you receive.

ACCESSING LISTSERVS

Users must subscribe to the Listservs they want to join. To subscribe to a Listserv, you have to have the electronic address of the group (you can find a list of addresses at http://www.lszt.com). Once you have the electronic address, send an E-mail to the Listserv with the following message:

```
Subscribe <name of the list> <your first
name> <your last name>
```

Many Listserv groups will then send you an E-mail message saying that your subscription has been accepted.

(4) FTP

FTP (File Transfer Protocol) enables users to transfer documents at high speed from one computer to another. (Note that because many FTP files are compressed—transferred in a nonreadable form—you must have a program such as StuffIt Expander™ to make them readable.) There are two kinds of FTP—*full-service* and *anonymous*. **Full-service** FTP enables you to access a host computer and transfer documents from it to your own computer if you have a password. **Anonymous** FTP enables anyone (without a password) to access thousands of computers on the Internet.

With FTP, you can get full texts of books and articles, as well as pictures. In addition, you can download **freeware**—software that is in the public domain—and **shareware**—software that developers allow people to use for a fee.

ACCESSING FTP FILES

You need an access program such as *Archie* to search the Internet for FTP files. You can also download FTP files through a World

continued on the following page

continued from the previous page
Wide Web browser, certain Gopher sites, or an FTP transfer program such as *Fetch* for the Macintosh.

(5) Gopher

Gopher is a tool that enables users to navigate the Internet. By presenting items as a series of menu choices, Gopher gives you access to a wide variety of resources all over the world. You can get information about business, medicine, and engineering as well as up-to-the-minute information about the weather. Gopher is also able to provide material from archived newsgroups and electronic books and magazines. (Note that Gopher can display only text, not graphics or sound; Gopher will ask you if you want to download nontext files.)

Gopher can be used by individuals who are connected to a mainframe or campus **server** (a computer that provides information to other computers) and can retrieve FTP files. It enables users to retrieve menu information from any server that is in the worldwide Gopher network. Because it can display only text, Gopher is being displaced by the World Wide Web, which is easier to use and has a much more dynamic visual format. Even so, the amount of information to which Gopher has access makes it a valuable research tool.

 ACCESSING GOPHER

The tool *Veronica* enables you to do a key-word search of the various menus on the Gopher network. After a key word (or words) is entered into *Veronica*, it creates a menu of items that contain the key word or words. When you select an item on the *Veronica* menu, you are sent to the Gopher site that contains the key word.

(6) World Wide Web (the Web)

Like Gopher, the **World Wide Web** is a way of navigating the Internet. But unlike Gopher, the World Wide Web presents information in documents with *hypertext* links. **Hypertext** is a term that refers to the way information in a group of related documents is cross referenced or "linked" together. When you use a mouse to click on hypertext elements—usually words or images underlined in blue, like the cross-reference terms in this book—you are connected to other related documents. Thus, the World Wide Web provides an easy and stimulating way of accessing the Internet.

The Web enables you to connect to a vast variety of documents. For example, you can call up a **home page** or **Web page** (an individual document), a **Website** (a collection of Web pages), a newsgroup, or an FTP site. Although the Web does not give you access to the entire Internet, it does offer you a great deal of information. Government agencies, businesses, universities, libraries, newspapers and magazines, journals, and public interest groups, as well as individuals, all operate their own Websites. Each of these sites contains hypertext links that in turn will take you to other relevant sites. By using these links, you can "surf the Net," following your interests as you move from one document to another.

Web sites vary greatly in quality and reliability. Those operated by well-known institutions—the Smithsonian or the Library of Congress, for example—tend to have highly reliable information. Those operated by individuals—private Web pages or commercial advertisements, for example—are less reliable. Remember to <u>evaluate</u> each Website on the quality of its information, not on the quality of its graphics.

See
40d

ACCESSING THE WORLD WIDE WEB

You access the Web by means of a program called a **browser** that enables you to find information on the Internet by clicking on icons or buttons instead of by typing commands. Two of the most popular Web browsers, which display the full range of **hypermedia** (some combination of text, photos, graphics, sound, and video files integrated into a document) on the Web, are *Netscape Navigator* and *Microsoft Internet Explorer*.

40c Searching the Web

Begin your World Wide Web search by clicking on your Web browser icon or by selecting the browser from the list of programs on your computer. After the program has loaded, you will see a screen that looks similar to the *Netscape* home page shown in Figure 1.

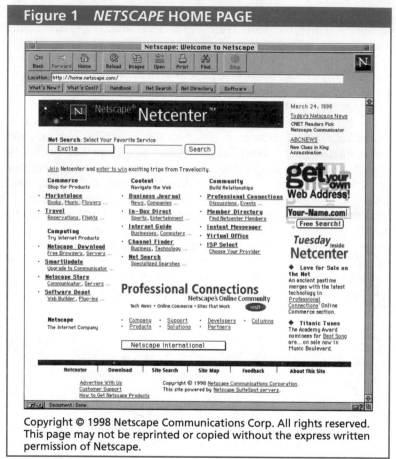

Figure 1   *NETSCAPE* HOME PAGE

There are two ways you can proceed: (1) you can search for an *address* or (2) you can search for *key words*.

(1)   Searching for an Address

The first way to access information on the Web is to enter a specific electronic address called a URL (uniform resource locator). (This is like looking for a book in the library once you have its call number.) You use this technique when you know a Web address and want to connect directly to it. Click the **Open** button at the top of the *Netscape* home page screen, and a dialogue box will open (see Figure 2).

Figure 2 DIALOGUE BOX FOR ELECTRONIC ADDRESS

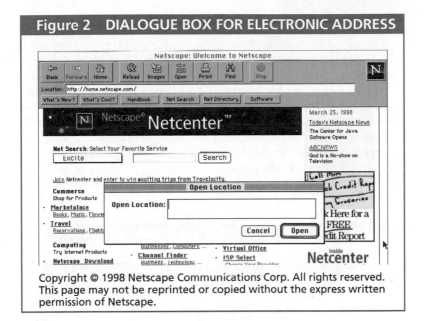

Then, enter the address (typically, a combination of letters, numbers, and symbols):

http://www.harbrace.com/english/

Click **Open** on the dialogue box, and *Netscape* will connect you to the page located at that address. From there, you use hypertext links to go to other parts of the document or to other sites that are related to the one you are exploring.

NOTE: Make sure you type the URL exactly as it appears, adding no spaces or punctuation marks that are not part of the address.

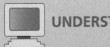 UNDERSTANDING URLs

The first section of the URL indicates the type of file being accessed. In the address above, *http* indicates that the file is in hypertext transfer protocol. After the colon and the two slashes is the name of the host site where the file is stored (www.harbrace.com/). The *www* tells the user that the Web site is on the World Wide Web, *harbrace* is the domain name, and *com* shows that this is a commercial institution. Following this section is the directory path to the file (english/).

(2)   Searching for Key Words

The second way to locate information on the Web is to do a **key-word search.** (This is like looking through the subject catalog in your college library.) You use this technique when you have a specific topic you want to explore. Begin your key-word search by connecting to a list of **search engines**—key-word search sites on the Web. When you click on the **Net Search** button at the top part of your Web browser's screen, the button will call up a page that lists some of the major Web search engines—for example, *Yahoo!, Excite, Infoseek,* and *Lycos.* Once you connect to the search engine by clicking on the one you want, type in one or more key words and click on the **Search** button. Figure 3 illustrates the *Excite* search engine.

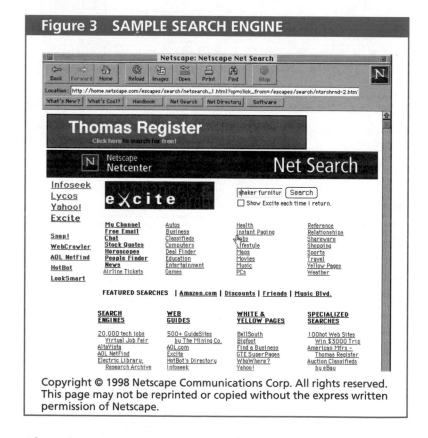

Figure 3   SAMPLE SEARCH ENGINE

After a short time, the search engine will generate a list of sites that contain your key word or words. Note that the screen pictured in Figure 4 displays the top 10 sites for information about Shaker furniture. To the left of each result is *Excite's* relevancy rating (represented as a percentage). The higher the percentage the more likely the site is relevant to your key-word search. You can reduce the number of sites (or hits) by customizing your search—for example, by using words such as *and, or,* or *not* to restrict your search (*Shaker furniture and museums*).

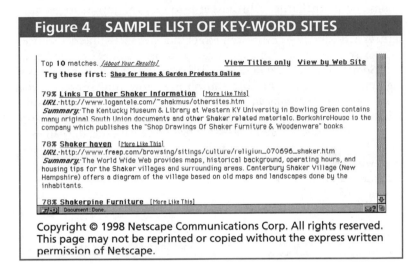

Figure 4   SAMPLE LIST OF KEY-WORD SITES

Copyright © 1998 Netscape Communications Corp. All rights reserved. This page may not be reprinted or copied without the express written permission of Netscape.

After connecting to the documents you want by clicking on them, you can evaluate their content and explore hypertext links to other pages.

ACCESSING SUBJECT-TREE DIRECTORIES

If you are interested in a general topic, such as health or education, *subject-tree directories* can be an alternative to search engines for finding information on the World Wide Web. **Subject-tree directories** organize Web sites through menus of topics and increasingly specific subtopics. Many search engines, such as *Yahoo!, Infoseek, Excite, Lycos, WebCrawler,* and the *World Wide Web Virtual Library,* offer subject-tree directories on their main pages. (For an example of a subject-tree directory, see Figure 3.)

40d Evaluating Internet Sources

Critical evaluation of material on the Internet is even more important than evaluation of more traditional sources of information, such as books and journal articles, because it is so easy for anyone to get anything, regardless of quality, published on the Internet. Because of the Internet's accessibility—anyone can establish a Website—Internet sources may present theories, rumors, hearsay, wild speculation, or even lies as fact. Sometimes it is hard to distinguish such unfounded opinions from legitimate information because you do not know your source as you would if you were dealing with a reputable magazine or journal. To complicate matters further, unscrupulous individuals can (and do) represent themselves as respected authorities—sometimes even using the names of other people—and make claims that seem credible but are not. Therefore, whenever you find information on the Internet that seems useful for your research, you must do some detective work to determine its legitimacy.

✔ CHECKLIST: EVALUATING INTERNET SOURCES

✔ **Where does the information come from?** An article, for example, may come from a scholarly source, or it may be the personal opinion of an individual with no expertise in the area he or she is discussing.

✔ **Is the author of the source identified, or is the source anonymous?** Even though you should approach any source with skepticism, you should be especially skeptical of an anonymous source.

✔ **Is the sponsoring institution reputable?** Can you trust the institution to be fair and impartial?

✔ **Is the author of the Web page trying to sell something?** Is the information biased, slanted, or intentionally misleading?

✔ **Is the text itself credible?** Does it contain evidence to support its claims? If authorities are quoted or paraphrased, does the text supply information about the credentials of the authorities?

✔ **Do slick graphics, sound, or video mask uninformed opinion or faulty logic?** Don't be misled by technologically sophisticated sites that do not offer you any way to evaluate the accuracy of the information presented.

DETERMINING THE LEGITIMACY OF AN INTERNET SOURCE

Sometimes—for example, when an Internet source is anonymous or when you are not familiar with the sponsoring institution—you have to take measures to determine the legitimacy of a source. The following strategies can help you to get information about a questionable document.

Post a Query To help you evaluate information from a newsgroup or a Listserv, ask others in the group what they know about the source and its author.

Follow the Links Follow the hypertext links in a document to other documents. If the links take you to legitimate sources of information, you know that the writer is aware of these sources.

Do a Web Search Do a search using the name of the writer or the writer's affiliation as key words. Other documents by the same writer or citations in other works can give you an idea of the legitimacy of your source.

 40e Netiquette

Proper behavior is as necessary on the Internet as it is in face-to-face interactions. The term **netiquette**—coined from the words *net* and *etiquette*—refers to the guidelines that responsible users of the Internet follow. When you use the Internet—especially E-mail—keep the following rules in mind.

✔ CHECKLIST: OBSERVING NETIQUETTE

✔ **Don't Shout** All-uppercase letters indicate that a person is SHOUTING. Not only is this immature, but it is also distracting and irritating.

✔ **Watch Your Tone** Make sure you actually send the message you intend to convey. What may sound humorous to you may seem sarcastic or impolite to someone else.

continued on the following page

continued from the previous page

✔ **Be Careful What You Write** Remember, anything you put in writing will be instantly sent to the address or addresses you have designated. Once you hit *Send* it's too late to call back your message. For this reason, you should treat an E-mail message or a posting as you would a written letter. Take the time to proofread and to consider carefully what you have written.

✔ **Respect the Privacy of Others** Do not forward or post a message that you have received unless you have permission from the sender to do so.

✔ **Do Not Flame** When you **flame,** you send an insulting electronic message. At best this response is immature; at worst it is disrespectful.

✔ **Make Sure You Use the Correct Electronic Address** Be certain that your message goes to the right person. Nothing is more embarrassing than sending a communication to the wrong address.

✔ **Use Your Computer Facility Ethically and Responsibly** Do not use computers in public labs for personal communications or for entertainment. Not only is this a misuse of the facility, but it also ties up equipment that others may be waiting to use.

40f Selected Research Sites

City.Net—http://www.city.net Information on travel, entertainment, business, government, and community services for over two thousand cities worldwide, accessed alphabetically by region or country.

Electronic Frontier Foundation—http://www.eff.org Information on Internet-related issues such as freedom of speech, censorship and privacy issues, computers and academic freedom, free expression, and social responsibility. Weekly online newsletter and links to other online publications and information.

The English Server—http://english-server.hss.cmu.edu Features academic resources for students and faculty in fiction, drama, film and television, history, technical communication, government, philosophy, music, languages, race, rhetoric, gender and sexuality, and feminism.

Internet Public Library—http://ipl.sils.umich.edu/ Librarians in the Reference Center answer research questions, providing factual information and reference to online and print sources. Also offers Youth Services, Teen Services, Services for Librarians and Information Professionals, a Classroom, Exhibit Hall, and Reading Room.

Library of Congress—http://lcweb.loc.gov Searchable LOCIS (Library of Congress Information System) index of books published worldwide, publications, online historical collections, research links, and searchable indexes for federal, state, foreign, and international government.

The Monster Magazine List—http://enews.com/monster/ index. html Links to popular magazines online. Titles can be accessed by key-word searching or by subject list.

Online Dictionaries—http://www.bucknell.edu/~rbeard/diction. html Comprehensive list of online dictionaries that allows the user to choose the language, links to acronym dictionaries, *Roget's Thesaurus,* synonym/antonym/homonym dictionaries, multilingual dictionary sites, and an Index of Dictionary Indexes.

Pathfinder—http://pathfinder.com Time Warner's comprehensive site of online versions of its publications, including news, world events, TV and film, entertainment, business, sports, health, travel, and technology.

Purdue University Online Writing Lab (OWL)—http://owl. english.purdue.edu Covers all the grammar basics, including punctuation, sentence structure, parts of speech, research papers, citing sources, spelling, English as a second language, general writing concerns, résumés, and business and professional writing.

Research-It!—http://www.iTools.com/research-it/research-it. html Provides a table with search engines for a dictionary, thesaurus, acronyms, quotations, language translators, King James Bible, currency exchange, stocks, postal ZIP codes, and package tracking for UPS and Federal Express. Links to online maps, the *CIA Factbook,* and telephone directories.

THOMAS—http://thomas.loc.gov Current congressional legislation and documents; includes the *Congressional Record,* the Constitution, links to sites for the House of Representatives and Senate, the Government Printing Office (GPO), and the General Accounting Office (GAO).

Virtual Computer Library—http://www.utexas.edu/computer/ vcl Comprehensive guide to information about computers on the Internet. Searchable database. Links to academic computing centers at major universities and journals with full-text articles.

The World Fact Book—http://www.odci.gov/cia/publications/ nsolo/wfb-all.html Compiled by the Central Intelligence Agency (CIA); has information on geography, international disputes, climate, terrain, environment, people, government, legal systems, economy, transportation, communications, and defense systems for nearly every country in the world. Reference maps for major world regions.

40g Important Computer Terms

archive   A collection of several files compressed and combined into one file. Used to save storage space and file transfer time.

ASCII   Acronym for "American Standard Code for Information Interchange." The dominant character set encoding of modern computers.

back up   To duplicate a document, usually on a portable disk. You should always back up your documents.

baud   In popular use (although not technically correct) as data transfer speed measured in bits per second. A 2,400-baud connection will transfer 2,400 bits per second, a 9,600-baud connection will transfer 9,600 bits per second, etc.

BBS   Abbreviation for "bulletin board system," an electronic bulletin board system; that is, a message database where people can log in and leave messages for others grouped into topic groups. The thousands of local BBS systems in operation throughout the United States are usually operated as a hobby.

bells and whistles   Features added to a program or system to make it more fun to use.

bit   Binary digit, the smallest unit of information in a binary computer, usually represented by *on* or *off*, or numerically by *0* or *1*.

BITNET   Acronym for "Because It's Time NETwork," a collection of IBM mainframe computers located mostly at universities and connected via a wide area network.

boot   To start a computer and initialize the operating system.

bug   A problem in a software application or system program that causes malfunctions.

copy   A command that makes it possible for the user to reproduce either a whole file or part of a file.

crash   A sudden, catastrophic system or program failure.

cursor   The blinking marker on a computer screen. The cursor is the entry point for all text you create on a computer screen. As you type, text will appear immediately to the left of the cursor.

delete   A command that permanently removes a portion of text from a document or a complete *file* from a *disk*.

document   A series of computer-generated characters—usually letters and numbers—stored on a *disk*. Each document is given a name so the computer can find it when commanded to do so. When you write an essay (or part of an essay) and *save* it, you create a *document* (sometimes called a *file*) that remains on the floppy disk as well as in the computer's hard drive and can be accessed again later to change, display, or print.

download   To transfer a file or other data from a remote system to the local system; a means of receiving data or files.

E-mail   Abbreviation for "electronic mail."

emoticons   Symbols used in E-mail communication to indicate emotions.

Fidonet   A worldwide network of personal computers for the exchange of E-mail.

forum   A BBS discussion group.

hard copy   The printed version of material produced on a computer. A hard copy enables you to reconstruct your work if you lose or damage your floppy disk or accidentally erase or destroy your file.

hard drive   The internal storage medium in a computer.

insert   A command that adds text to a document.

Internet   A worldwide network of computers at educational, corporate, and government and military sites.

modem   Modulator-demodulator; a device used to transmit data over telephone lines.

mouse   A hand-held device for moving the cursor around on the screen in order to execute certain commands.

move   A command that relocates text from one place to another in the same document or from one document to another document.

MS-DOS   Abbreviation for "Microsoft Disk Operating System." The operating system that underlies virtually all IBM compatible and DOS systems.

network   Two or more computers connected to one another so users can exchange information.

PC   Abbreviation for "personal computer."

post   To send a public message to a mailing list or newsgroup on a public bulletin board system.

RAM   Acronym for "Random Access Memory."

replace   The command—usually used along with the *search* or *find* command—that substitutes one character string for another. The *replace* command allows you to make quick, systematic changes in your writing. For example, if you decided to change the name of a character in a short story, you could instruct the computer to replace every instance of *Jim* with *Frederick*.

save   The command that makes a permanent copy of a document on either a floppy or hard disk. Until you save a document, it exists only as electronic impulses in the memory of your computer. If there should be an accidental power failure, all text produced since the last time you saved will be permanently lost. Get in the habit of using the *save* command regularly.

search   A command that looks for a designated character string—usually a word or a group of words chosen by the user—in a file. The command can help you find places in your writing where you might want to make changes or check for errors. For example, you can tell your computer to search for the pronouns *he, him,* and *his* so that you can be sure you have avoided sexist language.

server   A computer that performs a service for other computers, such as file storage and distribution of E-mail.

software   A program, written in a computer language, that tells a computer what to do and how to do it.

upload   To transfer a file or other data from the local system to a remote system; a means of sending data or files.

WYSIWYG   Acronym for "what you see is what you get." A graphic interface that shows documents as they will appear printed, with all special characters and fonts, on the screen.

SOME ABBREVIATIONS CURRENTLY USED ON E-MAIL

CIS   Consumer Information Service (of CompuServe)
RTFM   Read the forgotten manual

continued on the following page

600

continued from the previous page

PITA	Pain in the acronym
BTW	By the way
BFN	Bye, for now
TSR	Terminate-and-stay-resident program
OTOH	On the other hand
FWIW	For what it's worth
RSN	Real soon now
OIC	Oh, I see!
IMHO	In my humble opinion [the speaker is never humble]
IMCO	In my considered opinion
G,D,&R	Grinning, ducking, and running
OOTB	Out of the box

CHAPTER 41

SUMMARIZING, PARAPHRASING, QUOTING, AND SYNTHESIZING

See
7a
Once you have located sources of information for your paper, your next step is to begin to take notes. At this point, your emphasis shifts from looking *for* sources to looking *at* sources. In the process, you use **active reading** strategies to identify and highlight key ideas and to record significant relationships. As you do so, you make judgments about the writer's ideas so you can formulate a critical response to the material.

41a Taking Notes

Although it may seem like a sensible strategy, copying down the words of a source is the least efficient way to take notes. Experienced researchers know that a better strategy is to take notes that combine summary and paraphrase with direct quotation. By doing so, they make sure they understand both the material and its relevance to their research. This in turn makes it possible for them to synthesize their sources by combining borrowed material with their own ideas in an original and coherent piece of writing.

(1) Writing a Summary

A **summary** (sometimes called a *précis*) is a brief restatement in your own words of the main idea of a passage, article, or book. When you write a summary, you condense the writer's ideas into a few concise sentences, taking care not to misrepresent his or her views. You do not, however, include your own interpretations or opinions of the writer's ideas.

A summary is always much shorter than the original because it omits the examples, asides, analogies, and rhetorical strategies that writers use to add emphasis and interest. Just how short a summary should be depends on the length and complexity of the source and on the use you are going to make of it in your paper.

Before you write your summary, read your source until you understand it, paying particular attention to its thesis statement, topic sentences, and supporting details. Sometimes—especially with complicated material—you will find it helpful to highlight the source or list its key points.

Once you have isolated a source's key points, try to summarize its main idea in a single sentence. This is not always easy. You may have to write several versions of the sentence before you find one that accurately summarizes the original source.

Next, draft the summary, beginning with this sentence. As you write, use your own words, not the exact language or phrasing of the source or the writer's specific examples or analogies. If you think it is necessary to quote a distinctive word or phrase, place it within quotation marks; if you do not do so, you will be committing **plagiarism**. Finally, remember that your summary should include only the ideas of your source, not your own interpretations or opinions.

See 42a

After you have written a draft of your summary, make sure that it conveys both the meaning and spirit of the original. Make certain you have not inadvertently used any of the author's exact words without quotation marks. (As a rule you can use the proper nouns, simple words, or technical terms found in the original source without enclosing them within quotation marks.) Then, check to see that you have included smooth transitions. When you are finished, add documentation to identify the source you have summarized.

✔ Reread your source until you understand it.
✔ Write a one-sentence restatement of the main idea.
✔ Draft your summary, beginning with this sentence. Use your own words, not the words or phrasing of the source. Include quotation marks where necessary.
✔ Revise your summary, making sure that it accurately reflects the source and that you have not included any of your own ideas or opinions.
✔ Add transitions where necessary.
✔ Add appropriate documentation.

Compare the following three passages. The first is an original source, the second is an unacceptable summary, and the third is an acceptable summary.

ORIGINAL SOURCE: Sudo, Phil, "Freedom of Hate Speech?" *Scholastic Update* 124.14 (1992) 17–20.

Today, the First Amendment faces challenges from groups who seek to limit expressions of racism and bigotry. A growing number of legislatures have passed rules against "hate speech"—[speech] that is offensive on the basis of race, ethnicity, gender, or sexual orientation. The rules are intended to promote respect for all people and protect the targets of hurtful words, gestures, or actions.

Legal experts fear these rules may wind up diminishing the rights of all citizens. "The bedrock principle [of our society] is that government may never suppress free speech simply because it goes against what the community would like to hear," says Nadine Strossen, president of the American Civil Liberties Union and professor of constitutional law at New York University Law School. In recent years, for example, the courts have upheld the right of neo-Nazis to march in Jewish neighborhoods; protected cross-burning as a form of free expression; and allowed protesters to burn the American flag. The offensive, ugly, distasteful, or repugnant nature of expression is not reason enough to ban it, courts have said.

But advocates of limits on hate speech note that certain kinds of expression fall outside of First Amendment protection. Courts have ruled that "fighting words"—words intended to provoke immediate violence—and speech that creates a clear and present danger are not protected forms of expression. As the classic argument goes, freedom of speech does not give you the right to yell "Fire!" in a crowded theater.

UNACCEPTABLE SUMMARY: Today, the First Amendment faces challenges from lots of people. Some of these people are legal experts who want to let Nazis march in Jewish neighborhoods. Other people have the sense to realize that some kinds of speech fall outside of First Amendment protection because they create a clear and present danger (Sudo 17).

The unacceptable summary above uses words and phrases from the original without placing them in quotation marks. This use constitutes plagiarism. In addition, the summary expresses its writer's opinion ("Other people have the sense to realize . . .").

Compare the unacceptable summary with the following acceptable summary. Notice that the acceptable summary presents an accurate, objective overview of the original without using its exact language or phrasing. (The one distinctive phrase borrowed from the source is placed within quotation marks.)

ACCEPTABLE SUMMARY: The right to freedom of speech, guaranteed by the First Amendment, is becoming more difficult to defend. Some people think that stronger laws against the use of "hate speech" weaken the First Amendment. But others argue that some kinds of speech remain exempt from this protection (Sudo 17).

(2) Writing a Paraphrase

A summary conveys just the essence of a source; a **paraphrase** gives a *detailed* restatement of all a source's important ideas. It not only indicates the source's key points, but it also reflects its order, tone, and emphasis. Consequently, a paraphrase can be as long as the source. Like a summary, a paraphrase should present the source's ideas, not your own opinions or interpretations of those ideas.

The purpose of a paraphrase is to restate a source's ideas in order to clarify its meaning. You use a paraphrase only when you want to present a comprehensive explanation of a source to readers. For this reason, you should summarize—not paraphrase—extremely long passages or entire books or articles. A side-by-side comparison of a summary and a paraphrase of the passage discussed in the previous section appears below.

SUMMARY

The right to freedom of speech, guaranteed by the First Amendment, is becoming more difficult to defend. Some people feel that stronger laws against "hate speech" weaken the First Amendment. But others argue that some kinds of speech remain exempt from this protection (Sudo 17).

PARAPHRASE

Many groups want to limit the right of free speech guaranteed by the First Amendment to the Constitution. They do this to protect certain groups of people from "hate speech." Women, people of color, and gay men and lesbians, for example, may find that hate speech is used to intimidate them. Legal scholars are afraid that even though the rules against hate speech are well intentioned, such rules undermine our freedom of speech. As Nadine Strossen, president of the American Civil Liberties Union, says, "The bedrock principle [of our society] is that government may never suppress free speech simply because it goes against what the community would like to hear" (Sudo 17). People who support speech codes point out, however, that certain types of speech are not protected by the First Amendment—for example, words that create a "clear and present danger" or that would lead directly to violence (Sudo 17).

Before you begin to draft your paraphrase, carefully read the original. Because a paraphrase restates the *exact* points of the source, you may wish to outline the source before you start to write.

Next, draft your paraphrase, following the order, tone, and emphasis of the original. Make certain you use your own words, except when you want to quote to give readers a sense of the original. If you do include quotations, circle the quotation marks so you will not forget to include them when you revise your paraphrase. Try not to look at the source when you write—use the language and syntax that come naturally to you—and avoid duplicating the wording or sentence structure of the original.

Once you finish writing a draft of your paraphrase, revise it carefully, making sure that it is accurate and complete and that you have not inadvertently used the language, phrasing, or sentence patterns of the source. Make certain you have covered all important points and included quotation marks where they are required. As you revise, add transitions where necessary to make your paraphrase clear and coherent. Remember to document all quotations from your source as well as the entire paraphrase.

✔ CHECKLIST: WRITING A PARAPHRASE

✔ Reread your source until you understand it.
✔ Outline your source if necessary.
✔ Draft your paraphrase, following the order, tone, and emphasis of the original.
✔ Revise your paraphrase, making sure it reflects the order and emphasis of the original. Be sure you do not use the words or phrasing of the original without quoting them.
✔ Add transitions where necessary.
✔ Add appropriate documentation.

Following are an original passage, an unacceptable paraphrase, and an acceptable paraphrase.

ORIGINAL SOURCE: Turkle, Sherry. *The Second Self: Computers and the Human Spirit.* New York: Simon & Schuster, 1984: 83–84.

When you play a video game, you enter into the world of the programmers who made it. You have to do more than identify with a character on a screen. You must act for it. Identification through action has a special kind of hold. Like playing a sport, it puts people into a highly focused and highly charged state of mind. For many people, what is being pursued in the video game is not just a score, but an altered state.

606

The pilot of a race car does not dare to take . . . attention off the road. The imperative of total concentration is part of the high. Video games demand the same level of attention. They can give people the feeling of being close to the edge because, as in a dangerous situation, there is no time for rest and the consequences of wandering attention [are] dire. With pinball, a false move can be recuperated. The machine can be shaken, the ball repositioned. In a video game, the program has no tolerance for error, no margin for safety. Players experience their every movement as instantly translated into game action. The game is relentless in its demand that all other time stop and in its demand that the player take full responsibility for every act, a point that players often sum up [with] the phrase "One false move and you're dead."

UNACCEPTABLE PARAPHRASE: Playing a video game, you enter into a new world—one the programmer of the game made. You can't just play a video game; you have to identify with it. Your mind goes to a new level, and you are put into a highly focused state of mind.

Just as you would if you were driving a race car or piloting a plane, you must not let your mind wander. Video games demand complete attention. But the sense that at any time you could make one false move and lose is their attraction—at least for me. That is why I like video games more than pinball. Pinball is just too easy. You can always recover. By shaking the machine or quickly operating the flippers, you can save the ball. Video games, however, are not so easy to control. Usually, one slip means that you lose (Turkle 83–84).

The unacceptable paraphrase above does little more than echo the phrasing and syntax of the original, borrowing words and expressions without enclosing them in quotation marks. This constitutes **plagiarism**. In addition, the paraphrase digresses into a discussion of the writer's own views about the relative merits of pinball and video games.

See 42b

Although the acceptable paraphrase below follows the order and emphasis of the original—and even quotes a key phrase—its wording and sentence structure are very different from those of the source. It conveys the key ideas of the source and maintains an objective tone.

ACCEPTABLE PARAPHRASE: The programmer defines the reality of the video game. The game forces a player to merge with the character who is part of the game. The character becomes an extension of the player, who determines how he or she will think and act. Like sports, video games put a player into a very intense "altered state" of mind that is the most important part of the activity (Turkle 83).

The total involvement they demand is what attracts many people to video games. These games can simulate the thrill of participating in a dangerous activity without any of the risks. There is no time for rest and no opportunity to correct errors of judgment. Unlike video games, pinball games are forgiving. A player can—within certain limits—manipulate a pinball game to correct minor mistakes. With video games, however, every move has immediate consequences. The game forces a player to adapt to its rules and to act carefully. One mistake can cause the death of the character on the screen and the end of the game (Turkle 83–84).

(3) Recording Quotations

When you **quote**, you copy a writer's remarks exactly as they appear in a source, word for word and punctuation mark for punctuation mark, enclosing the borrowed words in quotation marks.

 RECORDING QUOTATIONS

When recording quotations in your notes, be careful not to leave out quotation marks. In fact, you should circle the quotation marks so you will notice them when you transfer them from your notes to your paper.

As a rule, you should not quote extensively in a research paper. The use of one quotation after another interrupts the flow of your discussion and gives readers the impression that your paper is just a collection of other people's ideas. Quote only when something vital would be lost otherwise, and then use only those words and phrases that obviously support your points. Before you include any quotation, ask yourself whether your purpose would be better served if you used your own words.

✔ CHECKLIST: WHEN TO QUOTE

✔ Quote when a source's wording or phrasing is so distinctive that a summary or paraphrase would diminish its impact.
✔ Quote when a source's words lend authority to your presentation. (If a writer is a recognized expert on your subject, his or her words are as convincing as expert testimony at a trial.)

continued on the following page

continued from the previous page
✔ Quote when a writer's words are so concise that paraphrase would create a long, clumsy, or incoherent passage or would change the meaning of the original.
✔ Quote when you are going to disagree with a source. Using a source's exact words assures readers you are being fair.

EXERCISE 1

Choose a debatable issue from the following list.

- Noncitizens' rights to free public education
- Helmet requirements for motorcycle riders
- Community service requirements for high school students
- Making English the official language of the United States
- The use of animals in medical experiments
- A constitutional amendment prohibiting the defacing of the American flag

Write a one-sentence *summary* of your own position on the issue; then, interview a classmate and write a one-sentence *summary* of his or her position on the same issue. Be sure each sentence includes the reasons that support the position. Next, locate a source that discusses your issue, and write a *paraphrase* of the writer's position, quoting a few distinctive phrases. Finally, write a single sentence that compares and contrasts the three positions.

EXERCISE 2

Assume that in preparation for a paper on the effects of the rise of the suburbs, you read the following passage from the book *Great Expectations: America and the Baby Boom Generation* by Landon Y. Jones. Reread the passage, and then write a brief summary. Next, paraphrase one paragraph, quoting only those words and phrases you consider especially distinctive.

As an internal migration, the settling of the suburbs was phenomenal. In the twenty years from 1950 to 1970, the population of the suburbs doubled from 36 million to 72 million. No less than 83 percent of the total population growth in the United States during the 1950s was in the suburbs, which were growing fifteen times faster than any other segment of the country. As people packed and moved, the national mobility rate leaped by 50 percent. The only other comparable influx was the wave of European immigrants to the United States around the turn of the century. But as

Fortune pointed out, more people moved to the suburbs every year than had ever arrived on Ellis Island.

By now, bulldozers were churning up dust storms as they cleared the land for housing developments. More than a million acres of farmland were plowed under every year during the 1950s. Millions of apartment-dwelling parents with two children were suddenly realizing that two children could be doubled up in a spare bedroom, but a third child cried loudly for something more. The proportion of new houses with three or more bedrooms, in fact, rose from one-third in 1947 to three-quarters in 1954. The necessary *Lebensraum* could only be found in the suburbs. There was a housing shortage, but young couples armed with VA and FHA loans built their dream homes with easy credit and free spending habits that were unthinkable to the babyboom grandparents, who shook their heads with the Depression still fresh in their memories. Of the 13 million homes built in the decade before 1958, 11 million of them—or 85 percent—were built in the suburbs. Home ownership rose 50 percent between 1940 and 1950, and another 50 percent by 1960. By then, one-fourth of *all* housing in the United States had been built in the fifties. For the first time, more Americans owned homes than rented them.

We were becoming a land of gigantic nurseries. The biggest were built by Abraham Levitt, the son of poor Russian-Jewish immigrants, who had originally built houses for the Navy during the war. The first of three East Coast Levittowns went up on the potato fields of Long Island. Exactly $7900—or $60 a month and no money down—bought you a Monopoly-board bungalow with four rooms, attic, washing machine, outdoor barbecue, and a television set built into the wall. The 17,447 units eventually became home to 82,000 people, many of whom were pregnant or wanted to be. In a typical story on the suburban explosion, one magazine breathlessly described a volleyball game of nine couples in which no less than five of the women were expecting.

41b Integrating Your Notes into Your Writing

Summaries, paraphrases, and quotations cannot simply be dropped into your paper. You must weave them smoothly into your discussion, adding analysis or explanation to show why you are using each source's words or ideas. As you integrate borrowed material into your paper, be sure to differentiate your ideas from those of your sources.

(1) Integrating Quotations

Quotations should be smoothly worked into your sentences and introduced by **identifying tags**. They should never be awkwardly dropped into the paper, leaving the exact relationship between the quotation and the point you are making unclear, as in the following example.

See
29e1

> UNACCEPTABLE: For the Amish, the public school system represents a problem. "A serious problem confronting Amish society from the viewpoint of the Amish themselves is the threat of absorption into mass society through the values promoted in the public school system" (Hostetler 193).

Instead, use a brief introductory remark to provide a context for each quotation, quoting only those words you need to make your point.

> ACCEPTABLE: For the Amish, the public school system is a problem because it represents "the threat of absorption into mass society" (Hostetler 193).

Whenever possible, use a **running acknowledgment** to introduce the source of the quotation into the text. Running acknowledgments are particularly helpful when you are using several sources in the same section of your paper.

> RUNNING ACKNOWLEDGMENT: As John Hostetler points out, the public school system represents "the threat of absorption into mass society" (193).

NOTE: Whenever you use a quotation by an expert to support your opinion, you can lend authority to your statement by establishing his or her expertise in the running acknowledgment (According to John A. Hostetler, a noted authority on Amish life . . .).

Trying to integrate quotations seamlessly into your writing can create problems. Solutions for some of these problems are discussed below.

Substitutions or Additions within Quotations   When you have to change or add a word to make a quotation fit your paper, acknowledge your changes by enclosing them in brackets (not parentheses).

> ORIGINAL QUOTATION: "Immediately after her wedding, she and her husband followed tradition and went to visit almost everyone who attended the wedding" (Hostetler 122).

> QUOTATION REVISED TO MAKE VERB TENSES CONSISTENT: Nowhere is the Amish dedication to tradition more obvious than in the events surrounding marriage. Right after the wedding celebration the Amish

bride and groom "[follow] tradition and [go] to visit almost everyone who [has attended] the wedding" (Hostetler 122).

QUOTATION REVISED TO SUPPLY AN ANTECEDENT FOR A PRONOUN: "Immediately after her wedding, [Sarah] and her husband followed tradition and went to visit almost everyone who attended the wedding" (Hostetler 122).

QUOTATION REVISED TO CHANGE A CAPITAL TO A LOWERCASE LETTER: The strength of the Amish community is illustrated by the fact that "[i]mmediately after her wedding, she and her husband followed tradition and went to visit almost everyone who attended the wedding" (Hostetler 122).

See
33f1
Omissions within Quotations When you delete unnecessary or irrelevant words, substitute an **ellipsis** (three spaced periods) for the deleted words.

ORIGINAL: "Not only have the Amish built and staffed their own elementary and vocational schools, but they have gradually organized on local, state, and national levels to cope with the task of educating their children" (Hostetler 206).

QUOTATION REVISED TO ELIMINATE UNNECESSARY WORDS: "Not only have the Amish built and staffed their own elementary and vocational schools, but they have gradually organized . . . to cope with the task of educating their children" (Hostetler 206).

NOTE: When you omit a word or phrase at the *beginning* of a quoted passage, do not use an ellipsis to indicate the omission.

 CLOSE-UP OMISSIONS WITHIN QUOTATIONS

Be sure you do not misrepresent quoted material when you shorten it. The material you delete should not change the meaning of the passage you are using. For example, do not say, "the Amish have managed to maintain . . . their culture" when the original quotation is "the Amish have managed to maintain *parts of* their culture."

See
32d2
Long Quotations Occasionally, you may want to quote a **long prose passage** from a source. Set off a quotation of more than four typed lines by indenting it ten spaces (or one inch) from the margin. Double-space,

do not use quotation marks, and introduce the long quotation with a colon. If you are quoting a single paragraph, do not indent the first line. If you are quoting more than one paragraph, indent the first line of each complete paragraph an additional three spaces (or one-quarter inch).

According to Hostetler, the Amish were not always hostile to public education:

> The one-room rural elementary school served the Amish community well in a number of ways. As long as it was a public school, it stood midway between the Amish community and the world. Its influence was tolerable, depending upon the degree of influence the Amish were able to bring to the situation. (196)

 CLOSE-UP

USING LONG QUOTATIONS

Long quotations can be distracting, so you should use them sparingly. They interrupt your discussion and, when used excessively, give the impression that you have relied too heavily on the words of others. Use long quotations only when you want to reproduce an author's style or thought process.

(2) Integrating Paraphrases and Summaries

Introduce your paraphrases and summaries with running acknowledgments and end them with appropriate documentation. By integrating your notes into your paper in this way, you make certain that your readers are able to differentiate your ideas from those of your sources.

MISLEADING (IDEAS OF SOURCE BLENDED WITH IDEAS OF WRITER.): Art can be used to uncover many problems that children have at home, in school, or with their friends. For this reason, many therapists use art therapy extensively. Children's view of themselves in society is often reflected by their art style. A cramped, crowded art style using only a portion of the paper shows their limited role (Alschuler 260).

REVISED WITH RUNNING ACKNOWLEDGMENT (IDEAS OF SOURCE DIF-FERENTIATED FROM IDEAS OF WRITER.): Art can be used to uncover many problems that children have at home, in school, or with their friends. For this reason, many therapists use art therapy extensively. <u>According to William Alschuler in *Art and Self-Image*,</u> children's view of themselves in society is often reflected by their art style. A cramped, crowded art style using only a portion of the paper shows their limited role (260).

As you integrate paraphrases and summaries into your paper, make the relationship between your ideas and the ideas of your sources clear by using appropriate transitional words and phrases. Not only will such words and phrases ensure that your paraphrases and summaries are smoothly woven into your discussion, they will also clarify your reason for using them.

CONFUSING: The chain of events that led to Richard Nixon's resignation is well known. According to Woodward and Bernstein, both Alexander Haig and Henry Kissinger urged Nixon to cut his ties with his aides (366).

REVISED: The chain of events that led to Richard Nixon's resignation is well known. <u>First,</u> according to Woodward and Bernstein, both Alexander Haig and Henry Kissinger urged Nixon to cut his ties with his aides (366). <u>Next,</u> . . .

 CLOSE-UP **INTEGRATING YOUR NOTES INTO YOUR WRITING**

To avoid monotonous sentence structure, experiment with different methods of integrating source material into your paper.

- Vary the verbs you use for attribution.

acknowledges	discloses	implies
suggests	observes	notes
concludes	believes	comments
insists	explains	claims
predicts	summarizes	illustrates
reports	finds	proposes
warns	concurs	speculates
admits	affirms	indicates

continued on the following page

continued from the previous page

- Vary the placement of the identifying tag. Instead of always putting it at the beginning of the quoted, paraphrased, or summarized material, try placing it in the middle or at the end.

QUOTATION WITH ATTRIBUTION IN MIDDLE: "A serious problem confronting Amish society from the viewpoint of the Amish themselves," observes Hostetler, "is the threat of absorption into mass society through the values promoted in the public school system" (193).

PARAPHRASE WITH ATTRIBUTION AT END: The Amish are also concerned about their children's exposure to the public school system's values, notes Hostetler (193).

EXERCISE 3

Look back at the summary and paraphrase you wrote for Exercise 2. Write three possible running acknowledgments for each, varying the verbs you use for attribution and the placement of the identifying tag. Be sure to include appropriate documentation at the end of each passage.

(3) Synthesizing Ideas

A **synthesis** combines ideas from two or more sources, along with your own ideas, to express an original view of a subject. (In this sense, an entire **research paper** is a synthesis.) You begin your synthesis by comparing your sources and determining how they are alike and different, where they agree and disagree, and whether they reach the same conclusions. As you identify connections between the ideas of one source and the ideas of another or between a source's ideas and your own, you develop an original perspective on your subject. It is this view, summarized in a thesis statement (in the case of an essay) or in a topic sentence (in the case of a paragraph), that becomes the main focus of your synthesis.

See Ch. 44

As you write your synthesis, make your points one at a time, and use information from your sources to support your statements. This information can be summarized, paraphrased, or quoted. Make certain that you use running acknowledgments as well as the transitional words and phrases that your readers will need to follow your discussion. Finally, remember that your ideas, not those of your sources, should be central to your discussion.

Following is a synthesis written by a student as part of a research paper.

Computers have already changed our lives. They carry out (at incredible speed) many of the everyday tasks that make our way of life possible. For example, computer billing, with all its faults, makes modern business possible, and without computers we would not have access to the telephone services or television reception that we take for granted. But computers are more than fast calculators. According to one computer expert, they are well on their way to learning, creating, and someday even thinking (Raphael 21). Another computer expert, Douglas Hofstadter, agrees, saying that someday a computer will have both "will . . . and consciousness" (423). It seems likely, then, that as a result of the computer, our culture will change profoundly (Turkle 15).

EXERCISE 4

Write a paragraph that synthesizes the three positions you worked with in Exercise 1. (If you like, you may use the sentence comparing the three positions, drafted in response to Exercise 1, as your topic sentence.)

CHAPTER 42

AVOIDING PLAGIARISM

42a Defining Plagiarism

Plagiarism is presenting another person's words or ideas as if they are your own. Some writers plagiarize deliberately, copying passages word for word or even presenting another person's entire work as their own. Other writers do so accidentally because they are not aware of what constitutes plagiarism or because they forget that a note they jotted down is really a direct quotation or that an idea they are using is actually someone else's. Even so, accidental plagiarism is still plagiarism, and it is not taken lightly in education, business, or anyplace else. *Plagiarism is theft.*

In general, you must provide **documentation** for all direct quotations, opinions, judgments, and insights of others that you summarize or paraphrase. You must also document information that is not well known, is open to dispute, or is not commonly accepted. Finally, document tables, graphs, charts, and statistics taken from a source.

See Ch. 43

 PLAGIARISM AND INTERNET SOURCES

Any time you download text that you can cut and paste, you have the potential to commit unintentional plagiarism. To avoid the possibility of plagiarism, follow these guidelines.

- Download information into individual files so that you can keep track of your sources.
- Do not simply cut and paste blocks of downloaded text into your paper; take the time to summarize or paraphrase this

continued on the following page

continued from the previous page
material, copying it into your notes (which may be stored in another file) before you use it in a paper.

- If you do record the exact words of your source, enclose them in quotation marks.
- Whether your information is from E-mail, discussion groups, Listservs, or World Wide Web sites, you must give proper credit by documenting the source.

Common knowledge, facts that are widely available in encyclopedias, textbooks, newspapers, and magazines, need not be documented. Information that is in dispute, however, or that one particular person has discovered or theorized about, must be acknowledged. For example, you need not document the fact that John F. Kennedy graduated from Harvard in 1940 or that he was elected president in 1960. You must, however, document a historian's analysis of Kennedy's performance as president or a researcher's recent discoveries about his private life.

42b Revising to Eliminate Plagiarism

You can avoid plagiarism by using documentation wherever it is required and by following these guidelines.

(1) Enclose Borrowed Words in Quotation Marks

ORIGINAL: Historically, only a handful of families have dominated the fireworks industry in the West. Details such as chemical recipes and mixing procedures were cloaked in secrecy and passed down from one generation to the next. . . . One effect of familial secretiveness is that, until recent decades, basic pyrotechnic research was rarely performed, and even when it was, the results were not generally reported in scientific journals. (Conkling, John A. "Pyrotechnics." *Scientific American* July 1990: 96)

PLAGIARISM: John A. Conkling points out that until recently, little scientific research was done on the chemical properties of fireworks, and when it was, <u>the results were not generally reported in scientific journals</u> (96).

Even though the student writer documented the source of his information, he did not acknowledge that he borrowed the source's exact words. To correct this problem, the student should use quotation marks to acknowledge his borrowing or should paraphrase the source's words.

CORRECT (BORROWED WORDS IN QUOTATION MARKS): John A. Conkling points out that until recently, little scientific research was done on the chemical properties of fireworks, and when it was, "the results were generally not reported in scientific journals" (96).

CORRECT (PARAPHRASE): John A. Conkling points out that research conducted on the chemical composition of fireworks was seldom reported in the scientific literature (96).

(2) Do Not Imitate a Source's Syntax and Phrasing

ORIGINAL: Let's be clear: this wish for politically correct casting goes only one way, the way designed to redress the injuries of centuries. When Pat Carroll, who is a woman, plays Falstaff, who is not, casting is considered a stroke of brilliance. When Josette Simon, who is black, plays Maggie in *After the Fall*, a part Arthur Miller patterned after Marilyn Monroe and which has traditionally been played not by white women, but by blonde white women, it is hailed as a breakthrough.

But when the pendulum moves the other way, the actors' union balks. (Quindlen, Anna. "Error, Stage Left." *New York Times* 12 Aug. 1990, sec. 1:21)

PLAGIARISM: Let us be honest. The desire for politically appropriate casting goes in only one direction, the direction intended to make up for the damage done over hundreds of years. When Pat Carroll, a female, is cast as Falstaff, a male, the decision is an inspired one. When Josette Simon, a black woman, is cast as Maggie in *After the Fall*, a role Arthur Miller based on Marilyn Monroe and which has usually been played by a woman who is not only white but also blonde, it is considered a major advance.

But when the shoe is on the other foot, the actors' union resists (Quindlen 21).

Although this student documents the passage and does not use the exact words of her source, she closely imitates the original's syntax and phrasing. In fact, all she has done is substitute synonyms for the author's words. The student could have avoided plagiarism by changing the syntax as well as the individual words of the original.

CORRECT (PARAPHRASE IN STUDENT'S OWN WORDS; ONE DISTINCTIVE PHRASE PLACED IN QUOTATION MARKS): According to Anna Quindlen, the actors' union supports "politically correct casting" (21) only when it means casting a woman or a minority group member in a role created for a male or a Caucasian. Thus, it is acceptable for actress Pat Carroll to play Falstaff or for black actress Josette Simon to play Marilyn Monroe; in fact, casting decisions such as these are praised. But when it comes to casting a Caucasian in a role intended for an African-American, Asian, or Hispanic, the union objects (21).

(3) Document Statistics Obtained from a Source

ORIGINAL: From the time they [male drivers between sixteen and twenty-four] started to drive, 187 of these drivers (almost two-thirds) reported one or more accidents, with an average of 1.6 per involved driver. Features of 303 accidents are tabulated in Table 2. Almost half of all first accidents occurred before the legal driving age of 18, and the median age of all accidents was 19. (Schuman, Stanley, et al. "Young Male Drivers: Accidents and Violations." *JAMA* 50 [1983]:1027)

PLAGIARISM: By and large male drivers between the ages of sixteen and twenty-four accounted for the majority of accidents. Of 303 accidents recorded in Michigan, almost one-half took place before the drivers were legally allowed to drive at eighteen.

The student who used this information incorrectly assumed statistics are common knowledge. But statistics are usually the result of original research, and therefore they deserve acknowledgment. (Besides, readers may need to locate the source of the statistics in order to assess their reliability.) For these reasons, you should always document statistics.

CORRECT: According to one study, male drivers between the ages of sixteen and twenty-four accounted for the majority of accidents. Of 303 accidents recorded, almost one half took place before the drivers were legally allowed to drive at eighteen (Schuman et al., 1027).

(4) Differentiate Your Words and Ideas from Those of Your Source

ORIGINAL: At some colleges and universities traditional survey courses of world and English literature . . . have been scrapped or diluted. At others they are in peril. At still others they will be. What replaces them is sometimes a mere option of electives, sometimes "multicultural" courses introducing material from Third World cultures and thinning out an already thin sampling of Western writings, and sometimes courses geared especially to issues of class, race, and gender. Given the notorious lethargy of academic decision-making, there has probably been more clamor than change; but if there's enough clamor, there will be change. (Howe, Irving. "The Value of the Canon." *The New Republic* 2 Feb. 1991: 40–47)

PLAGIARISM: Debates about expanding the literary canon take place at many colleges and universities across the United States. At many universities the Western literature survey courses have been edged out by courses that emphasize minority concerns. These courses are "thinning out an already thin sampling of Western writings" in favor of courses geared especially to issues of "class, race, and gender" (Howe 40).

Because the student who wrote this passage does not differentiate his ideas from those of his source, it appears that only the quotations in his last sentence are borrowed, but actually, his second sentence also borrows ideas from Howe. The student should have clearly defined the boundaries of the borrowed material with a running acknowledgment and documentation. In the following correct example, notice that both the summary and the quotation (which always requires a separate parenthetical reference) are documented.

CORRECT: Debates about expanding the literary canon take place at many colleges and universities across the United States. According to the noted critic Irving Howe, at many universities the Western literature survey courses have been edged out by courses that emphasize minority concerns (40). These courses, says Howe, are "thinning out an already thin sampling of Western writings" in favor of "courses geared especially to issues of class, race, and gender" (40).

✔ CHECKLIST: AVOIDING PLAGIARISM

✔ **Take careful notes.** Be sure you have recorded information from your sources carefully and accurately.

✔ **In your notes, put all words borrowed from sources inside circled quotation marks** and enclose your own comments within brackets.

✔ **In your paper, differentiate your ideas from those of your sources** by clearly introducing borrowed material with a running acknowledgment and by following it with documentation.

✔ **Enclose all direct quotations** used in your paper within quotation marks.

continued on the following page

continued from the previous page

✔ **Review paraphrases and summaries in your paper** to make certain they are in your own words and that any distinctive words and phrases from a source are quoted.

✔ **Document all quoted material and all paraphrases and summaries** of your sources.

✔ **Document all facts** that are open to dispute or are not common knowledge.

✔ **Document all opinions, conclusions, figures, tables, statistics, graphs, and charts** taken from a source.

EXERCISE

This student paragraph uses material from three sources, but its author has neglected to cite them. After reading the paragraph and the three sources that follow it, identify material that has been quoted directly from a source. Compare the wording to the original for accuracy and insert quotation marks where necessary, being sure the quoted passages fit smoothly into the paragraph. Next, paraphrase any passages the student did not need to quote, and, after consulting **Chapter 43,** document each piece of information that requires it.

Student Paragraph

Oral history became a legitimate field of study in 1948, when the Oral History Research Office was established by Allan Nevins. Like recordings of presidents' fireside chats and declarations of war, oral history is both oral and historical. But it is more: oral history is the creation of new historical documentation, not the recording or preserving of documentation that already exists. Oral history also tends to be more spontaneous and personal and less formal than ordinary tape recordings. Nevins's purpose was to collect and prepare materials to help future historians to better understand the past. Oral history has enormous potential to do just this because it draws on people's memories of their own lives and deeds and of their associations with particular people, periods, or events. The result, when it is recorded and transcribed, is a valuable new source.

Source 1

When Allan Nevins set up the Oral History Research Office in 1948, he looked upon it as an organization that in a systematic way could obtain from the lips and papers of living Americans who had led significant lives a full record of their participation in the political, economic, and cultural affairs of the nation. His purpose was to prepare such material for the use of future historians. It was his conviction that the individual played an important role in history and that an individual's autobiography might in the future serve as a key to an understanding of contemporary historical movements. (Excerpted from Benison, Saul. "Reflections on Oral History." *The American Archivist* 28.1 [January 1965]:71)

Source 2

Typically, an oral history project comprises an organized series of interviews with selected individuals or groups in order to create new source materials from the reminiscences of their own life and acts or from their association with a particular person, period, or event. These recollections are recorded on tape and transcribed on a typewriter into sheets of transcript. . . . Such oral history may be distinguished from more conventional tape recordings of speeches, lectures, symposia, etc., by the fact that the former creates new sources through the more spontaneous, personal, multitopical, extended narrative, while the latter utilizes sources in a more formal mode for a specific occasion. (Excerpted from Rumics, Elizabeth. "Oral History: Defining the Term." *Wilson Library Bulletin* 40 [1966]:602)

Source 3

Oral history, as the term came to be used, is the creation of new historical documentation, not the recording or preserving of documentation—even oral documentation—that already exists. Its purpose is not, like that of the National Voice Library at Michigan State University, to preserve the recordings of fireside chats or presidential declarations of war or James Whitcomb Riley reciting "Little Orphan Annie." These are surely oral and just as surely the stuff of history; but they are not oral history. For this there must be the creation of a new historical document by means of a personal interview. (Excerpted from Hoyle, Norman. "Oral History." *Library Trends* [July 1972]:61)

CHAPTER 43

DOCUMENTATION

Documentation, the formal acknowledgment of the sources you use in your paper, enables readers to judge the quality and originality of your work and to determine how authoritative and relevant each source you cite is. Different academic disciplines use different documentation styles. This chapter explains and illustrates the documentation styles recommended by the Modern Language Association (MLA), *The Chicago Manual of Style* (CMS), the American Psychological Association (APA), and the Council of Biology Editors (CBE).

✔ CHECKLIST: WHAT TO DOCUMENT

DO DOCUMENT
- ✔ Direct quotations
- ✔ Opinions, judgments, and insights of others that you summarize or paraphrase
- ✔ Information that is not widely known
- ✔ Information that is open to dispute
- ✔ Tables, charts, graphs, and statistics taken from a source

DO NOT DOCUMENT
- ✔ Your own ideas, observations, and conclusions
- ✔ Common knowledge (information that is widely available in reference books, newspapers, and magazines)
- ✔ Familiar quotations

 PLACEMENT OF DOCUMENTATION

Take the following steps to make sure that each parenthetical reference you use clearly identifies the source of the information it documents.

continued on the following page

continued from the previous page
- Avoid using a single reference to cover several pieces of information from a variety of different sources. Place documentation after each quotation as well as at the end of each passage of paraphrase or summary.

- Place documentation so that it will not interrupt your discussion—ideally, at the end of a sentence.

- Differentiate your ideas from those of your sources by placing running acknowledgments before, and documentation after, all borrowed material.

43a Using MLA Format*

MLA format is recommended by the Modern Language Association and is required by many teachers of English and other languages as well as teachers of other humanities disciplines. (Student papers illustrating the use of MLA format appear in **45l** and **47d1.**)

(1) Parenthetical References in the Text

MLA documentation uses parenthetical references within the text keyed to a Works Cited list at the end of the paper. A typical reference consists of the author's last name and a page number. (A reference to an electronic source may cite a paragraph number.)

The colony's religious and political freedom appealed to many idealists

in Europe (Ripley 132).

To distinguish two or more sources by the same author, shorten the title of each work to one or two key words, and include this shortened title in the parenthetical reference after the author's name.

Penn emphasized his religious motivation (Kelley, <u>William Penn</u> 116).

*MLA documentation format follows the guidelines set in the *MLA Handbook for Writers of Research Papers,* 4th ed. New York: MLA, 1995 with updates from the *MLA Style Manual and Guide to Scholarly Publishing,* 2nd ed. New York: MLA, 1998.

If you state the author's name or the title of the work in your sentence, do not include it in the parenthetical reference.

Penn's political motivation is discussed by Joseph P. Kelley in <u>Pennsylvania, the Colonial Years, 1681–1776</u> (44).

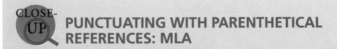

CLOSE-UP PUNCTUATING WITH PARENTHETICAL REFERENCES: MLA

Paraphrases and summaries Parenthetical references are placed *before* the sentence's end punctuation.

Penn's writings epitomize seventeenth-century religious thought (Dengler and Curtis 72).

Quotations run in with the text Parenthetical references are placed *after* the quotation but *before* the end punctuation.

As Ross says, "Penn followed this conscience in all matters" (127).

According to Williams, Penn's utopian vision was informed by his Quaker beliefs . . ." (72).

Quotations set off from the text When you quote a <u>long prose passage</u> or more than three lines of <u>poetry</u>, parenthetical references are placed one space *after* the end punctuation.

According to Arthur Smith, William Penn envisioned a state based on his religious principles:

> Pennsylvania would be a commonwealth in which all individuals would follow God's truth and develop according to God's law. For Penn this concept of government was self-evident. It would be a mistake to see Pennsylvania as anything but an expression of Penn's religious beliefs. (314)

See
32d2–3

DIRECTORY OF MLA PARENTHETICAL REFERENCES

1. A work by a single author
2. A work by two or three authors
3. A work by more than three authors
4. A work in multiple volumes
5. A work without a listed author
6. A work that is one page long
7. An indirect source
8. More than one work
9. A literary work
10. An entire work
11. Two or more authors with the same last name
12. A government document or a corporate author
13. Tables and illustrations

Sample MLA Parenthetical References

1. A Work by a Single Author

Fairy tales reflect the emotions and fears of children (Bettelheim 23).

2. A Work by Two or Three Authors

The historian's main job is to search for clues and solve mysteries
(Davidson and Lytle 6).

With the advent of behaviorism, psychology began a new phase of
inquiry (Cowen, Barbo, and Crum 31–34).

3. A Work by More than Three Authors

List only the first author, followed by *et al.* ("and others").

The European powers believed they could change the fundamentals of
Moslem existence (Bull et al. 395).

4. A Work in Multiple Volumes

If you list more than one volume of a multivolume work in your
Works Cited list, include the appropriate volume and page number (separated by a colon).

The French Revolution had a great influence on William Blake (Raine
1: 52).

If you use only one volume of a multivolume work and have included the volume number in the Works Cited list, include just the page number in the parenthetical reference.

(Raine 17)

5. A Work without a Listed Author

Use a shortened version of the title in the parenthetical reference, beginning with the word by which it is alphabetized in the Works Cited list.

In spite of political unrest, Soviet television remained fairly

conservative, ignoring all challenges to the system ("Soviet").

6. A Work That Is One Page Long

Do not include a page reference for a one-page article.

Sixty percent of Arab-Americans work in white-collar jobs (El-Badru).

7. An Indirect Source

If you must use a statement by one author that is quoted in the work of another author, indicate that the material is from an indirect source with the abbreviation *qtd. in* ("quoted in").

Wagner stated that myth and history stood before him "with opposing

claims" (qtd. in Thomas 65).

8. More than One Work

Cite each work as you normally would, separating one from another with a semicolon.

The Brooklyn Bridge has been used as a subject by many American

artists (McCullough 144; Tashjian 58).

Long parenthetical references distract readers. Whenever possible, present them as **content notes**.

See
43a3

9. A Literary Work

When citing a literary work, it is often helpful to include more than just the author's name and the page number.

In a parenthetical reference to a prose work, begin with the page number, follow it with a semicolon, and then add any additional information that might be necessary.

In <u>Moby-Dick</u> Melville refers to a whaling expedition funded by Louis
XIV of France (151; ch. 24).

In parenthetical references to long poems, cite both division and line
numbers, separating them with a period. For example, in the following
citation the reference is to book 8, line 124 of the *Aeneid.*

In the <u>Aeneid</u> Virgil describes the ships as cleaving the "green woods

reflected in the calm water" (8.124).

In citing classic verse plays, include the act, scene, and line numbers,
separated with periods.

(*Macbeth* 2.2.14–16)

In biblical citations include chapter, verse, and an abbreviated title (Gen.
5.12).

10. An Entire Work

When citing an entire work, include the author's name and the work's
title in the text of your paper rather than in a parenthetical reference.

Herbert Gans's <u>The Urban Villagers</u> is a study of an Italian-American

neighborhood in Boston.

11. Two or More Authors with the Same Last Name

To distinguish authors with the same last name, include their first initials in the parenthetical references.

Recent increases in crime have probably caused thousands of urban

homeowners to install alarms (Weishoff, R. 115). Some of these alarms

use sophisticated sensors that were developed by the Army (Weishoff,

C. 76).

12. A Government Document or a Corporate Author

Cite such works using the organization's name followed by the page
number.

(American Automobile Association 34)

You can avoid long parenthetical references by working the organization's name into the text of your paper.

According to the President's Commission for the Study of Ethical

Problems in Medicine and Biomedical and Behavioral Research, the

issues relating to euthanasia are complicated (76).

13. Tables and Illustrations

See
A1d

Tables and other visuals are documented in the text of your paper but not in parenthetical references. If you use a **table** or other type of visual, provide full source information directly below it, preceded by *source* for a table or *fig.* and an arabic numeral for other visual material.

Source: Robert Hughes, <u>The Fatal Shore</u> (London: Pan, 1988) 72.

NOTE: Because full source information is included in the text of your paper, it does not appear in the Works Cited list.

(2) Works Cited List

The **Works Cited list,** which appears at the end of your paper, gives publication information for the sources you cite. If your instructor tells you to list all the sources you read, whether you actually cited them or not, give this list the title *Works Consulted.*

✔ CHECKLIST: PREPARING THE MLA WORKS CITED LIST

✔ Begin the Works Cited list on a new page after the last page of text or content notes, numbered as the next page of the paper.

✔ Each item has three divisions—author, title, and publication information. The separation between major divisions is marked by a period and one space.*

✔ List entries alphabetically according to the author's last name. List the author's full name as it appears on the title page. Alphabetize unsigned sources by the first main word of the title.

✔ Type the first line of each entry flush left; indent subsequent lines five spaces (or one-half inch).

✔ Double-space within and between entries.

*The 1995 *MLA Handbook* shows one space but permits students to use two spaces if their instructors prefer this format.

Works Cited Format: MLA

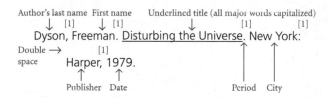

Author's last name   First name   Underlined title (all major words capitalized)
   ↓ [1]   ↓ [1]   ↓   [1]   [1]
   Dyson, Freeman. <u>Disturbing the Universe</u>. New York:
Double →   [1]   ↑   ↑
space   Harper, 1979.   Period   City
                 ↑   ↑
          Publisher Date

DIRECTORY OF MLA WORKS CITED ENTRIES

Entries for Books

1. A book by one author
2. A book by two or three authors
3. A book by more than three authors
4. Two or more books by the same author
5. An edited book
6. An essay in an anthology
7. More than one essay from the same anthology
8. A multivolume work
9. The foreword, preface, or afterword of a book
10. A short story, play, or poem in an anthology
11. A short story, play, or poem in a collection of an author's work
12. A book with a title within its title
13. A translation
14. A reprint of an older edition
15. A dissertation (published/unpublished)
16. An article in a reference book (signed/unsigned)
17. A pamphlet
18. A government publication

Entries for Articles

19. An article in a scholarly journal with continuous pagination through an annual volume
20. An article in a scholarly journal with separate pagination in each issue
21. An article in a weekly magazine (signed/unsigned)
22. An article in a monthly magazine
23. An article that does not appear on consecutive pages
24. An article in a newspaper (signed/unsigned)
25. An editorial
26. A letter to the editor

continued on the following page

Sample MLA Works Cited Entries: Books   Book citations include the following information.

- The author's name (last name first)
- The book title (underlined)
- Publication information (place, publisher, date)

NOTE: Capitalize all major words of a book title except articles, prepositions, coordinating conjunctions, and the *to* of an infinitive (unless such a word is the first or last word of the title or subtitle).

1. A Book by One Author

Use a short form of the publisher's name. *Alfred A. Knopf, Inc.*, for example, is shortened to *Knopf,* and *Oxford University Press* becomes *Oxford UP.*

> Bettelheim, Bruno. The Uses of Enchantment: The Meaning and
>
> Importance of Fairy Tales. New York: Knopf, 1976.

When citing an edition other than the first, indicate the edition number as it appears on the work's title page.

> Gans, Herbert J. The Urban Villagers. 2nd ed. New York: Free, 1982.

2. A Book by Two or Three Authors

List the first author's last name first. Subsequent authors are listed first name first in the order in which they appear on the title page.

> Davidson, James W., and Mark Hamilton Lytle. After the Fact: The Art
>
> of Historical Detection. New York: Knopf, 1982.

3. A Book by More than Three Authors

List only the first author, followed by *et al.* ("and others").

> Bull, H., et al. The Near East. New York: Oxford UP, 1990.

4. Two or More Books by the Same Author

List books by the same author in alphabetical order by title. Three unspaced hyphens, followed by a period, take the place of the author's name after the first entry.

> Thomas, Lewis. The Lives of a Cell: Notes of a Biology Watcher. New
>
> York: Viking, 1974.
>
> ---. The Medusa and the Snail: More Notes of a Biology Watcher. New
>
> York: Viking, 1979.

If the author is the editor or translator of the second entry, place a comma and the appropriate abbreviation after the hyphens (---, ed.).

5. An Edited Book

An edited book is a work that has been prepared for publication by a person other than the author. If your emphasis is on the *author's* work, begin your citation with the author's name. After the title, include the abbreviation *Ed.* ("Edited by") followed by the name of the editor or editors.

> Bartram, William. <u>The Travels of William Bartram</u>. Ed. Mark Van Doren.
>
> New York: Dover, 1955.

If your emphasis is on the *editor's* work, begin your citation with the editor's name followed by the abbreviation *ed.* ("editor") if there is one editor or *eds.* ("editors") if there is more than one.

> Van Doren, Mark, ed. <u>The Travels of William Bartram</u>. By William
>
> Bartram. New York: Dover, 1955.

6. *An Essay in an Anthology*

Include the *full* span of pages on which the whole essay appears, even though you may cite only one page in your paper.

> Lloyd, G. E. R. "Science and Mathematics." <u>The Legacy of Greece</u>. Ed.
>
> Moses I. Finley. New York: Oxford UP, 1981. 256–300.

NOTE: If you cite an essay that appears in a collection of the author's work, use the format illustrated in number 11.

7. *More than One Essay from the Same Anthology*

List each essay from the same anthology separately, followed by a cross-reference to the entire anthology. List complete publication information for the anthology itself in a separate entry.

> Bolgar, Robert R. "The Greek Legacy." Finley 429–72.
>
> Finley, Moses I., ed. <u>The Legacy of Greece</u>. New York: Oxford UP, 1981.
>
> Williams, Bernard. "Philosophy." Finley 202–55.

8. *A Multivolume Work*

When all volumes of a multivolume work have the same title, include the number of the volume you are using.

> Raine, Kathleen. <u>Blake and Tradition</u>. Vol. 1. Princeton: Princeton UP,
>
> 1968.

If you use two or more volumes, cite the entire work.

Raine, Kathleen. <u>Blake and Tradition</u>. 2 vols. Princeton: Princeton UP,

1968.

If the volume you are using has an individual title, you may cite the title without mentioning any other volumes.

Durant, Will, and Ariel Durant. <u>The Age of Napoleon</u>. New York:

Simon, 1975.

If you wish, however, you may include supplemental information such as the number of the volume, the title of the entire work, the total number of volumes, and the inclusive publication dates.

Durant, Will, and Ariel Durant. <u>The Age of Napoleon</u>. New York:

Simon, 1975. Vol. 11 of <u>The Story of Civilization</u>. 11 vols.

1935–75.

9. *The Foreword, Preface, or Afterword of a Book*

Taylor, Telford. Preface. <u>Less than Slaves</u>. By Benjamin B. Ferencz.

Cambridge: Harvard UP, 1979. xiii–xxii.

10. *A Short Story, Play, or Poem in an Anthology*

Chopin, Kate. "The Storm." <u>Literature: Reading, Reacting, Writing</u>. Ed.

Laurie G. Kirszner and Stephen R. Mandell. 3rd ed. Fort Worth:

Harcourt, 1997. 146–50.

Shakespeare, William. <u>Othello, The Moor of Venice</u>. <u>Shakespeare: Six</u>

<u>Plays and the Sonnets</u>. Ed. Thomas Marc Parrott and Edward

Hubler. New York: Scribner's, 1956. 145–91.

11. *A Short Story, Play, or Poem in a Collection of an Author's Work*

Walcott, Derek. "Nearing La Guaira." <u>Selected Poems</u>. New York:

Farrar, 1964. 47–48.

12. *A Book with a Title within Its Title*

If the work you are citing contains a title that you would normally underline to indicate italics (a novel, play, or long poem, for example), do *not* underline the interior title.

Knoll, Robert E., ed. Storm Over The Waste Land. Chicago: Scott,

1964.

If the book you are citing contains a title that is normally enclosed within quotation marks, keep the quotation marks.

Herzog, Alan, ed. Twentieth Century Interpretations of "To a Skylark."

Englewood Cliffs: Prentice, 1975.

13. A Translation

García Márquez, Gabriel. One Hundred Years of Solitude. Trans.

Gregory Rabassa. New York: Avon, 1991.

14. A Reprint of an Older Edition

Include the original publication date after the title.

Wharton, Edith. The House of Mirth. 1905. New York: Scribner's, 1975.

15. A Dissertation (Published/Unpublished)

For dissertations published by University Microfilms International (UMI), include the order number.

Peterson, Shawn. Loving Mothers and Lost Daughters: Images of

Female Kinship Relations in Selected Novels of Toni Morrison.

Diss. U of Oregon, 1993. Ann Arbor: UMI, 1994. 9322935.

NOTE: University Microfilms, which publishes most of the dissertations in the United States, also publishes in CD-ROM. You will find the proper format for citing CD-ROMs on pages 641–42.

Use quotation marks for the title of an unpublished dissertation.

Romero, Yolanda Garcia. "The American Frontier Experience in

Twentieth-Century Northwest Texas." Diss. Texas Tech U, 1993.

16. An Article in a Reference Book (Signed/Unsigned)

For a signed article, begin with the author's name. When citing relatively unfamiliar encyclopedias, give full publication information.

Drabble, Margaret. "Expressionism." The Oxford Companion to

English Literature. 5th ed. New York: Oxford UP, 1985.

Enter the title of an unsigned article just as it is listed in the reference book. No volume or page numbers are needed. When citing familiar encyclopedias, do not include publication information.

"Cubism." The New Encyclopaedia Britannica: Micropaedia. 1991.

17. A Pamphlet

If no author is listed, enter the underlined title first.

Existing Light Photography. Rochester: Kodak, 1989.

18. A Government Publication

If the publication has no listed author, begin with the name of the government, followed by the name of the agency.

United States. President's Commission for the Study of Ethical Problems

in Medicine and Biomedical and Behavioral Research. Deciding to

Forgo Life-Sustaining Treatment: Ethical, Medical, and Legal

Issues in Treatment Decisions. Washington: GPO, 1989.

Sample MLA Works Cited Entries: Articles Article citations include the following information.

- The author's name (last name first)
- The title of the article (in quotation marks)
- The name of the periodical (underlined)
- The month and the year
- The pages on which the full article appears (without the abbreviations *p.* or *pp.*)

NOTE: Abbreviate names of months (except for May, June, and July) in the Works Cited list: Jan., Feb., Mar., Apr., Aug., Sep. or Sept., Oct., Nov., Dec.

19. An Article in a Scholarly Journal with Continuous Pagination through an Annual Volume

For an article in a journal with continuous pagination—for example, one issue ends on page 172 and the next issue begins with page 173—include the volume number, followed by the date of publication (in parentheses). Follow the publication date with a colon, a space, and the page numbers.

Huntington, John. "Science Fiction and the Future." College English 37

(1975): 340–58.

20. An Article in a Scholarly Journal with Separate Pagination in Each Issue

For a journal in which each issue begins with page 1, add a period and the issue number after the volume number.

> Sipes, R. G. "War, Sports, and Aggression: An Empirical Test of Two
>
> Rival Theories." American Anthropologist 4.2 (1973): 65–84.

21. An Article in a Weekly Magazine (Signed/Unsigned)

In dates, the day precedes the month. For unsigned articles, start with the title of the article.

> Traub, James. "The Hearts and Minds of City College." New Yorker
>
> 7 June 1993: 42–53.

> "Solzhenitsyn: A Candle in the Wind." Time 23 Mar. 1970: 70.

22. An Article in a Monthly Magazine

> Roll, Lori. "Careers in Engineering." Working Woman Nov. 1982: 62.

23. An Article That Does Not Appear on Consecutive Pages

When, for example, an article begins on page 15, continues on page 16, and then skips to page 86, include only the first page number and a plus sign.

> Griska, Linda. "Stress and Job Performance." Psychology Today Nov.-
>
> Dec. 1995: 120+.

24. An Article in a Newspaper (Signed/Unsigned)

> Oates, Joyce Carol. "When Characters from the Page Are Made Flesh
>
> on the Screen." New York Times 23 Mar. 1986, late ed.: C1+.

> "Soviet Television." Los Angeles Times 13 Dec. 1990, sec. 2: 3+.

25. An Editorial

> "Tough Cops, Not Brutal Cops." Editorial. New York Times 5 May
>
> 1994, late ed.: A26.

26. A Letter to the Editor

> Bishop, Jennifer. Letter. Philadelphia Inquirer 10 Dec. 1995: A17.

27. A Book Review

Begin with the reviewer's name, followed by the title of the review (if any), the title and author of the book reviewed, and the date on which the review appeared.

> Fox-Genovese, Elizabeth. "Big Mess on Campus." Rev. of <u>Illiberal</u>
>
> > <u>Education: The Politics of Race and Sex on Campus</u>, by Dinesh
> >
> > D'Souza. <u>Washington Post</u> 15 Apr. 1991, ntnl. weekly ed.: 32.

28. An Article with a Title within Its Title

Use single quotation marks for the enclosed title.

> Nash, Robert. "About 'The Emperor of Ice Cream.'" <u>Perspectives</u>
>
> > 7 (1954): 122–24.

If an article includes a title that would normally be underlined, underline it in your Works Cited entry.

> Leicester, H. Marshall, Jr. "The Art of Impersonation: A General
>
> > Prologue to <u>The Canterbury Tales</u>." <u>PMLA</u> 95 (1980): 213–24.

Sample MLA Works Cited Entries: Nonprint Sources

29. A Lecture

> Sandman, Peter. "Communicating Scientific Information."
>
> > Communications Seminar, Dept. of Humanities and
> >
> > Communications. Drexel U, 26 Oct. 1994.

30. A Personal Interview

> West, Cornel. Personal interview. 28 Dec. 1993.
>
> Tannen, Deborah. Telephone interview. 8 June 1994.

31. A Published Interview

> Stavros, George. "An Interview with Gwendolyn Brooks."
>
> > <u>Contemporary Literature</u> 11.1 (Winter 1970): 1–20.

32. A Personal Letter

> Tan, Amy. Letter to the author. 7 Apr. 1990.

33. A Published Letter

Joyce, James. "Letter to Louis Gillet." 20 Aug. 1931. James Joyce. By

Richard Ellmann. New York: Oxford UP, 1965. 631.

34. A Letter in a Library's Archives

Stieglitz, Alfred. Letter to Paul Rosenberg. 5 Sept. 1923. Stieglitz

Archive. Yale, New Haven.

35. A Film

Include the title of the film (underlined), the distributor, and the date, along with other information of use to readers, such as the names of the performers, the director, and the writer.

Citizen Kane. Dir. Orson Welles. Perf. Orson Welles, Joseph Cotten,

Dorothy Comingore, and Agnes Moorehead. RKO, 1941.

If you are focusing on the contribution of a particular person, begin with that person's name.

Welles, Orson, dir. Citizen Kane. . . .

36. A Videotape

Interview with Arthur Miller. Dir. William Schiff. Videocassette. The

Mosaic Group, 1987.

37. A Radio or Television Program

"Prime Suspect 3." Writ. Lynda La Plante. Perf. Helen Mirren. Mystery!

WNET, New York. 28 Apr. 1994.

38. A Recording

List the composer, conductor, or performer (whichever you are emphasizing), followed by the title (and, when citing jacket notes, a description of the material), manufacturer, and year of issue.

Boubill, Alain, and Claude-Michel Schönberg. Miss Saigon. Perf. Lea

Salonga, Claire Moore, and Jonathan Pryce. Cond. Martin Koch.

Geffen, 1989.

Marley, Bob. "Crisis." Lyrics. Bob Marley and the Wailers. Kava Island

Records, 1978.

Sample MLA Works Cited Entries: CD-ROMS and Other Portable Databases   CD-ROM databases may contain material for which there is also a print source or material for which there is no print counterpart.

FORMAT: CD-ROM DATABASE

Author's Last Name, First Name. "Article Title." <u>Title of Print Source</u> date of print publication: pages. <u>Title of CD-ROM</u>. Publication medium (CD-ROM). Producer of CD-ROM. Electronic publication date.

---

39. CD-ROM: *Article from a Magazine with a Print Version*

Ingrassia, Michele, and Karen Springen. "She's Not Baby Jessica Anymore." <u>Newsweek</u> 21 Mar. 1994: 60–65. <u>InfoTrac Magazine Index Plus</u>. CD-ROM. Information Access. Aug. 1995.

If no author is listed, begin with the article title. This CD-ROM is updated monthly, so the date includes the month and the year.

40. CD-ROM: *Article from a Journal with a Print Version*

Gram, Lars F. "Drug Therapy: Fluoxetine." <u>New England Journal of Medicine</u> 331 (1994): 1354–61. <u>Biology Digest</u>. CD-ROM. Newsbank. Dec. 1995.

41. CD-ROM: *Article from a Newspaper with a Print Version*

Klein, Judy L. "The Ghosts of Octobers Past." <u>Wall Street Journal</u> 28 Sept. 1995: A18+. <u>InfoTrac Magazine Index Plus</u>. CD-ROM. Information Access. Aug. 1995.

42. CD-ROM: *Book with a Print Version*

Dickens, Charles. <u>David Copperfield</u>. <u>World's Greatest Classic Books</u>. CD-ROM. Corel World Library. 1995.

This CD-ROM is not updated, so the date includes only the year it was first issued.

43. CD-ROM: Material with No Print Version

"Psychology." <u>Encarta 1996</u>. CD-ROM. Redmond: Microsoft, 1996.

<u>A Music Lover's Multimedia Guide to Beethoven's 5th</u>. CD-ROM.

Spring Valley: Interactive, 1993.

The first citation above refers to an article from a CD-ROM; the second, to an entire CD-ROM.

44. Diskette: A Software Program

<u>Reunion: The Family Tree Software</u>. Diskette. Vers. 2.0. Lester

Productions, 1994.

NOTE: If you cannot find full information about a software program—the city of publication, for example—include just the information you have.

Sample MLA Works Cited Entries: Online Databases   Like CD-ROM sources, some online source material has a print counterpart, and some does not.

FORMAT: ONLINE DATABASE

Computer Network (Internet, World Wide Web, etc.)

Author's Last Name, First Name. "Article Title." <u>Title of Print</u>

<u>Source</u> Publication information and date of original

publication: number of pages or paragraphs (if available).

<u>Title of database</u> (if applicable). Date of electronic

publication or update or posting. Name of list, forum, or

sponsoring institution (if applicable). Date accessed

<Electronic address or URL>.

Computer Service (America Online, Prodigy, etc.)

Author's Last Name, First Name. "Article Title." <u>Title of Print</u>

<u>Source</u> Publication information: number of pages or

paragraphs (if available). Name of list or forum (if applicable).

Date accessed. Computer Service (America Online, etc.).

---

45. Online: Article from a Magazine with a Print Version

> Weiser, Jay. "The Tyranny of Informality." <u>New Republic</u> 26 Feb. 1996.
>
> > 1 Mar. 1996 <http://www.enews.com/magazines/tnr/current/
> >
> > 022696.3.html>.
>
> Lacayo, Richard. "Long Distance Calling." <u>Time</u> 17 July 1995: 7 pars.
>
> > 20 Nov. 1995. CompuServe.

This article was accessed from the CompuServe computer service, so it does not have an electronic address.

46. Online: Article from a Journal with a Print Version

> Maxwell, Catherine. "Browning's Pygmalion and the Revenge of
>
> > Galatea." <u>ELH</u> 60 (1993): 989–1011. 4 May 1996 <http://muse.
> >
> > jhu.edu/journals/elh/v060/60.4maxwell.html>.

47. Online: Article from a Newspaper with a Print Version

> Kleiman, Carol. "Footing the Bill for Welfare Reform." <u>Chicago Tribune</u>
>
> > 13 Dec. 1995. 10 Feb. 1996 <http://www.chicago.tribune.com/
> >
> > articles/kleiman/yourjob/yourjob_1213>.

If the author's name is not listed, begin with the article title.

48. Online: Book with a Print Version

> Twain, Mark. <u>The Adventures of Huckleberry Finn</u>. <u>The Writings of</u>
>
> > <u>Mark Twain</u>. Vol. 13. New York: Harper, 1991. <u>Wiretap.spies</u>.
> >
> > 13 Jan. 1996 <http://www.sci.dixie.edu/DixieCollege/Ebooks/
> >
> > huckfinn.html>.

The electronic edition was accessed from *Wiretap.spies*, an electronic database. A period is required between the title and the publication information of a book.

49. Online: Material with No Print Version

> "Psychology." <u>Compton's Encyclopedia</u>. Jan. 1996. 6 Feb. 1996.
>
> > America Online.

This entry shows that the material was posted in January of 1996 and accessed on February 6, 1996.

50. Online: Electronic Newsletter

"Unprecedented Cutbacks in History of Science Funding." <u>AIP Center</u>

<u>for History of Physics</u> 27.2 (Fall 1995). 26 Feb. 1996 <http://

www.aip.org/history/fall95/fall95.html>.

No author is listed for this article, so the entry begins with the article title.

51. Online: World Wide Web Site

Swofford, Jennifer. <u>The Complete Guide to Keeping Green Iguanas in</u>

<u>Captivity</u>. 28 July 1995. 5 Mar. 1996 <http://gto.ncsa.uiuc.edu/

pingleto/herps/iguanacare.html>.

The last update of this Website was July 28, 1995. The material was accessed on March 5, 1996.

52. Online: E-mail

Shienvold, Adrianne. "Information on Physical Therapy." E-mail to the

author. 12 Dec. 1995.

53. Online: Newsgroups

Newsgroups are online gathering places for groups of people with similar interests in which the users post comments and questions. On the Internet, newsgroups are sometimes called *forums*.

Dudley, Viva. "Is Catnip Safe to Eat?" Online posting. 4 Feb. 1996.

17 Feb. 1996 <news:alt.animals.felines>.

CLOSE-UP   ALLIANCE FOR COMPUTERS AND WRITING (ACW) DOCUMENTATION STYLE

Some writers prefer to follow ACW guidelines for electronic sources. However, this style has not been endorsed by the MLA, so be sure to check with your instructor before using ACW documentation style instead of MLA documentation style.

continued on the following page

continued from the previous page

Format

Author's Last Name. First Name. "Title of Document." Title of
Complete Work (if applicable). Version or file number (if
applicable). Document date or date of last revision (if
different then access date). Electronic address. Date of
access (in parentheses).

Sample Citations

1. File Transfer Protocol (FTP) Site

Frendi, Scott. "Discourse in Virtual Communities." Dec. 1996.
ftp://ftp.media.mit.edu/pub/asp/papers/deviance-chi97.txt
(19 Feb. 1997).

2. World Wide Web Site

Walker, Janice R. "MLA-Style Citations of Electronic Sources."
Jan. 1995. http://www.cas.usf.edu/english/walker/mla.html
(22 Jan. 1997).

3. Telnet Site

Rigg, Doreen. "Lesson Plan for Teaching about the Hubble
Telescope." Space News. 11 Oct. 1996. telnet://spacelink.
msfc.nasa.gov.guest (2 Dec. 1996).

4. Gopher Site

Still, David. "Laser." The ACRONYMs Dictionary. 6 Mar. 1996.
gopher://info.mcc.ac.uk, port: 70. select: 1/miscellany/
acronyms (11 Jan. 1997).

5. Listserv

Johnson, Sarah. "Traditional Amish Quilt Patterns."
quilt@cornell.edu (11 Mar. 1997).

continued on the following page

continued from the previous page

6. Newsgroup (USENET)

Provizor, Norman. "Jazz in the 1990s." 2 Mar. 1997.

alt.music.jazz. (4 Apr. 1997).

7. E-mail Citation

Gorenstein, Seth. "Joke of the Week." Personal E-mail. (27 Feb.

1997).

(3) Content Notes

Content notes—multiple bibliographical citations or explanations or other material that does not fit smoothly into the text—are indicated by a superscript (raised numeral) in the paper. Notes can appear either as footnotes at the bottom of the page or as endnotes on a separate page entitled *Notes*, placed after the last page of the paper and before the Works Cited list. Content notes are double-spaced within and between entries.

For Multiple Bibliographical Citations

In the Paper

Many researchers emphasize the necessity of having dying patients

share their experiences.[1]

In the Note

[1]Kübler-Ross 27; Stinnette 43; Poston 70; Cohen and Cohen

31–34; Burke 1:91–95.

For Explanations

In the Paper

The massacre of the Armenians during World War I is an event the

survivors could not easily forget.[2]

In the Note

[2]Many accounts of the Armenian massacre have been published.

For a firsthand account of this event, see Bedoukian 178–81. For a

fictional account, see Werfel.

43b Using CMS Format

The *Chicago Manual of Style** (CMS) is used in history and some social science and humanities disciplines. (Excerpts from a student research paper illustrating the use of CMS format appear in **47d2.**) **CMS format** has two parts: notes at the end of the paper (endnotes) and a list of bibliographic citations. (Although Chicago style encourages the use of endnotes, it also allows the use of footnotes at the bottom of the page.)

(1) Endnotes and Footnotes

The notes format calls for a superscript (raised numeral) in the text after source material you have either quoted or referred to. This numeral, placed after all punctuation marks except dashes, corresponds to the numeral that accompanies the note.

✔ CHECKLIST: PREPARING THE CMS ENDNOTES

✔ Begin endnotes on a new page after the last page of the paper.
✔ Number the page on which the endnotes appear as the next page of the paper.
✔ Type and number notes in the order in which they appear in the paper, beginning with number 1.
✔ Type the note number on the line, followed by a period and one space.
✔ Indent the first line of each note three spaces; type subsequent lines flush with the left-hand margin.
✔ Double-space within and between entries.

Endnote and Footnote Format: CMS

In the Text

By November of 1942, the Allies had proof that the Nazis were engaged in the systemic killing of Jews.[1]

In the Note

   1. David S. Wyman, *The Abandonment of the Jews: America and the Holocaust 1941–1945* (New York: Pantheon Books, 1984), 65.

---

*The Chicago format follows the guidelines set in *The Chicago Manual of Style*, 14th ed. Chicago: University of Chicago Press, 1993.

(2) Bibliography

In addition to the heading *Bibliography*, Chicago style allows *Selected Bibliography*, *Works Cited*, *Literature Cited*, *References*, and *Sources Consulted*.

✔ CHECKLIST: PREPARING THE CMS BIBLIOGRAPHY

✔ Type entries on a separate page after the endnotes.
✔ List entries alphabetically according to the author's last name.
✔ Type the first line of each entry flush with the left-hand margin; indent subsequent lines three spaces.
✔ Double-space the bibliography within and between entries.

Bibliography Format: CMS

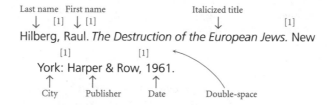

Last name   First name   Italicized title
  ↓ [1] ↓ [1]   ↓   [1]
Hilberg, Raul. *The Destruction of the European Jews.* New
    [1]   [1]
    York: Harper & Row, 1961.
    ↑   ↑   ↑
   City   Publisher   Date   Double-space

DIRECTORY OF CMS ENDNOTE AND BIBLIOGRAPHY ENTRIES

Entries for Books
1. A book by one author
2. A book by two or three authors
3. A book by more than three authors
4. An edited book
5. A chapter in a book or an essay in an anthology
6. A multivolume work
7. A dissertation
8. An article in a reference book
9. A government publication

continued on the following page

continued from the previous page

Entries for Articles

10. An article in a scholarly journal with continuous pagination through an annual volume
11. An article in a scholarly journal with separate pagination in each issue
12. An article in a weekly magazine
13. An article in a monthly magazine
14. An article in a newspaper

Entries for Nonprint Sources

15. A personal interview
16. A published interview
17. A letter
18. A film or videotape
19. A recording

Entries for Electronic Sources

20. Computer software
21. An electronic document

Subsequent References

Sample Chicago Manual of Style Endnote and Bibliography Entries Although underscoring to indicate italics is acceptable, Chicago style recommends the use of italics for titles.

Sample CMS Entries: Books

1. A Book by One Author

Endnote

1. Herbert J. Gans, *The Urban Villagers,* 2d ed. (New York: Free Press, 1982), 100.

Bibliography

Gans, Herbert J. *The Urban Villagers.* 2d ed. New York: Free Press, 1982.

2. A Book by Two or Three Authors

Endnote

2. James W. Davidson and Mark Hamilton Lytle, *After the Fact: The Art of Historical Detection* (New York: Alfred A. Knopf, 1982), 54.

Bibliography

Davidson, James W., and Mark Hamilton Lytle. *After the Fact: The Art of Historical Detection.* New York: Alfred A. Knopf, 1982.

3. A Book by More than Three Authors

Endnote

3. Robert E. Spiller et al., eds., *Literary History of the United States* (New York: Macmillan, 1974), 24.

Bibliography

Spiller, Robert E., et al., eds. *Literary History of the United States.* New York: Macmillan, 1974.

4. An Edited Book

Endnote

4. William Bartram, *The Travels of William Bartram,* ed. Mark Van Doren (New York: Dover Press, 1955), 85.

Bibliography

Bartram, William. *The Travels of William Bartram.* Edited by Mark Van Doren. New York: Dover Press, 1955.

5. A Chapter in a Book or an Essay in an Anthology

Endnote

5. Peter Kidson, "Architecture and City Planning," in *The Legacy of Greece,* ed. M. I. Finley (New York: Oxford University Press, 1981), 376–400.

Bibliography

Kidson, Peter. "Architecture and City Planning." In *The Legacy of Greece,* ed. M. I. Finley, 376–400. New York: Oxford University Press, 1981.

6. A Multivolume Work

Endnote

6. Kathleen Raine, *Blake and Tradition* (Princeton: Princeton University Press, 1968), 1: 143.

Bibliography

Raine, Kathleen. *Blake and Tradition.* Vol. 1. Princeton: Princeton
University Press, 1968.

7. A Dissertation

Endnote

7. Shawn Peterson, "Loving Mothers and Lost Daughters: Images
of Female Kinship Relations in Selected Novels of Toni Morrison" (Ph.D.
diss., University of Oregon, 1993), abstract in *Dissertation Abstracts
International* 53 (1994): 9322935.

Bibliography

Peterson, Shawn. "Loving Mothers and Lost Daughters: Images of
Female Kinship Relations in Selected Novels of Toni Morrison."
Ph.D. diss., University of Oregon, 1993. Abstract in *Dissertation
Abstracts International* 53 (1994): 9322935.

8. An Article in a Reference Book

Endnote

8. *The Focal Encyclopedia of Photography,* 1995 ed., s.v.
"Daguerreotype."

Bibliography

The Focal Encyclopedia of Photography. 1995 ed., s.v. "Daguerreotype."

NOTE: The abbreviation *s.v.* stands for *sub verbo* ("under the word").

9. A Government Publication

Endnote

9. President's Commission for the Study of Ethical Problems in
Medicine and Biomedical Research, *Deciding to Forgo Life-Sustaining
Treatment: Ethical, Medical, and Legal Issues in Treatment Decisions*
(Washington, D.C.: GPO, 1989), 75.

Bibliography

President's Commission for the Study of Ethical Problems in Medicine and Biomedical Research. *Deciding to Forgo Life-Sustaining Treatment: Ethical, Medical, and Legal Issues in Treatment Decisions.* Washington, D.C.: GPO, 1989.

Sample CMS Entries: Articles

10. An Article in a Scholarly Journal with Continuous Pagination through an Annual Volume

Endnote

10. John Huntington, "Science Fiction and the Future," *College English* 37 (fall 1975): 341.

Bibliography

Huntington, John. "Science Fiction and the Future." *College English* 37 (fall 1975): 340–58.

11. An Article in a Scholarly Journal with Separate Pagination in Each Issue

Endnote

11. R. G. Sipes, "War, Sports, and Aggression: An Empirical Test of Two Rival Theories," *American Anthropologist* 4, no. 2 (1973): 80.

Bibliography

Sipes, R. G. "War, Sports, and Aggression: An Empirical Test of Two Rival Theories." *American Anthropologist* 4, no. 2 (1973): 65–84.

12. An Article in a Weekly Magazine

Endnote

12. James Traub, "The Hearts and Minds of City College," *New Yorker,* 7 June 1993, 45.

Bibliography

Traub, James. "The Hearts and Minds of City College." *New Yorker,* 7 June 1993, 42–53.

13. An Article in a Monthly Magazine

Endnote

13. Lori Roll, "Careers in Engineering," *Working Woman,* November 1982, 62.

Bibliography

Roll, Lori. "Careers in Engineering." *Working Woman,* November 1982, 62.

14. An Article in a Newspaper

Endnote

14. Raymond Bonner, "A Guatemalan General's Rise to Power," *New York Times,* 21 July 1982, 3(A).

Bibliography

Bonner, Raymond. "A Guatemalan General's Rise to Power." *New York Times,* 21 July 1982, 3(A).

Sample CMS Entries: Nonprint Sources

15. A Personal Interview

Endnote

15. Cornel West, interview by author, tape recording, St. Louis, Mo., 8 June 1994.

Bibliography

West, Cornel. Interview by author. Tape recording. St. Louis, Mo., 8 June 1994.

16. A Published Interview

Endnote

16. Gwendolyn Brooks, interview by George Stravos, *Contemporary Literature* 11, no. 1 (winter 1970): 12.

Bibliography

Brooks, Gwendolyn. Interview by George Stravos. *Contemporary Literature* 11, no. 1 (winter 1970): 1–20.

17. A Letter

Endnote

17. Amy Tan, letter to author, 7 April 1990.

Bibliography

Tan, Amy. Letter to author. 7 April 1990.

18. A Film or Videotape

Endnote

18. *Interview with Arthur Miller,* dir. William Schiff, 17 min., The Mosaic Group, 1987, videocassette.

Bibliography

Miller, Arthur. *Interview with Arthur Miller.* Directed by William Schiff. 17 min. The Mosaic Group, 1987. Videocassette.

19. A Recording

Endnote

19. Bob Marley, "Crisis," on *Bob Marley and the Wailers,* Kava Island Records compact disk 423 095-3.

Bibliography

Marley, Bob. "Crisis." On *Bob Marley and the Wailers.* Kava Island Records compact disk 423 095-3.

Sample CMS Entries: Electronic Sources

20. Computer Software

Endnote

20. *Reunion: The Family Tree Software,* vers. 2.0 for Macintosh, Lester Productions, Cambridge, Mass.

Bibliography

Reunion: The Family Tree Software. Vers. 2.0 for Macintosh. Lester Productions, Cambridge, Mass.

21. An Electronic Document

The *Chicago Manual of Style* recommends following the guidelines developed by the International Standards Organization (ISO). List the authors, the title, the electronic medium (electronic bulletin board, for example), information about a print version, access dates, and electronic address or location information.

Endnote

21. Arthur Sklar, "Survey of Legal Opinions Regarding the Death Penalty in New Jersey," in NL-KR (Digest vol. 3, no. 2) [electronic bulletin board] (Newark, N. J., 1995 [cited 17 March 1997]); available from nl-kr@cs.newark.edu; INTERNET.

Bibliography

Sklar, Arthur. "Survey of Legal Opinions Regarding the Death Penalty in New Jersey." In NL-KR (Digest vol. 3, no. 2) [electronic bulletin board]. Newark, N. J., 1995 [cited 17 March 1997]. Available from nl-kr@cs.newark.edu; INTERNET.

Sample CMS Entries: Subsequent References In the first reference to a work, use the full citation; in subsequent references to the same work, list only the author's last name, followed by a comma and a page number.

First Note on Espinoza

1. J. M. Espinoza, *The First Expedition of Vargas in New Mexico, 1692* (Albuquerque: University of New Mexico Press, 1949), 10–12.

Subsequent Note

5. Espinoza, 29.

NOTE: *The Chicago Manual of Style* allows the use of the abbreviation *ibid.* ("in the same place") for subsequent references to the same work as long as there are no intervening references. *Ibid.* takes the place of the author's name and the work's title—but not the page number.

First Note on Espinoza

1. J. M. Espinoza, *The First Expedition of Vargas in New Mexico, 1692* (Albuquerque: University of New Mexico Press, 1949), 10–12.

Subsequent Note

2. Ibid., 23.

Keep in mind, however, that the use of *Ibid.* is giving way to the use of the author's last name and the page number in subsequent notes.

43c Using APA Format*

APA format, which is used extensively in the social sciences, relies on short parenthetical citations consisting of the last name of the author, the year of publication, and—for direct quotations—the page number. These references are keyed to an alphabetical list of references that follows the paper. APA format also permits content notes placed after the last page of the text. (A student paper illustrating the use of APA format appears in **48d.**)

(1) Parenthetical References in the Text

When introducing a *quotation,* include the author's name and the date in the introductory phrase, and include just the page number in the parenthetical reference after the quotation.

> According to Weston (1996), children from single-parent homes read
>
> at "a significantly lower level than those from two-parent homes"
>
> (p. 58).

When introducing a *paraphrase or summary,* include the author's name and the date either in the introductory phrase or in the parenthetical reference at the end of the paraphrase or summary.

> According to Zinn (1995), this program has had success in training
>
> teenage fathers to take financial and emotional responsibility for their
>
> offspring.

> This program has had success in training teenage fathers to take
>
> financial and emotional responsibility for their offspring (Zinn,
>
> 1995).

Although APA style does not require a page number for a paraphrase or summary, it encourages writers to provide one, especially when referring to a long, complex passage.

---

*APA documentation format follows the guidelines set in the *Publication Manual of the American Psychological Association,* 4th ed. Washington, DC: APA, 1994.

DIRECTORY OF APA IN-TEXT CITATIONS

1. A work by a single author
2. A work by two authors
3. A work by three to five authors
4. A work by six or more authors
5. A work by a corporate author
6. A work with no listed author
7. A personal communication
8. An indirect source
9. A specific part of a source
10. Two or more works within the same parenthetical reference
11. A long quotation
12. A table

Sample APA In-Text Citations

1. A Work by a Single Author

Supporters of bilingual education programs often speak about the psychological well-being of the child (Bakka, 1992).

NOTE: When the author's name and date appear in the parenthetical reference, APA style requires a comma between the name and the date.

2. A Work by Two Authors

When a work has two authors, cite both names every time you refer to it.

There is growing concern over the use of psychological testing in elementary schools (Albright & Glennon, 1982).

3. A Work by Three to Five Authors

If a work has more than two but fewer than six authors, mention all names in the first reference, and in subsequent references cite the first author followed by *et al.* and the year.

(Sparks et al., 1984).

4. A Work by Six or More Authors

When a work has six or more authors, cite the name of the first author followed by *et al.* and the year in all references.

(Miller et al., 1995).

 CITING WORKS BY MULTIPLE AUTHORS

When referring to multiple authors in the text of your paper, join the last two names with *and*.

According to Rosen, Wolfe, and Ziff (1988). . . .

When referring to multiple authors in parenthetical references, however, use an ampersand.

(Rosen, Wolfe, & Ziff, 1988).

---

5. A Work by a Corporate Author

Spell out the name of a corporate author each time you cite it. If the name is long, you may abbreviate it after the first citation.

First Reference

(National Institute of Mental Health [NIMH], 1994)

Subsequent Reference

(NIMH, 1994)

6. A Work with No Listed Author

If a work has no listed author, cite the first two or three words of the title (capitalized) and the year. Use quotation marks around the title of an article, and underline the title of a periodical or book.

("New Immigration," 1994).

7. A Personal Communication

Cite letters, memos, telephone conservations, personal interviews, E-mail, messages from electronic bulletin boards, and the like only in the text of your paper (not in the reference list). Give the initials and last name of the person with whom you communicated and the date.

(R. Takaki, personal communication, October 17, 1996).

8. An Indirect Source

Identify statements by one author mentioned in the work of another with the phrase *as cited in.*

Cogan and Howe offer very different interpretations of the problem (as

cited in Swenson, 1990).

9. A Specific Part of a Source

Use abbreviations for the words *page* (p.), *chapter* (chap.), and *section* (sec.).

These theories have an interesting history (Lee, 1966, chap. 2).

10. Two or More Works within the Same Parenthetical Reference

List works by different authors in alphabetical order. Use semicolons between citations.

This theory was supported by several studies (Barson & Roth, 1985;

Rose, 1987; Tedesco, 1982).

List works by the same author or authors in order of date of publication.

This theory was supported by several studies (Weiss & Elliot, 1982,

1984, 1985).

Distinguish works by the same author that appeared in the same year by designating the one whose title comes first alphabetically *a*, the one whose title comes next *b*, and so on; repeat the year in each citation.

This theory was supported by several studies (Hossack, 1985a, 1985b).

11. A Long Quotation

Long quotations (forty words or more) are double-spaced and indented five spaces from the left margin. If the quotation is more than one paragraph long, indent the first line of the second and subsequent paragraphs an additional five spaces from the margin of the quotation. Place parenthetical documentation after the final punctuation mark.

Todd Gitlin (1987) sees a change in left-wing politics beginning in 1969:

> Women had been the cement of the male-run movement; their
> "desertion" into their own circles completed the dissolution of
> the old boys' clan. While men outside the hard-line factions were
> miserable with the crumbling of their onetime movement,
> women were riding high. (p. 374)

12. A Table

See
Ald

If you use a **table** from a source, give credit to the author in a note at the bottom of the table.

Note. From "Predictors of Employment and Earnings among JOBS

Participants," P. A. Neenan and D. K. Orthner, 1996, Social Work

Research, 20(4), p. 233.

(2) Reference List

The list of all the sources cited in your paper falls at the end on a new numbered page headed *References* (or *Bibliography* if you are listing all the works you consulted, whether or not you cited them).

✔ CHECKLIST: PREPARING THE APA REFERENCE LIST

- ✔ Begin the reference list on a new page after the last page of the paper or after the content notes.
- ✔ Number the page on which the reference list appears as the next page of the paper.
- ✔ List the items on the reference list alphabetically (with author's last name first). Spell out the author's last name, and use initials for the first and middle names.
- ✔ Indent the first line of each entry five to seven spaces; type subsequent lines flush with the left-hand margin. This format, called a *paragraph indent,* is now recommended by the APA for all manuscripts submitted for publication. (If your instructor prefers, you may instead use a *hanging indent,* typing the first line of each entry flush with the left margin and indenting subsequent lines three spaces.)
- ✔ Separate the major divisions of each entry with a period and one space.
- ✔ Double-space the reference list within and between entries.

Reference List Format: APA

Last name   Initials   Date   Underlined title (only first word capitalized)
↓   ↓ [1] ↓   [1]   ↓   [1]
Morgan, C. T. (1986). Introduction to psychology. New

York: Knopf.
↑ [1] ↑
City   Publisher   Double-space

✔ CHECKLIST: ARRANGING WORKS IN THE APA REFERENCE LIST

✔ Single-author entries precede multiple-author entries that begin with the same name.

Field, S. (1987).

Field, S., & Levitt, M. P. (1984).

✔ Entries by the same author or authors are arranged according to date of publication, starting with the earliest date.

Ruthenberg, H., & Rubin, R. (1985).

Ruthenberg, H., & Rubin, R. (1987).

✔ Entries with the same author or authors and date of publication are arranged alphabetically according to title, with the first designated *a*, the second *b*, and so on. These entries include lowercase letters after the year.

Wolk, E. M. (1986a). Analysis . . .

Wolk, E. M. (1986b). Hormonal . . .

DIRECTORY OF APA REFERENCE LIST ENTRIES

Entries for Books
1. A book by a single author
2. A book by more than one author
3. An edited book
4. A book with no listed author or editor

continued on the following page

continued from the previous page

5. A work in several volumes
6. A work by a corporate author
7. A government report
8. One selection from an anthology
9. An article in a reference book
10. The foreword, preface, or afterword of a book

Entries for Articles

11. An article in a scholarly journal with continuous pagination through an annual volume
12. An article in a scholarly journal with separate pagination in each issue
13. A magazine article
14. A newspaper article (signed/unsigned)

Entries for Nonprint Sources

15. A letter to the editor
16. A published letter

Entries for Electronic Sources

17. Online article
18. Abstract on CD-ROM
19. Abstract online
20. Computer software
21. E-mail and messages from electronic bulletin boards

Sample APA Reference List Entries: Books   Capitalize only the first word of the title and the first word of the subtitle. Underline the entire title, including punctuation, and enclose the date, volume number, and edition number in parentheses. Write out the publisher's name in full.

1. A Book by a Single Author

> Maslow, A. H. (1974). <u>Toward a psychology of being.</u> Princeton: Van Nostrand.

2. A Book by More Than One Author

List all the authors—by last name and initials—regardless of how many there are. (Do not use *et al.*) All authors are cited last name first. Use an ampersand (not *and*) before the last author's name.

Wolfinger, D., Knable, P., Richards, H. L., & Silberger, R. (1990). The chronically unemployed. New York: Berman Press.

3. An Edited Book

Lewin, K., Lippitt, R., & White, R. K. (Eds.). (1985). Social learning and imitation. New York: Basic Books.

4. A Book with No Listed Author or Editor

Writing with a computer. (1993). Philadelphia: Drexel Publications.

5. A Work in Several Volumes

Jones, P. R., & Williams, T. C. (Eds.). (1990–1993). Handbook of therapy (Vols. 1–2). Princeton: Princeton University Press.

6. A Work by a Corporate Author

League of Women Voters of the United States. (1991). Local league handbook. Washington, DC: Author.

NOTE: When the author and publisher are the same, list *Author* at the end of the citation instead of repeating the publisher's name.

7. A Government Report

National Institute of Mental Health. (1987). Motion pictures and violence: A summary report of research (DHHS Publication No. ADM 91-22187). Washington, DC: U.S. Government Printing Office.

8. One Selection from an Anthology

Lorde, A. (1984). Age, race, and class. In P. S. Rothenberg (Ed.), Racism and sexism: An integrated study (pp. 352–360). New York: St. Martin's.

NOTE: A title of a selection in an anthology is treated as an article. Therefore, it is not underscored or enclosed in quotation marks. If you cite two or more selections from the same anthology, give the full citation for the anthology in each entry.

9. An Article in a Reference Book

> Edwards, P. (Ed.). (1987). Determinism. In The encyclopedia of philosophy (Vol. 2, pp. 359–373). New York: Macmillan.

10. The Foreword, Preface, or Afterword of a Book

> Taylor, T. (1979). Preface. In Less than slaves by Benjamin B. Ferencz. Cambridge: Harvard University Press.

Sample APA Reference List Entries: Articles   Capitalize only the first word of the title and the first word of the subtitle. Do not underline the title of the article or enclose it in quotation marks. Give the periodical title in full; underline the title and capitalize all major words. Underline the volume number but not the issue number in parentheses. Give inclusive page numbers. Use *pp.* when referring to page numbers in newspapers, but omit this abbreviation when referring to page numbers in periodicals with volume numbers.

11. An Article in a Scholarly Journal with Continuous Pagination through an Annual Volume

> Miller, W. (1969). Violent crimes in city gangs. Journal of Social Issues 27, 581–593.

12. An Article in a Scholarly Journal with Separate Pagination in Each Issue

> Williams, S., & Cohen, L. R. (1984). Child stress in early learning situations. American Psychologist, 21(10), 1–28.

13. A Magazine Article

> McCurdy, H. G. (1983, June). Brain mechanisms and intelligence. Psychology Today, pp. 61–63.

14. A Newspaper Article (Signed/Unsigned)

> James, W. R. (1993, November 16). The uninsured and health care. The Wall Street Journal, pp. A1, A14.

NOTE: Article appears on two separate pages; it begins on A1 and continues on A14.

Study finds many street people mentally ill. (1993, June 7). New York Times, p. A7.

15. A Letter to the Editor

Williams, P. (1993, July 19). Self-fulfilling stereotypes [Letter to the editor]. Los Angeles Times, p. A22.

16. A Published Letter

Joyce, J. (1931). Letter to Louis Gillet. In Richard Ellmann, James Joyce (p. 631). New York: Oxford University Press.

NOTE: Personal letters and interviews are cited in the text of the paper but not included in the reference list.

Sample APA Reference List Entries: Electronic Sources

FORMAT: ELECTRONIC SOURCES

Author, I. (date). Title of Article [number of paragraphs]. Name of Periodical [Online], xx. Available: Specify path

NOTE: APA recommends Li Crane's *Electronic Style: A Guide to Citing Electronic Information* (1993) for formats not covered here.

---

17. Online Article

Farrell, P. D. (1997, March). New high-tech stresses hit traders and investors on the information superhighway [14 paragraphs]. Wall Street News [Online serial]. Available: http:wall-street-news.com/forecasts/stress/stress.html

NOTE: There is no period after the electronic address.

18. Abstract on CD-ROM

Guiot, A., & Peterson, B. R. (1995). Forgetfulness and partial cognition. [CD-ROM]. Memory & Cognition, 23, 643–652. Abstract from: SilverPlatter File: PsycLIT Item: 90-14321

19. Abstract Online

>Guiot, A., & Peterson, B. R. (1995). Forgetfulness and partial
>
>cognition. [Online]. <u>Memory & Cognition, 23,</u> 643–652. Abstract from:
>
>DIALOG File: PsycINFO Item: 90-14321

20. Computer Software

>Sharp, S. (1995). Career Selection Tests (Version 5.0) [Computer
>
>software]. Chico, CA: Avocation Software.

21. E-Mail and Messages from Electronic Bulletin Boards

E-mail and messages from electronic bulletin boards are not included in the reference list. They are cited only in the text of the paper.

(3) Content Notes

APA format allows, but does not encourage, the use of content notes, indicated by superscripts (raised numerals) in the text. The notes are listed on a separate numbered page, entitled *Footnotes,* following the last page of text. Double-space all notes, indenting the first line of each note five to seven spaces and beginning subsequent lines flush left.

In the Text

Skinner's behaviorist theories fell into disfavor and were displaced by

the ideas of cognitive psychologists.[1]

In the Note

>[1]Skinner himself remained largely unconvinced by the cognitive
>
>theorists. In a <u>New York Times</u> interview just two weeks before his
>
>death in 1990, he affirmed his belief in his model of human behavior.

43d Using CBE Format*

Documentation formats recommended by the Council of Biological Editors (CBE) and published by Cambridge University Press are used by authors, editors, and publishers in biology, botany, zoology, physiology,

---

*CBE documentation format follows the guidelines set in *Scientific Style and Format: The CBE Manual for Authors, Editors, and Publishers,* 6th ed. Cambridge: Cambridge UP, 1994.

anatomy, and genetics. The *CBE Style Manual* recommends several documentation styles, including the number-reference format described below. This format calls for either raised numerals in the text of the paper (the preferred form) or numerals inserted parenthetically in the text to correspond to a list entitled *References, Literature Cited,* or *References Cited* at the end of the paper.

In the Paper

One study[1] has demonstrated the effect of low dissolved oxygen. Cell walls of. . . .

In the Reference List

1. White, RP. An introduction to biochemistry. Philadelphia: W. B. Saunders; 1994, 570 p.

NOTE: You can refer to more than one source in a single note. The numbers are separated by a dash if they are in sequence and by a comma if they are not.

✔ CHECKLIST: PREPARING THE CBE REFERENCE LIST

✔ Begin the reference list on a new page after the last page of the paper.

✔ Number the page on which the reference list appears as the next page of the paper.

✔ List the items in the order in which they appear in the paper, not alphabetically. (Each entry in the reference list should be cited at least once in the body of your paper.) Spell out the author's last name, and use initials for the first and middle names.

✔ Number the entries consecutively; type the note numbers on (not above) the line, followed by a period.

✔ Type the first line of each entry flush with the left-hand margin; align subsequent lines directly beneath the first letter of the author's last name.

✔ Double-space within and between entries.

Reference List Format: CBE

Name   Initials   Title not underlined, only first word capitalized
 ↓   ↓[2]   ↓   [2]
1. White, RP. An introduction to biochemistry.

Philadelphia: W. B. Saunders; 1994.
 ↑   ↑   ↑
City   Publisher   Date   Double-space

DIRECTORY OF CBE REFERENCE LIST ENTRIES

1. A book by a single author
2. A book by more than one author
3. An edited book
4. A specific section of a book
5. A chapter in a book or an essay in an anthology
6. An article in a scholarly journal with continuous pagination through an annual volume
7. An article in a scholarly journal with separate pagination in each issue
8. An article with no listed author
9. An electronic source

Sample CBE Reference List Entries: Books   List the author or authors (last name first), the title (not underlined, and with only the first word capitalized), the place of publication (followed by a colon), the full name of the publisher (followed by a semicolon), the year (followed by a period), and the total number of pages (followed by a period).

1. A Book by a Single Author

> 1. Key, K. Plant biology. Fort Worth: Harcourt Brace; 1995. 437 p.

2. A Book by More Than One Author

> 2. Krause, KF, Paterson, MK. Tissue culture: methods and application. New York: Academic Press; 1993. 217 p.

3. An Edited Book

> 3. Marzacco, MP, editor. A survey of biochemistry. New York: Bowker; 1985. 523 p.

4. A Specific Section of a Book

> 4. Baldwin, LD, Rigby, CV. A study of animal virology. New York: Wiley; 1984: p 121–133.

5. A Chapter in a Book or an Essay in an Anthology

> 5. Brydon, RB, Ellis, J, Scott, CD. Cell division and cancer treatment. In Gotlieb, JM. editor. Current research in cancer treatment. New York: Springer-Verlag; 1996: p 34–47.

Sample CBE Reference List Entries: Articles List the author or authors (last name first), the title of the article (with only the first word capitalized), the abbreviated name of the journal (with all major words capitalized, but not underlined), the year (followed by a semicolon), the volume number (followed by a colon), and inclusive page numbers. No spaces separate the year, the volume, and the page numbers.

6. *An Article in a Scholarly Journal with Continuous Pagination through an Annual Volume*

6. Bensley, KR. Profiling women physicians. Medica 1985;1:140–145.

7. *An Article in a Scholarly Journal with Separate Pagination in Each Issue*

7. Paul, DR, Wang, AR, Richards, L. The human genome project. Sci Am 1995 Sept;285(2):43–52.

8. *An Article with No Listed Author*

8. [Anonymous]. Developments in microbiology. Int J Microbiol 1987;6:234–248.

9. *An Electronic Source*

List the author or authors, the title (followed by the journal title, along with the date and volume number, in the case of journal articles), the electronic medium [*serial online* for periodicals and *monograph online* for books], the date of publication, the words *Available from* followed by a colon and the electronic address, and the date of access.

9. Bensley, KR. Profiling women physicians. Medica [serial online] 1985;1. Available from: ftp.lib.nscu.edu via the INTERNET. Accessed 1997 Feb 18.

 43e Using Other Documentation Styles

The following **style manuals** describe documentation formats different than the ones already discussed.

Chemistry

American Chemical Society. *The ACS Style Guide. A Manual for Authors and Editors.* Janet S. Dodd, editor. Washington: American Chemical Soc., 1997.

Government Documents

Garner, Diane L. *The Complete Guide to Citing Government Information Resources: A Manual for Writers and Librarians.* Rev. ed. Bethesda: Congressional Information Service, 1993.

Geology

United States Geological Survey. *Suggestions to Authors of the Reports of the United States Geological Survey.* 7th ed. Washington: GPO, 1991.

History

The Chicago Manual of Style. 14th ed. Chicago: U of Chicago P, 1993.

Journalism

Associated Press Staff. *Associated Press Stylebook and Libel Manual.* Reading, MA: Addison, 1992.

Law

The Bluebook: A Uniform System of Citation. Comp. Editors of *Columbia Law Review* et al. 15th ed. Cambridge: Harvard Law Review, 1991.

Linguistics

Linguistic Society of America. "LSA Style Sheet." Published annually in December issue of the *LSA Bulletin.*

Mathematics

American Mathematical Society. *A Manual for Authors of Mathematical Papers.* Rev. ed. Providence: AMS, 1990.

Medicine

Iverson, Cheryl, et al. *American Medical Association Manual of Style.* 8th ed. Baltimore: Williams and Wilkins, 1989.

Music

Kirn, Holman D., ed. *Writing about Music: A Style Sheet from the Editors of 19th-Century Music.* Berkeley: U of California P, 1988.

Physics

American Institute of Physics. *AIP Style Manual.* 4th ed. New York: Am. Inst. of Physics, 1990.

Scientific and Technical Writing

Rubens, Philip, ed. *Science and Technical Writing: A Manual of Style.* Fort Worth: Harcourt, 1992.

NOTE: For other guides to style see John Bruce Howell. *Style Manuals of the English-Speaking World: A Guide.* Phoenix: Oryx, 1983.

43f Using Abbreviations

Many of the abbreviations that once made documenting sources so tedious have been eliminated from the latest editions of style manuals. Because you may still encounter such abbreviations, however (and because some are still in use), you should be familiar with them.

COMMONLY USED SCHOLARLY ABBREVIATIONS

anon.	anonymous
bk.	book
c., ca.	circa ("about"). Used with dates that are approximate, as in *c. 1920* (approximately 1920).
cf.	*confer* ("compare")
ch.	chapter
col.	column
colloq.	colloquial
comp., comps.	compiled by, compiler(s)
diss.	dissertation
ed.	edition, editor, edited by
e.g.	*exempli gratia* ("for example")
et al.	*et alia* ("and others")
ff.	and the following pages, as in *pp. 88 ff.*
i.e.	*id est* ("that is")
illus.	illustrated by, illustration
l., ll.	line(s)
ms., mss.	manuscript(s)
n., nn.	note(s), as in *p. 12, n. 1*
NB	*nota bene* ("take notice")

continued on the following page

---

continued from the previous page

n.d.	no date (of publication)
n.p.	no place (of publication), no publisher
n. pag.	no pagination
p., pp.	page(s)
rev.	revision, revised by; review, reviewed by
rpt.	reprint, reprinted by
sec.	section
supp.	supplement
trans.	translated by, translator, translation
vol.	volume

EXERCISE

The following notes identify sources used in a paper on censorship and the Internet. Following the proper format for MLA parenthetical documentation, create a parenthetical reference for each source, and then arrange the sources in the proper order for the Works Cited list. (If your instructor requires a different method of documentation, use that style instead.)

1. Page 72 in a book called Banned in the USA by Herbert N. Foerstel. The book has 231 pages and was published in 1994 by Greenwood Press, located in Westport, Connecticut. The author's name appears in the text of your paper.

2. A statement made by Esther Dyson in her keynote address at the Newspapers 1996 Conference. Her statement is quoted in an article by Jodi B. Cohen called Fighting Online Censorship. The speech has not been printed in any other source. The article is in the April 13, 1996, edition of the weekly business journal Editor & Publisher. Dyson's quotation appears on page 44. The article begins on page 44 and continues on page 60. Dyson's name is mentioned in the text of your paper.

3. If You Don't Love It, Leave It, an essay by Esther Dyson in the New York Times Magazine, July 15, 1995, on pages 26 and 27. Your quotation comes from the second page of the essay. No author's name is mentioned in the text of your paper.

4. An essay by Nat Hentoff entitled Speech Should Not Be Limited on pages 22–26 of the book Censorship: Opposing Viewpoints, edited by Terry O'Neill. The book is published by Greenhaven Press in St. Paul, Minnesota. The publication year is 1985. The quotation you have used is from page 24, and the author is mentioned in the text of your paper.

5. An essay on the Internet called A Parent's Guide to Supervising a Child's Online and Internet Experiences. The document is by Robert Cannon, Esq., and you have Version 1.0 of the essay, which was updated May 10, 1996. Though the essay prints out on four pages, the pages are not numbered. In your paper you summarize information from the second and third pages of the document. You accessed the information on January 20, 1997, through the library's Internet provider. The author's name is mentioned in the text of your paper.

6. The first page of the introduction to Censorship: Opposing Viewpoints. The introduction is on pages 13 and 14. The author's name is mentioned in the text of your paper.

7. Page 89 in Foerstel's book. No author mentioned in the text of your paper.

8. An editorial by Robert A. Sirico, entitled Don't Censor the Internet, appears in Forbes Magazine, July 29, 1996, on page 48. The author's name appears in the text of your paper.

9. The Cyber Cops, which you found in Ms. magazine. The article is by Sandy M. Fernandez. It appears in the May-June issue on pages 22 and 23. You paraphrase a paragraph on page 22. The author's name is mentioned in the text of your paper.

10. Page A17 of an article in the Chronicle of Higher Education by Thomas J. DeLoughry and Jeffrey R. Young. The title of the article is Internet Restrictions Ruled Unconstitutional. It runs on pages A17, A19, and A20 in the June 21, 1996, edition. You do not mention the authors in the text of your paper.

11. A passage from the second page of the article in the New York Times Magazine. No authors mentioned in the text of your paper.

12. An essay in the Village Voice entitled The Speech Police Invade Cyberspace by Nat Hentoff. It was published on July 11, 1995, on pages 22 and 23. You mention the author's name in the text of your paper.

13. A book written by Jonathan Wallace and Mark Mangan entitled Sex, Laws, and Cyberspace. It was published in 1996 by M&T Books in New York. The quotation you have used is from page 42. The authors' names are mentioned in the text of your paper.

CHAPTER 44

WRITING A RESEARCH PAPER

Research involves more than absorbing the ideas of others; when you undertake a research project, you begin a process that requires you to think critically, evaluating and interpreting the ideas in your sources and developing ideas of your own. In addition, research requires strategic planning, careful time management, and a willingness to rethink ideas and reshape discussions.

The research process can be demanding, time consuming, and frustrating, but it offers great rewards. It tests and reinforces your critical thinking skills, exposes you to new ideas, and gives you an opportunity to explore a single subject in depth. For these reasons, a research project is an important part of many college courses.

The following schedule can help you manage your time.

THE RESEARCH PROCESS

	Activity	Date Due	Date Completed
Planning Your Paper	**Moving from Assignment to Topic**		
	• understanding your assignment **44a1**	___	___
	• choosing a topic **44a2**	___	___
	• keeping a research notebook **44a3**	___	___
	Doing Exploratory Research and Focusing on a Research Question		
	• mapping out a search strategy **44b1**	___	___
	• doing exploratory research **44b2**	___	___

continued on the following page

continued from the previous page

	Activity	Date Due	Date Completed
	• focusing on a research question **44b3**	_____	_____
	Assembling a Working Bibliography **44c**		
	Developing a Tentative Thesis **44d**		
	Doing Focused Research		
	• reading sources **44e1**	_____	_____
	• distinguishing between primary and secondary sources **44e2**	_____	_____
	• evaluating sources **44e3**	_____	_____
	Taking Notes **44f**	_____	_____
Shaping Your Material	*Deciding on a Thesis* **44g**	_____	_____
	Preparing a Formal Outline **44h**	_____	_____
Writing and Revising	*Writing a Rough Draft* **44i**	_____	_____
	Revising the Drafts **44j**	_____	_____
	Preparing a Final Draft **44k**	_____	_____

44a Moving from Assignment to Topic

(1) Understanding Your Assignment

Every research paper begins with an assignment. Before you can find a direction for your research, you must be sure you understand the exact requirements of this assignment.

| ✔ | CHECKLIST: UNDERSTANDING YOUR ASSIGNMENT |

- ✔ Has your instructor provided a list of possible topics, or are you expected to select a topic on your own?
- ✔ Is your purpose to explain or to persuade?
- ✔ Is your audience your instructor? Your fellow students? Both?
- ✔ Can you assume your audience knows a lot (or just a little) about your topic?
- ✔ When is the completed research paper due?
- ✔ About how long should it be?
- ✔ Will you be given a specific research schedule to follow, or are you expected to set your own schedule?
- ✔ Is collaborative work permitted? Is it encouraged? If so, at what stages of the research process?
- ✔ Does your instructor expect you to take notes on note cards? In a computer file?
- ✔ Does your instructor expect you to prepare a formal outline?
- ✔ Are instructor-student conferences required?
- ✔ Will your instructor review notes, outlines, or drafts with you at regular intervals?
- ✔ Does your instructor require you to do research only in the library, or can you also gather information outside the library?
- ✔ Are you expected to use your library's electronic resources?
- ✔ Are you encouraged to do research on the Internet?
- ✔ Does your instructor require you to keep a research notebook?
- ✔ What paper format and documentation style are you to use?
- ✔ What help is available to you—from your instructor, other students, experts in the field your paper will explore, community resources, your library?

(2) Choosing a Topic

Once you understand the requirements and scope of your assignment, you need to find a direction for your research. You begin this task by focusing on a topic you can explore within the boundaries of your assignment.

In many cases, your instructor will help you to choose a topic, either by providing a list of suitable topics or by suggesting a general subject area—a famous trial, an event that happened on the day you were born, a problem on your college campus. Even in these instances, you will still need to choose one of the topics or narrow the subject area: decide on one trial, one event, one problem.

If your instructor prefers that you select a topic entirely on your own, your task is somewhat more difficult: you must consider a number of different topics and weigh both their suitability for research and your interest in them. You decide on a topic for your paper in much the same way you decide on a topic for a short essay: you brainstorm, ask questions, talk to people, and read. With a research paper, however, you know from the start that you will examine not only your own ideas on a topic but also the ideas of others.

As you look for a suitable topic, keep the following guidelines in mind.

✔ CHECKLIST: CHOOSING A RESEARCH TOPIC

✔ **Are you genuinely interested in your research topic?** Remember that you will be deeply involved with the topic you select for weeks—perhaps even for an entire semester. If you lose interest in your topic, you are likely to see your research as a tedious chore rather than as an opportunity to discover new information, new associations, and new insights.

✔ **Is your topic suitable for research?** Topics limited to your personal experience and those based on value judgments are not suitable for research. For example, "The superiority of Freud's work to Jung's" might sound promising, but no amount of research can establish that one person's work is "better" than another's.

✔ **Are the boundaries of your research topic appropriate?** A research topic should be neither too broad nor too narrow. "Julius and Ethel Rosenberg: Atomic Spies or FBI Scapegoats?" is far too broad a topic for a ten-page—or even a one hundred-page—treatment, and "One piece of evidence that played a decisive role in establishing the Rosenbergs' guilt" would probably be too narrow for a ten-page research paper. But how two different newspapers reported the Rosenbergs' espionage trial or how a particular group of people (government employees, peace activists, or college students, for example) reacted at the time to the couple's 1953 execution might work well.

✔ **Can your topic be researched in a library to which you have access?** For instance, the library of an engineering or business school may not have a large collection of books of literary criticism; the library of a small liberal arts college may not have extensive resources for researching technical or medical topics. (Of course, if you have access to the Internet or to specialized databases, your options are greatly increased.)

(3) Keeping a Research Notebook

Keeping a **research notebook,** a combination journal of your reactions and log of your progress, is an important part of the research process. A research notebook maps out your direction and keeps you on track; throughout the research process it helps you define and redefine the boundaries of your assignment.

In this notebook you can record lists of things to do, sources to check, leads to follow up on, appointments, possible community contacts, questions to which you would like to find answers, stray ideas, possible thesis statements or titles, and so on. Be sure to date your entries and to check off and date work completed.

Some students use a spiral notebook that includes pockets to hold notes and bibliography cards. Others find a small assignment book more convenient. Still others prefer to use a special computer file for this purpose. Whatever form your research notebook takes, it can serve as a useful record of what has been done and what is left to do.

EXERCISE 1

Using your own instructor's guidelines for selecting a research topic, choose a topic for your paper. Then, start a research notebook by entering information about your assignment, schedule, and topic.

44b Doing Exploratory Research and Focusing on a Research Question

(1) Mapping Out a Search Strategy

See
39a

The key to successful research lies in finding out what questions to ask. Your research should be guided by a **search strategy**, a plan for systematically gathering and evaluating potential source material, moving from general to specific sources. At your first meeting your instructor can help you map out a tentative search strategy for researching the topic you have in mind and direct you to appropriate sources. Keep in mind, though, that as you continue your research, you will probably modify your search strategy to fit your changing priorities.

(2) Doing Exploratory Research

See
39b1

Exploratory research helps you get an overview of your topic and an understanding of its possibilities. One way to explore your topic is to discuss your ideas with others. Teachers, librarians, family, and friends may all suggest possible sources—sometimes unexpected or unconventional ones—for your paper. Another way to explore your topic is to skim general reference works—encyclopedias, for example—in your college library or online.

(3) Focusing on a Research Question

As you do exploratory research, your goal is to formulate a **research question,** the question you want your research paper to answer. A research question helps you to decide which sources to seek out, which to examine first, which to examine in depth, and which to skip entirely. The answer to this question will be your paper's **thesis statement.**

See
2b

Your assignment determines whether your paper will explain something to readers or persuade them, and your research question should reflect this general purpose. For example, the question "What characteristics do horror movies of the 1990s have in common?" calls for an informative paper. However, the question "Does the explicit violence in horror movies of the 1990s affect the behavior of adolescent viewers?" calls for a persuasive paper.

 44c **Assembling a Working Bibliography**

As you assess the value of potential sources, be sure to record complete bibliographic information and a brief evaluation for each source. You can enter this information directly into your research notebook or copy it on to individual index cards or into a computer file designated "Bibliography." (For examples of formats you can use to record bibliographic information, **see 45c.**)

CLOSE-UP **ASSEMBLING A WORKING BIBLIOGRAPHY**

As you record bibliographic information for your sources, you should include the following information.

Book   Author(s); Title (underlined or in italics); Call number (for further reference); City of publication; Publisher; Date of publication; Brief evaluation

continued on the following page

continued from the previous page
Article　Author(s); Title of article (in quotation marks); Title of journal (underlined or in italics); Volume number; Date; Inclusive page numbers; Electronic address (if applicable); Brief evaluation

See 43a2

Using complete bibliographic information in your notes now will decrease your chance of error and thus make your job of preparing your **Works Cited list** easier later on. Remember, bibliographic information should be *full* and *accurate;* if it is not, you may be unable to locate sources later.

In addition to keeping records of books and articles, you should also keep records of interviews (including telephone interviews), meetings, lectures, films, and other nonprint sources of information, as well as of electronic sources. Here too you should include not only basic identifying details—such as the date of an interview, the Web address (URL) of an Internet source, or the author of an article accessed from a database—but also a brief evaluation

See 44e3

of each source. This **evaluation** should include the kind of information the source contains, the amount of information offered, its relevance to your topic, and its limitations—whether it is biased or outdated, for instance.

As your research progresses, review your working bibliography regularly. Keeping your research question in mind, look over your list of sources and reevaluate them. Identify those that seem most useful, and make plans to reexamine them. (Retain notes on *all* the sources you have found, however, even those that do not seem very promising. You may decide to use a rejected source later on when you have a more definite direction for your research.) If you identify areas where additional sources are needed, plan to do further research.

CLOSE-UP　MANAGING SOURCES

Making informed choices early in the research process will save you a lot of time in the long run, so don't collect sources first and assess their usefulness later. Before you check a book out of the library, photocopy a journal article, or download a block of text, take the time to consider its relevance to your topic. Resist the temptation to check out every book that mentions your subject, photocopy page after page of perhaps only marginally useful articles, or download material from every electronic source to which
continued on the following page

continued from the previous page
you have access. After all, you will eventually have to read all these sources and take detailed notes on them. If you have too many sources, you will be overwhelmed, unable to remember why a particular idea or a certain article seemed important.

EXERCISE 2

Do exploratory research to find a research question for your paper, carefully evaluating the relevance and usefulness of each source. Then, compile a working bibliography for your research paper in progress by making a bibliographic record of each source. When you have finished, reevaluate your sources and plan additional research if necessary.

44d Developing a Tentative Thesis

Your **tentative thesis** is a preliminary statement of what you think your research will support. This statement, which you will eventually refine into a **thesis**, should be the answer to your research question.

See 2b

As you move through the research process, your tentative thesis and even your research question may change considerably. A line of inquiry may lead to a dead end, a key source may not be available, or an idea you uncover in your research may encourage you to branch out in a new direction. But whatever adjustments you make to your tentative thesis, it should grow increasingly more precise.

DEVELOPING A TENTATIVE THESIS

Subject Area
Computer technology

Topic	Research Question	Tentative Thesis
The possible negative effects of computer games on adolescents	Do computer games have any negative effects on adolescents?	Computer games interfere with adolescents' ability to learn.

continued on the following page

681

continued from the previous page
Subject Area
Feminism

Topic	Research Question	Tentative Thesis
The relationship between the feminist movement and the use of sexist language	What is the relationship between the feminist movement and the use of sexist language?	The feminist movement is largely responsible for the decline of sexist language.

Subject Area
Mood-altering drugs

Topic	Research Question	Tentative Thesis
The use of mood-altering drugs in state mental hospitals	How has the use of mood-altering drugs affected patients in state mental hospitals?	The use of mood-altering drugs has changed the population of state mental hospitals.

EXERCISE 3

Following your instructor's guidelines, develop a tentative thesis for your research paper.

44e Doing Focused Research

Once you have decided on a tentative thesis, you are ready to begin your focused research and note taking.

(1) Reading Sources

As you read, use **active reading** strategies: preview each source, skimming it quickly; then read it carefully, highlighting potentially useful material. Be sure to **read critically**: distinguish fact from opinion and evaluate writers' support carefully. Remain alert to bias, faulty reasoning, logical fallacies, and unfair appeals.

See 7b

It is important to **evaluate** the potential usefulness of each source as quickly as possible so you do not waste time reading irrelevant material. Before you begin, survey the work carefully. Check a book's index and the headings and subheadings in the table of contents to determine which pages to read thoroughly and which to skim, and look carefully at abstracts and headings of articles. These strategies will enable you to evaluate each source's usefulness to you as efficiently as possible.

See 44e3

As you look for sources, explore as many different viewpoints as possible. (Reading just the sources that present a single viewpoint will not give you the perspective you need to develop a balanced view of your topic.) You should also locate more sources than you actually intend to use in your paper because one or more of the sources you find may turn out to be one sided, outdated, unreliable, biased, superficial, or irrelevant—and therefore unusable. To be safe, then, you should collect about twice the number of sources you think you will need.

(2) Distinguishing Between Primary and Secondary Sources

An important part of evaluating a source is determining whether you are reading a **primary** or a **secondary source**—that is, whether you are considering original documents and observations or interpretations of those documents and observations.

PRIMARY SOURCE: United States Constitution, Amendment XIV (Ratified July 9, 1868). Section I.

All persons born or naturalized in the United States, and subject to the jurisdiction thereof, are citizens of the United States and the state wherein they reside. No state shall make or enforce any law which shall abridge the privileges or immunities of citizens of the United States; nor shall any state deprive any person of life, liberty, or property, without the process of law; nor deny to any person within its jurisdiction the equal protection of the laws.

SECONDARY SOURCE: Paula S. Rothenberg, *Racism and Sexism: An Integrated Study.*

Congress passed the Fourteenth Amendment . . . in July 1868. This amendment, which continues to play a major role in contemporary legal battles over discrimination, includes a number of important provisions. It explicitly extends citizenship to all those born or naturalized in the United States and guarantees all citizens due process and "equal protection" of the law.

For many research projects, primary sources such as letters, speeches, and data from questionnaires are essential. However, secondary sources, which provide the critical comments of scholars who know a good deal about the area you are studying, can also be valuable. Keep in mind, though, that the further you get from the primary source, the more chances exist for inaccuracies caused by researchers' inadvertent distortion and misinterpretation of material.

PRIMARY AND SECONDARY SOURCES

Primary Source	Secondary Source
Novel, poem	Literary criticism
Diary, autobiography	Biography
Letters, historical documents, oral testimony	Historical commentary
Newspaper report	Editorial
Raw data from questionnaires	Social science article
Observations/experiment	Scientific article
Television show/film	Review
Interview	Case study

---

(3) Evaluating Sources

Print Sources   One efficient way to evaluate a print source and its author is to ask a librarian or your instructor for an opinion. Remember, though, that even if a source is highly recommended, it may not suit your needs.

To assess the usefulness of a print source, ask the following questions.

Is the Source Relevant to Your Topic?   How detailed is its treatment of your subject? Skim a book's table of contents and index for references to your topic. To be of any real help, a book should devote a section or chapter to your topic, not simply a footnote or a brief mention. For articles, read the abstract, or skim the entire article for key facts, looking closely at section headings, information set in boldface type, and topic sentences. An article should have your topic as its central subject, or at least as a major concern.

Is the Source Current?   The date of publication tells you whether the information in a book or article is up to date. Scientific and technological subjects usually demand up-to-date treatment. A discussion of computer languages written in 1966, for instance, will now be obsolete. Even in the humanities, new discoveries and new ways of thinking lead scholars to reevaluate and modify their ideas.

Some classic works, however, never lose their usefulness. For example, although Edward Gibbon wrote *The History of the Decline and Fall of the Roman Empire* in the eighteenth century, the book still offers a valuable discussion of the events it describes. Contemporary historians may have newer information or may interpret events differently, but Gibbon's information is sound, and the book is required reading for anyone studying Roman history. If a number of your sources cite earlier works, you should consult those works, regardless of their publication dates. Do, however, be alert for out-of-date information in such sources.

Is the Source Reliable? Is a piece of writing largely fact or unsubstantiated opinion? Does the author support his or her conclusions thoroughly and appropriately? Is the supporting information balanced? Is the author objective? Here biographical information can be helpful. The source itself may contain such information, sometimes in a separate section, or you can consult a biographical dictionary. Skim the preface to see what the author says about purpose and methods. What do other sources say about the author? Do they consider the author fair? Biased? Compare a few statements with a fairly neutral source— a textbook or an encyclopedia, for instance—to see whether an author seems to be slanting facts.

Is the Source Respected? A contemporary review of a source can help you make this assessment. *Book Review Digest,* available in the reference section of your library, lists popular books that have been reviewed in at least three newspapers or magazines and includes excerpts from representative reviews. A larger number of books are indexed in *Book Review Index.* Although this index contains no excerpts, it does include citations that refer you to the periodicals in which books were reviewed. Book reviews are also available from the *New York Times Book Review*'s Website (http://www.nytimes.com/books), which includes text of book reviews it has published since 1980.

You can also find out about the standing of a source in the scholarly community by consulting a special class of indexes called **citation indexes.** These books list all scholarly articles published in a given year that mention a particular source. Information is listed under the original article, the author of the article in which the original article is mentioned, or the subject. Seeing how often an article is mentioned can help you determine how influential it is. Citation indexes are available for the humanities, the sciences, and the social sciences.

EVALUATING PRINT SOURCES

Use articles from popular periodicals such as *Newsweek* and *Sports Illustrated* with care. Assuming they are current and written by reputable authors, they may be appropriate for your research. But remember that they are aimed at a general audience, and not all adhere to the same kind of rigorous standards as scholarly publications. Although some popular periodicals—such as *Atlantic Monthly* and *Harper's*—generally contain articles that are reliable and carefully researched, others may not.

Nonprint Sources **Nonprint sources**—interviews, telephone calls, films, lectures, and so on—must also be evaluated. Here too you should consider the *relevance* of the source—the extent to which it addresses your needs. An expert on family planning who knows little about adolescent health problems may be an excellent source if your paper will focus on changing trends in birth control methods, but not if your paper is about teenage pregnancy.

The *currency* of a nonprint source is also a factor. A 1970 television documentary on the topography of a Pacific island may still be accurate, but a documentary on the lives of its people may not reflect today's conditions at all.

Reliability is important too. Is a radio feature on energy conservation part of a balanced news program or a thinly veiled commercial sponsored by a public utility or a special interest group? Is the material presented by experts in the field or by actors? Check the credits and acknowledgments and read reviews to see which sources were consulted. Do the participants in a panel discussion on global warming agree on the magnitude of the problem, or do they represent different points of view? Is the person you plan to interview fair and impartial or biased on some issues? Try to find out by consulting an instructor in a related field or by reading the person's writings before your interview.

EVALUATING INTERNET SOURCES

Evaluating the great variety of sources available on the Internet requires some special guidelines because the quality and reliability
continued on the following page

continued from the previous page
of these sources vary so dramatically. For specific advice on evaluating Internet sources, **see 40d.**

✔ CHECKLIST: EVALUATING SOURCES

✔ Are you considering a primary or a secondary source?

✔ How relevant is your source to your needs?
   How detailed is its treatment of your subject?
   Is your topic a major focus of your source?

✔ How current is your source?
   Have recent developments made any parts of your source dated?

✔ Does your source cite information from an earlier work? Is this information still sound?

✔ How reliable is your source?
   • Is your source largely fact or opinion? Are its opinions based on fact?
   • Is the **supporting evidence** accurate? Does the author present enough evidence to support his or her position? Does the author select representative examples?
   • Is your source meant to inform or to persuade?
   • Does the author of your source show any bias?
   • How respected is your source?
   • Do other scholars mention your source favorably?

See
7b2

EXERCISE 4

Read the following paragraphs carefully, paying close attention to the information provided about their sources and authors as well as to their content. Decide which sources would be most useful and reliable in supporting the thesis "Winning the right to vote has (or has not) significantly changed the role of women in national politics." Which sources, if any, should be disregarded? Which would you examine first? Be prepared to discuss your decisions.

1. Almost forty years after the adoption of the Nineteenth Amendment, a number of promised or threatened events have failed to materialize. The millennium has not arrived, but neither has the country's social

fabric been destroyed. Nor have women organized a political party to elect only women candidates to public office. . . . Instead, women have shown the same tendency to divide along orthodox party lines as male voters. (Eleanor Flexner, *Century of Struggle*, Atheneum 1968. *A scholarly treatment of women's roles in America since the* Mayflower, *this book was well reviewed by historians.*)

2. Woman has been the great unpaid laborer of the world, and although within the last two decades a vast number of new employments have been opened to her, statistics prove that in the great majority of these, she is not paid according to the value of the work done, but according to sex. The opening of all industries to women, and the wage question as connected with her, are the most subtle and profound questions of political economy, closely interwoven with the rights of self-government. (Susan B. Anthony; first appeared in Vol. I of *The History of Woman Suffrage;* reprinted in *Voices from Women's Liberation*, ed. Leslie B. Tanner, NAL 1970. *An important figure in the battle for women's suffrage, Susan B. Anthony* [1820–1906] *also lectured and wrote on abolition and temperance.*)

3. Women . . . have never been prepared to assume responsibility; we have never been prepared to make demands upon ourselves; we have never been taught to expect the development of what is best in ourselves because no one has ever expected *anything* of us—or for us. Because no one has ever had any intention of turning over any serious work to us. (Vivian Gornick, "The Next Great Moment in History Is Ours," *Village Voice* 1969. *The* Voice *is a liberal New York City weekly.*)

4. With women as half the country's elected representatives, and a woman President once in a while, the country's *machismo* problems would be greatly reduced. The old-fashioned idea that manhood depends on violence and victory is, after all, an important part of our troubles. . . . I'm not saying that women leaders would eliminate violence. We are not more moral than men; we are only uncorrupted by power so far. When we do acquire power, we might turn out to have an equal impulse toward aggression. (Gloria Steinem, "What It Would Be Like If Women Win," *Time* 1970. *Steinem, a well-known feminist and journalist, is one of the founders of* Ms. *magazine.*)

5. Nineteen eighty-two was the year that time ran out for the proposed equal rights amendment. Eleanor Smeal, president of the National Organization for Women, the group that headed the intense 10-year struggle for the ERA, conceded defeat on June 24. Only 24 words in all, the ERA read simply: "Equality of rights under the law shall not be denied or abridged by the United States or by any state on account of sex." Two major opinion polls had reported just

weeks before the ERA's defeat that a majority of Americans continued to favor the amendment. (June Foley, "Women 1982: The Year
That Time Ran Out," *The World Almanac & Book of Facts,* 1983.)

6. A chastened Senate yesterday bowed to Senator Carol Moseley-
Braun, its only African-American member, and reversed a vote that
would have given what an infuriated Moseley-Braun describes as an
"imprimatur" to an insignia that features the confederate flag.

   After an extraordinary emotional debate in which senators
talked with candor about racism in America, the Senate voted
75–25 to kill a proposal to renew a design patent for the insignia of
the United Daughters of the Confederacy (UDC). It featured the
original flag of the Confederacy encased in a wreath.

   Only a few hours before, the Senate signaled its intention to approve the proposal, sponsored by Senator Jesse Helms (R–NC), on
a procedural vote of 50–48.

   Helms contended the 24,000 UDC members were "delightful
gentleladies" engaged in charitable endeavors and deserving of the
largely honorific patent protection that Congress almost routinely
confers on national groups.

   What happened in between the two votes was Moseley-Braun
(D–IL), the first black woman in the history of the Senate, whose
voice was eloquent and angry as she spoke of the legacy of slavery and
the Confederacy's fight to preserve it. (Helen Dewar, "Senate Bows to
Pressure," *Philadelphia Inquirer* 7 Jan. 1993. *Dewar is a columnist for
the* Washington Post, *a daily newspaper published in Washington, DC.*)

7. When you think about it, right-wing victories have almost always depended *on turning on* the conservative minority, and *turning off*
everybody else. This was done categorically by denying suffrage to
black men and to women of all races; physically, by implementing
poll taxes and literacy tests; and procedurally, by creating barriers that
still make registration and voting a more daunting task here than in
any other democracy. It's interesting that the psychological turnoff—
the idea that politics is a dirty game, and voting doesn't matter—
began to be pushed just as the 1960s civil rights movement was
showing the nation that voting could be meaningful. (Gloria Steinem,
"Voting as Rebellion," *Ms.* magazine, Sept./Oct. 1996.)

8. From the 1950s, when women began voting in significant numbers,
through the '70s, women basically leaned Republican (women have
been a majority of voters since 1964). But in the 1980 election won
by Ronald Reagan, exit polls for the first time showed women
leaned toward the Democrats. [Eleanor] Smeal, who says she was
devastated by Reagan's victory, recalls how she was poring through
data looking for a "silver lining" when the gender gap leapt out at
her. Primarily male political scientists and pundits resisted her

unique analysis (though Reagan's pollster Richard B. Wirthlin says he used the phrase "gender gap" during his extensive polling among female voters in the late 1970s).

What was clear, however, is that women, who are more likely to be swing voters, were emerging as a new variable. "Political science had masked the importance of the women's vote because everyone assumed women didn't like politics and voted like their husbands," Smeal says. "But look at their life's experiences: Social Security? More women are dependent on it. Abortion? Nearly half of all women have one. Why do more women care about education? Women tend to be teachers." ("Feminism's Future," *CQ Researcher,* Feb. 28, 1997, Editor, Sandra Steel. CQ Researcher *reports on a variety of issues currently debated in Washington. It draws from a variety of sources for its reports.*)

44f Taking Notes

Take careful notes as you do research, and be sure to take notes on nonprint as well as print sources. And remember, if you discover a promising new source during the note-taking process, record full source information in your **working bibliography** immediately.

See
44c

As you take notes, your goal is flexibility; you want to be able to arrange and rearrange information easily and efficiently. If you take notes by hand, use one index card for each note rather than jotting comments down in the margins of photocopied pages or running several notes together on a single card. If you do your note-taking on a computer, keep your notes distinct from one another rather than collecting all information from a single source under one general heading. (Examples of two formats for notes appear in **45f.**)

Each note should include a short descriptive heading at the top that indicates its relevance to a specific aspect of your topic. Because you will use these headings to guide you as you construct your outline and organize your notes, they should be as specific as possible. Labeling every note for a paper on athletic scholarships *scholarships* or *financial aid,* for example, will not prove very helpful later on. More focused headings— *recruitment of athletes* or *benefits of athletic scholarships,* for instance— will be much more useful.

Each note should accurately identify the source of the information you are recording. You need not write out the complete citation, but you must include enough information to identify your source. For example, *Durrant 62* would be enough to send you back to your working bibliography, where you can find the complete documentation for Sue M. Durrant's

"Title IX—Its Powers and Its Limitations." If you use more than one source by the same author, however, you should include a shortened title for each. You might, for instance, use *Blum, "Graduation Rate" 42* if you were working with more than one source by Debra Blum. Be sure to provide information to identify each nonprint source as well—for example, *E-mail from Coach Walker.*

The body of the note should include the information from the source that you plan to use in your paper. Your **notes** may be in the form of **summary, paraphrase,** or **quotation.** In addition, you should include a brief comment that makes clear your reasons for recording the information and identifies what you think it will contribute to your paper. This comment (placed in brackets so you will know it expresses your own ideas, not those of your source) should establish the purpose of your note—what you think it can explain, support, clarify, describe, or contradict—and perhaps suggest its relationship to other notes or other sources. Any questions you have about the source information can also be included in your comment.

See
41a

 TAKING NOTES

Note-taking software can make it easy for you to record and organize information, allowing you to enter notes (quotations, summaries, paraphrases, or your own comments), pictures, or tables; to sort and categorize your material; and even to print out the information in order on computerized note cards. If you do not have access to such software, type each note under an appropriate heading on a separate page. When you finish taking notes and print out the individual pages, you will find that keeping notes distinct from one another makes it easy for you to sort notes into categories as well as to add and delete bits of information and to experiment with different sequences of ideas.

✔ CHECKLIST: TAKING NOTES

✔ Identify the source of each note clearly and completely.
Even if the source is on your bookshelf or downloaded in your computer, include full source information with each note.

continued on the following page

continued from the previous page

✔ **Include everything now that you will need later** to understand your note—names, dates, places, connections with other notes—and to help you remember why you recorded it.

✔ **Distinguish quotations from paraphrases and summaries, and distinguish your own ideas from those of your sources.** If you copy a source's words, place them in quotation marks. (If you take notes by hand, circle the quotation marks; if you type your notes, put the quotation marks in boldface.) If you write down your own ideas, enclose them in brackets—and, if you are taking notes on a computer, italicize them as well. (Sometimes an entire note may record your own thoughts; if this is the case, set off the complete note.)

✔ **Put an author's comments into your own words whenever possible,** summarizing and paraphrasing material as well as adding your own observations and analysis. Not only will this strategy save you time later on, but it will also help you understand your sources and evaluate their usefulness to you now, when you still have time to find additional sources to substitute for or complement them if necessary. If you do record an author's comments, be sure to copy them accurately, using the exact words, spelling, punctuation marks, and capitalization.

Photocopies   Many researchers routinely photocopy useful portions of sources. As long as you are careful to accurately record the bibliographic information for the source, this is a useful and time-saving strategy. As you prepare to photocopy material, however, keep the following guidelines in mind.

✔ CHECKLIST: WORKING WITH PHOTOCOPIES

✔ Record full and accurate source information, including the page numbers, on the first page of each copy.

✔ Clip or staple together consecutive pages of a single source.

✔ Do not copy a source without reminding yourself—*in writing*—why you are doing so. In pencil or on removable self-stick notes, record your initial responses to the source's ideas, jot down

continued on the following page

continued from the previous page
cross-references to other works or notes, and highlight important sections.

✔ Photocopying can be time consuming and expensive, so try to avoid copying material that is only marginally relevant to your paper.

✔ Keep photocopied material in a file so you'll be able to find it when you need it.

Photocopied information is not a substitute for notes. In fact, photocopying is only the first step in the process of taking thorough, careful notes on a source. In some cases—for example, for a short paper that uses only one or two sources—the **annotating** and highlighting you do on copies may be enough to guide your draft. But in most research assignments, it is unwise to use photocopies as a substitute for detailed notes. You should be especially careful not to allow the ease and efficiency of photocopying to encourage you to postpone decisions about the usefulness of your information. Remember, you can easily accumulate so many photocopied pages that it will be almost impossible to keep track of all your information.

See 7c

You should also keep in mind that photocopies do not have the flexibility of notes you take yourself because a single page of text may include information that should be earmarked for several different sections of your paper. This lack of flexibility makes it virtually impossible for you to arrange photocopied source material into any meaningful order.

Finally, remember that the annotations you make on photocopies are usually not focused or polished enough to be incorporated directly into your paper. You will still have to paraphrase and summarize your source's ideas and make connections among them. Therefore, you should approach a photocopy just as you approach any other print source—as material that you will read, highlight, annotate, and take notes about.

EXERCISE 5

Begin focused research for your paper, taking careful notes from your sources. Remember, your notes should include paraphrase, summary, and your own observations and analysis as well as quotations.

44g Deciding on a Thesis

After you have finished your focused research and note-taking, you must refine your tentative thesis into a **thesis statement,** a carefully worded sentence that expresses a conclusion your research can support. This **thesis statement** should be more detailed than your tentative thesis, accurately conveying the direction, emphasis, and scope of your paper.

See
2b2

DECIDING ON A THESIS

Tentative Thesis	Thesis Statement
Computer games interfere with adolescents' ability to learn.	Because they interfere with concentration and teach players to expect immediate gratification, computer games interfere with adolescents' ability to learn.
The feminist movement is responsible for the decline of sexist language.	By raising public awareness of careless language habits and changing the image of women, the feminist movement has helped to bring about a decline of sexist language.
The development of mood-altering drugs has changed the population of state mental hospitals.	It is the development of psychotropic (mood-altering) drugs, not advances in psychotherapy, that has made possible the release of large numbers of patients from state hospitals into the community.

If your thesis statement does not express a conclusion your research can support, you should try to revise it. Reviewing your notes carefully, perhaps grouping information in different ways, may help you to decide on a suitable thesis. Or you may try other techniques—for instance, brainstorming or freewriting with your research question as a starting point, or asking questions about your topic. The thesis you finally decide on should be consistent with the kind and amount of source material you have collected and the ideas you have developed in response to this material.

EXERCISE 6

Read the following passages. Assume you are writing a research paper on the influences that shaped young writers in the 1920s. What possible thesis statements could be supported by the information in these passages?

1. Yet in spite of their opportunities and their achievements the generation deserved for a long time the adjective [lost] that Gertrude Stein had applied to it. The reasons aren't hard to find. It was lost, first of all, because it was uprooted, schooled away and almost wrenched away from its attachment to any region or tradition. It was lost because its training had prepared it for another world that existed after the war (and because the war prepared it only for travel and excitement). It was lost because it tried to live in exile. It was lost because it accepted no older guides to conduct and because it formed a false picture of society and the writer's place in it. The generation belonged to a period of transition from values already fixed to values that had to be created. (Malcolm Cowley, *Exile's Return*)

2. The 1920s were a time least likely to produce substantial support among intellectuals for any sound, rational, and logical program. Pre-war stability and convention were condemned because all evidences of stability seemed illusory and artificial. The very lively and active interest in science was perhaps the decade's most substantial contribution to modern civilization. Yet in this case as well, achievement became a symbol of disorder and a source of disenchantment. (Frederick J. Hoffman, *The 20's*)

3. Societies do not give up old ideals and attitudes easily; the conflicts between the representatives of the older elements of traditional American culture and the prophets of the new day were at times as bitter as they were extensive. Such matters as religion, marriage, and moral standards, as well as the issues over race, prohibition, and immigration were at the heart of the conflict. (Introduction to *The Twenties*, ed. George E. Mowry)

EXERCISE 7

Carefully read over all the notes you have collected during your focused research and develop a thesis statement for your paper.

44h Preparing a Formal Outline

By the time you have completed your focused research and note-taking, you will have accumulated a good many notes. These notes will probably be arranged haphazardly, perhaps in the order in which you took them—and perhaps in no order at all. Before you can write a rough draft, you will need to make some sense out of all these notes, and you do this by sorting and organizing them. By identifying categories and sub-categories of information, you begin to see the emerging shape of your paper and are able to construct a formal outline that reflects this shape.

Although most students will not prepare an outline when planning a short essay, a formal outline is essential for a longer or more complex writing project. A **formal outline** indicates not only the order in which you will present your ideas but also the relationship of main ideas to supporting details.

See
3c3

Whether they are **topic outlines** or **sentence outlines,** formal outlines conform to specific conventions of structure, content, and style. (An example of a topic outline appears in **45h;** a sentence outline appears at the beginning of the sample student research paper in **45l.**) If you follow the conventions of outlining carefully, your outline can help you to plan a research paper in which you cover all relevant ideas in an effective order, with appropriate emphasis, and within a logical system of classification.

✔ CHECKLIST: PREPARING A FORMAL OUTLINE

✔ Make sure that each note expresses only one general idea. If this is not the case, recopy any unrelated information, creating a separate note.

✔ Check that the heading for each note specifically characterizes the information it includes. If it does not, change the heading.

✔ Sort your notes according to their headings.

✔ Check your categories for balance. If most of your notes fall into one or two categories, rewrite some of your headings to create narrower, more focused categories. If you have only one or two notes in a category, you will need to do additional research or treat that topic only briefly—or perhaps drop it entirely.

✔ Organize the individual notes within each group, adding more specific subheads to your headings and arranging ideas in an order that highlights the most important points and deemphasizes

continued on the following page

continued from the previous page

lesser ones. Set aside any notes that do not fit into your emerging scheme.

✔ Decide on a logical order in which to discuss your paper's major points.

✔ Write out your formal outline with divisions and subdivisions corresponding to your headings.

✔ Review your completed outline to determine whether you have placed too much emphasis on a relatively unimportant idea, whether ideas are illogically placed, or whether overlapping discussions turn up at different points.

Remember that the outline you construct at this stage is only a guide for you to follow as you draft your paper; it is likely to change as you write and revise. The final outline, written after your paper is complete, will reflect what you have written and serve as a guide for your readers.

EXERCISE 8

Review your notes carefully. Then, sort and group them into categories and construct a topic outline for your paper. (**3c3** explains and illustrates the specific conventions of topic outlines.)

44i Writing a Rough Draft

When you are ready to write your rough draft, arrange your notes in the order in which you intend to use them. Follow your outline as you write, using your notes as you need them.

To facilitate revision later on, triple-space your **rough draft**, and copy your source information fully and accurately *on this and every subsequent draft*, placing documentation as close as possible to the material it identifies.

See 3a

Once you begin drafting, you'll find that the time you spent taking careful, accurate notes and preparing an outline will pay off. Even so, do not expect to write the whole draft in a single sitting. Developing one major heading from your outline is a realistic goal for a morning or afternoon of writing.

Each paragraph will probably correspond to one major point of your outline, at least in this draft. (Later on, you may make changes.) As you write, supply transitions between sentences and paragraphs. These transitions need not be polished; you will refine them in subsequent drafts. But if you leave them out entirely at this stage, you may lose track of the logical and sequential links between ideas, and this will make revision difficult.

If words do not come easily, freewriting for a short period may help. Sometimes leaving your paper for five or ten minutes gives you a fresh view of your material. Another strategy for avoiding writer's block is beginning your drafting with the section for which you have the most material.

See
3b

Remember, the purpose of the first draft is to get ideas down on paper so that you can react to them. You should *expect* to **revise**, so postpone making precise word choices and refining style. As you draft, jot down questions to yourself, and note points that need further clarification (you can bracket those ideas or print them in boldface on a typed draft, or you can write them on self-stick notes). Leave space for material you plan to add, and bracket phrases or whole sections that you may later decide to move or delete. In other words, lay the groundwork for a major revision. Remember that even though you are guided by an outline and notes, you are not bound to follow their content or sequence exactly. As you write, new ideas or new connections among ideas may occur to you. If you find yourself deviating from your thesis or outline, reexamine them to see whether the departure is justified.

(1) Shaping the Parts of the Paper

Like any other essay, the research paper has an introduction, a body, and a conclusion, but in the rough draft you should concentrate on developing the body of your paper. You should not spend time planning an introduction or conclusion at this stage. Your ideas will change as you write, and you will want to revise your opening and closing paragraphs later to reflect your revisions.

See
6f2

Introduction In your **introduction** you identify your topic and establish how you will approach it. Your **introduction** also includes your thesis statement, which expresses the position you will support in the rest of the paper. Sometimes the introductory paragraphs briefly summarize your major supporting points (the major divisions of your outline) in the order in which you will present them. Such a preview of your thesis and support provides a smooth transition into the body of your paper. Your introduction can also present an overview of the problem you will discuss or summarize research already done on your topic. In your rough draft, however, an undeveloped introduction is perfectly acceptable; in fact, your thesis statement alone can serve as a placeholder for a more polished introduction.

Body   As you draft the **body** of your paper, indicate its direction with strong **topic sentences** that correspond to the divisions of your outline.

See 6b1

> Despite their obvious advantages, college athletic programs
>
> have problems.

You can also use **headings** if they are a convention of the discipline in which you are writing.

See A1b

> Problems of Athletic Programs
>
> Despite their obvious advantages, college athletic programs
>
> have problems.

Even in your first draft, descriptive headings and topic sentences will help you keep your discussion under control.

Use different **patterns of development** to shape the individual sections of your paper, and be sure to connect ideas with clear transitions. If necessary, connect two sections of your paper with a **transitional paragraph** that shows their relationship.

See 6e

See 6f1

Conclusion   The **conclusion** of a research paper often restates the thesis. This is especially important in a long paper because by the time your readers get to the end, they may have lost sight of your paper's main point. Your **conclusion** can also include a summary of your key ideas, a call for action, or perhaps an apt quotation. In your rough draft, however, your concluding paragraph can be very brief.

See 6f3

(2) Working Source Material into Your Paper

In the body of your paper, you evaluate and interpret your sources, comparing different ideas and assessing conflicting points of view. As a writer, your job is to draw your own conclusions, **synthesizing** information from various sources into a paper that presents a coherent, original view of your topic to your readers.

See 41b3

Your source material must be smoothly **integrated** into your paper, with the relationships among various sources (and between those sources' ideas and your own) clearly and accurately identified. If two sources present conflicting interpretations, you must be especially careful to use precise language and accurate transitions to make the contrast apparent (for instance, "Although Durrant believes the situation has

See 41b

changed, a later study suggests ...". When two sources agree, you should make this clear (for example, "Like Blum, Durrant believes ..." or "Coach Walker's statistics confirm those reported in Dealy"). Such phrasing will provide a context for your own comments and conclusions. If different sources present complementary information about a subject, blend details from the sources *carefully,* keeping track of which details come from which source, to reveal the complete picture.

EXERCISE 9

Write a draft of your paper, being careful to incorporate source material smoothly and to record source information accurately. Begin with the section for which you have the most material.

44j Revising the Drafts

See
3c3

A good way to start revising is to check to see that your thesis is still appropriate for your paper. Make an **outline** of your completed draft, and compare it with the outline you made before you began the draft. If you find significant differences, you will have to revise your thesis or rewrite sections of your paper.

See
3b, c

As you review your drafts, follow the **revision** procedures that apply to any paper. In addition, you should try to answer the following questions that apply specifically to research papers.

✔ CHECKLIST: REVISING A RESEARCH PAPER

✔ Should you do more research to find support for certain points?
✔ Do you need to reorder the major sections of your paper?
✔ Should you rearrange the order in which you present your points within those sections?
✔ Do you need to add section headings? Transitional paragraphs?
✔ Have you integrated your notes smoothly into your paper?
✔ Do you introduce source material with running acknowledgments?
✔ Are quotations blended with paraphrase, summary, and your own observations and reactions?

See
Ch. 42

✔ Have you avoided **plagiarism** by carefully documenting all borrowed ideas?

continued on the following page

---

continued from the previous page

✔ Have you analyzed and interpreted the ideas of others rather than simply stringing those ideas together?
✔ Do your own ideas—not those of your sources—define the focus of your discussion?

If your instructor allows **collaborative revision**, take advantage of it. As you move from rough to final draft, you should think more and more about your readers' reactions. Testing out others' reactions to a draft can be extremely helpful.

See
3c1

 REVISING THE DRAFTS

You will probably take your paper through several drafts, changing different parts of it each time or working on one part over and over. After revising each draft, type or print out a corrected version and make additional corrections by hand on that draft before typing your next version.

 EXERCISE 10

Following the guidelines in **44i** and **3c,** revise your research paper until you are ready to prepare a final draft.

 Preparing a Final Draft

Before you type or print out the final version of your paper, you will have to prepare your **Works Cited list**. In addition, you may have to prepare a detailed formal outline (usually a sentence outline) to hand in with your paper. After you have finished these tasks, you will edit all your material—paper, outline, documentation, Works Cited list, and so on.

See
43a2

At this point, stop for a moment to consider your paper's **title.** It should be descriptive enough to tell your readers what your paper is about, and, ideally, it should create interest in your subject. Your title should also be consistent with the purpose and tone of your paper. (You would hardly want a humorous title for a paper about the death penalty or world hunger.) Finally, your title should be engaging and to the point—and perhaps even provocative. Often a quotation from one of your sources will suggest a likely title.

Now you can proceed to type your final draft. Before you hand in your manuscript, read it through one last time, proofreading for grammar, spelling, or typing errors you may have missed. Pay particular attention to parenthetical documentation and Works Cited entries. (Remember that every error undermines your credibility.) Once you are satisfied that your manuscript is as accurate as you can make it, you are ready to hand it in.

EXERCISE 11

Prepare a sentence outline and Works Cited list for your research paper. (**3c3** explains and illustrates the specific conventions of sentence outlines; **43a2** illustrates MLA Works Cited list format.) Then, edit your paper, outline, and Works Cited list; decide on a title; and type your paper according to the format your instructor requires. Proofread your typed copy carefully before you hand it in.

CHAPTER 45

RESEARCH NOTEBOOK: A STUDENT'S PROCESS

Marion Duchac, a student in a composition class, was given this assignment:

Write a ten- to fifteen-page research paper that takes a persuasive stance on one issue that affects students on our campus.

This was a full-semester project, so Marion had fourteen weeks in which to research and write the paper. This chapter traces her progress, reproducing (in italics) the comments she made in her research notebook at various stages of the project as well as some examples of her work in progress.

Marion's instructor, Dr. Mary Ann Potter, required regular conferences at which she reviewed students' progress and checked their research notebooks; a segment of the assignment was due at each meeting. At various points in the process, she required collaborative work, and she expected students to use a variety of print, electronic, and nonlibrary sources. With these general guidelines in mind, Marion began to think about her assignment.

45a Moving from Assignment to Topic

For my comp class, I was assigned to do a research paper about an issue that affects students on my campus. At first I thought I might write about need vs. merit in financial aid to college students, but that topic didn't have the right edge. Besides, according to the two articles I found, the federal government is overhauling the system, and the facts keep changing. I talked to a financial aid officer and to some students, whose most common complaint was that financial aid forms are too hard to fill out. This topic just wasn't producing a thesis I could support, so I had to abandon it. But I did talk to a student whose athletic scholarship may be cancelled next year because of new NCAA regulations, and as a result I became interested in exploring some of the problems associated with athletic scholarships.

Assignment	Topic
Defend a position on an issue that affects students on campus.	Problems associated with athletic scholarships

I started this research notebook by copying down my assignment on the first page and taping Dr. Potter's research schedule to the inside front cover, so I could check off each stage of my research as I completed it. Next, I jotted down the assignment's other requirements and the time of my first conference with Dr. Potter. Then, I wrote down my topic and listed a few people I thought might be able to help me get started. At this point I felt I was ready to move on to the next stage of my assignment.

Doing Exploratory Research and Focusing on a Research Question

(1) Mapping Out a Search Strategy

Before I started writing about athletic scholarships, I spent some time in the library and even more time on the Internet. My research was frustrating at first because I couldn't find much objective information about athletic scholarships. I did find plenty about the controversial aspects of athletic scholarships and their place in the world of academics, though, and I thought that a lot of this material could be useful.

(2) Doing Exploratory Research

Consulting Experts

When I thought I understood some of the basic issues of my topic, I talked to Dr. Potter about how to continue my research. I had already planned to interview student athletes on campus, but she suggested that I also try to arrange a few personal or telephone interviews with coaches from local schools. Unfortunately, only one of the coaches I contacted was willing to let me use his name. Another coach said he would talk to me but preferred to remain anonymous. Dr. Potter didn't think it would be ethical to cite an anonymous source, so I decided I wouldn't rely on information from coaches to the extent I'd hoped to. But as I continued my reading, I started to feel that I was clarifying the direction of my search and developing my own opinions on my subject.

Asking Questions

My preliminary research suggested a number of questions I think I should explore as I continue my research.

- *What is the purpose of athletic scholarships?*
- *What percentage of schools offer them?*
- *What percentage of college students receive them?*
- *What kinds of students receive athletic scholarships?*
- *In what sports are scholarships awarded?*
- *What is the relationship between athletics and academics?*
- *What should this relationship be?*
- *Who should determine what this relationship should be?*
- *What are the advantages and disadvantages of athletic scholarships?*
- *What are some of the problems and controversies associated with athletic scholarships?*

(3) Focusing on a Research Question

As I was thinking about these questions, I realized my primary question, the one I wanted my paper to answer, was really quite simple: given the problems they create, should athletic scholarships be continued?

Now that I knew what I wanted to find, I had to plan my research. I decided to go to the library to do a key-word search on one of the databases, looking for articles on my topic. I also thought I might try to talk to someone in the financial aid or admissions office who might help me find statistics, and I wanted to try to get hold of a recruitment brochure so I could see how schools sell themselves to athletes. I really felt, though, that my first priority should be to contact Coach Walker, who had agreed to talk to me about my paper. (I decided to E-mail him so he wouldn't feel pressured or put on the spot. I also figured this could save me some time.) Meanwhile, I planned to talk informally with students, especially student athletes, about my research question.

45c Assembling a Working Bibliography

As I did my exploratory research, I recorded bibliographic information and evaluations of all my source material. I found it convenient to use index cards for books and articles I located in the library and for recording information about people I talked to, but I used my computer to record information I got from E-mail and other electronic sources. (I printed these out so Dr. Potter could check them along with my cards.)

As Dr. Potter looked over my bibliography, she noticed that I'd found some sources on women's athletic programs. She reminded me that 1997 was the twenty-fifth anniversary of Title IX, the law that said men and women should have equal access to sports programs, and so she thought I would find some useful material on women's athletic programs in 1997 sources.

INFORMATION FOR WORKING BIBLIOGRAPHY (ON INDEX CARD)

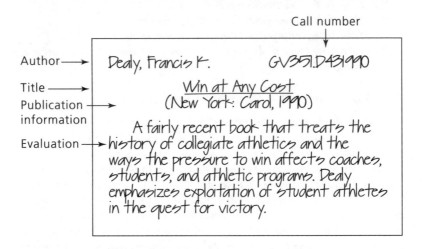

Call number

Author → Dealy, Francis F.   GV351.D431990

Title → Win at Any Cost
Publication information → (New York: Carol, 1990)

Evaluation → A fairly recent book that treats the history of collegiate athletics and the ways the pressure to win affects coaches, students, and athletic programs. Dealy emphasizes exploitation of student athletes in the quest for victory.

INFORMATION FOR WORKING BIBLIOGRAPHY (IN COMPUTER FILE)

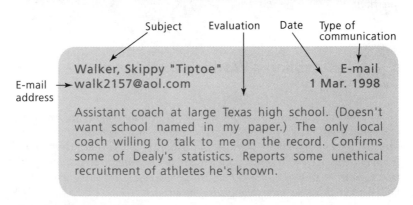

Subject   Evaluation   Date   Type of communication

Walker, Skippy "Tiptoe"   E-mail
E-mail address → walk2157@aol.com   1 Mar. 1998

Assistant coach at large Texas high school. (Doesn't want school named in my paper.) The only local coach willing to talk to me on the record. Confirms some of Dealy's statistics. Reports some unethical recruitment of athletes he's known.

45d Developing a Tentative Thesis

My answer to my research question became the tentative thesis for my paper.

Athletic scholarships should be retained because athletic teams add something vital to college life.

45e Doing Focused Research

(1) Reading Sources

At this point I felt ready to choose the best books and articles from the key-word search I had done earlier. As I began to read these sources, I discovered that many of them stress the reform of existing athletic programs. The problems discussed most often are unfair recruiting practices; inequities in support of men's and women's sports, "major" and "minor" sports, and winning and losing teams; and neglect of student athletes' academic obligations. I began to think I might need to revise my tentative thesis to emphasize needed reform of college athletic programs.

(2) Evaluating Sources

As I read, I tried to decide which sources I could trust and which I ought to question. Although I wanted a wide variety of sources, I didn't want to rely on information I had from popular sources like Sporting News *or from old newspaper columns or unrestricted chat lines or Listservs. A librarian recommended the* Chronicle of Higher Education *and the* New York Times *as reliable periodicals, so I looked carefully at articles I'd found in those sources.*

45f Taking Notes

As I read, I made myself take careful notes. (Dr. Potter checked five note cards to make sure I was being thorough and accurate, but I took most of my notes on my computer.)

NOTE (ON NOTE CARD)

Author and
page number ↓

Short → heading

Information → from source (summary, paraphrase, or quotation)

Comments → (opinions, reactions, purpose of note, connections with other sources, etc.)

Recruitment of athletes   Dealy 180

Surprisingly, "of the 265,000 seniors play-ing high school football, only 2,253, one out of every 118 high school senior football players, receive scholarships."

[This is an important statistic. It helps to explain the pressure and competition for these scholarships among high school athletes—and suggests how important recruitment is. It might also explain why there are so many recruiting violations.]

NOTE (IN COMPUTER FILE)

Information from source   Short heading   Note   Source

Recruitment of athletes   E-mail from Coach Walker

"When our players are recruited we have seen some methods that peo-ple might consider unethical. . . . Most of our players don't get schol-arships. Actually, we've only had two receive scholarships in the last ten years—and remember, those were ten years in which we scored high in our division."

[His statistic about scholarship students is consistent with Dealy's numbers.]

Comments

45g Deciding on a Thesis

As I read, I also continued to talk with different people about my topic. One of the student athletes I spoke to, a tennis player, mentioned that our campus wheelchair basketball team won a national championship a few years ago. I hadn't been aware of this team at all because I wasn't a student here the year they won the championship. But I was intrigued by the whole idea and decided to attend one of their games. The team was really good, and the gym was packed. I later found out that crowds of local people follow this team wherever they play, but none of the players are on scholarship. I think they should be. I don't know if I can use this experience in my paper, but it's certainly affected my thinking about athletic scholarships.

After I attended the wheelchair basketball game, I knew I had to revise my thesis. When I began my research, I'd wanted to write a paper in support of retaining athletic scholarships, but now I wanted to call for reforming the system to provide equal support for athletic and academic efforts, men's and women's sports, major and minor sports, and winning and losing teams. This change, in my opinion, would mean shifting the focus of athletic programs away from winning at all costs toward enriching campus life and the lives of individual student athletes. As a result, I decided on the following thesis statement.

Athletic scholarships should be continued, but college athletic programs should be reformed to deemphasize winning at all costs and to ensure that all student athletes are treated fairly.

45h Preparing a Formal Outline

After finally deciding exactly what I would write about and what position I would take, I reread my notes and sorted them into related groups, breaking my topic down into parts I could handle. Then, to see how all the parts were related and to decide on a logical order for the parts, I made a topic outline. (Later, I'll have to do a more detailed sentence outline to hand in with my paper.)

Thesis statement: Athletic scholarships should be continued, but college athletic programs should be reformed to deemphasize winning at all costs and to ensure that all student athletes are treated fairly.

I. Advantages of Athletic Programs

   A. School Spirit

   B. Money

   C. Balanced Education

II. Disadvantages of Athletic Programs

   A. Unequal Support of Sports

      1. Football and basketball vs. other sports

      2. Men's sports vs. women's sports

   B. Treatment of Student Athletes

      1. Acceptance of unqualified students

      2. Little academic support

      3. Heavy schedules

III. Causes of Problems

   A. Dishonest and Exploitive Athletic Directors

   B. Concentration on Winning

IV. Historical Background

   A. Harvard-Yale Contest

   B. Competition for Students

   C. Efforts to Control Violence and Standardize Rules

      1. Early organizations

      2. NCAA

V. Abuses in Athletic Programs and Scholarships

   A. Recruitment

      1. Before 1980s

continued on the following page

continued from the previous page

    2. NCAA intervention

    3. Continuing violations

  B. Sexism

    1. Concentration on men

    2. Title IX

    3. NCAA study

  C. Academics

    1. Proposition 48

    2. Controversy

    3. Recent developments

VI. Suggested Changes

  A. Fair Recruitment and Academic Support Programs

  B. Clear Priorities

  C. Balanced Treatment of Students

  D. Responsible Recruitment

45i   Writing a Rough Draft

Following my outline, I wrote a rough draft of my paper, concentrating on the body paragraphs.

45j   Revising the Drafts

As I revised, I made a lot of changes. For example, in the first draft of my paper I tried to explain the effects of Title IX by using my own words to paraphrase and summarize Durrant. But a student who read my draft in a collaborative revision session asked me what the regulation actually says, so I decided to add the exact wording of a portion of Title IX (quoted in Durrant) in my final draft.

Rough Draft

Since the introduction of Title IX in 1972, however, such a focus could be interpreted as illegal. Sue M. Durrant reports that although Title IX encompasses nearly all facets of education, it is mainly associated with increased opportunities for women in the area of athletics (60).

Revised (from ¶11)

Since the introduction of Title IX in 1972, however, this focus on men's teams is illegal. According to Title IX, "No person in the United States shall, on the basis of sex, be excluded from participation in, be denied the benefits of, or be subjected to discrimination under any program or activity receiving Federal financial assistance" (qtd. in Durrant 60).

Someone else pointed out that one of my paragraphs seemed unfocused. He said the first two sentences of the paragraph didn't seem to go with the rest of the sentences. I decided to delete the first two sentences of this paragraph and add a new topic sentence that accurately stated the main idea.

Rough Draft

Francis X. Dealy points out that as long as there have been human civilizations, there have been athletes and their competitions. Spanning from the ancient Greek games to last year's Super Bowl, human beings have organized contests to celebrate athletes and sports. Dealy reports that the first American intercollegiate spectacle was held in 1852 in New Hampshire when a rowing contest between Harvard and Yale was staged. Harvard won, and so began a fierce rivalry between the two schools (56). As Dealy observes, "Judging from the intensity of the spectators and the participants, the stakes included which school had the more beautiful campus, the smarter faculty, the brighter student body, and the more successful alumni" (59).

Revised (from ¶16)

This concentration on winning has led to some of the worst abuses in college athletic programs. Francis X. Dealy reports that this competitive attitude existed even in the first American intercollegiate competition, an 1852 rowing contest between Harvard and Yale. Harvard won, and so began a fierce rivalry between the two schools (56). As Dealy observes, "Judging from the intensity of the spectators and the participants, the stakes included which school had the more beautiful campus, the smarter faculty, the brighter student body, and the more successful alumni" (59).

45k Preparing a Final Draft

After struggling to finish everything Dr. Potter required—title page, Works Cited list, sentence outline—and editing and proofreading my paper, I had to choose a title. Looking over my sources in search of an appropriate quotation, I considered using the title of Dealy's book (Win at Any Cost), *but I decided instead to use the more focused "Athletic Scholarships: Who Wins?"*

45l The Completed Paper

Marion Duchac's completed research paper, "Athletic Scholarships: Who Wins?" appears on the pages that follow. The paper, which uses MLA documentation style, is accompanied by a title page, a sentence outline, a notes page, and Works Cited list. Annotations opposite each page of the manuscript comment on the style and structure of the paper; explain the format for proper documentation; illustrate various methods of incorporating source material into the paper; and explain some of the choices Marion made as she moved from notes to rough draft to completed paper.

If your instructor does not require a title page, include all identifying information—your name, the name of the course, your instructor's name, and the date—in the upper left-hand corner of your paper's first page, one inch from the top and flush with the left-hand margin. Your title should be centered two spaces below the last line of this heading. Type your name and the number *1* in the upper right-hand corner, one-half inch from the top.

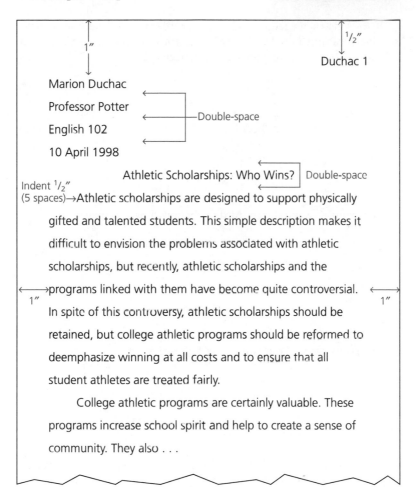

Duchac 1

Marion Duchac

Professor Potter ←

←————————Double-space

English 102 ←

10 April 1998

Athletic Scholarships: Who Wins? | Double-space

Indent ¹/₂″
(5 spaces)→Athletic scholarships are designed to support physically

gifted and talented students. This simple description makes it

difficult to envision the problems associated with athletic

scholarships, but recently, athletic scholarships and the

←——→programs linked with them have become quite controversial. ←——→

1″ In spite of this controversy, athletic scholarships should be 1″

retained, but college athletic programs should be reformed to

deemphasize winning at all costs and to ensure that all

student athletes are treated fairly.

College athletic programs are certainly valuable. These

programs increase school spirit and help to create a sense of

community. They also . . .

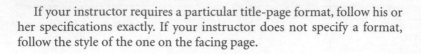

If your instructor requires a particular title-page format, follow his or her specifications exactly. If your instructor does not specify a format, follow the style of the one on the facing page.

Type your title about one-third of the way down the page.

Type your name about two inches below the title.

Type your course number, your instructor's name, and the date about two inches below your name. Double-space between these lines.

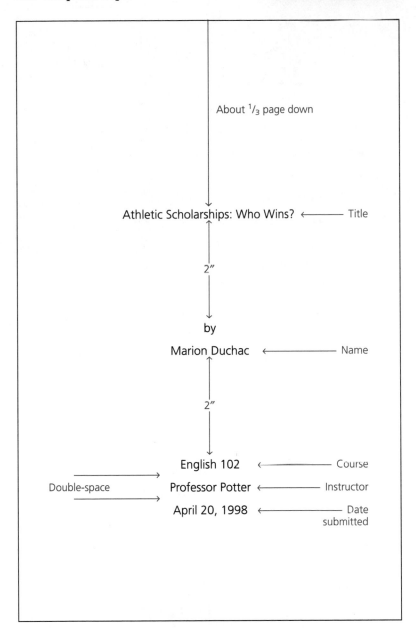

About ⅓ page down

Athletic Scholarships: Who Wins? ⟵——— Title

2″

by

Marion Duchac ⟵——————— Name

2″

English 102 ⟵———————— Course

Double-space ⟶ Professor Potter ⟵————— Instructor

April 20, 1998 ⟵—————— Date submitted

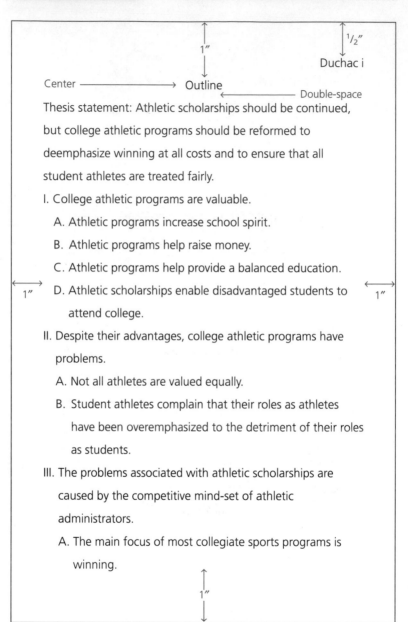

½″

Duchac i

Center ⟶ Outline

⟵ Double-space

Thesis statement: Athletic scholarships should be continued, but college athletic programs should be reformed to deemphasize winning at all costs and to ensure that all student athletes are treated fairly.

I. College athletic programs are valuable.

   A. Athletic programs increase school spirit.

   B. Athletic programs help raise money.

   C. Athletic programs help provide a balanced education.

   D. Athletic scholarships enable disadvantaged students to attend college.

II. Despite their advantages, college athletic programs have problems.

   A. Not all athletes are valued equally.

   B. Student athletes complain that their roles as athletes have been overemphasized to the detriment of their roles as students.

III. The problems associated with athletic scholarships are caused by the competitive mind-set of athletic administrators.

   A. The main focus of most collegiate sports programs is winning.

1″

Duchac ii

B. To the alumni, the administrators, and the fans, the only measure of a program's success is its win/loss record.

IV. The concentration on winning has led to the worst abuses in college athletic programs and scholarships.

A. American intercollegiate sports began in 1852 with a rowing contest between Harvard and Yale, which began a fierce rivalry.

B. The emphasis on winning encouraged the recruitment of the best athletes, regardless of cost.

C. The history of college athletics has been marked by violence and controversy.

V. Recruitment of student athletes, a large and controversial part of the athletic scholarship process, is often unethical.

A. Until the late 1980s, recruiters openly enticed high school football players with generous financial aid.

B. After several instances of unethical recruitment practices became public, the NCAA intervened.

C. Perhaps due to the intense competition for positions and scholarships, unethical recruitment has not been eliminated.

VI. Sexism is another serious problem in college athletic programs.

A. The economics of college sports encourages sexism.

Duchac iii

B. Title IX was enacted to increase opportunities for female athletes in elementary schools, high schools, and colleges.

C. A March 1992 NCAA study of gender equity in colleges found that more resources were allotted to men's teams than to women's.

D. For progress to be made, the NCAA should continue surveys like the gender equity study, and complaints should continue to be filed.

VII. Admissions irregularities have also plagued college athletics.

A. Proposition 48 was instituted when it was made public that some of America's star athletes were unable to read.

B. In 1989 the NCAA passed a series of controversial reforms.

C. Preliminary results indicate that athletes are getting the message.

D. Changes may or may not indicate improvement.

VIII. Colleges should retain athletic scholarships--with certain changes.

A. Academic support programs should be fair to all student athletes.

Duchac iv

B. Academics--not sports--must be given first priority.

C. Students who receive athletic scholarships should not
be exploited.

D. Recruitment should be responsible.

Beginning with the first page of your paper, type your last name and the page number one-half inch from the top in the upper right-hand corner. Do not use punctuation before or after the page number. Leave one-inch margins.

Type the title one inch from the top of the page. Leave two spaces between the title and the first line of the paper.

¶1 Introduction presents background information and thesis statement.

¶2 (Outline point I): Paragraph presents background on value of athletic programs and need for athletic scholarships. First four sentences of paragraph support student's opinion with information available in several sources; therefore, no documentation is required.

Here the identifying tag *as Alvin Sanoff observes* introduces material summarized from a source. Introducing the summary with the author's name and following it with parenthetical documentation clearly identifies the boundaries of the borrowed material.

Duchac 1

Athletic Scholarships: Who Wins?

Athletic scholarships are designed to support physically gifted and talented students. This simple description makes it difficult to envision the problems associated with athletic scholarships, but recently, athletic scholarships and the programs linked with them have become quite controversial. In spite of this controversy, athletic scholarships should be retained, but college athletic programs should be reformed to deemphasize winning at all costs and to ensure that all student athletes are treated fairly.

College athletic programs are certainly valuable. These programs increase school spirit and help to create a sense of community. They also help to raise money: winning teams spark alumni contributions, and athletic events raise funds through ticket sales. In addition, athletic programs--like programs in the performing arts and music--help to provide a rewarding, balanced education for all students. Student athletes make important academic, social, and cultural contributions to their schools and thus enrich the college experience for others. Finally, without athletic scholarships, many students would not be able to attend college because, as Alvin Sanoff observes, the aid for which many economically deprived student athletes are eligible does not

Parenthetical reference indicates material is from paragraph 5 of an electronic source.

¶3 (Outline point IIA): Paragraph's discussion of disparities in athletic programs is supported by source material, which combines paraphrase with quotation.

¶4 (Outline point IIB): Student's point is supported by her own observations as well as by a source whose ideas she summarizes (to convey general ideas rather than specific details). Because the author's name is mentioned in the paragraph, it is not included in the parenthetical documentation.

Duchac 2

cover the expense of a college education the way athletic scholarships do (par. 5).

Despite their obvious advantages, college athletic programs have problems. First, not all athletes--or all programs--are valued equally. On many campuses money, equipment, and facilities have traditionally been allotted to football and basketball at the expense of less visible sports such as swimming, tennis, and field hockey. Men's sports have been given a disproportionate amount of support, and "winning" teams and coaches have been compensated accordingly. In fact, according to Sue M. Durrant, until recently it was not unusual for women's teams to use "hand-me-down" gear while men's teams played with new "state of the art" equipment or for women's teams to travel by bus while men's teams traveled by plane (60).

Another problem is that college athletes at all levels complain that their roles as athletes are overemphsized, to the detriment of their roles as students. According to Francis X. Dealy, some college athletic departments have become little more than glorified training camps for professional sports teams. This problem is compounded by overzealous recruiting practices, with colleges accepting academically unqualified students solely because of their athletic skills. These students

¶5 (Outline points IIIA and IIIB): Two quotations identify emphasis on winning, introducing student's point that this emphasis is a significant cause of the abuses her paper will discuss.

Note that the Lombardi quotation is so well known that it does not require documentation.

Qtd. in indicates that the Santayana quotation appears in Dealy.

are exploited and overworked, treated as commodities rather than as students, and given little academic support; many fail to graduate (106). With the demands of heavy travel and practice schedules, many student athletes, even those with strong academic backgrounds, risk falling behind in their studies. Moreover, their grueling schedules tend to isolate them from other students, excluding them from the college community. Given these difficulties, college athletic programs are under considerable pressure to institute reforms.

The problems associated with athletic scholarships are numerous and complex, but they have less to do with the scholarships themselves than with the way dishonest and exploitive athletic administrators run their programs. It is understandable that the main focus of most collegiate sports programs is winning. According to Vince Lombardi, the famous football coach, "Winning isn't everything; it's the only thing." To the alumni, the administrators, and the fans, the only measure of an athletic program's success is its win/loss record. A winning record attracts money and students; a losing record does not. They seem to believe, as the philosopher George Santayana has observed, "In athletics, as in all performances, only winning is interesting. The rest has value only as leading to it or reflecting it" (qtd. in Dealy 61).

¶6 (Outline points IVA and IVB): Paragraph provides background to explain roots of today's problems. Three parenthetical references cite the same source (Dealy).

¶7 (Outline point IVC): Paragraph continues tracing background, summarizing problems historically associated with collegiate athletics and steps taken to address those problems.

Quotation is introduced by a running acknowledgment ("Fleisher, Goff, and Tollison report . . .").

Duchac 4

This concentration on winning has led to some of the worst abuses in college athletic programs. Francis X. Dealy reports that this competitive attitude existed even in the first American intercollegiate competition, an 1852 rowing contest between Harvard and Yale. Harvard won, and so began a fierce rivalry between the two schools (56). As Dealy observes, "Judging from the intensity of the spectators and the participants, the stakes included which school had the more beautiful campus, the smarter faculty, the brighter student body, and the more successful alumni" (59). The emphasis on winning encouraged the recruitment of the best athletes, no matter what the cost. In fact, Dealy observes that the first athletic scholarships were in the form of salaries paid to professional athletes to perform in the name of a particular school. Without regulation, athletic scholarships were like shady financial deals arranged in smoky back rooms (56). Athletes became commodities to be bought and sold.

Fleisher, Goff, and Tollison report that until the late 1870s, collegiate games were generally "marked by violence . . . and controversy over eligibility requirements. Athletes moved from school to school, . . . and club members hired professional athletes to participate in intercollegiate events" (37). Several organizations were formed to help control violence and to

Fleisher, Goff, and Tollison 38–41 indicates summary of four pages of material from a source.

¶8 Transitional paragraph identifies the three principal abuses on which the paper will focus (unethical recruitment practices, sexism, and admissions irregularities).

¶9 (Outline points VA–B): Paragraph introduces first abuse (unethical recruitment practices).

standardize rules, but all had spotty participation and were short-lived. In December 1905, in order to deal with violence and to standardize rules of play, the National Collegiate Athletic Association (NCAA) was formed in response to the concerns of Theodore Roosevelt, then president of the United States. Even though the scope of the NCAA has widened tremendously in the last ninety years, one of its main concerns remains the equitable distribution of financial aid and scholarships (Fleisher, Goff, and Tollison 38–41).

Today the NCAA continues to address abuses associated with athletic programs and scholarships, including aggressive and often unethical recruitment techniques, a disproportionate amount of money being awarded to men over women, and academically underprepared athletes being admitted to and retained by colleges and universities. The organization's task is a difficult one, however, because the problems have deep roots.

Recruitment of student athletes, a large and controversial part of the athletic scholarship process, is often unethical. Understandably, colleges and universities want to recruit the finest athletes for their teams, but sometimes this quest for the best has led to overly aggressive recruitment practices. Dealy reports, for example, that until the late 1980s,

Dealy 173–80 indicates that paragraph summarizes several pages of a source. Concluding citation includes Dealy's name because parenthetical reference is far from running acknowledgment ("Dealy reports, for example . . .").

¶10 (Outline point VC): Paragraph continues discussion of unethical recruitment practices, blending information from three sources, one of which is an E-mail communication.

Superscript (raised numeral) at end of second sentence of paragraph refers readers to a content note. (See notes following text of paper.)

Marion's notes for information from Dealy and Coach Walker appear on page 708; her working bibliography entries for these two sources appear on page 706.

Duchac 6

recruiters openly enticed talented high school football players with promises of generous financial aid and merchandise, including cars or expensive athletic clothing and shoes. After several instances of unethical recruitment practices became public, most notably the fact that one university had been paying its football players salaries to play ball, the NCAA intervened and became more vigorous in its attempt to regulate the recruitment process. Recruitment is still the principal means of matching students with available funds. For this reason, violations continue to account for 60 to 70 percent of all NCAA infractions (Dealy 173–80).

Perhaps due to the intense competition for positions and scholarships, unethical recruitment has not been eliminated. Skippy "Tiptoe" Walker, assistant football coach at a large Texas high school, reports that some of his athletes have been recruited in ways that could be considered unethical.[1] Walker is quick to point out, though, that most of his athletes do not receive scholarships. In fact, only two football players from his high school have received athletic scholarships during the past ten years. This statistic is in line with statistics from the rest of the country. As reported by Dealy, very few high school seniors--one out of every 118--actually receive athletic scholarships (180). Understandably, competition for funds and

Title alone (abbreviated) is used in parenthetical reference because source does not specify an author's name. No page number is given for a one-page article.

¶11 (Outline point VIA): Paragraph introduces second major abuse to be discussed in paper (sexism in college sports programs).

Note that quotation is used rather than paraphrase or summary. Using the exact wording from a key piece of legislation is important because it conveys the law's ideas clearly and eliminates any possibility of readers' misinterpreting its intent.

¶12 (Outline point VIB): Paragraph continues discussion of sexism in college sports programs.

Duchac 7

positions is stiff. Some students try to locate their own athletic scholarships by paying a nominal fee to an independent search service, which enters the student's name into a national database and also provides the student with a list of available scholarships and schools seeking recipients ("You C.A.N.").

Sexism is another serious problem in college athletic programs. In fact, the economics of college sports almost ensures that female athletes will not be recruited as aggressively as male athletes are. The strongest teams, in the view of colleges, are the ones that generate the greatest amount of interest (and revenue). In general, the money-making teams are the men's teams. Because the emphasis is on winning and making money, it is not surprising that colleges and recruiters concentrate on men when building and maintaining their sports programs. Since the introduction of Title IX in 1972, however, this focus on men's teams is illegal. According to Title IX, "No person in the United States shall, on the basis of sex, be excluded from participation in, be denied the benefits of, or be subjected to discrimination under any program or activity receiving Federal financial assistance" (qtd. in Durrant 60).

Sue M. Durrant reports that although Title IX encompasses nearly all facets of education, it is mainly

Paragraph includes three parenthetical references to a single source (Durrant). Note that each quotation requires its own parenthetical reference. Paragraph also cites a newspaper article and a television documentary (using a shortened form of the title).

¶13 (Outline point VIC): Paragraph continues discussion of sexism in college sports programs, using a pie graph to illustrate disparities in spending between men's and women's sports.

Duchac 8

associated with increased opportunities for women in the area of athletics (60). In fact, Durrant notes, "Title IX tilted the balance of power. Title IX granted acceptability and status to elementary school, high school, and college female athletes" (61). During the first decade that Title IX was in place, the number of women athletes in colleges doubled, and there was rapid growth in female athletic programs at all levels of education, particularly in colleges and universities (Durrant 61). Since this ten-year-span of compliance to the law, however, there has been an obvious slowing of the movement toward equality between men and women in collegiate sports programs. Even as recently as 1997--ironically, the twenty-fifth anniversary of Title IX--parity had not been achieved. As Secretary of Health and Human Services Donna Shalala commented in a documentary film that year, "In twenty-five years, Title IX has still not been fully realized" ("Breaking Through"). One of the areas in which this lack of progress is most visible and measurable is athletic financial aid and scholarships.

A 1992 NCAA study of gender equity in colleges that play big-time sports showed the degree to which men's sports received more money than women's sports. The following graph illustrates this disparity in spending.

Note that full source information for the **graph** is included directly below it. Two quotations from a recent newspaper article bring the discussion up to date.

¶14 (Outline point VID): Paragraph continues discussion of sexism in college sports programs, blending paraphrases from two different sources.

Duchac 9

Scholarship Money Operating Money Recruiting Money

Fig. 1. Summary of Comparative Spending for Men's and Women's Sports. Based on information from Douglas Lederman, "Men Get 70 Percent of Money Available for Athletic Scholarships and Colleges That Play Big-Time Sports Programs," <u>Chronicle of Higher Education</u> 18 Mar. 1992: A1.

The NCAA study found that men's teams received almost 70 percent of the athletic scholarship money, 77 percent of the operating money, and 83 percent of the recruiting money. And, as a 1997 <u>New York Times</u> article reports, "for all the progress women have made, they are still far behind men on the playing fields" (Chambers A1). In fact, the 1992 NCAA gender equity study found that "the finding for men's athletics continues to dwarf the money spent on women's sports" (Chambers A1).

  Supporters of women's programs argue that the distribution of money should be based on enrollment, which, as reported in a <u>Chronicle of Higher Education</u> study of

Note that shortened title is included in parenthetical reference because paper cites more than one source by Lederman.

¶15 (Outline point VIIA): Paragraph introduces discussion of third major abuse (admissions irregularities in college sports programs).
Paragraph begins with a transitional sentence that moves readers from one problem (sexism) to another (admissions irregularities).

Running acknowledgment ("Alvin Sanoff reports that. . . .") introduces paraphrase of a source.

Note that paraphrase includes quotation of a key term ("partial qualifier") that cannot be accurately paraphrased.

gender equality, would give women a slight edge over men
(Lederman, "Men Outnumber" A1). In order for progress to
be made in gender equity in college sports, it is important for
the NCAA and other independent organizations to continue
surveys like the NCAA gender equity study. And, as Durrant
points out, it is also important that complaints continue to be
filed when discrimination is suspected or encountered (63).

Admissions irregularities have also plagued college
athletics. Proposition 48 was an effort by the NCAA to address
the problems. When it was made public that some of
America's star college athletes were unable to read (Dealy 111),
the NCAA was forced into action. Proposition 48, the result of
much compromise and maneuvering during the NCAA's 1983
convention, required that athletes meet two basic academic
requirements before they could receive athletic scholarships.
Alvin Sanoff reports that the potential recipients had to score
at least 700 out of a possible 1,600 points on the Scholastic
Aptitude Test (or 15 out of 36 on the American College Test) or
attain a C average in eleven core academic courses. If the
student achieved only one of these requirements, he or she
was a "partial qualifier" and, although eligible for an athletic
scholarship, would not be allowed to participate in sports
during his or her first year (68). Since Proposition 48 went into

¶16 (Outline point VIIB): Paragraph continues discussion of admissions irregularities, introducing a controversy associated with athletes' admissions and scholarships and a discussion of the NCAA's role in the controversy.

Author Lederman is named in the paragraph; an abbreviated title is included in the parenthetical reference to distinguish source from other sources by Lederman. (Superscript refers to content note.)

¶17 (Outline points VIIB–D): Paragraph continues discussion and analysis of the controversial reforms and their impact, blending direct quotation and paraphrase from two sources.

Qtd. in indicates that Chaney and Ashe quotations were found in Sanoff.

Duchac 11

effect in 1986, approximately six hundred students per year have received athletic scholarships under the "partial qualifier" umbrella. Of these students, 90 percent were African-American football or basketball players (Sanoff, par. 6).

In 1989, however, the NCAA voted to enact a series of reforms, the most stringent of which was to take effect in August 1995, when, as reported by Lederman, first-year athletes would be required to achieve a 2.5 grade-point average in thirteen academic core courses rather than 2.0 in eleven courses as previously required. Students would also have to score a minimum of 700 on the SAT in addition to the GPA requirement ("NCAA Votes" A1).[2]

Because underprivileged athletes are most affected by these rule changes, the proposed reforms were extremely controversial. John Chaney, the men's basketball coach at Temple University, called the new rule "an insane, inhuman piece of legislation that will fill the streets with more of the disadvantaged" (qtd. in Sanoff, par. 7). The late tennis player Arthur Ashe believed, however, that "any time educational standards have been raised, the athletes have gotten the message" (qtd. in Sanoff, par. 7). Preliminary results of ongoing studies have indicated that the athletes are indeed getting the message: the graduation rate of Division I scholarship athletes

Parenthetical reference includes title because paper cites two articles by Blum.

Over four lines long, this quotation is typed as a block, indented ten spaces (or one inch) from the left martin, and double-spaced, with two spaces above and below. No quotation marks are used. Because the quotation is a single paragraph, no paragraph indentation is needed. (In a quotation of more than one paragraph, the first line of each complete paragraph, including the first, is indented three additional spaces.)

Note that in a long quotation the parenthetical reference is placed one space *after* the final punctuation. Author's name is cited in text, so parenthetical reference does not include it.

¶18 (Outline point VIII): Paragraph introduces concluding remarks, which make recommendations about reforms. Because all ideas in this paragraph are the student's original conclusions, no documentation is necessary.

entering college in 1986 was six percentage points higher than the average graduation rates of athletes who enrolled at those same colleges three years before Proposition 48 took effect (Blum, "Graduation" A42). Other study results show that the number of academically underprepared athletes enrolling in Division I colleges dropped in 1991. As reported by Debra Blum, however, these statistics do not necessarily indicate improvement:

> The decline in the number of academically underqualified athletes going to Division I and II colleges may mean that more athletes are meeting the standard, as supporters of the standard contend. On the other hand, the decline may suggest that the underprepared students are simply moving in greater numbers into junior colleges or preparatory schools or, as some critics fear, that they are not continuing their education at all. ("More Freshmen" A39)

Despite the problems, colleges should retain athletic scholarships--with certain changes. Academic support programs should be reformed so that they are fair to all student athletes--men and women, football players and tennis players, winners and losers. Academics--not sports--must be

¶19 (Conclusion): Student presents further recommendations for re-forming abuses in college athletic programs.

Paper closes with an emphatic final sentence that echoes the title, re-minding readers of what the paper has identified as the cause of the problems in college athletics programs: the focus on winning.

given first priority. Students who receive athletic scholarships should not be exploited; they should be treated like other scholarship recipients. Recruitment should be responsible, academic standards should be maintained, and promises made to athletes should be realistic.

In short, the scholarship athlete should be treated like any other exceptional student on campus who loves his or her subject and takes joy in the process of learning. Athletic programs clearly benefit educational institutions, and athletic scholarships should certainly be a part of any college system; however, the focus of sports programs should expand to encompass the personal enrichment of the whole student. Shifting the focus of athletics away from winning will ultimately benefit not only college athletes and the scholarship programs that support them, but also the colleges themselves.

This page is numbered.

Content notes provide supplementary information to the reader. Because the information is a digression, including it in the body of the paper would be distracting.

1″

¹/₂″

Duchac 14

Center ————————→ Notes

←————————— Double-space

Indent → ¹I also interviewed another high school coach who asked
5 spaces
(or   that he not be identified. He admitted that several of his star
¹/₂″)

athletes over the past few years had been lured with

expensive dinners and generous financial packages into big-

time colleges. When I asked the coach if he had reported

these infractions to the proper authorities, he said he had not.

²When the SATs were reformed in 1995, the minimum

test score was raised to 820.

Every page of the Works Cited section is numbered. List entries in alphabetical order, indenting the second and subsequent lines of every entry five spaces (or one-half inch). Double-space within and between entries.

The first entry illustrates the correct form for a signed newspaper article by a single author. Note that it indicates both section and page numbers and provides inclusive pagination.

The Works Cited list includes two works by Debra E. Blum. Note that the author's name is not repeated in the second entry; instead, three unspaced hyphens, followed by a period, are used.

Entry identifies a television documentary.

Entry identifies a newspaper article. A1+ indicates an article that begins on page 1 of Section A and skips to a nonconsecutive page.

Entry identifies a book by a single author.

Entry identifies a journal article by a single author.

Entry identifies a book with more than one author.

Entry identifies a newspaper article by a single author. (The two entries that follow list additional articles by the same author.)

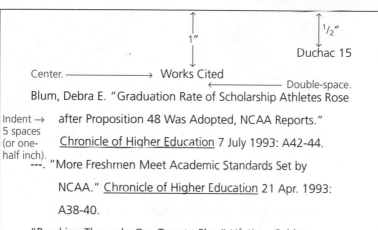

1"   ¹/₂"

Duchac 15

Center. ──────→ Works Cited

←────────── Double-space.

Blum, Debra E. "Graduation Rate of Scholarship Athletes Rose

Indent → after Proposition 48 Was Adopted, NCAA Reports."
5 spaces
(or one-   Chronicle of Higher Education 7 July 1993: A42-44.
half inch).
---. "More Freshmen Meet Academic Standards Set by

NCAA." Chronicle of Higher Education 21 Apr. 1993:

A38-40.

"Breaking Through: Our Turn to Play." Lifetime Cable

Network. 19 June 1997.

Chambers, Marcia. "For Women, 25 Years of Title IX Has Not

Leveled the Playing Field." New York Times 16 June

1997: A1+.

Dealy, Francis X. Win at Any Cost. New York: Carol, 1990.

Durrant, Sue M. "Title IX--Its Power and Its Limitations."

Journal of Physical Education, Recreation and Dance 45

(1992): 60-64.

Fleisher, Arthur A., Brian L. Goff, and Robert D. Tollison. The

National Collegiate Athletic Association. Chicago: U of

Chicago P, 1992.

Lederman, Douglas. "Men Get 70% of Money Available for

Athletic Scholarships and Colleges That Play Big-Time

Sports, New Study Finds." Chronicle of Higher Education

18 Mar. 1992: A1+.

Entry identifies a signed periodical article accessed through Compu-Serve, a computer service.

Entry identifies an electronic communication.

Entry identifies an unsigned periodical article (alphabetized by title).

Duchac 16

---. "Men Outnumber Women and Get Most of Money in Big-Time Sports Programs." <u>Chronicle of Higher Education</u> 8 Apr. 1992: A1+.

---. "NCAA Votes Higher Academic Standards for College Athletes." <u>Chronicle of Higher Education</u> 15 Jan. 1992: A1+.

Sanoff, Alvin P. "When Is the Playing Field Too Level?" <u>U.S. News & World Report</u> 30 Jan. 1989. 10 pars. CompuServe. 3 Mar. 1994.

Walker, Skippy "Tiptoe." E-mail to the author. 1 March 1998.

"You C.A.N. Get Help with a Scholarship." <u>Scholastic Coach</u> Aug. 1992: 56.

PART 9

WRITING IN THE DISCIPLINES

CHAPTER 46

UNDERSTANDING THE DISCIPLINES

All instructors, regardless of academic discipline, have certain expectations when they read a paper. They expect to see standard English, correct grammar and spelling, logical thinking, and clear documentation of sources. In addition, they expect to see sensible organization, convincing support, and careful editing. Despite these similarities, however, instructors in various disciplines have different expectations about a paper.

One way of putting these differences into perspective is to think of the various disciplines as communities of individuals who exchange ideas about issues that concern them. Just as in any community, scholars who write within a discipline have agreed to follow certain practices—conventions of style and vocabulary, for example. Without these conventions it would be difficult or even impossible for them to communicate effectively with one another. If, for example, everyone writing about literature used a different documentation format or a different specialized vocabulary, the result would be chaos. To a large extent, then, learning to write in a particular discipline involves learning the conventions that govern a discourse community.

46a Research Sources

Gathering information is basic to all disciplines, but not all disciplines rely on the same kinds of resources. In the humanities, for example, print sources—whether found on shelves in the library or accessed from a database—are central to most studies. Although some historians will conduct interviews and some literary scholars will collect quantifiable data, most people who do research in the humanities spend a great amount of time reading **primary and secondary sources**.

See 44e2

Those who work in the social sciences also spend a lot of time examining the literature on a particular topic. But they also rely heavily on primary source information—observation of behavior, interviews, and surveys, for example. Because of the kind of data they generate, social scientists often use statistical methodology and record their results in charts, graphs, and tables. Those who work in the natural sciences (such as biology, chemistry, and physics) and the applied sciences (engineering and computer science, for example) rely almost exclusively on **empirical data**—information obtained through controlled laboratory experiments or from mathematical models. They use the data they collect to formulate theories that try to explain their observations.

The information you gather from print and electronic resources in the library, in the field, on the Internet, or in the laboratory will help you support the conclusions you formulate when you write. Whether you want to make a point about the color gray in a work by Herman Melville or about the effect of a particular amino acid on the respiratory system, your intent is the same: to find the support you need to explain something to readers or to convince them of something.

The kind of support that is acceptable and persuasive, however, varies from discipline to discipline. Students of literature often use quotations from fiction or poetry to support their statements, whereas historians are likely to refer to original documents and court or church records. Social scientists frequently rely on statistics to support their conclusions; those in the natural sciences use the empirical data they derive from controlled experiments.

Although all scholars will use the opinions of recognized experts to support their ideas, the weight given to these opinions varies from discipline to discipline. A historian developing a Marxist analysis of Western industrialism, for example, will use the ideas of Karl Marx to support his or her conclusions; a feminist literary critic will cite the work of other feminist critics. However, although scientists frequently begin papers with a literature survey, they base their conclusions on data they themselves generate.

46b Writing Assignments

Because each discipline has a different set of concerns, writing assignments vary from course to course. A sociology course, for example, may require a statistical analysis; a literature course may require a literary analysis. Therefore, it is not enough simply to know the material about which you are asked to write. You must also be aware of what the instructor in a particular discipline expects of you. For example, when your art history instructor asks you to write a paper on the Brooklyn Bridge, she does not expect you to write an analysis of Hart Crane's poem *The Bridge* (a topic suitable for a literature class) nor does she want a detailed discussion of the steel cables used in bridge building (a topic suitable for a materials engineering class). What she might expect is for you to discuss the use of the bridge as an artistic subject—as it is in the paintings of Joseph Stella and the photographs of Alfred Stieglitz, for example.

When you get any assignment, be sure you understand exactly what you are being asked to do; if you have any doubt, ask your instructor for clarification. Then, try to acquaint yourself with the ideas that are of interest to those who publish on your topic. Take the time to look through your text and class notes or do some exploratory research to get a sense of the theories, concerns, and controversies pertinent to your topic. (See **47a, 48a,** and **49a** for lists of specialized research sources used in each discipline.) Keep in mind, however, that you should not limit yourself to topics that researchers have explored exhaustively. On the contrary, papers that explore new ideas, move in new directions, or make new connections between disciplines—for example, quoting a few lines from the poem *The Bridge* in your art history paper to shed some light on the power of the bridge as a literary and artistic symbol—are often valuable and enlightening.

46c Conventions of Style, Format, and Documentation

(1) Style

Specialized Vocabulary Learning the vocabulary of a discipline is like learning a new language. At first, you observe native speakers from a distance. Eventually, as you learn a few words, you begin to communicate—if only slightly—with the natives. Finally, after you can speak the language well, you become actively involved with those around you and, if you are lucky, participate in the life of the community. Only by learning the specialized vocabulary of a field can you communicate with those who work in it. Once you know this vocabulary, you can begin to participate in the discussions and debates that define the discipline.

When you write a paper for a particular course, you use the specialized vocabulary of those who publish in the discipline. When you write a paper for a literature course, for example, use the literary terms you hear in class and read in your textbook—*point of view, persona, imagery,* and so on. Do the same for assignments in your other classes. It makes no sense to use inexact words or colloquial phrases when the discipline offers a vocabulary that will enable you to express concepts accurately and concisely. What other words, for example, would you use to denote *ecosystem, conditioned reflex,* or *metaphor*?

 WRITING IN THE DISCIPLINES

See 20c1

Although technical terms facilitate communication within a discipline, outside that discipline they become **jargon** and do exactly the opposite. Moreover, in most disciplines, particularly in the sciences, scholars are often so narrowly specialized that even those in the same field may have difficulty understanding their colleagues' technical vocabulary. Therefore, some basic definitions may be helpful.

See 20a

Level of Diction   Within any field, particular assignments call for different **levels of diction**. Regardless of discipline, research papers tend to be formal: they contain learned words, are grammatically correct, avoid contractions and colloquialisms, and use third-person pronouns. Proposals—whether they are in the humanities, social sciences, or natural sciences—also are relatively formal.

Other assignments, by their very nature, are less formal than proposals and research papers. For example, because its purpose is to present an individual's personal reactions, a response statement uses subjective language, first person, and active voice ("I see a lot of weaknesses I didn't notice last time"). A lab report is also informal, but because its purpose is to report the observations themselves—not the observer's reactions—it frequently uses objective language and passive voice ("The acid was poured" rather than "I poured the acid"). For the most part, then, it is an assignment's purpose and audience, not its discipline, that determines its level of diction.

(2) Format

See App. A

Each discipline has certain formatting conventions that govern the way written information is presented on the page. A **format** is an accepted way of displaying material in a document. A format may govern the arrangement of an entire document (such as a lab report, which has certain prescribed sections) determining, for example, whether or not writers use internal headings in their papers. Formatting conventions also determine how certain kinds of information are presented or displayed *within* a document. For example, social scientists expect statistical data to be presented in tables or graphs. Specific mechanical concerns, such as whether to spell out a **number** or use numerals, also differ from discipline to discipline.

See
Ch. 38

Professional organizations, such as the Modern Language Association, define the guidelines that govern document formats within their disciplines. Typically, a professional organization will issue or recommend a handbook or style sheet that defines the standards for spelling, mechanics, punctuation, and capitalization. This style sheet also gives explicit guidelines for the use and placement of information in diagrams, graphs, tables, and photographs within a paper as well as for typing conventions, such as the placement of page numbers and the arrangement of information on a title page. In addition, style sheets explain and illustrate the documentation style they recommend for research papers. Because significant differences in format exist between disciplines, you should consult the appropriate style sheet before you begin your paper.

(3) Documentation

Different disciplines use different styles of **documentation**. Four of the most widely used styles are those recommended by the Modern Language Association (MLA), the American Psychological Association (APA), *The Chicago Manual of Style* (CMS), and the Council of Biology Editors (CBE).

See
Ch. 43

Instructors in the humanities usually prefer MLA style, which uses parenthetical references within the text to refer to a Works Cited list at the end of the paper, or CMS style, which uses footnotes or endnotes keyed to bibliographic citations at the end of the paper. Instructors in some of the social sciences, such as psychology and education, prefer APA style, which uses parenthetical references that differ from MLA references. Other disciplines—the physical and biological sciences and medicine, for example—prefer a number-reference format, such as CBE style, which uses raised numbers or numbers in parentheses in the text that refer to a numbered list of works at the end of the paper.

Because of the lack of uniformity among the disciplines, it is especially important that you consult your instructor to see which documentation style he or she requires. Your instructor may expect you to use a certain style sheet that he or she will place on reserve in the library or ask you to purchase. If this is not the case, however, it is your responsibility to determine which style to use—possibly by looking at an important journal in the field and following its documentation style.

✔ CHECKLIST: DOCUMENTATION

✔ Make sure you understand what information must be documented **(see 43a).**

✔ Do not assume the documentation style you use in one class is appropriate for another.

✔ Use one documentation style consistently throughout the paper.

✔ Make sure you have a copy of the appropriate style sheet or journal so that you can consult it as you write.

✔ Follow *exactly* the conventions of the style you decide to use.

✔ When you proofread the final draft of your paper, make certain that you have documented all information that needs documentation and that you have punctuated all entries correctly.

WRITING IN THE DISCIPLINES

	Discipline	Research Sources	Assignment

HUMANITIES	Languages
	Literature
	Philosophy
	History
	Linguistics
	Religion
	Art history
	Music
		Library sources
		  (print and
		  electronic)
		Interviews
		Observations
		  (museums,
		  concerts)
		Oral history
		Internet
			Response
			  statement
			Book review
			Art, music, dance,
			  or film review
			Bibliographic
			  essay
			Annotated
			  bibliography
			Literary analysis
			Research paper

SOCIAL SCIENCES	Anthropology
	Psychology
	Economics
	Business
	Education
	Sociology
	Political science
	Social work
	Criminal justice
		Library sources
		  (print and
		  electronic)
		Surveys
		Observation
		  (behavior of
		  groups and
		  individuals)
		Internet
			Experience paper
			Case study
			Literature review
			Proposal
			Research paper

continued on the following page

continued from the previous page

NATURAL AND APPLIED SCIENCES

<u>Natural sciences</u>
Biology
Chemistry
Physics
Astronomy
Geology
Mathematics

<u>Applied sciences</u>
Engineering
Computer science
Nursing
Pharmacy

Library sources
  (print and
   electronic)
Observations
Experiments
Surveys
Internet

Abstract
Literature survey
Laboratory report
Research paper

Style and Format	Documentation

HUMANITIES

Style
Specialized vocabulary
Direct quotations

Format
Little use of internal
  headings, visuals, etc.

English, languages, philosophy:
  MLA
History, art: CMS

SOCIAL SCIENCES

Style
Specialized vocabulary,
  including statistical
  terminology

Format
Internal headings
Use of visuals (graphs, maps,
  flow charts, photographs)
Numerical data (in tabular
  form)

APA

NATURAL AND APPLIED SCIENCES

Style
Frequent use of passive voice
Few direct quotations

Format
Internal headings
Use of tables, graphs, and
  illustrations (exact formats
  vary)

Biology: CBE
Other scientific disciplines use
  a variety of different
  <u>documentation styles</u>.

See
43e

CHAPTER 47

WRITING IN THE HUMANITIES

The humanities encompass a variety of disciplines, such as art, music, literature, languages, religion, and philosophy. In these disciplines, research is often conducted in order to analyze or interpret a **primary source**—a literary work, a historical document, a musical composition, or a painting or piece of sculpture—or to make connections between one work and another. Scholars in humanities disciplines may also examine **secondary sources**—commentaries on primary sources—in order to make critical judgments and, sometimes, to develop new theories.

See
44e2

47a Research Sources

Library research is an important part of study in many humanities disciplines. When you begin your research in any subject area, the *Humanities Index* is one general source you can use. This index lists articles from more than two hundred scholarly journals in areas such as history, language, literary criticism, and religion. It is available in print—with entries arranged alphabetically in yearly volumes according to author and subject—and in electronic form.

Many specialized sources are also available to help you with your research.

(1) Specialized Library Sources

The following reference sources are used in various humanities disciplines.

Art

Art Index
Contemporary Artists

The Dictionary of Art
Encyclopedia of World Art
Index to Art Reproductions in Books
New Dictionary of Modern Sculpture
Oxford Companion to Art
Praeger Encyclopedia of Art

Drama

The Crown Guide to the World's Great Plays from Ancient Greece to Modern Times
A Guide to Critical Reviews
International Dictionary of Theatre
McGraw-Hill Encyclopedia of World Drama
Modern World Drama: An Encyclopedia
New York Times Theater Reviews
Oxford Companion to the Theatre

Film

The Film Encyclopedia
Guide to Critical Reviews
International Dictionary of Film and Filmmakers
International Index to Film Periodicals
International Index to Multimedia Information
Magill's Survey of Cinema
New York Times Film Reviews
Oxford History of World Cinema

History

America: History and Life (United States)
Cambridge Ancient History
Cambridge Medieval History
CRIS (Combined Retrospective Index to Journals in History, 1838–1974)
Dictionary of American History
Encyclopedia of Latin American History and Culture
Guide to Historical Literature (AHA)
Harvard Guide to American History

Historical Abstracts (Europe)
New Cambridge Modern History

Language and Literature

Annual Bibliography of English Language and Literature
Biography Index
Book Review Digest
Book Review Index
Cassell's Encyclopaedia of World Literature
Children's Literature Review
Contemporary Authors
Current Biography
Dictionary of Literary Biography
Essay and General Literature Index
European Writers
Language and Language Behavior Abstracts (LLBA)
Literary History of the United States (LHUS)
MLA International Bibliography
Oxford Companion to American Literature
Oxford Companion to Classical Literature
Oxford Companion to English Literature
Oxford English Dictionary
New Princeton Encyclopedia of Poetry and Poetics
Reference Guide to Short Fiction
Salem Press Critical Surveys of Poetry, Fiction, Long Fiction, and Drama
Twentieth Century Authors
World Literature Criticism

Music

Music Article Guide
Music Index
New Grove Dictionary of Music and Musicians
New Harvard Dictionary of Music
New Oxford Companion to Music

Philosophy

The Concise Encyclopedia of Western Philosophy and Philosophers
Dictionary of the History of Ideas
Encyclopedia of Philosophy
Oxford Companion to Philosophy
Philosopher's Index

Religion

Encyclopedia of Ethics
Encyclopaedia of Judaica
Encyclopaedia of Islam
Encyclopedia of Religion
The Hutchinson Encyclopedia of Living Faiths
New Catholic Encyclopedia
Oxford Dictionary of the Christian Church
Religion Index

(2) Specialized Databases for Computer Searches

Many of the indexes that appear on the preceding list of specialized library sources are widely available on CD-ROM or online as well as in bound volumes. Some of the most helpful databases for humanities disciplines include *Art Index, MLA Bibliography, Religion Index, Philosopher's Index, Music Literature International (RRM), Essay and General Literature Index, Artbibliographies Modern, Historical Abstracts,* the *LLBA Index, Dissertation Abstracts, Arts and Humanities Search,* and *OnLine.* Ask your librarian about the availability of these and other databases.

(3) Other Sources of Information

Research in the humanities is not limited to the library. Historians may do interviews or archival work or consult records collected in town halls, churches, or courthouses; art historians may visit museums and galleries; and music scholars may attend concerts. The **Internet** can also be a rich resource for sources in a variety of humanities disciplines.

See
Ch. 40

In addition, nonprint sources, such as the oral history **interview** excerpted below, can be important resources for a paper in any humanities discipline.

See
39c5

Excerpt from Interview with Arturo Tapia, a Registered Tigua Indian

My daddy never used to say he was Tigua Indian. . . . We never talked about it. . . . Other Indians never liked us, and the white people never allowed us in their bars or stores. I have gone up to people and told them I am Tigua, and they say, "What a low-class Indian," or "Them down there, the Mexicans, they sold out."

The student who recorded this interview chose to use it in her paper's conclusion.

As many of the sources examined in this paper have demonstrated, the history of the Tiguas is full of misconceptions. The New Mexico version of the Tiguas' migration is that they fled with a Spanish party to El Paso during the Indian uprising of August 10, 1680. (The Tigua version of their migration is quite different.) The New Mexico Indians have portrayed the Tiguas of Isleta as a "Judas tribe" who turned against their own people to ally themselves with the Spanish. As one registered Tigua Indian points out, even today the Tiguas face discrimination from other Indians as well as from whites and feel they are considered "low class" (Tapia).

47b Assignments in the Humanities

(1) The Response Statement

In some disciplines, particularly literature, you may write a **response statement,** in which you express (usually informally) your reactions to a literary work, a painting, a film, a dance performance, or a concert. Such an assignment requires you to write a first-person account of your feelings and to explore the factors that influenced your reactions. The following response statement was written for a journal kept for an Introduction to Literature course.

Sample Response Statement

Rereading The Catcher in the Rye after two years, I see a lot of weaknesses I didn't notice last time. The style is too cute and too repetitive, and it calls attention to itself. Salinger has Holden Caulfield say things like "I mean" and "if you know what I mean" too many times, and he seems to use bad language for no particular reason. Also, I don't like Holden as much as I did the first time I read the book. Before I saw him as isolated and misunderstood, a pathetic character who could have been happy if only he had stayed a child forever. Now he gets on my nerves. I keep thinking he could do something to help himself if he didn't have to blame everything on the "phonies." All this probably says more about how I've changed in two years than about how good or bad the book is.

(2) The Book Review

A **book review,** which may be assigned in any humanities discipline, asks you to **respond critically** to a book, judging it according to a partic- ular set of standards. (Reviews of performances or nonprint works are similar to book reviews in that they present judgments that assess the worth of a work or an artist.) Before you begin your evaluation of the work, you should provide some context to enable readers to follow your discussion—for example, a brief summary or overview of the work or an outline of the author's key points or arguments. After you summa- rize the book, you should evaluate its content (the writer's central idea and supporting information) and the way in which the material is pre- sented (the book's style and organization). End your book review with a statement that summarizes your critical evaluation of the text. The book review that follows was written for a cross-disciplinary composi- tion class.

See
Ch. 7

Excerpt from a Book Review

In his thought-provoking book Chaos: Making a New Science, James Gleick presents the events of recent years that have shaped this new science and introduces the individuals responsible for those events.

He begins with what is considered the starting point of the new science, Edward Lorenz's Butterfly Effect, and ends with a comprehensive discussion of the newest discoveries and the future of chaos. Most importantly, he explains the equations, theories, and concepts that are the heart of chaos. One example of how this new science is applied is Mitchell Feigenbaum's theory of universality. Using only a hand-held calculator, this physicist proved that simple equations from a simple system can be applied to a totally unrelated system to produce a complicated solution. Although Feigenbaum's theory was at first greeted with skepticism, it soon became the basis for finding order in otherwise unrelated irregularities. Gleick's clear analysis of this and other theories makes his explanation of chaos appropriate for readers with little scientific background as well as for more knowledgeable readers.

(3)   The Bibliographic Essay

A **bibliographic essay** surveys research in a field and assesses the usefulness of various sources on a particular subject. Several publications in various humanities specialties publish annual bibliographic essays to inform scholars of recent developments in a field. Students in advanced literature or history classes may also prepare this type of essay. The following excerpt, written by a student in an American literature class, comes from a bibliographic essay on Mark Twain's novel *Pudd'nhead Wilson*.

Excerpt from a Bibliographic Essay

Most early critics analyze the novel in terms of racial issues and the doctrine of environmental determinism. Langston Hughes, for instance, writes that "the basic theme [of <u>Pudd'nhead Wilson</u>] is slavery . . . and its main thread concerns the absurdity of man-made differentials, whether of caste or 'race'" (viii). James M. Cox also focuses on the racial issue, specifically on miscegenation, but in a more symbolic vein than does Hughes. Cox's analysis of the novel is very similar to Fiedler's. Like Fiedler,

Cox believes that the novel deals with American guilt; it is a "final unmasking of the heart of darkness beneath the American dream" (361). Tom serves as the white man's nemesis, spawned by the guilt of miscegenation, a violation of the black race. According to Cox, he is "the instrument of an avenging destiny which has overtaken Dawson's Landing" (353).

(4) The Annotated Bibliography

Each entry in an **annotated bibliography** includes full source information and a *brief* summary of the source's main points or arguments. The following example is an entry from a student's annotated bibliography of *Pudd'nhead Wilson*.

Excerpt from an Annotated Bibliography

Chellis, Barbara A. "Those Extraordinary Twins: Negroes and Whites."
American Quarterly 21 (1969): 100-12. Chellis sees
Pudd'nhead Wilson as an exposure of "the fiction of law and
custom" that has justified distinctions between blacks and whites.
Twain develops his theme through his characterizations of Roxy, Tom,
and Chambers. According to Chellis, Roxy's "crime"--condemning the
real Tom to slavery--stems not from the influence of her race but from
that of her white values. Tom is spoiled and selfish--the kind of person
produced by white society's values. The invalidity of race distinctions is
further pointed out through the servility of Chambers, who is white.
Black "servility" is ultimately seen to be nothing more than the result
of training.

(5) The Literary Analysis

Students in literature classes are frequently called on to analyze poems, plays, short stories, or novels. For a detailed discussion of how to write a **literary analysis,** as well as three sample papers—illustrating an analysis of a short story, a poem, and a one-act play—see **Chapter 51.** See **47d1** for an example of a literary analysis that uses secondary source material.

47c Conventions of Style, Format, and Documentation

(1) Style and Format

Each humanities discipline has its own specialized vocabulary, and you should use the key terms used in the field; be careful, however, not to overuse technical terminology. You can use the first person (*I*) when you are expressing your own reactions and convictions—for example, in a response statement. In other cases, use the third-person point of view.

Although papers in the humanities have traditionally not included abstracts, internal headings, tables, or graphs, this situation is gradually changing. Be sure you know what your instructor expects.

NOTE: When you write papers about literature, you should follow the special conventions of literary analysis. These conventions are explained in **51c.**

(2) Documentation

See
43a, b   Literature and modern and classical language scholars use **MLA format**; history scholars use **The Chicago Manual of Style**.

47d Sample Humanities Research Papers

(1) Modern Language Association (MLA) Format: A Literary Analysis

The following literary analysis, "Assertive Men and Passive Women: A Comparison of Adrienne Rich's 'Aunt Jennifer's Tigers' and 'Mathilde in Normandy,'" is based on two of Adrienne Rich's poems. It uses MLA documentation style and cites several critical articles. Because the instructor did not require a separate title page, the student included identifying information on the first page of her paper. For a detailed discussion of the process of writing a research paper in the humanities, see **Chapter 44;** for an annotated student paper, see **Chapter 45.**

Thomason 1

Cathy Thomason

Composition 102

Dr. Alvarez-Goldstein

9 May 1998

Assertive Men and Passive Women: A Comparison

of Adrienne Rich's "Aunt Jennifer's Tigers" and

"Mathilde in Normandy"

Center title

Double-space

Adrienne Rich began her poetic career in the 1950s as an

undergraduate at Radcliffe College. The product of a

conservative Southern family, Rich was greatly influenced by her

Background

father, who encouraged the young poet to seek higher

standards for her work. However, her early work shows evidence

of Rich's future struggle with this upbringing. Although she used

styles and subjects that gained approval from both her father

and the almost all-male literary world, some of her early works

suggest an inner struggle with the status quo of male

Thesis statement

dominance (Bennett 178). "Aunt Jennifer's Tigers" and

"Mathilde in Normandy" clearly reflect this struggle.

Both "Aunt Jennifer's Tigers" and "Mathilde in Normandy"

tell the story of women living in the shadow of men's

Paragraph summarizes similarities between two poems

accomplishments. The central figures of the two poems display

their creativity and intelligence through a traditional female

occupation, embroidery. Although the poems are set in different

Thomason 2

time periods ("Mathilde in Normandy" in the Middle Ages and "Aunt Jennifer's Tigers" in the 1950s), their focus is the same: both are about women who recognize their subordinate positions to men but are powerless to change their situations. The difference between the two, however, lies in the fact that Mathilde does not suffer the inner conflict that Aunt Jennifer does.

"Aunt Jennifer's Tigers" is the story of a woman trapped in a conventional and apparently boring marriage. Her outlet is her needlework; through her embroidery she creates a fantasy world of tigers as an escape from her real life. In 1972, in her essay "When We Dead Awaken," Rich said, "In writing this poem, composed and apparently cool as it is, I thought I was creating a portrait of an imaginary woman" (469). What she later discovered was that Aunt Jennifer was probably typical of many married women in the 1950s. These women, Rich observed, "didn't talk to each other much in the fifties-- not about their secret emptiness, their frustrations . . ." (470).

Standing in opposition to the timid and frustrated Aunt Jennifer are the tigers in the first stanza:

> Aunt Jennifer's tigers prance across a screen,
>
> Bright topaz denizens of a world of green.
>
> They do not fear the men beneath the tree;
>
> They pace in sleek chivalric certainty. (1-4)

Running acknowledgement introduces quotation

Parenthetical documentation

Long quotation indented 10 spaces (1") from left-hand margin; no quotation marks necessary

Parenthetical documentation identifies quoted lines

Unlike Aunt Jennifer, the tigers move with confidence and "chivalric certainty." They are not dominated by men, as Aunt Jennifer is. According to Claire Keyes, this stanza contains the dominant voice (24). Although Aunt Jennifer is not assertive or forceful, her creations--the tigers--are. In other words, Aunt Jennifer's work is more interesting than she is. Even so, the tigers are a part of Aunt Jennifer's imagination, and they show there is more to Aunt Jennifer than her existence as a housewife would suggest.

"Mathilde in Normandy" is based on the folktale that William the Conqueror's wife, Queen Mathilde, created the Bordeaux Tapestry to tell the story of the Norman invasion of England (Keyes 24). The men in this poem are as powerful as the men who dominate Aunt Jennifer, showing their masculinity in their attack on another country. Although Rich acknowledges Mathilde's position as a woman who may never see her husband again--"Say what you will, anxiety there too / Played havoc with the skein" (21-22)--Mathilde, unlike Aunt Jennifer, has no problem with the notion that women should stay home. According to the speaker, "Yours was a time when women sat at home" (17). Therefore, Mathilde does not suffer inner turmoil about her role in life as a subordinate wife.

Mathilde is separated from her husband's world because she is female and considered unable to fight, to compete in a

Short quotation run in with text; slash separates two lines of poetry

Thomason 4

male world. Aunt Jennifer, however, is held back from the
male world by a different barrier:

> Aunt Jennifer's fingers fluttering through her wool
>
> Find even the ivory needle hard to pull.
>
> The massive weight of Uncle's wedding band
>
> Sits heavily upon Aunt Jennifer's hand. (5-8)

Her marriage is not a happy one; her wedding band holds her
down (Keyes 23). In accepting her role as housewife, Aunt
Jennifer is denied a satisfying existence. She is reduced to
maintaining a household for a husband who dominates all
aspects of her life. Even Aunt Jennifer's pursuit of art is made
difficult by her marriage. The "weight" of her wedding band
makes it difficult to embroider.

For Mathilde, life is objectionable only because she fears
that her husband and the men of the kingdom will not return.
She identifies with her husband's cause and accepts the fact
that the life men lead is dangerous, "Harsher hunting on the
opposite coast" (16). Unlike Mathilde, Aunt Jennifer sees her
marriage as imprisonment; she will be free only when she dies:

> When Aunt is dead, her terrified hands will lie
>
> Still ringed with the ordeals she was mastered by.
>
> The tigers in the panel that she made
>
> Will go on prancing, proud and unafraid. (9-12)

Thomason 5

Aunt Jennifer's hands are "terrified," overwhelmed by the power that her husband, and society, have over her. Aunt Jennifer, who is "mastered" by her situation, stands in opposition to the tigers, who flaunt their independence, forever "prancing, proud and unafraid." Mathilde's experience with male power is also terrifying. She is in the vulnerable position of being a queen whose husband and court are away at war. If her husband does not return, she can be subjugated by another man, one wishing to take over the kingdom.

Both "Aunt Jennifer's Tigers" and "Mathilde in Normandy" present stories of women bound to men. Although both poems suggest that conventional relationships between men and women are unsatisfactory, Mathilde does not struggle against her role as Aunt Jennifer does. Claire Keyes points out that although these poems are "well mannered and feminine on the surface," they "speak differently in their muted stories" (28). Although only "Aunt Jennifer's Tigers" openly criticizes the status quo, both poems reflect the inner conflicts of women and express their buried desires subtly, but nonetheless powerfully.

Conclusion

Thomason 6

Works Cited ← Center
← Double-
space

Bennett, Paula. "Dutiful Daughter." <u>My Life a Loaded Gun:</u>

Indent ⟶
5 spaces
(or ½")
<u>Female Creativity and Feminist Poetics</u>. Boston: Beacon,

1986. 171-76.

Keyes, Claire. <u>The Aesthetics of Power: The Story of Adrienne</u>

<u>Rich</u>. Athens: U of Georgia P, 1986.

Rich, Adrienne. "Aunt Jennifer's Tigers." <u>Poems: Selected and</u>

<u>New</u>. New York: Norton, 1974. 81.

---. "Mathilde in Normandy." <u>Poems: Selected and New</u>. New

York: Norton, 1974. 94-95.

Three ⟶
unspaced
hyphens
used instead
of repeating
author's
name
---. "When We Dead Awaken." <u>Ways of Reading: An</u>

<u>Anthology for Writers</u>. Ed. David Bartholomae and

Anthony Petrowsky. Boston: Bedford, 1993. 461-76.

(2) Chicago Manual of Style (CMS) Format: Excerpts from a History Research Paper

The following pages are excerpted from a history research paper, "Native Americans and the Reservation System," which uses **Chicago style**. Because the instructor did not require a separate title page, the student included the necessary identifying information in a heading on the first page of her paper.

See
43b

1   Page number
on every page

Angela M. Womack

American History 301

December 3, 1997

Double-space   Native Americans and the Reservation System

It is July 7th, and ten thousand Navajo Indians make

ready to leave land in Arizona that they have called home for

generations. This land has been assigned to the Hopi tribe by

the U.S. government to settle a boundary dispute between the

two tribes.[1] Ella Bedonie, a member of the Navajo tribe, says,

"The Navajo and the Hopi people have no dispute. It's the

government that's doing this to us. I think the Hopis may have

the land for a while, but then the government . . . will step

in."[2] The Hopis are receiving 250,000 acres to compensate

them for the 900,000 acres they will lose in this land deal;

however, the groundwater on this land is suspect because of

possible contamination by a uranium mine upstream. To

mitigate this situation the government has sweetened the deal

with incentives of livestock.[3]

        This was the fate many Native Americans faced as

western expansion swept across the North American

Superscripts
(raised
numerals)
refer to
endnotes
listed on
"Notes" page

2

continent. Now consider that the incident mentioned occurred

not on July 7, 1886, but on July 7, 1986. Indian relations with

the U.S. government are as problematic today as ever before,

for the federal government's administration of the reservation

system both promotes and restricts the development of the

Native American culture.

A reservation is an area of land reserved for Indian use.

There are approximately 260 reservations in the United States

at present.[4] The term *reservation* can be traced back to the

time when land was "reserved" for Indian use in treaties

between whites and Native Americans. Figures from 1978 by

the Bureau of Indian Affairs show that 51,789,249 acres of

land are in trust for Native Americans; 41,678,875 acres of

this are for tribes, and 10,110,374 acres are for individuals.[5]

The Native Americans are by no means restricted to these

areas, although this assumption is commonly made. They are

as free as any other citizen to leave these areas.

10

Notes

1. Trebbe Johnson, "Indian Land, White Greed," *Nation,* 4 July 1987, 15.

2. Johnson, 17.

3. Johnson, 16.

4. Ted Williams, "On the Reservation: America's Apartheid," *National Review,* 8 May 1987, 28.

5. U.S. Bureau of Indian Affairs, "Information About . . . The Indian People" (Washington, D.C.: GPO, 1981), 6, mimeographed.

Sources listed in order in which they appear in paper. Second and subsequent references to sources include only author's last name and page number.

11

Bibliography ⟵ Center
⟵ Double-
space

"Adrift in Their Own Land." *Time,* 6 July 1987, 89.

Entries are listed alphabetically according to author's last name

Arrandale, Tom. "American Indian Economic Development."

   Editorial Research Reports, 17 Feb. 1984, 127-142.

Battise, Carol. Personal interview, 25 Sept. 1987.

Cook, J. "Help Wanted--Work, Not Handouts." *Forbes,* 4 May

   1987, 68-71.

Horswell, Cindy. "Alabama-Coushattas See Hope in U.S.

   Guardianship." *Houston Chronicle,* 26 May 1987, 11.

First line of each entry is flush with left-hand margin; subsequent lines indented 3 spaces

Johnson, Trebbe. "Indian Land, White Greed." *Nation,* 4 July

   1987, 15-18.

Martin, Howard N. "Alabama-Coushatta Indians of Texas:

   Alabama-Coushatta Historical Highlights." Brochure,

   Alabama-Coushatta Indian Reservation: Livingston,

   Tex., n.d.

Article has no listed author; alphabetized according to first significant word of title

"A New Brand of Tribal Tycoons." *Time,* 16 March 1987, 56.

Philp, K. R. "Dillon S. Myer and the Advent of Termination:

   1950-1953." *Western Historical Quarterly* 3 (January

   1988): 37-59.

U.S. Bureau of Indian Affairs. "Information About . . . The

   Indian People." Washington, D.C.: GPO, 1981.

   Mimeographed.

12

Williams, Ted. "On the Reservation: America's Apartheid."

National Review, 8 May 1987, 28-30.

Young, J., and Williams T. *American Realities: Historical*

Realities from the First Settlements to the Civil War. Boston:

Little, Brown, 1981.

CHAPTER 48

WRITING IN THE SOCIAL SCIENCES

The social sciences include anthropology, business, criminal justice, economics, education, political science, psychology, social work, and sociology. When you approach an assignment in the social sciences, your purpose is often to study the behavior of individuals or groups. You may be seeking to understand causes; predict results; define a policy, habit, or trend; draw an analogy between one group and another; or analyze a problem. Before you can approach a problem in the social sciences, you must develop a **hypothesis,** an educated guess about what you believe your research will suggest. Then you can go on to gather the data that you hope will support that hypothesis. Data may be quantitative or qualitative. **Quantitative data** are essentially numerical—the "countable" results of surveys and polls. **Qualitative data** are less exact and more descriptive—the results of interviews or observations, for example.

48a Research Sources

Although library research is an important component of research in the social sciences, researchers also engage in field work. In the library, social scientists consult print and electronic versions of compilations of statistics, government documents, and newspaper articles, in addition to scholarly books and articles. Outside the library, social scientists conduct interviews and surveys and observe individuals and groups. Because so much of their data are quantitative, social scientists must know how to analyze statistics and how to read and interpret tables.

(1) Specialized Library Sources

The following reference sources are useful in a variety of social science disciplines.

African American Encyclopedia

American Statistics Index (ASI)

Bibliografia Chicana: A Guide to Information Sources

CQ Researcher

Dictionary of Mexican American History

Encyclopedia of Black America

Handbook of North American Indians

Harvard Encyclopedia of American Ethnic Groups

Human Resources Abstracts

Index to International Statistics (IIS)

International Bibliography of the Social Sciences

International Encyclopedia of the Social Sciences

PAIS (Public Affairs Information Service)

Population Index

Reference Encyclopedia of the American Indian

Reference Library of Black America

Social Sciences Citation Index

Social Sciences Index

Statistical Reference Index (SRI)

Women's Studies: A Guide to Information Sources

The following are the reference sources most often used for research in specific disciplines.

Anthropology

Abstracts in Anthropology

Anthropological Literature

Dictionary of Anthropology

Encyclopedia of Cultural Anthropology

Business and Economics

Accountants' Index

Business Information Sources

Business Periodicals Index

Dictionary of Economics

The Encyclopedia of Banking and Finance

The Encyclopedia of Management
Journal of Economic Literature
The McGraw-Hill Dictionary of Modern Economics
Personnel Management Abstracts
Wall Street Journal Index

Criminal Justice

Criminology, Penology, and Police Science Abstracts
Criminal Justice Abstracts
Dictionary of Crime
Encyclopedia of Crime and Justice
Encyclopedia of World Crime
Index to Legal Periodicals

Education

Critical Dictionary of Educational Concepts
Current Index to Journals in Education
Dictionary of Education
Education Index
Encyclopedia of Educational Research
Facts on File
Resources in Education

Political Science

ABC Political Science
American Political Dictionary
CIS Index (Congressional Information Service)
CRIS: The Combined Retrospective Index to Journals in Political Science
Dictionary of Modern Politics
Dictionary of Political Thought
Encyclopedia of Modern World Politics
Encyclopedia of the Third World
Encyclopedia of the United Nations and International Agreements
Europa World Year Book
Foreign Affairs Bibliography
ISLA (Information Services on Latin America)

International Political Science Abstracts

Worldmark Encyclopedia of the Nations

Psychology

Biographical Dictionary of Psychology

Contemporary Psychology

Encyclopedia of Psychology

International Encyclopedia of Psychiatry, Psychology, Psychoanalysis and Neurology

Psychological Abstracts

Sociology and Social Work

Encyclopedia of Social Work

Encyclopedia of Sociology

Poverty and Human Resources Abstracts

Sage Family Studies Abstracts

Social Work Research and Abstracts

Sociological Abstracts

Government Documents   Government documents are important resources for social scientists because they contain complete and up-to-date facts and figures on a wide variety of subjects.

Government documents can be located through the *Monthly Catalog,* which contains the list of documents (in print, microfiche, and electronic formats) published each month. Other useful indexes include *The Congressional Information Service Index, The American Statistics Index,* and *The Index to U.S. Government Periodicals.*

Newspaper Articles   Newspaper articles are particularly good sources for researching subjects in political science, economics, and business. For information from newspapers from across the country, a useful source is *Newsbank,* which provides subject headings under the appropriate government agencies. For instance, articles on child abuse are likely to be listed under "Health and Human Services." Another useful source of information from newspapers is *InfoTrac's National Newspaper Index.*

(2) Specialized Databases for Computer Searches

Many of the print sources cited above are also available as CD-ROMs or online. Some of the more widely used databases for social science disciplines include *Cendata, Business Index ASAP, Social Sciences Index,*

PsycINFO, ERIC, Social Scisearch, Sociological Abstracts, Information Science Abstracts, PAIS International, Population Bibliography, Economic Literature Index, ABI/INFORM, Legal Resource Index, Management Contents, Trade & Industry Index, PTSF + S Indexes, and *Facts on File.* Check with your librarian about the availability of these and other databases in your library.

Lexis/Nexis is a powerful database that enables you not only to survey thousands of newspapers from across the country but also to view and reprint the articles. *Lexis/Nexis* also has a special library that contains articles focusing on legal matters and tax issues.

(3) Other Sources of Information

Interviews, surveys, and observation of the behavior of various groups and individuals are important nonlibrary sources for social science research. Assignments may ask you to use your classmates as subjects for surveys or interviews. For example, in a political science class, your teacher may ask you to interview a sample of college students and classify them as conservative, liberal, or moderate. You may be asked to poll each group to find out college students' attitudes on issues such as acquaintance rape, affirmative action, or the problems of the homeless. If you were writing a paper on educational programs for the mentally gifted, in addition to library research you might want to observe two classes—one of gifted students and one of average students. You might also want to interview students, teachers, or parents. Similarly, research in psychology and social work may rely on your observations of clients and their families.

48b Assignments in the Social Sciences

(1) The Experience Paper

See 39c

Instructors in the social sciences often ask students to do hands-on research **outside the library**; one typical assignment is the **experience paper,** in which students record their observations and reactions to a field trip or site visit. For example, students in an education class might write up their observations of a class of hearing-impaired students, criminal justice students might record their reactions to a juvenile detention facility, business majors might write about their impressions of how a particular small business operates, and students in a psychology class could write an experience paper about a visit to a state-run psychiatric facility.

The following excerpt, written by a student in a sociology of religion class, describes visits to two different churches.

Excerpt from an Experience Paper

The Pentecostal church service I observed was full of self-expression, movement, and emotion. People sang and praised the Lord in loud voices. In an atmosphere similar to that of a revival, people spontaneously expressed their joy and their reactions to the sermon. Each word the preacher spoke elicited responses like "Praise the Lord," "Hallelujah," "Thank the Lord," and "Amen." Rather than focusing on religious doctrine, the sermon focused on the problems of everyday life. The Presbyterian service I observed was very different. Compared to the Pentecostal service it seemed orderly, structured, and traditional. The sanctuary was quiet; organ music was the only sound. Worshippers did not shout or clap. They conducted silent, almost whispered, prayers; even their hymns were restrained and solemn. Finally, the sermon was less practical than the Pentecostal sermon; it focused on the interpretation of theological doctrine and only tangentially discussed the doctrine's relevance to everyday life.

(2) The Case Study

The **case study** is important for the presentation of information in psychology, sociology, anthropology, and political science, where it can examine an individual case, the dynamics of a group, or the operations of a political organization. Case studies are usually informative rather than persuasive, describing a problem and suggesting solutions or treatments. They generally follow a set format, including the statement of the problem, the background of the problem, the observations of the behavior of the individual or group being studied, the conclusions arrived at, and suggestions for improvement or future recommendations.

Different disciplines use case studies in different ways. In political science, case studies can examine foreign policy negotiations or analyses of issues such as "Should government control the media?" In psychology, social work, and educational psychology or counseling, the case study typically focuses on an individual and his or her interaction with peers or with agency professionals. Such a case study usually describes behavior and outlines the steps that should be taken to solve the problem that the caseworker or researcher observes.

Excerpt from a Case Study (Social Work)

Mona Freeman, a 14-year-old girl, was brought to the Denver Children's Residential Treatment Center by her 70-year-old, devoutly religious adoptive mother. Both were personable, verbal, and neatly groomed. The presenting problem was seen differently by various members of the client system. Mrs. Freeman described Mona's "several years of behavior problems," including "lying, stealing, and being boy crazy." Mona viewed herself as a "disappointment" and wanted "time to think." She had been expelled from the local Seventh-day Adventist School for being truant and defiant several months earlier and had been attending public school. The examining psychiatrist diagnosed a conduct disorder but saw no intellectual, physical, or emotional disabilities. He predicted that Mona probably would not be able to continue to live in "such an extreme disciplinary environment" as the home of Mrs. Freeman because she had lived for the years from seven until twelve with her natural father in Boston, Massachusetts--a situation that was described as a "kidnapping" by Mrs. Freeman. The psychiatrist mentioned some "depression" and attributed it to Mona's inability to fit into her current environment and to the loss of her life with her father in Boston.

(3) The Literature Review

See
47b3

The **literature review** (similar in purpose and format to the **bibliographic essay** assigned in the humanities) is often part of the background section of a social science research paper. By reading, summarizing, and commenting on recent scholarship on a particular topic, students demonstrate a knowledge of a topic as well as an understanding of different critical approaches to that topic. The following excerpt, written for an introductory psychology class, is from a literature review on depression among college students.

Excerpt from a Literature Review

Negative events and outlook are not the only causes of depression among college students (Brown & Silberschatz, 1988; Cochran & Hammen, 1985). In fact, some students do not become depressed in the presence of one or more negative events, while others are depressed even if no negative event takes place (Billings et al., 1983). Depression can appear to arise from a range of social and environmental factors, which can appear as a combination of stressful life events, poor coping style, and a lack of social resources (Cochran & Hammen, 1985; Vrendenburg et al., 1985).

(4)   The Proposal

A **proposal,** often the first stage of a research project, can help clarify and focus the project's direction and goals. In a proposal, you make a convincing case for your idea. To do so, you define your research project and defend it. In the process you must adhere strictly to any specifications outlined by your instructor or in the request for proposals issued by the grant-giving agency.

Along with a proposal you usually send a letter, called a *letter of transmittal,* and a **résumé,** which lists your specific qualifications for the project. This **résumé** summarizes your relevant work experience and accomplishments and reinforces your qualifications.

See
52b2

Many proposals include some or all of the following components.

Cover Sheet   The cover sheet includes your name, the title of your project, and the person or agency to which your proposal is submitted. It also provides a short title that expresses your subject concisely. Usually another line on this sheet states the reason for the submission of the proposal—for example, to satisfy a course requirement or to request funding or facilities.

Cover Sheet Format

Advantages of the Maquiladora Project

in El Paso

Submitted to: Professor Lawrence Howley

For: Fulfillment of Research Requirement

for Sociology 412

by Laura Talamantes

Abstract   Usually on a separate page, the abstract provides a short summary of your proposal. (See **49b1** for information on writing abstracts; for a sample, see the abstract accompanying the social science research paper in **48d**.)

Statement of Purpose   Your statement of purpose tells why you are conducting your research and what you hope to accomplish—for example, "The Maquiladora Project is an industrial development program that relies on international cooperation with Mexican industries to utilize Mexican labor while boosting the employment of US white-collar workers."

Background of the Problem   This section summarizes previous research and indicates the need for your specific study.

Rationale   In this section, you explain as persuasively as possible why your research project is necessary and what makes it important at this time.

Statement of Qualification   This section demonstrates why you are qualified to carry out the research and enumerates the special qualifications you bring to your work.

See
48b3

Literature Review   The **literature review** contains a brief survey of each source you have consulted. Because it helps to establish your credibility as a researcher, this section should be thorough.

Research Methods   This section describes the exact methods you will use in carrying out your research and the materials you will need; its purpose is to demonstrate the soundness of your method.

Timetable   This section states the time you will need to carry out the project.

Budget   This section estimates the costs for carrying out the research.

Conclusion   In this section you restate the importance of your project.

 Conventions of Style, Format, and Documentation

(1)   Style and Format

Like other disciplines, social science uses a technical vocabulary. For instance, the social work case study excerpted in **48b2** identifies "the presenting problem"—that is, the reason the "subject," Mona, was brought to the Denver Children's Facility. Because you are addressing specialists, you should use the specialized vocabulary of the discipline and, when you describe charts and tables, you should use statistical terms, such as *mean, percentage,* and *chi square.* Keep in mind, however, that you should use plain English to explain what percentages, means, and standard deviations signify in terms of your analysis.

A social science research paper includes **page headers,** an abbreviated title printed at the top of each page of a paper. It also includes **internal headings** (for example, *Method, Results, Background of Problem, Description of Problem, Solutions,* and *Conclusion*). Each section of a social science paper is a complete unit with a beginning and an end so that it can be read separately, out of context, and still make sense. The body of the paper may present and discuss graphs, maps, photographs, or flow charts. Finally, a social science paper frequently presents numerical data in tabular form.

(2)   Documentation

Many of the journals in the various social science disciplines use the documentation style of the American Psychological Association's *Publication Manual.*

 American Psychological Association (APA) Format: Social Science Research Paper

The following psychology research paper, "Impression Formation in Customer-Clerk Interactions," uses APA documentation style.

Page header,
page number

|

Type running
head flush
with left-hand
margin

|

Center

Impression Formation   1

Running head: IMPRESSION FORMATION

Impression Formation in

Customer-Clerk Interactions

Jennifer Humble

Dr. Barbara Bremer

December 11, 1997

Page header
and number
on every page

Abstract

Center

The present study examined the extent to which physical appearance and dress affect the quality of customer-clerk interactions. An observational study was conducted in which a well-dressed actor and a poorly dressed actor posed as customers and engaged in customer-clerk interactions at nine different stores in a suburban shopping mall. The sociability of the clerk, time of initiation of interaction, duration of interaction, and prices of the first two watches shown were recorded. In support of the proposed hypothesis that dress and physical appearance will affect the quality of social interactions, the results indicated that the sociability of each clerk was significantly higher when interacting with the well-dressed actor than when interacting with the poorly dressed actor.

Impression Formation in

Customer-Clerk Interactions

In an attempt to understand the factors that influence the quality of social interactions between customers and clerks, some theorists have proposed that the sociability of the customer is the critical factor in determining the sociability of the interaction (Hester, Koger, & McCauley, 1985). Hester et al. (1985) reported that the customer's sociability will determine the sociability of the salesperson because the salesperson appears to adapt to and mimic the sociability of the customer. Furthermore, Segal and McCauley (1986) reported that sociability of customer-clerk interactions is only minimally affected by factors such as urbanism of location of interaction and business of the location. Thus, they too indicated that customer sociability plays a crucial role in determining the quality of customer-clerk interactions.

Although customer sociability is believed to be a key factor in determining the quality of social interactions, one must also consider the effect of first impressions as a determinant of the quality of these interactions. Past research indicates that individuals tend to form impressions and make judgments of others on the basis of cues, including facial

Left margin annotations:

Full title (centered)

Introduction

Literature review (¶s 1–3)

Authors' names in parentheses when not mentioned in text

Year in parentheses, authors' names in text

expression, gestures, and dress (Hamid, 1972). Hamid examined the effects of glasses and makeup on impression formation and judgments and discovered that female actors who wore glasses and no makeup were perceived as being conservative while actors who wore makeup and no glasses were perceived as intelligent, neat, and self-confident. These stereotypical responses occurred despite the fact that the subjects had neither seen nor communicated with the actors before. This indicates that individuals tend to make intrinsic judgments about a person based on external cues. Francis and Evans (1987) further demonstrated the significant effects of personal coloring and garment style on the assessment of personality trait factors such as emotional, sociable, adaptable, and scientific. Additional research has also confirmed that there is an overall general tendency to form impressions of strangers primarily on the basis of physical/biological traits (e.g., being well dressed and physically attractive) (Lennon & Davis, 1989).

     The impressions that individuals form of others, although at times accurate judgments of intrinsic characteristics, nevertheless often prove to be inaccurate. In addition, once individuals integrate external information into their impression of a person it is very difficult to discount such information (Tetlock, 1983). One can see how impression formation can play a critical role in determining the quality of social interactions, for individuals tend to make intrinsic trait assumptions of others based on external cues. This tendency in turn alters their behavior toward the individual according to their preconceived perception of the individual. Furthermore, social interactions can be greatly hindered when the impressions one forms are inaccurate.

The purpose of the present study is to examine the effects of physical appearance and dress on impression formation and to determine how the formed impression of a customer will consequently affect the quality of customer-clerk interactions. Based on the previous research indicating the effect of dress cues on impression formation, it is proposed that the manipulation of dress and physical appearance will have a significant effect on the sociability of customer-clerk interactions.

Hypothesis

Method

Internal headings; see **A1b** *for format*

Subjects

The study included nine salespersons employed at various stores located in a large suburban shopping center.

The subjects were unaware of the fact that an observational study was in progress.

Materials

A previously developed observational measure of sociability or friendliness of public interaction was used to determine the sociability of each clerk (Segal & McCauley, 1986). The clerk's sociability was scored based on the following six behaviors: (a) greeting; (b) conversation; (c) farewell (0 = none; 1 = routine, conversational; 2 = friendly, personal recognition); (d) smiles; (e) facial regard (0 = none; 1 = one or two briefly; 2 = three or more; 3 = more or less continuous); and (f) overall tone (1 = unfriendly; 2 = functional, routine; 3 = friendly; 4 = personal recognition, willingness to go beyond business at hand). In addition, the time taken to initiate the interaction (minutes), the duration of the interaction (minutes), and the prices of the first two watches shown were recorded.

Procedure

The study was conducted by three experimenters (one male and two females) at a large suburban shopping center on a Sunday afternoon between 11 a.m. and 4 p.m. The two female experimenters (Actor 1 and Actor 2) posed as customers in a customer-clerk interaction while the male experimenter served as the Stable Observer of the interaction. Additionally, Actor 1 and Actor 2 served as observers when not directly participating in the interaction.

To test the effects of dress and appearance cues on impression formation and the quality of customer-clerk interactions, Actor 1 was at first dressed in a beige tailored suit, wore high-heeled shoes, and carried a leather handbag. In addition, she wore gold jewelry and makeup and had her hair neatly arranged. Actor 2 wore an old blue hooded sweatshirt, blue sweatpants, and old running sneakers. In addition, she wore glasses, no makeup, and no jewelry and had her hair combed straight back. In each interaction Actor 1 entered a store, approached a jewelry counter, and began to look at watches. A jewelry counter was chosen as a site for the interaction because of the ease of observation of the interaction and the high probability of obtaining the same clerk for both Actor 1 and Actor 2. Actor 2 and the Stable Observer also approached the jewelry counter or surrounding areas (within 10–20 feet of Actor 1) in order to record the sociability of the clerk.

The basic scenario involved the salesperson's approaching Actor 1 and inquiring if she needed assistance, to which Actor 1 was instructed to respond that she was interested in purchasing a watch. If Actor 1 was asked if she had a price range in mind, she was to respond that she had no price range. This measure was taken to allow the clerk to make a decision as to the price of the watch that Actor 1 could afford based on his or her impression of Actor 1. After being shown a minimum of two watches, Actor 1 thanked the salesperson for his or her help and departed.

After the interaction, Actor 2 and the Stable Observer scored the sociability of the clerk on small notepads that had been concealed in their pockets during the interaction. Actor 2 and the Stable Observer were on opposite sides of Actor 1; thus, each was unaware of the degree of sociability recorded by the other. After the interaction involving Actor 1 was complete and the data recorded, approximately five minutes elapsed before Actor 2 approached the same jewelry counter. Actor 2 then engaged in an interaction with the clerk using the same dialogue as Actor 1. The Stable Observer and Actor 1 scored the sociability of the clerk. The Stable Observer also timed the initiation of each interaction and the duration of each interaction. This procedure was repeated in five large department stores and four smaller jewelry stores. This measure was taken to determine whether the clerk's sociability would vary according to store type.

Impression Formation   9

Results

Analysis of the results of the sociability scale indicated significant differences in each of the six behavioral ratings of the clerk's sociability with respect to Actor 1 and Actor 2. In Actor 1/Actor 2 evaluation of the clerk's interaction with both Actor 1 and Actor 2, significant differences were seen with

Statistical findings reported.

respect to the clerk's greeting ($\underline{t}(16) = 4.81$, $\underline{p}<.000$), conversation ($\underline{t}(16) = 2.98$, $\underline{p}<.009$), farewell ($\underline{t}(16) = 3.58$, $\underline{p}<.003$), smile ($\underline{t}(16) = 5.41$, $\underline{p}<.000$), facial regard ($\underline{t}(16) = 8.50$, $\underline{p}<.000$), and overall tone ($\underline{t}(16) = 3.50$, $\underline{p}<.008$), using two-tailed $\underline{t}$-tests for independent samples. Each clerk's sociability rating tended to be higher when interacting with Actor 1 than when interacting with Actor 2. Means and standard deviations of the six behavioral scores are presented in Table 1.

*Tables, included as appendix, are referred to in text. See **A3** for format.*

The results of the Stable Observer's evaluation of the clerk's behavior when interacting with Actor 1 and Actor 2 also indicated significant differences in the clerk's greeting ($\bar{t}(16) = 4.81$, $\bar{p}<.001$), conversation ($\bar{t}(16) = 2.98$, $\bar{p}<.009$), farewell ($\bar{t}(16) = 4.37$, $\bar{p}<.000$), smile ($\bar{t}(16) = 6.43$, $\bar{p}<.000$), facial regard ($\bar{t}(16) = 8.50$, $\bar{p}<.000$), and overall tone ($\bar{t}(16) = 4.38$, $\bar{p}<.000$), using two-tailed $\bar{t}$-tests for independent

Impression Formation   10

samples. The Stable Observer also rated the clerk as being more sociable when interacting with Actor 1 than when interacting with Actor 2. Means and standard deviations of the six behavioral scores are presented in Table 1.

Interrater reliability was shown to be significant in each of the six behaviors rated: greeting ($\bar{r} = .94$), conversation ($\bar{r} = 1.00$), farewell ($\bar{r} = .94$), smile ($\bar{r} = .98$), facial regard ($\bar{r} = 1.00$), and overall tone ($\bar{r} = .93$), $\bar{p}<.001$, one-tailed, for all correlations.

The overall evaluations by Actor 1/Actor 2 and the Stable Observer of clerk sociability in six behaviors over 18 interactions were shown to be strikingly similar. Means and standard deviations are presented in Table 2.

Significant differences were also noted in the prices of the first two watches shown to Actor 1 and Actor 2 ($\bar{t}(14) = 5.73$, and 2.95, respectively, $p<.01$, two-tailed $\underline{t}$-test for independent samples). Actor 1 tended to be shown higher priced watches (watch #1, $\bar{x} = \$433.33$; S.D. = 98.68; watch #2, $\bar{x} = \$730.00$; S.D. = 457.24) than Actor 2 (watch #1, $\bar{x} = \$196.42$; S.D. = 51.94; watch #2, $\bar{x} = \$215.00$; S.D. = 38.30).

The amount of time until the initiation of the interaction (minutes) was also shown to be significantly shorter

($\underline{t}(16) = -3.91$, $\underline{p} < .001$) and the duration of the interaction significantly longer ($\underline{t}(16) = 2.98$, $\underline{p} < .009$; two-tailed $\underline{t}$-tests for independent samples) for interactions involving Actor 1 as opposed to Actor 2. Means and standard deviations are presented in Table 3.

Discussion

The results of the study clearly support the proposed hypothesis that physical appearance and dress influence impression formation, which will consequently affect the quality of social interactions, namely customer-clerk interactions. It was demonstrated that each salesperson tended to be more sociable to the well-dressed Actor 1 than he or she was to the poorly dressed Actor 2 despite the lack of variation in behavior or dialogue between the two actors.

Analysis of findings

Both the Stable Observer and Actor 1/Actor 2 rated each salesperson as generally exhibiting a more friendly greeting ($\bar{x} = 1.78$; S.D. $= .44$) and conversation ($\bar{x} = 1.67$; S.D. $= .50$) when interacting with Actor 1 as opposed to Actor 2. In addition, a higher degree of smiles ($\bar{x} = 2.67$; S.D. $= .50$) and facial regard ($\bar{x} = 2.67$; S.D. $= .50$) was recorded in each clerk's interaction with Actor 1. This suggests that each salesperson tended to form different impressions about Actor 1 and Actor 2 based on dress and physical appearance cues because these two factors were the only intended differences between the interactions. The role of dress could be confirmed in future studies through the use of a single actor posing as both a poorly dressed customer and a well-dressed customer, thus eliminating the influence of differing personality factors of each actor on the clerk's sociability. Nevertheless, the differences in impressions formed led each clerk to behave in a more sociable manner to the well-dressed, physically attractive Actor 1.

The degree to which dress cues can influence impression formation and judgment is further demonstrated by the prices of the watches shown to Actor 1 (watch #1, $\bar{x}$ = $433.33; watch #2, $\bar{x}$ = $730.00) and Actor 2 (watch #1, $\bar{x}$ = $196.43; watch #2, $\bar{x}$ = $215.00). The salesperson in each case clearly made the assumption that a well-dressed customer would be interested in a more expensive watch, whereas a poorly dressed customer would be interested in a less expensive watch. The impression formation was so strong in one case that the clerk recommended Actor 2 visit a store that sold less expensive watches. Thus, each clerk made judgments about each Actor despite a lack of information about the person's socioeconomic status. The physical appearance of each Actor also influenced the amount of time taken for service. In all cases the well-dressed Actor was waited on sooner. In fact, in two stores the poorly dressed Actor could not get waited on for 15 minutes and therefore left the store. The duration of the interaction was also shorter for Actor 2, and in most cases the conversation was very routine, involving no friendliness or personal recognition.

The results further indicated a high interrater reliability in the subjective measurement of each clerk's behavior. It must be noted that a potential weakness in the results exists due to the fact that each observer was previously aware of the hypothesis being tested. Thus, the potential for biased observations does exist. However, this factor appears not to have significantly influenced the results because the objective measurements (i.e., price of watches shown, time of initiation of interaction, and duration of interaction) also indicated the tendency of each clerk to form different impressions of each Actor based on appearance.

The results of the present study support previous research indicating the effects of physical appearance and dress on impression formation (Francis & Evans, 1987; Hamid,

Impression Formation   14

1972). This noted importance of dress cues on impression
formation and resulting social interactions can have important
implications in situations other than customer-clerk
interactions because dress is an integral part of one's
appearance; thus, one must pay particular attention to mode
of dress when trying to convey a given impression, particularly
in situations such as job interviews.

Conclusion

References
page
numbered
consecutively

Center

Double-space

Journal article
by two
authors

Items listed
alphabetically
by first
author's last
name. Use
initials for
first names

Indent first
line of each
entry 5 to 7
spaces.* Type
subsequent
lines flush
with left-
hand margin.

Impression Formation   15

References

Francis, S. K., & Evans, P. K. (1987). Effects of hue, value, and style of garment and personal coloring of model on person perception. Perceptual and Motor Skills, 64, 383–390.

Hamid, P. N. (1972). Some effects of dress cues on observational accuracy, a perceptual estimate, and impression formation. Journal of Social Psychology, 86, 279–289.

Hester, L., Koger, P., & McCauley, C. (1985). Individual differences in customer sociability. European Journal of Social Psychology, 15, 453–456.

Lennon, S. J., & Davis, L. L. (1989). Categorization in first impressions. Journal of Psychology, 123(5), 439–446.

Segal, M. E., & McCauley, C. R. (1986). The sociability of commercial exchange in rural, suburban, and urban locations: A test of the urban overload hypothesis. Basic and Applied Social Psychology, 7(2), 115–135.

Tetlock, P. E. (1983). Accountability and the perseverance of first impressions. Social Psychology Quarterly, 46(4), 285–292.

*This format is now recommended by the APA for all manuscripts submitted for publication. If your instructor prefers, you may instead type the first line of each entry flush with the left-hand margin and indent subsequent lines three spaces.

Impression Formation   16

Table 1
Mean (S.D.) Scores and Correlations of Interrater Reliability of Actor 1/Actor 2 and Stable Observer's Rating of Salesperson Sociability

| | Actor 1/Actor 2 Rating | | | | Stable Observer's Rating | | | | Interrater Reliability |
| | Clerk 1 | | Clerk 2 | | Clerk 1 | | Clerk 2 | | |
	$\bar{x}$	S.D.	$\bar{x}$	S.D.	$\bar{x}$	S.D.	$\bar{x}$	S.D.	Correlation Coefficient
Greeting	1.78	0.44	0.78	0.44	1.78	0.44	0.78	0.44	0.87
Conversation	1.67	0.50	0.89	0.60	1.67	0.50	0.89	0.60	1.00
Farewell	1.78	0.44	0.89	0.60	1.89	0.33	0.89	0.60	0.94
Smile	2.56	0.53	0.78	0.83	2.56	0.53	0.67	0.71	0.98
Facial regard	2.67	0.50	0.78	0.44	2.67	0.50	0.78	0.44	1.00
Overall tone	2.78	0.67	1.44	1.13	2.89	0.60	1.22	0.97	0.93

N = 9 for both Clerk 1 and Clerk 2.

Table 2

Mean (S.D.) Scores of Actor 1/Actor 2 and Stable Observer's
Overall Evaluation of Clerk Sociability

	Actor 1/Actor 2 Evaluation		Stable Observer's Evaluation	
	$\bar{x}$	S.D	$\bar{x}$	S.D.
Greeting	1.28	0.67	1.28	0.67
Conversation	1.28	0.67	1.28	0.67
Farewell	1.33	0.67	1.39	0.70
Smile	1.67	1.14	1.61	1.14
Facial regard	1.72	1.07	1.72	1.07
Overall tone	2.11	1.13	2.06	1.16

$N = 18$.

All means are significantly different, $p<.001$, by two-tailed
t-test for paired samples.

Table 3

Mean (S.D.) Scores of Prices of Watches, Time to Approach, and Time of Interaction

	Price of Watch #1		Price of Watch #2		Time to Approach (minutes)		Time of Interaction (minutes)	
	$\bar{x}$	S.D.	$\bar{x}$	S.D.	$\bar{x}$	S.D.	$\bar{x}$	S.D.
Actor 1	$433.33	98.68	$730.00	457.24	5.11	2.03	3.11	0.78
Actor 2	$196.43	51.94	$215.00	38.30	10.11	3.26	1.78	1.09

N = 9 for all cases except for Actor 2 price of watch #1 and watch #2 (n = 7).

All means differ significantly, $p < .01$, by two-tailed t-test for independent samples.

CHAPTER 49

WRITING IN THE NATURAL AND APPLIED SCIENCES

Writing in the natural and applied sciences relies on **empirical data**—information derived from observations or experiments. Although science writing is usually concerned with accurately reporting observations and experimental data, it may also be persuasive.

Basic to research in the natural and applied sciences is the **scientific method,** a process by which scientists gather and interpret information.

✔ CHECKLIST: THE SCIENTIFIC METHOD

✔ Define a problem you want to solve or an event you want to explain. Conduct a literature search to find out what previous work has been done on the problem.

✔ Formulate a hypothesis that attempts to explain the problem.

✔ Plan a method of investigation that will allow you to test your hypothesis.

✔ Carry out your experiment. Make careful observations, and record your data.

✔ Analyze the results of your experiment, and determine whether or not they support your initial hypothesis. Revise your hypothesis, if you can, to account for any discrepancies. If you cannot, plan further research that may help you explain the phenomena you have observed.

49a Research Sources

The data used in the sciences are the result of observation and experimental research. In addition to being discussed, most results are tabulated and displayed graphically. In addition, scientists often carry out literature searches to determine what other work has been done in their areas of interest.

(1) Specialized Library Sources

Because scientists are interested in the number of times and the variety of sources in which a study is cited, they frequently consult the *Science Citation Index*. The following specific sources are also useful.

General Science

Applied Science and Technology Index

CRC Handbook of Chemistry and Physics (and other titles in the CRC series of handbooks)

Current Contents

General Science Index

McGraw-Hill Encyclopedia of Science and Technology

Reference Sources in Science, Engineering, Medicine, and Agriculture

Scientific and Technical Information Sources

Van Nostrand's Scientific Encyclopedia

Chemistry

Analytical Abstracts

Chemical Abstracts

Chemical Technology

A Dictionary of Chemistry

Dictionary of Organic Compounds

Kirk-Othmer Encyclopedia of Chemical Technology

McGraw-Hill Encyclopedia of Chemistry

Engineering

Engineering Index

Environment Abstracts

Government Reports Announcements and Index (NTIS)

Pollution Abstracts

Selected Water Resources Abstracts

Earth Sciences

Abstracts of North American Geology

Annotated Bibliography of Economic Geology

Bibliography and Index of Geology
Bibliography of North American Geology
Climatology and Data (US Environmental Data Service)
Encyclopedia of Earth System Science
Geological Abstracts
Geophysical Abstracts
Guide to USGA Publications

Life Sciences

G. Zimek's Animal Life Encyclopedia
Bibliography of Agriculture
Cumulative Index to Nursing and Allied Health Literature
Biological Abstracts
Biological and Agricultural Index
Biology Digest
A Dictionary of Genetics
Encyclopedia of Bioethics
Encyclopedia of the Biological Sciences
Encyclopedia of Environmental Biology
Environment Abstracts Annual
Hospital Literature Index
Index Medicus
International Dictionary of Medicine and Biology
International Nursing Index
Zoological Record

Mathematics

Computer and Control Abstracts
Current Index to Statistics
Encyclopedia of Mathematics
Encyclopedia of Statistical Sciences
Encyclopedic Dictionary of Mathematics
Mathematical Reviews
Universal Encyclopedia of Mathematics

Physics

Astronomy and Astrophysics Abstracts
Encyclopaedia of Physics
Encyclopedic Dictionary of Physics
Physics Abstracts
Solid State and Superconductivity Abstracts

(2) Specialized Databases for Computer Searches

As in other disciplines, many print indexes are available on CD-ROM or online. Some databases are available only in electronic format. Helpful databases for research in the sciences include *BIO-SIS Previews, CASearch, SCISEARCH, Agricola, CAB Abstracts, CINAHL, Compendex, Environmental Route Net, NTIS, Inspec, MEDLINE, MATHSCI, Life Sciences Collection, GEOREF, Zoological Record Online, Wildlife Review and Fisheries Review,* and *World Patents Index.* Check with your librarian about the availability of these databases in your library.

(3) Other Sources of Information

Opportunities for research outside the library vary widely because of the many ways in which scientists can gather information. In agronomy, for example, researchers collect soil samples; in toxicology, they test air or water quality. In marine biology, they might conduct research in a particular aquatic environment, and in chemistry they conduct experiments to identify an unknown substance. Scientists also conduct surveys: epidemiologists study the spread of communicable diseases, and cancer researchers question populations to determine how environmental or dietary factors influence the likelihood of contracting cancer. The Internet can be an important source of up-to-date scientific information. In fact, scientists have used the Internet for years to communicate and share information about their research.

49b Assignments in the Sciences

Many writing assignments in the sciences are similar to those assigned in other disciplines. Three assignments that are common in (but not limited to) scientific disciplines are the *abstract,* the *literature survey,* and the *laboratory report.*

(1) The Abstract

Most scientific articles begin with **abstracts,** highly condensed summaries that serve as guides for readers. In addition, many scientific indexes provide abstracts of articles so researchers can determine whether an article is of use to them. An **indicative abstract** gives a general sense of the content of an article, helping readers decide whether they want to read it in full. (An annotated bibliography includes short indicative abstracts following each complete citation.) An **informative abstract** includes enough detail so that readers can obtain essential information without reading the article itself. (Some scientific abstracts, called **structured abstracts,** include internal headings.)

When writing an abstract, follow the organization of your paper, devoting a sentence or two to each of its major sections. In two hundred to five hundred words, state the purpose, method of research, results, and conclusion in the order in which they appear in the paper, but include only essential information. Avoid quoting from your paper or repeating its title.

Abstract: Biology

"Purification to Near Homogeneity of Bovine Transforming Epithelial Growth Factor," by Stephen McManus, Cooperative Education Student, Smith, Kline & French Labs.

The control of cellular proliferation is known to be mediated at an extracellular level by polypeptide growth factors; examples include epidermal growth factor (EGF), platelet-derived growth factor (PDGF), and transforming growth factors alpha and beta (TGF-a, TGF-ß). The transforming growth factors are so called because of their ability to induce anchorage-independent growth of selected target cell lines. Our studies have identified an apparently novel growth factor activity associated with epithelial cells and tissues. This activity, called epithelial transforming growth factor (TGFe), is identified by the anchorage-independent growth of the SW13 epithelial cell line, derived from human adrenocortical carcinoma. The purification of this factor was accomplished by a multistep chromatography and electrophoretic process. The total purification was estimated as

6×10^5-fold with 1% recovery, corresponding to a yield of 0.1 μg TGf-e/kg bovine kidney.

(2) The Literature Survey

Literature surveys are common in the sciences, most often appearing as a section of a proposal or as part of a research paper. Unlike an abstract, which summarizes a single source, a literature survey summarizes a number of studies and sometimes compares and contrasts them. By doing so, the literature survey provides a theoretical context for the paper's discussion.

Literature Survey: Parasitology

Ultrastructural studies of micro- and macrogametes have included relatively few of the numerous Eimerian species. Major early studies include the following (hosts are listed in parentheses): micro- and macrogametes of E. performans (rabbits), E. stiedae (rabbits), E. bovis (cattle), and E. auburnensis (cattle) (Hammond et al., 1967; Scholtyseck et al., 1966), macrogametogenesis in E. magna (rabbits) and E. intestinalis (rabbits) (Kheysin, 1965), macrogametogony of E. tenella (chickens) (McLaren, 1969), and the microgametocytes and macrogametes of E. neischulzi (rats) (Colley, 1967). More recent investigations have included macrogametogony of E. acervulina (chickens) (Pitillo and Ball, 1984).

(3) The Laboratory Report

A laboratory report is the most common assignment for students taking courses in the sciences. It is divided into sections that reflect the stages of the scientific method, and it generally conforms to the specifications for the laboratory report outlined below. Not every section will be necessary for every experiment, and some experiments may call for additional components, such as an abstract or a reference list. In addition, lab experiments may include tables, charts, graphs, and illustrations. The exact format of a student lab report is usually defined by the specific course's lab manual.

A lab report is an explanation of a process. Because its purpose is to enable readers to understand a complex series of tasks, it must present stages clearly and completely, in exact chronological order, and illustrate the purpose of each step. In addition, a lab report must provide descriptions of the equipment used in an experiment.

Laboratory Report: Chemistry

Purpose   In this section you describe the goal of the experiment, presenting the hypothesis you tested or examined.

> The purpose of this lab experiment is to determine the iron content of an unknown mixture containing an iron salt by titration with potassium permanganate solution.
>
> Equation to find % of Fe: $5Fe^{2+} + MnO_4- + 8H^+ = 5Fe^{3+} + Mn^{2+} + 4H_2O$

Equipment   In this section you list the equipment you used in the experiment. Often this section also identifies and explains your methodology.

> Equipment includes two 60 ml beakers, a graduated cylinder, a scale, 600 ml of distilled water, 2 grams of H_2SO_4, 5 grams of $KMnO_4$, 100 ml of $H_2C_2O_4 \cdot 2H_2O$, and a Bunsen burner.

Procedure   In this section you describe the steps of the experiment in the order in which they occur, usually numbering the steps.

> 1) A $KMnO_4$ solution was prepared by dissolving 1.5 grams of $KMnO_4$ in 500 ml of distilled water.
>
> 2) Two samples $H_2C_2O_4 \cdot 2H_2O$ of about 0.2 grams each were weighed.
>
> 3) Each sample was dissolved in 60 ml of H_2O and 30 ml of H_2SO_4 in a 250 ml beaker.
>
> 4) The mixture was heated to 80°C and titrated slowly with $KMnO_4$ until the mixture turned pink.
>
> 5) The procedure was repeated twice.

Results   In this section you present the results—observations, measurements, or equations—that you obtained from your experiments.

Percentage of iron: 1st run = 12.51 ml

2nd run = 11.2 ml

Conclusion or Discussion of Results   In this section you explain your results or justify them in terms of the initial questions asked in the *Purpose* section.

Calculation for % of iron

$$\frac{12.5 \text{ ml} \times .0894 \text{ M}}{100 \text{ ml/1}} \times \frac{5 \text{ moles Fe}}{1 \text{ mole MnO}_4} \times \frac{55.85 \text{ g/mol}}{.5g} \times 100 = \frac{66.11}{500}$$

$$= 13.22\% \text{ Fe}$$

49c Conventions of Style, Format, and Documentation

(1) Style and Format

Because writing in the sciences focuses on the experiment itself, not on those conducting the experiment, writers often use the passive voice. For example, in a lab report, you would say, "The mixture was heated for forty-five minutes" rather than "I heated the mixture for forty-five minutes." (You would use the first person, however, if you were asked to write a reaction statement or to give your opinion about something.) Another stylistic convention to remember concerns verb tense: a conclusion or a statement of generally accepted fact should be in the **present tense** ("Objects in motion *tend* to stay in motion"); a summary of a study, however, should be in the past tense ("Watson and Crick *discovered* the structure of DNA"). Finally, note that direct quotations are seldom used in scientific papers.

See 25c1

Because you are writing to inform or persuade other scientists, you should write clearly and concisely. Remember to use technical terms only when they are necessary to convey your meaning. Too many terms can make your paper difficult to understand—even for scientists familiar with your discipline. Often a scientific paper will include a glossary that lists and defines terms that may be unfamiliar to readers.

Tables and illustrations are an important part of most scientific papers. Be careful to place tables as close to your discussion of them as possible and to number and label any type of illustration or diagram so you can refer to it in your text. Keep in mind that each professional society prescribes formats for **tables** and other visuals and the way they are to be presented. Therefore, you cannot use a single format for all your scientific writing.

See
A1d

Remember that different scientific journals follow different conventions of style and use different paper formats and documentation styles. For example, although the *CBE Style Manual* governs the overall presentation of papers in biology, the *Journal of Immunology* might have a different format from the *Journal of Parasitology*. (The *CBE Style Manual* lists the different journals that use their own paper formats.) Your instructor may ask you to prepare your paper according to the style sheet of the journal to which you might wish to submit your work. Although publication may seem a remote possibility to you, following a style sheet reminds you that writing in the sciences involves writing for a specific audience.

You should also learn the various abbreviations by which journals are referred to in the reference sections of science papers. For example, *The American Journal of Physiology* is abbreviated "Amer. J. Physiol.," and *The Journal of Physiological Chemistry* is abbreviated "J. of Physiol. Chemistry." Note that in CBE style, the abbreviated forms of journal titles are *not* underlined in the reference list.

(2) Documentation

See
43e

Documentation style varies from one scientific discipline to another; even within each discipline, **documentation style** may vary from one journal to another. For this reason, ask your instructor which documentation format is required. Most disciplines in the sciences use a number-reference format prescribed by their professional societies. For instance, electrical engineers use the format of the Institute for Electronics and Electrical Engineers, chemists use the format of the American Chemical Society, physicists use the format of the American Institute of Physics, and mathematicians use the format of the American Mathematical Society.

49d Council of Biology Editors (CBE) Format: Excerpts from a Science Research Paper

The following excerpts from a biology research paper, "Maternal Smoking: Deleterious Effects on the Fetus," uses a number-reference format recommended by the *CBE Style Manual.*

Maternal Smoking

1

June M. Fahrman

Biology 306

April 17, 1997

Maternal Smoking: Deleterious

Effects on the Fetus

Introduction

The placenta, lifeline between fetus and mother, has been the
subject of various studies aimed at determining the mechanisms
by which substances in the mother's bloodstream affect the
fetus. For example, cigarette smoking is clearly associated with
an increased risk in the incidence of low-birthweight infants,[1]
due both to prematurity and to intrauterine growth
retardation.[2]

Development of the Placenta

At the morula stage of development, less than one week after
fertilization, two types of cells can be distinguished. . . .

Maternal Smoking

10

Conclusion

In summary, abundant evidence exists as to the harmful

effects maternal smoking may have on the fetus. These

include low birthweight, low IQ scores, minimal brain

dysfunction, shorter stature, prenatal mortality, and premature

birth. . . .

References

1. Rakel, Robert E. Conn's current therapy 1988. Philadelphia: W. B. Saunders; 1988. 360 p.

2. Meberg, A.; Sande, H.; Foss, O. P.; Stenwig, J. T. Smoking during pregnancy--effects on the fetus and on thiocyanate levels in mother and baby. Acta. Paediatr Scand 1979; 68:547 552.

3. Lehtovirta, P.; Forss, M. The acute effect of smoking on intervillous blood flow of the placenta. Brit Obs Gyn 1978; 85:729–731.

4. Phelan, Jeffrey P. Diminished fetal reactivity with smoking. Amer Obs Gyn 1980; 136:230–233.

5. VanDerVelde, W. J. Structural changes in the placenta of smoking mothers: a quantitative study. Placenta 1983; 4:231–240.

6. Asmussen, I. Ultrastructure of the villi and fetal capillaries in placentas from smoking and nonsmoking mothers. Brit Obs Gyn 1980; 87:239–245.

7. Meyer, M. Perinatal events associated with maternal smoking during pregnancy. Amer Epid 1976; 103(5):464–476.

CHAPTER 50

WRITING ESSAY EXAMINATIONS

Taking examinations is a skill, one you have been developing throughout your life as a student. Although both short-answer and essay examinations require you to study, to recall what you know, and to budget your time carefully as you write your answers, only essay questions ask you to synthesize information and to arrange ideas in a series of clear, logically connected sentences and paragraphs. To write an essay examination, or even a paragraph-length answer, you must do more than memorize facts; you must see the relationships among them. In other words, you must **think critically** about your subject.

See
Pt. 2

50a Planning an Essay Examination Answer

Because you are under pressure during an examination and tend to write quickly, you may be tempted to skip the planning and revision stages of the writing process. But if you write in a frenzy and hand in your examination without a second glance, you are likely to produce a disorganized or even incoherent answer. With careful planning and editing, you can write an answer that demonstrates your understanding of the material.

(1) Review Your Material

Be sure you know beforehand the scope and format of the examination. How much of your text and class notes will the examination cover—the entire semester's work or only the material covered since the last test? Will you have to answer every question, or will you be able to choose among alternatives? Will the examination be composed entirely of fill-in, multiple-choice, or true/false questions, or will it call for sentence-, paragraph-, or essay-length answers? Will the examination test your ability to recall specific facts, or will it require you to demonstrate your understanding of the course material by drawing conclusions?

Examinations challenge you to recall and express in writing what you already know—what you have read, what you have heard in class, what you have reviewed in your notes. Before you even begin any examination, then, you must study: reread your text and class notes, highlight key points, and perhaps outline particularly important sections of your notes. When you prepare for a short-answer examination, you may memorize facts without analyzing their relationship to one another or their relationship to a body of knowledge as a whole: the definition of *pointillism*, the date of Queen Victoria's death, the formula for a quadratic equation, three reasons for the fall of Rome, two examples of conditioned reflexes, four features of a feudal economy, six steps in the process of synthesizing Vitamin C. When you prepare for an essay examination, however, you must do more than remember bits of information; you must also make connections among ideas.

When you are sure you know what to expect, see if you can anticipate the essay questions your instructor might ask. Try out likely questions on classmates, and see whether you can do some collaborative brainstorming to outline answers to possible questions. If you have time, you might even practice answering one or two in writing.

(2) Consider Your Audience and Purpose

The audience for any examination is the instructor who prepared it. As you read the questions, think about what your instructor has emphasized in class. Although you may certainly arrange material in a new way or use it to make an original point, keep in mind that your purpose is to demonstrate that you understand the material, not to make clever remarks or introduce irrelevant information. In addition, you should make every effort to use the vocabulary of the particular academic discipline for which you are writing and to follow any discipline-specific stylistic **conventions** your instructor has discussed.

See
46c

(3) Read through the Entire Examination

Your time is usually limited when you take an examination, so plan carefully. How long should a "short-answer" or "one-paragraph" or "essay-length" answer be? How much time should you devote to answering each question? The question itself may specify the time allotted for each answer, so look for that information. More often the point value of each question or the number of questions on the examination will indicate how much time to spend on each answer. If an essay question is worth 50 out of 100 points, for example, you will probably have to spend at least half of your time planning, writing, and proofreading your answer.

Before you begin to write, read the entire examination carefully to determine your priorities and your strategy. First, be sure your copy of the test is complete and that you understand exactly what each question requires. If you need clarification, ask your instructor or proctor for help. Then, decide where to start. Responding first to short answers (or to questions whose answers you are sure of) is usually a good strategy. This tactic ensures that you will not become bogged down in a question that baffles you and left with too little time to write a strong answer to a question you understand well. Moreover, starting with the questions you are sure of can help build your confidence.

(4) Read Each Question Carefully

To write an effective answer, you need to understand the question. As you read any essay question, you may find it helpful to underline key words and important terms.

SOCIOLOGY: Distinguish among Social Darwinism, instinct theory, and sociobiology, giving examples of each.

MUSIC: Explain how Milton Babbitt used the computer to expand Schoenberg's twelve-tone method.

PHILOSOPHY: Define existentialism and identify three influential existentialist works, explaining why they are important.

Look carefully at the wording of each examination question. If the question calls for a *comparison and contrast* of *two* styles of management, then a *description* or *analysis* of *one* style, no matter how comprehensive, will not be acceptable. If the question asks for causes *and* effects, then a discussion of causes alone will not do.

The wording of the question suggests what you should emphasize. For instance, an American history instructor would expect very different answers to the following two examination questions:

- Give a detailed explanation of the major causes of the Great Depression, noting briefly some of the effects of the economic collapse on the United States.

- Give a detailed summary of the effects of the Great Depression on the United States, briefly discussing the major causes of the economic collapse.

Although the preceding questions look somewhat alike, the first calls for an essay that stresses *causes*, whereas the second calls for one that stresses *effects*.

The following question on a literature exam also requires a very specific treatment of the topic.

826

QUESTION: Identify three <u>differences</u> between the hard-boiled detective story and the classical detective story.

The response below, which simply *identifies* three characteristics of *one* kind of detective story, is not acceptable.

UNACCEPTABLE ANSWER: The hard-boiled detective story, popularized in *Black Mask* magazine in the 1930s and 1940s, is very different from the classical detective stories of Edgar Allan Poe or Agatha Christie. The hard-boiled stories feature a down-on-his-luck detective who is constantly tempted and betrayed. His world is dark and chaotic, and the crimes he tries to solve are not out-of-the-ordinary occurrences; they are the norm. These stories have no happy endings; even when the crime is solved, the world is still corrupt.

The answer below, which *contrasts* the *two* kinds of detective stories, is acceptable.

ACCEPTABLE ANSWER: The hard-boiled detective story differs from the classical detective story in its characters, its setting, and its plot. The classical detective is usually well educated and well off; he is aloof from the other characters and therefore can remain in total control of the situation. The hard-boiled detective, on the other hand, is typically a decent but down-on-his-luck man who is drawn into the chaos around him, constantly tempted and betrayed. In the orderly world of the classical detective, the crime is a temporary disruption. In the hard-boiled detective's dark and chaotic world, the crimes he tries to solve are not out-of-the-ordinary occurrences; they are the norm. In the classical detective story, order is restored at the end, but hard-boiled stories have no happy endings; even when the crime is solved, the world is still corrupt.

 CLOSE-UP **KEY WORDS IN EXAMINATION QUESTIONS**

Pay careful attention to the words used in exam questions.

• Explain	• Clarify	• Classify
• Compare	• Relate	• Identify
• Contrast	• Justify	• Illustrate
• Trace	• Analyze	• Define
• Evaluate	• Interpret	• Support
• Discuss	• Describe	• Summarize

(5) Brainstorm to Find Ideas

See
1c2

Once you understand the question, you need to **find something to say**. Begin by **brainstorming,** quickly listing all the relevant ideas you can remember. Then, identify the most important points on your list, and delete the others. A quick review of the exam question and your supporting ideas should lead you toward a workable thesis for your essay answer.

50b Shaping an Essay Examination Answer

(1) Stating a Thesis

See
2b3

Often you can rephrase the examination question as a **thesis statement**. For example, the American history examination question "Give a detailed summary of the effects of the Great Depression on the United States, briefly discussing the major causes of the economic collapse" suggests the following thesis.

EFFECTIVE THESIS STATEMENT: The Great Depression, caused by the American government's economic policies, had major political, economic, and social effects on the United States.

An effective thesis statement addresses all aspects of the question but highlights only relevant concerns. The following thesis statements are not effective.

VAGUE THESIS STATEMENT: The Great Depression, caused largely by profligate spending patterns, had a number of very important results.

INCOMPLETE THESIS STATEMENT: The Great Depression caused major upheaval in the United States.

IRRELEVANT THESIS STATEMENT: The Great Depression, caused largely by America's poor response to the 1929 stock market crash, had more important consequences than World War II did.

(2) Making an Informal Outline

See
2c

Because time is limited, you should plan your answer before you write it. Therefore, once you have decided on a suitable thesis, you should make an **informal outline** of your major points.

See
Ch. 5

Write on the inside cover of your exam book or on its last sheet. Use the **pattern of development** suggested by the question—definition, comparison and contrast, or cause and effect, for instance—to shape your outline, and list your supporting points in the order in which you plan to discuss them. Once you have completed your outline, check it against the exam question to make certain it covers everything the question calls for—and *only* what the question calls for.

An informal outline for an answer to the American history question ("Give a detailed summary of the effects of the Great Depression on the United States, briefly discussing the major causes of the economic collapse.") might look like this.

> THESIS STATEMENT: The Great Depression, caused by the American government's economic policies, had major political, economic, and social effects on the United States.
>
> SUPPORTING POINTS:
> *Causes*
> American economic policies: income poorly distributed, factories expanded too much, more goods produced than could be purchased
> *Effects*
> 1. Economic situation worsened—farmers, businesses, workers, and stock market all affected.
> 2. Roosevelt elected—closed banks, worked with Congress to enact emergency measures.
> 3. Reform—TVA, AAA, NIRA, etc.
> 4. Social Security Act, WPA, PWA

An answer based on this outline will follow a **cause-and-effect** pattern, with an emphasis on effects, not causes.

See
5e

50c Writing and Revising an Essay Examination Answer

Referring to your outline, you can now begin to draft your answer. Don't bother crafting an elaborate or unusual **introduction;** your time is precious, and so is your reader's. A simple statement of your thesis that summarizes your answer is your best introductory strategy: this approach is efficient, and it reminds you to address the question directly.

To develop the **body** of the essay, follow your outline point by point, using clear topic sentences and transitions to indicate your progression and to help your instructor see that you are answering the question in full. Such signals, along with parallel sentence structure and repeated key words, make your answer easy to follow.

The most effective **conclusion** for an essay examination is a clear, simple restatement of the thesis or a summary of the essay's main points.

Essay answers should be complete and detailed, but they should not contain irrelevant material. Every unnecessary fact or opinion increases your chance of error, so don't repeat yourself or volunteer unrequested information, and don't express your own feelings or opinions unless such information is specifically called for. In addition, be sure to support all your general statements with specific examples.

Leave enough time to reread and revise what you have written. Try to view your answer from a fresh perspective. Is your thesis statement clearly worded? Does your essay support your thesis and answer the question? Are your facts correct, and are your ideas presented in a logical order? Review your topic sentences and transitions. Check sentence structure and word choice, spelling and punctuation. If a sentence—or even a whole paragraph—seems irrelevant, cross it out. If you suddenly remember something you want to add, you can insert a few additional words with a caret (^). Neatly insert a longer addition at the end of your answer, box it, and label it so your instructor will know where it belongs. Finally, be sure that you have written legibly and that you have not inadvertently left out any words.

The following one-hour essay answer was written in response to the question outlined in **50b2.** Notice how the student restates the question in her thesis statement and keeps the question in focus by repeating key words like *cause, effect, result, response,* and *impact.*

QUESTION: Give a detailed summary of the effects of the Great Depression on the United States, briefly discussing the major causes of the economic collapse.

EFFECTIVE ESSAY EXAM ANSWER

Introduction—thesis statement rephrases exam question

The Great Depression, caused by the American government's economic policies, had major political, economic, and social effects on the United States.

Summarizes policies leading to Depression (causes)

The Depression was precipitated by the stock market crash of October 1929, but its actual causes were more subtle: they lay in the US government's economic policies. First, personal income was not well distributed. Although production rose during the 1920s, the farmers and other workers got too little of the profits; instead, a disproportionate amount of income went to the richest 5 percent of

continued on the following page

continued from the previous page

the population. The tax policies at this time made inequalities in income even worse. A good deal of income also went into development of new manufacturing plants. This expansion stimulated the economy but encouraged the production of more goods than consumers could purchase. Finally, during the economic boom of the 1920s the government did not attempt to limit speculation or impose regulations on the securities market; it also did little to help build up farmers' buying power. Even after the crash began, the government made mistakes: instead of trying to counter the country's deflationary economy, the government focused on keeping the budget balanced and making sure the United States adhered to the gold standard.

The Depression, devastating to millions of individuals, had a tremendous impact on the nation as a whole. Its political, economic, and social consequences were great.

> Transition from causes to effects

Between October 1929 and Roosevelt's inauguration on March 4, 1932, the economic situation grew worse. Businesses were going bankrupt, banks were failing, and stock prices were falling. Farm prices fell drastically, and hungry farmers were forced to burn their corn to heat their homes. There was massive unemployment, with millions of workers jobless and humiliated, losing skills and self-respect. President Hoover's Reconstruction Finance Corporation made loans available to banks, railroads, and businesses, but he felt state and local funds (not the federal government) should finance public works programs and relief. Confidence in the president declined as the country's economic situation worsened.

> Early effects (paragraphs 4 to 8 summarize important results in chronological order)

One result of the Depression was the election of Franklin Delano Roosevelt. By the time of his inauguration, most American banks had closed, thirteen million workers were unemployed, and millions of

> Additional effects: Roosevelt's emergency measures

continued on the following page

continued from the previous page

farmers were threatened by foreclosure. Roosevelt's response was immediate: two days after he took office, he closed all banks and took steps to support the stronger ones with loans and to prevent the weaker ones from reopening. During the first hundred days of his administration, he kept Congress in special session. Under his leadership, Congress enacted emergency measures designed to provide "Relief, Recovery, and Reform."

Additional effects: Roosevelt's reform measures

In response to the problems caused by the Depression, Roosevelt set up agencies to reform some of the conditions that had helped to cause the Depression in the first place. The Tennessee Valley Authority, created in May of 1933, was one of these. Its purposes were to control floods by building new dams and improving old ones and to provide cheap, plentiful electricity. The TVA improved the standard of living of area farmers and drove down the price of power all over the country. The Agricultural Adjustment Administration, created the same month as the TVA, provided for taxes on basic commodities, with the tax revenues used to subsidize farmers to produce less. This reform measure caused prices to rise.

Additional effects: NIRA, other laws, etc.

Another response to the problems of the Depression was the National Industrial Recovery Act. This act established the National Recovery Administration, an agency that set minimum wages and maximum hours for workers and set limits on production and prices. Other laws passed by Congress between 1935 and 1940 strengthened federal regulation of power, interstate commerce, and air traffic. Roosevelt also changed the federal tax structure to redistribute American income.

Additional effects: Social Security, WPA, etc.

One of the most important results of the Depression was the Social Security Act of 1935, which established unemployment insurance

continued on the following page

continued from the previous page

and provided financial aid for the blind and disabled and for dependent children and their mothers. The Works Progress Administration (WPA) gave jobs to over two million workers, who built public buildings, roads, streets, bridges, and sewers. The WPA also employed artists, musicians, actors, and writers. The Public Works Administration (PWA) cleared slums and created public housing. In the National Labor Relations Act (1935), workers received a guarantee of government protection for their unions against unfair labor practices by management.

As a result of the economic collapse known as the Great Depression,   Conclusion
Americans saw their government take responsibility for providing immediate relief, for helping the economy recover, and for taking steps to ensure that the situation would not be repeated. The economic, political, and social impact of the laws passed during the 1930s is still with us today, helping to keep our government and our economy stable.

Notice that the student does not include any irrelevant material: she does not, for example, describe the conditions of people's lives in detail, blame anyone in particular, discuss the president's friends and enemies, or consider parallel events in other countries. She covers only what the question asks for. Notice too how topic sentences ("One result of the Depression . . ."; "In response to the problems caused by the Depression . . ."; "One of the most important results of the Depression . . .") keep the primary purpose of the discussion in focus and guide her instructor through the essay.

A well-planned essay like the preceding one is not easy to write. Consider the following ineffective answer to the same question.

INEFFECTIVE ESSAY EXAM ANSWER

The Great Depression is generally considered to have begun with the stock market crash of October 1929 and to have lasted until

continued on the following page

continued from the previous page

the defense buildup for World War II. It was a terrible time for millions of Americans, who were not used to being hungry or out of work. Perhaps the worst economic disaster in our history, the Depression left its scars on millions of once-proud workers and

No clear thesis. Vague, subjective impressions of the Depression

farmers who found themselves reduced to poverty. We all have heard stories of businessmen committing suicide when their investments failed, of people selling apples on the street, and of farmers and their families leaving the Dust Bowl in desperate search of work. My own grandfather, laid off from his job, had to support my grandmother and their four children on what he could make from odd carpentry jobs. This was the Depression at its worst.

What else did the Depression produce? One result of the Depression was the election of Franklin Delano Roosevelt. Roosevelt immediately closed all banks. Then Congress set up the Federal Emergency Relief Administration, the Civilian Conservation Corps, the Farm Credit Administration, and the Home Owners' Loan Corporation. The Reconstruction Finance Corporation and the Civil Works Administration were two other agencies designed to provide "Relief,

Gratuitous summary

Recovery, and Reform." All these agencies helped Roosevelt in his efforts to lead the nation to recovery while providing relief and reform.

Along with these emergency measures, Roosevelt set out to reform some of the conditions he felt were responsible for the economic collapse. Accordingly, he created the Tennessee Valley Authority (TVA) to control floods and provide electricity in the Tennessee Valley. The Agricultural Adjustment Agency levied taxes and got the farmers to grow less, causing prices to rise. Thus, these

Unsupported generalization

agencies, the TVA and the AAA, helped to ease things for the farmers.

continued on the following page

continued from the previous page

The National Industrial Recovery Act established the National Recovery Administration, which was designed to help workers. It established minimum wages and maximum hours, both of which made conditions better for workers. Other important agencies included the Federal Power Commission, the Interstate Commerce Commission, the Maritime Commission, and the Civil Aeronautics Authority. Changes in the tax structure at about this time made the tax system fairer and eliminated some inequities. Roosevelt, working smoothly with his cabinet and with Congress, took many important steps to ease the nation's economic burden.

> Why were these agencies important? What did they do?

Despite the fact that he was handicapped by polio, Roosevelt was a dynamic president. His fireside chats, which millions of Americans heard on the radio every week, helped to reassure Americans that things would be fine. This increased his popularity. But he had problems too. Not everyone agreed with him. Private electric companies opposed the TVA, big business disagreed with his support of labor unions, the rich did not like the way he restructured the tax system, and many people saw him as dangerously radical. Still, he was one of the most popular presidents ever.

> Digression: discussion of Roosevelt is irrelevant to topic.

--Social Security Act: unemployment insurance, aid to blind and
   disabled and children

--WPA: built public projects

--PWA: public housing

--National Labor Relations Act: strengthened labor unions

> Undeveloped information

This essay only indirectly answers the examination question. It devotes too much space to unnecessary elements: an emotional introduction, needlessly repeated words and phrases, gratuitous summaries, and unsupported generalizations. Without a thesis statement to guide her, the writer slips into a discussion of only the immediate impact of the Depression and never discusses its causes or long-term effects. Although the body paragraphs do provide the names of many agencies created by the Roosevelt administration, they do not explain the purpose of most of them. Consequently, the student seems to consider the formation of the agencies, not their contributions, to be the Depression's most significant result.

Because the student took a time-consuming detour, she had to list points at the end of the essay without discussing them fully; moreover, she was left with no time to sum up her main points, even in a one-sentence conclusion. Although it is better to include undeveloped information than to skip it altogether, an undeveloped list has shortcomings. Many instructors will not give credit if you do not write out your answer in full. More importantly, you cannot effectively show logical or causal relationships in a list.

50d Writing Paragraph-Length Essay Examination Answers

Some essay questions ask for a paragraph-length answer, not a full essay. A paragraph should be just that: not one or two sentences, not a list of points, not more than one paragraph.

See
6b

See
6c

See
6d

A paragraph-length answer should be **unified** by a clear topic sentence. Just as an essay answer begins with a thesis statement, a paragraph answer opens with a topic sentence that summarizes what the paragraph will cover. You should generally word this sentence so that it echoes the examination question. The paragraph should also be **coherent**—that is, its statements should be linked by transitions that move the reader along. And the paragraph should be **well developed**, with enough relevant detail to convince your reader that you know what you are talking about.

QUESTION: In one paragraph, define the term *management by objectives,* give an example of how it works, and briefly discuss an advantage of this approach.

EFFECTIVE PARAGRAPH-LENGTH EXAMINATION ANSWER

Definition   As defined by Horngren, <u>management by objectives</u> is an

approach by which a manager and his or her superior together

formulate goals, and plans by which they can achieve these goals, for

Example   a forthcoming period. For example, a manager and a superior can

continued on the following page

836

continued from the previous page

formulate a responsibility accounting budget, and the manager's

performance can then be measured according to how well he or she

meets the objectives defined by the budget. The advantage of this   Advantage

approach is that the goals set are attainable because they are not

formulated in a vacuum. Rather, the objectives are based on what the

entire team reasonably expects to accomplish. As a result, the burden

of responsibility is shifted from the superior to the team: the goal

itself defines all the steps needed for its completion.

In this answer, key phrases ("As *defined* by . . ."; "For *example* . . ."; "The *advantage* of this approach . . .") clearly identify the various parts of the question being addressed. The writer includes just what the question asks for, and no more. His use of the wording of the question helps make the paragraph orderly, coherent, and emphatic.

The student who wrote the following response may know what *management by objectives* is, but his paragraph sounds more like a casual explanation to a friend than an answer to an exam question.

INEFFECTIVE PARAGRAPH-LENGTH EXAMINATION ANSWER

Management by objectives is when managers and their bosses   Sketchy, casual definition

get together to formulate their goals. This is a good system of

management because it cuts down on hard feelings between   No example given

managers and their superiors. Because they set the goals together,

they can make sure they're attainable by considering all possible

influences, constraints, etc., that might occur. This way neither the   Vague

manager nor the superior gets all the blame when things go wrong.

Remember, no response to an exam question will be effective unless you take the time to read the question carefully, plan your response, and outline your answer before you begin to write. It is always a good idea to use the wording of the question in your answer and to reread your answer to make sure it explicitly answers the question.

CHAPTER 51

WRITING ABOUT LITERATURE

51a Approaching Literature

When writers create works of imaginative literature, they work within certain **genres:** short stories, novels, plays, poems, and the like. Each of these literary genres has its own special characteristics. If you recognize these genres and understand their distinctive characteristics, literary works will be more accessible to you.

51b Reading Literature

See
7a

See
7c

When you read a literary work about which you plan to write, use the same critical thinking skills and **active reading** strategies you apply to other works you read: **preview** the work, and **highlight** it to identify key ideas and cues to meaning; then, **annotate** it carefully.

As you read and take notes, focus on the special concerns of literary analysis, considering elements like a short story's plot, a poem's rhyme or meter, or a play's characters. Look for *patterns,* related groups of words, images, or ideas that run through a work. Look for *anomalies,* unusual forms, unique uses of language, unexpected actions by characters, or unusual treatments of topics. And look for *connections,* links with other literary works, with historical events, or with biographical information.

READING LITERATURE

When you read a work of literature, keep in mind that you do not read to magically discover the one correct meaning the writer has hidden between the lines. The "meaning" of a literary work is created by the interaction between a text and its readers. Do not assume, however, that a work can mean whatever you want it to mean; ultimately, your interpretation must be consistent with the stylistic signals, thematic suggestions, and patterns of imagery in the work.

51c Writing about Literature

When you have finished your reading and annotating, **brainstorm** to discover material to write about; then, organize your material. As you arrange related material into categories, you should begin to see a structure for your paper. At this point, you will be ready to start drafting your essay.

When you write about literature, your goal is to make a point and support it with appropriate references to the work under discussion or to related works or secondary sources. (For an example of a **literary analysis** that uses outside sources, see **47d1.**) As you write, you observe the conventions of literary criticism, which has its own specialized vocabulary and formats. You also respond to discipline-specific assignments. For instance, you may be asked to **analyze** a work, to take it apart and consider one or more of its elements—perhaps the plot or characters in a story or the use of language in a poem. Or, you may be asked to **interpret** a work, to try to explore its possible meanings. Less often, you may be called on to **evaluate** a work, to judge its strengths and weaknesses.

More specifically, you may be asked to trace the critical or popular reception to a work; to compare two works by a single writer (or by two different writers); to consider the relationship between a work of literature and a literary movement or historical period. You may be asked to analyze a character's motives or the relationship between two characters, or to comment on a story's setting or tone. In any case, understanding exactly what you are expected to do will make your writing task easier.

✔ CHECKLIST: WRITING ABOUT LITERATURE

✔ Use present-tense verbs when discussing works of literature: "The character of Mrs. Mallard's husband *is* not developed. . . ."

✔ Use past-tense verbs only when discussing historical events ("Owen's poem conveys the destructiveness of World War I, which at the time the poem *was* written *was* considered to be . . ."), when presenting historical or biographical data ("Her first novel, *published* in 1811 when Austen *was* thirty-six, . . ."), or when identifying events that occurred prior to the time of the story's main action ("Miss Emily is a recluse; since her father *died* she has lived alone except for a servant").

✔ Support all points with specific, concrete examples from the work you are discussing, briefly summarizing key events, quoting dialogue or description, describing characters or setting, or paraphrasing ideas.

See 41a1–3

✔ Combine **summary, paraphrase, and quotation** with your own interpretations, weaving quotations smoothly into your paper.

✔ Be careful to acknowledge all sources, including the literary work or works under discussion. Check to see that you have introduced the words or ideas of others with a reference to the source and followed borrowed material with appropriate parenthetical documentation. Also, be sure you have quoted accurately and enclosed the words of others in quotation marks.

See 43a

✔ Use parenthetical documentation and include a Works Cited list in accordance with **MLA** documentation style.

See 32d2–3

✔ When citing a part of a short story or novel, supply the page number (168); for a poem, give the line numbers (2–4); for a classic verse play, include act, scene, and line numbers (1.4.29–31). For other plays, supply act and/or scene numbers. When quoting more than four lines of **prose** or three lines of **poetry**, follow MLA guidelines.

✔ Avoid subjective expressions like *I feel, I believe, it seems to me,* and *in my opinion.* These weaken your paper by suggesting that its ideas are "only" your opinion and have no validity in themselves.

✔ Avoid unnecessary plot summary. Your goal is to draw a conclusion about one or more works and to support that conclusion with pertinent details. If a plot detail supports a point you wish to make, a *brief* summary is acceptable. But plot summary is no substitute for analysis.

See 51g

✔ Use **literary terms** accurately. For example, be careful to avoid confusing *narrator* or *speaker* with *author;* feelings or opinions

continued on the following page

continued from the previous page

expressed by a narrator or character do not necessarily represent those of the author. You should not say, "In the poem's last stanza, *Frost* expresses his indecision" when you mean that the poem's *speaker* is indecisive.

✔ Underline <u>titles</u> of novels and plays; place titles of short stories and poems within quotation marks.

See
32b;
35a

51d Writing about Fiction

When you write a **literary analysis** of a work of fiction, you follow the same process you use when you write any paper about literature. However, you concentrate on elements—such as plot, character, setting, and point of view—characteristic of works of fiction.

✔ CHECKLIST: WRITING ABOUT FICTION

✔ **Plot** What happens in the story? What conflicts can you identify? Are they resolved? How are the events arranged? Why are they arranged in this way?

✔ **Character** Who is the protagonist? The antagonist? What role do minor characters play? What are each character's most striking traits? Does the protagonist grow and change during the story? Are the characters portrayed sympathetically? How do characters interact with one another?

✔ **Setting** Where and when is the story set? How does the setting influence the plot? How does it affect the characters?

✔ **Point of View** Is the story told by an anonymous third-person narrator or by a character, using first-person (*I* or *we*) point of view? Is the first-person narrator trustworthy? Is the narrator a participant in the action or just a witness to the story's events? How would a different point of view change the story?

✔ **Style, Tone, and Language** Is the level of diction formal? Informal? Is the style simple or complex? Is the tone intimate or distant? What kind of imagery is used?

✔ **Theme** What central theme or themes does the story explore?

Carla Watts, a student in an introductory literature course, was asked to select a short story from the literature anthology her class was using and to write an essay about it, basing her analysis solely on her own reactions to the story, not on literary criticism. The following story, written in 1983 by Gary Gildner, is the one she decided to write about.

SLEEPY TIME GAL

In the small town in northern Michigan where my father lived as a young man, he had an Italian friend who worked in a restaurant. I will call his friend Phil. Phil's job in the restaurant was as ordinary as you can imagine—from making coffee in the morning to sweeping up at night. But what was not ordinary about Phil was his piano playing. On Saturday nights my father and Phil and their girlfriends would drive ten or fifteen miles to a roadhouse by a lake where they would drink beer from schooners and dance and Phil would play an old beat-up piano. He could play any song you named, my father said, but the song everyone waited for was the one he wrote, which he would always play at the end before they left to go back to the town. And everyone knew of course that he had written the song for his girl, who was as pretty as she was rich. Her father was the banker in their town, and he was a tough old German, and he didn't like Phil going around with his daughter.

My father, when he told the story, which was not often, would tell it in an offhand way and emphasize the Depression and not having much, instead of the important parts. I will try to tell it the way he did, if I can.

So they would go to the roadhouse by the lake, and finally Phil would play his song, and everyone would say, Phil, that's a great song, you could make a lot of money from it. But Phil would only shake his head and smile and look at his girl. I have to break in here and say that my father, a gentle but practical man, was not inclined to emphasize the part about Phil looking at his girl. It was my mother who said the girl would rest her head on Phil's shoulder while he played, and that he got the idea for the song from the pretty way she looked when she got sleepy. My mother was not part of the story, but she had heard it when she and my father were younger and therefore had that information. I would like to intrude further and add something about Phil writing the song, maybe show him whistling the tune and going over the words slowly and carefully to get the best ones, while peeling

continued on the following page

continued from the previous page

onions or potatoes in the restaurant; but my father is already driving them home from the roadhouse, and saying how patched up his tires were, and how his car's engine was a gingerbread of parts from different makes, and some parts were his own invention as well. And my mother is saying that the old German had made his daughter promise not to get involved with any man until after college, and they couldn't be late. Also my mother likes the sad parts and is eager to get to their last night before the girl goes away to college.

So they all went out to the roadhouse, and it was sad. The women got tears in their eyes when Phil played her song, my mother said. My father said that Phil spent his week's pay on a new shirt and tie, the first tie he ever owned, and people kidded him. Somebody piped up and said, Phil, you ought to take that song down to Bay City—which was like saying New York City to them, only more realistic—and sell it and take the money and go to college too. Which was not meant to be cruel, but that was the result because Phil had never even got to high school. But you can see people were trying to cheer him up, my mother said.

Well, she'd come home for Thanksgiving and Christmas and Easter and they'd all sneak out to the roadhouse and drink beer from schooners and dance and everything would be like always. And of course there were the summers. And everyone knew Phil and the girl would get married after she made good her promise to her father because you could see it in their eyes when he sat at the old beat-up piano and played her song.

That last part about their eyes was not, of course, in my father's telling, but I couldn't help putting it in there even though I know it is making some of you impatient. Remember that this happened many years ago in the woods by a lake in northern Michigan, before television. I wish I could put more in, especially about the song and how it felt to Phil to sing it and how the girl felt when hearing it and knowing it was hers, but I've already intruded too much in a simple story that isn't even mine.

Well, here's the kicker part. Probably by now many of you have guessed that one vacation near the end she doesn't come home to see Phil, because she meets some guy at college who is good-looking and as rich as she is and, because her father knew about Phil all along and was pressuring her into forgetting about him, she gives in to this new guy and goes to his hometown during the vacation and falls in love with him. That's how the people in town figured it, because after she

continued on the following page

continued from the previous page

graduates they turn up, already married, and right away he takes over the old German's bank—and buys a new Pontiac at the place where my father is the mechanic and pays cash for it. The paying cash always made my father pause and shake his head and mention again that times were tough, but here comes this guy in a spiffy white shirt (with French cuffs, my mother said) and pays the full price in cash.

And this made my father shake his head too: Phil took the song down to Bay City and sold it for twenty-five dollars, the only money he ever got for it. It was the same song we'd just heard on the radio and which reminded my father of the story I just told you. What happened to Phil? Well, he stayed in Bay City and got a job managing a movie theater. My father saw him there after the Depression when he was on his way to Detroit to work for Ford. He stopped and Phil gave him a box of popcorn. The song he wrote for the girl has sold many millions of records, and if I told you the name of it you could probably sing it, or at least whistle the tune. I wonder what the girl thinks when she hears it. Oh yes, my father met Phil's wife too. She worked in the movie theater with him, selling tickets and cleaning the carpet after the show with one of those sweepers you push. She was also big and loud and nothing like the other one, my mother said.

Carla began by reading the story through quickly. Then she reread it more carefully, highlighting and annotating as she read. A portion of the highlighted and annotated story appears below.

When do events take place?

In the small town in northern Michigan where my father lived as a young man, he had an Italian friend who worked in a restaurant. I will call his friend Phil. Phil's job in the restaurant was as ordinary as you can imagine--from making coffee in the morning to sweeping up at night. But what was not ordinary about Phil was his piano playing. On Saturday nights my father and Phil and the girlfriends would drive ten or fifteen miles to a roadhouse by a lake where they would drink beer from schooners and dance and Phil would play an old beat-up piano. He could play any song you named, my father said, but the song everyone waited for was the one he wrote, which

Sat. nights = special—dancing, beer, etc.

?

continued on the following page

continued from the previous page

he would always play at the end before they left to go back to the town. And everyone knew of course that he had written the song for his girl, who was as pretty as she was rich. Her father was the banker in their town, and he was a tough old German, and he didn't like Phil going around with his daughter.

Sounds like fairy tale

My father, when he told the story, which was not often, would tell it in an offhand way and emphasize the Depression and not having much, instead of the important parts. I will try to tell it the way he did, if I can.

Carla's next task was to brainstorm to find ideas. As she searched for a topic for her essay, she found it helpful to brainstorm separately on plot, character, setting, point of view, tone and style, and theme to see which suggested the most promising possibilities.

Brainstorming List

Plot
Flashback — narrator remembers story father told.
Story: Phil loved rich banker's daughter, wrote song for
        her, girl married someone else, Phil sold song for
        $25.00, married another woman.
Ordinary, predictable story of "star-crossed lovers" from
        different backgrounds ("Probably by now many of
        you have guessed . . ."), but what actually happened
        isn't important.

Character
Phil — Italian, never went to high school, ordinary job in
        restaurant, extraordinary piano player.
Girl — no name, pretty, rich, educated
Narrator — ?
Mother — romantic
Father — mechanic; gentle, practical

Setting
"small town in northern Michigan"
Past — when narrator's father was a young man

In woods — near lake
Roadhouse — dancing, drinking, beat-up piano

Point of View
Narrator tells story to reader, but there's a story
    inside the story.
Father tells his story, mother qualifies his version (she's
    "not part of the story" but has heard it), narrator
    tells how they told it.
Point of view keeps shifting — characters compete to tell
    the story ("I would like to intrude further. . . .").
Father's version: stresses Depression, hard times
Mother's version: stresses relationship, "sad parts"
Readers encouraged to find own point of view; narrator of
    story addresses readers.
Three characters invent and reinvent and embellish story
    each time they tell it.

Tone and Style
Conversational style — narrator talks to reader ("Well,
    here's the kicker part.").
Like a fairy tale (girl = "as pretty as she was rich";
    father = "a gentle but practical man")
Casual speech: contractions; "Well," "some guy," etc.

Theme
Which is "real" story?
    Subject of Phil's story = missed chances, failure.
    Subject of narrator's story = the past?
    Values of different characters? Conflict between real
    events and memory?

When Carla looked over her brainstorming list, she saw at once that character and point of view suggested the most interesting possibilities for her paper. Still, she found herself unwilling to start drafting her essay until she could find out more about the story's title, which she thought must be significant. She asked around until she found someone who told her that the title was the name of an actual song—and supplied the lyrics. She recorded her reactions to this information in a journal entry.

Journal Entry

"Sleepy Time Gal" = name of song
Mother says Phil got inspiration for song from the way
    his girl looked when she got sleepy. ✳✳ Does title of
    story refer to girl or to song? ✳✳
Song = fantasy about the perfect married life that should
    follow the evenings of dancing: in a "cottage for two"
    wife will be happy cooking and sewing for her husband
    and will end her evenings early. She'll be happy to
    forget about dancing and be a stay-at-home wife.
Maybe lyrics describe what Phil wants and never gets?

At this point Carla decided to arrange some of the most useful material from her brainstorming list, journal entry, and annotations into categories. She gave these categories headings that corresponded to the three versions of Phil's story presented in "Sleepy Time Gal," and she added related supporting details as they occurred to her.

Three Versions of Phil's Story

Mother's Version
("Likes the sad parts") and the details of the romance: the
    way the father made the daughter promise not to get
    involved with a man until she finished college, the way the
    women got tears in their eyes when Phil played his song.
Remembers girl's husband had french cuffs.
Remembers Phil's wife = "big and loud."
Notes people were trying to cheer Phil up.
Remembers girl resting head on Phil's shoulder, and how he
    got idea for song.

Father's Version
Depression/money: mentions Phil's patched tires and engine,
    how he spent a week's pay on new clothes, how girl's
    husband pays cash for a new Pontiac.
("Times were tough")

Narrator's Version
Facts of story — but wants to add more about Phil's
    process of writing song (because he, like Phil, = artist?),

more about romance ("you could see it in their eyes"). Wants to embellish story. ("I wish I could put more in . . .")

Carla's notes and lists eventually suggested the following thesis statement for her paper: "'Sleepy Time Gal' is a story that is not about the 'gal' of the title or about the man the narrator calls Phil but rather about the different viewpoints of its three narrators." Guided by this tentative thesis statement, she went on to write and revise her paper, following the process detailed in **Chapter 3.** The final draft of Carla's paper begins on the following page. Annotations have been added to identify the conventions that apply to writing essays about works of fiction. (Note that because all students in the class selected stories from the same text, Carla's instructor did not require a Works Cited page.)

Watts 1

Carla Watts

Professor Sierra

English 1001

12 March 1998

Whose Story?

Midway through Gary Gildner's short story "Sleepy Time Gal" the narrator acknowledges, "I've already intruded too much in a simple story that isn't even mine" (215). But whose story is "Sleepy Time Gal"? It is presented as the tale of Phil, an ordinary young man of modest means who falls in love with a rich young woman, writes a song for her, and loses both the woman and the song, as well as the fame and fortune the song could have brought him, apparently because he is unwilling to fight for either. But actually, "Sleepy Time Gal" is not Phil's story, and it is not the story of the girl he loves; the story belongs to the three characters who compete to tell it.

The story these characters tell is a simple one; it is also familiar. Phil is a young man with an ordinary job. He has little education and no real prospects of doing anything beyond working in a restaurant doing menial jobs. He is in love with a girl whose father is a rich banker, a girl who goes to college. Phil has no more chance of marrying the girl than he has of becoming educated or becoming a millionaire. He has written

---

Paper title is centered

Title is in quotation marks

Parenthetical documentation identifies page on which quotation appeared

Thesis statement

Brief plot summary is combined with interpretation

Watts 2

a song for her, but he is doomed to sell the rights to it for twenty-five dollars. Phil may be a man with dreams and expectations that go beyond the small Michigan town and the roadhouse, but he does not seem to be willing to struggle to make his dreams come true. Ironically, he never achieves the happy married life his song describes; his dreams remain just dreams, and he settles for life in the dream world of a movie theater.

Father's perspective

|

Past tense used to identify events that occurred before story's main action

The character who seems to be the author of Phil's story is the narrator's father: he is the only one who knew Phil and witnessed the story's events, and he has told it again and again to his family. But the story he tells reveals more than just what happened to Phil; it says a lot about his own life too. The father is a mechanic who eventually leaves his small Michigan town for Detroit. As the narrator observes, he is "a gentle but practical man" (214). We can assume he has seen some hard times; he sees Phil's story only in the context of the times, and "times were tough" (216). The narrator says,

Ellipsis indicates words omitted from quotation

"My father, when he told the story, . . . would tell it in an offhand way and emphasize the Depression and not having much, instead of the important parts" (214). In the father's version, seemingly minor details are important: Phil's often-mended car engine, "a gingerbread of parts from different

Watts 3

makes" (215), and incidents like how Phil spent a week's pay on a new shirt and tie, "the first tie he ever owned" (215), and how the girl's husband paid cash for a new Pontiac. These details are important to the father because they have to do with money. He sees Phil's story as more about a particular time (the Depression era) than about particular people. Whenever he hears Phil's song on the radio, he remembers that time.

The narrator's mother, however, sees Phil's story as a romantic, timeless story of hopelessly doomed lovers. She did not witness the story's events, but she has heard the story often. According to the narrator, she "likes the sad parts and is eager to get to their last night before the girl goes away to college" (215). She remembers how the women in the roadhouse got tears in their eyes when Phil played the song he wrote. The mother's selective memory helps to characterize her as somewhat romantic and sentimental, interested in people and their relationships (the way the girl's father made her promise to avoid romantic entanglements until after college; the way Phil's friends tried to cheer him up) and in visual details (the way the girl rested her head on Phil's shoulder; the French cuffs on her husband's shirt). In the interaction between the characters she sees drama and even

Mother's perspective

Point is supported by specific references to story

Watts 4

tragedy. The sentimental story of lost love appeals to her just as the story of lost opportunity appeals to the father.

The narrator knows the story only through his father's telling and retelling of it, and he says, "I will try to tell it the way he did, if I can" (214). But this is impossible: as he tells the story, he embellishes it, and he makes it his own. He is the one who communicates the story to readers, and he ultimately decides what to include and what to leave out. His story reflects both his parents' points of view: the focus on both characters and events, both romance and history. In telling Phil's story, he tells the story of a time, re-creating a Depression-era struggle of a man who could have made it big but wound up a failure; however, he also recounts a story about people, a romantic, sentimentalized story of lost love. And, he tells a story about his own parents.

The narrator, like Phil, is creative; he needs to convey the facts of the story, but he must struggle to resist the temptation to add to them--to add more about how Phil went

about writing the song, "maybe show him whistling the tune and going over the words slowly and carefully to get the best ones" (214-15), more about the romance itself. The narrator is clearly embellishing the story--for instance, when he says everyone knew Phil and the girl would get married because

Watts 5

"you could see it in their eyes" (215), he admits that this detail is not in his father's version of the story--but he is careful to identify his own contributions, explaining, "I couldn't help putting it in there" (215). The narrator cannot help wondering about the parts his father did not tell, and he struggles to avoid rewriting the story to include them. Sometimes he cannot help himself, and he apologizes for his lapses with a phrase like "I have to break in here. . . ." (214). But, for the most part, the narrator knows his place, knows it is not really his story to tell: "I wish I could put more in, especially about the song and how it felt to Phil to sing it and how the girl felt when hearing it and knowing it was hers, but I've already intruded too much in a simple story that isn't even mine" (215).

Phil's story is, as the narrator acknowledges, a simple one, almost a cliché. But Gary Gildner's story, "Sleepy Time Gal," is more complex. In it, three characters create and re-create a story of love and loss, ambition and failure, each contributing the details they feel should be stressed and, in the process, revealing something about themselves and about their own hopes and dreams.

Conclusion reinforces thesis

Carla's paper focuses on the story's shifting point of view and the contributions of the three central characters to Phil's story. She supports her thesis with specific references to "Sleepy Time Gal"—in the form of quotation, summary, and paraphrase—and interprets the story's events in light of the points she is making. Her paper does not include every idea in her notes, nor should it: she selects only those details that support her thesis.

51e Writing about Poetry

When you write a paper about poetry, you follow the same process discussed in **51d.** However, you concentrate on the elements poets use to create and enrich their work—for example, voice, form, sound, meter, language, and tone.

✔ CHECKLIST: WRITING ABOUT POETRY

- ✔ **Voice** Who is the poem's speaker? What is the speaker's attitude toward the poem's subject? How would you characterize the speaker's tone?
- ✔ **Word Choice and Word Order** What words seem important? Why? What does each word say? What does it suggest? Are any words repeated? Why? Is the poem's diction formal or informal? Is the arrangement of words conventional or unconventional?
- ✔ **Imagery** What images are used in the poem? To what senses (sight, sound, smell, taste, or touch) do they appeal? Is one central image important? Why? Is there a pattern of related images?
- ✔ **Figures of Speech** Does the poet use simile? Metaphor? Personification? What do figures of speech contribute to the poem?
- ✔ **Sound** Does the poem include rhyme? Where? Does it have regular meter (that is, a regular pattern of stressed and unstressed syllables)? Does the poem include repeated consonant or vowel sounds? What do these elements contribute to the poem?
- ✔ **Form** Is the poem written in open form (with no definite pattern of line length, rhyme, or meter) or in closed form (conforming to a pattern)? Why do you think this kind of form is used?
- ✔ **Theme** What central theme or themes does the poem explore?

Daniel Johanssen, a student in an introductory literature course, followed this process as he planned an essay about Delmore Schwartz's

1959 poem "The True-Blue American," which follows. Daniel's essay appears on pages 856–58. (Note that because all students in the class selected poems from the same text, Daniel's instructor did not require a Works Cited page.)

THE TRUE-BLUE AMERICAN

Jeremiah Dickson was a true-blue American,
For he was a little boy who understood America, for he felt that he must
Think about *everything;* because that's all there is to think about,
Knowing immediately the intimacy of truth and comedy,
5 Knowing intuitively how a sense of humor was a necessity
For one and for all who live in America. Thus, natively, and
Naturally when on an April Sunday in an ice cream parlor Jeremiah
Was requested to choose between a chocolate sundae and a banana split
He answered unhesitatingly, having no need to think of it
10 Being a true-blue American, determined to continue as he began:
Rejecting the either-or of Kierkegaard,[1] and many another European;
Refusing to accept alternatives, refusing to believe the choice of between;
Rejecting selection; denying dilemma; electing absolute affirmation:
      knowing
15   in his breast
            The infinite and the gold
            Of the endless frontier, the deathless West.
"Both: I will have them both!" declared this true-blue American
In Cambridge, Massachusetts, on an April Sunday, instructed
20   By the great department stores, by the Five-and-Ten,
Taught by Christmas, by the circus, by the vulgarity and grandeur of
      Niagara Falls and the Grand Canyon,
Tutored by the grandeur, vulgarity, and infinite appetite gratified and
      Shining in the darkness, of the light
25 On Saturdays at the double bills of the moon pictures,
The consummation of the advertisements of the imagination of the light
Which is as it was—the infinite belief in infinite hope—
      of Columbus, Barnum, Edison, and Jeremiah Dickson.

---

[1] Søren Kierkegaard (1813–1855)—Danish philosopher who greatly influenced twentieth-century existentialism. *Either-Or* (1841) is one of his best-known works.

Daniel Johanssen

Professor Stang

English 1001

8 April 1998

Paper title is
centered

Title of poem
is in quotation
marks

Thesis
statement

Parenthetical
documen-
tation
indicates line
numbers

Irony in "The True-Blue American"

The poem "The True-Blue American" by Delmore Schwartz
is not as simple and direct as its title suggests. In fact, the title is
extremely ironic. At first, the poem seems patriotic, but actually
the flag-waving strengthens the speaker's criticism. Even though
the poem seems to support and celebrate America, it is actually
a bitter critique of the negative aspects of American culture.

According to the speaker, the primary problem with
America is that its citizens falsely believe themselves to be
authorities on everything. The following lines introduce the
theme of the "know-it-all" American: "For he was a little boy
who understood America, for he felt that he must / Think
about <u>everything</u>; because that's <u>all</u> there is to think about"
(2-3). This theme is developed later in a series of parallel
phrases that seem to celebrate the value of immediate
intuitive knowledge and a refusal to accept or to believe
anything other than what is American (4-6).

Americans are ambitious and determined, but these
qualities are not seen in the poem as virtues. According to the
speaker, Americans reject sophisticated "European" concepts

Johanssen 2

like doubt and choices and alternatives and instead insist on

"absolute affirmation" (13)--simple solutions to complex

problems. This unwillingness to compromise translates into

stubbornness and materialistic greed. This tendency is

illustrated by the boy's asking for <u>both</u> a chocolate sundae

<u>and</u> a banana split at the ice cream parlor--not "either-or"

(11). Americans are characterized as pioneers who want it all,

who will stop at nothing to achieve "The infinite and the gold

/ Of the endless frontier, the deathless West" (16-17). For the

speaker, the pioneers and their "endless frontier" are not

noble or self-sacrificing; they are like a greedy little boy at an

ice cream parlor.

 According to the speaker, the greed and materialism of

America began as grandeur but ultimately became mere

vulgarity. Similarly, the "true-blue American" is not born a vulgar

parody of grandeur; he learns it from his true-blue fellows:

<blockquote>

instructed

 By the great department stores,

  by the Five-and-Ten,

Taught by Christmas, by the circus, by

  the vulgarity and grandeur of

Niagara Falls and the Grand Canyon,

Tutored by the grandeur, vulgarity, and

  infinite appetite gratified. . . . (19-23)

</blockquote>

More than 3 lines of poetry are set off from text. Quotation is indented 10 spaces (or 1") from left margin; no quotation marks are used.

Among the "tutors" the speaker lists are American institutions such as department stores and national monuments. Within these institutions, grandeur and vulgarity coexist; in a sense, they are one and the same.

The speaker's negativity climaxes in the phrase "Shining in the darkness, of the light" (24). This paradoxical statement suggests the negative truths hidden beneath America's glamorous surface. All the grand and illustrious things of which Americans are so proud are personified by Jeremiah Dickson, the spoiled brat in the ice cream parlor.

Conclusion
reinforces
thesis

Like America, Jeremiah has unlimited potential. He has native intuition, curiosity, courage, and a pioneer spirit. Unfortunately, however, both America and Jeremiah Dickson are limited by their willingness to be led by others, by their greed and impatience, and by their preference for quick, easy, unambiguous answers rather than careful philosophical analysis. Regardless of his--and America's--potential, Jeremiah Dickson is doomed to be hypnotized and seduced by glittering superficialities, light without substance, and to settle for the "double bill of the moon pictures" (25) rather than the enduring truths of a philosopher like Kierkegaard.

51f Writing about Drama

When you write a paper about a play, you focus on the special conventions of drama. Here, for example, you might consider not just the play's plot and characters but also its staging.

✔ CHECKLIST: WRITING ABOUT DRAMA

✔ **Plot** What happens in the play? What conflicts are developed? How are they resolved? Are there any subplots? What events, if any, occur offstage?

✔ **Character** Who are the major characters? The minor characters? What relationships exist among them? What are their most distinctive traits? What do we learn about characters from their words and actions? From the play's stage directions? From what other characters tell us? Does the main character change or grow during the course of the play?

✔ **Staging** When and where is the play set? How do the scenery, props, costumes, lighting, and music work together to establish this setting? What else do these elements contribute to the play?

✔ **Theme** What central theme or themes does the play explore?

Kimberly Allison, a student in an introductory literature class, was assigned to write a short paper on one element—plot, character, staging, or theme—in a one-act play. She chose to write about the characters in Susan Glaspell's 1916 play *Trifles*. Her completed paper, annotated to highlight some conventions of writing about drama, appears on pages 860–65. (Note that because all students in the class selected plays from the same text, Kimberly's instructor did not require a Works Cited page.)

Kimberly Allison

English 1013

Professor Johnson

March 1, 1998

Double-space

Breaking through the Boundaries:

Acts of Defiance in <u>Trifles</u>

Opening
sentence
identifies
author and
work

Susan Glaspell wrote her best-known play, <u>Trifles</u>, in

1916, at a time when women were beginning to challenge

their socially defined roles, realizing that their identities as

wives and domestics kept them in a subordinate position in

society. Because women were demanding more autonomy,

Introduction
places play in
historical
context

traditional institutions such as marriage, which confined

women to the home and made them mere extensions of their

husbands, were beginning to be reexamined.

As a married woman, Glaspell was evidently touched by

these concerns, perhaps because when she wrote <u>Trifles</u> she

was at the mercy of her husband's wishes and encountered

barriers in pursuing her career as a writer because she was a

woman. But for whatever reason, Glaspell chose as the play's

protagonist a married woman, Minnie Foster (Mrs. Wright),

who has challenged society's expectations in a very extreme

way: by murdering her husband. Minnie's defiant act has

occurred before the action begins, and as the play unfolds

two women, Mrs. Peters and Mrs. Hale, who accompany their

Allison 2

husbands on an investigation of the murder scene, piece
together the details of the situation surrounding the murder.
As the events unfold, however, it becomes clear that the focus
of <u>Trifles</u> is not on who killed John Wright, but rather on the
themes of the subordinate role of women, the confinement of
the wife in the home, and the commonality of women's
experiences.

The subordinate role of women, particularly Minnie's role
in her marriage, becomes evident in the first few minutes of
the play when Mr. Hale observes that the victim, John Wright,
had little concern for his wife's opinions: "I didn't know as
what his wife wanted made much difference to John" (956).
Here Mr. Hale suggests that Minnie was powerless against the
wishes of her husband. Indeed, as these characters imply,
Minnie's every act and thought were controlled by her
husband, who strove to break her spirit by forcing her to
perform repetitive domestic chores alone in the home. Minnie
only had power in her kitchen, and Mrs. Peters and Mrs. Hale
understand this situation because their behavior is controlled
by their husbands. Therefore, when Sheriff Peters condemns
Minnie's concern about her preserves, saying, "Well, can you
beat the women! Held for murder and worrying about her
preserves" (958), he is, in a sense, condemning all three of the
women for worrying over domestic matters rather than about

Thesis
statement

Topic
sentence
identifies first
point paper
will discuss:
women's
subordinate
role

Allison 3

the murder that has been committed. Indeed, the sheriff's

comment suggests that he assumes women's lives are trivial,

an assumption that pervades the thoughts and dialogue of all

three men.

Topic
sentence
introduces
second point
paper will
discuss:
women's
confinement

Mrs. Peters and Mrs. Hale are similar to Minnie in

another way as well: throughout the play, they are confined to

the kitchen of the Wrights' house. Therefore, the kitchen

becomes the focal point of the play. The women find that the

kitchen holds the clues to Mrs. Wright's loneliness and to the

details of the murder. Mrs. Peters and Mrs. Hale remain

confined to the kitchen while their husbands enter and exit

the house at will. This scenario mirrors Minnie's daily life, as

she remained in the home while her husband went to work

and into town. The two women discuss Minnie's isolation in

being housebound: "Not having children makes less work--

but it makes a quiet house, and Wright out to work all day,

and no company when he did come in" (963). Beginning to

identify with Minnie's loneliness, Mrs. Peters and Mrs. Hale

recognize that, busy in their own homes, they have, in fact,

participated in isolating and confining Minnie. Mrs. Hale

declares, "I wish I had come over once in a while! That was a

crime! That was a crime! Who's going to punish that? . . . I

might have known she needed help" (965)!

Allison 4

Soon the two women discover that Minnie's only connection to the outside world was her bird, the symbol of her confinement; Minnie was a caged bird who was kept from singing and communicating with others because of her restrictive husband. And piecing together the evidence--the disorderly kitchen, the poorly stitched quilt pieces, and the dead canary--the women come to believe that John Wright broke the bird's neck just as he had broken Minnie's spirit. Likewise, Mrs. Peters and Mrs. Hale discern the connection between the dead canary and Minnie's situation. The stage directions describe the moment when the women become aware of the truth behind the murder: "Their eyes meet," and the women share "A look of growing comprehension, of horror" (964).

Through their observations and discussions in Mrs. Wright's kitchen, Mrs. Hale and Mrs. Peters come to understand the commonality of women's experiences. Mrs. Hale speaks for both of them when she says, "I know how things can be--for women. . . . We all go through the same things--it's all just a different kind of the same thing" (965). And, once the two women realize the experiences they share, they begin to recognize that they must band together in order to challenge a male-oriented society; although their experiences may seem trivial to the men, the "trifles" of their

Transitional paragraph discusses women's observations and conclusions

Topic sentence introduces third point paper will discuss: commonality of women's experiences

lives are significant to them. They realize that Minne's independence and identity were crushed by her husband and that their own husbands have asserted that women's lives are trivial and unimportant as well. Thus, the revelation that Mrs. Peters and Mrs. Hale experience is one that urges them to commit an act as defiant as the one that has gotten Minnie into trouble: they conceal their discovery from their husbands and from the law.

Significantly, Mrs. Peters does acknowledge that "the law is the law," but she also understands that because Mr. Wright treated his wife badly, Minnie is justified in killing him. They also realize, however, that for men the law is black and white and that an all-male jury will not take into account the extenuating circumstances that prompted Minnie to kill her husband. And even if Minnie were allowed to communicate to the male-dominated court the abuses she has suffered, the law would undoubtedly view her experience as trivial because a woman who complained about how her husband treated her would be considered ungrateful.

Nevertheless, because Mrs. Hale and Mrs. Peters empathize with Minnie's condition, they suppress the evidence they find, enduring their husbands' condescension rather than standing up to them. And, through this action, the women

Allison 6

attempt to break through the boundaries of their social role, just as Minnie has done. Although Minnie is imprisoned for her crime, she has freed herself; and, although Mrs. Peters and Mrs. Hale appear to conceal their knowledge, fearing the men will laugh at them, these women are really challenging society and freeing themselves as well.

Susan Glaspell addressed many of the issues important to early twentieth-century women in <u>Trifles</u>, including women's subordinate status, the wife's confinement in the home, and the experiences that all women have in common. In order to emphasize the pervasiveness of these issues, Glaspell does more than focus on the plight of the woman who has ended her isolation and loneliness by committing a heinous crime against society. By presenting three male and two female characters who demonstrate the vast differences between male and female experience, she illustrates how men define the roles of women and how women can challenge these roles in search of their own significance in society and their eventual independence.

Conclusion places play in historical context

51g Using Literary Terms

When you write about literature, you use a vocabulary appropriate to the discipline. The following glossary defines some of the terms you will use.

alliteration   Repetition of initial sounds in a series of words, as in "<u>d</u>ark, <u>d</u>amp <u>d</u>ungeon."

allusion   A reference to a historical event, a work of literature, a biblical passage, or the like that the author expects readers to recognize.

antagonist   The character who is in conflict with or in opposition to the *protagonist*. Sometimes the antagonist is a force or situation, such as war or poverty.

assonance   Repetition of vowel sounds in a series of words, as in "f<u>i</u>ne sl<u>i</u>de on the <u>i</u>ce."

blank verse   Lines of unrhymed iambic pentameter in no particular stanzaic form; approximates the rhythms of ordinary English speech.

character   The fictional representation of a person. Characters may be *round* (well developed) or *flat* (undeveloped stereotypes), *dynamic* (changing and growing during the course of the story) or *static* (remaining essentially unchanged by the story's events).

climax   The point of greatest tension or importance in a play or story; the point at which the story's decisive action takes place.

closed form   A kind of poetic structure characterized by a consistent pattern of rhyme, meter, or stanzaic form.

conflict   The opposition between two or more characters, between a character and a natural force, or between contrasting tendencies or motives or ideas within one character.

consonance   Repetition of consonant sounds in a series of words, as in "the g<u>n</u>arled fi<u>n</u>gers of his <u>n</u>ervous ha<u>n</u>ds."

denouement   The point in the plot of a work of fiction or drama at which the action comes to an end and loose ends are tied up.

end-stopped line   A line of poetry that ends with a full stop, usually at the end of a sentence.

enjambment   A line of poetry ending with no punctuation or natural pause so that it runs over into the next line.

exposition   The initial stage of the plot of a work of fiction or drama, in which the author presents basic information readers need to understand the story's characters and events.

figurative language   Language whose meaning is not to be taken literally. The most commonly used figures of speech are *metaphor, personification,* and *simile.*

free verse   Poetry that does not follow a fixed meter or rhyme scheme.

hyperbole   Intentional overstatement or exaggeration.

imagery   Use of sensory description (description that relies on sight, sound, smell, taste, or touch) to make what is being described more vivid. A *pattern of imagery* combines a group of related images in order to create a single effect.

irony   Language that suggests a discrepancy or incongruity between what is said and what is meant (*verbal irony*), between what actually happens and what we expected to happen (*situational irony*), or between what a character knows or believes and what the reader knows (*dramatic irony; also* called *tragic irony*).

lyric poetry   Poetry that expresses a speaker's mood or feelings. Lyric poems are usually short.

metaphor   A comparison that equates two things that are essentially unlike. Unlike a *simile,* a metaphor does not use *like* or *as.*

meter   The pattern of stressed and unstressed syllables in a line of poetry; each repeated unit of meter is called a *foot.* An *anapest* has three syllables, the first two unstressed and the third stressed; a *dactyl* has three syllables, the first stressed and subsequent ones unstressed; an *iamb* has two syllables, of which the second is stressed; a *spondee* has two syllables, both stressed; and a *trochee* has two syllables, the first stressed and the second unstressed. A poem's meter is described by the kind of foot (iamb, dactyl, and so on) and the number of feet in each line (one foot per line = monometer, two feet per line = dimeter, three feet = trimeter, four = tetrameter, five = pentameter, and so on). Thus, a poetic line containing five feet, each of which contains an unstressed syllable followed by a stressed syllable, would be described as *iambic pentameter.*

monologue   An extended speech by one character.

narration   The recounting of events—for example, in a work of fiction. When an event that has already occurred is recounted in a later sequence of events, it is called a *flashback;* when something that will occur later in a narration is suggested earlier, the suggestion is called a *foreshadowing.*

open form   A kind of poetic structure not characterized by any consistent pattern of rhyme, meter, or stanzaic form.

paradox   A seemingly contradictory statement.

persona   The narrator or speaker of a story or poem; the persona's attitudes and opinions are not necessarily those of the author.

personification   The assigning of human qualities to nonhuman things.

plot   The arrangement of events in a work of literature.

point of view   The perspective from which a story is told. A story may have a *first-person narrator,* who may be a major or minor character in the story. Alternatively, a story may have a *third-person narrator,* who is not a character in the story. Such a narrator may be an *omniscient narrator,* who knows the thoughts and motives of all the story's characters, or a *limited omniscient narrator,* who sees into the minds of only some of the characters. A narrator who cannot be trusted—because he or she is naive, evil, stupid, or self-serving—is called an *unreliable narrator.* The objective perspective that presents only information an audience would get from watching the action unfold on stage is called the *dramatic* point of view.

protagonist   The principal character of a work of drama or fiction.

rhyme   The repetition of the last stressed vowel sound and all subsequent sounds. *End rhyme* occurs at the ends of poetic lines; *internal rhyme* occurs within a line of poetry.

rhythm   The regular repetition of stresses and pauses.

setting   The background against which the action of a work of literature takes place: the historical period, locale, season, time of day, etc.

simile   A comparison that equates two essentially unlike things using the words *like* or *as.*

soliloquy   A convention of drama in which a character speaks directly to the audience, revealing thoughts and feelings that the play's other characters, even if they are present on the stage, are assumed not to hear.

stanza   A group of lines in a poem, separated from others by a blank space on the page, which forms a unit of thought, mood, or meter. Common stanzaic forms include the *couplet* (two lines), *tercet* (three lines), *quatrain* (four lines), *sestet* (six lines), and *octave* (eight lines).

stock character   A character who behaves consistently and predictably and who is instantly recognizable and familiar to the audience.

symbol   An image whose meaning transcends its literal or denotative sense in a complex way. Its multiple associations give it significance beyond what it could carry on its own.

theme   An idea expressed by a work of literature.

tone   The attitude of the speaker toward a work's subject, characters, or audience, conveyed by the work's word choice and arrangement of words.

understatement   Intentional downplaying of a situation's significance, often for ironic effect.

CHAPTER 52

WRITING FOR THE WORKPLACE

52a Writing Business Letters

Business letters should be brief and to the point, with important information placed early in the letter. Be concise, avoid digressions, and try to sound as natural as possible.

The first paragraph of your letter should introduce your subject and mention any pertinent previous correspondence. The body of your letter should present the facts readers will need in order to understand your points. (If your ideas are complicated, present your points in a bulleted or numbered **list**.) Your conclusion should reinforce your message.

See
A1c

 BUSINESS LETTER SALUTATIONS

If you are writing to a woman, consult previous correspondence, and use the title she uses. If you do not know her preference, use *Ms.* If you know a person's last name and first initial and do not know whether the person is male or female (or if you do not have a specific person to whom to address your letter), call the company and ask for the full name of the person who should receive your letter. If you are unable to determine the name of the person who will receive your letter, use a neutral form of address—*Dear Editor* or *Dear Personnel Director,* for example. Keep in mind that generic salutations such as *Gentlemen, Dear Sirs,* and *Dear Madam* are both **sexist** and outdated. Whenever possible, use a person's name.

See
20f2

SAMPLE LETTER

Heading
6732 Wyncote Avenue
Houston, TX 77004
May 3, 1997

Inside address
Mr. William S. Price, Jr., Director
Division of Archives and History
Department of Cultural Resources
109 East Jones Street
Raleigh, NC 27611

Salutation
Dear Mr. Price:

Thank you for sending me the material I requested about pirates in colonial North Carolina.

Body
Both the pamphlets and the bibliography were extremely useful for my research. Without your help, I am sure my paper would not have been so well received.

I have enclosed a copy of my paper, and I would appreciate any comments you may have. Again, thank you for your time and trouble.

Complimentary close
Sincerely yours,

Written signature
Kevin Wolk

Typed signature
Kevin Wolk

Copy sent
cc: Dr. N. Provisor, Professor of History

Additional data
Enc.: Research paper

SENDING MESSAGES BY FAX AND E-MAIL

The standards for electronic messages are the same as those for any other form of business correspondence.

Faxes Remember that faxes are often received not by an individual but at a central location, so you must include a cover sheet that contains the recipient's name and title, the date, the company and department, the fax and telephone numbers, and the total number of pages faxed. In addition, supply your own name and telephone and fax numbers. (It is also a good idea to call ahead to alert the addressee that a fax is coming.)

E-mail Although E-mail can be quite informal, you should treat your E-mail message as if it were a standard written business letter. Include a salutation and a subject line, and be sure to state your purpose and to present your ideas clearly and succinctly. Avoid slang and imprecise diction, and proofread carefully. Also keep in mind that E-mail composed at work is the property of the employer, who has the right to access it. For this reason, E-mail is never completely secure.

52b Writing Letters of Application and Résumés

When you apply for employment, your primary objective is to obtain an interview. The **letter of application** summarizes your qualifications for a specific position; the **résumé** provides a general overview of your accomplishments.

(1) Letters of Application

Begin your letter of application by identifying the job you are applying for and stating where you heard about it—in a newspaper, in a professional journal, on the Internet, or from your school's job placement service, for example. Be sure to include the date of the advertisement and the exact title of the position. End your introduction with your thesis: a statement of your ability to do the job.

SAMPLE LETTER OF APPLICATION

Heading

246 Hillside Drive
Urbana, IL 61801
October 20, 1997
kr237@metropolis.105.com

Inside address

Mr. Maurice Snyder, Personnel Director
Guilford, Fox, and Morris
Eckerd Building
22 Hamilton Street
Urbana, IL 61822

Salutation

Dear Mr. Snyder:

Body

My college advisor, Dr. Raymond Walsh, has told me that you are interested in hiring a part-time accounting assistant. I believe that my academic background and my work experience qualify me for this position.

I am presently a junior accounting major at the University of Illinois. During the past year, I have taken courses in taxation, trusts, and business law. I have worked extensively with a personal computer, and I am proficient in *Lotus* and *ClarisWorks*. Last spring, I gained practical accounting experience by working in our department's tax clinic.

After I graduate, I hope to get a master's degree in taxation and then return to the Urbana area. I believe that my experience in taxation as well as my familiarity with the local business community would enable me to contribute to your firm.

I have enclosed a résumé for your examination. I will be available for an interview any time after midterm examinations, which end October 25. I look forward to hearing from you.

Complimentary close

Sincerely yours,

Typed signature

Sandra Kraft

Sandra Kraft

Additional data

Enc.: Résumé

In the body of your letter, provide the information that will convince your reader of your qualifications—for example, relevant courses you have taken and pertinent job experience. Be sure to address any specific criteria mentioned in the advertisement. Above all, emphasize your strengths, and explain how they relate to the specific job for which you are applying.

Conclude by saying that you have enclosed your résumé. State that you are available for an interview, noting any dates on which you cannot be available.

EXERCISE 1

Look through the employment advertisements in your local paper or in the files of your college placement service. Choose one job, and write a letter of application in which you outline your achievements and discuss your qualifications for the position.

(2) Résumés

A résumé lists relevant information about your education, your job experience, your goals, and your personal interests. When you prepare your résumé, select the information that is most appropriate for the job you want, emphasizing the accomplishments that differentiate you from other candidates. For example, if you have received academic honors or awards, or if you have financed your own education, include this information.

There is no single correct format for a résumé. You may decide to arrange your résumé in **chronological order,** listing your education and work experience in sequence (beginning with the most recent), or in **emphatic order,** presenting first the material (for example, a particular job) that will be of most interest to an employer. Whatever a résumé's arrangement, it should be brief—one page is sufficient for an undergraduate—easy to read, and clearly and logically organized.

✔ CHECKLIST: COMPONENTS OF A RÉSUMÉ

- ✔ The **heading** includes your name, school address, home address, telephone number, and E-mail address.
- ✔ A statement of your **career objective** (optional), placed at the top of the page, identifies your professional goals.
- ✔ The **education section** includes the schools you have attended, starting with the most recent one and moving back in time.

continued on the following page

continued from the previous page

(After graduation from college, do not list your high school un-less you have a compelling reason to do so—for instance, if it is nationally recognized for its academic standards or it has an ac-tive alumni network in your field.)

✔ The **summary of work experience** generally starts with your most recent job and moves backward in time.

✔ The **background** or **interests section** lists your most important (or most relevant) special interests and community activities.

✔ The **honors section** lists academic achievements and awards.

✔ The **references section** lists the full names and addresses of at least three references. If your résumé is already one full page long, a line saying that your references will be sent upon request is sufficient.

RÉSUMÉS

Increasingly, résumés are posted on electronic bulletin boards or at sites that list résumés for a number of employment cate-gories. The format of the electronic résumé is often similar to the ones described in this section, with one notable difference: spe-cific words and phrases can be **hypertext links** to other sites. (These links are highlighted in blue on the résumé.) For example, your name could be a link to your home page, which might in-clude a detailed biographical sketch as well as pictures and sound. Or, a company's name in your "Work Experience" section could be a link to that company's Website. Finally, the title of your se-nior thesis could be a link to a site that contains a copy of the the-sis itself. So far, the majority of résumés are still submitted on paper, but in the future, electronic résumés will most likely gain in popularity.

EXERCISE 2

Prepare a résumé to include with the letter of application you wrote for Exercise 1.

SAMPLE RÉSUMÉ: CHRONOLOGICAL ORDER

KAREN L. OLSON

SCHOOL
3312 Hamilton St. Apt. 18
Philadelphia, PA 19104
215-382-0831
olsonk@durm.ocs.drexel.edu

HOME
110 Ascot Ct.
Harmony, PA 16037
412-452-2944

EDUCATION

DREXEL UNIVERSITY, Philadelphia, PA 19104
Bachelor of Science in Graphic Design
Anticipated Graduation: June 1998
Cumulative Grade Point Average: 3.2 on a 4.0 scale

COMPUTER SKILLS AND COURSE WORK

HARDWARE
Operate both Macintosh computer and PCs.
SOFTWARE
Adobe Illustrator, Photoshop, and *TypeAlign; QuarkXPress; CorelDRAW; Micrografx Designer*
COURSES
Corporate Identity, Environmental Graphics, Typography, Photography, Painting and Printmaking, Sculpture, Computer Imaging, Art History

EMPLOYMENT EXPERIENCE

UNISYS CORPORATION, Blue Bell, PA 19124
June–September 1997, Cooperative Education
Graphic Designer. Designed interior pages as well as covers for target marketing brochures. Created various logos and spot art designed for use on inter-office memos and departmental publications.

CHARMING SHOPPES, INC., Bensalem, PA 19020
June–December 1996, Cooperative Education
Graphic Designer/Fashion Illustrator. Created graphics for future placement on garments. Did some textile designing. Drew flat illustrations of garments to scale in computer. Prepared presentation boards.

THE TRIANGLE. Drexel University, Philadelphia, PA 19104
January 1997–present
Graphics Editor. Design all display advertisements submitted to Drexel's student newspaper.

DESIGN AND IMAGING STUDIO, Drexel University, Philadelphia, PA 19104
October 1995–June 1996
Monitor. Supervised computer activity in studio. Answered telephone. Assisted other graphic design students in using computer programs.

ACTIVITIES AND AWARDS

The Triangle, Graphics Editor: 1997–present
Kappa Omicron Nu Honor Society, vice president: 1997–present
Dean's List: Spring 1996, fall and winter 1997
Graphics Group, vice president: 1997–present

REFERENCES AND PORTFOLIO

Available upon request.

SAMPLE RÉSUMÉ: EMPHATIC ORDER

Michael D. Fuller

SCHOOL
27 College Avenue
University of Maryland
College Park, MD 20742
(301) 357-0732
mful532@aol.com

HOME
1203 Hampton Road
Joppa, MD 21085
(301) 877-1437

Restaurant Experience

McDonald's Restaurant, Pikesville, MD. Cook.
Prepared hamburgers. Acted as assistant manager for two weeks while manager was on vacation. Supervised employees, helped prepare payroll and work schedules. Was named employee of the month. Summer 1998.

University of Maryland Cafeteria, College Park, MD. Busboy.
Cleaned tables, set up cafeteria, and prepared hot trays. September 1997–May 1998.

Other Work Experience

University of Maryland Library, College Park, MD. Reference assistant.
Filed, sorted, typed, shelved, and catalogued. Earnings offset college expenses. September 1996–May 1997.

Education

University of Maryland, College Park, MD (sophomore).
Biology major. Expected date of graduation: June 2000.
Forest Park High School, Baltimore, MD.

Interests

Member of University Debating Society.
Tutor in University's Academic Enrichment Program.

References

Mr. Arthur Sanducci, Manager
McDonald's Restaurant
5712 Avery Road
Pikesville, MD 22513

Mr. William Czernick, Manager
Cafeteria
University of Maryland
College Park, MD 20742

Ms. Stephanie Young, Librarian
Library
University of Maryland
College Park, MD 20742

52c Writing Memos

Unlike letters, memos communicate information *within* a business organization, transmitting brief messages of a paragraph or two or short reports or proposals. Their function is either to convey information or to persuade.

WRITING MEMOS

In many places of employment, virtually all internal communications—including memos—circulate via E-mail. E-mail should not be an occasion for sloppy, informal writing and does not eliminate the need for careful revising and editing. In general, treat all electronic communications as if they were hard copy.

EXERCISE 3

Your duties at your summer job with a public utility include reading correspondence sent from your division to the public. While reading a pamphlet that discusses energy conservation, you notice repeated use of the word *repairmen,* and you come across the sentences "Each consumer must do *his* part" and "*Mothers* should teach their children about conservation." With the approval of your supervisor, you decide to write a memo to John Durand, public relations manager, explaining that some customers might perceive this language as <u>sexist</u>—and therefore offensive. In your memo, explain to Mr. Durand why the language should be changed and suggest some words and phrases he could use in their place. Mr. Durand is your superior, so maintain a reasonable and respectful tone.

See 20f2

SAMPLE MEMO

Opening
component

TO: Ina Ellen, Senior Counselor
FROM: Kim Williams, Student Tutor Supervisor
SUBJECT: Construction of a Tutoring Center
DATE: November 10, 1997

Purpose
statement

This memo proposes the establishment of a tutoring center in the Office of Student Affairs.

BACKGROUND
Under the present system, tutors must work with students at a number of facilities scattered across the university campus. As a result, tutors waste a lot of time running from one facility to another and are often late for appointments.

NEW FACILITY
Body

I propose that we establish a tutoring facility adjacent to the Office of Student Affairs. The two empty classrooms next to the office, presently used for storage of office furniture, would be ideal for this use. We could furnish these offices with the desks and file cabinets already stored in these rooms.

BENEFITS
The benefits of this facility would be the centralizing of the tutoring services and the proximity of the facility to the Office of Student Affairs. The tutoring facility could also use the secretarial services of the Office of Student Affairs.

RECOMMENDATIONS
Conclusion

To implement this project we would need to do the following:

1. Clean up and paint rooms 331 and 333
2. Use folding partitions to divide each room into five single-desk offices
3. Use stored office equipment to furnish the center

I am certain these changes would do much to improve the tutoring service. I look forward to discussing this matter with you in more detail.

APPENDIX A

DOCUMENT DESIGN AND MANUSCRIPT GUIDELINES

This appendix presents general principles of document design as well as specific guidelines for preparing manuscripts in the humanities and the social sciences as specified by MLA and APA, respectively.

A1   Document Design

Document design refers to the conventions that affect the way a document looks on a page. A well-designed document is convincing because it is pleasing to the eye, it is easy to read, and it highlights important information. However, a document can conform to the appropriate manuscript guidelines of a discipline and still not be well designed. In general, well-designed documents—whether they are research papers, memos, reports, business letters, or résumés, for example—have an effective format, clear headings, useful lists, and attractive visuals.

(a)   Creating an Effective Format

Margins   Your document should be visually simple and uncluttered—double-spaced (unless your instructor tells you otherwise), with at least 1 1/2-inch margin on all sides. If you are using a computer you can either leave a ragged edge on the right, or you can *justify* your text so that all the words will align evenly on the right. A ragged edge helps you vary the visual landscape of your document, making it easier to read.

Font   The font you select should make your document as readable as possible. In general, you should use either a 10- or 12-point font (a smaller font will make your writing difficult to read and give your document a crowded appearance). Avoid typefaces that will distract readers (script or cursive fonts, for example).

Typographical Emphasis   You can emphasize important words and phrases, such as headings, by using **boldface** or *italics* or ALL CAPITAL LETTERS. Used in moderation, these distinctive typefaces make a text more readable. (Notice, for example, how these typefaces are used in this handbook.) Used excessively, however, they slow readers down and make reading more difficult.

(b) Using Headings

Headings act as visual cues that enable readers to retrieve information easily. They tell readers what to expect in a section before they actually read it; they also enable readers to locate particular sections of a document so they can read material that interests them and skip material that does not. In addition, by breaking up a text and eliminating long passages of prose, headings make a document inviting and easy to read.

Number of Headings   Although there is no hard and fast rule about how many headings you need in a document, you should have enough to highlight the most important points of your discussion. A long, complicated document will need more headings than a shorter, less complex one. (A very short document, less than a page in length, usually needs no headings.) Keep in mind that whereas too few headings may not be of much use, too many headings will make your document look like an outline.

Phrasing   Headings should be brief, descriptive, specific, and to the point. They can be single words—*Summary, Introduction, Methods, Results,* and *Conclusions,* for example. Headings can also be phrases (always stated in **parallel** terms):

> See
> Ch. 18

Choosing a dog

Caring for the dog

Housebreaking the dog

Headings can be questions:

How do you file your receipts?

How do you calculate your deductions?

How do you determine your tax liability?

How do you determine if you are entitled to a refund?

How do you file electronically?

Or they can be statements:

Begin with stretching.

Do twenty minutes of aerobics.

Work out with light weights.

End with stretching.

 USING HEADINGS

Headings and subheadings may be *centered*, placed *flush left*, or *indented*. The most important thing to remember is that headings at the same level should have the same format—for example, if one first-level heading is boldfaced and centered, all other first-level headings must also be boldfaced and centered.

Centered, Boldfaced, Uppercase and Lowercase

<u>Flush Left, Underlined, Uppercase and Lowercase</u>

<u>Indented, underlined, lowercase paragraph heading ending with a period.</u>

CENTERED, ALL CAPITAL LETTERS

(c) Constructing Lists

A list separates material out of a text and arranges it in a format that enables readers to see the material easily. A list can also reduce complicated statements to a series of key ideas. Lists are most easy to read when all the elements are parallel and about the same length. Make sure you introduce a list with a complete sentence followed by a colon.

When rank is important, number the items on the list.

There are several steps we should take to reduce our spending:

1. We should cut our workforce by 10 percent.
2. We should utilize less expensive vendors.
3. We should decrease overtime.
4. We should replace our present health plan with a less expensive HMO.

Notice that because the items on the list above are complete sentences, each ends with a period.

When rank is not important, use bullets (not numbers) before items on the list.

By playing an active role in politics, the scientific community aims to exert influence in three areas:

- Public opinion
- Public policy
- Allocation of funds for research

Notice that periods are not used if the items are not sentences.

NOTE: Lists are useful because they make items stand out from the text around them. Too many lists, however, have the opposite effect, obscuring logical connections and making the text difficult to understand.

(d) Using Visuals: Tables, Graphs, Diagrams, and Photographs

Visuals—tables, graphs, diagrams, and photographs—enable you to present a great deal of information in a limited space. You can create your own tables and graphs by using a computer program like *Excel* or *Lotus,* and you can draw your own diagrams and take your own photographs. You can also get diagrams and photographs by photocopying or scanning them from a print source, by downloading them from the Internet, or by cutting them from CD-ROM encyclopedias such as the *Grolier Multimedia Encyclopedia* and pasting them into your documents.

See
43a1,
43c1

NOTE: If you use visuals from a source, you must use the appropriate documentation **format**.

Tables   Tables present data in a condensed, visual format—arranged in rows and columns. The advantages of a table are that it can present numerical data more concisely than text can and that it can provide more detail than a graph can. When you plan your table, make sure you include only the data that you will need; discard data that are too detailed or difficult to understand (this information is best presented in an appendix). Keep in mind that tables may distract readers, so include only those that are necessary to support your discussion. The following table from a report is not documented because it presents the writer's own data.

As the following table shows, the Madison location now employs more workers in every site than the St. Paul location.

Table 1 — Heading
Number of Employees at Each Location — Descriptive caption

Employees	Location	
	Madison	St. Paul
Plant	461	254
Warehouse	45	23
Outlet Stores	15	9

Data

Because the Madison location has grown so quickly, steps must be taken to. . . .

Graphs and Charts   Like tables, graphs and charts present data in visual form. Whereas tables present specific numerical data, graphs and charts convey the general pattern or trend that the data suggest. Because graphs and charts tend to generalize, they are usually less accurate than tables. For this reason, graphs and charts are frequently accompanied by tables. Following is an example of a bar graph. (**See 45l** for an example of a pie graph.)

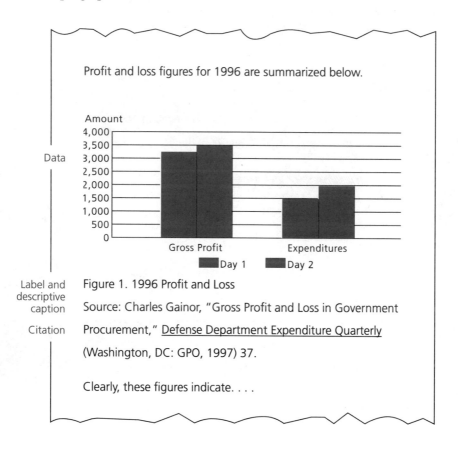

Profit and loss figures for 1996 are summarized below.

Data

Label and descriptive caption

Figure 1. 1996 Profit and Loss

Citation

Source: Charles Gainor, "Gross Profit and Loss in Government Procurement," <u>Defense Department Expenditure Quarterly</u> (Washington, DC: GPO, 1997) 37.

Clearly, these figures indicate. . . .

Diagrams A diagram enables you to emphasize one part of a mechanism or object and to eliminate parts that are not relevant to your discussion. Diagrams are often used in scientific and technical writing to clarify concepts while at the same time eliminating paragraphs of detailed and confusing description. They can also be used in humanities papers, as the following example illustrates.

The design of the ancient Greek theater is similar to that of a present-day sports stadium, as figure 2 illustrates.

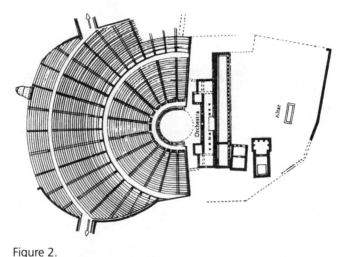

Label   Figure 2.

The Theater of Dionysus at Athens. Redrawn from a drawing   Descriptive
                                                                   caption
Citation   by R. C. Flickinger, <u>The Greek Theater and Its Drama</u> (1918).

This design, with its tiered seats, enabled the audience to view the actors onstage as well as. . . .

Photographs   Photographs enable you to show exactly what something or someone looks like—an animal in its natural habitat, a work of fine art, or an actor in costume, for example. Although computer technology that allows a writer to paste photographs directly into a text is widely available, you should use it with care. Not every photograph will support or enhance your written text; in fact, an irrelevant photograph will distract readers.

Robes 3

In the later years of his life, Twain was seen more as a personality than as a writer. Figure 3 shows him in a characteristic pose.

Figure 3.

Mark Twain, on porch with kitten.

The white suit he wears in this photograph. . . .

✔ CHECKLIST: INCLUDING VISUALS IN THE TEXT

✔ Use a visual only when it contributes something important to the discussion, not for embellishment.

✔ Include the visual in the text only if you plan to discuss it in your paper. (Place the visual in an appendix if you do not.)

✔ Introduce each visual with a complete sentence.

✔ Follow each visual with a discussion of its significance.

✔ Leave wide margins around each visual.

✔ Label each visual appropriately. See **A2** and **A3**.

✔ Make sure you document any visual that you did not create yourself. (Remember that each discipline has its own conventions for documenting visuals.)

A2 MLA Manuscript Guidelines

MLA guidelines are used for papers in the humanities. The following information is based on the *MLA Handbook for Writers of Research Papers* (4th ed.). For an example of a paper that uses MLA manuscript format, see **Chapter 45.**

1. Type your paper with a one-inch margin at the top and bottom and on both sides. Indent five spaces (or one-half inch) for each new paragraph and ten spaces (or one inch) for a long prose quotation set off from the text. Double-space your paper throughout.

2. If your instructor does not require a separate title page, type your name, the course number, your instructor's name, and the date (all double-spaced) one inch from the top of the first page of the paper, flush with the left-hand margin. Double-space again, and center the title. If the title is longer than a single line, double-space and center the second line below the first. Capitalize all important words in the title, but not prepositions, coordinating conjunctions, articles, or the *to* in infinitives, unless they begin or end the title. Do not underline the title or enclose it in quotation marks, but do underline words in the title if they would normally be underlined (for example, book titles). Never put a period after a title, even if it is a sentence. Double-space between the last line of the title and the first line of your paper.

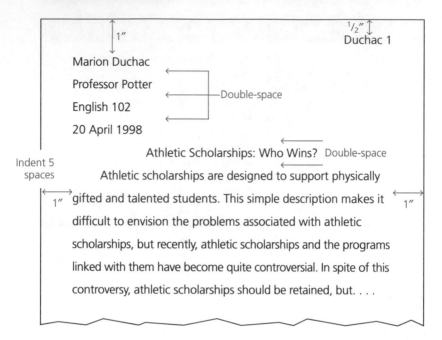

3. If your instructor requires a separate title page, use a format like the one used in the paper in **45l.** The title page includes the title; your name, course, and section number; your instructor's name; and the date you submitted your paper. When you use a title page, repeat your title on the first page of your manuscript, centered one inch below the top of your page and one-half inch below the page number.

4. Number all pages of your paper consecutively—including the first— in the upper right-hand corner, one-half inch from the top, flush right. Do not put *p.* before the page numbers and do not put periods or any other punctuation after them. Type your name before the page number on every page.

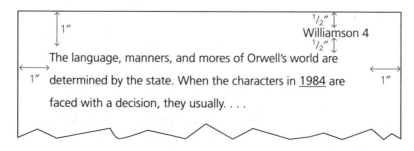

5. The *MLA Handbook* does not mention **headings**. Traditionally, papers in the humanities do not use headings; instead, strong topic sentences or transitional paragraphs introduce ideas. This trend does seem to be changing, however. If you want to use internal headings in your paper, check with your instructor to make sure this format is acceptable.

See A1b

6. Tables and other visuals should be placed as close as possible to the part of the paper in which they are discussed.

   Tables should be headed *Table* and given an arabic numeral and a descriptive caption. Type the heading and the descriptive caption flush left on a separate line *above* the table. Capitalize the heading and the caption as if they were titles. If the table is borrowed from a source, give the full citation below the table beginning at the left-hand margin. Double-space the table's text and the caption.

See A1d

   Other visuals, such as graphs, diagrams, and photographs, should be labeled *Figure* (abbreviated *Fig.*) and given an arabic number. The label, descriptive caption, and the full citation are typed *below* the visual beginning at the left-hand margin.

7. If you use source material in your paper, consult the section on MLA documentation format in **43a.**

A3 APA Manuscript Guidelines

APA guidelines are used for papers in the social sciences. The following information is based on the *Publication Manual of the American Psychological Association* (4th ed.). For an example of a paper that uses APA manuscript format, see **48d.**

1. Type your paper with at least a one-inch margin at the top, bottom, and sides of the paper. Double-space between all lines of the manuscript. (You may use triple- or quadruple-spacing before and after a table.)

2. Indent the first line of every paragraph, as well as the first line of every item on the Reference List, five to seven spaces. Set off quotations of forty or more words in a block format indented five to seven spaces from the left-hand margin. If the quotation is one paragraph or less, do not indent; if it is more than one paragraph, indent the first line of the second and subsequent paragraphs five to seven spaces from the new margin.

3. The title page should include a page header (a shortened title that will appear in the upper right-hand corner of each page of the paper, including the title page), the running head for publication, the title of

the paper, and your name as well as other pertinent information. Type the running head in all UPPERCASE letters flush left at the top of the title page, preceded by the phrase *Running head.* Type the title in uppercase and lowercase letters, centered on the page. Type your name and other relevant information one double-space below the title.

4. A social science paper often contains an **abstract,** a short summary of approximately one hundred words. If your instructor requires an abstract, it should appear as a separate numbered page (labeled *Abstract*) after the title page.

5. Number all pages of your paper consecutively. Each page should include the page header as well as the page number in the upper right-hand corner. (If your paper includes an abstract, the first page of text will be page 3; if it doesn't, the first page will be page 2.) Begin the text of your paper on a new page. Center the title of the paper at the top of the page; if the title is more than one line, double-space between the lines and center. Skip two spaces and begin typing the text.

See A1b

6. **Headings** are often included in papers in the social sciences in order to convey the sequence and the relative importance of ideas. Most student papers use only one or two levels of headings. Major headings should be centered and typed with uppercase and lowercase letters. Minor headings should be flush left, typed with uppercase and lowercase letters and underlined.

See A1c

7. Items in a series should be formatted as a numbered **list.**

See A1d

8. **Tables** (numerical values displayed in columns and rows) should be numbered consecutively in the order in which they are mentioned in the paper (Table 1, Table 2, and so on). Double-space each table and include a brief identifying title—(*Table 1. Population Figures for 1995*)—directly *above* it. Begin each table on a separate page after the reference list. Refer to each table by number in the text of your paper—for example, "Table 3 summarizes this study."

Other types of visuals—graphs, diagrams, and so on—are also numbered consecutively. The label *Figure* and an identifying caption are typed *below* the visual beginning at the left-hand margin.

APA recommends that tables and your other visuals be placed in an appendix at the end of the paper; however, your instructor may want this material to be included in the text of the paper.

9. If you use source material in your paper, citations should be consistent with APA documentation format (see **43c**).

APPENDIX B

ENGLISH FOR SPEAKERS
OF OTHER LANGUAGES (ESOL)

B1   Writing for Native English Speakers

Writing for a native English-speaking audience involves much more than writing correct English sentences. Native and nonnative speakers of English may have very different expectations about logic, organization, support, and even purpose and audience. In order to meet the expectations of your English-speaking audience, you need to understand these differences. Scholars in the field of **contrastive rhetoric,** which is devoted to the study of the contrasting rhetorical and stylistic characteristics of various languages, have identified some of these differences.

Native English speakers are direct. English speakers tend to follow a straight line of logic, from clear statement to supporting examples, without irrelevancies or digressions. Compared to speakers of other languages, native speakers of English can seem curt and businesslike, perhaps even blunt and rude. Whereas business letters in many Asian languages may begin with observations about the weather or even with inquiries about the health of the recipient's family, business letters in English usually begin by stating the main point of the letter. Many English sayings express the direct quality of the language: "Get to the point," "Say what you mean," "Stop beating around the bush."

Native speakers of English prize originality. In many cultures, the point of speaking in public or writing for an audience is to imitate the style of famous orators and writers, both ancient and modern. Native speakers of English, however, generally expect writers to be original in their opinions, choice of supporting details, and even style. Readers of English want to see new twists on old ideas and original uses of language. Therefore, they label overly familiar language trite and object to the use of clichés.

Native speakers of English expect audiences to disagree. In many cultures, audiences are expected to agree with the speaker or writer. By contrast, writers in English may invite questions, criticism, or even disagreement from the audience. In some cultures, such responses by the audience might be considered inappropriate or rude, but they show English-speaking writers that the audience is reading closely and taking their ideas seriously.

Native speakers of English question authority. Native speakers of English assume they are operating within a democratic society that encourages open debate. Every belief the audience holds, no matter how ancient or cherished, can be challenged. The English speaker's skeptical attitude may disturb some members of some cultural groups. To them, English speakers may appear to have no firm beliefs of their own at all and may seem not to respect the beliefs of their audience. However, English speakers often use skepticism not to destroy belief, but rather to investigate it, refine it, and reinforce it.

EXERCISE 1

Newspaper editorials or letters to the editor are often good examples of the qualities of English discussed in this section. Find a letter or editorial in a local newspaper and see how many of these qualities it displays. (For example, does it come to the point immediately? Does it challenge the truth of accepted ideas?) Does it display qualities that are different from those of a writer discussing the same subject in your native language?

B2 Choosing a Topic

See
1c1

What **topics** do native speakers of English choose to write about? In general, they try either to *inform* their readers, giving new information that readers may not already know, or to *persuade* their readers, offering opinions that may not be popular and then convincing their readers to accept these opinions as valid. Therefore, they will choose a topic about which they believe they know more than their audience does, or they will choose a controversial topic about which there is public debate.

Such topics may be quite different from those chosen by nonnative speakers of English. In some cultures, it is rude for a writer to claim to know more than an audience about a topic; a writer must be humble and perhaps even apologize to the audience for not knowing enough. In other cultures, controversial topics are intentionally avoided for complex social and political reasons. However, too much humility may cause English audiences to lose their trust in the writer; avoiding controversial topics may make the writer seem indecisive.

B3 Stating and Supporting a Thesis

(a) Stating a Thesis

When writing in English, state your **thesis**—your main idea or point of view—as quickly as possible. You need not worry about offending or insulting your readers by doing this; in fact, your readers expect you to state your thesis as soon as you can.

You should also be quite specific in <u>stating your thesis</u>. You may begin with general statements, but keep in mind that an English-speaking audience will look for a specific thesis statement that expresses what you have to say about the topic.

> **CLOSE-UP** STATING A THESIS
>
> An <u>effective thesis statement</u> has the following characteristics.
>
> - It is a statement of opinion or conjecture, not a self-evident statement or a statement of fact.
>
> - It is not a familiar platitude such as "Honesty is the best policy" or "Look before you leap," but a more original, even unique, idea.
>
> - It is narrow enough to be supported within the scope of the essay.
>
> - It can be supported with concrete examples.

See 2b3

See 2b2

(b) Supporting a Thesis

Native speakers of English usually demand a very tight connection between <u>thesis and support</u>: the thesis states the writer's main point, and the support answers the question "Why?" or "How?" by giving reasons or examples. English speakers expect that all the support will be directly related to the thesis.

Native speakers of English may have little patience for what they see as digressions or indirect discussions of the subject. In the classic essay patterns of many languages—the *ba-gu-wen* pattern of Chinese rhetoric, for example—the writer is supposed to digress. In the eyes of Chinese essay writers, English essays may seem less imaginative, less creative, than

See 2b1

A-15

the Chinese ideal. Nevertheless, it is important that you meet the native-speaking audience's expectations of a direct, businesslike discussion.

Native speakers of English support a thesis statement in one of two ways:

- With *facts and figures*   Native English speakers reject the strategy of supporting one personal opinion only with other personal opinions (which is an accepted pattern of logic in many cultures).

- With the *opinions of authorities*   The criteria that make a person an authority for English speakers may be different from those used in other cultures. It is not simply a person's social status or position as a political or religious leader that matters, but rather the person's expertise in the subject. Even the highest-ranking officials still must support their beliefs with factual information.

 CLOSE-UP   SUPPORTING A THESIS

- Examples must be real and not hypothetical. It is better to point to the experiences of real people than to make up examples. It is better to say, "Eighty-six percent of Americans on welfare say they would prefer to have a job" than to say, "Few people would choose welfare over working if they had a choice."

- Examples must be relevant to the thesis. Speakers of English want to see a direct connection between factual evidence and the position the writer is taking. If a writer asserts, for example, that cats make better pets than dogs, it makes no sense to say that pigs are also becoming popular pets in America. Instead, the writer can point out that cats are quieter and easier to care for than dogs.

- Examples must be sufficient to convince readers that a statement is true. Beware of false generalizations based on too few details. For example, the fact that your friend got a good job without going to college does not mean that no one needs to go to college to get a good job. Do enough people who do not go to college get good jobs to justify the assertion that college is not necessary?

EXERCISE 2

After each of the following thesis statements are statements of fact meant to support it. In each group, which factual statements best support the writer's position? Why?

1. Eating too much beef is bad for your health.
   a. People who eat a lot of beef have more heart attacks than people who do not.
   b. American beef in particular is full of unhealthful chemicals.
   c. Raising animals just to eat them is cruel.
   d. People who eat a lot of beef tend not to eat other foods that they need, such as grains and vegetables.
2. Standardized tests are a poor means of determining a student's academic abilities.
   a. Many students who perform well at other academic tasks do poorly on standardized tests.
   b. Standardized tests are too difficult.
   c. Other kinds of academic work are much more important than standardized tests.
   d. The conditions under which students takes standardized tests may damage their performance.
   e. Standardized tests may have content that is unfamiliar to some groups of otherwise able students.
3. Engineering is a very good field to enter today.
   a. There are too many doctors.
   b. There are many jobs open to engineers.
   c. Engineering is fun.
   d. Engineers are well paid.
   e. Engineers build things.

EXERCISE 3

For each of the following thesis statements, write at least three statements of fact that support it. If you disagree with any of the statements, rewrite it so that you can better support it.

1. American women are the freest women in the world.
2. Knowing English well is a very important business skill.
3. Americans do not know enough about other countries.
4. Recycling alone will not solve our pollution problems.

B4   Organizing Ideas

(a)   Using an Introduction, Body, and Conclusion

Native speakers of English are likely to expect to find a **thesis-and-support** organization of ideas. In addition, most native speakers learn to use a very specific organizational pattern in their essays.

- The **introduction** introduces the topic and states the thesis.
- The **body** presents the support for the thesis statement.
- The **conclusion** sums up the writer's position.

Introduction   Thesis statement: Languages contain a lot of cultural information.

Body

> Support: For example, a language can tell a lot about social relations among the people who speak it.
>
> Support: A language can also reveal the social values of particular groups.
>
> Support: Learning a language can even tell us about the material possessions of its speakers.
>
> Support: On the deepest level, a language can contain ingrained cultural attitudes about time and space.

Conclusion   Summary: Therefore, when we study a language, we are also studying the cultural attitudes of the people who speak it.

EXERCISE 4

Is there a specific strategy for organizing essays in your native language? If so, what is it? Is it similar to the English method for organizing ideas, or is it quite different from it? Make a list of similarities and differences.

(b) Writing in Paragraphs

See
Ch. 6

   The **paragraph** is a basic unit of communication in English. Many other languages use paragraphs, of course, but some do not. Some languages are not even written, as English is, horizontally from left to right. In some other languages, even those that are written as English is, there is no convention of bringing together groups of sentences into a paragraph.

CLOSE-UP   WRITING IN PARAGRAPHS

An English paragraph is immediately recognizable.

- The first line of a paragraph is indented, giving a paragraph its characteristic shape on a page.

continued on the following page

continued from the previous page
- Paragraphs vary in length, from a single sentence to many sentences, from a few lines to a page or more. Regardless of the paragraph's length, however, all its sentences focus on a single idea.

- A paragraph's main idea is often stated explicitly as a topic sentence, most often (though not always) at the beginning.

- All the other sentences in the paragraph provide further explanation of the topic sentence or concrete examples to illustrate the topic sentence.

- The sentences in a paragraph are often linked by connecting devices such as the repetition of key words and the use of <u>transitional words or phrases</u>.

See
6c2

EXERCISE 5

In each of the following paragraphs, look for the elements listed in the box above: a clearly stated main idea, examples that illustrate the topic sentence, connecting devices such as transitional phrases. If the main idea is not clearly stated, try stating it in your own words. Is every sentence in the paragraph clearly focused on that main idea?

1. Asian Americans are not one people but several—Chinese Americans, Japanese Americans, and Filipino Americans. Chinese and Japanese Americans have been separated by geography, culture, and history from China and Japan for seven and four generations, respectively. They have evolved cultures and sensibilities distinctly not Chinese or Japanese and distinctly not white American. Even the Asian languages as they exist today in America have been adjusted and developed to express a sensitivity created by a new experience. In America, Chinese and Japanese American culture and history have been inextricably linked by confusion, the popularization of their hatred for each other, and World War II. (Frank Chin, Jeffery Paul Chan, Lawson Fusao Inada, Shawn Wong, Preface to *Aiiieeeee*)

2. The sex differences in personality formation that Chodorow describes in early childhood appear during the middle childhood years in studies of children's games. Children's games are considered by George Herbert Mead and Jean Piaget as the crucible of social development during the school years. In games, children learn to take the role of the other and come to see themselves through another's eyes. In games, they learn respect for rules and come to understand the ways rules can be made and changed. (Carol Gilligan, *In a Different Voice*)

B5 | Writing Correct English

Grammatical errors can become a serious problem for native as well as nonnative speakers when such errors get in the way of efficient communication. Therefore, although you may not be able to eliminate all grammatical errors from your English, you should try to make it as correct as possible.

In addition to the cultural and logical patterns discussed so far, English differs from other languages in its grammar. The study of grammatical differences among various languages is called **contrastive linguistics.** Scholars in the field of contrastive linguistics have identified a number of differences between English and other languages.

In English, words may change their form according to their function. In some languages, words never change form, or they change form according to rules different from those of English. In English, for example, verbs change form to communicate whether an action is taking place in the past, in the present, or in the future, whereas in Chinese, other words may be added to the sentence to indicate when in the past the action took place, but the verb itself does not change form.

In English, context is extremely important in understanding function. Sometimes it is impossible to identify the function of an English word without noting its context. In the following sentences, for instance, the very same words perform different functions according to their relation to other words.

Juan and I are taking a <u>walk</u>. (*Walk* is a noun, a direct object of the verb *taking,* with an article, *a,* attached to it.)

If you <u>walk</u> instead of drive, you will help conserve the earth's resources. (*Walk* is a verb, the predicate of the subject *you.*)

Jie was <u>walking</u> across campus when she met her chemistry professor. (*Walking* is part of the verb, the predicate of the subject *Jie.*)

<u>Walking</u> a few miles a day will make you healthier. (*Walking* is a noun, the subject of the verb *will make.*)

Next summer we'll take a <u>walking</u> tour of southern Italy. (*Walking* is an adjective describing *tour.*)

See
Ch. 22

<u>Spelling</u> **in English is not perfectly phonetic and may sometimes seem illogical.** In many languages that use a phonetic alphabet or syllabary, such as Japanese, Korean, or Persian, words are spelled exactly as they are pronounced. Spelling in English, however, is often a matter of memorization, not sounding out the words phonetically. For example,

the "ough" sound in the words *tough, though,* and *thought* is pronounced quite differently in each case. In fact, spelling in English is related more to the history of the word and its origins in other languages than to the way the word is pronounced.

Word order is extremely important in English sentences.

See
B11

EXERCISE 6

As a nonnative speaker of English, you may have more conscious knowledge of English grammar than a native speaker who has never studied it as a foreign language. Moreover, as a speaker of at least two languages, you probably have a good sense of grammatical differences between languages.

Make a list of a few major differences between the grammar of English and the grammar of your native language and of any other languages you know. Be prepared to explain these differences to your classmates.

B6 | Nouns

A **noun** *names* things: people, objects, places, feelings, ideas.

Nouns can be quite different in different languages. In some languages nouns have gender; that is, they may be *masculine* or *feminine*. In Spanish, the word for *moon* (*la luna*) is feminine, whereas the word for *sun* (*el sol*) is masculine. In other languages, there is no difference between the singular and plural forms of nouns. In Japanese, one person is *hito,* whereas many people are still *hito*. In some languages (including English), nouns may be used as adjectives: "She ate a *cheese* sandwich."

See
23a

See
27f

(a) Singular, Plural, and Noncount Nouns

In English nouns may have number; that is, they may change in form according to whether they name one thing or more than one thing. If a noun names only one thing, it is a *singular* noun; if a noun names more than one thing, it is a plural noun.

Some English nouns, called **noncount nouns,** do not have a plural form because the things they name—qualities such as love and justice, for example—cannot be counted. (**Count nouns** name items that can be counted, such as books or children.) Understanding the distinction between count and noncount nouns is important in determining the correct use of articles with nouns.

See
22b8

See
B6b

CLOSE-UP   NONCOUNT NOUNS

The following commonly used nouns are noncount nouns. These words have no plural forms. Therefore, you should never add *s* to them.

advice	evidence	knowledge
clothing	furniture	luggage
education	homework	merchandise
equipment	information	revenge

EXERCISE 7

Underline all the nouns in the following passage. Then list the nouns in three columns (singular, plural, noncount).

The highway took me through Danville, where I saw a pillared antebellum mansion with a trailer court on the front lawn. Route 127 ran down a long valley of pastures and fields edged by low, rocky bluffs and split by a stream the color of muskmelon. In the distance rose the foothills of the Appalachians, old mountains that once separated the Atlantic from the shallow inland sea now the middle of America. The licks came out of the hills, the fields got smaller, and there were little sawmills cutting hardwoods into pallets, crates, and fenceposts. The houses shrank, and their colors changed from white to pastels, to iridescents, to no paint at all. The lawns went from Vertagreen bluegrass to thin fescue to hard-packed dirt glinting with fragments of glass, and the law ornaments changed from birdbaths to plastic flamingos and donkeys to broken-down automobiles with raised hoods like tombstones. On the porches stood long-legged wringer washers and ruined sofas, and, by the front doors, washtubs hung like coats of arms. (William Least Heat Moon, *Blue Highways*)

EXERCISE 8

Each of the following sentences has one number error in a noun. Underline each noun in the sentence. Then locate the noun that has the incorrect number and correct it. Be prepared to explain the error and how you corrected it.

1. Donald arrived in New York with three suitcase and his aunt's telephone number.
2. Where is the magazines I lent you last month?
3. The United States has fifty state, one special district, and territories such as the Virgin Islands, Guam, and American Samoa.

4. There are more woman in the American military today than at any time in the past.
5. When Françoise came back from vacation, she was filled with happinesses.
6. The journey of a thousand mile begins with just one step.
7. John F. Kennedy was president of the United States for only three year.
8. Why do so many man say they are superior to women?
9. Most rock-and-roll bands have three guitar and one set of drums.
10. Except for the Native Americans, every American citizens is the descendant of immigrants or slaves.

(b) Using Articles with Nouns

English has two **articles:** *a* and *the.* In some cases *a* is replaced by *an* purely for reasons of sound: if the word that follows begins with a vowel (*a, e, i, o,* or *u*) or a vowel sound, then the *a* is changed to *an* (<u>a</u> book, <u>an</u> apple, <u>an</u> honor). Note that a word may begin with a vowel and still not begin with a vowel sound (<u>a</u> unique event), whereas another word may not begin with a vowel but still begin with a vowel sound (<u>an</u> honest mistake).

The primary function of articles is to signal to the audience whether the noun being referred to is new to the discussion or has already been mentioned.

The indefinite article: *a* Use *a* with a noun when readers have no reason to be familiar with the noun you are naming—when you are introducing the noun for the first time, for example. To say, "The car was in front of <u>a</u> building" signals to the audience that you are introducing the idea of the building into your speech or writing for the first time. The building is *indefinite,* or not specific, until it has first been identified.

The definite article: *the* Use *the* with a noun when readers have already been introduced to the noun you are naming. Use of the *definite* article indicates that the noun introduced may already be familiar to readers. To say, "The car was in front of <u>the</u> building" signals to readers that you are referring to the same building you mentioned earlier. The building has now become specific and may be referred to by the definite article.

 USING ARTICLES WITH NOUNS

There are two main exceptions to the rules governing the use of articles with nouns.

continued on the following page

continued from the previous page

1. Plural nouns do not require indefinite articles: "I love horses," not "I love a horses." (Plural nouns do, however, require definite articles: "I love the horses in the national park near my house.")
2. Noncount nouns may not require articles: "Love conquers all," not "A love conquers all" or "The love conquers all."

EXERCISE 9

In the following passage, underline every noun and circle the article that accompanies it. Do your best to explain why the noun requires that article, or, if there is no article, why it does not require one.

Close about the plaza and the cathedral were the townhouses that intrigued me greatly. These were the homes of the rich, *los ricos*. The high front walls were neatly painted brown, grey, pink, or light cream. The street windows were even with the sidewalk with long iron bars that reached also to the roof. Lace curtains, drapes, and wooden screens behind the bars kept people from looking in. Every townhouse had a *zaguán* and a driveway cutting across the sidewalk, ramped and grooved so the carriages could roll in and out. On hot days the *zaguanes* were left wide open, showing a part of the patios with their fountains, rose gardens, and trees. The walls and the floors of the corridors were decorated with colored tile in solid colors and complicated designs. Between the open *zaguán* and the patio there was the *cancel*, a grill of wrought iron that was always kept closed and locked. (Ernesto Galarza, *Barrio Boy*)

(c) Using Other Determiners with Nouns

Determiners are words that limit or qualify the meaning of nouns. In addition to articles, nouns may be identified by other determiners that function in ways similar to articles, such as **demonstrative pronouns, possessive nouns and pronouns, numbers** (both **cardinal** and **ordinal**), and other words indicating amount and order.

1. **Demonstrative pronouns** (*this, that, these, those*) communicate

   • the relative nearness or farness of the noun from the speaker's position (*this* and *these* for things that are *near, that* and *those* for things that are *far*): *this* book on my desk, *that* book on your desk; *these* shoes on my feet, *those* shoes in my closet

- the *number* of things indicated (*this* and *that* for *singular* nouns, *these* and *those* for *plural* nouns): *this* (or *that*) flower in the vase, *these* (or *those*) flowers in the garden.

2. **Possessive nouns** and **possessive pronouns** (*Ashraf's, his, their*) show who or what the noun belongs to: *Maria's* courage, *everybody's* fears, the *country's* natural resources, *my* personality, *our* groceries.

3. **Cardinal** numbers (*three, fifty, a thousand*) and **ordinal** numbers (*first, tenth, thirtieth*) indicate how many of the noun you mean and in what order the noun appears among other items: *seven* continents, *third* planet.

4. Words other than numbers may indicate **amount** (*many, few*) and **order** (*next, last*) and function in the same ways as cardinal and ordinal numbers: *few* opportunities, *last* chance.

For information on the order of determiners and other modifiers within a sentence, see **B9b**.

B7 Pronouns

Any English noun may be replaced by a **pronoun.** <u>Pronouns</u> enable you to avoid repeating the same noun over and over. For example, *doctor* may be replaced by *he* or *she, books* by *them,* and *computer* by *it.*

See Ch. 24

Pronouns must be in proper grammatical **case:** *subjective, objective,* or *possessive.* (Possessive <u>case</u> in nouns is often indicated by an apostrophe followed by an *s: Philip's* beard, *England's* weather, a *computer's* keyboard. These nouns too can be replaced by pronouns called *possessive pronouns: my, his/her/its, your, their.*)

See 24a

Pronouns must <u>agree</u> with the nouns they replace; that is, they must be the same *number* (singular or plural) and *gender* (male, female, or neuter).

See 26b

Finally, pronouns must clearly <u>refer</u> to the nouns they replace.

See 24c

EXERCISE 10

Underline all the pronouns in the following passage. Identify the noun each pronoun replaces.

In the olden days, both Land and Heaven were tight friends as they were once human-beings. So one day, Heaven came down from heaven to Land his friend and he told him to let them go to the bush and hunt for the bush animals; Land agreed to what Heaven told him. After that they went into a bush with their bows and arrows, but after they had reached the bush, they were hunting for animals from morning till 12 o'clock a.m., but nothing was killed in that bush, then they left that bush and went to a big field and were hunting till 5 o'clock in the evening and nothing was killed there as well. After that, they left there again to go to a forest and it was 7 o'clock before they could find a mouse and started to hunt for another, so that they might share them one by one, because the one they had killed already was too small to share, but they did not kill any more. After that they came back to a certain place with the one they had killed and both of them were thinking how to share it. But as this mouse was too small to divide into two and these friends were also greedy, Land said that he would take it away and Heaven said that he would take it away. (Amos Tutuola, *The Palm-Wine Drunkard*)

EXERCISE 11

There are no pronouns in the following passage. The repetition of the nouns again and again would seem strange to a native speaker of English. Rewrite the passage, replacing as many of the nouns as possible with appropriate pronouns. Be sure that the connection between the pronouns and the nouns they replace is clear.

The young couple seated across from Daniel at dinner the night before were newlyweds from Tokyo. The young couple and Daniel ate together with other guests of the inn at long, low tables in a large dining room with straw mat flooring. The man introduced himself immediately in English, shook Daniel's hand firmly, and, after learning that Daniel was not a tourist but a resident working in Osaka, gave Daniel a business card. The man had just finished college and was working at the man's first real job, clerking in a bank. Even in a sweatsuit, the man looked ready for the office: chin closely shaven, bristly hair neatly clipped, nails clean and buffed. After a while the man and Daniel exhausted the man's store of English and drifted into Japanese.

The man's wife, shy up until then, took over as the man fell silent. The woman and Daniel talked about the new popularity of hot springs spas in the countryside around the inn, the difficulty of finding good schools for the children the woman hoped to have soon, the differences between food in Tokyo and Osaka. The woman's husband ate busily with an air of tolerating the woman's prattling. From time to time the woman refilled the man's beer glass or served the man radish pickles from a china bowl in the middle of the table, and then returned to the conversation.

B8 Verbs

Although verbs in different languages perform similar functions, they differ in form and usage from language to language perhaps more than any other speech or grammatical unit. **Verbs** are words that describe *states of being* or *actions*. Although all languages use verbs to express **states of being**, some languages use two different verbs to describe permanent and impermanent states of being—for example, *ser* and *estar* in Spanish. Other languages use two different verbs to describe animate and inanimate objects—for example, *aru* and *iru* in Japanese. With its single verb *be*, English is in this respect simpler than many other languages.

Languages may also differ in the ways they use verbs to communicate **action.** In Arabic, verbs change form to indicate whether the action they describe is complete or not. In Japanese, verbs can be conjugated to communicate the speaker's feelings about the action of the verb—for example, whether the action was overdone or "too much." Again, because English communicates such concepts in other words, the forms of its action verbs are simpler in these contexts than the forms of action verbs in other languages are.

(a) Tense, Person, and Number

English verbs change their form according to *tense, person,* and *number.* <u>Tense</u> refers to when the action described by the verb takes place. <u>Person</u> refers to who or what is performing the action described by the verb (*I, you, she*), and <u>number</u> refers to how many people or things are performing the action (one or more than one).

See 25b

See 19d

In other languages, verbs may change their appearance according to different rules. In Japanese, for example, verbs are not conjugated according to the person performing the action, but rather according to the social relationship between the speaker and the listener. In Chinese, verbs themselves do not change form to express tense; the time when the action is performed is communicated through other words.

Many <u>irregular</u> English verbs do not change their form according to the usual rules governing tense and person, but instead change in idiosyncratic ways. Unless you use the correct forms of the verbs in your sentences, you will confuse your English-speaking reader by communicating meanings you do not intend.

See 25a2

(b) Subject–Verb Agreement

The **subject** of a verb is the person or thing that performs the action expressed by the verb. Verbs must match, or <u>agree</u> with, their subjects in

See 26a

person (I, you, he) and *number* (he, they) so that in English we say *I read* but *she reads*. Be especially careful with irregular verbs: "I *am*, it *is*, they *are*."

(c) Auxiliary Verbs

Meaning is also communicated in English by **auxiliary verbs** (also known as *helping verbs*), such as forms of the verbs *be* and *have*: "Julio *is taking* a vacation." These auxiliary verbs change form to indicate tense, person, and number: "Julio and Ana *were taking* a vacation." Other auxiliary verbs, called **modal auxiliaries**, include *would, should,* and *can*. Modal auxiliaries do not change form to indicate tense, person, and number: "I *should save* some money"; We *should have saved* some money."

See 23c1

(d) Verb Tense

See 25b

Some nonnative speakers of English use **verb tenses** that are more complicated than they need to be. Such speakers may do this because their native language uses a more complicated tense where English does not, or because they "overcorrect" their verbs into complicated tenses.

See 25c–e

Specifically, nonnative speakers tend to use **progressive** (present and past) verb forms instead of **simple** (present and past) verb forms, and **perfect** (present and past) verb forms instead of simple (present and past) verb forms. To communicate your ideas clearly to an English-speaking audience, you should choose the simplest possible verb tense.

(e) Double Negatives

The meaning of a verb may be made negative in English in a variety of ways, chiefly by adding the words *not* or *does not* to the verb (is, *is not*; can ski, *can't* ski; drives a car, *does not* drive a car).

See 27e

A tendency among nonnative speakers (and some native speakers of English) is the use of the **double negative**. A double negative occurs when the meaning of a verb is negated not just once but twice. In some languages, a double structure is actually required in order to negate a verb; for example, the French phrase "Je ne sais pas" ("I don't know") uses the double structure *ne + pas* around the verb *sais*. However, a double negative is incorrect in English.

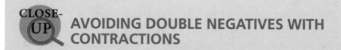

CLOSE-UP AVOIDING DOUBLE NEGATIVES WITH CONTRACTIONS

Be especially careful to avoid using double negatives with contractions that include the word *not*.

continued on the following page

continued from the previous page

> INCORRECT: Henry <u>doesn't</u> have <u>no</u> friends at all.
>
> CORRECT: Henry <u>doesn't</u> have <u>any</u> friends at all.
>
> CORRECT: Henry has <u>no</u> friends at all.
>
> INCORRECT: I looked for articles in the library, but there <u>weren't none</u>.
>
> CORRECT: I looked for articles in the library, but there <u>weren't any</u>.
>
> CORRECT: I looked for articles in the library, but there were <u>none</u>.

(f) Verbs as Nouns and Adjectives

In some cases English verbs may be used as nouns or adjectives, and this can confuse speakers of other languages, particularly if in their native language words do not change their function according to the way they are used in a sentence. Two particular verb forms may be used as nouns: **infinitives** (which always begin with *to*) and **gerunds** (which always end in *ing*). **Present participles** (which also end in *ing*) and **past participles** (which often end in *ed, t,* or *en*) are frequently used as adjectives.

<u>To bite</u> into this steak takes better teeth than mine. (infinitive used as noun)

<u>Cooking</u> is one of my favorite hobbies. (gerund used as noun)

Some people think raw fish is more healthful than <u>cooked</u> fish. (past participle used as adjective)

According to the Bible, God spoke to Moses from a <u>burning</u> bush. (present participle used as adjective)

EXERCISE 12

Identify all the infinitives (*to* _____), gerunds (_____ *ing*), present participles (_____ *ing*), and past participles (_____ *ed*, _____ *t*, _____ *en*) in the following passage. Define their function as either noun or adjective.

The car is the quintessential American possession. The car, not the home, is the center of American life. Despite its central place in the mystique of the American Dream, the individually owned home is actually anti-American in many ways. Owning a car means freedom, progress, and individual initiative, the most basic American values. To own a house means rusting pipes and rotting roof beams. Staying in one place implies stagnation and decay, whereas moving (always "forward") connotes energy, creativity, never-ending youth: "Moss doesn't grow on a rolling stone." And the way Americans move is in their cars, their personalized, self-contained, mobile units.

B9 Adjectives and Adverbs

See 27a

Adjectives and adverbs are words that modify other words, such as nouns and verbs.

See 27b

Adjectives describe the qualities of nouns or modify other adjectives. A book might be *large* or *small, blue* or *red, difficult* or *easy, expensive* or *cheap.* Unlike adjectives in other languages, English adjectives change their form only to indicate degree (*fast, faster, fastest*). In English, adjectives do not have to agree in gender with the noun they describe, as adjectives must in French and German, for example. In Japanese, some adjectives are conjugated in past and present tenses, something English adjectives do not require.

See 27c

Adverbs describe the qualities of verbs and sometimes help describe adjectives, other adverbs, and even whole clauses. Most adverbs in English end in *ly,* making them easily identifiable. A person may walk *slowly* or *quickly, shyly* or *assuredly, elegantly* or *clumsily.*

(a) Position of Adjectives and Adverbs

In Arabic and in Romance languages such as Spanish, French, and Italian, adjectives typically follow the nouns they describe. In other languages, such as Japanese, Chinese, and English, adjectives usually appear before the nouns they describe. A native speaker of English would not say, "Cars red and black are involved in more accidents than cars blue, green, or white," but would say instead, "Red and black cars are involved in more accidents than blue, green, or white cars."

Adverbs may appear before or after the verbs they describe, but they should be placed as close to the verb as possible: not "I *told* John that I couldn't meet him for lunch *politely,*" but "I *politely told* John that I couldn't meet him for lunch" or "I *told* John *politely* that I couldn't meet him for lunch." When an adverb modifies an adjective, it usually comes before the adjective: "The logic is *basically sound.*"

EXERCISE 13

Each sentence below is followed by a list of adjectives and adverbs that can be used in the sentence. Place the adjectives and adverbs where they belong in each sentence. (Adjectives and adverbs are listed in the order in which they should appear in the sentences.)

1. Researchers believe that tests are not reliable. (most, now, IQ, entirely)
2. Just as culture is derived from Greece, culture is derived from China. (European, ancient, Asian, ancient)
3. According to the Japanese proverb, for a lid there's a pot. (old, cracked, chipped)
4. The people of Louisiana play a music called zydeco. (Cajun, southern, lively)
5. When you begin to exercise, start and build up to levels. (slowly, steadily, strenuous)
6. Because I transferred credits from my school, I was able to graduate. (many, previous, early)
7. Signers of the Declaration of Independence, which proclaimed the rights of people, owned slaves. (many, American, "unalienable," all, African)
8. Often, feminists feel they are describing the condition of women in the world, when they are describing women in America. (too, American, all, really, only)
9. I work hours on essays, but I remember to take breaks. (usually, many, periodic)
10. The word can have meanings in contexts. (same, different, different)

(b) Adjectives in a Series

A single noun may be modified by more than one adjective, perhaps even by a whole list of adjectives in a row. Given a list of three or four modifiers, most native speakers would arrange them in a sentence in the same order. If shoes are to be described as *green* and *big*, numbering *two*, and of the type worn for playing *tennis*, a native speaker would say "two big green tennis shoes." However, determining the order in which these modifiers should be listed before the noun can be troublesome for speakers of languages other than English.

Generally, the modifiers that are most important in completing the meaning of the noun are placed closest to that noun. For example, the most important fact in characterizing the shoes described above is that they are tennis shoes; their size and color are less important. Details about size generally precede details about color and texture. Details about number nearly always precede all others.

Another way of determining the correct order of modifiers is to make sure that each word describes all the words that follow. For example, in the phrase *fat black cat, black* describes *cat*, whereas *fat* describes *black cat*.

 ORDER OF MODIFIERS

1. articles (*a, the*), demonstratives (*this, those*), and possessives (*his, our, Maria's, everybody's*)
2. amounts (*one, five, many, few*), order (*first, next, last*)
3. personal opinions (*nice, ugly, crowded, pitiful*)
4. sizes and shapes (*small, tall, straight, crooked*)
5. age (*young, old, modern, ancient*)
6. colors (*black, white, red, blue, dark, light*)
7. nouns functioning as adjectives to form a unit with the noun (*soccer* ball, *cardboard* box, *history* class)

 EXERCISE 14

Write five original sentences in which two or three adjectives describe one noun. Be sure that the adjectives are in the right order.

 B10 **Prepositions**

See
23f

In English, **prepositions** (such as *to, at, from, with,* and *between*) give meaning to nouns by linking them with other words and other parts of the sentence: "I got a book *of* poetry *for* my birthday." **Prepositions** convey several different kinds of information.

- relations of **time** (*at* nine o'clock, *in* five minutes, *for* a month)
- relations of **place** (*in* the classroom, *at* the library, *beside* the chair) and **direction** (*to* the market, *onto* the stage, *toward* the freeway)
- relations of **association** (go *with* someone, the tip *of* the iceberg)
- relations of **purpose** (working *for* money, dieting *to* lose weight)

Learning to use prepositions correctly may cause problems for speakers of languages other than English. Prepositions may be used in quite different ways in other languages, or may exist in forms quite different from English, or may not exist at all.

For speakers of languages with prepositions very similar to those in English, there are different problems. Because speakers of Romance languages such as Italian and Romanian use prepositions in ways very similar to English, speakers of these languages may be tempted to translate prepositional phrases from their own languages directly into English, though idiomatic uses of prepositions can vary widely.

 PREPOSITIONS IN IDIOMATIC EXPRESSIONS

Nonnative speakers of English may have trouble with prepositions in the following expressions.

Common nonnative speaker usage	*Native speaker usage*
according *with*	according *to*
apologize *at*	apologize *to*
appeal *at*	appeal *to*
apply *with*	apply *to*
believe *at*	believe *in*
different *to*	different *from*
for least, *for* most	*at* least, *at* most
refer *at*	refer *to*
relevant *with*	relevant *to*
similar *with*	similar *to*
subscribe *with*	subscribe *to*

Remember also that more than one preposition may be combined with a given word, but the combinations create different expressions with different meanings.

agree *with*, agree *to*
care *for*, take care *of*
from the beginning, *at* the beginning
look *for*, look *at*, look *after*
talk *to*, talk *with*
to the end, *at* the end
unfamiliar *with*, unfamiliar *to*

There is one construction incorporating a preposition that is peculiar to English. Infinitive forms of verbs are formed in English by adding *to* to the base form of the verb: *to write, to read, to sleep, to eat*. When these verbs are combined with other verbs, confusion may result. In the sentence, "Ali is learning to read Braille," *to* is part of the verb *read,* not part of the verb *learning.* Thus, a native speaker would know to say, "Ali is learning Braille," not "Ali is learning to Braille," but a nonnative speaker might not.

EXERCISE 15

Identify as many prepositions as you can in the following passage. Note their position and their use. How might similar information be communicated in your native language?

In retrospect, the distinguishing feature of the post-World War II era was its remarkable affluence. From 1950 through 1970, by fits and starts, the American Gross National Product grew at an average annual rate of 3.9 percent, perhaps the best performance in the nation's history. Autos, chemicals, and electrically powered consumer durables were the leading sectors driving the economy forward in the 1950s; housing, aerospace, and the computer industry, in the 1960s. In consequence, the average American commanded 50 percent more real income at the end of the period than at the beginning. Exuberant growth and dramatic changes in the standard of living were hardly novel in the American experience, and it was possible to view postwar economic developments as a mere extension of historic trends. But in one crucial respect the era was indeed different. Past increases in real income had mainly purchased improvements in the necessities of life—more and better food, clothing, shelter. After 1950 rising income meant that the mass of Americans, including many blue-collar workers, could, for the first time, enjoy substantial amounts of discretionary income—i.e., income spent not for essentials but for amenities. (Allen J. Matusow, *The Unraveling of America*)

EXERCISE 16

In the following passage, provide appropriate prepositions in the positions indicated.

Everyone knows what is supposed to happen when two Englishmen who have never met before come face _____ face _____ a railway compartment—they start talking _____ the weather. _____ some cases this may simply be because they happen to find the subject interesting. Most people, though, are not particularly interested _____ analyses _____ climatic conditions, so there must be other reasons _____ conversations _____ this kind. One explanation is that it can often be quite embarrassing to be alone _____ the company _____ someone you are not acquainted _____ and *not* speak to them. If no conversation takes place the atmosphere can become rather strained. However, by talking _____ the other person _____ some neutral topic like the weather, it is possible to strike up a relationship _____ him without actually having to say very much. Railway compartment conversations _____ this kind—and they do happen, although not of course as often as the popular myth supposes—are good examples of the sort _____ important social function that is often fulfilled _____ language. Language is not simply a means of communicating information _____ the weather or any other subject. It is also a very important means _____ establishing and maintaining relationships _____ other people. (Adapted from Peter Trudgill, *Sociolinguistics: An Introduction to Language and Society*)

B11 Word Order

(a) Standard Word Order

The importance of word order varies from language to language. In English, word order is extremely important, contributing a good deal to the meaning of a sentence. Like Chinese, English is an "SVO" language, or one in which the most typical sentence pattern is "subject-verb-object." (Arabic, by contrast, is a "VSO" language.) A native speaker of English will understand that in the sentence "Dog bites man," the dog is doing the biting and the man is getting bitten, whereas in the sentence "Man bites dog," the opposite is true.

Of course, there is some flexibility in the word order of English sentences. For example, modifying words, such as adjectives and adverbs (or phrases that function as adjectives or adverbs), may be placed in various positions in a sentence, depending upon the sentence's intended emphasis or meaning.

(b) Word Order in Questions

Word order in questions can be particularly troublesome for speakers of languages other than English, partly because there are so many different ways to form questions in English. For sentences using the verb *be*, simply inverting the order of the subject and verb creates a question that elicits a *yes* or *no* answer:

> Rasheem *is researching* the depletion of the ozone layer.
>
> *Is Rasheem researching* the depletion of the ozone layer?

Inverting the subject and verb and then using a negative form of the verb can indicate that the person asking the question thinks that the answer to the question is probably *yes*.

> *Isn't Rasheem researching* the depletion of the ozone layer?

To ask for more information, you can use an interrogative word as well as invert the subject and verb.

> *What* is Rasheem researching?
>
> *Why* is Rasheem researching the depletion of the ozone layer?

To create a yes/no question from a statement using a verb other than *be*, you can use a form of the auxiliary verb *do* before the sentence without inverting the subject and verb.

> *Does* Rasheem want to research the depletion of the ozone layer?
>
> *Do* Rasheem's friends want to help him with his research?
>
> *Did* Rasheem's professor approve his research proposal?

You can also form a question by adding a **tag question** to the end of a declarative sentence.

> Rasheem is researching the depletion of the ozone layer, *isn't he?*
>
> Rasheem will write his dissertation about the depletion of the ozone layer, *won't he?*

EXERCISE 17

Write five declarative sentences. Then write as many questions as you can based on each one. Pay particular attention to the word order of the questions.

B12 Common Sentence Errors

Even native speakers of English make errors in their writing—in particular, common errors such as **sentence fragments, comma splices, fused sentences,** and excessive or unnecessary passive constructions.

For information on some of the most common sentence errors in English, see **Chapter 15,** "Revising Sentence Fragments"; **Chapter 16,** "Revising Comma Splices and Fused Sentences"; and **25j,** "Changing from Passive to Active Voice."

GLOSSARY

GLOSSARY OF USAGE

This glossary of usage lists words and phrases that often present problems for writers.

a, an   Use *a* before words that begin with consonants or words that have initial vowels that sound like consonants.

> *a* primitive artifact   *a* one-horse carriage

Use *an* before words that begin with vowels and words that begin with a silent *h*.

> *an* aqueous solution   *an* honest person

accept, except   *Accept* is a verb that means to "to receive." *Except* is a preposition or conjunction that means "other than." As a verb *except* means "to leave out."

> The auditors will *accept* all your claims *except* the last two.

> Aliens who have lived in the United States for more than five years are *excepted* from the regulation.

advice, advise   *Advice* is a noun meaning "opinion or information offered." *Advise* is a verb that means "to offer advice to."

> The king sent a messenger to the oracle to ask for *advice.*

> The broker *advised* her client to stay away from speculative stocks.

affect, effect   *Affect* is a verb meaning "to influence." *Effect* can be a verb or a noun. As a verb it means "to bring about," and as a noun it means "result."

> A severe cutback in federal funds for student loans could *affect* his plans for graduate school.

> The arbitrator tried to *effect* a settlement that would satisfy both the teachers and the school board.

> The most notable *effect* of the German bombing of London was to strengthen the resolve of the British.

afraid, frightened   See **frightened, afraid.**

aggravate, irritate   *Aggravate* means "to worsen." *Irritate* means "to annoy." Avoid using *aggravate* as a colloquial term for *irritate.*

> The malfunction of the computer system *irritated* the project leaders, who worried that the breakdown would *aggravate* an already tense situation.

all ready, already   *All ready* means "wholly prepared." *Already* means "by or before this or that time."

> During the thirties President Roosevelt made the country feel that it was *all ready* for any challenge that might confront it.

> By the time Horatius decided to call for help, it was *already* too late.

all right, alright   Although there is a tendency in the direction of *alright*, current usage calls for *all right.*

allusion, illusion   An *allusion* is a reference or hint. In literature it is a brief reference to a person, place, historical event, or other literary work with which a reader is expected to be familiar. An *illusion* is something that is not what it seems.

> In *The Catcher in the Rye* the main character makes an *allusion* to *The Return of the Native,* a novel by Thomas Hardy.

> The *Viking* landing proved that the canals of Mars are an *illusion* caused by atmospheric and topographical conditions.

a lot   *A lot* is always two words. It is used colloquially as a substitute for "many" or "a great deal."

although, while   Do not use *while* for *although* if there is any chance of confusion.

> *Although* (not *while*) Ellen hurt her foot, Amy continued going to aerobics class.

a.m., p.m   Use these abbreviations after specific times, never as synonyms for *morning* or *evening.*

> Tomorrow I have to get up early in the *morning* (not *in the a.m.*).

among, between   *Among* refers to groups of more than two things. *Between* refers to just two things.

> The three parties agreed *among* themselves to settle the question out of court.

> By the time of his death in 323 BC, Alexander's empire included all the territory *between* Macedon and India.

amoral, immoral   *Amoral* means "neither moral nor immoral" or "not having a sense of morality." *Immoral* means "contrary to or against existing morality."

Wolf Larson, the main character in Jack London's *The Sea-Wolf*, is *amoral.*

White-collar crime is *immoral.*

amount, number   *Amount* refers to a quantity that cannot be counted. *Number* refers to things that can be counted. Always use *number* when referring to groups of people.

Because he had missed several payments, the bank called in the full *amount* of the loan.

Seeing their commander fall, a large *number* of troops ran to his aid.

an, a   See **a, an.**

and/or   In business or technical writing, use *and/or* when either or both of the items it connects can apply. In college writing, however, the use of *and/or* should generally be avoided.

The data recorder can print *and/or* display the temperature.

ante-, anti-   *Ante-* is a prefix meaning "before." *Anti-* is a prefix meaning "opposing" or "against." Use a hyphen with *anti-* when it precedes a capital letter or a word beginning with *i.*

A pronoun must point clearly to its *antecedent.*

During the 1950s many innocent people were accused of being *anti-American.*

apt to, liable to, likely to   *Apt to* implies a natural tendency. *Liable to* implies that something undesirable is about to occur. *Likely to* suggests a strong chance that something might happen.

Old books are *apt to* increase in value if you protect them from heat and moisture.

If we do not do something to correct the poor drainage in this area, we are *liable to* have a repeat of last year's flooding.

Medical researchers feel that in fifty years human beings are *likely to* have a life span of more than a hundred years.

as . . . as . . .   In such constructions, *as* signals a comparison; therefore, you must use the second *as.*

AWKWARD: John Steinbeck's *East of Eden* is as long if not longer than *The Grapes of Wrath.*

CLEAR: John Steinbeck's *East of Eden* is *as* long *as* if not longer than *The Grapes of Wrath.*

as, like   *As* can be used as a conjunction or a preposition. As a conjunction, *as* is used to introduce a complete clause.

In *The Scarlet Letter* Hawthorne uses imagery *as* (not *like*) he does in his other works.

When used as a preposition, *as* indicates equivalency or identity.

> After classes he works *as* a manager of a fast-food restaurant.

Like should be used as a preposition only. It indicates resemblance but never identity.

> Writers *like* Carl Sandburg appear once in a generation.

as, than   When making comparisons, either objective or subjective case pronouns can follow *as* or *than*. To determine case, you must know whether the things being compared are subjects or objects of verbs. A simple way to test this is to add the missing verb.

> Nassim was as tall *as* he (is tall).

> I have walked farther *than* he (has walked).

> I like Jim more *than* (I like) *him*. (*Him* is the object of the missing verb *like*.)

assure, ensure, insure   *Assure* means "to tell confidently or to promise." *Ensure* and *insure* can be used interchangeably to mean "to make certain." Always use *insure* (not *ensure*) to mean "to protect people or property against loss."

> Caeser wished to *assure* the people that if they surrendered, he would not plunder their city.

> To *ensure* (or *insure*) the smooth operation of the mechanism, you should oil it every six months.

> It is extremely expensive for physicians to *insure* themselves against malpractice suits.

at, to   Many people use the prepositions *at* and *to* after *where* in conversation. These prepositions should not be used in this context in college writing.

> **Colloquial:** *Where* are you working *at?*
> *Where* are you going *to?*

> **Revised:** Where are you working?
> Where are you going?

bad, badly   *Bad* is an adjective, and *badly* is an adverb.

> The school board decided that *Huckleberry Finn* was a *bad* book and deleted it from the high school reading list.

> For the past five years American automobile makers have been doing *badly*.

After verbs that refer to any of the senses or any other linking verb, use the adjective form.

> He looked *bad*. He felt *bad*. It seemed *bad*.

being as, being that   These awkward phrases, used colloquially to mean "because," add unnecessary words and weaken your writing.

Because (not *being that*) the climate was getting colder, a great number of animals migrated south.

beside, besides   *Beside* is a preposition meaning "next to" and occasionally "apart from." *Besides* can be either a preposition or an adverb. As a preposition, *besides* means "except" or "other than." As an adverb it means "in addition to."

Beside the tower was a wall that ran the length of the old section of the city.

The judge pointed out to the lawyer that his argument was *beside* the point.

Besides its industrial uses, laser technology has many other applications.

Edison invented not only the lightbulb and the ticker tape, but the phonograph *besides*.

between, among   See **among, between.**

bring, take   *Bring* means to transport from a farther place to a nearer place. *Take* means to transport from a nearer place to a farther place.

In the late nineteenth century many immigrants were able to *bring* to this country only the clothes they wore.

Take this message to the general and wait for a reply.

but, however, yet   *But, however,* and *yet* should be used alone, not in combination.

She thought her essay was adequate, *but* (not *but yet* or *but however*) she continued to revise.

can, may   *Can* denotes ability, and *may* indicates permission.

Can (are they *able* to?) first-year students participate in the work-study program?

May (do they have permission to?) registered aliens collect unemployment benefits?

capital, capitol   *Capital* is a noun meaning "the official seat of government." *Capitol* means "a building in which the legislature meets" or (capitalized) "the building in which the US Congress meets."

Washington, DC, is the *capital* of the United States. When we were there, we visited the *Capitol*.

censor, censure   To *censor* is to label as undesirable passages of books, plays, films, news broadcasts, essays, etc. To *censure* is to condemn or criticize harshly.

Many recording artists are concerned that their albums will be *censored*.

In 1633 Galileo was *censured* by the Inquisition for holding that the sun was the center of the universe.

center around   This common colloquialism is acceptable in speech and informal writing but not in college writing.

The report *centers on* (not *around*) the effects of cigarette smoking on the circulatory system.

cite, site   *Cite* is a verb meaning "to quote an authority" or "to mention as support or as an example." *Site* is a noun meaning "a place or setting."

Jeff *cited* five sources in his research paper.

The builder cleared the *site* for the new bank.

climactic, climatic   *Climactic*, derived from *climax*, means "building to a climax." *Climatic* means "of or related to climate."

The *climactic* moment of the movie occurred when the tornado passed right over the heads of the main characters.

If scientists are correct, the *climatic* conditions of earth are changing.

coarse, course   *Coarse* is an adjective meaning "inferior" or "having a rough, uneven texture." *Course* is a noun meaning "a route or path," "an area on which a sport is played," or "a unit of study."

Coarse sandpaper is used to smooth out the surface.

The *course* of true love never runs smoothly.

Last semester I had to drop one of my *courses*.

compare to, compare with   *Compare to* means "to liken to" or "to represent as similar." *Compare with* means "to examine to find ways in which two things are similar or different."

Let me *compare* you *to* a summer's day.

Jane *compared* the Cézanne painting at the Philadelphia Museum of Art *with* the one at the Barnes Foundation.

complement, compliment   *Complement* means "to complete or add to." *Compliment* means "to give praise."

A double-blind study would *complement* their preliminary work on this anticancer drug.

Before accepting the 1949 Nobel Prize for literature, William Faulkner *complimented* the people of Sweden for their courtesy and kindness.

conscious, conscience   *Conscious* means "having one's mental faculties awake." *Conscience* is the moral sense of right and wrong.

With a local anesthetic a patient remains *conscious* during the procedure.

During the American Civil War, the Copperheads followed the dictates of *conscience* and refused to fight.

consensus "Consensus of opinion" is redundant because *consensus* means an "agreement of the majority." Write "they reached a consensus," or use "they agreed" or "the majority view was."

continual, continuous *Continual* means "recurring at intervals." *Continuous* refers to an action that occurs without interruption.

A pulsar is a star that emits a *continual* stream of electromagnetic radiation. (It emits radiation at regular intervals.)

A small battery allows the watch to run *continuously* for five years. (It runs without stopping.)

could of, would of In speech, the contractions *could've* and *would've* sound like the nonstandard constructions *could of* and *would of*. Spell out *could have* and *would have* in college writing.

Macbeth *would have* (not *would of*) defied his wife if he *could have* (not *could of*).

council, counsel A *council* is "a body of people who serve in a legislative or advisory capacity." *Counsel* means "advice" or "guidance." A *counselor* is "a person who counsels" or "a lawyer."

The city *council* argued about whether to ban smoking in all municipal buildings.

The judge *counseled* the couple to seek the help of a marriage *counselor*.

couple of *Couple* means "a pair," but *a couple of* is a vague expression that means "several" or "a few." In your college writing, specify "four points," "three reasons," or "two examples" rather than "a couple of."

criterion, criteria *Criteria*, from the Greek, is the plural of *criterion*, meaning "standard for judgment."

Of all the *criteria* for hiring graduating seniors, class rank is the most important *criterion*.

data *Data* is the plural of the Latin *datum*, meaning "fact." In everyday speech and writing *data* is used for both singular and plural. In college writing, however, you should preserve the distinction.

The *data* discussed in this section *are* summarized in the graph in Appendix A.

different from, different than *Different than* is used extensively in American speech. In college writing, use *different from*.

His test scores were not much *different from* (not *than*) mine.

discreet, discrete *Discreet* means "careful or prudent." *Discrete* means "separate or individually distinct."

Because Madame Bovary was not *discreet,* her reputation suffered.

Current research has demonstrated that atoms can be broken into hundreds of *discrete* particles.

disinterested, uninterested　*Disinterested* means "objective" or "capable of making an impartial judgment." *Uninterested* means "indifferent or unconcerned."

The narrator of Ernest Hemingway's "A Clean, Well-Lighted Place" is a *disinterested* observer of the action.

Finding no treasure after leading an expedition from Florida to Oklahoma, Hernando de Soto was *uninterested* in going farther.

don't, doesn't　*Don't* is the contraction of *do not. Doesn't* is the contraction of *does not.* Do not confuse the two.

My dog *doesn't* (not *don't*) like to walk in the rain.

due to the fact that　*Due to the fact that* is a wordy substitute for *because.*

Classes were cancelled *because* (not *due to the fact that*) it snowed.

effect, affect　See **affect, effect.**

e.g.　*E.g.* is a Latin abbreviation meaning "for example" or "for instance." In college writing do not use *e.g.* Instead, use its English equivalent.

The colonists faced many hardships—*for example* (not *e.g.*), disease and drought.

emigrate, immigrate　*To emigrate* is "to leave one's country and settle in another." *To immigrate* is "to come to another country and reside there." The noun forms of these words are *emigrant* and *immigrant.*

In 1887 my great-grandfather *emigrated* from the Russian city of Minsk and traveled by ship to Boston. During that year many other *emigrants* made the same trip.

The potato famine of 1846–47 caused many Irish to *immigrate* to the United States. These *immigrants* became builders, politicians, and storekeepers.

eminent, imminent　*Eminent* is an adjective meaning "standing above others" or "prominent." *Imminent* means "about to occur."

Oliver Wendell Holmes, Jr., was an *eminent* jurist.

In ancient times, a comet signaled *imminent* disaster.

ensure, assure, insure　See **assure, ensure, insure.**

enthused　*Enthused,* a colloquial form of *enthusiastic,* should never be used in college writing.

President John F. Kennedy was *enthusiastic* (not *enthused*) about the US space program.

especially, specially   *Especially* means "particularly" or "very." *Specially* means "for a particular reason or purpose."

He was *especially* proud of his daughter's athletic abilities when he learned a scholarship had been created in her honor. The *specially* created college scholarship was earmarked for athletically gifted women.

etc.   *Etc.*, the abbreviation of *et cetera*, means "and the rest." Do not use it in your college writing. Instead, write "and so on" or, better, specify exactly what *etc.* stands for.

UNCLEAR: Before beginning to draft your research paper, you should have paper and pencil, *etc.*

REVISED: Before beginning to draft your research paper, you should have a pencil or pen, paper, and your note cards.

everyday, every day   *Everyday* is an adjective that means "ordinary" or "commonplace." *Every day* means "occurring daily."

In the *Gettysburg Address,* Lincoln used *everyday* words to create a model of clarity and conciseness.

In *The Canterbury Tales* Chaucer describes a group of pilgrims who tell stories *every day* as they ride from London to Canterbury.

everyone, every one   *Everyone* is an indefinite pronoun meaning "every person." *Every one* means "every individual or thing in a particular group."

Everyone seems happier in the spring.

Every one of these packages had been opened.

except, accept   See **accept, except.**

explicit, implicit   *Explicit* means "expressed or stated directly." *Implicit* means "implied" or "expressed or stated indirectly."

The director *explicitly* warned the actors to be on time for rehearsals.

Her *implicit* message was that lateness would be grounds for dismissal from the play.

farther, further   *Farther* designates distance, and *further* designates degree.

I have traveled *farther* from my hometown than any of my relatives.

Critics of the welfare system charge that government subsidies to the poor encourage *further* dependence.

fewer, less   Use *fewer* with nouns that can be counted: *fewer* books, *fewer* people, *fewer* dollars. Use *less* with quantities that cannot be counted: *less* pain, *less* power, *less* enthusiasm.

figuratively, literally   *Literally* means "following the letter" or "in a strict sense." *Figuratively* means "metaphorically" or "not literally."

Literally, the Declaration of Independence is a list of grievances that the English colonists had against their king. *Figuratively,* the Declaration of Independence is a document that elevates the rights of common people above the divine right of kings.

firstly (secondly, thirdly, . . .)   Archaic forms meaning "in the first . . . second . . . third place." Use *first, second, third.*

former   *Former* as an adjective means "preceding" or "previous." As a noun it means "the first of two things mentioned previously" and is often used in conjunction with *latter.*

The *former* residents of this area, the Delaware Indians, were forced to cede their land in 1795.

Two books mark the extremes of Herman Melville's career: *Typee* and *Moby-Dick.* The *former* was a best-seller; the *latter* was generally ignored by the public.

further, farther   See **farther, further.**

good, well   *Good* is an adjective, never an adverb.

The townspeople thought the proposal for a new municipal water plant was a *good* one.

Well can function as an adverb or an adjective. As an adverb it means "in a good manner": "He did *well* (not *good*) on the test" and "She swam *well* (not *good*) in the meet."

Well is used as an adjective with verbs that denote a state of being or feeling. Here *well* can mean "in good health": "I feel *well.*"

good and . . .   This colloquial phrase meaning "very" is not appropriate in college writing.

After escaping from the Iroquois, Natty Bumppo was *very* (not *good and*) tired.

got to   *Got to* is not suitable in college writing. To indicate obligation use *have to, has to,* or *must.*

COLLOQUIAL: Anyone who takes a literature course has *got to* get a copy of *A Glossary of Literary Terms* by M. H. Abrams.

REVISED: Anyone who takes a literature course *has to* get a copy of *A Glossary of Literary Terms* by M. H. Abrams.

hanged, hung   Both *hanged* and *hung* are past participles of *hang. Hanged* is used to refer to executions. *Hung* is used in all other senses meaning "suspended" or "held up."

Billy Budd was *hanged* from the mainyard of the ship for killing the master-at-arms.

The pictures in the National Gallery were *hung* to take advantage of the natural lighting in the various rooms.

he, she Traditionally *he* has been used in the generic sense to refer to both males and females. To acknowledge the equality of the sexes, however, avoid the generic *he*. Use plural pronouns whenever possible.

TRADITIONAL: Before registering, *each student* should be sure *he* has received *his* student number.

REVISED: Before registering, *students* should receive *their* student numbers.

hopefully The adverb *hopefully* should modify a verb, an adjective, or another adverb.

During the 1930s many of the nation's jobless looked *hopefully* to the federal government for relief. (*Hopefully* modifies *looked*.)

Do not use *hopefully* as a sentence modifier meaning "it is hoped."

AMBIGUOUS: *Hopefully,* scientists will discover a cure for AIDS within the next five years. (Who is hopeful? Scientists or the writer?)

REVISED: Scientists *hope* they will discover a cure for AIDS within the next five years.

however See **but, however, yet.**

if, whether When asking indirect questions or expressing doubt, use *whether*.

He asked *whether* (not *if*) the flight would be delayed because of the fog.

The attendant was not sure *whether* (not *if*) the fog would delay the flight.

Use *whether* or *not* when expressing alternatives.

He did not know *whether or not* to change his travel plans.

illusion, allusion See **allusion, illusion.**

immigrate to, emigrate from See **emigrate from, immigrate to.**

implicit, explicit See **explicit, implicit.**

imply, infer *Imply* means "to hint" or "to suggest." *Infer* means "to conclude from." When you *imply,* you *send out* a suggestion; when you *infer,* you *receive* or draw a conclusion.

Mark Antony *implied* that Brutus and the other conspirators had wrongfully killed Julius Caesar. The crowd *inferred* his meaning and called for the punishment of the conspirators.

in, into Use *in* when you want to indicate position. Use *into* when you want to indicate motion to a point within a thing.

As he stood *in* the main burial vault of the tomb of Tutankhamen, Howard Carter saw a wealth of artifacts.

Before he walked *into* the cave, Tom Sawyer grasped Becky Thatcher's hand.

In 1828 Russia and Persia entered *into* the Treaty of Turkmanchai.

infer, imply See **imply, infer.**

ingenious, ingenuous *Ingenious* means "clever at inventing or organizing." *Ingenuous* means "open" or "artless."

Ludwig van Beethoven is recognized as one of the most *ingenious* composers who ever lived.

For a politician the mayor was surprisingly *ingenuous.*

inside of, outside of *Of* is unnecessary when *inside* and *outside* are used as prepositions.

He waited *inside* (not *inside of*) the coffee shop.

Inside of is colloquial in references to time.

He could run a mile in *under* (not *inside of*) eight minutes.

insure, ensure, assure See **assure, ensure, insure.**

irregardless, regardless *Irregardless* is a nonstandard version of *regardless.* The suffix *-less* means "without" or "free from," so the negative prefix *ir-* is unnecessary.

Regardless (not *irregardless*) of what some people might think, drunk drivers kill more than twenty-five thousand people a year.

irritate, aggravate See **aggravate, irritate.**

is when, is where These constructions are often incorrectly used in definitions.

A play-off *is* an additional game played (not *"is when an additional game is played. . . ."*) to establish the winner of a tie.

its, it's *Its* is a possessive pronoun. *It's* is a contraction of *it is.*

The most obvious characteristic of a modern corporation is the separation of *its* management from *its* ownership.

It's not often that you see a collection of rare books such as the one housed in the Library of Congress.

-ize, -wise The suffix *-ize* is used to change nouns and adjectives into verbs: *civilize, industrialize, immunize.* The suffix *-wise* is used to change a noun or adjective into an adverb: *likewise, otherwise.* Some people use these suffixes carelessly, making up words as they please: *prioritize, tastewise, weatherwise,* and *policywise,* for example. Be sure to look up suspect *-ize* and *-wise* words in the dictionary to be sure they are standard forms.

kind of, sort of *Kind of* and *sort of* to mean "rather" or "somewhat" are colloquial and should not be used in college writing.

COLLOQUIAL: The countess was surprised to see that Napoleon was *kind of* short.

REVISED: The countess was surprised to see that Napoleon was *rather* short.

Reserve *kind of* and *sort of* for occasions when you categorize.

Willie Stark, a character of Robert Penn Warren's *All the King's Men,* is the *kind of* man who begins by meaning well and ends by being corrupted by his success.

lay, lie *Lay* is a transitive verb (one that takes an object) meaning "to put" or "to place."

Base Form	Past	Past Participle	Present Participle
lay	laid	laid	laying

The Federalist Papers *lay* the foundation for the American conservative movement.

In October of 1781 the British *laid* down their arms and surrendered to George Washington at Yorktown.

After he had *laid* his money on the counter, he walked out of the restaurant.

We watched the Amish stonemasons *laying* a wall without using mortar.

Lie is an intransitive verb (one that does not take an object) that means "to recline."

Base Form	Past	Past Participle	Present Participle
lie	lay	lain	lying

Each afternoon she would *lie* in the sun and listen to the surf.

As I Lay Dying is a novel by William Faulkner.

In 1871 Heinrich Schliemann unearthed the city of Troy, which had *lain* undisturbed for two thousand years.

The painting *Odalisque* by Eugene Delacroix shows a nude *lying* on a couch.

leave, let *Leave* means "to go way from" or "to let remain." *Let* means "to allow" or "to permit."

Many missionaries were forced to *leave* China after the Communist revolution in 1948.

As the liquid boils away, it will *leave* a dark brown precipitate at the bottom of the flask.

In London it is illegal to *let* dogs foul the footpath.

less, fewer See **fewer, less.**

let, leave See **leave, let.**

liable to   See **apt to, liable to, likely to.**

lie, lay   See **lay, lie.**

like, as   See **as, like.**

likely to   See **apt to, liable to, likely to.**

literally, figuratively   See **figuratively, literally.**

loose, lose   *Loose* is an adjective meaning "not rigidly fastened or se-
curely attached." *Lose* is a verb meaning "to misplace."

The marble facing of the building became *loose* and fell to the sidewalk.

After only two drinks, most people *lose* their ability to judge distance.

lots, lots of, a lot of   These words are colloquial substitutes for "many,"
"much," or "a great deal of." Avoid their use in college writing.

The students had several (not *lots of* or *a lot of*) options for essay topics.

When using these words informally, be careful to use correct subject-
verb agreement.

There are (not *is*) *lots of* possible topics.

majority, plurality   *Majority* denotes more than half. *Plurality* means a
larger number but not necessarily a majority. A candidate with a *majority* has over 50 percent of the votes cast. A candidate with a *plurality* has more votes than any of the other candidates, but not over 50
percent of the total. Use *most* rather than *majority* when you do not
know the exact numbers.

INCORRECT: The soprano got the *majority* of the applause.

REVISED: The soprano got *most* of the applause.

man   Like the generic pronoun *he, man* has been used in English to denote members of both sexes. This usage is being replaced by *human
beings, people,* or similar terms that do not specify gender.

The dinosaur was extinct long before *human beings* (not *man*) walked
the earth.

may, can   See **can, may.**

may, might   The distinction between the two modal auxiliaries *may* and
might is a subtle one. Use *may* to express a probable condition and
might to express a less likely one.

I *may* vote on Tuesday. (I probably will vote.)

I *might* vote on Tuesday. (It is possible, but not very likely.)

may be, maybe   *May be* is a verb phrase. *Maybe* is an adverb meaning
"perhaps."

She *may be* older than the other students, but she is more enthusiastic
than they are.

Maybe her experience in the corporate world will give her an advantage in the management courses.

medium, media   *Medium,* meaning a "means of conveying or broadcasting something," is singular. *Media* is the plural form.

Television has replaced print and film as the *medium* of communication that has the most profound effect on our lives.

A good business presentation uses a number of different *media* to make its point.

might, may   See **may, might.**

might have, might of   *Might of* is a nonstandard construction, not the written form for the contraction of *might have.*

John F. Kennedy *might have* (not *might of*) been a great president had he not been assassinated.

number, amount   See **amount, number.**

OK, O.K., okay   All three spellings are acceptable, but this term should be avoided in college writing. Use a more specific word or words instead.

The instructor's lecture was *adequate* (not *okay*), if uninspiring.

on account of   Use *because of.*

The computer malfunctioned *because of* (not *on account of*) a faulty circuit board.

outside of, inside of   See **inside of, outside of.**

passed, past   *Passed* is the past tense of the verb *pass. Past* means "belonging to a former time" or "no longer current."

The car must have been doing eighty when it *passed* us.

In the envelope was a bill marked "*past* due."

percent, percentage   *Percent* indicates a part of a hundred when a specific number is referred to: "10 *percent* of his weekly salary"; "5 *percent* of the monthly rent." *Percentage* is used when no specific number is referred to: "a *percentage* of the people"; "a *percentage* of next year's receipts." In technical and business writing it is permissible to use the percent sign (%) after percentages you are comparing. Write out *percent* in college writing.

phenomenon, phenomena   A *phenomenon* is a single observable fact or event. It can also refer to a rare or significant occurrence. *Phenomena* is the plural form.

Metamorphosis is a *phenomenon* that occurs in many insects, mollusks, amphibians, and fish.

Solar eclipses are celestial *phenomena* that have been regarded with awe and terror and were once seen as omens of unfavorable events.

plenty   *Plenty,* when used as a noun followed by *of,* means "abundance" or "a large amount." Avoid using *plenty* as a colloquial substitute for "very" or "quite."

There are *plenty* of benefits to recycling plastic.

Recycling can be *quite* (not *plenty*) time consuming, but it is well worth the trouble.

plus   As a preposition, *plus* means "in addition to." Avoid using *plus* as a substitute for *and.*

Include the sum of the principal, *plus* the interest, in your calculations.

The amount you quoted was too high, and (not *plus*) it was inaccurate.

precede, proceed   *Precede* means "to go or come before." *Proceed* means "to go forward in an orderly way."

Robert Frost's *North of Boston* was *preceded* by another volume of poetry, *A Boy's Will.*

In 1532 Francisco Pizarro landed at Tumbes and *proceeded* south until he encountered the Incas.

principal, principle   As a noun, *principal* means "a sum of money (minus interest) invested or lent" or "a person in the leading position." As an adjective it means "most important." A *principle* is a rule of conduct or a basic truth.

If you cash the bond before maturity, a penalty can be subtracted from the *principal* as well as the interest.

The *principal* of the high school is a talented administrator who has instituted a number of changes.

Women are the *principal* wage earners in many American households.

The Constitution embodies the fundamental *principles* upon which the American republic is founded.

quote, quotation   *Quote* is a verb meaning "to repeat or copy the words of another." *Quotation* is a noun referring to the passage quoted. In college writing situations, do not use *quote* as a shortened form of *quotation.*

He used several *quotations* (not *quotes*) from experts to support his arguments.

raise, rise   *Raise* is a transitive verb, and *rise* is an intransitive verb—that is, *raise* takes an object, and *rise* does not.

A famous photograph taken during World War II shows American Marines *raising* the flag on Iwo Jima.

When it *rises,* the planet Venus is brighter than any light in the sky except the sun or the moon.

real, really *Real* means "genuine" or "authentic." *Really* means "actually." In your college writing, do not use *real* as an adjective meaning "very."

COLLOQUIAL: The planarian is a *real* flat worm that we studied in biology class.

REVISED: The planarian is a *very* flat worm that we studied in biology class.

reason is that, reason is because *Reason* should be used with *that* and not with *because,* which is redundant.

The *reason* he moved out of the city *is that* (not *is because*) property taxes rose sharply.

regardless, irregardless See **irregardless, regardless.**

respectably, respectfully, respectively *Respectably* means "worthy of respect." *Respectfully* means "giving honor or deference." *Respectively* means "in the order given."

Even though Abraham Lincoln ran his campaign for the US Senate quite *respectably,* he was defeated by Stephen Douglas in 1858.

When being presented to Queen Elizabeth of England, foreigners are asked to bow *respectfully.*

"The Sisters" and "The Dead" are the first and the last stories, *respectively,* in James Joyce's collection *Dubliners.*

rise, raise See **raise, rise.**

set, sit To *set* means "to put down" or "to lay." To *sit* means "to assume a sitting position."

Base Form	Past Tense	Past Participle	Present Participle
set	set	set	setting
sit	sat	sat	sitting

After rocking the baby, he *set* her down carefully in her crib.

Research has shown that many children *sit* in front of the television five to six hours a day.

shall, will *Will* has all but replaced *shall* to express all future action.

simple, simplistic *Simple* means "not involved or complicated." *Simplistic* means "oversimplified."

The math problem was *simple.*

His interpretation of the problem was *simplistic.*

since Do not use *since* for *because* if there is any chance of confusion.

Because (not *since*) President Nixon made a historic trip to China, trade between China and the United States increased. (In this sentence, *since* could mean either "from the time that" or "because.")

sit, set See **set, sit.**

so   Avoid using *so* alone as a vague intensifier meaning "very" or "extremely." Follow *so* with *that* and a clause that describes the result.

> She was *so* pleased with their work *that* she took them out to lunch (not *She was so pleased with their work*).

sometime, sometimes, some time   *Sometime* means "at some time in the future." *Sometimes* means "now and then." *Some time* means "a period of time."

> In his essay "The Case against Man," Isaac Asimov says that *sometime*, far in the future, human beings will not be able to produce enough food to sustain themselves.

> All automobiles, no matter how well constructed, *sometimes* need repairs.

> At the Battle of Gettysburg, General Meade's failure to counterattack gave Lee *some time* to regroup his troops.

sort of   See **kind of, sort of.**

specially, especially   See **especially, specially.**

stationary, stationery   *Stationary* means "staying in one place." *Stationery* means "materials for writing" or "letter paper."

> When viewed from the earth, a communications satellite traveling at the same speed as the earth appears to be *stationary* in the sky.

> The secretaries are responsible for keeping departmental offices supplied with *stationery*.

supposed to, used to   Both *supposed to* and *used to* require the final *d* to indicate past tense.

> She was *supposed to* (not *suppose to*) turn in her paper yesterday.

> She always *used to* (not *use to*) turn in her papers on time.

take, bring   See **bring, take.**

than, as   See **as, than.**

than, then   *Than* is a conjunction used to indicate a comparison, and *then* is an adverb indicating time.

> The new shopping center is bigger *than* the old one.

> He did his research; *then* he wrote a report.

that, which, who   Use *that* or *which* when referring to a thing. In general, use *who* when referring to a person.

> In *How the Other Half Lives*, Jacob Riis described the conditions *that* existed in working-class slums in nineteenth-century America.

> *The Wonderful Wizard of Oz*, *which* was published in 1900, was originally entitled *From Kansas to Fairyland*.

Anyone *who* (not *that*) visits Maine cannot help being impressed by the beauty of the scenery and the ruggedness of the landscape.

their, there, they're   *Their* is a possessive pronoun. Use *there* to indicate place and in the expressions *there is* and *there are. They're* is a contraction of *they are.*

James Watson and Francis Crick did *their* work on the molecular structure of DNA at the Cavendish Laboratory at Cambridge University.

I have always wanted to visit the Marine Biological Laboratory in Woods Hole, Massachusetts, but I have never gotten *there.*

There is nothing we can do to resurrect a species once it becomes extinct.

White sharks and mako sharks are dangerous to human beings because *they're* good swimmers and especially sensitive to the scent of blood.

themselves, theirselves, theirself   *Theirselves* and *theirself* are nonstandard variants of *themselves* and are never acceptable in your writing.

Pioneer families had to build their homes and clear their land by *themselves* (not *theirself* or *theirselves*).

then, than   See **than, then.**

thus, therefore   *Thus* means "in this way"; *therefore* means "as a result."

In Joseph Conrad's *Heart of Darkness,* Kurtz becomes a man-god to the natives. *Thus,* he is able to collect a fortune in ivory.

INCORRECT: Throughout the past year, interest rates have dropped dramatically. *Thus,* businesses are able to buy the equipment they need to modernize their operations.

REVISED: Throughout the past year, interest rates have dropped dramatically. *Therefore,* businesses are able to buy the equipment they need to modernize their operations.

till, until, 'til   *Till* and *until* have the same meaning, and both are acceptable. *Until* is preferred in college writing. *'Til,* a contraction of *until,* should be avoided.

to, at   See **at, to.**

to, too, two   *To* is a preposition that indicates direction. *Too* is an adverb that means "also" or "more than is needed." *Two* expresses the number 2.

Last year we flew from New York *to* California.

"Tippecanoe and Tyler *too*" was William Henry Harrison's campaign slogan during the 1840 presidential election.

The plot was *too* complicated for the average reader.

Just north of *Two* Rivers, Wisconsin, is a petrified forest.

try to, try and   *Try and* is the colloquial equivalent of the more formal *try to*.

> COLLOQUIAL: Throughout most of his career E. R. Rutherford was determined to *try and* discover the structure of the atom.

> REVISED: Throughout most of his career E. R. Rutherford *tried to* discover the structure of the atom.

-type   Deleting this empty suffix eliminates clutter and clarifies meaning.

> COLLOQUIAL: Found in the wreckage of the house was an *incendiary-type* device.

> REVISED: Found in the wreckage of the house was an *incendiary* device.

uninterested, disinterested   See **disinterested, uninterested.**

unique   *Unique* means "the only one," not "remarkable" or "unusual."

> COLLOQUIAL: Its undershot lower jaw makes the English bulldog *unique* among dogs.

> REVISED: Its undershot lower jaw makes the English bulldog unusual among dogs.

> CORRECT USAGE: In their scope and unity, Michelangelo's paintings are *unique*.

Because *unique* means "the only one," it can take no intensifiers. Never use constructions like "the most unique" or "very unique."

until   See **till, until, 'til.**

used to   See **supposed to, used to.**

utilize   In most cases, it is best to replace *utilize* with *use* (*utilize* often sounds pretentious).

> Students are able to *use* (not *utilize*) the computer lab until midnight.

wait for, wait on   To *wait for* means "to defer action until something occurs." To *wait on* means "to act as a waiter."

> COLLOQUIAL: I am *waiting on* dinner.

> REVISED: I am *waiting for* dinner.

> CORRECT: The captain *waited on* the head table himself.

weather, whether   *Weather* is a noun meaning "the state of the atmosphere." *Whether* is a conjunction used to introduce an alternative.

> The *weather* outside is frightful, but the fire inside is delightful.

> I wonder *whether* or not we will be able to ski tomorrow.

well, good   See **good, well.**

whether, if   See **if, whether.**

whether, weather   See **weather, whether.**

which, who, that   See **that, which, who.**

while, although   See **although, while.**

who, whom   When a pronoun serves as the subject of its clause, use *who* or *whoever;* when it functions as an object in a clause, use *whom* or *whomever.*

Sarah, *who* is studying ancient civilizations, would like to visit Greece.

Sarah, *whom* I haven't seen in a year, wants me to travel to Greece with her.

To determine which to use at the beginning of a question, use a personal pronoun to answer the question.

Who tried to call me? *He* tried to call. (subject)

For *whom* is the package? It is for *her.* (object of a preposition)

Whom do you want for the job? I want *her.* (object)

who's, whose   Use *who's* when you mean *who is.* Use *whose* when you want to indicate possession.

Who's going to take calculus?

The writer *whose* book was in the window was autographing copies in the store.

will, shall   See **shall, will.**

-wise, -ize   See **-ize, -wise.**

would of   See **could of, would of.**

yet   See **but, however, yet.**

your, you're   Because these words are pronounced alike they are often confused. *Your* indicates possession, and *you're* is the contraction of *you are.*

You can improve *your* stamina by jogging two miles a day.

You're certain to be impressed the first time you see the Golden Gate Bridge spanning San Francisco Bay.

GLOSSARY OF GRAMMATICAL AND RHETORICAL TERMS

absolute phrase   See **phrase.**

abstract noun   See **noun.**

acronym   A word formed from the first letters or initial sounds of a group of words: <u>NATO</u> = <u>N</u>orth <u>A</u>tlantic <u>T</u>reaty <u>O</u>rganization.

active voice   See **voice.**

adjective   A word that describes, limits, qualifies, or in any other way modifies a noun or pronoun. A **descriptive adjective** names a quality of the noun or pronoun it modifies: <u>junior</u> year. A **proper adjective** is formed from a proper noun: <u>Hegelian</u> philosophy. **27a**

adjective clause   See **clause.**

adverb   A word that describes the action of verbs or modifies adjectives, other adverbs, or complete phrases, clauses, or sentences. Adverbs answer the questions "How?" "Why?" "Where?" "When?" and "To what extent?" Adverbs are formed from adjectives, many by adding *ly* to the adjective form (*dark/darkly, solemn/solemnly*), and may also be derived from prepositions (*Joe carried <u>on</u>.*). Other adverbs that indicate time, place, condition, cause, or degree are not derived from other parts of speech: *then, never, very,* and *often,* for example. The words *how, why, where,* and *when* are classified as **interrogative adverbs** when they ask questions (*<u>How</u> did we get into this mess?*). See also **conjunctive adverb. 23e; 27c**

adverb clause   See **clause.**

adverbial conjunction   See **conjunctive adverb.**

agreement   The correspondence between words in number, person, and gender. Subjects and verbs must agree in number (singular or plural) and person (first, second, or third): <u>Soccer</u> <u>is</u> a popular European sport.; <u>I</u> <u>play</u> soccer too. **26a** Pronouns and their antecedents must agree in number, person, and gender (masculine, feminine, neuter): <u>Lucy</u> loaned Charlie <u>her</u> car. **26b** *allusion* A reference to a well-known historical, literary, or biblical person or event that readers are expected to recognize.

analogy A kind of comparison in which the writer explains an unfamiliar idea or object by comparing it to a more familiar one: *Sensory pathways of the central nervous system are bundles of nerves rather like telephone cables that feed information about the outside world into the brain for processing.*

antecedent The word or word group to which a pronoun refers: <u>*Brian*</u> *finally bought the stereo he had always wanted.* (*Brian* is the antecedent of the pronoun *he.*)

appositive A noun or noun phrase that identifies or renames the noun or pronoun it follows: *Columbus,* <u>*the capital of Ohio,*</u> *is in the central part of the state.* Appositives may be used without special introductory phrases, as in the preceding example, or they may be introduced by *such as, or, that is, for example,* or *in other words: Japanese cars,* <u>*such as Hondas,*</u> *now have a large share of the US automobile market.* **10c6** In a restrictive appositive, the appositive precedes the noun or pronoun it modifies: <u>*Singing cowboy*</u> *Gene Autry became the owner of the California Angels.* **29d1**

article The word *a, an,* or *the.* Articles signal that a noun follows and are classified as **determiners. B6b–c**

auxiliary verb See **verb.**

balanced sentence A sentence neatly divided between two parallel structures. Balanced sentences are typically **compound sentences** made up of two parallel clauses (*The telephone rang, and I answered.*), but the parallel clauses of a **complex sentence** can also be balanced. **12c**

cardinal number A number that expresses quantity—*seven, thirty, one hundred.* (Contrast **ordinal.**)

case The form a noun or pronoun takes to indicate how it functions in a sentence. English has three cases. A pronoun takes the **subjective** (or **nominative**) **case** when it acts as the subject of a sentence or a clause: <u>*I*</u> *am an American.* **24a1** A pronoun takes the **objective case** when it acts as the object of a verb or of a preposition: *Fran gave* <u>*me*</u> *her dog.* **24a2** Both nouns and pronouns take the **possessive case** when they indicate ownership: <u>*My*</u> *house is brick,* <u>*Brandon's*</u> *T-shirt is red.* This is the only case in which nouns change form. **24a3**

clause A group of related words that includes a subject and a predicate. An **independent** (main) **clause** may stand alone as a sentence (*Yellowstone is a national park in the West.*), but a **dependent** (subordinate) **clause** must always be accompanied by an independent clause (*Yellowstone is a national park in the West* <u>*that is known for its geysers.*</u>).

Dependent clauses are classified according to their function in a sentence. An **adjective clause** (sometimes called a **relative clause**) modifies nouns or pronouns: *The philodendron, which grew to be twelve feet tall, finally died* (the clause modifies *philodendron*). An **adverb clause** modifies single words (verbs, adjectives, or adverbs) or an entire phrase or clause: *The film was exposed when Bill opened the camera* (the clause modifies *exposed*). A **noun clause** acts as a noun (as subject, direct object, indirect object, or complement) in a sentence: *Whoever arrives first wins the prize* (the clause is the subject of the sentence). An **elliptical clause** is grammatically incomplete—that is, part or all of the subject or predicate is missing. If the missing part can be easily inferred from the context of the sentence, such a construction is acceptable: *When (they are) pressed, the committee will act.* **10b2**

climactic word order The writing strategy of moving from the least important to the most important point in a sentence and ending with the key idea. **12a2**

collective noun See **noun.**

comma splice An error created when two independent clauses are incorrectly joined by a comma. **16a–d**

COMMA SPLICE: The Mississippi River flows south, the Nile River flows north.

REVISED: The Mississippi River flows south. The Nile River flows north.

REVISED: The Mississippi River flows south; the Nile River flows north.

REVISED: The Mississippi River flows south, and the Nile River flows north.

REVISED: Although the Mississippi River flows south, the Nile River flows north.

common noun See **noun.**

comparative/superlative The forms taken by an adjective or an adverb to indicate degree. The **positive degree** describes a quality without indicating comparison (*Frank is tall.*). The **comparative degree** indicates comparison between two persons or things (*Frank is taller than John.*). The **superlative degree** indicates comparison between one person or thing and two or more others (*Frank is the tallest boy in his scout troop.*). **27d**

complement A word or word group that describes or renames a subject, an object, or a verb. A **subject complement** is a word or phrase that follows a linking verb and renames the subject. It can be an adjective (called a **predicate adjective**) or a noun (called a **predicate**

nominative): *Clark Gable was a movie star.* An **object complement** is a word or phrase that describes or renames a direct object. Object complements can be either adjectives or nouns: *We call the treehouse the hideout.*

complex sentence   See **sentence.**

compound   Two or more words that function as a unit, such as **compound nouns:** *attorney-at-law; boardwalk;* **compound adjectives:** *hardhitting editorial;* **compound prepositions:** *by way of, in addition to;* **compound subjects:** *April and May are spring months.;* **compound predicates:** *Many try and fail to climb Mount Everest.*

compound adjective   See **compound.**

compound noun   See **compound.**

compound predicate   See **compound.**

compound preposition   See **compound.**

compound sentence   See **sentence.**

compound subject   See **compound.**

compound-complex sentence   See **sentence.**

conjunction   A word or words used to connect single words, phrases, clauses, and sentences. **Coordinating conjunctions** (*and, or, but, nor, for, so, yet*) connect words, phrases, or clauses of equal weight: *crime and punishment* (coordinating conjunction *and* connects two words). **Correlative conjunctions** (*both . . . and, either . . . or, neither . . . nor,* and so on), always used in pairs, also link items of equal weight: *Neither Texas nor Florida crosses the Tropic of Cancer.* **Subordinating conjunctions** (*since, because, although, if, after,* and so on) introduce adverb clauses: *You will have to pay for the tickets now because I will not be here later.* **23g**

conjunctive adverb   An adverb that joins and relates independent clauses in a sentence (*also, anyway, besides, hence, however, nevertheless, still,* and so on): *Howard tried out for the Yankees; however, he didn't make the team.* **23e**

connotation   The emotional associations that surround a word. (Contrast **denotation.**) **20b1**

contraction   The combination of two words with an apostrophe replacing the missing letters: *We + will = we'll; was + not = wasn't.*

coordinate adjective   One of a series of adjectives that modify the same word or word group: *The park was quiet, shady, and cool.* **29b2**

coordinating conjunction   See **conjunction.**

coordination   The pairing of similar elements (words, phrases, or clauses) to give equal weight to each. Coordination is used in simple sentences to link similar elements into compound subjects, predicates, complements, or modifiers. It can also link two independent clauses to form a compound sentence: *The sky was cloudy, and it looked like rain.* (Contrast **subordination.**)

correlative conjunction   See **conjunction.**

cumulative sentence   A sentence that begins with a main clause followed by additional words, phrases, or clauses that expand or develop it: *On the hill stood a schoolhouse, paint peeling, windows boarded, playground overgrown with weeds.* **12b1**

dangling modifier   A modifier for which no logical headword appears in the sentence. To correct dangling modifiers, either create a new subject that can logically service as the headword of the dangling modifier, or change the dangling modifier into a dependent clause. **17b**

DANGLING: Pumping up the tire, the trip continued.

REVISED: After pumping up the tire, they continued the trip.

dead metaphor   A metaphor so overused that it has become a meaningless cliché. **20e1**

declarative sentence   See **sentence.**

deductive argument   An argument that begins with a general statement or proposition and establishes a chain of reasoning that leads to a conclusion. **8b**

demonstrative pronoun   See **pronoun.**

denotation   The dictionary meaning of a word. (Contrast **connotation.**) **20b1**

dependent clause   See **clause.**

descriptive adjective   See **adjective.**

determiner   **Determiners** are words that function as adjectives to limit or qualify nouns. Determiners include **articles** (*a, an, the*): the book, a peanut; **possessive nouns** (*Janet's*): *Janet's* dog; **possessive pronouns** (*my, your, his,* and so on): *their* apartment, *my* house; **demonstrative pronouns** (*this, these, that, those*): *that* table, *these* chairs; **interrogative pronouns** (*what, which, whose,* and so on): *Which* car is yours?; **indefinite pronouns** (*another, each, both, many,* and so on): *any* minute, *some* day; **relative pronouns** (*what, whatever, which, whichever, whose, whosoever*): Bed rest was *what* the doctor ordered.; and **numbers** (*one, two, first, second,* and so on): Claire saw *two* robins. **23d; 27a**

direct object   See **object.**

direct quotation   See **quotation.**

documentation   The formal acknowledgment of the sources used in a piece of writing. **43a–f** *documentation style*   A format for providing information about the sources used in a piece of writing. Documentation formats vary from discipline to discipline. **43a–f**

double negative   A nonstandard combination of two negative words:

DOUBLE NEGATIVE: *She <u>didn't</u> have <u>no</u> time.*

REVISED: *She had <u>no</u> time* or *She <u>didn't</u> have any time.* **27e; B8e**

ellipsis   Three spaced periods used to indicate the omission of a word or words from a quotation: "*The time has come . . . and we must part.*" **33f**

elliptical clause   See **clause.**

embedding   A strategy for varying sentence structure that involves changing some sentences into modifying phrases and working them into other sentences. **14b3**

enthymeme   A syllogism in which one of the premises—usually the major premise—is implied rather than stated. **8b2**

expletive   A construction in which *there* or *it* is used with a form of the verb *be*: <u>*There is*</u> *no one here by that name.*

faulty parallelism   See **parallelism.**

figurative language   Language that departs from the literal meaning or order of words to create striking effects or new meanings. Types of figurative language (called **figures of speech**) include **simile, metaphor,** and **personification. 20d**

finite verb   A verb that can serve as the main verb of a sentence. Unlike **participles, gerunds,** and **infinitives** (see **verbal**), finite verbs do not require an auxiliary in order to function as the main verb: *The rooster <u>crowed</u>.*

fragment   See **sentence fragment.**

function word   An article, preposition, conjunction, or auxiliary verb that indicates the function of and the grammatical relationships among the nouns, verbs, and modifiers in a sentence.

fused sentence   A type of **run-on sentence** that occurs when two independent clauses are joined without punctuation. Correct fused sentences by separating the independent clauses with a period, a semicolon, or a comma and a coordinating conjunction, or by using subordination. **16a–d**

FUSED SENTENCE: Protein is needed for good nutrition lipids and carbohydrates are too.

REVISED: Protein is needed for good nutrition. Lipids and carbohydrates are too.

REVISED: Protein is needed for good nutrition; lipids and carbohydrates are too.

REVISED: Protein is needed for good nutrition, but lipids and carbohydrates are too.

REVISED: Although protein is needed for good nutrition, lipids and carbohydrates are too.

gender   The classification of nouns and pronouns as masculine (*father, boy, he*), feminine (*mother, girl, she*), or neuter (*radio, kitten, them*).

gerund   A special form of verb ending in *ing* that is always used as a noun: <u>Fishing</u> is <u>relaxing</u> (gerund *fishing* serves as subject; gerund *relaxing* serves as subject complement). Note: When the *ing* form of a verb is used as a modifier, it is considered a **present participle.** See also **verbal.**

gerund phrase   See **phrase.**

headword   The word or phrase in a sentence that is described, defined, or limited by a modifier.

helping verb   See **auxiliary verb.**

idiom   An expression that is characteristic of a particular language and whose meaning cannot be predicted from the meaning of its individual words: *lend a hand.*

imperative mood   See **mood.**

indefinite adjective   See **adjective.**

indefinite pronoun   See **pronoun.**

independent clause   See **clause.**

indicative mood   See **mood.**

indirect object   See **object.**

indirect question   A question that tells what has been asked but, because it does not report the speaker's exact words, does not take quotation marks or end with a question mark: *He asked whether he could use the family car.*

indirect quotation   See **quotation.**

inductive argument   An argument that begins with observations or experiences and moves toward a conclusion. **8a**

infinitive   The base form of the verb preceded by *to,* an infinitive can serve as an adjective (*He is the man <u>to watch</u>.*), an adverb (*Chris hoped <u>to break</u> the record.*), or a noun (*<u>To err</u> is human.*). See also **verbal.**

infinitive phrase   See **phrase.**

intensifier   A word that adds emphasis but not additional meaning to words it modifies. *Much, really, too, very,* and *so* are typical intensifiers.

intensive pronoun   See **pronoun.**

interjection   A grammatically independent word, expressing emotion, that is used as an exclamation. An interjection can be set off by a comma, or, for greater emphasis, it can be punctuated as an independent unit, set off by an exclamation point: *Ouch! That hurt.* **23h**

interrogative adverb   See **adverb.**

interrogative pronoun   See **pronoun.**

intransitive verb   See **verb.**

irregular verb   A verb that does not form both its past tense and past participle by adding *d* or *ed* to the base form of the verb. **25a2**

isolate   Any word, including **interjections,** that can be used in isolation: *Yes. No. Hello. Good-bye. Please. Thank you.*

linking verb   A verb that connects a subject to its complement: *The crowd became quiet.* Words that can be used as linking verbs include *seem, appear, believe, become, grow, turn, remain, prove, look, sound, smell, taste, feel,* and forms of the verb *be.*

main clause   See **clause.**

main verb   See **verb.**

mass noun   See **noun.**

metaphor   A form of **figurative language** in which the writer makes an implied comparison between two unlike items, equating them in an unexpected way: *The subway coursed through the arteries of the city.*

misplaced modifier   A modifier that has no clear relationship with its headword, usually because it is placed too far from it. **17a**

MISPLACED: By changing his diapers, Dan learned much about his new baby son.

REVISED: Dan learned much about his new baby son by changing his diapers.

mixed construction   A sentence made up of two or more parts that do not fit together grammatically. **19f**

MIXED: The Great Chicago Fire caused terrible destruction was what prompted changes in the fire code. (independent clause used as a subject)

REVISED: The terrible destruction of the Great Chicago Fire prompted changes in the fire code.

REVISED: Because of the terrible destruction of the Great Chicago Fire, the fire code was changed.

mixed metaphor   The combination of two or more incompatible images in a single figure of speech: *During the race John kept a stiff upper lip as he ran like the wind.* **20e2** *modal auxiliary*   See **verb.**

modifier   A word, phrase, or clause that acts as an adjective or an adverb, describing, limiting, or qualifying another word or word group in the sentence.

mood   The verb form that indicates the writer's basic attitude. There are three moods in English. The **indicative mood** is used for statements and questions: *Nebraska became a state in 1867.* **25g** The **imperative mood** specifies commands or requests and is often used without a subject: (*You*) *Pay the rent.* **25g** The **subjunctive mood** expresses wishes or hypothetical conditions: *I wish the sun were shining.* **25h**

nominal   A word, phrase, or clause that functions as a noun.

nominative case   See **case.**

nonfinite verb   See **verbal.**

nonrestrictive modifier   A modifying phrase or clause that does not limit or particularize the words it modifies, but rather supplies additional information about them. Nonrestrictive modifiers are set off by commas: *Oregano, also known as marjoram or suganda, is a member of the mint family.* **29d1** (Contrast **restrictive modifier.**)

noun   A word that names people, places, things, ideas, actions, or qualities. A **common noun** names any of a class of people, places, or things: *lawyer, town, bicycle.* A **proper noun,** always capitalized, refers to a particular person, place, or thing: *Anita Hill, Chicago, Schwinn.* A **count noun** names something that can be counted: *a dozen eggs, two cats in the yard.* A **noncount noun** names a quantity that is not countable: *sand, time, work.* An **abstract noun** refers to an intangible idea or quality: *bravery, equality, hunger.* A **collective noun** designates a group of people, places, or things thought of as a unit: *Congress, police, family.* **23a**

noun clause   See **clause.**

noun phrase   See **phrase.**

number   The form taken by a noun, pronoun, or verb to indicate one (**singular**): *car, he, this, boast,* or many (**plural**): *cars, they, those, boasts.* **19d**

object   A noun, pronoun, or other noun substitute that receives the action of a **transitive verb, verbal,** or **preposition.** A **direct object** indicates where the verb's action is directed and who or what is affected by it: *John caught a butterfly.* An **indirect object** tells to or for whom the verb's action was done: *John gave Nancy the butterfly.* An **object of a preposition** is a word or word group introduced by a preposition: *John gave Nancy the butterfly for an hour.*

object complement   See **complement.**

object of a preposition   See **object.**

objective case   See **case.**

ordinal number   A number that indicates position in a series: *seventh, thirtieth, one-hundredth.*

parallelism   The use of similar grammatical elements in sentences or parts of sentences: *We serve <u>beer</u>, <u>wine</u>, and <u>soft drinks</u>.* Words, phrases, clauses, or complete sentences may be parallel, and parallel items may be paired or presented in a series. When elements that have the same function in a sentence are not presented in the same terms, the sentence is flawed by **faulty parallelism. 12c; 18a–b**

participial phrase   See **phrase.**

participle   A verb form that generally functions in a sentence as an adjective. Virtually every verb has a **present participle,** which ends in *ing* (*breaking, leaking, taking*), and a **past participle,** which usually ends in *d* or *ed* (*agreed, walked, taken*). (See also **verbal.**) **Present participle:** *The <u>heaving</u> seas swamped the dinghy* (present participle *heaving* modifies noun *seas*); **past participle:** *<u>Aged</u> people deserve respect* (past participle *aged* modifies noun *people*).

parts of speech   The eight basic building blocks for all English sentences: *nouns, pronouns, verbs, adjectives, adverbs, prepositions, conjunctions,* and *interjections.*

passive voice   See **voice.**

past participle   See **participle.**

periodic sentence   A sentence that moves from a number of specific examples to a conclusion, gradually building in intensity until a climax is reached in the main clause: *Wan and pale and looking ready to crumble, the marathoner headed into the last mile of the race.* **12b2**

person   The form a pronoun or verb takes to indicate the speaker (**first person**): *I am/we are;* those spoken to (**second person**): *you are;* and those spoken about (**third person**): *he/she/it is; they are.* **19d**

personal pronoun   See **pronoun.**

personification   A form of **figurative language** in which the writer describes an idea or inanimate object in terms that imply human attributes, feelings, or powers: *The big feather bed beckoned to my tired body.* **20d**

phrase   A grammatically ordered group of related words that lacks a subject or a predicate or both and functions as a single part of speech. A **verb phrase** consists of an auxiliary (helping) verb and a main verb: *The wind <u>was blowing</u> hard.* A **noun phrase** includes a noun or pronoun plus all related modifiers: *She broke <u>the track record</u>.* A

prepositional phrase consists of a preposition, its object, and any modifiers of that object: *The ball sailed over the fence.* A **verbal phrase** consists of a verbal and its related objects, modifiers, or complements. A verbal phrase may be a **participial phrase** (*Undaunted by the sheer cliff, the climber scaled the rock.*), a **gerund phrase** (*Swinging from trees is a monkey's favorite way to travel.*), or an **infinitive phrase** (*Wednesday is Bill's night to cook spaghetti.*). An **absolute phrase** usually consists of a noun or pronoun and a participle, accompanied by modifiers: *His heart racing, he dialed her number.* **10b1**

positive degree See **comparison.**

possessive case See **case.**

predicate A verb or verb phrase that tells or asks something about the subject of a sentence is called a **simple predicate:** *Well-tended lawns grow green and thick.* (*Grow* is the simple predicate.) A **complete predicate** includes all the words associated with the predicate: *Well-tended lawns grow green and thick.* (*Grow green and thick* is the complete predicate.) **Ch. 10**

predicate adjective See **complement.**

prefix A letter or group of letters put before a root or word that adds to, changes, or modifies it. **21e3**

preposition A part of speech that introduces a noun or pronoun (or a phrase or clause functioning in the sentence as a noun), linking it to other words in the sentence: *Jeremy crawled under the bed.* **23f**

prepositional phrase See **phrase.**

present participle See **participle.**

principal parts The forms of a verb from which all other forms can be derived. The principal parts are the **base form** (*give*), the **present participle** (*giving*), the **past tense** (*gave*), and the **past participle** (*given*).

pronoun A word that may be used in place of a noun in a sentence. The noun for which a pronoun stands is called its **antecedent.** There are eight types of pronouns. Some have the same form but are distinguished by their function in the sentence. A **personal pronoun** stands for a person or thing: *I, me, we, us, my,* and so on (*They broke his window.*). A **reflexive pronoun** ends in *self* or *selves* and refers to the subject of the sentence or clause: *myself, yourself, himself,* and so on (*They painted the house themselves.*). An **intensive pronoun** ends in *self* or *selves* and emphasizes a preceding noun or pronoun (*Custer himself died in the battle.*). A **relative pronoun** introduces an adjective or noun clause in a sentence: *which, who, whom,* and so on (*Sitting Bull was the Sioux chief who defeated Custer.*). An **interrogative pronoun** introduces a question: *who, which, what, whom,* and so on

(*Who won the lottery?*). A **demonstrative pronoun** points to a particular thing or group of things: *this, that, these, those* (*Who was that
masked man?*). A **reciprocal pronoun** denotes a mutual relationship:
each other, one another (*We still have each other.*). An **indefinite pronoun** refers to persons or things in general, not to specific individuals. Most indefinite pronouns are singular—*anyone, everyone, one,
each*—but some are always plural—*both, many, several* (*Many are
called, but few are chosen.*). **23b**

proper adjective   See **adjective.**

proper noun   See **noun.**

quotation   The use of the written or spoken words of others. A **direct
quotation** is a passage borrowed word for word from another source.
Quotation marks (" ") establish the boundaries of a direct quotation:
"These tortillas taste like cardboard," complained Beth. **32a** An **indirect
quotation** reports someone else's written or spoken words without
quoting that person directly. Quotation marks are not used: *Beth
complained that the tortillas tasted like cardboard.*

reciprocal pronoun   See **pronoun.**

reflexive pronoun   See **pronoun.**

regular verb   A verb that forms both its past tense and past participle by
the addition of *d* or *ed* to the base form of the verb. **25a1**

relative clause   See **clause.**

relative pronoun   See **pronoun.**

restrictive appositive   See **appositive.**

restrictive modifier   A modifying phrase or clause that limits the meaning of the word or word group it modifies. Restrictive modifiers are
not set off by commas: *The Ferrari that ran over the fireplug was red.*
29d1 (Contrast **nonrestrictive modifier.**)

root   A word from which other words are formed. An understanding of
a root word increases a reader's ability to understand unfamiliar
words that incorporate the root.

run-on sentence   An incorrect construction that results when the
proper connective or punctuation does not appear between independent clauses. A run-on occurs either as a **comma splice** or as a **fused
sentence.**

sentence   An independent grammatical unit that contains a subject and
a predicate and expresses a complete thought: *Carolyn sold her car.* A
simple sentence consists of one subject and one predicate: *The season
ended.* **10a;** a **compound sentence** is formed when two or more simple sentences are connected with coordinating conjunctions, conjunctive

adverbs, semicolons, or colons: *The rain stopped, and the sun began to shine.* **11a;** a **complex sentence** consists of one simple sentence, which functions as an independent clause in the complex sentence, and at least one dependent clause, which is introduced by a subordinating conjunction or a relative pronoun: *When he had sold three boxes* [dependent clause], *he was halfway to his goal.* [independent clause] **11b;** and a **compound-complex sentence** consists of two or more independent clauses and at least one dependent clause: *After he prepared a shopping list* [dependent clause], *he went to the store* [independent clause], *but it was closed.* [independent clause]. **11c**

sentence fragment   An incomplete sentence, phrase, or clause that is punctuated as if it were a complete sentence. **15a–c**

shift   A change of *tense, voice, mood, person, number,* or *type of discourse* within or between sentences. Some shifts are necessary, but problems occur with unnecessary or illogical shifts. **19a–e**

simile   A form of **figurative language** in which the writer makes a comparison, introduced by *like* or *as,* between two unlike items on the basis of a shared quality: *Like sands through the hourglass, so are the days of our lives. The wind was as savage as his neighbor's Doberman.* **20d**

simple predicate   See **predicate.**

simple sentence   See **sentence.**

simple subject   See **subject.**

split infinitive   An infinitive whose parts are separated by a modifier. **17a4**

Split: She expected *to* ultimately *swim* the channel.

Revised: She expected ultimately *to swim* the channel.

squinting modifier   A modifier that seems to modify either a word before it or one after it and that conveys a different meaning in each case. **17a1**

Squinting: The task completed simply delighted him.

Revised: He was delighted to have the task completed simply.

Revised: He was simply delighted to have the task completed.

subject   A noun or noun substitute that tells who or what a sentence is about is called a **simple subject:** *Healthy thoroughbred horses run like the wind.* (*Horses* is the simple subject.) The **complete subject** of a sentence includes all the words associated with the subject: *Healthy thoroughbred horses run like the wind.* (*Healthy thoroughbred horses* is the complete subject.) **Ch. 10**

subject complement   See **complement.**

subjective case   See **case.**

subjunctive mood   See **mood.**

subordinate clause   See **clause.**

subordinating conjunction   See **conjunction.**

subordination   Making one or more clauses of a sentence grammatically dependent upon another element in a sentence: *Preston was only eighteen when he joined the firm.* (Contrast **coordination.**) **11b**

suffix   A syllable added at the end of a word or root that changes its part of speech. **21e3**

superlative degree   See **comparison.**

suspended hyphen   A hyphen followed by a space or by the appropriate punctuation and a space: *The wagon was pulled by a two-, four-, or six-horse team.*

syllogism   A three-part set of statements or propositions, devised by Aristotle, that contains a major premise, a minor premise, and a conclusion. **8b1**

tag question   A question, consisting of an auxiliary verb plus a pronoun, that is added to a statement and set off by a comma: *You know it's going to rain, don't you?*

tense   The form of a verb that indicates when an action occurred or when a condition existed. **25b–f**

transitive verb   See **verb.**

verb   A word or phrase that expresses action (*He painted the fence.*) or a state of being (*Henry believes in equality.*). A **main verb** carries most of the meaning in the sentence or clause in which it appears: *Winston Churchill smoked long, thick cigars.* A main verb is a **linking verb** when it is followed by a **subject complement:** *Dogs are good pets.* An **auxiliary verb** (sometimes called a **helping verb**) combines with the main verb to form a **verb phrase:** *Graduation day has arrived.* The auxiliaries *be* and *have* are used to indicate the tense and voice of the main verb. The auxiliary *do* is used for asking questions and forming negative statements. Other auxiliary verbs, known as **modal auxiliaries** (*must, will, can, could, may, might, ought (to), should,* and *would*), indicate necessity, possibility, willingness, obligation, and ability: *It might rain next Tuesday.* A **transitive verb** requires an **object** to complete its meaning in the sentence: *Pete drank all the wine* (*wine* is the direct object). An **intransitive verb** has no direct object: *The candle flame glowed.* **23c1; 25a–k**

verb phrase   See **phrase.**

verbal   (nonfinite verb) Verb forms—**participles, infinitives,** and **gerunds**—that are used as nouns, adjectives, or adverbs. Verbals do not behave like verbs. Only when used with an auxiliary can such verb forms serve as the main verb of a sentence. *The wall painted* is not a sentence; *The wall was painted* is. **23c2**

verbal phrase See **phrase.**

voice The form that determines whether the subject of a verb is acting or is acted upon. When the subject of a verb performs the action, the verb is in the **active voice:** *Tiger Woods sank a thirty-foot putt.* When the subject of a verb receives the action—that is, is acted upon—the verb is in the **passive voice:** *A thirty-foot putt was sunk by Tiger Woods.* **12e; 19b; 25i–k**

ACKNOWLEDGMENTS

INDEX

Blue page numbers refer to definitions of terms.

Index

Index

Index

Index

Index

Insure, assure, ensure, G-4
Intensifier(s), G-28
Intensive pronoun(s), 386, G-32
Interjection(s)
  capitalization of *O,* 533
  comma with, 393–394
  definition of, 393, G-29
  exclamation point with, 394
Interlibrary loan(s), 576
Internal heading(s), 793
International students
  adjectives, guidelines for, A-30–A-32
  adverbs, guidelines for, A-30–A-32
  common sentence errors, A-37
  compared with writing for nature
    English speakers, A-13–A-14
  English compared with other
    languages, A-20–A-21
  idiom and, 358, A-33
  nouns, guidelines for, A-21–A-25
  organizing ideas, A-17–A-19
  paragraph writing, A-18–A-19
  prepositions, guidelines for,
    A-32–A-35
  pronouns, guidelines for, A-25–A-26
  thesis and support, A-15–A-16
  thesis statement, A-15
  topic choice, A-14
  verbs, guidelines for, A-27–A-30
  word order, A-35–A-36
Internet. *See also* E-mail
  definition of, 584, 599
  evaluation of Internet sources,
    594–595, 686–687
  for finding information for essays, 14
  FTP (File Transfer Protocol), 587–588
  Gopher, 588
  for humanities research, 767
  information available on, 584–585
  Listservs, 579, 586–587
  netiquette, 595–596
  newsgroups, 579, 586
  organizations and groups on World
    Wide Web, 578
  plagiarism and, 617–618
  for research, 563, 565
  research sites on, 596–598
  résumés posted on, 874
  searching the Web, 589–593
  server, 588

Internet *(cont.)*
  terminology on, 598–600
  using, 585–589
  World Wide Web, 578, 588–593
Interrogative adverb(s), 391, G-22
Interrogative pronoun(s), 386, 390,
    G-26, G-32–G-33
Interruption, dashes for, 516
Interview(s)
  CMS Works Cited list, 653
  for humanities research, 767–768
  MLA Works Cited list, 639
  as research method, 580–581
  for social science research, 788
Into, in, G-11–G-12
Intransitive verb(s)
  definition of, 215, G-35
  labeled in dictionary, 356
  in simple sentences, 216–217
Introduction(s)
  of argumentative essays, 201
  of essay examination answers, 829
  of essays, 21–22, 134, 135–138,
    141–142, A-18
  of research paper, 698
Introductory elements, commas with,
    465–467
Intrusive modifier(s), 305–307
Inverted subject-verb order, 430
Inverted word order, 272
Irony, 867
Irregardless, regardless, G-12
Irregular comparative forms, 443
Irregular plural noun(s), apostrophe
    with, 492
Irregular superlative forms, 443
Irregular verb(s), 405–408, A-27, G-29
Irritate, aggravate, G-2
Is when, is where, 328, G-12
Isolate(s), 394, G-29
Italics
  aircraft, 538
  books, 536
  clarity, 539
  films, 537
  foreign words and phrases, 538
  journals, 537
  letters, numerals, words, and phrases
    referred to as themselves, 538–539
  magazines, 537

Index